D1551563

JAMES W. WADSWORTH, Jr.

The Gentleman from New York

A NEW YORK STATE STUDY

JAMES W. WADSWORTH, Jr.

The Gentleman from New York

Martin L. Fausold

SYRACUSE UNIVERSITY PRESS   1975

Excerpts from *The Wadsworths of the Genesee,* by Alden Hatch, reprinted by permission of G. P. Putnam's Sons, copyright © 1959 by Alden Hatch.

Library of Congress Cataloging in Publication Data

Fausold, Martin L.   1921–
   James W. Wadsworth, Jr.

   Includes bibliographical references and index.
   1. Wadsworth, James Wolcott, 1877–1952.
E664.W13F38   328.73'092'4 [B]   75-6111
ISBN 0-8156-2171-X

To Sherry, Cindy, Marti, Sammy

who grew up with

The Gentleman from New York

Martin L. Fausold, professor of history at State University of New York College at Geneseo, received the A.B. degree from Gettysburg College and the Ph.D. from Syracuse University.

He is the author of *Gifford Pinchot, Bull Moose Progressive* (1961) and is editor of *The Hoover Presidency: A Reappraisal* (1974). His articles have appeared in many professional journals.

Contents

Illustrations

Acknowledgments

A WORK as extended as this biography can be accomplished only with the help of hundreds of people. There were conversations with more than fifty people who were quite willing to give their time to the author. And the staffs of numerous libraries in the eastern United States gave their services unstintingly, as is always the case with librarians. Then, too, there were all those, lay people and historian alike, who gave the author much encouragement to push on with the work, particularly: Alfred B. Rollins, former Professor of History, State University of New York (SUNY) college at Binghamton, and currently Vice-President of the University of Vermont; Donald R. McCoy, University Distinguished Professor of History, University of Kansas; Blake McKelvey, former City Historian, Rochester, New York; Walter Harding, Distinguished Professor of English, SUNY College at Geneseo; Harold Peterson, Distinguished Professor Emeritus of History, SUNY College at Buffalo.

Certain individuals gave so much of their time and qualifications as, at times, to be embarrassing to the author. Special thanks go to Richard Quick, Head Librarian, and William Lane and his reference staff at the Milne Library, SUNY College at Geneseo, for continuing assistance to the author. The following individuals read the manuscript *in toto* and commented extensively on it: Donald R. McCoy, Blake McKelvey and Walter Harding, as mentioned above; Stow Persons, Professor of History, University of Iowa; Marguerite J. Fisher, Professor Emeritus, Maxwell Graduate School of Citizenship And Public Affairs, Syracuse University; Robert Heussler, Professor of History, SUNY College at Geneseo; Alan Cywar, Assistant Professor of History, SUNY College at Geneseo; the Honorable James J. Wadsworth, the distinguished son of the subject of this biography; Porter Chandler, cousin of James W. Wadsworth and attorney of the New York City Bar. Reverdy Wadsworth, son of the Senator, read more than half of the manuscript prior to his untimely death. Other individuals read those parts of the manuscript which were related to their areas of expertise: Selig Adler, SUNY College at Buffalo, foreign policy specialist;

Robert Wesser, SUNY College at Albany, definitive historian of the Charles Evans Hughes governorship in New York; Ralph Adams Brown, SUNY College at Cortland, long the author's mentor; George Mazuzan, SUNY College at Geneseo, diplomatic historian and the author's office mate. Any errors in this manuscript, of course, are solely those of the author and in no way attributable to the scholars listed above.

I wish also to thank James Wadsworth's successor to New York's thirty-seventh Congressional District, Barber Conable, for permitting me to spend time with him in Washington, getting the feeling for the office.

Then there were those who did yeoman service in helping with the book. Mrs. Maxine Callan, who had typed the author's Gifford Pinchot manuscript, typed much of this biography in its early stages. Mrs. Joyce Parfitt, the author's secretary during the important final three years of the writing phase, was indispensable in both her editorial suggestions and her fine typing.

Much of the cost of the research and the manuscript was borne by several generous grants and fellowships awarded to the author by the Research Foundation of the State University of New York. It is a pleasure to pay tribute to the chancellor of the University and the Research Foundation for maintaining a faculty fellowship and grant-in-aid program which is unique in higher education in the United States. I also appreciate the aid extended by various members of Geneseo's administrative staff, particularly President Robert MacVittie, Arthur Hatton, Roger Smith, and Gordon Miller.

If anyone suffers when a book is being writtten, it is the author's family. If they did, they were always gracious and never complained. Frequently, the book's time was that of my wife, Daryl, and my children. As noted on the dedication page, the latter grew up with *The Gentleman From New York*.

Geneseo, New York   MARTIN L. FAUSOLD
Spring 1975

Introduction

REVERDY WADSWORTH, the younger son of James W. Wadsworth, Jr., suggested the subtitle of this book, *The Gentleman from New York,* for three reasons. First, his father was long addressed in the Congress of the United States as "the gentleman from New York." Second, Reverdy knew that his father was a gentle man. And third, in the generic sense of that word, James Wadsworth was a gentleman. Representative Helen Gahagan Douglas of California underscored the application of *gentleman* to Wadsworth. Reminiscing about his congressional days, she poignantly spoke of him as "a noble man," perhaps unaware of the dual meaning of that word—a high station and high quality of life.

Stow Persons, the historian of American gentility, correctly describes Wadsworth's life as combining political and gentry-elite qualities. A prominent political leader, the New Yorker possessed gentlemanly traits: virtue, a distinctive style and breeding, financial and personal security and self-reliance, republicanism, and an aversion to both ostentatiousness and aloofness from the crowd. Like his forebears in his class and in his family, James Wadsworth also was committed to aristocratic concepts of integrity, education, leisure, class, family, and military and public service. Whereas most recent forebears of his class succumbed to the crass materialism of the gilded age, and were shattered or absorbed by plutocrats and political elites, the Wadsworths remained both political and gentry-elites in an American aristocratic tradition.

Few American political leaders in the twentieth century possessed gentry qualities of James W. Wadsworth, Jr. Some few did, among them the Tafts of Ohio, Henry L. Stimson and Elihu Root of New York, and Gifford Pinchot of Pennsylvania. Some political figures, emanating from the post–Civil War plutocracy, intermingled with gentry-elites in the exclusive clubs and academies and in the twentieth century manifested near-gentry qualities, as in the case of Nelson Rockefeller and Averell Harriman of New York. Some possessed the aristocratic potential but lacked firm commitment to principle and became more political elites than gentry, as did Theodore Roosevelt and his cousin, Franklin. Others, such as the du Ponts of Deleware, possessed the heritage but became more economic than gentry-elites. But few political families were so consistently and for so long republican gentlemen in an American aristocratic tradition as the Wadsworths of New York. Strange as it may seem to Democrats who wearied of James Wadsworth's long life, he could probably trace a more direct lineage from their alleged patron saint, Thomas Jefferson, than could they.

The reader, of course, need not be reminded that there is no fixed aristocracy in America. The leaving of the canon and feudal law behind in Europe, the rigors of the American frontier, the coming of a polyglot immigration, and the rise of industrialism denied the nation a firm foundation for a ruling and a serving class. The nation did not hold still long enough to agree on tolerance, order, and authority. Today the scholarly literature on the American scene is almost totally devoid of any evidence of an aristocratic role in American politics. Yet, while gentry and aristocratic tenets are viewed as aberrations, as monuments to a genteel past, Americans have been, albeit only rarely, under the political influence of the gentry qualities of a James Wadsworth. Such political leaders, often possessing an education in the finest of America's academies, leisure time to pursue intellectual and philanthropic interests, an economic independence which precludes bribery, an influence premised on frequent interaction with decision-makers, a commitment to public service, and an integrity of long standing have counterbalanced and juxtaposed politicos who emerged in electoral politics with an unhealthy dependence on the interest group or the party machine.

Of Americans combining the qualities of gentry and the politically elite, none have served both halls of Congress for as long in the twentieth century as did James Wolcott Wadsworth, Jr. In a manner more intriguing than in fiction, as he approached the eve of his long legislative career, the egalitarian House of Representatives applauded him as its most valuable member.

The Wadsworth lineage of the Genesee Valley manifested in prototype the criteria for making the American aristocracy—a family which in two centuries of development was nurtured relatively undisturbed by frontier hazards and plutocratic urges. Four generations of Wadsworths watched over vast tracts of land in the Genesee Valley. The constant attention demanded by. landed wealth and its nonliquid form precluded precipitous investment in less stable and industrial property. Yet, each generation of Wadsworths, true to the classic aristocratic principle of service, fought in America's wars and stood for important public office, passing the torch of service to successive generations, including that of James W. Wadsworth, Jr.

Befitting his station, young Wadsworth's preparation for his life was in the exclusive private eastern institutions, Fay School, St. Mark's, and Yale, and at an early age, just out of Yale, the young landowner entered the race for the New York State Assembly, the first of some seventeen campaigns for public service. In each race and in each office, Wadsworth manifested the security and position of his class. True to it, however, he seldom sought to govern at the sacrifice of principle. Defeat in 1926, when he lost his United States Senate seat on the wet issue, was secondary to his commitment to the principle inherent in the repeal of prohibition. And nowhere was his adherence to principle more apparent than in his aristocratic concept of the state—a decentralized balancing by worthy leaders of democratic and plutocratic elements and always in accord with constitutional principle.

The aristocratic principles to which Wadsworth was born, and to which he adhered, were re-enforced by his conservative thought. Such thought reflected the ideas of prescription, the goodness of property, adherence to classical economics, the need for variety in the nation, the essentialness of harmony, and the organic nature of society. Coincidentally, the conservative tradition in America received its most shattering blows during Wadsworth's adolescence, the period of post–Civil War industrialism, and its most sympathetic reception during the latter years of his life, in the New Conservatism of the post-World War II period. Despite the ill-repute of conservatism during the interim, the New Yorker's was constant, particularly where conservative and aristocratic tenets converged in his life.

The convergence of aristocratic and conservative tenets, strikingly illustrated by a number of episodes in which Wadsworth was intimately involved over his long life, is the thread of this biography. Almost as if by design, the episodes appeared chronologically as tests, each building on the prior experience. In 1906, as the young man launched his important legislative career, he observed and learned from his father's fight against Theodore Roosevelt's Meat Inspection Act over a matter of constitutional principle. A consequence of the act, the creation of a regulatory state premised on the commerce clause of the Constitution, was too excessive for both father and son. Although frequently opposed to Charles Evans Hughes's progressive governorship, 1907–1910, Wadsworth, as Speaker of the Assembly, reacted with responsibility to the Governor's proposals—at a time when most Republican "bosslets" in the State were obstructionists. In 1910, the young James Wadsworth was involved in an important republican fight against Theodore Roosevelts' direct primary issue, a form of democratization which Wadsworth felt would make political parties less responsible. The struggle led directly to the national Republican split of 1912. In 1916, he, as Elihu Root's successor in the United States Senate, continued the rear-guard conservative defense against Woodrow Wilson's progressive programs. In 1919, Wadsworth, as a strong reservationist regarding the proposed League of Nations, defended the nation's sovereignty by deploring Article X of the League Covenant which might have committed the nation economically and militarily without the consent of Congress or the President. In 1920, James Wadsworth made his first important contribution to America's military preparedness as the author of the National Defense Act of that year. Throughout his life, military legislation would be his first concern. His co-authorship of the Conscription Act of 1940 was perhaps the high point of his congressional career. Commitment to principle, an important aristocratic tenet, has seldom been so dramatically illustrated in American political history as when James Wadsworth literally sacrificed his senate seat in 1926 by refusing to bow to the Republican demands that he hedge on the issue of prohibition. Wadsworth's view of the United States Constitution absolutely precluded negative and statist amendments such as the Eighteenth Amendment. Wadsworth's anti-statist role was most significantly played in his leadership of the American Liberty League of 1935 and 1936. As the only national Republican officeholder in its leadership, he exposed himself to intense public criticism by identifying with plutocrats like John J. Raskob and the duPonts, who obviously appeared more fearful of Roosevelt's anti-corporate efforts than the New Deals' adverse effects on the liberty of Americans. (Wadsworth, at times in his long political life, notably in 1935 and 1936, gave plutocrats undeserving credit when he found himself allied with them.) Above all, Wadsworth's political career was marked by his internationalism, a twentieth-century tenet adhered to by the cosmopolitans of the aristocracy, e.g., John Hay, Elihu Root, and Henry L. Stimson. Almost alone as a Republican in the Congress in the 1930s, Wadsworth saw and fought for America's salvation by early identification with the English in their struggle against Nazi Germany.

James W. Wadsworth, Jr., was indeed a gentleman and a conservative. Each characterization so complemented the other that both were accentuated. Yet his aristocratic bearing overshadowed the general view of his conservatism. Helen Gahagan Douglas saw Wadsworth's nobility. Former Congressman (and Senator) Kenneth Keating described for the author Wadsworth's integrity as the essential characteristic of his life. The liberal Keating stressed it to the total exclusion of the Geneseoan's conservatism. Carl Hallauer, chairman of the Board of Bausch & Lomb, Incorporated, who professed political intimacy with Richard Nixon, thought along the same lines and made the implausible suggestion to the future president that he pattern his political life after that of James Wadsworth.

Perhaps the quality of Wadsworth's political life was due to the nobility and integrity which attended its conservatism, no better illustrated than by the fact that the "Gentleman from New York" was viewed by Helen Gahagan Douglas and by Kenneth Keating in terms of the former, principles, and not the latter, ideology. The unique amalgam of the two manifestations is the focus of this biography.

JAMES W. WADSWORTH, Jr.

The Gentleman from New York

1

The Education of
James W. Wadsworth, Jr.

1

The family heritage of James W. Wadsworth, Jr., was steeped in the traditions of America. While other men might see the heritage as awesome or irrelevant, this scion—perhaps the family's most eminent —seemed to draw quietly from the experiences and lessons of his forebears.[1]

Wadsworth's ancestor, William Wadsworth, was, in 1634, among the first selectmen in the newly-founded Massachusetts Bay Colony, prior to accompanying the Reverend Thomas Hooker in the settlement of Connecticut. Fifty-one years later, William's sons, John and Joseph, were among those who confronted the King's representative, Sir Edmund Andros, Royal Governor of the Dominion of New England, when the crown attempted to revoke the charter and its attendant liberties. It is reported that John eloquently defended Connecticut's independence and that Sir Edmund deferred by noting that, "England has few better names . . . [and] no better soldiers than the Wadsworths."[2] Deference would dissuade neither the Wadsworth brothers nor their compatriots. According to tradition, Connecticut loyalists, fearing confiscation of the charter lying on the table before them, doused the lights while Joseph ran off with the great document, preserving it in the hollow of a tree, thereafter known as the Charter Oak.[3] Three decades later he was voted a sum of money for his deed.[4]

1. See partial Table of Descendants of William Wadsworth of Hartford, Appendix A.
2. W. H. Gocher, *Wadsworth of the Charter Oak* (Hartford, Conn.: W. H. Gocher, 1904), pp. 327–328.
3. *Ibid.*, pp. 333–337; Wayne Andrews, ed., *Concise Dictionary of American History* (New York: Charles Scribner's Sons, 1962), p. 233.
4. Henry Greenleaf Pearson, *James S. Wadsworth of Geneseo* (New York: Charles Scribner's Sons, 1913), p. 2.

Joseph Wadsworth had no children, but John had nine, two of whom produced particularly eminent families. One of the families gave the nation Colonel Jeremiah Wadsworth, Washington's Commissary General; the other, the ancestral line of James W. Wadsworth, Jr., immediately produced James Wadsworth of Durham, Connecticut, a graduate of Yale College, Class of 1748, and a major-general of the Connecticut line. Of Jeremiah Wadsworth, Washington said, "He has been indefatigable in his exertions to provide for the army, and since his appointment our supplies of provisions have been good and ample." [5] General James Wadsworth's most noted act was his opposition, in 1788, to the ratification of the proposed federal Constitution. He feared its consequence of centralization of power, a concern expressed by future generations of Wadsworths, but by none more impressively than by the subject of this biography in the twentieth century.

The families of Colonel Jeremiah and General James Wadsworth became inextricably intertwined in the 1790s. Very early in the decade, James, a nephew of the general and the son of John Noyes Wadsworth of Durham, visited Jeremiah at Hartford en route home from a year's teaching at Montreal. While there he was offered lands in western New York on which to settle. Colonel Wadsworth held a dominant interest in the Phelps and Gorham purchase which encompassed more than 2,000,000 acres of land bounded on the north and south by Lake Ontario and the Pennsylvania line, and on the east and west by longitudinal lines through Geneva and a point approximately fifteen miles west of Rochester. Jeremiah offered James, at a cost of eight cents per acre, 2,000 acres of choice land within his own purchase, "township number six in range seven," bordering on the Genesee River, an unusually rich territory. In return for Jeremiah's offer, James was to till the land, settle in the territory and serve as an agent for the sale of land in the Phelps-Gorham tract.[6]

James Wadsworth, more fitted for the sedentary life of teaching, business, or law, than the active life of the frontier, persuaded his older brother, William, to join him. It was fortunate that he did, for William proved to be a leader of pioneers, and nicely complemented James in the western settlement.

In early 1790 the brothers set out from Durham. Professor James Renwich of Columbia College has described the movement westward:

5. Worthington Ford, ed., *Writings of George Washington*, VII (Boston: G. P. Putnam's Sons, 1889, 1893), p. 141.

6. Alden Hatch, *The Wadsworths of the Genesee* (New York: Coward-McCann, Inc., 1959), Chapter III, *passim*; Pearson, *op. cit.*, Ch. I, *passim*; Lockwood Doty, *History of Livingston County, New York* (Jackson, Mich.: W. J. Van Deusen, 1905), pp. 227–230.

The brothers hired a small band of hardy axmen in Connecticut, purchased provisions to maintain them until the first crops should ripen, and provided agricultural implements sufficient for their proposed farm. The whole party, with its heavy incumbrances, ascended the Hudson to Albany, then often the voyage of a week; made the long portage through the pines to Schenectady; embarked in bateaux upon the Mohawk . . . and followed its tortuous course until they reached the limit of continuous settlement. Here cattle were purchased to serve as the foundation of a future stock and for temporary support, and the party was divided into two bands. James continued the laborious task of threading nameless streams, encumbered by wood-drifts and running in narrow channels, while William undertook the still more difficult duty of driving the stock through the pathless forest. Finally the party was again united upon a small savannah upon the bank of the Genesee. . . . A house having been built by the aid of no other implement than the ax, crops were planted and the cattle turned out to graze in the rich savannah. . . . With the autumn came the enervating and unmanning attacks of the ague. This, to the natives of a country where it was unknown, presented such terrors that the hired men broke the conditions of their engagement and hurried as they best could to the older settlements, leaving the two brothers almost if not quite alone in their log-built cabin. In this position even mere passiveness on the part of their neighbour Big Tree, the chief of the Indian village on the Genesee, immediately opposite to the settlement of the Wadsworths, might have compelled them to follow their servants; but they now obtained from him ready and efficient aid. . . . With the opening of a new spring, a fresh supply of white laborers was obtained, and whether they were acclimatized, or had been familiarized to the endemic disease, no further interruption occurred in the progress of the clearing.[7]

During the early 1790s William managed the farm—which meant largely the raising of stock—and James departed for New York and London, seeking buyers for the great tract. James was only moderately successful in executing sales in London, although his stay there confirmed in him the worth of a well-ordered and plentiful life. The large English estates had great appeal and upon his return to Big Tree, shortly to be called Geneseo, he would emulate them.

For a helpmate in establishing his large estate James took a bride, Naomi Wolcott, a cousin of Oliver Wolcott, who had been Secretary of the Treasury in Washington's administration. William remained a bachelor to the end of his days.

The Wadsworth brothers fared well by raising cattle, growing grain,

7. Pearson, *op. cit.*, pp. 8–10.

buying land—always buying land. The affluence of living was never permitted to curb the purchase of additional land; so extensive were their holdings that, reportedly, the brothers could ride from Geneseo to Rochester on their own land, a distance of twenty-eight miles. Yet life in Geneseo was bountiful. A Spanish traveller described it as follows:

Genesee [sic] August 4 [1835]. We left Avon yesterday at one-thirty, bound for this town, where I was brought by the desire of becoming acquainted with some of the large farming and stock-raising estates of this region, with which object my friend D. Leonardo Santo Suarez had furnished me in New York a letter of introduction to Mr. Wadsworth, a rich proprietor of this place. The trip was one of the most agreeable which I made, because of the beauty and the variety of the views which were enjoyed. Extensive and luxurious pasture-fields covered with herds, leafy woods, placid flower gardens, fields of golden wheat, recreation country estates [i.e., the country homes of persons who made their living in the city], whose white and yellow houses stand out against the green of the countryside, and in the distance a horizon of columns of smoke resulting from the burning-off of the hills, signs of the progress of the people and precursors of cultivation. Such is the picture which the delightful Genesee Valley offers, seen from the height which dominates the town.

After dining, I went to the residence of Mr. Wadsworth, who was not found in it, but his son Mr. Williams [William] was, who told me with great amiability and courtesy: "My father, who has been expecting you for some days, should not be long in returning from his walk with my sister Elizabeth." Scarcely had he pronounced these words when the father and his daughter appeared and gave me the most cordial welcome. Mr. Wadsworth is an elderly gentleman of notable and venerable appearance, whose goodness of character reveals itself at the first glance. His daughter, young and beautiful, seems the image of sweetness and candor. As soon as she learned that my wife was accompanying me, she asked to be excused to change her clothing and to go out to look for her. . . .

Returning to his house and during the evening, we entertained each other with various conversations, which the father sustained with his knowledge of matters agricultural, and the daughter with her varied information. Among her distractions in the solitude of the country, which they live in during the summer, one is the making of an herbarium of beautiful plants. She speaks French very well, and the store of angelic goodness of her soul and the tender love which she professes for her father —sweet compensation for the wife whom he has lost!—contribute to making more interesting her conversation.[8]

8. "Part I—Foreign Travelers' Notes on Rochester and the Genesee Country before 1840," The Rochester Historical Society Publications, XVIII (Rochester, N.Y.: The Rochester Historical Society, 1940), pp. 111–112.

The fulfillment of life to James lay not only in farming, the buying of land, and living in a great house. He read considerably and concerned himself with the education of his neighbors. He established a high school for six hundred students, importing three young Harvard scholars as teachers, one of whom, Cornelius C. Felton, later became president of Harvard. Although he was the institution's guiding force, James Wadsworth kept to the background as he did in political matters, where he was very active behind the scenes with Whig leaders William H. Seward and Thurlow Weed.

Five children were born to James and Naomi Wadsworth—Harriet, James Samuel, William Wolcott, Cornelia and Elizabeth. While James Samuel, the grandfather of J. W. Wadsworth, Jr., is of particular interest, his brother and sisters warrant comment. William W. Wadsworth settled in his father's house, the Homestead, a great white clapboard place of Greek style, south of the village of Geneseo. The many-gabled mansion, clearly visible to the south and west, would mark the center of the famous valley fox hunts. In 1852, at forty-two years of age, William W. Wadsworth sustained a fatal fall on the ice, leaving at the Homestead his wife, Emmeline Austin, and one son, William Austin. William Austin became heir to the Homestead. His grandson is today the head of the rambling home.

Cornelia Wadsworth, James Wadsworth's eldest daughter, died in 1831 at nineteen years of age, to be followed by her sister Harriet two years later. Elizabeth, the remaining sister, cared for her father until his death in 1844. She later married an Englishman, Charles Murray. Her father's anti-British prejudice had prevented the marriage prior to his death. Elizabeth at first refused Charles Murray's hand after her father's death, fearing that he was only being chivalrous. By chance they met six years later and were married "within a week." Tragically, she died a year later with the birth of her first child.

By 1852, of the brothers and sisters, only James Samuel survived. James had attended Harvard College without graduating, and afterward "read law" in the office of Daniel Webster. In 1829–30 he studied at Yale Law School and was admitted to the bar in 1833. In the following year he married Mary Craig Wharton, of the Quaker merchant family of Philadelphia. Befitting a young man of his family station, James and his bride honeymooned in Europe.

In Europe the newlyweds were welcomed into the great mansions of England and France. Like his father, James S. loved the large estates and the style of life they epitomized. He was so taken by Lord Hertford's villa in Regent's Park that exact plans were procured for a like structure to be built in the Genesee Valley in 1835. Hartford House, as it came to be called, commanded a view of the valley from north of the village. The widow of Reverdy Wadsworth, a great-grandson of James S. Wadsworth, currently presides over the great house.

James S. Wadsworth, while engaging mostly in farming, distinguished himself in the political and military affairs of his state and his nation. Although his father was a committed Whig, James S. was a Democrat, a radical Democrat and a close associate of "Prince John" VanBuren, the son of the former president. Radical Democrats were ardent opponents of the extension of slavery. Conservative Democrats supported their southern brethren on the slave question and in New York were called Hunkers because they hankered after public office. The radicals became so enraged by the Hunker position and arrogance that, like the farmer burning his barn to be rid of the rat plague, they were willing to destroy the Democratic party to be rid of the Hunkers. Thus James S. Wadsworth became a Barnburner, and with his radical colleagues, seceded from the Democratic party on the issue of slavery.

When the New York radicals arrived at the national Democratic convention in the summer of 1848, half of their number was admitted, including Wadsworth. The rest of the delegates from New York accepted by the national convention were, of course, Hunkers. But Barnburner representation in the convention could not prevent the nomination of a slavery advocate, whereupon Wadsworth and associates departed and convened in New York a separate state convention which nominated Martin VanBuren.

In the late summer of 1848 other New York groups assembled in Buffalo to endorse VanBuren's candidacy. Such a diverse grouping—Free Soilers, Conscience Whigs, Barnburners and Liberty men—united on the motto: "Free soil, free speech, free labor, and free men." Similar assemblages in other states endorsed VanBuren. As a consequence of the Free Soil effort—the splitting of the Democratic ticket—Americans turned their backs on the Democratic candidate, Lewis Cass, and elected the Whig candidate, Zachary Taylor, to the presidency.

With the defeat of Cass, Wadsworth and his friends hoped to make over the Democratic party as one of protest against the institution of slavery. They achieved some success, at least in New York. The New York Democrats in their 1855 state convention condemned pro-slavery excesses in Kansas. But in 1856, the southern Democrats dominated the national convention and nominated for the presidency one of their persuasion, James Buchanan.

On July 24, 1856, at Syracuse, New York, Wadsworth presided at a state Democratic-Republican convention. There Wadsworth declared that "one of the corner-stones of the Democracy of New York, a stone of Jefferson granite [was] opposition to the extension of slavery." [9] Such, he noted, had been well established by the VanBuren Free Soil race in New York in 1848. The convention supported the candidate of the "new" national Republican party, J. C. Fremont.

By 1860 James S. Wadsworth and many anti-slavery Democrats were Republicans but with questionable commitment. It was not easy for former Democratic leaders, like Wadsworth, and former Whig leaders, like Thurlow Weed, to harmonize, particularly on Weed's ambition to put the former Whig, William H. Seward, into the presidency. At the national convention in Chicago Wadsworth circulated letters among delegates from various states opposing the Seward nomination. Largely due to New York opposition, such as Wadsworth's, Seward was not nominated. Instead, the convention chose Abraham Lincoln. In November he was elected.

In April 1861, war broke out between the North and the South, but not to Wadsworth's surprise. He had seen the futility of the peace attempt as a delegate to the Virginia Peace Convention in February. Shortly after the President's declaration of war, Wadsworth was asked by Governor Morgan of New York to serve as a major general of volunteers. The Geneseo patrician pleaded lack of qualification and instead asked for assignment to the staff of General Irwin McDowell, the commander of the Union Army of Virginia. There Wadsworth served competently until given field command of the First New York Brigade in August, 1861, with the rank of brigadier general. In March of the following year he was appointed military governor of Washington by the President. In the fall of the same year Wadsworth acceded to Republican overtures to run for the governorship of New York. Although his election against the Democratic candidate, Horatio Seymour, was expected, the criticism of the national war effort in 1862 brought defeat. Wadsworth returned to the field.

On December 22, 1862, Wadsworth succeeded General A. Doubleday as commander of the I Division of the I Corps. Having just suffered defeat at Fredericksburg, Wadsworth's division wintered at Belle Plain, near the Potomac, and in the spring moved south to join General Hooker at Chancellorsville. Union defeat there came without engagement by Wadsworth's two brigades, which General Hooker never committed.

9. Pearson, *op. cit.*, p. 45. Also, see pp. 35–54 for general discussion of James S. Wadsworth's political activity.

By early summer, the I Corps, to which Wadsworth's division belonged, moved north to cover Washington while Lee marched up the Shenandoah Valley to invade the North. As Lee moved through southern Pennsylvania, the I Corps, with the II, XI and XII Corps, rushed north from Washington to meet him. On July 1, 1863, Wadsworth's I Division arrived in Gettysburg only after General Buford, with two brigades of Union cavalry, contacted the enemy arriving from Chambersburg. As battle lines formed west of the village, Wadsworth's division relieved General Buford's brigade on Seminary Ridge, "meeting Heth's attack with a furious counterattack which wrecked the latter's two leading brigades." [10] By evening the Union forces fell east and south of the village, taking a position on Seminary Ridge. Wadsworth's division of two brigades, half decimated by the day's fighting, took up a position on Culp's Hill, northeast of the ridge. There his division stood for the two remaining days of the battle, until defeat came to Lee's forces late in the afternoon of July 3.

After Gettysburg, President Lincoln sent Wadsworth to the Mississippi Valley to check on the arrangements for the care and recruitment of the freed slaves. Between journeys into the southland Wadsworth made a last trip home to Washington, D.C. His son, James Wolcott Wadsworth, subsequently described the moving event for the *Rochester Museum Bulletin*:

Those were the days when every boy and girl had to have a "finished" education. The finish consisted of mainly learning to speak French and to dance and acquire certain graces and conduct. Everyone was military minded. Our boys' school was disciplined like a junior West Point.

Ordinarily I went home every night, but on that particular day, I had failed to study my French lesson and as a punishment I was ordered to remain at school overnight. I knew that my beloved father was coming home for that one day, so I sneaked out and went home.

When I reached our brownstone house, he was there in all the splendor of his blue uniform with his medals on his breast and the golden stars of a major general on his shoulder straps. He was the most magnificent sight I had ever seen.

We talked together happily for a while, and then Father began to question me about school. He soon sensed that something was wrong. When he asked me directly I told him the story. He got to his feet and so did I, both of us stiffly at attention. My father asked, "What is the first duty of a soldier?"

10. Col. Vincent J. Esposito, *The West Point Atlas of American Wars*, I, *1689–1900* (New York: Frederick A. Praeger, 1959), Map 96: The Civil War.

Saluting I replied, "Sir, the first duty of a soldier is to obey."

Then my magnificent father burst into tears and so did I. Weeping, we kissed each other. Then I went back to school. I never saw my father again.[11]

In the spring of 1864 Wadsworth again requested field duty and was given command of his old division, designated as the Fourth Division of the First Corps. General U. S. Grant now commanded the Union armies and pursued Lee into southern Virginia. There, at the Battle of the Wilderness, Wadsworth's brigades broke through two lines of Confederate battle but soon were overwhelmed.

After two days of interminable fighting, a fatal shot felled the division's commander as he desperately directed a withdrawal of his troops from the Confederate pocket. A Confederate officer described these last moments:

Near the edge of the woods I saw stretched under the shade of the bushes, which had been raised over him, Major General Wadsworth of the Federal Army, who commanded a Division in the battle. A ball had penetrated his brain and he was insensible. He was a fine looking, portly man, about sixty years old, bald and gray. Our men had gone through him before his rank was discovered by our officers, who would have prevented it. His hat and boots were gone and every button cut off his coat. I heard afterwards that the Sixth Regiment boys, Mahone's Brigade, in whose front he must have fallen, had ministered on his effects very summarily. Bob Archer, of Company G, got his pocketbook with ninety dollars in greenbacks; some one got his elegant field glasses; another got his silver spurs and John Belote, of Norfolk, got his gold watch. Belote told me that after the War he sent the watch to Mrs. Wadsworth, who made him a very handsome acknowledgment of it. General Wadsworth was, I believe, a prominent man in the State of New York and possessed of great wealth. As soon as his rank was known he was sent to our Brigade Hospital. (Mahone's Brigade, A, N. Va.) I saw him next when he was still alive, but insensible. He was lying in a tent to himself and received the attention of our surgeons and nurses which was due his rank. He lingered until the afternoon, when he died, and his body was sent through the lines under a flag of truce.[12]

11. Hatch, op. cit., pp. 93–94.

12. Westwood A. Todd, Reminiscences of Westwood A. Todd (written in 1880–1886), Wadsworth MSS, Library of Congress, Washington, D.C.

Colonel Jeremiah Wadsworth,
1743–1804.

General William Wadsworth,
1761–1833.

James Wadsworth, 1768–1844.

General James S. Wadsworth,
1807–1864.

2

Aside from his widow, now the mistress of Hartford House, the general, at his death, left two sons in the Union's service, one in boarding school, and two daughters, one of whom was married to a Union officer. Charles, the eldest son, had been educated at the École des Mines in the *Quartier Latin* in Paris, and later served as a captain in the One Hundred Sixteenth New York Volunteers, participating in the siege of Port Hudson in Louisiana. Cornelia, the elder daughter, had married Montgomery Ritchie of Boston, who also participated in the siege of Port Hudson, as aide-de-camp to a division commander. Craig Wharton Wadsworth, the general's second son, served variously as aide to the First Corps commander, Major General J. F. Reynolds; to his father at Gettysburg; and, in the latter months of the war, to a division commander in the Cold Harbor campaign, Brigadier-General A. T. A. Tarbert. James Wolcott Wadsworth, General Wadsworth's youngest son, a student at the Hopkins Grammar School in Massachusetts at the time of his father's death, volunteered for service and was appointed an aide on the staff of Major General G. K. Warren whom he served as a captain until the end of the war. Elizabeth remained in Hartford House with her mother.[13]

Because James Wolcott Wadsworth became the father of the subject of this biography, he is of particular interest to the reader. Following his honorable discharge as a brevet major, young Wadsworth tutored at Yale College, in the Class of '68. There he roomed in Old South Middle and was elected to Delta Kappa Epsilon and Book and Snake, a scientific society. After Yale—he did not graduate—the young Civil War veteran went west where he joined archeologists in digging for bones, accompanied a United States Cavalry unit chasing Indians, and became a close friend of Buffalo Bill Cody. (In subsequent years when Buffalo Bill brought his Wild West Show to Rochester, Wadsworth rode the "Deadwood Coach.") When in 1872 "Jimmy's" mother died, she left him Hartford House and 8,000 acres of the valley's richest land. (Charles had "taken to liquor," and Craig was in ill health.) Shortly after settling into the big house, the young master took a bride—Marie Louisa Travers, of New York City. Miss Travers was the daughter of William R. Travers, a Wall Street tycoon, and a granddaughter of Reverdy Johnson, a former attorney general of the United States.

13. Pearson, *op. cit.*, Ch. III–Ch. IX, *passim.*

In the tradition of his father and grandfather, James Wolcott Wadsworth became interested in public affairs. In 1878 he was elected to the New York State Assembly and served two terms before being elected comptroller. Following a brief tenure in that office, he was elected to the national House of Representatives where he served two terms before being gerrymandered out of office. Shortly thereafter the former congressman was re-elected and, in 1896, became chairman of the House Committee on Agriculture. From that powerful position—the nation was very much agrarian then—the New Yorker ruled conservatively, frequently siding with large economic interests. For ten years his conservatism prevailed until he opposed the meat inspection legislation of the progressive president, Theodore Roosevelt.[14]

James W. Wadsworth, known in the Genesee Valley as the "Boss," never sacrificed his role as farmer—for all of his winters in Albany and Washington where he enjoyed prominent political and social success. On the contrary, he built considerably on the 8,000-acre inheritance. In addition, he relied far less heavily than his father had on tenant farmers, personally overseeing the operations of most of his farms.

> All the long summer days he would be riding through the fields on his gaited saddle horse, his white suit as crisp as though freshly laundered, his tiny boots mirror-bright, overseeing the work; judging the weight of steers with an expert eye; mentally selecting which lambs to slaughter and which to keep to strengthen the flock; poking into the dairy barns to make sure the straw was fresh and the milk cleanly handled; appraising the wheat and corn, the young peas, beans and sweet corn for the canning factories which sprang up around Geneseo, Avon, and Mount Morris, making suggestions, giving orders, planning repairs and improvements.[15]

3

James Wolcott Wadsworth, Jr., was born at Hartford House on August 12, 1877, after two days of his mother's traumatic labor. The family

14. Hatch, op. cit., Ch. VII; J. W. Wadsworth, Jr., Autobiography (unpublished), pp. 7–11, Wadsworth MSS.; J. W. Wadsworth, Jr., The Reminiscences of James W. Wadsworth, Jr. (Columbia University, Oral History Research Office, 1952), Ch. I.

15. Hatch, op. cit., p. 105.

would be grateful henceforth to young Doctor Walter F. Lauderdale for saving mother and son.

The newly arrived James Wadsworth, the sixth generation of that given name, was born with a "silver spoon" in his mouth. He was to enjoy the comforts of his legacy. Yet, during his son's youth, the Boss seemed to compensate, almost purposely, for the boy's favored position. He did so in a variety of ways. For all the elegance of Hartford House there was little ostentation—"no solemn butler, no uniformed secondman, no liveried coachman—'just three maids.'" And the Boss saw to it that young James, like himself and his forebears got close to the soil. At six years of age he was given his own horse to groom and care for, and not many years later, Herb Hanby, an employee, furthered Jim's education—"Harnessing work-horses, greasing axles, mowing, cocking up or bunching hay, pitching on, loading the wagon, pitching off, moving away or stacking." And what can be more leveling than manure? Jim learned at first hand its origin and that it went back on the land as the best of all fertilizers. (It was little wonder that in future years his farmer constituents would recall how easily their congressman tramped around barnyards.) And Herb Hanby could put the young heir straight: "Hey boy!" he would shout, "drive those staples so they'll straddle the grain. Then they won't pull out easy!"

When Jim arrived at sixteen years of age, the Boss put him on one of his largest farms, The Street farm. For two and one-half months it was "up at five-thirty, do the chores, breakfast at six-thirty and out in the fields shortly after seven o'clock, one hour for dinner, back to work, lay off at six p.m., and then supper, and a good one. In bed by nine o'clock." [16]

The education of James W. Wadsworth was rooted not only in the soil. Indeed, it included playing with village kids, placing coins on railroad tracks, shooting arrows into tin roofs, and great family picnics on Conesus Lake. It meant learning early in life the game of baseball. His father, a baseball "crank," spent hours instructing Jim on how to cup his hand properly and pull it back on the ball's impact. Education also included reading, first *The Boys of '61* and other books by Charles Coffin, and still more books, particularly about American history. And, of course, education encompassed riding to the hounds and racing, although his sister, Harriet, four years younger, soon surpassed him in that quarter; she became a superb rider. Jim's education required going to Sunday School and the Episcopalian church, although the religious convictions of the family were not "strictly denominational." For much of this educa-

16. Wadsworth, Jr., *Autobiography*, pp. 15–19.

tion in his youth, James Wadsworth was eternally grateful to his father—
a gratitude at times not felt because of the firmness by which his father
directed his son. Yet the son, with true affection, called his father the
Boss. This is not to say that his mother's role in his life was of little
consequence. Her warmth and wit were always cherished. And within
the confines of Hartford House, she was the boss.[17]

Formal schooling, of course, comprised an important part of the
education of James Wadsworth, although it is questionable whether the
impact of its formal instruction surpassed the influence of his parents.
Parental influence in the case of James Wadsworth was unusual, particularly in view of his early attendance at boarding school, requiring a
separation by five hundred miles, commencing when he was eleven.

Two years of village schooling was making Jim tough, so his mother
thought.[18] Then, too, he seemed to be taking on a village twang.[19] So,
in the autumn of 1887, the Boss and Louisa took him to Fay School, in
Southborough, Massachusetts, the nation's oldest elementary boarding
school. Episcopalian in form, Fay School was founded by two sisters
who were first cousins of the founder of St. Mark's, a Southborough
secondary boarding school which young Wadsworth would also attend.
Then, as now, Fay School was comfortable, its pupils made up of the
children of wealthy Americans. Its way of life has changed little in a
century, emphasizing "the good manners of unobtrusive gentlemanliness
toward one's fellows as a preparation for adult living." Manners and
behaving like "young Christian gentlemen should" seemed to surpass
intellectual pursuit at Fay.[20] Jim remembered little about his two years
at Fay School except that his roommate there was Frederic Kernochan.
The two also roomed together for five years at St. Mark's and four years
at Yale.

Wadsworth and Kernochan were in the Class of 1894 at St. Mark's.
There the values inculcated were much like those at Fay. Jim remembered
particularly how the headmaster, Mr. William E. Peck, instilled integrity
"into youngsters—not perfection of performance so much as integrity of
motive and conduct." [21] Although an indifferent scholar—of forty honor
bulletins he was never on one—Jim did deliver the traditional year's end

17. See footnote 14, *passim.*

18. Hatch, *op. cit.,* p. 131.

19. Conversation with Harriet Wadsworth Harper, The Plains, Virginia,
summer 1967.

20. *Fay School Catalog,* 1968–69, p. 1.

21. Wadsworth, Jr., *Reminiscences,* p. 18.

"cart speech" which the *Vindex* described as "very amusing." He was best remembered for his playing first base on the baseball team. Then Jim and Fred Kernochan were Yale bound.

The college town of old New Haven was "beautiful and decorous." A fellow Yaleman reports that "the elm-shaded streets . . . were lined by sedate houses which in various modes still kept the impress of the Greek revival of the early nineteenth century," [22] only to be occasionally broken by great brick mansions of the eighties or the shuttered homes of the colonial day. Old New Haven, the heart of the city, however, impressed the new Eli less than the sight of the College Green. Despite rather decrepit halls of Gothic and Byzantine style, freshmen, crossing the Green, were moved by the simple colonial brick structures. That they were as old as Yale was not lost on the entering students. Perhaps young Wadsworth saw there shades of that far earlier day when his forebear of early Connecticut fame, General James Wadsworth, crossed the same Green a century and a half previously.

About 350 young men from across the nation marched with Wadsworth and Fred Kernochan to a torch-lite meeting where freshmen mingled with "Strong Silent Men" and the "Big Men" of Yale, the athletes and the powers behind college life.[23] Not a few of those assembled classmates were the beneficiaries of great trusts—oil, steel, and lumber. Practically all by "birth and breeding" were elite young Americans. Such station was reflected by Wadsworth's particular circle of fellow Eli—Frederic Kernochan, who roomed with Jim for four years at 12 Vanderbilt Hall, Gouverneur Morris, Jr., James Otis Rodgers, Isaac Newton Swift, Robert James Turnbell, Jr., J. H. Scranton, R. T. Garrison, Adelbert S. Hay and Payne Whitney. Whitney and Wadsworth were to marry sisters of young Hay, the son of the eminent Secretary of State, John Hay.

Wadsworth's life as a freshman at Yale hardly differed from that of others. Undoubtedly, he too enjoyed the "breakaway from the moral platitudes and conventional discipline of boarding school." [24] He too, on a Thursday or Saturday night, sat at the long table "with steins and pretzels," singing about the Richard Peck, a ship of great fame which ran nightly from New Haven to New York. The hour was 11:00 p.m., a time when steins of beer made Yalemen neither drunk nor sober. Choruses rang across the table. Wadsworth sang bass:

22. Henry Seidel Canby, *Alma Mater, The Gothic Age of the American College* (New York: Farrar and Rinehart, 1936), p. 5.

23. *Ibid.*, p. 26.

24. *Ibid.*, p. 32.

> I will tell you of a little scheme I've got
> And I hope sirs, that you will refuse it not,
> To go down upon the Richard Peck tonight,
> And have fun aplenty in the moo-oon light.

And from the other side:

> We accept your generous invitation
> Since having pleasure is our occupation.
> We will meet you on the dock at twelve o'clock
> And to get the dough we'll put our watch and chain in hock.[25]

Sophomores hazed Wadsworth as they did others. His requirement was to hail a street car on Chapel Street, rest his foot on a lower step, tie his shoe, tip his hat to the conductor, and walk away. More constructively, the young New Yorker played freshman baseball and sang first bass in the freshman Glee Club. Both activities were more engaging than the freshman curriculum. Of the required fare, Jim cared little for mathematics, literature, and languages but liked history.[26]

In the fall of 1895 Wadsworth returned to Vanderbilt Hall, to lounge "whole evenings through under the wisteria blooms that swung inward over our window seat," to tell of summer adventures.[27] In Jim's case it was of summer baseball in Geneseo and of how his father imported college varsity men to put the village on the baseball map.

The sophomore year went well for Wadsworth until scarlet fever struck in mid-winter. Young Jim barely made Hartford House. He arrived with a fever of 105° after an all-night journey on the Lackawanna Railroad. During his long convalescence his mother read Nicolay and Hay's great biography of Abraham Lincoln to him. Upon his return to New Haven, only the tutoring of Jim Moore, a Genesee Valley farmer's son of modest means, saved Wadsworth his sophomore status.

What strength Jim lacked by the summer of 1896 was restored by farm labors and more baseball in Geneseo. Now the Boss looked for a professional to run the village team. The Brooklyn Robins released Billy Earle, a drug addict, to captain the Geneseo nine. Although Earle failed to jell the team, he did discover that Jim's "shy foot" disappeared when he batted left handed. Yale was to gain an All-American.[28]

25. *Ibid.*, pp. 31–32.

26. Wadsworth, Jr., *Autobiography*, pp. 22–23.

27. Canby, *op. cit.*, p. 35.

28. Wadsworth, Jr., *Autobiography*, p. 27; conversation with Reverdy Wadsworth, summer 1968.

The young Eli of Wadsworth's class remembered best the visit of William Jennings Bryan in the fall of 1896. Throughout the presidential campaign, the Democratic candidate had nailed the rich to his "cross of gold" and certainly New Haven was to be no exception. But only "the dull adult population" was stirred. Not Yalemen. When the Great Commoner boomed out that "ninety-nine out of a hundred of the students in this University are the sons of the idle rich," the same sons took up the cheer "Ninety-nine! Nine-nine-ninety-nine." Henry Coffin, standing next to Wadsworth, loudly pleaded his father's honesty. The Eli picked up the cheer again. "Ninety-nine! Nine-nine-ninety-nine." In the sway of exuberance, down came the speaker's platform, the Great Commoner and all. Years later, Bryan remembered the incident well. He could not be persuaded that it was the style of college life and "not the bias of the idle rich which drowned his speech in mirth and yelling." Wadsworth did feel a second cheer should have been omitted.[29]

All was not mirth at Yale. While Wadsworth, as a typical Yaleman, hardly expected a distinguished academic record, he did appreciate the great men on the Yale faculty. William Graham Sumner, the father of American sociology, made an indelible impression on him. Jim would never forget his lecture on the "Forgotten Man," probably because he so wholeheartedly agreed. Unlike Franklin Roosevelt's "Forgotten Man" of another age, the ill-fed and ill-clothed, Sumner's was "honest, industrious and thrifty, who married, built himself a modest home, raised a family, paid his taxes, took part modestly in public or semi-public activities, and demanded nothing from society save freedom." Wadsworth would always prefer Sumner's "Forgotten Man" to that of Franklin Roosevelt. Only once did the great sociologist have to call Jim to task. "This class will begin, Mr. Wadsworth," chided Professor Sumner to the back row student, "when you have completed reading the morning paper."[30] Others on the faculty who impressed Jim were Billy Phelps, a young assistant professor of English, and Arthur Hadley, the economist who became one of Yale's great presidents. History, however, was Wadsworth's forte. He took every course available when electives were plentiful in his junior and senior years. The high point of Jim's junior year, however, was not a history course nor a course from Professor Sumner, Phelps or Hadley. It was his election to Skull and Bones, a prestigious club, one of the three "holy of holies."

As well as Skull and Bones, Wadsworth made Walter Camp's All-

29. Wadsworth, Jr., *Autobiography*, pp. 27–30; Canby, *op. cit.*, pp. 27–28.
30. Wadsworth, Jr., *Autobiography*, pp. 34–37.

American baseball team in his senior year. The Boss had contributed to that. During Jim's third summer at Yale, the Boss brought to Geneseo college baseball greats from Cornell, Wesleyan, Princeton, Brown, Dartmouth and Lafayette. The Geneseo Collegians gained something of a national reputation, playing in such distant places as Canada, Atlantic City, and Chicago. With that experience Wadsworth led the Yale team in fielding and was second in batting. In one three-game series he earned ten hits.

Jim Wadsworth's academic achievements were less illustrious. He barely squeaked through his senior examinations. Yet he epitomized the best of the Eli. He was one of the "Big Men"—athlete and clubman; he also sang first bass in the university Glee Club. Graduation day was all the sweeter because his alma mater chose to give his father, congressman and patron of Yale baseball, an honorary master's degree on the same day.

Wadsworth's college life was much like that of fellow student Henry S. Canby of the next year's class, who years later wrote of his Yale experience: "It was like a vigorous kick of a football, too high, too aimless, into a drift of adverse winds. Yet that kick, if it was not like the shot at Concord Bridge, heard round the world, was felt throughout America. Behind it was the college spirit—naïve intellectually but emotionally vigorous, the still youthful soul of the last great age of romantic individualism." [31]

5

True to family tradition, Wadsworths answered the call to the colors upon the President's declaration of war against Spain on April 4, 1898. Austin Wadsworth left the Homestead to serve in the Quartermaster Corps. First cousin Craig Wharton Wadsworth became a cavalryman and charged up San Juan Hill with Roosevelt's Rough Riders. The Boss also served. President McKinley sent him on a special mission to Cuba. There he sat under the "Surrender Tree" at Santiago with old General Wheeler, "listening to the discussion of the surrender terms with the Spanish General." [32] Jim, however, was admonished by his father to finish both college and his Yale baseball career. He did, and then rushed home to announce his enlistment, only to find his father not there. Unaware that

31. Canby, op. cit., p. 55; Wadsworth, Jr., Reminiscences, p. 23.
32. Wadsworth, Jr., Autobiography, p. 43.

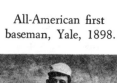

All-American first
baseman, Yale, 1898.

At St. Mark's School, 1893. Jim, fourth from left,
front row; Fred Kernochan, sixth from left, front row.
By permission of the Library of Congress.

Private Wadsworth, 1898. *By
permission of the Library of
Congress.*

Father and son at Hartford House,
about 1898.

the Boss was in Cuba, Wadsworth hurried down to Newport News, Virginia, to join Battery A, Pennsylvania Field Artillery-Volunteers. Fred Kernochan and two other classmates had already enlisted and called him to join. "Socially," Wadsworth recalled a half-century later, "the outfit was elite, intellectually excellent, physically superb." [33] Ninety percent were college graduates and many were college athletes. Most were over six feet tall.

After several weeks of close order drill and some training as "driver of the swingteam of the guns of the fourth section," Jim and the battery were assigned to General Nelson Miles's expedition to Puerto Rico, but not without misgivings. Young Wadsworth sensed that "something was wrong, something lacking:" [34] there had been no orderly recruitment of the battery; there had been no sound basic training. His misgivings portended a lifetime concern about military policy.

The Pennsylvania Field Artillery-Volunteers were joined on the transport by troops from Brooklyn and Harrisburg, a detachment from two Kentucky infantry regiments, and 800 horses and mules. The trip was uneventful until at Ponce, Puerto Rico, the ship hit a sand bar. On the third day of the struggle to free her, Wadsworth stood on the deck watching a small boat put off from a nearby cruiser. As the boat approached the transport, Jim made out two people in the stern—one a navy captain, the other a civilian. There sat the Boss. Jim later reported in his memoirs that the President had sent the congressman on another mission. It is not unlikely, however, that the Boss was in Puerto Rico because his son was there.

With the transport finally dislodged, the Boss returned to the cruiser and Jim's battery moved into the hills beyond the city. There the battery camped in A tents through the sizzling hot and wet summer, without fresh meat and vegetables, but with large quantities of flies. Still, the battery did have coffee, hardtack bread, canned meat and vegetables. And fortunately, they avoided yellow fever.

The hill on which Wadsworth's battery camped reverberated with no shots; the island was secured without their services. Only talk filled the air. There, for example, Jim listened to an infantryman, Lieutenant Oswald Latrobe, describe Frederic Funston who served the Cuban insurrectionists by blowing up a Spanish block-house and becoming Chief of Artillery of the Army of Cuba Libre. Wadsworth was to meet both again, Funston in the Philippine Islands as the heroic leader of the Twentieth Kansas Division and Latrobe as President Coolidge's military aid.

33. *Ibid.*, p. 44.
34. *Ibid.*, p. 45.

With the end of "the splendid little war" by August, the Pennsylvania Volunteers headed for New York, leaving ammunition and horses behind. En route to New York, Jim ate more than his share of some fresh meat and fell seriously ill. As the transport approached the Narrows outside of New York, the port's health officer, Dr. Alvah Doty, formerly of Geneseo, and the Boss boarded the ship, took Jim in hand and rushed him to Geneseo. There he regained his health sufficiently to join his battery in a great Peace Jubilee Parade in Philadelphia, prior to his discharge from service. In later years he would have the distinction of being the only member of Congress "who, having enlisted in the U.S. Army as a private came out a private."

By January of 1899 the Boss and three highly-placed Republicans in the nation's capitol—Secretary of State John Hay, Senator Eugene Hale of Maine, and Congressman John Dalzell of Pennsylvania—had "pressured" the War Department into giving their sons a trip around the world. Jim, in his autobiography, pleads "guilty to being the beneficiary—a very real beneficiary—of 'influence.'" [35] He, Del Hay, Bill Hale and Sam Dalzell accompanied the Third Regular Infantry Division and a battalion of Seventeenth Regulars being sent on to the Philippines to relieve volunteers.

On February 2, 1899, the USS Sherman, with sister transports, the *Grant* and the *Sheridan*, sailed from New York for Manila by way of the Mediterranean, the Red Sea, and the Indian Ocean. Just at a time when calm waters at port calls were being appreciated after the stormy Atlantic crossing, word was received at Gibraltar that the Philippine leader, Aguinaldo, had begun his insurrection. The ships hurriedly prepared to get under way. Shore liberties were cut short, but not before Del Hay employed diplomatic finesse in rescuing from Spain three hundred American soldiers who had wandered from Gibraltar into the enemy country. So tense did the situation of American troops in Spain become that only a civilian could be sent to extricate them. The young Mr. Hay began his short-lived diplomatic career.

Wadsworth and Sam Dalzell partially earned their keep on the *Sherman* by selling commissary stores for three hours each day—cigars, cigarettes, pipe tobacco, pipes, candy and toilet goods. The lower hold from which they sold the stores was not too much less preferable to conditions topside, particularly when in certain Mediterranean ports. Jim thought Port Said was "the toughest, rottenest community one can imagine." [36] The Suez Canal provided "monotonous . . . scenery." Aden, the Arabian port on the southern end of the Red Sea, was avoided because of cholera raging

35. *Ibid.*, p. 54.
36. *Ibid.*, p. 58.

there. Colombo, Ceylon, in the Indian Ocean was different, however. The country surrounding that city was beautiful and a hotel downtown provided a "wide covered porch" on which to enjoy a "cooling drink." There Wadsworth talked baseball with a young army medical officer, only to be interrupted by a half drunk beachcomber who staggered over from an adjoining table to inquire: "Did I hear you say Geneseo a while ago?" When Jim answered yes to that and to his name being Wadsworth, the beachcomber exclaimed: "I saw you play at Auburn, New York, in 1897." [37]

As the *Sherman* entered Manila, Colonel Page, the Third Infantry commander, asked Wadsworth if he would care to serve as a volunteer aide. Wadsworth was delighted and sought necessary permission from General Otis, the Manila area commander. As soon as the *Sherman* tied abreast the *Olympia*, Admiral Dewey's flag ship, Wadsworth went ashore and "crashed" the general's headquarters. "He was exceedingly kind," Jim reports, and after some friendly banter, gave his consent.[38]

Jim's aide duties consisted of helping the commissary officer issue three days' field rations to troops in the "northern advance." The divisions of the Second Oregon, First Nebraska, the Tenth Pennsylvania, the Twentieth Kansas, the First Montana, the Third Heavy Artillery, the Twenty-Second Infantry, the Third Infantry and four troops of the Ninth Cavalry, under the command of General Arthur MacArthur, headed for Malolos, Aguinaldo's rebel capital. Keeping the "advance" supplied proved difficult, involving much traveling from the rear to the front lines. On one occasion, Wadsworth was sent through Caloocan to ascertain the needs of a battalion of the Third Infantry. The search for the battalion meant crossing bamboo thickets, rivers, blown-up bridges and old ruins. Jim found it and that night reported back to Manila. On the following morning, seventeen two-wheeled carts, each drawn by a *carabao*, were loaded and turned over to Wadsworth to get to Caloocan. On the next day, he arrived there in front of a great church, the inside floor of which provided for blessed sleep. Such was Jim's contribution to the forces which brought Aguinaldo's forces to bay. Among those pursuing the insurrectionist, Wadsworth noticed particularly Colonel Frederick Funston, formerly Cuba's chief artillery officer.

Having fulfilled its mission of delivering American regulars to pursue Aguinaldo, the *Sherman* headed home. After a stop at Nagasaki, the great transport plowed across the Pacific. There were no ships' stores for Wadsworth and Dalzell to sell. The four sons of influential Americans idled

37. *Ibid.*, p. 59.
38. *Ibid.*, p. 61.

away their time, contemplating their lives' directions. Their station afforded many alternatives, yet the directions were quite predictable. Those of Jim's life were set by his forebears and pointed to the soil, the military, politics, and, foremost, well-placed marriage.

6

Any thought of not returning to the soil faded as Jim's father drove him from the station at Avon to Hartford House, down the side of the "beautiful valley" in the freshness of the springtime. As the two passed the family farms—Street, York, North, Maple, Orchard, The Nations—the Boss reflected a contagious enthusiasm. Jim knew his work was farming; it "had been decided on August 12, 1877," he reports in his autobiography, "and I was . . . glad." [39]

In the library of Hartford House, his father turned over to Jim "in fee simple" the Kemp farm, five miles south of the village. One half of its 725 acres straddled the Canaseraga Creek in the valley flats, the other half lying on the eastern slopes. In addition, the Boss deeded to him the Hampton farm next door, once the property of the great landholding Fitzhugh family.

Just off the bend in the road to Mt. Morris, known as "Hampton Corners," stood a pleasant, rambling, summery-looking mansion built by the Fitzhughs only a few years before to replace their federalist home which unfortunately had burned to the ground. Such would be the seat of Jim's holding, with additional purchases, soon to be increased to 1400 acres. For the seat and acreage, the Boss gave Jim $20,000, and an additional $8,000 to be gradually "worked off." [40]

Wadsworth "got down to work." Through the summer of 1899 he directed the repairs of tenant houses, rebuilt fences, bought steers to fatten, selected breeding ewes, picked teams of working horses. Soon the farms were operative. Jim busied himself "buying [more] young steers, grazing, feeding and selling them, sheering sheep, selling wool, weaning and selling lambs, raising wheat, corn oats, beans and sweet corn for the canners; and of course a lot of clover, alfalfa and mixed hay." [41] During that first summer Jim lived with one of his hands in a tenant house, going home to Hart-

39. *Ibid.*, p. 69.

40. Harriet Wadsworth to Nancy Wadsworth Rogers, Oct. 19, 1902, Wadsworth MSS.

41. Wadsworth, Jr., *Autobiography*, p. 75.

ford House only on Saturday night, for "a great bath" and church on Sunday morning. In the winter when his family was back in Washington, Jim boarded at the Big Tree Inn in the village.

Also, during the winter months Jim worked at the local bank, doing simple bookkeeping, attending a teller's window, and delivering bills of lading to village merchants. From this experience, Wadsworth learned something of business and village psychology. He inadvertently learned much from the wise cashier, Theodore Olmsted, because the man talked loudly as a result of being hard of hearing.

In off times Jim would occasionally ride with his cousin Austin Wadsworth's hounds. At times, he attended the hunt balls in one or other of the country houses, where the young Wadsworth heir attracted the attention of debutantes. During the winter holidays Jim visited his parents in Washington.

While in Washington, Wadsworth enjoyed particularly visiting the Hay residence on LaFayette Square, across from the White House. The Hay and the Wadsworth families were extremely close. John Hay, the Secretary of State, had known young Jim's grandfather when both served President Lincoln, Mr. Hay as the President's secretary and General Wadsworth as Lincoln's military governor in the district. When the Boss came to Washington as a congressman in the 1880s, the families naturally came together. Jim and Del had been, of course, classmates at Yale. Another classmate, Payne Whitney, courted Helen, Del's sister.

Late afternoon teas at the Hay residence attracted Jim Wadsworth particularly. There he was fascinated by jocular yet frequently profound conversations between Hay and Henry Adams, the great historian and descendent of presidents. Since the tragic suicide of Adams's wife, the afternoon dialogues were almost religiously adhered to. The discussions between John Hay and Henry Adams were intense, all the more so because of the confidence each had in the other's affection, thus inviting unguarded comment. In reality, John Hay perplexed Adams. The historian viewed cynically most members of Hay's aristocratic class, believing that in rewarding them the American society deferred to the mediocre and illbred. Try as he might, Adams, in young Wadsworth's mind, could never disparage Hay. Jim would always esteem John Hay as he did only two other men— the Boss and Elihu Root, Hay's successor as Secretary of State.[42]

42. Professor Frank Ray, SUNY College at Cortland, notes in letter to author, Nov. 18, 1968, that John Hay filled a curious role for Henry Adams. From references in the Education of Henry Adams (an autobiography published by Houghton Mifflin in 1918) and Volume II of Adams' letters, Ray points out that while Adams exaggerates Hay's success as Secretary of State, he makes disparaging

James W. Wadsworth, Sr.,
about 1920.

Secretary of State John Hay.

Hampton Corners, Mt. Morris, the Wadsworth home, 1902–1932.

Wadsworth's real attraction at the great brick home on 16th and H Streets proved to be Alice Hay, the Secretary's youngest daughter. Although only eighteen at the time of Wadsworth's Washington visits in 1899, Alice possessed for him appealing qualities. Tall and handsome, she was well-traveled and educated and made her mark in almost any company. Yet her tastes were basically simple, as manifested by her dress and her frequent eschewing of Washington society. Wadsworth's appeal for Alice was apparent. Physically attractive, well educated, personable, and of very proper social station, the young scion and Alice Hay were completely compatible. "Jimmy was funny," said Alice, "and sang well. He loved music and all the same things I did." [43]

In addition to seeing one another in Washington during winter holidays, Alice and Jim enjoyed each other's company during the summer when Wadsworth managed a week's reprieve from the farms to visit the Hays at their summer home, "The Fells," at Newberry, New Hampshire. The rambling "cottage" off Lake Sunapee, with a great veranda and large airy windows, was a place of complete happiness for the Hays and their many guests. There in the summers of 1899 and 1900 Jim caught the spirit of "The Fells." He was much at home at the place of the Secretary, classmates Del and Payne Whitney, and the sisters Helen and Alice, particularly Alice. At "The Fells" Alice and Jim realized the meaning of their love for one another, and in the second summer agreed to an early marriage.

Only tragedy could interrupt Alice's plans to marry Jim Wadsworth, and tragedy struck in 1901. The event seemed all the more tragic because of the subjects' good fortunes—Wadsworth successfully launched in carrying on his family tradition in the valley, now buoyed by his imminent marriage to Alice; and Del Hay recently returned as a highly successful consul-general in Pretoria, the capital of the Boer Republic, and just appointed secretary to President McKinley. All was to change when Jim and Del attended their third reunion at Yale and Del, seeking relief from the New Haven heat, sat on a dormitory windowsill, fell fast asleep, and dropped down to his death.

The family was stricken by the tragedy of Del's death. The Secretary of State lamented to Henry Adams: "I do not know yet whether I shall get

---

remarks about Hay's career, saying, for example, at one point, "I never can take his public career seriously." Ray also notes that while Hay is one of the heroes of the *Education*, Adams was never comfortable with him; "hence," writes Ray, "he had to either glorify him or to tear him down."

43. Hatch, *op. cit.*, p. 156.

through or not." [44] Alice's love for her lost brother was too great to permit for the moment the bliss of marriage. The loss to Jim was nearly comparable. Gone for him was a classmate, sweet friend, and the anticipation of the closest of brothers-in-law. Alice and Jim postponed their marriage.

They were finally married at "The Fells" on September 30, 1902, almost a year following the wedding of Helen and Payne Whitney. Thirty house guests were present for the occasion, ushers, bridesmaids, relatives and Yalemen. Many had been there for several days. Jim's sister, Harriet, was annoyed that her brother's Yale cronies rather ignored the girls, except for Fred Kernochan who took them canoeing. On the day of the wedding, two special railroad cars came up from Boston. The Boss arrived in his own wedding suit, "a tight-waisted Prince Albert coat and a violent pair of black and white checked trousers." [45]

The wedding took place in the billiard room. "Alice looked lovely," wrote Harriet to Aunt Hattie, "really prettier than I've ever seen her, in a white lace dress, with very long train and tulle veil not over her face." Jim "looked pale and very delicate." A reception followed the ceremony. Harriet noted that it was not a "jovial affair, and I don't believe small house weddings ever are gay." [46]

Among the wedding gifts, John Hay gave his daughter "a spray of diamonds and rubys, with large bowknots at either end." From Jim's mother, Alice received the diamond rose which her mother had given her. The Boss gave the couple $10,000 in bonds and "paid off nearly all the debt on the farm."

Following the wedding the couple went to Stockbridge, Massachusetts, for ten days before settling down at Hampton House. Harriet thought Jim and Alice would be happy there. "You have never seen a couple so beamingly happy," she concluded to Aunt Hattie, "and crazy about their house and place. I think [Alice] . . . is going to like it up there, although she doesn't care anything about riding or sport. That will not make so much difference, as James isn't very keen about riding either. Then she has very simple tastes . . . and has never cared about going out in society much, so she will not miss city life!" [47]

In the following year, Jim and his bride, henceforth referred to as

44. William Roscoe Thayer, *The Life and Letters of John Hay* (Boston and New York: Houghton Mifflin Co., 1916), II, 263.

45. Hatch, *op. cit.*, p. 159.

46. Harriet Wadsworth to Nancy Wadsworth Rogers, Oct. 19, 1902, Wadsworth MSS.

47. *Ibid.*

AHW by her husband, took a previously postponed wedding trip to the West Indies. There they saw the *Maine* being raised and sat under the "Surrender Tree" as the Boss had five years before. They also saw where Craig had charged up San Juan Hill.

By April, the couple were back in the valley. The remainder of the year proved equally eventful. Evelyn was born in the summer. In the fall, Wadsworth made his first speech at Brooks Grove, about seven miles south of Mt. Morris. It was the last speech he would read. "I can't do it well," Wadsworth wrote in his autobiography, "it is a mean chore . . . [and] I much prefer just to talk." [48]

48. Wadsworth, Jr., *Autobiography*, p. 79.

II

Alpha and Omega

1

Aᴌᴛʜᴏᴜɢʜ it was unusual for young aristocrats to enter politics, Wadsworth's entry was quite predictable. His father, a town supervisor, member of the state Assembly, and New York State comptroller, prior to being elected to the House of Representatives in Washington, D.C., "drilled it into" him. Wadsworth, Sr.'s father before him had been a candidate for the governorship of New York and had served as military governor of the District of Columbia during the Civil War. Then too, important political affairs filled the home of "young Jim's" in-laws. There, in a great mansion on Lafayette Square, facing the White House, as noted, he frequently listened to John Hay and Henry Adams discourse over tea. Hay was a "black Republican" and Adams was a "mugwump." Not surprisingly, the Secretary of State, the Boss and AHW urged Wadsworth to run for the Assembly when, in 1904, the incumbent representative from Livingston County, W. Y. Robinson of Nunda, declined another term.[1]

Livingston County was Wadsworth country and Jim was nominated by a 51–3 vote in county convention and elected over Lewis H. Moses of Lima by 5,653 votes at the polls, out of some 9,500 votes cast.[2] The *Livingston Democrat* had bravely predicted his defeat, seeing no reason why the Wadsworths should have a monopoly on public office.[3]

Wadsworth's speeches, sincere and almost always extemporaneous,

1. James W. Wadsworth, Jr., *The Reminiscences of James W. Wadsworth, Jr.* (Columbia University, Oral History Research Office, 1952), pp. 43–47; James W. Wadsworth, Jr., *Autobiography* (unpublished, 1951), Wadsworth MSS, Library of Congress, Washington, D.C., pp. 124–126.

2. Henry F. Holthusen, *James W. Wadsworth, Jr., A Biographical Sketch* (New York: G. P. Putnam's Sons, 1926), p. 42.

3. *The Livingston Democrat,* Sept. 21, 1904.

29

were somewhat "husky" in tone and evinced a beginner's awkwardness. His canvass of delegates to the county nominating convention and of the votes was quite complete. His reputation as an all-American baseball player was helpful. The local press was generally admiring. "No one," commented one paper, "but a man of strong common sense could say so much in so few words." [4] That Wadsworth was somewhat naïve about it all was revealed by his "falling for" the suggestion of mischievous party elders that he campaign among the Covenanters in York who by act of their faith did not vote because of the absence of "God" in the Constitution.[5]

Rather than have AHW hold the fort at Hampton House for five days a week from January to May, while Jim attended the legislature, Wadsworth took his family and "a couple of good maids" to Albany in 1905. AHW wanted it that way. There the young couple began to develop their family; Evie was two years of age and Jerry (James Jeremiah) was born on June 12 of that year.[6]

Almost as if by design, 1905 was a time for reflective orientation, a time to quietly observe and learn before the large political push a year hence. One hundred and fifty souls, the majority guaranteed by the 1894 state constitution to be Republicans, sat in the ornate assembly chamber under the "absolute" control of Speaker S. Frederick Nixon. Such control, not unlike that of "Uncle" Joe Cannon in the federal lower house, was attributed variously to Nixon's forceful personality, great popularity, and his close identification with the Republican state chairman and former governor, Benjamin B. Odell. Nixon doled out the committee assignments, including the chairmanships, a power even greater than that of the federal Speaker. On minority assignments, Nixon readily cooperated with Tammany's leader in the Assembly.[7] A Democrat like Alfred Smith, out of the Tiger's "grace," would gain little solace from Speaker Nixon.

The Speaker's control of the Assembly could be a force for good and on occasion was, under Nixon's leadership—as in the consolidation of state departments, converting the Erie Canal to a barge canal, cutting state expenditures and controlling working conditions within the state.[8] Not infrequently, however, the leadership winked at the antics of the "Black Horse Cavalry," rough-riding legislature accustomed to "shaking" people down when possible (political blackmail). While Wadsworth had difficulty

4. Holthusen, op. cit., p. 42.
5. Wadsworth, Jr., Reminiscences, pp. 45–47.
6. Wadsworth, Jr., Autobiography, p. 125.
7. Wadsworth, Jr., Reminiscences, pp. 50–54.
8. David M. Ellis and Associates, A Short History of New York State (Ithaca, N.Y.: Cornell University Press, 1957), pp. 382–383.

identifying instances of "shake-downs," he frequently noticed the introduction of "strike bills." "Strike bills" were acts which, if enacted, would
hurt seriously a particular business or interest group. A pay-off from the
group would result in the bill being buried in one of many places along
the legislative route. Equally abusive was the "ripper bill," which, if
passed, would rip certain people out of office, to be replaced by those who
would "pay off." Then, too, Wadsworth got his eye full of lobbyists quite
openly paying for legislation. While much of what transpired in Wadsworth's first year in the Assembly was vague, he knew "that things were
going on that oughtn't." [9]

As important to understanding the "way" of the Assembly were the
political friendships formed there, on both sides of the "aisle." Edwin
Merritt, Jr., a fellow Yaleman, would later become Speaker. Sherman More-
land would become majority leader during Wadsworth's own speakership.
J. Mayhew Wainwright, a scion of Wadsworth's stature, would become
Assistant Secretary of War. John Lord O'Brian, of nearby Erie, would
preside over a future Republican state convention. Beverly Robinson, a
Harvard graduate, represented the decreasing Republican contingent from
New York City. On the other side of the aisle, Wadsworth appreciated
James "Jimmy" Walker, Robert Wagner and Alfred Smith. Walker was
a likeable "playboy." Wagner would later distinguish himself on the bench
and in the United States Senate, defeating Wadsworth in 1926. "Somehow
or other," writes Wadsworth, in his memoirs, "Al [Smith] and I got to be
close friends the first year I was there. I don't know how it happened. It
just happened. He came from the sidewalks, and I came from the soil.
We hadn't lived the same kind of lives at all. By comparison I had been
born into a very fortunate position. Al Smith made his own way, with
his wit, his honesty, his resourcefulness, and his good humor. I became
very fond of him. We were really friends before either of us became at
all prominent." [10]

Outside of the Assembly young Wadsworth saw who had power aside
from the state chairman and, of course, Governor Higgins. There was
Timothy Woodruff, Republican chairman from Brooklyn (Kings County);
Herbert Parsons, chairman from Manhattan (New York County); William F. Barnes, chairman from Albany County; John Raines, majority
leader in the Senate; and Julius Mayer, Higgins's attorney general. [11]

Wadsworth expectedly made little impact as a first-year assemblyman.

9. Wadsworth, Jr., *Reminiscences*, pp. 54–56.
10. *Ibid.*, p. 53.
11. *Ibid.*, pp. 50–54.

His committee assignments were respectable enough—Taxation and Retrenchment, and Villages—but he sat as a green legislator at the bottom of the tables. He did introduce a bill permitting the use of night lines in Hemlock Lake, only to be opposed by Assemblyman Ogden who feared polluting Rochester's water supply.[12] Wadsworth made two speeches, and got two bills passed over his name, one regulating fishing through the ice on Conesus Lake, described sarcastically by himself as "an epoch making measure"; and second, an act making compulsory uniform accounting in all townships, under the supervision of the state comptroller. The "Boss," a former state comptroller, probably influenced his son on the latter legislation.[13]

In late spring, 1905, Wadsworth returned to Geneseo to mend fences. Still "young," he somewhat "gilded the lilly" when addressing the Grand Army of the Republic at Mt. Morris. "It is assuredly a privilege," he began:

> for a young man of my age and generation who has seen so little of life and who has done nothing for his country, to be permitted to address a gathering of this sort, composed of men who have seen so much of life and who have helped save a mighty nation from destruction. The contrast between what you have done and what my generation has done is so great —the balance of achievement is so vastly in your favor—that I find it hard to excuse my presence here on my feet before you.[14]

Not surprisingly, Wadsworth was renominated and returned to the Assembly, by a margin comparable to that achieved in the previous year. His opponent, Donald A. Frazer from York, conceded defeat a week before the election.[15] Wadsworth's expenses filed with the county clerk were: railroad fares, $3.00; livery hire, $5.25; refreshments, $2.00; cigars, $2.00; central committee, $150.00; for a total of $162.25.[16]

2

The alpha of Wadsworth's public life, the elevation of the Assembly's youngest member to the speakership, was almost inexplicable. All the more

12. *Livingston Republican*, Feb. 9, 1905.
13. Wadsworth, Jr., *Reminiscences*, pp. 47–48.
14. Address by James W. Wadsworth, Jr., June 15, 1906, Wadsworth, MSS.
15. *Livingston Democrat*, Nov. 1, 1905.
16. *Livingston Republican*, Nov. 23, 1905.

so because the powerful Benjamin Odell, state chairman and former governor, determined to keep the state's second position in his grasp.

S. Frederick Nixon's death on October 5, 1905, at the age of forty-five, triggered a scramble for the speakership. In his attempt to replace Nixon with another of his men, Odell discovered that he did not run the party. His recent struggles with former governor Frank Black and "Easy Boss," Tom Platt, disenchanted their followers with Odell. Theodore Roosevelt, watching the New York situation anxiously, lumped Odell together with E. H. Harriman as a "malefactor of great wealth," one not fit to lead the party, particularly in view of recent exposés of the business community by the brilliant young legislative counsel, Charles E. Hughes.[17] And certainly many assemblymen wanted to be rid of the Black Horse Cavalry, an unlikely eventuality with another Odell man in the speakership. Lastly, Governor Higgins determined to be governor in fact as well as name and not permit the Republican state chairman to run the state. Knowing that Odell would be challenged on the speakership, it was little wonder that ambitious assemblymen sought the speakership for themselves.

Claims on the speakership came from around the state, each candidate having a coterie of sectional supporters. The candidates were Robert Lynn Cox, from Buffalo; George B. Agnew, from New York City; J. Mayhew Wainwright, from Westchester County; James T. Rogers, from Broome County; Edwin A. Merritt, from St. Lawrence County; Sherman Moreland, from Chemung County; and S. Percy Hooker, from nearby Genesee County. Wadsworth, of course, supported Hooker.[18] The candidates were well qualified. Rogers had been his party's majority leader in the Assembly. Merritt, in another administration, would achieve the speakership. Moreland would become majority leader. Wainwright would one day hold national cabinet office.

The second most powerful position in New York is not decided only by deliberation among assemblymen. Hauling and pulling by personalities and factions in the party is witnessed, usually in the glare of an attentive press. Such was certainly the case in 1905, particularly with the Governor and the President allied to put down the powerful State Chairman Odell, who himself had only recently wrested control of the party from the

17. Roscoe C. E. Brown, *History of the State of New York, Political and Governmental, Vol. IV, 1896–1920* (Syracuse, N.Y.: The Syracuse Press, Inc., 1922), Chapter VIII., *passim.*

18. *Ibid.,* p. 121; Alden Hatch, *The Wadsworths of the Genesee* (New York: Coward-McCann, Inc., 1959), p. 167–168; Wadsworth, Jr., *Reminiscences; Livingston Republican,* Dec. 28, 1905; *New York Times,* Jan. 1, 1906; *Rochester Democrat and Chronicle,* Jan. 1, 1906.

almost legendary boss, Tom Platt. To consolidate his power, Odell, during his governorship, also assumed the state chairmanship, an act viewed by critics as somewhat excessive.[19]

While pressures mounted and alignments formed prior to the convening of the Legislature in January, Wadsworth tramped over his farms, little concerned at the moment about the speakership. The contest intensified as the new year approached. Odell gave his considerable support to Merritt. Higgins threw down the gauntlet on December 15 in a face-to-face confrontation with Odell at New York's Manhattan Hotel. He would not "support Merritt or tell Odell whom he favored." Higgins had told the press that he would speak out against any candidate whom he disapproved. The two men never spoke again.[20]

With Merritt in the Odell camp, Majority Leader Rogers hoped, unrealistically, that the Assembly would be permitted to work its will and elect him. Observing, however, that Cox was granted an interview by Roosevelt, Rogers, from a sick bed in his Albany hotel, rushed word to the President. Pleadingly, he expressed concern about the President's interference. He also insisted that if the members of the Assembly really made their own decision "the marked tendency will be to do the rational and logical thing by electing me." Rogers concluded that if Roosevelt were going to participate, he would like to have an "honest man-fashion" talk with him.[21] Not surprisingly the President was besieged for support in the important contest. Civil Service Commissioner Alford Cooley, seeking to secure downstate dominance in the Assembly, interceded on Wainwright's behalf.[22]

Higgins knew, of course, that the anti-Merritt forces would have to concentrate on one candidate if Odell were to be checked. Leaders accepted Higgins's strategy but could not agree on the candidate. One can only conjecture reasons for disagreement. Cox was from Democratic country, Erie County. Wainwright was from downstate. Rogers had been too close to Nixon. Moreland, the strongest candidate, was unavailable because the Clerk of the Assembly also hailed from Chemung County. Hooker was from the "hinterland" and lacked committed sponsors. Finally, George W. Aldridge, Rochester leader with great longevity in the state leadership,

19. Brown, *op. cit.*, p. 92.

20. *Ibid.*, p. 120; *Rochester Democrat and Chronicle*, Dec. 14, 1905.

21. James T. Rogers to Theodore Roosevelt, Dec. 16, 1905, Roosevelt MSS, Library of Congress, Washington, D.C.

22. Alford Cooley to Theodore Roosevelt, Dec. 1, 1905, Roosevelt MSS.

brought forward the name of James W. Wadsworth, Jr., though he and the elder Wadsworth were often at odds.[23] The upstate leaders concurred. The decision was made.

From the snow-covered Geneseo farms, Wadsworth and his family had traveled to the comfortable Hay home in Washington for the Christmas holidays. While there, the Higgins "kitchen cabinet" in Albany decided Wadsworth's fate. The Governor summoned him to the mansion. Unaware of being the chosen one, Wadsworth crossed Lafayette Square to chat with the President and report his surmise that the call from the Governor probably had to do with party or legislative organization. The President agreed but the speakership was very much on his mind. "I hope Higgins runs this show," he imparted. "Tell [the Governor] . . . that it would be all right with me if he would name . . . Wainwright as Speaker." [24]

Wadsworth went to Albany, reporting at the Executive Mansion at about seven in the evening. To his astonishment he encountered his father. They quickly concluded that their man Hooker was the administration's choice for Speaker. Otherwise, why would both father and son be present?

Prior to going in for dinner, Wadsworth quietly delivered Roosevelt's message to the Governor that Wainwright was the President's choice for Speaker. "Well, never mind that, now," replied Higgins.

Sitting down to dinner with the Governor and the Wadsworths were Aldridge, Francis Hendricks of Syracuse, Superintendent of Public Works Nicholas Franchot, John Lord O'Brian of Erie County, Superintendent of Banks Frederick D. Kolburn, and Cuthbert Pound, the Governor's legal counsel.

"Now, Gentlemen," said the Governor after dinner had been served, "I would like to talk to you a little about the speakership." Higgins then went over the anti-Odell candidates and "in the most friendly fashion, and without abusing any of them," he eliminated them all, except Hooker. "My father winked at me across the table," reported Wadsworth, meaning Hooker was the choice.

The Governor then eliminated Hooker, and without pausing, turned to the younger Wadsworth at the end of the table, saying, "Assemblyman Wadsworth, we want you to be our candidate for the speakership."

"Good God, Governor! You don't mean that," the Boss blurted out.

23. Brown, op. cit., p. 121; Wainwright to Alford W. Cooley, Wainwright MSS, New York Historical Library. Wainwright thought the following concurred: William Barnes, Thomas Dunn, Nicholas Franchot, Francis Hendricks.

24. Wadsworth, Jr., Reminiscences, pp. 59–60.

"Yes, I do," replied Higgins. "In fact, all of these men here feel the same way about it."

Young Wadsworth was stunned. After gathering his wits, he claimed inexperience and said "I'm pledged to Percy Hooker." The Governor assured him that Hooker agreed to withdraw "if you are to be our candidate." Inwardly, Wadsworth was delighted. He rested comfortably that night in the Governor's Mansion.[25]

Louisa was proud. "We are all happy over the Governor's selection of James as Speaker—a great honor for one so young and inexperienced in public life, but a mark of the Governor's esteem and confidence in his integrity, and was not done without consultation with the heads of the party. So he will be elected without doubt."[26] What was pleasurable to Louisa worked consternation in other quarters. "Until I read it in the papers I had no idea that the Governor would pick Wadsworth or the man he would support," wrote Roosevelt to Herbert Parsons, the New York City leader, whose support was crucial. "I had seen Wadsworth the day before and found him in hearty sympathy with our views, and he had gone to the Governor to say he would himself support any good man such as Moreland, Hooker, or Wainwright. Of course, the thing to do now is to turn in with all possible zeal and try to elect Wadsworth." Admitting that he and Parsons had not had their way in choosing the candidate for Speaker, Roosevelt consoled the New York leader: "We can perfectly well afford to be beaten in the effort to elect a fearless, clean, honorable man, who is the candidate of no boss or ring." Roosevelt became somewhat apoplectic about the need to beat Odell: "we have Odell's own testimony to the effect that legislation which he controls is controlled in his own personal and financial interests, as well as in the interest of the wealthy individuals or corporations with whom he is on good terms. . . . I am a citizen of New York State and am interested . . . in having clean politics in Albany, and therefore in seeing some clean man, whoever he may be, given the highest position in the legislative body—a position which wields great influence in the party." Roosevelt concluded that supporting Wadsworth in his struggle against Odell's man was not just a revolt against a boss or machine "but in this instance . . . is a revolt against the cynical practice of corruption in public life and the prostitution of official place for the advancement of personal gain. Against such corruption and such prostitution of office, all honest men should set their faces like flint."[27]

25. *Ibid.*, pp. 60–62; Hatch, *op. cit.*, pp. 168–169; Wadsworth, Jr., *Autobiography*, pp. 133–136; Brown, *op. cit.*, p. 121.

26. Louisa Wadsworth to Mrs. Walter Gay, Dec. 19, 1905, Wadsworth MSS.

27. Theodore Roosevelt to Herbert Parsons, Dec. 20, 1905, Roosevelt MSS.

Parsons, who, with Roosevelt's help, had just won the New York County chairmanship, unseating the Odell faction, lacked enthusiasm for Wadsworth but could not gainsay Roosevelt's points. When, after Christmas, Wadsworth set up headquarters in the Manhattan Hotel in New York City, Parsons was there to gather the votes.[28] But Wadsworth had the votes before trekking down to New York. Roosevelt's pressure and that of Higgins's "kitchen cabinet" paid off. William Barnes, Albany's leader, initiated a lifetime of association with Wadsworth by bringing four assembly votes to him. Congressman Littauer, from Gloversville, assured the President that seven assemblymen from seven surrounding counties would support Wadsworth.[29] Woodruff would bring in at least nine from Brooklyn. Certainly, Aldridge had control of four votes from Monroe County. Francis Hendricks delivered Onondaga. Sloat Fassett would bring in support from the Southern Tier.[30] And so it went. The pressure was too much for most of the field of candidates. Only Wainwright and Merritt remained to oppose Wadsworth. Wainwright stayed in the race on principle, to maintain his independence in the next assembly. Merritt stayed in to win. He and Odell, from the Murray Hill Hotel, one block down Park Avenue, watched their machine disintegrate. Merritt could do no more harm than call Wadsworth "Little Lord Fauntleroy."[31] Odell could only say that Wadsworth was T. R.'s puppet.[32]

"I am afraid there is going to be a great deal of trouble over the Wadsworth matter," wrote Parsons to Roosevelt on December 30, "although he can be elected." It was difficult, he pointed out, for strong, independent men in New York City to "stand for a man whom they do not think is qualified by experience no matter how much they like him personally."[33] Wadsworth wasn't in yet. If Wainwright, with twenty-four New York City votes, could get the support of those backing Merritt, he, according to the New York Times, would have a majority in the Republican caucus. Parsons vetoed this strategy.[34] He stayed firmly with Wadsworth, even though previously he supported Wainwright. Furthermore, said Parsons, a Wainwright victory "now" would be an Odell victory.[35]

28. Hatch, op. cit., pp. 169–170; Wadsworth, Jr., Autobiography, p. 136; Wadsworth, Jr., Reminiscences, pp. 62–64.

29. Lucius N. Littauer to Theodore Roosevelt, Dec. 21, 1905, Roosevelt MSS.

30. Alfred Spring to Theodore Roosevelt, Dec. 23, 1905; Frank Higgins to Theodore Roosevelt, Dec. 22, 1905, Roosevelt MSS.

31. Holthusen, op. cit., p. 49.

32. Rochester Democrat and Chronicle, Dec. 29, 1905.

33. Herbert Parsons to Theodore Roosevelt, Dec. 30, 1905, Roosevelt MSS.

34. New York Times, Jan. 1, 1906.

35. Ibid., Jan. 2, 1906.

On January 1 the Merritt men saw slippage in the Wadsworth camp. If only they could get a secret ballot in the Republican caucus the following day, defection from the Roosevelt-Higgins organization might put Merritt over. Wadsworth objected. "Each member," he solemnly insisted, "owes it to his constituents to rise in his place and state his preference." Odell did not think much of Wadsworth's comment and had a heated exchange with Aldridge in the Ten Eyck lobby.[36]

On January 2, the day of decision, it was over before it began. Higgins's confidence, expressed to Roosevelt some ten days previously, was justified. Despite charges of a new federal regency throwing federal and state patronage around to name the Speaker, Wadsworth was elected in caucus by seventy-five votes. Wainwright received fifteen and Merritt fourteen. There was no secret ballot. Odell commented irrelevantly: "You will note that the total number of votes cast in protest against the election of Mr. Wadsworth was 29. That is the exact number of votes that were cast in favor of the return of Senators Conkling and Platt to the Senate the last time we had Federal interference with the politics of the State, and a Republican Governor was not elected for ten years thereafter." [37]

Merritt and Wainwright moved to make Wadsworth's election unanimous and escorted the successful candidate to the rostrum. "He is a mere boy in appearance," reported the *New York Times,* "but he has a manly bearing and he carried himself with dignity throughout the trying ordeal he had to face." Modestly, Wadsworth commented on the "difficulties and intricacies" of his task and asked for the help of all. "And so it is with this sense of responsibility and with the intention of freely seeking the advice of all loyal Republicans that I accept this nomination." [38] Wadsworth, at twenty-eight years of age, was elected Speaker of the Assembly against George M. Palmer, the Democratic candidate.

3

The new Speaker's baptism of fire came immediately. Hardly had Wadsworth ascended the rostrum in the Victorian chamber when George Palmer moved that the Rules Committee be denied its complete power

36. *Ibid.,* Jan. 2, 1906.
37. *Ibid.,* Jan. 3, 1906.
38. *Ibid.*

over legislation in the last ten days of the session. The threat was pointed, for the current procedure gave the Speaker great power. Much of a session's legislation came out of the Rules Committee in the last ten days, from a committee appointed by the Speaker. The young Speaker "stood grasping the gavel, surveying the 149 members, but making no effort to abate the storm." He did rebuke Mr. Merritt on one occasion for not addressing the chair. Mr. Merritt bowed and did as directed. James Rogers, of Broome, who had aspired to the speakership, finally brought order to the debate. He insisted that the Speaker be allowed "to work out this reform along with other processes of betterment." The Speaker's power was sustained. Wadsworth's first day showed him gaining the confidence of the Assembly, although many who opposed him had not decided whether to be "good." Committee assignments would affect their behavior.[39]

While Wadsworth faced his baptism in Albany, Roosevelt sent out contemplative notes from his White House office. (Might he now set New York politics aside?) "I congratulate you heartily," he wrote Higgins. "What a curious mood Odell seems to be in. The great fight was to prevent a secret ballot." In view of his fulminations "you may be interested to know that I have from him a letter urging in frantic terms the appointment of Hyde as Ambassador to France, saying that it would be the greatest personal favor I could do him. This letter offers rather interesting reading in connection with Hyde's testimony before the insurance investigating committee."[40] Higgins thanked the President for his suggestion that the association of Odell and James H. Hyde, the scandalous head of the Equitable Life Assurance Society, be used, if necessary, to check the state chairman.[41]

Roosevelt was more deliberate in writing Wadsworth, a new force now in New York politics.

My dear Mr. Speaker:
    Just a word of hearty congratulations. I believe that you possess to a marked degree the three qualities essential to a public servant if he is to be of use—courage, honesty, and commonsense. You will need all three. I cannot give you specific advice because I am not acquainted with the situation closely enough. I know you will encounter great difficulties. I have entire faith that you will overcome them.
    I wonder if you will mind an older man, who has a great belief in

39. *Ibid.*, Jan. 4, 1906.
40. Theodore Roosevelt to Frank W. Higgins, Jan. 3, 1906, Higgins MSS., George Arents Research Library, Syracuse University, Syracuse, N.Y.
41. Frank W. Higgins to Theodore Roosevelt, Jan. 11, 1906, Roosevelt MSS.

you, giving you two bits of general advice which will probably sound platitudinous? At any rate I shall venture to do so. Remember that in the long run, for a man of your instincts and of your ambitions, which are always strictly honorable, the only way in which he can help himself is by trying to make the party useful to the public and the State; and in order to do this he has got to try to [act] in accordance with high ideals, and yet by the aid of practical methods. In the second place, my own experience has been that both my pleasure and my usefulness in any office depended absolutely upon my refusal to let myself get to thinking about my own future political advancement; for I have always found that such thought merely tended to hamper me and impair my usefulness, without giving me the miserable offset of a continuance in place. I very early, while myself in the Legislature, became convinced that if I wished to have a good time in public life and to keep my self-respect by doing good service, it paid me to think only of the work that was actually up, to do it as well as I knew how, and to let the future absolutely take care of itself. I believe that you have a future before you, and this future will come not through scheming on your part but by giving first-class service, through your party, to the State. The Odell type of politician can advance himself by scheming and by practices which to you and me are impossible. We could not win by such methods because we should practice them so clumsily, and if we could win we would find the prize not worth having on such terms, while to fail would mean hideous disaster. Go ahead just as you have begun—fearlessly, honorably, and trying to show both your good judgment and good temper, neither flinching nor showing petty vindictiveness. I think you will win out, and even if you do not you will have nothing to regret, and you will have already achieved something substantial for the credit of your name.

Sincerely yours,
Theodore Roosevelt[42]

Wadsworth thanked the President profusely for his advice and encouragement, assuring him that he would "obliterate all thoughts of my future career while holding this job." He would have no time for scheming. Wadsworth then confessed that the appointment of committees was "a most perplexing problem." The assignment of James Rogers, the former majority leader under Nixon, proved "a very difficult one; he had behaved loyally and generously and deserves the best treatment."[43] Yet all who studied the situation, presumably Aldridge, Franchot, and Higgins,[44] felt

42. Theodore Roosevelt to James W. Wadsworth, Jr. (hereafter J.W.W.), Jan. 3, 1906, Wadsworth MSS.
43. J.W.W. to Theodore Roosevelt, Jan. 7, 1906, Wadsworth MSS.
44. New York Times, Jan. 5, 1906.

that "it is impossible to put him in his old place as Chairman of Ways and Means and leader on the floor." Without humiliating him, he "must suffer some reduction in rank." At the moment Wadsworth was inclined to put him in the chairmanship of the Committee on Insurance, to be a blue ribbon committee. "He is a desperately unhappy man and I am terribly sorry for him." [45] The President appreciated his first communication from the new Speaker. "I shall be delighted if you can come here next Saturday. Wire me if you will be here in time for dinner next Saturday night, and if so I shall ask your father and just one or two other men to meet you." [46]

The degree of independence manifested by Wadsworth in making committee assignments is difficult to assess. It probably lies somewhere between his oral *Reminiscences* statement that the Governor and the leaders made no suggestions and the press reports that the Speaker conferred heavily with the Higgins-Aldridge-O'Brian combination. Nor was a *New York Times* editorial accurate in assuming that the President sat in the Speaker's chair, although his fervent White House invitations to the Speaker and his father were not purely social.[47] Aside from any large suggestions, the President went so far as to suggest that his own Nassau County assemblyman be appointed chairman of the Committee on Villages.[48]

Wadsworth's announcement of the new organization of the Assembly on January 9 ushered in a new order. Rogers, the former majority leader, was replaced in that position by Sherman Moreland of Chemung County. As Wadsworth had assured the President, Rogers was made chairman of the Committee on Insurance. Moreland also assumed Rogers's important chairmanship of Ways and Means. Wainwright became chairman of the Committee on Banks. Hooker, a strong Wadsworth man, replaced Bedell, an Odell confidant, as chairman of the Committee on Railroads. Odell-Nixon chairmen of the Judiciary, the Electricity, Gas and Water Supply, and the Labor and Industry committees were replaced by Wadsworth appointees. Perhaps most importantly, William Barnes received two chairmanships for his Albany County "fief." [49]

Tammany recommendations of minority committee appointments were, as customary, accepted by Wadsworth, with one important exception. The Speaker insisted that Al Smith no longer suffer from inferior committee appointment merely because Tammany leader Charles Murphy had a

45. J.W.W. to Theodore Roosevelt, Jan. 7, 1906, Roosevelt MSS.
46. Theodore Roosevelt to J.W.W., Jan. 9, 1906, Wadsworth, MSS.
47. *New York Times,* Jan. 6, 1906.
48. Theodore Roosevelt to J.W.W., Jan. 10, 1906, Wadsworth MSS.
49. *New York Times,* Jan. 10, 1906.

difference with Tom Foley, Smith's local leader in the Second Assembly District. In an unprecedented way Wadsworth put Smith on the Committee on Insurance, an important assignment in view of recent insurance investigations. Smith was always grateful to Wadsworth. He himself dated the beginning of his active interest in government from this action.[50]

"Everybody is astounded at the way he has taken hold of a very difficult situation, and made himself known as a national character," wrote Louisa about her son.[51] "The Legislature is a mass of unrelated atoms that fly through space . . . without guidance, without purpose, without seeming to know what they are about," editorialized the New York Times.[52] Though the contrast of the two statements is striking, Wadsworth did effect a wholesale change in chairmanships. He did successfully counter Tammany's treatment of its most able son, Alfred E. Smith. He went far in eliminating "strike bills." He would not permit peddling of free Pullman passes in the Assembly. He stopped "the passing around of money on various bills."[53] In future years former assemblymen would look back at Wadsworth with high praise. "The situation was so bad in 1905 after I was out of the Assembly," wrote William Stiles Bennet, "that they just simply took over the situation and put Jim W. Wadsworth in as Speaker. That cleaned the situation up."[54] Another observer of Wadsworth's speakership, Beverly R. Robinson, insisted that Wadsworth never received credit for what he did for the assembly.[55]

Warren Isbell Lee, from Kings County, agreed that Wadsworth had "tremendous ability" and courage and was the "most outstanding of men he knew in the Legislature and in Congress," but he was no "so-called reformer."[56] Indeed, the young Speaker was an organization man. He identified with organization leaders and their economic conservatism, but not inflexibly nor at the sacrifice of his principles. Wadsworth guided through the Assembly seven bills reported by the 1905 Armstrong In-

50. Norman Hapgood and Henry Moskowitz, Up From the Streets, A Life of Alfred E. Smith (New York: Harcourt, Brace and Co., 1927), p. 56; Wadsworth, Jr., Autobiography, p. 136; Wadsworth, Jr., Reminiscences, pp. 66–67; Hatch, op. cit., p. 172.

51. Marie Louisa Wadsworth to Mrs. Walter Gay, Jan. 5, 1906, Wadsworth MSS.

52. New York Times, Jan. 12, 1906.

53. Beverly R. Robinson, Reminiscences of Beverly R. Robinson (Columbia University, Oral History Research Office, 1949), p. 85.

54. William Stiles Bennet, Reminiscences of William Stiles Bennet (Columbia University, Oral History Research Office, 1949–1950).

55. Robinson, op. cit.

56. Warren Isbell Lee, Reminiscences of Warren Isbell Lee (Columbia University, Oral History Research Office, 1950), pp. 2–3.

surance Committee to correct insurance abuses, regulate lobbying, and forbid corporations to contribute to political funds.[57] He supported the investigation of banks when Governor Higgins and the senate Republican leadership opposed the investigation.[58] Contrary to the wishes of Aldridge and O'Brian, important political friends, he called for itemized appropriations as opposed to much abused "lump-sum" appropriations.[59] He supported a reasonable gas ceiling bill for New York City. And, although he opposed transforming the frequently evaded mortgage tax to a more stringent recording tax, he permitted such legislation to come out of the Rules Committee at the session's end.[60] It was passed.

Only on new apportionment legislation did Wadsworth seem seriously to lose his aplomb. State Senator Frederick Stevens and the Speaker's father for some time supported an arrangement in which Stevens' senatorial district of Wyoming, Allegheny, and Livingston Counties would be assured of Livingston County's Wadsworth support and, in return, Wadsworth's congressional district of Livingston, Wyoming, Genesee, Orleans and Niagara counties would be assured of Stevens's support in Wyoming County. In the new apportionment legislation Allegheny County was taken from Stevens's senatorial district and replaced by Genesee County where Percy Hooker, after withdrawing from the speakership race, had no little claim on the Wadsworth support. When the legislation was passed, the congressman informed Stevens that the old alliance was dissolved. Later, the Wadsworths successfully supported Hooker to replace Stevens in the new senatorial district. Stevens's elephantine memory of this event would spell no little trouble for the Wadsworths.[61]

Of far more consequence to New York Republicanism than the Wadsworth-Stevens feud was that between Odell and the reorganization faction which so successfully put Wadsworth into the speakership. From January until the Republican convention in September, the reorganizers fumed about Odell's presence as the state Republican chairman. Roosevelt's dinner for the new Speaker on January 13 turned largely to ways of deposing the chairman. Important administration leaders attending the White House session, such as Secretary of State Elihu Root, Assistant Secretary of State Robert Bacon, Postmaster General George Cortelyou, Civil Service Commissioner Alford Cooley, and Congressman Parsons could not help the President. Subsequent strategy was of no avail,

57. Brown, *op. cit.*, p. 124.
58. *New York Times*, Jan. 25, 26; Feb. 2, 3, 10, 1906.
59. Holthusen, *op. cit.*, pp. 52–53; *New York Times*, Feb. 25, 1906.
60. Brown, *op. cit.*, p. 124.
61. *Ibid.*, pp. 124–125.

particularly when Higgins balked.[62] The Governor feared another large contest with Odell, especially on the eve of a governorship race in November. In addition, Higgins tired of Wadsworth's advances on behalf of the White House urging Higgins to act against Odell while being silent on Higgins's own renomination as governor.[63]

4

Of the butchers and floormen, the beef-boners and trimmers, and all those who used knives, you could scarcely find a person who had the use of his thumb; time and time again the base of it had been slashed, till it was a mere lump of flesh against which the man pressed the knife to hold it. . . . There were men who worked in the cooking rooms, in the midst of steam and sickening odors, by artificial light, in these rooms the germs of tuberculosis might live for two years, but the supply was renewed every hour. . . . There were the wool-pluckers, whose hands went to pieces even sooner than the hands of the pickle men. . . . Worst of any, however, were the fertilizermen, and those who served in the cooking rooms. These people could not be shown to the visitor—for the odor of a fertilizer man would scare any ordinary visitor at a hundred yards, and as for the other men, who worked in tank rooms full of steam, and in some of which there were open vats near the level of the floor, their peculiar trouble was that they fell into the vats; and when they were fished out, there was never enough of them left to be worth exhibiting— sometimes they would be overlooked for days, till all but the bones of them had gone out to the world as Durham's Pure Leaf Lard![64]

On the heels of Wadsworth's secure political beginning in Albany, came the Omega and the high point of his father's public life, an exemplary life to young Jim. Because the life of the father affected so much the son, it is necessary to describe the relationship of the Boss to *The Jungle*, recently published, and the President, who read it well. With poignant irony, the same Roosevelt who in January applauded the younger Wadsworth's ascendency to the New York speakership, in June would berate his father and in November would aid in his defeat. James

62. *New York Times,* Jan. 14, 1906.

63. *Ibid.,* Feb. 28; March 6, 1906.

64. Upton Sinclair, *The Jungle* (New York: Harper and Brothers, 1946 edition; originally published in 1905 by Sinclair Lewis), pp. 97–99.

W. Wadsworth, Sr. would no longer serve in the House of Representatives and as chairman of its Committee on Agriculture.

The Jungle was the foremost of the great muckraking works of the period, and probably the most effective of all American propaganda novels written to that date, excepting only Uncle Tom's Cabin. No novel had so exposed a great industry as it did the nation's large meat-packing houses in Chicago. Roosevelt was horrified. He called its author to the White House for a personal account. He sought further confirmation by sending his Commissioner of Labor and an associate to Chicago to investigate, even though the Department of Agriculture had conducted its own investigation.[65] The President suspected the department might be reluctant to criticize an industry which its employees daily inspected for the foreign market.

On May 22, 1906, Senator Beveridge, with the President's support, introduced meat inspection legislation as an amendment to the Agriculture Appropriation bill. Although few expected the passage of the amendment, three days later the public was surprised by the quick Senate action on what was considered one of the President's most harsh regulatory bills. The public was unaware that Roosevelt threatened to publish the report of his investigators, Charles P. Neill and James B. Reynolds, if the packers impeded congressional action.[66]

In essence, the bill called for a thorough on-going inspection of all cattle, sheep, swine, and goats after being killed in the packing process, "a post-mortem inspection." It mandated the labeling of all meats with date of packing. It provided for the destruction of all unfit carcasses. It brought sanitary conditions in packing houses under federal regulation. It required that clearance to outbound ships carrying meat products be given only after the issuance of a certificate by the Department of Agriculture. Most importantly, it required that the packing houses pay a fee for inspection. Those establishments denying inspection would be prohibited from trading in interstate and foreign commerce. Heavy penalties would be imposed on those bribing inspectors or in any way violating the law.[67]

65. Claude G. Bowers, Beveridge and the Progressive Era (Cambridge, Mass.: The Riverside Press, 1932), pp. 228–230. Hamlin Garland had some doubts about Sinclair's attempts to reform the industry—"I know a good deal about Sinclair's attempt to get the limelight," he wrote Roosevelt, "and I confess to a prejudice against him. However he seems to have done some good in this case."

66. Ibid.; New York Times, May 26, 1906.

67. Hearings Before the Committee on Agriculture, on the So-Called Beveridge Amendment to the Agricultural Appropriations Bill (HR 18537), (Washington: Government Printing Office, 1906), pp. 351–357.

"I am anxious to see you about the amendment to the agricultural appropriation bill," wrote Roosevelt to the senior Wadsworth the day after the Senate action.[68] The President suspected, correctly, that Wadsworth, as chairman of the House Agricultural Committee, might tamper with the Senate version of the bill. The large Wadsworth cattle grazing in the Genesee Valley had for years brought the family into close contact with the Chicago stockyards where they made annual purchases of young beef. Then, too, the Boss was quite ideologically identified with large enterprises, such as the Chicago packing houses.

Roosevelt informed Wadsworth of the Neill-Reynolds investigation of the Chicago situation. "It is hideous, and it must be remedied at once. I was at first so indignant that I resolved to send in the full report to Congress." The President continued to say, however, that the damage publication would do to the stock-growers and export-traders would be so great that "I am going to withhold the report," if the packers would not interfere with the Beveridge amendment. Again, Roosevelt asked to see him. Also, he asked, "can you not see Commissioner Neill?" [69] Wadsworth was to see much of Roosevelt and Neill in the coming weeks.

Roosevelt's strategy of threatening publication of the Neill-Reynolds report if the House did not speedily accept the Beveridge amendment almost worked. So quickly had the legislation passed the Senate that the Chicago lobbyists were not in Washington. And in a White House conference between the House leadership, the President, Commissioner Neill, and Speaker Joseph Cannon, the latter became momentarily convinced of the need for the bill.[70] On the following day, however, Cannon felt differently. The packers had arrived and talked about amendments to strike out the mandatory character of the legislation and to have the government assume the cost of inspection. The Speaker took a breathing spell. He sent the bill to Wadsworth's Committee on Agriculture.[71]

Wadsworth needed no instructions from lobbyists arriving from Chicago. He had already pointed out some weaknesses of the amendment to the President—that Chicago conditions were not universal in the industry, that avoidance of conflict of interests between packer and inspector required government payment of inspection fees, and that the competency of government to carry out such full inspection as demanded by the bill was questionable. Roosevelt replied by saying that Pennsylvania

68. Theodore Roosevelt to James W. Wadsworth, Sr., May 26, 1906, Wadsworth MSS.

69. *Ibid.*

70. *New York Times,* May 28, 1906.

71. *New York Times,* May 29, 1906.

conditions, for example, were as bad as those in Chicago, and that there would be competent inspection if directed by the Chief of Animal Industry, appointed by the President and confirmed by the Senate. On government payment of fees, Roosevelt weakened: "I do not regard as vital whether the packers or the Government pay." [72]

By May 29 the packers had made the nation's cattlemen aware of their stake in the Beveridge amendment. Certainly they made clear that if the packing houses paid for inspection, the cost would be passed on to the cattlemen. All contracts of cattle purchases would provide for the absorption of government costs. Cattlemen lost little time in informing their congressmen of the need for the government payment of inspection costs. The packers also were not averse to saying that the cost of meat to the public would go up. [73]

The lack of court review became the prime objection to the legislation on May 30. After all, the packers argued, where except to the courts could they appeal unjust inspection decisions. This criticism was particularly attractive to some packers for "broad" court review would not only tie up the inspection machinery but, given the courts' conservative stance, would probably result in sympathetic decisions. On the same day Wadsworth expressed emphatically his purpose of having the bill changed in several particulars, and so informed the President. [74]

The several particulars brought to the President's attention by Wadsworth very likely were suggestions mentioned more recently by the industry and incorporated into a so-called Wadsworth Substitute. The substitute called for discretionary ante-mortem inspection at the behest of the Secretary of Agriculture, the non-dating of labels, the use of certain preservatives, the converting of destroyed carcasses into fertilizer, the government payment of inspection fees, and "broad" court review.

Whatever the particular Wadsworth recommendations, the President expressed shock, but only after conferring with Agriculture Secretary Wilson, Senator Beveridge and Commissioners Neill and Reynolds. Prior to conferences with his advisors, Roosevelt actually approved many of Wadsworth's suggestions. "I am sorry to have to say," he wrote Wadsworth after the conference, "that it seemed to me that each change is for the worse and that in the aggregate they are ruinous, taking away every particle of good from the suggested Beveridge Amendment. In view of the wide difference of opinion developed by these proposed changes, and the evident likelihoods

72. Theodore Roosevelt to J. W. Wadsworth, Sr., May 29, 1906, Wadsworth MSS.

73. New York Times, May 29, 1906.

74. Ibid., May 31, 1906.

that there cannot be an agreement upon anything which would seem to me satisfactory, I do not feel warranted in longer withholding my message to Congress transmitting the reports as to the conditions in the Beef-packing establishments, and I shall send it in at an early date." The President concluded that he had erred in the government payment of inspection fees. He wrote that the Secretary of Agriculture "says that failure to appropriate sufficient money would at any time reduce the inspection under the proposed law to the force which it now is."[75] The President's letter came as no surprise to Wadsworth. Secretary Wilson had already informed him of the administration's adamant position on the legislation. The gauntlet thrown down twice by the administration was picked up by the chairman of the Committee on Agriculture.

Wadsworth appeared unruffled as battle lines formed. By now Speaker Cannon and the majority of the House appeared to support him. "We . . . shall settle on a new bill that will be what all concerned want," Wadsworth confidently informed the press. Roosevelt, incensed by Wadsworth's obdurance, was heavily advised by his "inner circle," not a few of whom counselled a campaign of "enlightenment" in Wadsworth's congressional district which would defeat him for reelection. "Society" friends of the congressman, however, could not believe that Roosevelt would move against the congressional seat "in view of his having ridden to the hounds with the Wadsworth fox-hunting parties at Geneseo."[76] Interestingly, Roosevelt continued a friendly correspondence with the Homestead Wadsworths, south of the village, while feuding with the Boss.

The first part of the Neill-Reynolds report, transmitted to the House on June 4, was referred by the Speaker to the Committee on Agriculture. Generally, the report confirmed Sinclair's findings. Specifically, it deplored the conditions of the stockyards, such as inadequate building materials, poor lighting and ventilation, unsanitary conditions in handling products, and incompetent inspection, before and after slaughtering.[77] The charges were particularly directed against canned meat processes and not the "fresh" processes. As Wadsworth prepared for hearings on the Neill-Reynolds report and the Beveridge amendment, Roosevelt informed him that the administration's investigations "are not yet through."[78]

On June 5, the day before Wadsworth's hearings, a break appeared in the packer ranks. Certain of them seemed "anxious" when Wadsworth ignored Roosevelt's threat to deny the packing houses the use of export

75. Theodore Roosevelt to J. W. Wadsworth, Sr., May 31, 1906, Wadsworth MSS.
76. New York Times, June 3, 1906.
77. Hearings Before the Committee on Agriculture, pp. 261–272.
78. Ibid., pp. 272–273.

labels if the Beveridge amendment failed passage. Also, they were wary of the stiffening of Wadsworth's position. His substitute bill now revealed the striking of the words "sound and healthful," to be replaced by the less stringent phraseology, "fit for human food." The Beveridge amendment was allegedly further weakened by having the industry prescribe sanitary codes to be approved by the Secretary of Agriculture rather than having the Secretary "prescribe." Chicago representatives talked compromise. For example, some suggested that packers and government split the inspection fees, that Agriculture Department scientists determine the use of preservatives, and that court review apply only to sanitation enforcement, not inspection of meat.[79]

On Wednesday, June 6, Chairman Wadsworth convened the Committee on Agriculture for purposes of public hearing. Thomas E. Wilson, representing Nelson Morris and Company and other Chicago packers, appeared to defend the industry. Present also were Secretary Wilson, Dr. Alonzo D. Melvin, Chief of the Bureau of Animal Industry, and Commissioner Neill. Critics of the packers suspected that by convening the public hearing and by considering committee investigation "on the ground" in Chicago, Wadsworth was stalling to avoid any passage in the congressional session.[80]

Thomas Wilson denied the charges in the Neill-Reynolds report, with no little encouragement from Chairman Wadsworth. The *New York Times* saw a striking resemblance between his testimony and the Wadsworth substitute, especially when the Chicago representatives listed recommended changes in the Beveridge amendment. Wilson boldly attacked the President and by implication questioned his motive. If it "was simply the obtaining of legislation to improve the inspection and the sanitary conditions, then I say the criticisms have been doubly unjust and unfair, for in the very inception of the investigation the commission and their superiors had the assurance of the packer's co-operation and their personal guarantee was given that any practical recommendations would be welcome and adopted." [81]

The following day saw a change of attitude on the committee's part. The Wadsworth side was somewhat subdued by Neill's testimony that the packers had pleaded with Neill that they be given thirty days to clean up their industry before a report was finalized and published.[82] Also, Neill stood up well under rather antagonistic questioning. Most

79. *New York Times,* June 6, 1906.
80. *New York Times,* June 7, 1906.
81. *Ibid.*
82. *New York Times,* June 8, 1906.

persistent were Republicans Franklin E. Brooks and William Lorimer, the latter a congressman from the Chicago area. Wadsworth's several colloquies with Neill were limited in time, but sharp. He questioned the report's credibility, first as related to a lack of any commendation, and specifically as to the report's descriptions of the "rottiness" of equipment, the inclusion of foreign matter in canned meats, the prevalence of tuberculosis spitting, and the fall of a dressed hog into a urinal.[83]

The fall of the hog became a recurring subject for discussion during the hearings. Neill and Reynolds, in their report, had described how, in their presence, a hog, already cleaned and inspected, had fallen off a rail into the men's urinal and was immediately placed back on the rail and, without being cleaned, sent on its way into the canning process. Wadsworth thought that such a situation was too extraordinary to believe. Neill agreed. Wadsworth pressed the matter, "because it seems to me that this goes into the credibility of the report." The chairman wondered if the report should not have said that no effort was made to clean it "in your presence" instead of "no effort being made to clean it." "Is not that pretty careless?" asked Wadsworth. In spite of the chairman's intense questioning, Neill stood firm in his contention that the hog had not been cleaned.[84]

Neill's forbearance was soon strained. "I think the way in which questions are being asked is not quite fair to me. . . . I feel like a witness under cross-examination." Republican John Lamb and Democrat C. R. David agreed with Neill.[85]

At 6:00 p.m. on June 13, Wadsworth brought down the gavel on all committee deliberations and reported out a bill. By a close 9–7 bipartisan vote the committee recommended the Beveridge amendment with several significant changes, most of which previously were reported to be in the Wadsworth substitute: non-dating of meat inspection, government assumption of inspection costs, use of certain preservatives, sanitation requirements by experts in the Department of Agriculture, non-Civil Service appointment of inspectors during the first year, use of condemned carcasses for fertilizer purposes, and court review.[86] The President was angered. The bill "is very, very bad . . . and I cannot even promise to sign it." In actuality, the President's case proved unsubstantial and in its main criticism, erroneous. Not referring to major changes, except for

83. *Hearings Before the Committee on Agriculture*, pp. 94–140.
84. *Ibid.*, pp. 120–121.
85. *Ibid.*, p. 128.
86. *Ibid.*, pp. 357–363.

court review, Roosevelt complained that "there is no provision for making [a] plant accessible at all hours to the inspectors." [87]

"You are wrong, very, very, wrong in your estimate of the Committee's bill," wrote Wadsworth to the President, engaging in his own hyperbole. "It is as perfect a piece of legislation to carry into effect your own views of this question as was ever prepared by a committee of Congress." Somewhat joyfully, Wadsworth then showed Roosevelt where he had erred on "nighttime" inspection: "turn to page 4, line 2 . . . [and] to page 6, line 16" of the bill. On court review, Wadsworth wrote: "The worst that can be said . . . is that it is perhaps unnecessary—that it is already covered by existing law." Wadsworth said the rest of the letter dealt with generalities. The chairman concluded by regretting that the President of the United States should impugn "the sincerity and the competency of a Committee of the House of Representatives. You have no warrant for it."[88]

The "fur flew" in the White House when Roosevelt discovered that Wadsworth was right on night and day inspection. The President was badly advised. Beveridge insisted it was the fault of Agricultural Department staff for having misinformed him.[89] To make matters worse Beveridge had badgered Roosevelt into making his erroneous letter public.[90] The President of the United States quickly responded to Wadsworth: "I wish promptly to acknowledge the one portion of your letter in which you are in the main right. I was in error in the statement, which I accepted from Senator Beveridge, that there was no provision for making the plants accessible at all hours to the inspectors." Roosevelt then launched into an attack on the court review provision, pointing out that such review of the decision of the Secretary of Agriculture would limit him to only ministerial functions and "if enacted into law will nullify the major part of the good." of the law. The President then concluded that, at the request of the Speaker, he had gone over with Agriculture Committeeman Henry C. Adams the specifics of the bill Wadsworth called for. Wadsworth was now *persona non grata* in the White House. Roosevelt reported that Adams agreed on the exclusion of court review and certain other "alterations." [91]

87. *New York Times,* June 16, 1906.

88. J. W. Wadsworth, Sr., to Theodore Roosevelt, June 15, 1906, Wadsworth MSS.

89. Albert J. Beveridge to Theodore Roosevelt, June 16, 1906, Roosevelt MSS.

90. Theodore Roosevelt to Albert J. Beveridge, June 15, 1906, Roosevelt MSS.

91. Theodore Roosevelt to J. W. Wadsworth, Sr., June 15, 1906, Roosevelt MSS.

Wadsworth and Speaker Cannon accepted the Roosevelt-Adams agreements. Compromise came on word changes, such as substituting "night and day" inspection for inspection "at all times," and most importantly on court review. Wadsworth accepted elimination of the review clause. Roosevelt agreed to dropping the clause designating the Secretary as the final authority. Thus, the act was silent on both court review and final authority.[92]

On June 19, the House addressed itself to the Meat Inspection bill. Wadsworth explained the changes of "verbiage," giving specific authority to the Secretary of Agriculture to withhold inspection if condemned carcasses were not destroyed, substituting "night and day" inspection for the words "at all times", and the elimination of the word "unclean." He further explained the dropping of the civil service and the court review clauses. Only the government assumption of the cost of inspection drew objectional comment. The minority leader, John Sharp Williams, wanted the packers to pay, claiming that they "have been poisoning our wives and our children." Still, Williams's concern did not affect his eulogizing Chairman Wadsworth with an extraordinary comment: "He is a worthy son of a noble sire, (Applause) and an honest man if God makes honest men, (Applause) and I believe He does. If the abbreviated disturbance between the two gentlemen from New York had come off, my reasoning would have been with the other gentleman from New York, but my affection and feelings would have been with this gentleman from New York. I think we have had entirely too much tolerance for the idea that when men honestly differ about a public measure their motives are to be impugned and their integrity to be attacked." [93]

The Senate concurred in the House action. The President signed the bill into law. The principal protagonists both succeeded and failed. Roosevelt achieved firm inspection of all meat products in foreign and interstate commerce. He failed in stemming the many changes in the Beveridge amendment effected by the House Agriculture Committee. That failure was Wadsworth's success. As chairman of the Agriculture Committee he achieved the use of preservatives, the use of condemned meat for fertilizers, the government payment of inspection fees, and the non-dating of labels. Although he did not succeed in getting court review, at least the Secretary of Agriculture was not designated as the final authority.

92. *New York Times,* June 18, 1906.

93. *New York Times,* June 20, 1906; *Congressional Record,* Vol. 40, 59th Congress, 1st Session, June 19, 1906, pp. 8720–8729.

The act, with the House changes, would stand for decades to come. Wadsworth's failure was his political demise, a high price.[94] It was to many an act of political courage, not to be lost on his son. The Boss's struggle hurt Louisa, especially as she saw him reviled by the press. She thought it dreadful to "blacken a man's character without any compunction or redress." She hoped it would come out all right in the end, "but I don't think we will be intimate at the White House next winter."[95] Two months later she was bitter. "The President read that horrid, untruthful book . . . [and] let his imagination run away with him." While Louisa sorrowed, the official White House family appeared amused. At some length, Secretary of State Elihu Root described how the President wrote excitedly about the birth of a daughter, Vera, to Her Imperial Highness the Grand Duchess Elizabeth Mavrikievna, Consort of His Imperial Highness the Grand Duke Constantin Constantinovitch. "Permit me," he wrote to Roosevelt, "to call your attention to the difference between your treatment of this interesting and important topic and the letter written by you when His Royal American Highness the Honorable James W. Wadsworth, Chairman of the Committee on Agriculture of the House of Representatives, was delivered a Beef Bill."[96]

The Boss lost little time in mending fences back home. In answer to the Genesee County resolution calling for his defeat he insisted that his committee had acted swiftly to support strong meat-inspection legislation but that certain changes were necessary. "As Chairman of the Committee on Agriculture, it is my duty to guard all the agricultural interests of the entire country."[97] But the farmers were not much interested in having Wadsworth defer to the packers. The most they could get from them was four cents a pound for beef on the hoof. Even the Groveland Grange, next door, voted not to support Wadsworth.[98] It was not only the meat legislation which bothered them. They did not like Wadsworth's position on either oleomargarine or federal aid to state roads. He supported oleomargarine as an agricultural product, which it was. He voted against federal road programs, fearing centralization of power in Washington.[99]

Throughout July and August, Wadsworth and his son scurried over the district trying to put the meat inspection legislation in the best possible

94. Statutes of the U.S.A., 59th Congress, 1st Session, Ch. 3913, 1906.
95. Louisa Wadsworth to Mrs. Walter Gay, June 16, 1906, Wadsworth MSS.
96. Elihu Root to Theodore Roosevelt, June 20, 1906, Roosevelt MSS.
97. J. W. Wadsworth, Sr., to J. W. Burke, June 21, 1906, Wadsworth MSS.
98. Livingston Democrat, October 17, 1906.
99. J. W. Wadsworth, Sr., to J. W. Burke, June 21, 1906, Wadsworth MSS.

light. The local press, unlike the press elsewhere, frequently helped, quoting the praises of congressmen, especially John Sharp Williams and Speaker Cannon.

By October 4, Wadsworth had most of the party organization in the congressional district with him, the principal support coming from Orleans, Genesee, and Livingston counties. Frederick Stevens, forced out of his state senate seat by the younger Wadsworth's reapportionment effort in the legislature, went after the Boss's seat but his Wyoming and Niagara efforts were not enough.[100] Nor was Peter Porter, a Buffalo contender, any more successful. In his speech accepting the Republican nomination, Wadsworth took on Porter, who ran as an independent Republican with Democratic support. In addressing the Genesee Grange, the Boss answered Porter's charges regarding meat inspection, oleomargarine and federal aid to roads. He concluded by stating his Republican belief: "I am a stand-patter on the tariff; I believe in the Gold Standard; I believe in the rights of the citizen and in the rights of property as opposed to the government ownership of railroads, of telegraph lines or any business which can be carried on by private enterprise and capital. I am not tainted with socialism or anarchism. On all party questions I bow willingly to my party's mandates as expressed by a majority. But on all other questions my conscience and my judgment must be my guides." [101]

Such was a legacy for a son; it was not enough to procure a victory in that November's election. The Boss had too much going against him. The President's wishes were well known. Federal office holders throughout the district were warned to lift no finger to help the incumbent congressman. Even in Livingston County, the farmers were angry with him.

"Jimmy was much pleased with your cable, but my dear, he was *not* elected!" [102] wrote Louisa to the Boss's sister in France. "In a district he carried last year by 13,000 he was beaten by about 4,000. So after twenty years of hard faithful service, he is kicked out."

From Melun, France, Tillie Gay consoled her brother-in-law. "You fought for the good cause as your brave father did before you, and were he here, he would be as proud of you as I am." [103]

Louisa had one consolation. "James had a good majority in this County for Assembly, and will no doubt be Speaker again." [104]

100. *New York Times*, June 5, 1906, June 17, 1906; *Picket Line Post*, Oct. 19, 1906, October 26, 1906; *Livingston Republican*, June 21, 1906.

101. *Livingston Republican*, Oct. 4, 1906; also, address in Wadsworth MSS.

102. Louisa Wadsworth to Martha Gay, Nov. 9, 1906, Wadsworth MSS.

103. Martha Gay to J. W. Wadsworth, Sr., Nov. 19, 1906, Wadsworth MSS.

104. Louisa Wadsworth to Mrs. Walter Gay, Nov. 9, 1906, Wadsworth MSS.

Most observers, of course, saw the Meat Inspection Act and the New York speakership as unrelated. Yet they were ironically and indelibly enmeshed. Literally, they marked the end and the beginning of significant political careers of father and son. And because the events occurred simultaneously, emotional, familial and ideological elements were accentuated. Of the three elements, the ideological was the most profound. Born to landed wealth, both the Boss and his son resented statist intrusion, New York or federal, in the industry tied closest to the product of their land—beef. While the Boss failed to foil the Meat Inspection Act and the commerce clause on which it was based, he at least blunted its provisions. He fought the good fight of constitutional principle against the rise of a regulatory state.

For the rest of his long life, young Wadsworth would remember and applaud his father's efforts in the meat inspection fight. During his own remaining years, the Boss would watch fondly Jim's political growth so auspiciously launched by his election to the speakership. And in common both would loathe Theodore Roosevelt. The speakership would give Jim particular cause to scorn the twenty-sixth President.

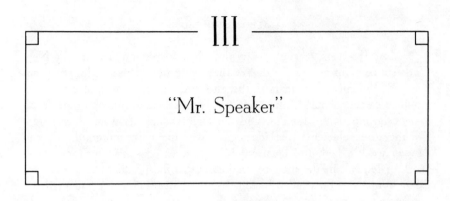

III

"Mr. Speaker"

1

While Congressman Wadsworth went down in defeat, and young Jim handily won re-election to the Assembly, a new political star arose to assume the governorship and the leadership of the state Republican party. Charles Evans Hughes, a brilliant counsel to two important joint legislative committees—the Armstrong and Stevens committees—was drafted to run as the Republican candidate for governor. As counsellor, he was principally responsible for unearthing great wrongdoing in the state's insurance and utilities industries. Governor Higgins's health did not permit his making the race, and although many of the party's leaders considered nominating Lieutenant Governor M. Lynn Bruce or former governor Frank S. Black, Hughes's nomination was inevitable. President Roosevelt and Herbert Parsons, the New York County Republican leader, insisted upon it and led the drive with the party. The party's image had been too much tarnished by Hughes's own insurance and utilities revelations, by recent Republican defeat in the New York City mayoralty race, and by Republican State Chairman Benjamin Odell's alleged "deals" with the Democratic leader, William Randolph Hearst.[1]

Hughes waged a vigorous and successful campaign against the flamboyant Democratic gubernatorial candidate, William R. Hearst. Although the newspaper magnate, an independence League candidate, had little delegate support in the Democratic convention which met in Buffalo on September 25, Charles Murphy used his candidacy to take over the state Democratic party from its George B. McClellan wing. The campaign be-

1. Robert F. Wesser, *Charles Evans Hughes, Politics and Reform in New York, 1905–1910* (Ithaca, N.Y.: Cornell University Press, 1967), pp. 58–66; Roscoe C. E. Brown, *History of the State of New York, Political and Governmental, Vol. IV, 1896–1920,* (Syracuse, N.Y.: The Syracuse Press, Inc., 1922), pp. 127–128.

tween Hearst and Hughes turned into a donnybrook, with Hearst attacking Hughes as a corporation attorney and the latter denouncing the former as a demagog. Had any Republican other than Hughes been the party's candidate, Hearst would have won in spite of his reputation as a political "adventurer" and yellow journalist. The Democrats swept all the state-wide offices except the governorship.[2]

Wadsworth justifiably attributed Hughes's victory to Democratic votes. Indeed, in addition to upstate Democratic support, he lost New York City, the Democratic bastion, by only 70,000 votes.[3] Factionalism within the Democratic party—New York City's Democratic mayor, George B. McClellan, supported Hughes—was juxtaposed by Roosevelt's steadying influence among varied Republicans. The President conciliated differences between "amateur" and "organization" Republicans down-state, and between progressive and conservative Republicans upstate. On one occasion, he became so upset with alleged Republican anti-Hughes efforts in Livingston County, Wadsworth's bailiwick, that he sent off a letter to State Chairman Woodruff: "Cannot you send up a man yourself who will see that everything is done for Hughes exactly the same as for the rest of the ticket."[4] The President was understandably gun-shy in Livingston County. Having scrapped so heatedly with Congressman Wadsworth, who was on the same ballot as Hughes, he feared retribution by the Wadsworth organization. His fears were apparently unwarranted for Livingston County gave Hughes a larger plurality than it had given Frank Higgins two years previously when Roosevelt himself had headed the ticket as the presidential candidate.

If Republican leaders in the state did not know what to make of "their" progressive governor-elect, they soon learned. Before Wadsworth, Barnes, Odell, Platt, Aldridge and other assembled leaders at a New York City Republican dinner, he sketched out his *modus operandi* as governor. "I shall be my own spokesman," he intoned, declaring his intent not to be hamstrung by the bosses. Among his listeners, only William Barnes, Albany County's "feudal Baron," did not get the message. He tried to tell Hughes that reform would not work—it might factionalize the party. Hughes then gave Barnes a lesson in good government: harmony was not the issue; "a disinterested view" of the public needs was.[5] Immediately upon

2. Brown, *op. cit.*, pp. 129–136; Wesser, *op. cit.*, Ch. IV, *passim.*
3. Wesser, *op. cit.*, p. 103.
4. Theodore Roosevelt to Timothy L. Woodruff, Oct. 27, 1906, Charles E. Hughes MSS, Library of Congress, Washington, D.C.
5. Wesser, *op. cit.*, pp. 104–106.

his inauguration the new governor specified the state's needs as he saw them. In his first message to the Legislature he called for reform of election and party nomination procedures, railway and public utility regulation, improvement of police and welfare services, labor department reorganization, more effective child-labor legislation, pure food legislation, expansion of the forest preserves, and prison reform.[6]

Republican leaders, including Wadsworth, were silent on the Governor's catalog of reforms. The Geneseoan, just returned to the speakership, busied himself organizing the new Assembly. While country members of the body practiced walking on the Assembly chamber's resplendent new carpet, Wadsworth appointed the new committees.[7] He consulted with Hughes and learned first hand of the Governor's independent *modus operandi*. Regarding the make-up of committees, Hughes told the press, "I made no suggestions whatsoever. I said to . . . [Wadsworth] that I supposed he would act upon his own best judgment and with a full realization of his great responsibility."[8]

Hughes could not have been disappointed by Wadsworth's appointment of Assembly committee chairmen, as well he might have been by the Senate appointments. Generally, the Speaker retained the previous year's chairmen, including such progressive Republicans as Sherman Moreland, James T. Rogers, and Jonathan M. Wainwright, respectively chairmen of the Ways and Means Committee, the Insurance Committee, and the Committee on Banking. In addition to appointing Moreland head of the important Ways and Means Committee, he made him his majority leader. Again, the public was impressed by the Speaker's own method of operation.[9] Professor Robert F. Wesser, the recognized historian of the Hughes administration, describes Wadsworth's leadership in 1906 and 1907 as a "stellar performance" and notes the contrast between the progressive Assembly and the "placid State Senate." There, the conservative leader, John Raines, when possible, replaced the progressive legislators with stand-pat Republicans.[10] With an eye to the Senate, the Governor commented, "If I get into difficulty . . . I shall appeal to the people of the State."[11]

The Governor's difficulty came even before the Legislature got down

6. *Ibid.*, pp. 111–112.

7. *New York Times*, Jan. 6, 1907.

8. *Rochester Democrat & Chronicle*, Jan. 11, 1907.

9. *New York Times*, Jan. 8, 9, 10, 1907. The *New York Times's* inference that conservatives were appointed to important legislative posts is belied by its own announcement of Wadsworth appointees in the Assembly.

10. Wesser, *op. cit.*, pp. 147–150.

11. *Rochester Democrat & Chronicle*, Jan. 11, 1907.

Speaker of the New York State Assembly, 1906. Wadsworth was twenty-nine years old. *By permission of the Library of Congress.*

to business. To the consternation of Herbert Parsons and State Chairman Woodruff, Hughes refused to accept their recommendation regarding the appointment of Lewis N. Swasey as Superintendent of Elections for New York City. Hours of discussion between the city leaders and the Governor did not dissuade Hughes, who became even more determined not to appoint a "mere tool of the machine" to the important position. Upon leaving the conference, Parsons, who should have known better, commented to the Governor, "I think we'll find a way." His way was to have Wadsworth call upon the President to bring the recalcitrant Governor into line. The Speaker journeyed to Washington, secured the President's approval of Swasey's appointment, and returned to Albany to tell the Governor that Roosevelt felt that he should appoint Swasey. "I am sorry to get this message," replied Hughes. "I would be very glad if it were possible to accept the President's advice. However, I wish you would tell the President that I have thought over this matter very carefully and that I'm sending in the nomination of William Leary this evening." In one fell swoop the Governor rebuffed the President, the Speaker, and the state Republican chairman of the State of New York and the New York County Republican Committee. It helped little that Leary was a loyal Republican regular, or that Hughes thought his independence was the best Republican politics. The incident, with similar confrontations to follow, festered, and in time seriously impaired the Governor's relations with the President and the state's important Republican leaders.[12]

The actions of the new governor strained his relations with no Republican leader more than with Speaker Wadsworth. Unlike the strain put on the Governor's relations with William Barnes—they were polls apart ideologically—the threats to the Hughes-Wadsworth relationship were frequently fortuitous. On the same day that the Governor announced Leary's appointment, he made public the appointments of Frederick C. Stevens as Superintendent of Public Works, and Charles Hollam Keep as Superintendent of Banking. The Keep appointment brought no criticism, but the Stevens appointment was almost beyond Wadsworth's belief. Only a few months previously, Stevens, former state senator and chairman of a specially-formed Gas Committee, bolted the Wyoming County GOP, in the heart of Wadsworth's territory, to aid Peter Porter in unseating the elder Wadsworth from his congressional seat. Bad blood flowed between the Stevenses and the Wadsworths. For years Stevens had balked at delivering Wyoming and Allegheny counties in his senatorial district to the

12. Wesser, op. cit., pp. 115–123; Brown, op. cit., p. 137; Henry C. Beerits, "Memorandum," p. 5, Charles E. Hughes MSS; New York Times, Jan. 14, 1907.

Wadsworths in exchange for Livingston County support. And when Stevens moved to share more political power in Wadsworth country, the Speaker gerrymandered him out of the Senate.[13]

Although Wadsworth was stunned, the Stevens appointment made sense. As a senator, he had chaired the important Gas Committee to which Hughes had served as counsel and on whose findings the new governor had recommended regulatory utilities legislation. Further, Hughes was unaware of the intensity of feeling between Stevens and the Wadsworths.

The press had a field day with the Stevens appointment. Reporters viewed the appointment as part of the Governor's campaign against the young Speaker and the Republican organization. And Wadsworth was inclined to agree. "Do you know, Governor," he said, "if you had used your great mind to discover the way in which you could have done me the most injury, you would have found no better way than appointing Mr. Stevens to this place?" "Then the statements which I read in the newspapers are true?" asked the Governor. "They are," said Wadsworth. "I never gave the subject a moment's consideration," replied Hughes.[14]

The Governor immediately made amends for what he had done, without, of course, withdrawing the appointment. He issued a statement disavowing any political intent in the appointment, noting the ability of the new superintendent and "particularly" emphasizing that the appointment should not be regarded as showing the slightest antagonism to Speaker Wadsworth, "for whom . . . [I have] the most unqualified esteem." The young Speaker swallowed his chagrin and in the spirit of fairness supported the appointment, bringing other organization leaders into line.[15]

Before two weeks elapsed, Governor Hughes again threatened the Republican organization, and especially Wadsworth, by calling in Otto Kelsey, the Superintendent of Insurance, and requesting his resignation. Having been counsel to the Armstrong Committee which exposed abuses in the state's insurance industry, Hughes naturally made insurance reform a priority consideration in his administration. He felt that Kelsey had not heeded Armstrong Committee suggestions which were necessary to prevent "a recurrence of evil practices" in the insurance industry.

Otto Kelsey lived on Main Street in Geneseo, only half a block from the Wadsworth Farms office. Under the elder Wadsworth's tutelage, he had quickly climbed the organizational ladder. He had served as Livings-

13. Wesser, op. cit., pp. 119–123; Brown, op. cit., pp. 124–125.

14. Burton J. Hendrick, "Governor Hughes," McClures Magazine, Vol. XXX, No. 5, pp. 521–536.

15. Wesser, op. cit., p. 122; Beerits, op. cit., p. 8; Rochester Democrat & Chronicle, Jan. 16, 1907.

ton County Assemblyman from 1894–1902; was appointed State Comptroller in 1903; and in 1905 became Superintendent of Insurance. Young Jim had "real affection" for Kelsey and, like all of his neighbors, viewed him as the "soul of honor." [16]

Hughes never questioned Kelsey's personal honesty or integrity, but he did think he had bungled the Armstrong Committee's recommendations. Given the furor created by the committee's exposures in 1905, and the fact that Senator Armstrong and Hughes had talked at length with Kelsey about the insurance industry when he had first become superintendent, the Governor could not understand why no vital changes had been effected by 1907.[17]

On January 31, Hughes summoned Kelsey to the Governor's Mansion and quietly asked for his resignation. Kelsey asked for time. Hughes acquiesced and in the meantime discussed the affair with the party leaders. The leadership, including the moderate Speaker and the more liberal Herbert Parsons, were displeased by the Governor's precedent-breaking dismissal and well understood Kelsey's position in not resigning. Taking great umbrage at the Governor's attack upon him, Kelsey released a preliminary annual insurance report in which he questioned the Hughes-sponsored legislation passed in 1906 as being too harsh and restrictive.[18]

Hughes then made public his request for the Insurance superintendent's resignation and took advantage of Kelsey's request for "justice" by calling Kelsey before him in his chambers for a public hearing. The Insurance superintendent, no match for Hughes, was nearly demolished. He complained about the formal nature of the hearing, wondered aloud if he should have legal counsel, admitted that he had not read thoroughly the Armstrong report, agreed that Insurance Department personnel responsible for insurance irregularities were still employed by the department, lamely suggested that such employees were only performing technical tasks, and offered the case burden of the San Francisco earthquake and fire as reasons for thus far not reforming the department. The Governor pursued his "prey" with detailed questions regarding the minutiae of Insurance Department operations and specifically wanted to know how the San Francisco fire precluded the institution of reform. Kelsey faltered. At the hearing's end, he requested that his counsel have time to examine the transcript.

16. Wesser, *op. cit.*, p. 126; Wadsworth, *Autobiography*, p. 146, Wadsworth MSS, Library of Congress, Washington, D.C.

17. Wesser, *op. cit.*, p. 126.

18. *Ibid.*, pp. 127–128.

"Now, Mr. Superintendent," responded Hughes coldly, "there is no indictment against you. . . . The sole object is to get out the facts." The Governor concluded: "But, I want you to supplement . . . [the transcript] and do anything that ought to be done to make it complete."[19]

Kelsey immediately supplemented the transcript, sending to the Governor a long letter, again emphasizing the additional work-load caused by the San Francisco earthquake. The Governor was, of course, unmoved and sent to the state Senate a harshly-worded indictment demanding the superintendent's removal from office. The issue was fast becoming the *cause célèbre* of the new administration.[20]

Wadsworth notes in his memoirs that he was only a spectator of the torrid events, "although deeply interested." One Hughes biographer credits Wadsworth with a "neutral position in the matter." Contemporary sources, however, demonstrate more than a spectator role on the part of the Speaker, and of his father. The *New York Press* reported, probably accurately, that while young Jim caucussed with western New York senators regarding a strategy to defend the superintendent, his father, by telephone from Washington, where he resided, pressured the same senators to make a stiff fight against the removal of the superintendent.[21]

Also, evidence that the young Wadsworth and his father were more than spectators was revealed by the solidarity with which western New York senators, representing 13 of 20 counties west of Syracuse, supported Kelsey. Their votes, with the votes of two downstate Republicans and an almost solid phalanx of Democrats, saved Kelsey from removal by a close 27–24 vote. Of course, the Speaker stayed clear of the senate chamber during weeks of hearings before the Senate Judiciary Committee and during debate on the senate floor. There, Majority Leader John Raines, himself a member of the Judiciary Committee, saw that Kelsey got a "fair hearing." He stalled the hearing by permitting former state Supreme Court Justice Edward G. Hatch, Kelsey's counsel, to question interminable numbers of witnesses while the superintendent effected the reforms which the San Francisco 'quake had supposedly precluded. Hatch skillfully corroborated Kelsey's point that departmental reform had perforce to await the adjustment of thousands of San Francisco claims. Evidence of very recent institution of reform were letters of resignation by the two most controversial

19. Wesser, *op. cit.*, pp. 128–130; *Proceedings Before the Senate of the State of New York on a Message from the Governor Recommending the Removal from Office of Mr. Otto Kelsey* (Albany, N.Y.: J. B. Lyon Co., 1908), pp. 11–48.

20. Wesser, *op. cit.*, pp. 130–131.

21. Wadsworth, Jr., *Autobiography*, pp. 146–147; *New York Press*, Feb. 12, 1907.

members of the department, Isaac Vanderpoel and Robert H. Hunter, dated January 17 and February 19, respectively. Although only Vanderpoel's resignation preceded Hughes's January 31 request for Kelsey's resignation, Hatch elicited from the Insurance superintendent his intent to relieve the two men since the summer of 1906. Hatch also called various officials to testify concerning the superintendent's ability as an administrator. The Hughes position was, of course, also aired before the Judiciary Committee. Although evidence elicited by the Governor when he took "proof" was still very substantial, Hatch's work made possible a "no recommendation" by the committee, except that the full Senate decide the issue. Then the Judiciary Committee asked that Hatch have the senate floor.[22]

Hatch again performed brilliantly in Kelsey's defense but now had the added assistance of western New York senators. Few were as persuasive as Wadsworth's Senator S. Percy Hooker, who particularly resented Hughes's threat to gerrymander out of the Senate recalcitrant Republicans if they did not vote for removal. Hooker claimed to have the courage of Roosevelt and Hughes. Differing honestly with the Governor, who he felt did not "represent all the honesty, integrity, courage and brains in the State," Hooker concluded, "I cannot and will not waive my own judgment, [and] become one of those who bend the pregnant knee to royalty and vociferously exclaim, 'the King can do no wrong.' "[23]

Hooker, Raines, and their fellow western New York senators could not have bailed out Kelsey without Democratic assistance. Tammany's Tom Grady and the Democratic leader for Kings County, Patrick McCarren, allied with the Republicans to defeat the twenty-two Hughes senators and the two Democrats who defected from the Democratic ranks.[24]

Wadsworth, needless to say, was pleased with the results. "His" victory was all the more remarkable in that the senators of most organization leaders stayed with the Governor—those from the senatorial districts of Parsons, Barnes, Woodruff, Aldridge, and O'Brian. Wadsworth and Hooker were probably the more justified in their stand. Although Kelsey was anything but a vigorous Insurance superintendent and should have tendered his resignation when Hughes came into office, the Governor's case did not warrant Kelsey's public removal by the Senate. Still, the Wadsworths were uneasy about their ward. The Boss, at various times, unsuccessfully tried to bring Kelsey home and make him the Livingston

22. *Proceedings Before the Senate,* pp. 89–710, *passim; New York Times,* May 1, 1907; Wesser, *op. cit.,* pp. 135–136.
23. *Proceedings Before the Senate,* pp. 778–780; Wesser, *op. cit.,* pp. 138–140; *New York Times,* Apr. 27, May 1, 2, 3, 1907.
24. Wesser, *op. cit.,* p. 138; *The Nation,* May 9, 1907.

County judge. Jim wondered how long he himself would "survive" the torrid events. "The best way," he wrote Aunt Tillie, "is to keep straight ahead and retain a clear conscience." [25]

It was not surprising that Wadsworth spoke of survival in the spring of 1907. While Stevens and the Governor seemed to be dismantling the Wadsworth machine, the President got into the act. On April 13, he demanded the resignation of Archie Sanders as Collector of Internal Revenue at Rochester. Sanders, from Genesee County, had long been loyal to the Wadsworth organization. In fact, he alone among federal office-holders in the district defied the President and vociferously supported the Boss for re-election to the Congress in 1906. For that reason, and because the President agreed with Stevens that Sanders' removal would aid the Governor's reform program, the collector was asked to step down. Excitement prevailed. The Boss called Roosevelt a "Fakir and humbug," and noted that "the country is fast awakening to the real character of this bloody hero of Kettle Hill." Louisa was right: "Jimmy [the Boss] bellows his opinions from the house tops" about T.R.'s attempt to "break up the Wadsworth power in western New York." As quickly as the Boss bellowed, Hughes disavowed the Roosevelt action, claiming no knowledge or interest in the Sanders removal. Roosevelt sheepishly retracted the demand. He would never forgive Hughes for his "thoraly [sic] selfish and cold-blooded" act of repudiation.[26] "There is no telling what will happen next," wrote Louisa on April 20.[27]

For all of Wadsworth's contention with the Governor on many issues in 1907, he largely supported the Hughes program in the Legislature. And given the conservative character of the state Senate, Hughes needed and appreciated the Speaker's support. On March 8, Wadsworth firmly supported the mainstay of Hughes's legislative program—the Page-Merritt public utility commission bill. The bill, stemming from the 1905 Senate investigation in which Hughes served as counsel, called for two five-member commissions, one to supervise public service corporations downstate, the other upstate. The commissions were to investigate complaints, assure adequate service, set rates, determine accounting procedures, and change schedules when necessary. Wadsworth's only *caveat* was understandably

25. *New York Times*, May 3, 1907; conversation with W. B. Sanders, summer 1966; J.W.W. to Mrs. Tillie Gay, March 4, 1907, Wadsworth MSS; Wadsworth, Jr., *Autobiography*, pp. 146–147.

26. Wesser, *op. cit.*, pp. 163–164; Brown, *op. cit.*, p. 141; *New York Times*, Apr. 19, 1907; Beerits, *op. cit.*, pp. 16–20.

27. Louisa Wadsworth to Tillie Gay, Wadsworth MSS; *New York Times*, Apr. 20, 1907.

the Governor's removal authority. He told the press, "I am unalterably opposed to vesting that power anywhere but in the Senate." As the Senate was saving Kelsey from removal at the very time Hughes was seeking "removal authority" in the Page-Merritt bill, the press saw Wadsworth, the Governor's "mainstay" in the bill, breaking away. But Wadsworth pushed the bill through the Assembly. He saw it out of committee, and in the final Republican caucus on it seemed so anxious to cut short debate on the bill, including the removal clause, that he jumped to his feet almost before the final vote and moved for adjournment. The Senate, however, balked. Its leader, John Raines, capitulated only after Roosevelt's Congressman William W. Cocks conferred with state leaders to pressure for passage. In short, although the efforts of Hughes, Roosevelt, and a sympathetic press principally explain the passage of the important utilities bill, Wadsworth's support was a contributing factor. Comparable factors seem to explain passage of other elements of the Hughes reform program in 1907 —New York City charter reform, limitation of campaign expenditures, reorganization of the New York City courts, New York City recount legislation, corrupt practices legislation, a water-power site bill, and a bill granting the Governor authority to investigate his Executive Department.[28]

"Affairs here at Albany are progressing most favorably," wrote Wadsworth to Roosevelt on May 29. "In fact, they have never been as bad as the newspaper reports through the winter have insinuated. When the session of the Legislature shall have finished I believe that the State Administration and the party in general will be in a strong position in this State." [29]

The letter is revealing of an equanimity which would frequently mark Wadsworth's long political life. While the Boss fumed over the President's role in his defeat a half-year previously; while Louisa feared for both her husband and her son in the Sanders affair; while both the Boss and Jim worked to save Kelsey; and while young Jim expressed no little annoyance at the Governor for his appointment of Stevens as Superintendent of Public Works, the Speaker assuaged both the President and the Governor.

The swirl of events in which Wadsworth was caught from January to May of 1907 was far from abated by the time of his reassuring letter to Roosevelt. For one thing, he became embroiled in a controversy concerning William Pryor Letchworth's gift of his 1,000-acre estate which included the incredibly beautiful gorge and falls in the Genesee River, south of

28. Wesser, op. cit., pp. 155–171; New York Times, May 1, 3, 4, 8, 9, 14, 1907; Livingston Republican, May 16, 1907.

29. J.W.W. to Theodore Roosevelt, May 29, 1907, Roosevelt MSS, Library of Congress, Washington, D.C.

Rochester. The Speaker had vigorously supported in the Legislature a renewal of a Genesee River Company charter which would have diverted waters from the falls. When Letchworth then gave his estate to the state on condition that the state effect no changes, Wadsworth still sought legislative permission to build a dam that would have, at times, reduced the falls' flow to 100 cubic feet per second. The press, ecstatic about Mr. Letchworth's gift, frequently reached a comparable pitch of opposition regarding Wadsworth's alleged tampering with the gift. With such an adverse reaction and with the work of Letchworth's attentive lawyers, Wadsworth lost. Allegations of his motives were numerous, the most frequently-mentioned being collusion between him and the River Company's Board of Directors. Such was never proved. However, the magnificent falls were threatened by the River Company's charter, and Wadsworth's involvement in the affair added no lustre to his reputation, then or now.[30]

Equally traumatic and bad, press-wise, was an unsuccessful fight against a legislative apportionment plan which was intended to transfer the Wadsworth hold on Genesee and Wyoming counties to Frederick Stevens, an old foe of the family. Many Hughes Republicans, like Herbert Parsons, felt that Wadsworth, who had given so much for Hughes, should not be so treated. Hughes, however, was loath to get involved in such matters and Wadsworth finally, after two Legislature sessions, gave in rather than have apportionment revert to an old law which would have stripped the family of its control of even their home county.[31]

2

In late 1907 the press was full of dire attempts to discredit Hughes when the new legislature convened early in the new year, and of charges

30. *New York Times,* May 10, 1907; *Livingston Republican,* June 6, 1907; see numerous clippings, Letchworth MSS (SUNY, Geneseo, N.Y.); Adelbert Moot to William P. Letchworth, Apr. 1, May 2, May 11, 1907, Edward Hagaman Hall to William P. Letchworth, Apr. 18, May 6, 11, 27, 1907, Letchworth MSS. Assumption of possible dam spoilage is based on conversation with Gordon Harvey, Supt. of Letchworth State Park. Flow of minimum of 100 cubic feet per second mandated in Schoeneck bill should have been only a "trickle" of water as compared to average flow of 2,000 cubic feet per second. Conversation, summer 1967.

31. *New York Times,* June 7, 8, 15, 17, 18, 20, 27, July 16, 17, 24, 1907; Wesser, *op. cit.,* p. 174; Herbert Parsons to Theodore Roosevelt, June 14, 17, Parsons MSS, Columbia University Library, New York, N.Y.; Beverly R. Robinson, *The Reminiscences of Beverly R. Robinson,* (Columbia University: Oral History Office, 1949), p. 52.

that Roosevelt would be a party to the process. One report had it that Wadsworth's re-election as Speaker was an important part of the discrediting effort on the presumption that few Republicans had more reason to be anti-Hughes than the Geneseoan. Another alleged anti-Hughes strategy was to make Jesse S. Phillips, a Wadsworth associate, the Assembly majority leader. *The New York Sun* reported that the election of Wadsworth and Phillips to the Assembly leadership would be a prelude to Wadsworth's nomination for the governorship in September of 1908.[32]

Such prognostications were, at best, ill-founded. While Wadsworth was firmly in control of the new Assembly and effected his own re-election as Speaker, he vigorously supported the progressive E. A. Merrit as majority leader. Also, Wadsworth expressed no interest in opposing the Governor's political ambitions, including any interest Hughes might have in the presidency. Somewhat ominous, however, was Wadsworth's comment that his duties as Speaker would preclude any political activity concerning the governorship. Such was, of course, absurd for the Speaker was knee-deep in New York Republican politics and publicly so by the summer of 1908.[33]

Throughout the spring of 1908, the young Speaker was publicly indifferent to both Hughes's political life and his legislative program. He might not have been so had the Governor pushed many of his reform programs, especially ballot reform and the direct primary. But Hughes avoided ballot reform and the direct primary and got caught up in racetrack gambling reform. Contrary to press reports, the Governor achieved the Assembly's cooperation in repeal of the then-current racing law which clearly flouted the Constitution. It was the Senate which defeated the Agnew-Hart bill, so enraging the Governor that in late spring he campaigned in a Niagara County senate by-election for a candidate committed to racetrack reform. The candidate won and gave Hughes the one necessary vote to get Senate passage of racetrack reform in a special session of the Legislature. As in January, the Governor had the cooperation of Wadsworth's Assembly in the final passage of the bill.[34]

Although Hughes's legislative record in 1908 was feeble as compared to that in 1907, the racetrack victory attracted such national attention that many progressive Republicans considered him a presidential contender. Of course, a year previously Roosevelt himself had considered Hughes a likely successor until the Governor became blatantly independent. Roose-

32. *Attica Observer*, Nov. 16, 1907; *Rochester Union*, Nov. 18, 1907; *New York Sun*, Nov. 18, 1907, Fuller Collection, New York Public Library.

33. *New York Times*, Jan. 1, 2, 14, 17, 20, 1908.

34. Wesser, *op. cit.*, pp. 191–201; Brown, *op. cit.*, pp. 144–145; Robinson, *op. cit.*; *New York Times*, May 9, 1908.

velt was deeply offended by Hughes's disavowal of the President's attempt to remove the Wadsworth liege in Rochester, Archie Sanders. Even after that "mugwumpism," T.R. waited "watchfully" before publicly supporting Secretary of War Taft as his first choice. While Hughes's racetrack fight and progressive pronouncements in the spring of 1908 conjured support in and out of the state, Roosevelt successfully concerted with the state's organization leaders to have Taft delegates appointed to the GOP state convention in April. That convention easily blocked a Hughes endorsement for the presidency, paving the way for a quick Taft presidential nomination at the Republican convention in June. In fact, New York's conservative anti-Hughes forces, including Wadsworth, proved so forceful at the national convention that they put over Utica Congressman James S. Sherman, long identified with their wing of the party, as the vice presidential candidate. Actually, Taft would have preferred a western Progressive as a running-mate. The *New York Times* thought the Sherman victory by the New York conservatives paved the way for replacing Hughes with Wadsworth in the New York governorship.[35]

Retirement from the governorship was an attractive thought to Hughes, but recent rebuffs—particularly the failure to achieve direct nominations legislation and an improved public service commission law, and the Sherman nomination—seemed to strengthen his political resolve. On July 24 he shocked his conservative opponents by announcing his desire for another term.[36]

Upon recovering from their state of shock, GOP stalwarts followed State Chairman Woodruff's lead in fighting the Governor's renomination. Even the moderate Herbert Parsons enlisted in the effort. But Woodruff met with resistance. The national GOP forces did not want a New York donnybrook that might lose the state for Taft. Besides, any Republican in his right senses knew Hughes would have far more support in a gubernatorial race than Wadsworth or other possible contenders.[37]

Still, Wadsworth, encouraged by Barnes, thought he had a chance to be governor. "He [Barnes]," Wadsworth wrote Alice on the eve of the Republican state convention, "says we can win and are going to. We figured that Hughes will have about 300 delegates when the convention meets—that's fairly liberal; that the opposition would have 500 almost sure, without counting Buffalo and Rochester on either side. It takes 505 to nominate. So you see, there is an excellent chance and there will be a

35. Wesser, *op. cit.*, Ch. IX, *passim*; *New York Times*, June 20, 1908.
36. Wesser, *op. cit.*, pp. 228–229.
37. *Boston Transcript*, Aug. 4, 1908; *Auburn Citizen*, Aug. 13, 1908.

big fight." [38] Barnes and Wadsworth deluded themselves. They could not get stalwarts to agree on the Geneseoan as their candidates—Kings County wanted William Berri, Brooklyn publisher, as their favorite-son candidate —let alone get the support of the federal Root-Taft-Roosevelt-Sherman crowd. When, at the state convention, David Jayne Hill, the former president of the University of Rochester and the ambassador to Germany, was suggested as a stalwart compromise, Elihu Root laughed and then in a no-nonsense fashion said that Taft and Roosevelt wanted Hughes. The conservatives capitulated, except Barnes who still pushed for Wadsworth and with great flourish and bitterness seconded his nomination. "If antiorganization leaders, like Hughes, are to discredit party effort," he exhorted, "and such a policy is to be established as Republican doctrine . . . why should . . . [not the loyal Republican] be admonished in advance that he must forever hold himself disbarred from the public service." The Barnes effort was futile exercise.

Hughes was nominated on the first ballot, receiving 827 votes to 151 for Wadsworth and 31 for John K. Stewart of Montgomery County. While federal forces had little difficulty putting over Hughes's renomination, the platform reflected more truly the tone of the state convention. It only perfunctorily endorsed the federal administration and was absolutely silent on the direct primary and the need to extend the jurisdiction of the Public Service Commission. Still, by election time the Republican organization supported their candidate and he beat the Democratic candidate, Lieutenant Governor Lewis Chanler, by a plurality of 69,462 votes.[39]

On January 1, 1909, the re-elected governor entered the Assembly chambers and ironically announced a program destined to firmly remove the Assembly Speaker from the moderate role he consistently played in the first Hughes administration. Heretofore, in a true aristocratic and conservative sense, Wadsworth had reacted responsibly to the Governor's principal programs, particularly the public utility commission bill and the racetrack gambling reform legislation, albeit, he had little enthusiasm for the gamut of progressive legislation sprouting in New York and other states. And, had he been more aware of the seething nature of the result, he might have protested more loudly. Yet, to date, the Speaker tolerated the Governor's important measures, surprising in view of many of the

38. J.W.W. to Alice Hay Wadsworth, Sept. 2, 1908, Wadsworth MSS.

39. Wesser, op. cit., pp. 231–251; Brown, op. cit., pp. 153–155; Taft to Theodore Roosevelt, Aug. 15, 16, Sept. 1, 1908, Roosevelt MSS; see numerous clippings re Wadsworth candidacy in Fuller Collection, New York Public Library; Beerits, op. cit., "Renomination and Re-election as Governor."

Cartoons, about 1908 and 1912. Photographed from the originals in the Wadsworth Farms office, Main Street, Geneseo, New York.

Governor's apparent anti-Wadsworth constraints such as the Swasey affair, the Stevens appointment, the attempted Kelsey purge, and reapportionment. Now, however, the Governor treaded heavily on the Speaker by demanding direct primary legislation. The proposal, a bane to Wadsworth, stood out in bold relief as compared to the Governor's treatment of conservation, highway maintenance, public health, agriculture, labor, education, utility regulation, insurance and state institutions.[40]

The Speaker, re-elected—Majority Leader Merritt described him as "untainted by criticism or innuendo—a man without blame or fear"—immediately took exception to the direct primary proposal.[41] While the Kelsey affair evoked Hughes's criticism of senate authority regarding removal of executive officers, it confirmed Wadsworth's belief in that power. On the direct primary, the young Speaker was adamant. Even more than Barnes, Raines, and other stalwarts, he viewed it as irresponsible. When shortly after the inauguration Hughes contended that three-fourths of the Assembly was constituted of men elected without contest, after having been nominated by local party bosses, Wadsworth fumed at the implication that "any sort of a man" could be sure of election to his Assembly.

"The Governor has suddenly discovered," he replied with no little hyperbole, "a state of affairs which has never occurred to anyone else. If the Governor is right," Wadsworth pointed out, "the legislative branch is rotten to the core." The press descended upon Wadsworth. The *New York Evening Post* called him a legislative sophomore. The *New York World* regretted that he had unwisely become the "champion" of the bosses who, if "virtuous" instead of "rotten," were only so for fear of "affronting public opinion" and losing the "plum tree" and "pork barrel" emanating from Republican victories at the state and national levels.[42]

The direct primary confrontation between Hughes and Wadsworth was honest and classic. The Governor believed that the convention system failed to name candidates favored by the rank and file members of the party; that therefore nominees considered themselves accountable to the party leaders and their party constituents. Just as sincerely, Wadsworth believed that party leaders should be held accountable for the party's candidates but not without the authority, in convention, to select such candidates. Especially did he think that party leaders in large judiciary and

40. Wesser, *op. cit.*, p. 259.

41. *New York Times*, Jan. 6, 1909; *Rochester Post Express*, Jan. 7, 1909.

42. J.W.W. to Nicholas Murray Butler, Jan. 15, 1909, Wadsworth MSS; *New York Times*, Jan. 26, 1909; *New York World*, Jan. 27, 1909; *New York Evening Post*, Jan. 26, 1909; Herbert Hillel Rosenthal, "The Progressive Movement in New York State, 1906–1914" (Harvard University: Ph.D. dissertation, 1955), p. 135.

statewide constituencies, where candidates for the Supreme Court and statewide offices, such as governor and lieutenant governor were to be selected, should represent their parties in nominating candidates, in preference to contenders for office going all over the state "shaking hands, kissing babies, slapping you on the back and making promises." If bosses unduly dominated nominating conventions, Wadsworth suggested, "control . . . the conventions by law." The Geneseoan did accept the idea of direct primary for selecting candidates for local offices where "we know the different candidates." [43]

The struggle of the two points of view focused on the Hinman-Green bill, a compromise bill, the key feature of which called for the state committee, in convention, to select candidates to challenge other contenders who, by petition, would have their names placed on the primary ballot. In the same fashion, other committees—the congressional district committee, the judicial district committee, the county committee, and so forth —would name candidates for their jurisdictions. Neither wing of the Republican party was happy about the compromise. Assemblyman Beverly R. Robinson of New York County said it merely "narrows down to the substitute of the State Committee with a membership of 37 for a convention of 1,000 delegates." [44]

Wadsworth led the conservative opposition to the Hinman-Green bill. Although pleased that it incorporated some of his ideas regarding enrollment procedures and an official primary ballot, he was sure it would strengthen, not weaken, the hold of the party organization over the nominating process. Also, he argued, opponents of the nominating committee would have to run in two primaries—the convention canvass and the primary itself—at prohibitive cost. Behind Wadsworth's public rhetoric on the bill lay his real opposition: regardless of how one sliced the Hinman-Green bill, it was a direct primary. With little public enthusiasm for the bill within the state, and a lack of pressure from Taft, Roosevelt, and Root, now New York's junior United States senator, Wadsworth led the Assembly to defeat it overwhelmingly. The New York Senate followed suit. As a sop, the Legislature passed the Meade resolution calling for a joint legislative committee, to be appointed by the Speaker and the Lieutenant Governor, to study various types of provisions. [45]

Hughes was, as he told the annual Legislative Correspondents' Asso-

43. James W. Wadsworth, Jr., *The Reminiscences of James W. Wadsworth, Jr.* (Columbia University: Oral History Research Office, 1952), pp. 70–73.

44. Wesser, *op. cit.*, p. 263.

45. Wadsworth, *Reminiscences*, pp. 70–73; Wesser, *op. cit.*, pp. 264–268; *New York Times*, Apr. 4, 1909.

ciation dinner in April, no quitter. Although he set aside the direct primary issue and other reforms for the remainder of the session, he directed his staff to organize a state-wide effort, in the guise of the Direct Primary Association, to defeat Hinman-Green opponents in the November elections and propagandize for a direct primary.[46]

Quite naturally, Speaker Wadsworth became the focal point for defeat at the polls. In late summer, the association's secretary, Frederick Cone, entered Livingston County and made an alliance with the Democratic candidate for the Assembly, Albert C. Olp, to defeat Wadsworth. The eyes of the state were on the "red-hot" race in Livingston County. Wadsworth, by his own account, had the fight of his life. By campaign's end on election day, his 1908 plurality of 2,000 was cut to under 300. Quite apparently, the long-standing Wadsworth influence in the county saved him. (Forty-six of the 112 assemblymen who voted against the Hinman-Green bill were not so fortunate. They were defeated.) There was another, though less apparent, explanation of the young Speaker's success. Ironically, Hughes himself saved his adversary. Although Cone effected a bi-partisan alliance with Olp to defeat Wadsworth, Hughes would not let his own staff leader, William H. Wadhams, enter Livingston County to aid the alliance. When Wadhams eagerly called Hughes from the Livingston County border for permission to enter, the Governor firmly replied: "Don't do it. Don't go into Livingston County. I don't want a campaign for the defeat of Wadsworth." Wadhams was aghast. His recollection some years later was that Hughes further replied, "Wadsworth is a very useful man. He's an honest man. He's a capable man and ought to be retained in public life. . . . I think men of education and of ability such as he has are few in public life and that he should continue to serve the State." [47]

By January of 1910 Hughes felt ready to push strenuously for the Hinman-Green bill. Unfortunately, the Senate got bogged down in electing a majority leader to replace the recently-deceased John Raines. Then, having settled on Jotham P. Allds, a Raines henchman, the Senate got snarled in a charge that he had some years previously accepted a $1,000 bribe to beat down a "strike" bill. For six weeks the Senate set aside all legislative matters, including the primary bill, and investigated Allds. Concurrent with the investigation, which considerably tarnished the GOP image, Taft pleaded with Hughes, Wadsworth, Chairman Woodruff, and

46. Wesser, op. cit., p. 268.

47. William H. Wadhams, The Reminiscences of William H. Wadhams (Columbia University: Oral History Research Office, 1950); Rosenthal, op. cit., pp. 152–163.

Senator Chauncey Depew to quit warring on the direct primary and get behind a leader. The President failed, for the Hughes and Wadsworth factions disagreed not only on a leader and the direct primary, but on the Allds investigation itself. While reformers wanted the senate investigation broadened to root out all possible evil-doers in the Legislature, Wadsworth thought that such an investigation was too much like a witch-hunt and would merely exacerbate the Republican situation. Allds was found guilty of wrong-doing and replaced by a new majority leader, George Cobb. Finally, the Senate could turn its attention to the Hinman-Green bill.[48]

In the meantime, the special legislative commission issued its final report, making proposals not surprisingly quite consistent with those made by Speaker Wadsworth in 1909: a uniform primary day, an official primary ballot, statewide enrollment of all voters, and the elimination of the current party management of primaries. Hughes, of course, was dissatisfied and, just as the public expected, the Governor and the Speaker did battle royal on the issue, until President Taft interrupted by appointing the Governor to the Supreme Court. Hughes insisted he would carry on the primary fight through September, but he did so with little success. Wadsworth had little difficulty in defeating the Hinman-Green bill, noting again that the proposed nominating committees would actually be less democratic than existing conventions and that having direct primaries for all elected officers across the state would only make for confusion. The young Speaker stood against all attempted compromises. Professor Wesser notes that, as if to rub salt in Hughes's wounds, the Assembly passed the Meade-Phillips bill which contained the minor changes recommended by the Direct Primary Commission and the "determined Speaker." [49]

In the remaining days of the session, Wadsworth did support the Governor's bills to tighten the 1908 racing legislation, to revise existing insurance restrictions, to establish a workmen's compensation law, and to strengthen the utilities laws. The Governor apparently misread such support as a weakening on the part of the Geneseoan and convened a special session of the Legislature to get the Hinman-Green bill passed. But the Geneseoan would not give in. The divided Republican party unhappily adjourned its Legislature and prepared for its state convention to convene at Saratoga on September 27. [50]

The convention at Saratoga was to be a battle.

48. Wesser, op. cit., pp. 276–290; Rosenthal, op. cit., pp. 153–175.
49. Wesser, op. cit., p. 292.
50. Ibid., pp. 293–296; Rosenthal, op. cit., pp. 174–176.

3

On June 16 Theodore Roosevelt returned a hero from a two-year stint in the jungles of Africa and the capitals of Europe. A compulsive politico, listening to all manner of Republicans, including Wadsworth, filling his ears at Oyster Bay—the principal contention being between stand-pat and progressive wings of the GOP—T.R. soon entered the fray. It was fortuitous, yet natural, that Wadsworth would become one of the former president's principal contenders.

Within two weeks of his return, Roosevelt broke a self-imposed silence to defend Hughes in his direct primary flight. Both attended the Harvard commencement on June 29, and there, under the elms of the college Yard, discussed the issue of the day, the direct primary. At first Roosevelt demurred from supporting the measure, but when Hughes insisted that "silence means opposition," T.R. exclaimed, "Opposition! Opposition! Silence means opposition! I'll speak."

Following the commencement exercise, Roosevelt addressed an alumni conference. "Our Governor has a very persuasive way with him," he told his audience. "I have intended to keep absolutely clear of any kind of public or political question after coming home, and I have carried my resolution out all right until I met the Governor this morning . . . and after a very brief conversation I put up my hands and agreed to help him." That evening the former governor publicly appealed to legislative leaders to accept the Cobb Direct Primary bill with minor modifications. In doing so, he swelled enormously Republican pressures in the state and the nation on the young Speaker of the Assembly.[51]

Wadsworth resisted the pressure. Although a majority of Republicans in the Assembly knuckled under and favored the Cobb bill, the Speaker successfully warded off a caucus to commit the Republicans to a party vote. Forty Republicans stayed with the Speaker and were joined by forty Democrats to defeat the bill. The Senate, taking the Assembly lead, also defeated the measure, but nearly acquiesced under the Roosevelt pressure. There the Cobb bill lost by one vote.

"The supreme issue," reported young Wadsworth to the press, "is whether the Assembly shall swallow its convictions and deliberately

51. Wesser, op. cit., pp. 297–298; Brown, op. cit., pp. 179–180.

reverse its honest judgment and thereby announce to the legislatures of the future that the legislative branch of the government . . . can be coerced and forced to occupy a secondary position in our system of government."[52]

If Wadsworth's reaction was viewed as heady by some, it was not by others. "It may interest you to know," wrote a *New York World* reporter to the Speaker, "that I have not seen a man in or out of politics—and I have looked up many—who does not regard the job you pulled off . . . as a splendid piece of work; a view that I fully endorse. The rest of the country, according to the sentiments reflected by the newspaper comments seems to have appreciated the extent and importance of the achievement."[53] Admirers from the hinterland were less staid. "You not only put the Governor to bed," wrote a lawyer from upstate, "but sent the President, Vice President, and Senator back to Washington . . . [and] you now returned the 'big stick with blood on it.'"[54] Louisa, in a letter to Aunt Tilly, summed up for the family. "[James] has just won his long battle with the Governor, and Teddy, who could not refrain from meddling, failed for the first time in public affairs, which means that Teddy's not now infallible or feared as he was."[55]

Feared or not, Roosevelt thrashed about for vindication. More was at stake than a confrontation with the young Speaker of the Assembly and his allies, Barnes and Woodruff. The former president was concerned about the national party and the incumbent president. The tension between Roosevelt and Taft, stemming from differences over policies and personnel, i.e., conservation policies and the President's firing of Gifford Pinchot, was common rumor.[56] If Roosevelt were to be a force in "straightening out" the GOP, his New York political base would be essential. To establish that base, Wadsworth, who most opposed the issue on which party control turned, would have to be brushed aside.

Roosevelt sought his vindication and control of the New York party at a Republican state committee meeting held on August 16, 1910. When some hours before the meeting, which was expected to be a routine affair, the former president heard that Wadsworth and associates were going to elect Vice President "Sunny Jim" Sherman of Utica temporary chairman

52. Rosenthal, *op. cit.*, p. 243; Wesser, *op. cit.*, p. 299.
53. Lional Siebold to J.W.W., July 4, 1910, Wadsworth MSS.
54. Charles L. Fellows to J.W.W., July 1, 1910, Wadsworth MSS.
55. Louisa Wadsworth to Mrs. Walter Gay, July 2, 1910, Wadsworth MSS.
56. George Mowry, *Theodore Roosevelt and the Progressive Movement* (Madison, Wis.: University of Wisconsin Press, 1946), Ch. IV and V, *passim*; Rosenthal, *op. cit.*, Ch. V, *passim*.

of the forthcoming state convention, Roosevelt was enraged. Sherman, a devoted Taftite and arch enemy of the Roosevelt forces in his Utica congressional district, would, as temporary chairman, keynote the convention along conservative and anti-direct primary lines. Roosevelt then, through Lloyd Griscom, consented to have his name put up for the same position. Hughes, very recently appointed to the Supreme Court, was happy to have Roosevelt fight the bosslets who had for so long opposed the direct primary. When the committee met, Sherman, with Taft's tacit approval, won, 20–15. Upon hearing the news of Sherman's election, Roosevelt was stunned. At first he could not believe it. By contrast, the White House was gleeful. Taft laughed as his secretary, Charles D. Norton, shouted: "We have got him—we've got him—we've got him." Organization leaders in Albany were beside themselves, convinced as they were that they had "exchanged [Roosevelt's] steam roller for a locomotive." [57]

By day's end on August 16, the former president determined upon a course of action and a rationale. Now that organization leaders had denied him his role in harmonizing the party, he could, with clear conscience, fight them for all he was worth. As if conscious of Roosevelt's new resolve, Taft sobered quickly. Although he relished writing to his brother, "They have defeated Theodore," the President on August 17 pressed Sherman to compromise with Roosevelt on the organization of the forthcoming state convention. Sherman reluctantly agreed, but Roosevelt rejected the overture. [58]

Roosevelt was to "fight" Sherman, Wadsworth, and company some six weeks later in the convention itself. In the interim, he moved on to the national stage and irrevocably into the insurgent camp. Encouraged by a host of anti-Taft Republicans and, most importantly, by the recently-fired Chief Forester, Gifford Pinchot, the former president made a swing around the country. At Osawatomie, Kansas, he announced his doctrine of New Nationalism, i.e., effective publicity of corporate affairs, prohibition of corporate funds spent for political purposes, the regulation of capitalization of corporations, government aid to agriculture, workmen's compensation, and the enactment of the direct primary legislation. Most importantly, the former president shocked eastern Republicans with a bitter denouncement of the courts as bulwarks of property. [59]

57. Rosenthal, op. cit., pp. 251–257; New York Times, Aug. 13, 14, 1910; Brown, op. cit., pp. 180–181.
58. Rosenthal, op. cit., pp. 256–258; Henry F. Pringle, The Life and Times of William Howard Taft (New York: Farrar and Rinehart, Inc., 1939), pp. 563–565.
59. Mowry, op. cit., Chapter V.

"There is an awful fight going on for control in politics in New York State between Teddy and James and his friends," wrote Louisa to Tilly, "and it will be fought out at the State Convention. . . . I am going to see the proceedings, the results of which mean much to James. Teddy has now started on a triumphal tour of the West in a private car, stirring up the people . . . a very dangerous man. He comes back to fight at Saratoga, and says it will be war to the knife." [60]

Louisa exaggerated only slightly. Under the veneer of jocular manifestations at Saratoga—at the time T.R. called it a "bully fight" and in his autobiography, Wadsworth described it as a good-natured "free-for-all"—the struggle was ominous and a portent of Republican things to come. "The Democrats were born lucky," observed Tammany's Thomas Tracey as he watched the proceedings get under way. Even before the convention convened, the bosses and T.R.'s man Griscom had it out in the state committee, the former insisting that the committee had not been deceived into believing that Taft had supported Sherman's election as temporary chairman at the August 16 meeting, and the latter accusing Wadsworth of lying about the meeting when the Speaker denied any prior knowledge of T.R.'s candidacy. (On August 16, Wadsworth had refused to support Griscom's request to postpone the meeting.) As the state committee concluded its pre-convention meeting by reaffirming its election of Sherman as temporary chairman, Griscom swore it would be the old guard's last victory. [61]

And so it was. While Griscom had little influence over the state committee, he had directed well the election of Roosevelt delegates in the September primary, with the help of Buffalo's Fred Greiner, New York's Herbert Parsons, Brooklyn's William Calder, and Oneida County's Frederick M. Davenport. As the first business of the convention, the delegates turned aside the commitee's recommendation for temporary chairman and elected T.R. by a vote of 567 to 445. Then Roosevelt as temporary chairman proceeded to appoint the various committees, ignoring the time-honored tradition of permitting congressional district leaders to name appointees. The temporary chairman wanted to make sure that his forces would dominate the convention, particularly the Resolutions Committee. From the floor, as the minority leader, Wadsworth objected, raising many points of order, but to no avail except to confuse the former president. "The Livingston from Gentleman is completely mistaken,"

60. Louisa Wadsworth to Mrs. Walter Gay, Sept. 1910, Wadsworth MSS.

61. New York Times, Sept. 27, 28, 1910; Alden Hatch, The Wadsworths of the Genesee (New York: Coward-McCann, Inc., 1959), p. 176; Rosenthal, op. cit., pp. 293–294.

shouted Roosevelt. Roosevelt had his way. The Resolutions Committee would recommend a direct primary plank.[62]

That evening Alice and Jim entered the plush dining room of Saratoga's United States Hotel. Roosevelt and his leaders were seated at a prominently placed table. The young Speaker and his wife, radiant in appearance, sauntered among the guests until they were seated. Then he rose and walked to the former president's table to pay his respects. "Jim Wadsworth," exclaimed T.R., refusing the young Speaker's hand, "you tried to mix me up in the Convention today! You did! You know you did!" Somewhat aghast, Wadsworth responded, "No, Colonel, you mixed yourself up."[63]

On the following morning, prior to the proceedings, Roosevelt sent for Wadsworth. As he entered the former president's crowded suite, T.R. said for all to hear: "Jim Wadsworth, I'm so glad to see you! What can I do for you?" Knowing the ways of T.R., the young Speaker replied, "Colonel Roosevelt, you sent for me." Whereupon Roosevelt ushered the Speaker into a lavatory where for twenty minutes they discussed their respective strategies. Wadsworth expressed interest only in fighting the Resolution Committee's direct primary plank. T.R., reporting little personal interest in the direct primary, noted his public commitment to the plank. They parted amicably, agreeing to a floor fight on the direct primary plank.[64]

Following a prayerful appeal by the chaplain that the delegates might have "trust and brotherly love for each other," T.R. banned smoking and introduced the permanent chairman of the convention, Elihu Root. Root bowed and made a speech in which he declared that the party would unite to elect a ticket to be named later. Then the platform was read and all planks were accepted with the exception of the one on the direct primary. On it, Speaker Wadsworth opened the debate: "We believe that as the party governs itself, so essentially shall the State govern itself, and that if we establish the principle of pure democracy in the government of the party, so eventually shall the State government govern itself . . . and abolish representative government."[65]

Wadsworth was persuasive, as were others in the minority—William Barnes, E. A. Merritt, J. Sloat Fassett, and Ezra P. Prentice. The majority

62. *New York Times*, Sept. 28, 1910; Wadsworth, Jr., *Reminiscences*, pp. 76–78; Wadsworth, Jr., *Autobiography*, pp. 157–163.

63. Hatch, *op. cit.*, p. 176; Wadsworth, Jr., *Autobiography*, p. 164.

64. Hatch, *op. cit.*, p. 176.

65. *New York Times*, Sept. 29, 1910.

included Seth Low, Senator Davenport, and William A. Prendergast, all vociferous champions of the direct primary but no debating match for the minorities. Only Roosevelt bailed them out with closing arguments, the moŝt important being a defense of the "pure democracy" Wadsworth feared. Noting that the Cobb bill protected the party and the convention system, the former president closed: "I ask you to put yourself un-equivocally on the side that says: 'We trust the people.'" Following roars of approval of Roosevelt's exhortation, the Wadsworth substitute plank failed, 606–403. Anti-climactic was the convention's nearly unani-mous nomination of Henry L. Stimson to run for governor.[66]

Wadsworth's failure on the direct primary plank in 1910 does not obscure the significance of the fight for his political beliefs and for the State of New York. It reflected importantly his gentry-elite conservative belief in republican as opposed to democratic government—that the former was deliberative and balanced and that the latter was shallow and dema-gogic. Furthermore, although the Democratic John Dix administration would shortly establish a statewide direct primary, it would be repealed a decade later, in 1922, and would not rise again until the participatory democratic days of the late 1960s.

Wadsworth was less discouraged by the Saratoga convention than one would think, given his almost months-on-end fight against the direct primary, the critical issue in the convention. Except for the direct primary plank, the platform was basically generally conservative, to the distress of many progressives in the state and across the country. For example, it had high praise for Taft and the recently-passed high tariff legislation. Ironically, it was Roosevelt who gave the platform its conservative twist. Through it, he hoped to strike a blow for national party unity, bringing together all shades of Republicans. The slate too served that purpose. It was acceptable to most Roosevelt and Taft men. Wadsworth saw it as "all right": "All we've got to do now is elect it."[67]

For some time Wadsworth had planned not to seek re-election to the Assembly. Louisa had been discussing it in her correspondence. Of course, had Republican fortunes been more propitious in 1910, the Speaker might have thought differently. Certainly he expected his respite to be temporary. In the closing hours of the Saratoga convention he accepted membership on the state Republican Committee and agreed to campaign for the head of the ticket. In the ensuing weeks he and Job Hedges accompanied Stimson as he campaigned upstate. As Wadsworth

66. *Ibid.;* Rosenthal, *op. cit.,* p. 297.
67. *New York Times,* Sept. 29, 1910; Brown, *op. cit.,* pp. 184–185.

was not standing for re-election to the Assembly from Livingston County, in 1911 he was succeeded by John C. Winter, Jr.

In the long swing across the state, the trio established a life-long relationship.[68] Early in the 1910 campaign Wadsworth realized that in Henry L. Stimson he "was travelling with a man of strong, clear character." A Yale graduate, and recently the United States Attorney for the southern district of New York, Stimson, with his sincerity and lack of flamboyance, two of Wadsworth's own traits, had profound impact on the young Geneseoan. Wadsworth struck Stimson comparably. Shortly after the election, in which the Democratic candidate, John Adams Dix, won, Stimson would support Wadsworth for the state chairmanship of the party.[69] The impression of one on the other expanded as they had important contact for nearly half a century.

4

In December of 1910, Wadsworth, AHW and the children, Jerry and Evie, enjoyed a good Christmas holiday with Mrs. Hay at the Lafayette Square home, interspersed with frequent visits with the Boss and Louisa in their K Street home. Following the Yuletide, Jim and AHW departed on an extended European and Middle East sojourn, first through the Mediterranean with stops in Algiers and then to Egypt with an impressive trip up the Nile. From Egypt, the couple sailed to the south of France and then motored through the "lovely" Pau Valley. Partway through the valley, they stayed with the Boss's sister, Nancy, married to one Edward Montezuma Rogers. Then to Paris, where they visited with Louisa's sister, Aunt Tillie, and her husband, the artist Walter Gay. The Gays lived in truly aristocratic style in their beautiful chateau, Le Breau. From Paris they went on to London and visited more aunts— Aunt Lilly, Lady Barrymore, the Boss's younger sister; and Aunt Neelie, Mrs. John Adair, the Boss's eldest sister. Jim and Alice became fast friends with cousin Nellie, Lady Barrymore's daughter. Jim and Aunt Neelie spent hours on end discussing a great Texas ranch her second

68. *New York Times*, Sept. 29, 1910; Brown, *op. cit.*, pp. 187–192; Rosenthal, *op. cit.*, pp. 319–324; Robert F. Wesser to author, May 15, 1972.

69. Wadsworth, Jr., *Reminiscences*, pp. 80–82; Wadsworth, Jr., *Autobiography*, p. 169.

husband left her. In addition, the Geneseo couple met and mingled with the flower of London society. Often they encountered the great names of English history: Herbert Asquith, Arthur Balfour, and young Winston Churchill.[70]

Of all those with whom Jim conversed in his sojourn abroad, none influenced his future more than Aunt Neelie. Her second husband, John Adair, had effected a partnership in 1876 with a scout of the American West, Charles Goodnight, and established one of America's largest ranches. Nearly the size of Rhode Island, the J. A. Ranch consisted of 525,000 acres and 700 miles of fence. Sixteen thousand head of Herefords, or "white-faces" as Texans called them, roamed the ranch. In winter months they grazed in the Red River' Palo Duro Canyon and in the summer months ascended to the great open flat lands. Upon John Adair's death, Aunt Neelie bought out Goodnight and hired managers to run the great ranch and periodically report to her. Little wonder that Jim talked to Aunt Neelie so much about the trade of raising beef in the Genesee Valley, and that Aunt Neelie talked so enthusiastically and intelligently about beef on the hoof.[71]

Not long after Jim and Alice returned to their home at Hampton Corners in the Genesee Valley, Aunt Neelie asked Jim to run her Texas ranch, to spend several years giving it the management and organization she knew it should have. Jim was enjoying the Genesee Valley but could not resist going to Texas. He did so and was soon established in the ranch headquarters not far from Clarendon, Texas, in the great panhandle. The ranch included a large Hudson Valley type mansion, spacious and comfortable, with "big open fireplaces, comfy furniture, lots of books, modern plumbing, central heating, and lighted by acetylene gas."[72]

Wadsworth did not ensconce himself in the big house. He truly became a ranch man. He described the life to AHW:

> Back from camp in the canyon. . . . Those cowboys keep terrific hours. In the saddle at 5 A.M. Back to the [chuck] wagon for dinner at noon. Then off until 6 or 7 P.M. . . . The heat Monday was terrific . . . slow work driving the cows and their calves out of the canyon. [The calves] get tired and lag behind. . . . I carried one in front of me on my saddle for an hour, a very warming task. Last year's calves are now yearlings and have to be cut out of the herd. But they hate to be separated

70. Wadsworth, Jr., *Autobiography*, pp. 171–174; Hatch, *op. cit.*, pp. 179–184.
71. Wadsworth, Jr., *Autobiography*, p. 173.
72. *Ibid.*, pp. 175–179.

from the old cows. . . . It takes a heap of breakneck riding to cut them out in rough country. . . .

[When] the work of clearing the canyon was finished, the outfit wound its way up the "Loop the Loop" trail—well named. I never have seen a more picturesque sight than this exodus from the canyon in the slanting rays of the sun. The trail from the river is about four miles long winding up about a thousand feet. I stayed below until the whole procession had started up. The herd was guided along the trail by 16 cow punchers. The men ride their horses up perfectly inaccessible peaks and they're silhouetted for a moment flanking the cattle. They and the long narrow file of cattle climb up and up, now disappearing from sight around projecting shoulders and re-appearing like tiny moving specks further up. After the cattle comes the herd of cow horses, 150 of them. They herd wonderfully, and one cow puncher, called the horse wrangler, looks after them. Last comes the big wagon with the four-horse team driven by the patient cook. . . . The great, crawling, winding, bawling, cussing procession is a wonderfully inspiring sight. . . .

The next two days were spent rounding up a herd of about 1200 cattle, sorting out the old cows and branding the calves. The sorting business was up to me and Reynolds. Tell the Boss all he has taught me about cattle exactly coincides with ideas on cattle down this away. . . .

I had no change of clothes for twelve days. I fully expected the Board of Health to be after me.[73]

Soon Jim proved himself, overhearing a ranch hand comment: "Say, he ain't so bad is he." More importantly, Wadsworth did what Aunt Neelie wanted done. He managed and organized well. He built new buildings, drove more wells, put up more water tanks, brought in northern pure bred bulls, and, most importantly, in the market he sold steers as yearlings rather than three-year olds—at the same price. Wadsworth made money for Aunt Neelie. Aside from his know-how, the times were quite prosperous for American farmers.[74]

The Texas years were the "good old days" for Jim Wadsworth. Even AHW, who came down for spells in the autumn weeks, had nostalgic memories of the period. In the cloak rooms of Congress in later years, Jim reminisced with westerners like Sam Rayburn, Dewey Short and Lyndon Johnson. When Aunt Neelie's grandson, Montgomery W. Richie, took over the great ranch in later years, Wadsworth never lost touch. He loved talk of Herefords, bulls, steers and yearlings, "cut-

73. Hatch, *op. cit.*, pp. 182–183.
74. Wadsworth, Jr., *Autobiograhy,* pp. 183–205.

outs," chuck-wagons, corrals, brands, stake-outs, "stink holes," and black leg disease.

During Wadsworth's three years in Texas he frequently traveled East for long extended stays with the family in Geneseo or Washington, but mostly to attend to political matters, especially on three occasions.

The first political interruption of Wadsworth's Texas stint was the National Republican Convention which met in Chicago in mid-June, 1912. From the Republican state convention in Saratoga in 1910 to the spring of 1912, relations between Theodore Roosevelt and Taft worsened, except for some months following Stimsons defeat in 1910. The former president had taken the defeat somewhat personally. But by the spring of 1912, Roosevelt was determined to take the Republican nomination and return to the White House. "What a fine lot of billingsgate our friend T.R. is indulging in these days!" wrote Wadsworth to AHW from Texas. "[I] was literally astounded at . . . [his] language. I haven't read Taft's attack on him. . . . Incidentally, the President wrote me a most civil and grateful letter." [75]

Wadsworth was, of course, for Taft in the fray; and Barnes, now the Republican state chairman in New York, kept the Geneseoan fully informed of T.R.'s anti-Taft maneuvers, at least what he knew of them. Barnes, although really respectful of T.R.'s vigor and imagination, could not stand his political ideology and his anti-organization stance, especially after Osawatomie. He kept the former president out of the New York organization and had much to do with keeping his hands off the national committee. Indeed, by the summer of 1942, Barnes was probably Taft's principal adviser, rather the first of the top echelon close to the President, most of whom were New Yorkers—Elihu Root, H. L. Stimson and C. D. Hilles. Not surprisingly, Barnes saw to it that the New York delegation to the 1912 national convention was in sound hands—Wadsworth's. The New York delegation supported Taft, 77–13. As chairman of the delegation, Wadsworth announced the several votes. On one important issue a delegate demanded a recount in the course of which there had been a change of one vote. A member of the gallery screeched: "Wadsworth, you're a crook."

The Boss, only one seat removed from the heckler, at Louisa's instigation—"Hit him Jimmy"—landed a left hook to the Roosevelt rooter's jaw. Both the Boss and his victim were led from the convention hall but the latter refused to press charges, especially upon learning the Boss's identity. The commotion gave some excitement to a dull convention in which stand-

75. J.W.W. to Alice Hay Wadsworth, Apr. 28, 1912, Wadsworth MSS.

patters easily put Taft over and T.R. took his walk to form the Progressive Party of America. Roosevelt's Bull Moose candidacy—he said he felt like a bull moose—split the Republican party, and the Democrats elected Woodrow Wilson, the first Democratic president since Cleveland had been elected twenty years previously.[76]

Of greater moment to Wadsworth than the three-way presidential race in 1912 was his own gubernatorial race in New York. The trio of Wadsworth, Stimson, and Hedges was determined that Bull Moosers would not dominate New York Republicanism and the former wanted to run for governor, but Hedges, also interested in the candidacy, worked harder to get it and did. Wadsworth gracefully stepped aside and assented to run for lieutenant governor. But just as national Bull Moosers caused Taft's defeat, a state Progressive slate, headed by Oscar Straus, did the same thing in New York, returning Democrats to the State House.[77] The Democratic candidate for governor defeated the Republican candidate. Still, the stand-pat Republicans retained control of their national and New York parties. With at least that consolation, Wadsworth returned to Texas.

76. Hatch, op. cit., p. 188.
77. Brown, op. cit., pp. 222–228.

IV

The Senator

1

WHILE lounging one summer evening in 1914 near a Texas "stink hole," thirty miles from headquarters, Wadsworth noticed a cowboy coming over the hill, outlined against the sky. He came with word that the Western Union office held an important message for the New Yorker. Characteristically, Wadsworth apologized for his messenger's hard ride. At daybreak he headed for camp. The wire, from Geneseo Republicans, requested their prominent citizen to seek the nomination for the United States Senate.[1] Behind County Chairman William A. Brodie's wire, of course, was William Barnes, the Republican state chairman, and Wadsworth's political mentor. To check the gain of any radical Roosevelt influence in the state party, Barnes was reaching for attractive anti-Roosevelt candidates. Charles Seymour Whitman, his gubernatorial choice, had investigated gambling and highway frauds spectacularly as New York County's district attorney. More important to Barnes, Roosevelt disliked Whitman most of all the possible Republican candidates.[2] Wadsworth was, of course, emphatically anti-Roosevelt, and in his own right would make an attractive senatorial candidate.

The former Assembly Speaker could not have been overly startled by the entreaty to seek senatorial office. For months Elihu Root's refusal to

1. James W. Wadsworth, Jr., *The Reminiscences of James W. Wadsworth, Jr.* (Columbia University: Oral History Research Office, 1952), pp. 104–108; Henry F. Holthusen, *James W. Wadsworth, Jr., A Biographical Sketch* (New York: G. P. Putnam's Sons, 1926), pp. 84–6; Alden Hatch, *The Wadsworths of the Genesee* (New York: Coward-McCann, Inc. 1959), pp. 185–6; telegram, William A. Brodie to J.W.W., July 6, 1914, telegram, J.W.W. to Wm. A. Brodie, July 6, 1914, Wadsworth MSS, Library of Congress, Washington, D.C.

2. Roscoe C. E. Brown, *History of the State of New York* (Syracuse, N.Y.: the Syracuse Press, 1922), p. 250; Frederick C. Tanner, *The Reminiscences of Frederick C. Tanner,* (Columbia University: Oral History Office, 1960).

seek re-election to the august Senate had been rumored and the names of numerous possible successors were bandied about in the press, Wadsworth's among them. Most contenders were impressive: Henry L. Stimson, the former Secretary of War; Nicholas Murray Butler, president of Columbia University; Herbert Parsons, New York County Republican leader; Harvey D. Hinman, prominent Hughes and Roosevelt confidant; Dr. David Jayne Hill, former president of the University of Rochester; and Judge Nathan L. Miller, associate judge of the New York Court of Appeals. A less impressive candidate was William M. Calder, a member of Congress and formerly a building contractor. Of all the candidates, Wadsworth was the most conservative and organization-minded; yet his image belied particularly his conservatism. Aside from his youthful appearance, it was well known that T.R. had supported him as a reform candidate in 1906 for the New York Assembly speakership. Opponents noted his youth as likely to be harmful to his possible nomination.[3]

Wadsworth, like Barnes, sincerely regretted Root's firm declination to seek re-election to the Senate. The young Geneseoan held the New Yorker from Clinton in awe. Root's commitment to public service had always impressed him. As Secretary of War, he had organized the modern army. As Secretary of State, he was a worthy successor to Wadsworth's own father-in-law, John Hay. Root's conservatism—his emphasis on efficient administration, a proper balance of power, a minimal alteration of the Constitution, and stability as opposed to change—could not have been more compatible with Wadsworth's ideology. Also, both perceived economic aspects of the law in comparable terms. Root surely put to the young Geneseoan what he wrote to Theodore Roosevelt in the latter's younger days: "It is not the function of law to enforce the rules of morality," wrote the learned attorney. "There is altogether too general an impression that it is immoral to acquire wealth, and far too little appreciation of the fact that the vast preponderance of great fortunes which now exist in this country have been amassed, not by injuring any living being, but as an incident to the conferring of great benefits on the Community." Wadsworth always approved such doctrine; he also followed quite successfully Root's example of integrity and courage.

Barnes also loved Root for his conservatism. Particularly did he appreciate the way he stood up to Roosevelt in 1912. But neither Barnes nor Wadsworth, nor others, could dissuade the eminent man from declining

3. *New York Times,* May 17, July 2, 7, 8, 1914; *Livingston Republican,* July 9, 1914.

another senate term. Root felt physically and mentally ill-equipped for six more years of conflict in that body.[4]

Ironically, the nomination could not come to Wadsworth in the tried convention manner. The direct primary, that instrument of democracy he fought so diligently, served as the only avenue to nomination. To add insult to injury, if he succeeded in the primary contest, he would suffer further direct democratization under the Seventeenth Amendment, the direct election of United States senators.

Although statewide contests were not foreign to Wadsworths—Jim's father ran for state comptroller and his grandfather for governor—anxiety struck the family. As Jim manfully prepared to enter the wider arena, Alice implored Root to "approve of him in some sort of statement that would come before the public." She rationalized that since the whole state wanted the great statesman, they would "take the man you would choose." [5] Root let Alice down easy, noting that he would like to make Jim Senator, but "it would simply be playing favorites." [6]

Young Wadsworth did not need Root's endorsement to achieve the nomination. For one thing, only William Calder and Dr. David Jayne Hill remained with him in the field. Henry L. Stimson and Herbert Parsons would have little to do with the state party under Barnes's chairmanship. In fact, Stimson viewed him as archaically conservative and tried to depose him from the chairmanship. Nicholas Murray Butler always eschewed public office.[7] Harvey Hinman and Nathan Miller lacked support to try for the nomination. Thus, only Calder and Hill, both lackluster candidates, remained in contention. The former had strong downstate support, the latter had the support of George Aldrich who did not care to ally himself with the Barnes-Wadsworth interests. Wadsworth won, but his plurality was much narrower than Whitman's win over gubernatorial contenders.[8]

For good reasons Wadsworth and Whitman won in November and

4. Phillip C. Jessup, *Elihu Root* (New York: Dodd, Mead and Company, 1938), Ch. X–XL, *passim*; Richard W. Leopold, *Elihu Root and the Conservative Tradition* (Boston; Little, Brown and Co., 1954), Ch. I, VIII, *passim*.

5. Alice H. Wadsworth to Elihu Root, July 11, 1914, Wadsworth MSS.

6. Elihu Root to Alice H. Wadsworth, July 15, 1914, Wadsworth MSS.

7. Herbert Parsons to William H. Waldhams, Parsons MSS, Columbia University Library, New York, N.Y.; William H. Wadhams, *The Reminiscences of William H. Wadhams* (Columbia University; Oral History Research Office, 1950); Henry L. Stimson and McGeorge Bundy, *On Active Service in Peace and War* (New York: Harper and Brothers, 1947), p. 63.

8. Tanner, *op. cit.*; *New York Times*, Sept. 29, 30, Oct. 1, 1914.

carried the Republican slate against their Democratic opponents, James W. Gerard, also a Geneseoan, and Martin H. Glynn. Divisiveness within state Democratic ranks more than equalled that of the Republican-Progressive schism. Only a year had passed since Tammany leader Charles F. Murphy had caused the impeachment of his own governor, William Sulzer, for showing his independence. The Republican schism, on the other hand, was much on the wane. Conservatives like Wadsworth prevailed across the nation in 1914. From the new senate class elected in that year, the New Yorker would be surrounded in his last row seat by standpatters Charles Curtis of Kansas, and Warren Harding of Ohio. Then too, the Barnes organizational efforts more than equalled those of the Tammany chieftain. The Albany leader hungered to strengthen his position as Republican state chairman and national committeeman. Helpful also to Wadsworth was Root's testimony which at least partially checked Roosevelt's attempt to discredit the young candidate. Root, after the primary, spoke of how young Jim's grandfather "laid down his life for his country in the Battle of the Wilderness" and how the Republican candidate "above all the able young men . . . [has] exhibited the greatest promise of useful public service of the highest order." [9] Roosevelt ranged Wadsworth with the dark forces of evil for championing big business and for having deserted Hughes during his governorship.[10] Issues also counted. The New Freedom, Wadsworth said, was unworkable. The new income tax had not reduced the cost of living, and the lowered tariff rates were responsible for pockets of economic depression. Worse yet, the federal government contemplated increased regulation of the railroads, the operation of ocean freight vessels, and the acquisition of the telegraph and telephone industry. Government was "punitive," especially in its relation to business—"the American business man is [viewed as] an object of suspicion . . . to be watched, restrained, and punished." [11] Nineteen-fourteen seemed to be the year to put the lid on Progressivism and Wadsworth did his part. Lastly, Wadsworth was helped by the physical absence of his opponent. James W. Gerard considered his tenure as ambassador to Germany more important than the senatorial campaign. Even so, Gerard believed he would have won had not the Wadsworth supporters spread circulars over western New York protesting Gerard's alleged Catholicism. The charge that Wadsworth

9. *New York Times*, Oct. 28, Nov. 4, 1914.

10. *Ibid*, Oct. 20, 1914. Theodore Roosevelt considered supporting Harvey D. Hinman as a fusion gubernatorial candidate until Hinman said he would support Republican candidates running in other races against Progressive party candidates.

11. *Ibid.*, Oct. 14, 1914.

would spread such anti-Catholic circulars was out of his character.[12]

Wadsworth could not take his senate seat until more than a year hence, December 6, 1915. As the Constitution stood prior to its Twentieth Amendment, adopted in 1933, lame-duck sessions were convened usually in December and carried on into the spring of the following year. In the interim, he settled down for a winter's stay in the Genesee Valley, frequently journeying to Lafayette Square in Washington and various places in the state to address his new constituents. (The family, including the senator-elect, spent much of the year doting over the baby Reverdy, born to Alice in November of 1914.)

In public statements, as expected, Wadsworth sounded a conservative note. He applauded the Congress for defeating recent Rivers and Harbor legislation which he saw as mostly "pork." He called for the defeat of the President's Ship Purchase bill which he thought "contrary to all our American beliefs in the viciousness of Government ownership." [13] True to his family's past, Wadsworth always agonized over government spending and ownership. He hoped the state's Constitutional Convention in the spring of 1915, dominated by conservative Republicans, would provide further opportunity to extol the virtues of conservatism.

New York's constitutional conventions are frequently grand affairs. At least every twenty years the eminent figures of the Empire State recommend changes to the citizens. Frequently the delegates are of national prominence. Such was the case in Albany on April 5, when Wadsworth joined Elihu Root; Seth Low, the former reform mayor of New York City; Henry L. Stimson and George W. Wickersham, both former cabinet members; and President Jacob Gould Schurman of Cornell University. There was a host of lesser figures, including William Barnes, Herbert Parsons, Alfred E. Smith, and Robert F. Wagner. The eminent Root presided as the delegates, without division on party lines, hammered out their recommendations, most of which were very progressive: adoption of the "short ballot" (reduction of the number of elective offices), the reduction of more than one hundred and fifty boards or positions into seventeen departments, the adoption of a systematic budget system, the creation of uniform assessment for taxation, and the granting of increased home-rule.[14]

12. James Gerard, The Reminiscences of James Gerard, (Columbia University: Oral History Research Office, 1950); James W. Gerard, The Memoirs of James W. Gerard, (New York: Doubleday, 1951), pp. 215–216; New York Times, Nov. 4, 1914.

13. New York Times, Jan. 22, 1915.

14. William A. Prendergast, The Reminiscences of William A. Prendergast (Columbia University: Oral History Research Office, 1951).

Wadsworth, stressing particularly the economies to be effected by the amended constitution, supported the recommendations. Indeed, he served as the chairman of the Committee for the Adoption of the Constitution. Yet it was defeated at the polls. Democrats were suspicious of the new appointing power of the Governor, the Governor's new budget authority, and the insufficiency of home-rule. Progressives, who should have been ecstatic, blindly suspected Root's chairmanship as representative of the "interests." Labor feared that the strengthening of the judiciary would turn judicial power against them. Some downstaters opposed it. Frank L. Polk, counsellor to the State Department and a native of New York City, saw little relief in the Assembly for his hometown. With more than one-half of the state's population, its representatives made up only 42 percent of the Assembly. Wadsworth blamed defeat largely on Root's demeanor at the convention, which appeared presumptuous, and his identification with the New York City delegates, known as the federal crowd. Both points of criticism were offensive to the upstate Republicans.[15]

On December 6, 1915, Vice President Marshall intoned that the Honorable James W. Wadsworth, Jr., had been properly chosen by his state's electors to represent them. Wadsworth, although youthful by senate standards, thirty-eight years of age, was little impressed by the installation. He must have felt the incongruity of the high drama revealed by the chamber's history as compared to the herding of new senators into the well to be sworn. The great of the nation had deliberated in the Senate—Thomas Jefferson, John C. Calhoun, Henry Clay, Daniel Webster, Stephen Douglas, Charles Sumner, and his own predecessor, Elihu Root. Yet here a Tammany hack, James O'Gorman, escorted, courteously enough, the new senator forward. Alice watched and overheard an observer comment about her husband: "He's very wealthy and a leader in Society!"[16] Colleagues were more attentive than the young senator from New York thought. Senator Henry F. Ashurst of Arizona noted much interest "manifested in two of the new Senators, viz., Warren Harding of Ohio and James Wadsworth of New York."[17] Wadsworth was little more impressed on the following day when the President addressed a joint session of Congress. He thought Wilson's profile Machiavellian: "long jaw (not a firm one), large pointed ears, thin prominent nose, rather receding forehead and a high point at the back of the head." The new senator "heard little [from

15. *Ibid.; New York Times*, Oct. 11, 1914.

16. James W. Wadsworth, Jr., *Diary*, Dec. 6, 1915, Wadsworth MSS.

17. Henry F. Ashurst, *A Many-Colored Toga; The Diary of Henry F. Ashurst* (University of Arizona Press, 1962), p. 43.

the President] that was concrete" and was amazed by such partisan signs in the chamber as "the shrill Southern yell."[18]

Jim, constraining his small disappointments about the "Hill," appeared affable and was received in kind. His office staff, all three, and his Negro messenger were attentive. The Republican Conference in the Senate elected him both secretary and party whip. Minority Leader William Gallinger soon thought the two positions were too many and suggested that Charles Curtis should take the whip post. Wadsworth was relieved. Warren Harding enjoyed sitting next to his senate colleague, and did so for five years as they edged up front. Henry Cabot Lodge of Massachusetts, an old friend of John Hay and Henry Adams, was particularly solicitous of the young senator. One senator, James Hamilton Lewis of Illinois, even advised him on ways to dress and stand in the senate well so as to attract the attention of the press.[19]

The young senator soon grew fond of the Senate and the men who made it. In his *Reminiscences,* transcribed three decades later, aside from Harding, Lodge and Lewis, he recalled well such Democrats as Vice President Thomas Marshall, one so fair, possessing "a delightful, friendly, comfortable sense of humor"; James P. Clarke of Arkansas, a "completely courageous man"; Oscar W. Underwood of Alabama, the low tariff advocate; Claude A. Swanson of Virginia, a born politician and a "great friend of the Navy"; Carter Glass of Virginia, the sponsor of the Federal Reserve Act; Benjamin Tillman of South Carolina, a picturesque "red neck"; John Sharp Williams of Mississippi, "a really brilliant man"; James Reed of Missouri, a protester; and William J. Stone, also of Missouri, an "isolationist." Among Republican colleagues, Jim noted Reed Smoot of Utah, "the watchdog of the Treasury"; William E. Borah of Idaho, a liberal on economic questions and a conservative on constitutional questions; Charles Curtis of Kansas, the Republican whip; Robert LaFollette, a rebel "at odds with most of us"; George Sutherland of Utah, a "great lawyer"; Albert B. Cummins of Iowa, a progressive proponent of railroad legislation; and Boies Penrose of Pennsylvania, the chairman of the Finance Committee and a "very influential" senator.[20] Time, of course, mutes feelings. Wadsworth had not always thought kindly of his colleagues. The welling-up of aristocratic contempt was no better expressed than when he wrote of John D. Works of California, who had just read a long diatribe against the army: "the poor little thing!"[21]

18. Wadsworth, Jr., *Diary,* Dec. 7, 1915.
19. Wadsworth, Jr., *Reminiscences,* Ch. VII, *passim.*
20. *Ibid.*
21. Wadsworth, Jr., *Diary,* Dec. 16, 1916.

James and Alice Wadsworth were attractive figures in Washington. Young, vivacious, secure, they were really already a part of the city. Only a decade previously, when America was still rural, the Boss presided over the Committee on Agriculture in the House of Representatives, and John Hay was viewed by most Washingtonians as the capital's eminent figure, the servant of the martyred presidents, Lincoln and McKinley. Although young Wadsworth might chastise Democrats in the senate cloakroom, in the press, or on the pages of his diary, he was welcome company among the Democratic elite, *i.e.*, the Franklin Lanes, the Frank Polks, the William Phillipses or the Franklin Roosevelts. Needless to say, good Republican doors were opened extremely wide to the new couple. They particularly enjoyed the repartee prevalent at the dining tables of the Nicholas Longworths and the Oliver Wendell Holmeses. Nor did Jim confine his social contact to after dark.[22] On summer afternoons he and Franklin Roosevelt frequently took off for a swim.[23] Jim and Nicholas Longworth, T.R.'s son-in-law, enjoyed morning walks together.[24]

The Wadsworth home on Lafayette Square was a Washington landmark. Alice had inherited a third of the famous Hay house, designed by the eminent architect, Henry H. Richardson. She and Jim bought her brother's and sister's shares. With its master, though young, once again in the councils of government, the home was to become the byway of the politically sophisticated. Its very appearance was inviting. A red brick adaptation of Romanesque design, its deeply recessed doors, shadowed by low arches, seemed to impose a discriminating hospitality which fitted well the mistress of the home.[25] Reticence often marked Alice's commitment to "entertain." [26] For those, however, who did settle in the panelled rooms, the famous old St. John's Church to the east and the White House to the south came into view. William Barnes, urbane, intelligent, and very conservative, fitted well into the surroundings when he came down from Albany. But then, so probably did Franklin Roosevelt, the young Assistant Secretary of the Navy, who crossed the Square en route to the Capitol from his home on N Street.[27]

22. *Ibid.*, *passim.*

23. Molly Berkeley, *Winking at the Brim* (Boston, Mass.: Houghton, Mifflin, 1967), p. 42.

24. Wadsworth, Jr., *Diary*, *passim*; Henry F. Holthusen, *op. cit.*, p. 156.

25. Tyler Dennett, *John Hay* (New York: Dodd, Mead and Co., 1934), p. 163.

26. Conversation with Miss Bessie Christian, Wadsworth residence secretary, summer 1965.

27. Jonathan Daniels, *Washington Quadrille* (New York: Doubleday and Co., Inc., 1968), pp. 162–3.

Wadsworth was fairly well pleased by his committee assignments, especially the Committee on Agriculture and Forestry, and its companion committee, that of Expenditures in the Department of Agriculture. Committees on Canadian Relations, Indian Depredations, Mississippi River and its Tributaries, Public Buildings and Grounds, and Claims were uninteresting. The young senator took the Claims assignment particularly seriously until he and Democrat Joseph Robinson of Arkansas failed to get their fellow committeemen to show up at meetings.[28]

Politics and senate concerns seemed equally important to Wadsworth in his first senate year. While sworn to duty as a United States senator, politics was the stuff of survival in office and the young senator loved it. Over the long haul of his legislative career, however, law-making took precedence over politics. If such was not the case in 1916, his Agriculture assignment was a partial explanation. Although always close to the soil, Wadsworth would develop his specializations in military, foreign, and financial policy, not agriculture. Such future assignments gelled well with his strong commitment to national defense, international affairs, and his laissez-faire economics. These areas were of early interest to Wadsworth even without such committee assignments. In 1916, his ears perked up at Agriculture Committee hearings only when Hoke Smith, of North Carolina, introduced a "visionary bill providing that the Government spend 15 million dollars constructing a great water power plant for the manufacture of atmosphere nitrogen—used in high explosives and as an ingredient in fertilizer." Wadsworth sloughed off the suggestion as another Democratic shot at "economic impossibilities and government ownership and operation of everything in sight." He was sure no committee in the New York legislature would be so impractical. The New Yorker would never buy Hoke Smith's idea even when, twenty years later, David Lilienthal made TVA a large and very permanent government corporation.[29]

Preparedness was the over-riding issue to Wadsworth in 1916. As war clouds drifted westward from Europe he feared for the nation's safety, and considered foreign affairs accordingly. He supported Wilson's programs for American protectorates in Nicaragua and Haiti because they helped make secure the Panama Canal. On Mexican policy the New Yorker differed with the President. Had the United States not engaged in weak-kneed "watchful waiting," the show of American force would have steered German U-Boats away from the *Lusitania*.[30] He saw the Philippine Islands'

28. Wadsworth, Jr., *Diary*, Dec. 13, 1915, March 14, 1916.
29. *Ibid.*, March 16, 1916.
30. *Ibid.*, Jan. 14, 1916.

demand for independence as unimportant. To him, it affected little our security. British interference with American shipping did not bother him. After all, England, in a real sense, was our first line of defense.[31] The Gore-McLemore resolution, a statement decrying American travel on belligerent ships, did bother him. When it came to a vote in the House of Representatives, Wadsworth went over to the other chamber to attempt to dissuade New York Republicans from supporting the resolution. Needless to say, Wadsworth strongly supported military legislation.[32]

Generally, Wilson's domestic programs were anathema to Wadsworth. River improvement, postal savings, the eight-hour day for railroad workers, tariff reduction, road surveys in Alaska, and an appropriation for a new Treasury building faced emphatic Wadsworth opposition,[33] as did the confirmation of Louis Brandeis as Justice of the United States Supreme Court. The Brandeis appointment went to the heart of contention between the New Freedom and the conservative Republicanism Wadsworth represented. "Our contention," noted Wadsworth, "is that Brandeis is an open, avowed, bitter radical on constitutional questions. He has more than once expressed his contempt for those provisions of the Constitution which are aimed at securing property rights. There is nothing judicial in his makeup —he has pre-judged pretty nearly every important question which can come before the Court for the next ten years." Brandeis was confirmed and received far more than the "four or five" Republican votes Wadsworth predicted. Twenty-two Republicans voted for the "Peoples' Attorney." The New York senator did accurately predict the consistency of Brandeisian liberalism in the coming decade, a consistency not unlike that of Wadsworth's conservatism.[34]

4

While only a freshman minority member of the United States Senate, Wadsworth was a key figure in New York politics. Three days after his installation, the new senator journeyed to New York City to dine with state Republican leaders, Dr. Nicholas Murray Butler, the president of Columbia University; Charles D. Hilles, the Republican national commit-

31. *Ibid.*, Jan. 20, 1916.
32. *Ibid.*, March 4, 1916.
33. *Congressional Record*, Vol. 55, 65th Congress, 1st Session, 1917, *passim.*
34. Wadsworth, Jr., *Diary*, Jan. 23, Feb. 1, 1916.

teeman; and Cornelius Bliss, James Sheffield, and Otto Bannard, other prominent Republicans. Prior to the dinner hosted by Butler, Wadsworth called on his old mentor, William Barnes, at his rooms. Barnes suspected that Butler would seek Wadsworth's support of Root for the Republican nomination for President at the Republican convention in the following summer. While both Barnes and Wadsworth were staunch Root supporters, they agreed that a precipitous candidacy would be harmful on two grounds —initial support coming from the federal crowd, always suspect to upstate Republicans, and the recent defeat of the state constitution, coming as it did from the convention over which Root presided. The pro-Root pressures came even before the dinner. En route to the affair, Wadsworth visited briefly with Henry L. Stimson in his Manhattan Hotel apartment. For twenty-five minutes Stimson pleaded with young Jim to "lead the way"; "sound the bugle." His last ploy was to note that Root wanted his young successor to "lead the way." [35]

Barnes was right. The Butler dinner conference was an attempt to launch a Root campaign. Wadsworth's position prevailed, perhaps mistakenly. Had he then "led the way," the very substantial support forthcoming from the state and the nation might have made the difference in the end. But the young senator believed that such an early presidential drive would hurt his idol. Root needed time, he felt, to dissipate the ill effects of the constitutional defeat and his identification with the federal crowd.[36]

Although Wadsworth's principal ties were with the conservative Barnes wing of the state party, as the Republican holding the highest national office he felt the pressures of the several factions, and kept all doors open. Barnes, of course, was always welcome. He and Wadsworth visited back and forth and drew on a great reservoir of common political efforts. The federal crowd, with which Charles D. Hilles, Henry L. Stimson, and Herbert Parsons were frequently associated, was important and earnestly listened to. Wadsworth, however, felt they over-emphasized their importance; there were far more Republicans upstate than in New York City. He mused that "Root's fortunes would be wrecked if left solely in the hands of Stimson, Parsons, and company, likewise the Republican party in N.Y.!"[37] Even within the federal crowd there were factions. Parsons, the

35. *Ibid.*, Dec. 10, 1915; Wadsworth, Jr., *Reminiscences*, Ch. IX, *passim.* Although it was doubtful that Root wanted anybody to "lead the way" to his nomination, he stood ready to run if friends thought he could rally the people against Wilson and his weak preparedness policy. See Philip C. Jessup, *Elihu Root* (New York: Dodd, Mead and Co., 1938), pp. 339–352.

36. Jessup, *op. cit.*, p. 337.

37. Wadsworth, Jr., *Diary*, Dec. 10, 1915.

New York County leader, thought Wadsworth was over-rated, and could never accept his conservatism. Stimson, on the other hand, saw Wadsworth as high-minded and very able. An important faction in 1916 was that element in the party tied to Governor Whitman's presidential aspirations. Lieutenant Governor Edward Schoeneck, and New York Insurance Commissioner Jesse Phillips, both intimate friends from old Assembly days, traveled to Washington with the Governor's private secretary to urge Wadsworth's support of Whitman for the Republican nomination, ostensibly to forestall the possibility of former Governor Charles E. Hughes being nominated.[38]

Wadsworth must have liked Schoeneck's idea of forestalling a Hughes presidential drive, but not at the price of a Whitman candidacy. Although believing Governor Whitman was entitled to his "day in court," the state Republican convention, the Senator knew that Whitman's support was narrow indeed. Besides, Root was still Wadsworth's man.

The Republican convention went as Wadsworth hoped. Root, as keynoter, gave a superb address, eloquently critical of Wilson's foreign policy. Wadsworth, as permanent chairman, gave his address, hardly a match for Root's. (Jim hated to write speeches.) Whitman had "his day," but in test voting on the selection of four delegates-at-large to the national convention, he failed to have his supporters elected or to have himself elected to the chairmanship of the delegation. Wadsworth received the honor. The new senator's only defeat, an important one, was his failure to commit State Chairman Tanner to the Root candidacy.[39]

Republican politics were mercurial in New York, as would be expected with prominent national figures like Roosevelt, Hughes, Root and, to a lesser degree, Whitman, casting shadows upon the state party. While the young senator controlled much of the Republican convention which had been convened in February, such was not the case with the state committee meeting in April. So futile had been Wadsworth's attempts at securing Tanner's support for Root, that he, with Barnes' urging, determined to replace him as state chairman.[40] (So suspicious had Wadsworth been of Tanner that when the state chairman visited Washington, the Senator placed him under surveillance.)[41] When, however, the committee convened at the Republican Club in New York City, Wadsworth's well laid plans failed to put over as chairman the wealthy Oneida farmer, Charles W.

38. Wadsworth, Jr., *Reminiscences*, Ch. IX, *passim.*

39. Wadsworth, Jr., *Diary*, Feb. 17, 1916; Brown, *op. cit.*, pp. 269–272; *New York Times*, Feb. 17, 1916.

40. *New York Times*, Apr. 8, 1916.

41. Tanner, *op. cit.*, *passim.*

Wicks. The Governor had the Republican patronage in the state, not Wadsworth. Although, by April, Whitman had abandoned his presidential hopes, he saw Wadsworth's control of the committee as a threat to his own renomination as governor. Thus, he supported the retention of Tanner as state chairman, as well as Root's only serious contender for the presidency, Charles E. Hughes.[42]

Wadsworth was beaten badly, Tanner thought. He had risked the prestige of his high office and lost. Jim felt betrayed. He thought the state chairman had been for Root but that in deference to the Governor's White House hopes, had withheld early support of Root. When the chairman did not come through for Root by April, however, the Senator tried to depose him, not knowing that Root had written to the chairman requesting that his nomination not be considered.[43] Still, Tanner's letter from Root, dated February 23, was outdated by events. Only the day before the April 8 committee meeting, seventy-five prominent Republicans endorsed Root for the presidency, with his reluctant concurrence.[44]

Jim returned to Washington and licked his wounds. His grand mentor, William Barnes, was through. The Albany editor had failed in a libel suit against Theodore Roosevelt and in June would be forced to resign as the New York national committeeman. His power gone, Barnes's immoderate life-style would soon overtake him. Elihu Root, Wadsworth's foremost political idol, lost his last chance to be president. Most important, New York party control slipped from his own hands. At the Chicago national convention, Governor Whitman would easily take the chairmanship of the Republican delegation, supported by Tanner and recipients of state patronage. In November he would be re-elected governor of the state. One gleam of light came through for Wadsworth. Theodore Roosevelt, despite valiant efforts, would not "sell his goods" at Chicago. Charles Evans Hughes would be nominated and Wadsworth, of course, would support him.

"Not, please God, the Bearded Lady," wrote AHW's brother about Hughes prior to the election. He would have preferred in 1916 T.R., "whose record's shady." He needn't have worried. Wilson carried enough independent Progressive votes and squeaked again into the presidency.[45] Wadsworth wondered whether the President could carry on through the European crisis. The cabinet particularly needed strengthening. Worse yet,

42. *New York Times,* Apr, 8, 1916.
43. Tanner, *op. cit., passim.*
44. *New York Times,* Apr. 9, 1916; Brown, *op. cit.,* p. 272.
45. Clarence Hay to J.W.W., June 5, 1915, Wadsworth MSS. See Arthur Link, *Wilson, Campaigns for Progressivism and Peace* (Princeton: Princeton University Press, 1947), p. 163.

the atmosphere was such that Republicans feared criticizing the President, for "their action would find its way into print through characteristic White House channels and . . . they would be placed in a false light." He wished Cleveland were President.[46] For once Wadsworth did balk over at least one presidential appointment: he thought Bainbridge Colby, the former Bull Mooser, did not know enough to be on the Shipping Board and so wrote the President, to no avail.[47]

5

Wadsworth had grave doubts about the various diplomatic notes the President exchanged with the belligerent governments. He viewed Wilson's late December 1916 note, requesting the objectives of the warring powers, as weak and harmful to the Allied cause. The support of the note by senate Democrats disgusted him. "On questions of foreign relations they never think. . . . Oh Lord, how long!" he wrote to Nicholas Murray Butler.[48] In the evening of his life, twenty-five years later, Wadsworth thought differently, and excused Wilson's cautiousness.[49]

When Wilson broke diplomatic relations with Germany on February 4, 1917, Wadsworth, as did most of the nation, defended the action. The New York senator hoped it would bring Germany to her senses.[50] It is to Wadsworth's credit that throughout 1917 and 1918 his public stance was non-partisan. With the President he deplored the senate filibuster in March by "wilful men" to block action to arm merchant ships. Pacifists, like Robert LaFollette, one of the "wilful men," were to Wadsworth more evil than the soft-liners advising the President. When the declaration of war did come on April 6, few Americans applauded the firm action as enthusiastically as did Wadsworth.

On April 2, 1917, Wadsworth entered his second Congress, the sixty-fifth. Appropriately, he was appointed to the Senate Committee on Military Affairs. In keeping with his family's military tradition, Jim helped organize Troop M of National Guard Cavalry in Geneseo in 1913 and maintained his active commission in the unit until it was ordered to the Mexi-

46. J.W.W. to Nicholas Murray Butler, Feb. 27, 1917, Butler MSS, Columbia University Library, New York, N.Y.

47. J.W.W. to Woodrow Wilson, July 31, 1917, Wadsworth MSS.

48. J.W.W. to Nicholas Murray Butler, Jan. 4, 1917, Wadsworth MSS.

49. Wadsworth, Jr., Reminiscences, Ch. XI.

50. Link, op. cit., pp. 301–2; New York Times, Feb. 4, 1917.

can border in 1915. The commanding general of the Division, John F. O'Ryan, then ordered Wadsworth to stay in the Senate. On Thanksgiving, however, the Geneseoan messed with Troop M, whether in this country or overseas.[51]

Wadsworth was completely at home on the Military Affairs Committee. No assignment in his long legislative career was so meaningful, nor contributed so much to his reputation. After his twenty-five years of military specialization, *The Saturday Evening Post* labeled him "Mr. National Defense." That journey began at the foot of the committee table. Chairman George E. Chamberlain of Oregon sat at the head, with nine Democrats on his left and seven Republicans on his right. The New York senator was impressed by the chairman's devotion. He thought Wilson fortunate to have such an able, yet non-partisan, defender of his military policy. Wadsworth looked particularly to Democrat James A. Reed of Missouri and Republican John Weeks of Massachusetts for guidance.[52]

No one, however, impressed the New Yorker on military matters as much as the Secretary of War, Newton D. Baker, appointed just prior to the entrance of the United States into the war. At first appearing unsure— his pacifist background mitigated against support of the military—his candidness and ability in time disarmed the committee, before which he frequently appeared. Baker grew with the increasing military dimension. At war's end he appeared very large. And when the Secretary left office, Wadsworth saw particularly a third attribute: courage. As President Harding concluded his inaugural address on March 4, 1920, Wadsworth slipped out and looked up Baker. He found him shining his shoes in his office. They talked. Baker liked Wadsworth and took the parting occasion to explain why the famous Republican, General Leonard Wood, was not given a war command overseas. Baker withheld the command on his own, not the President. General Wood, the former Chief of Staff, was so unalterably critical of General Pershing that Baker feared jeopardizing western "front" operations. The press had screamed politics. In the quiet of the Secretary's office, Wadsworth saw it was the work of a brave man.[53] When the *Encyclopaedia Britannica* shortly thereafter cast an aspersion on Baker, Wadsworth jumped to his defense with a public statement.

Immediately upon the declaration of war, the President asked Baker for a selective service law. Within hours of the President's request, the Committee on Military Affairs had the War Department's draft of the

51. Hatch, *op. cit.*, pp. 197–200.
52. Wadsworth, Jr., *Reminiscences*, Ch. XI, *passim.*
53. *Ibid.*, Chapter X; see Hermann Hagedorn, *Leonard Wood, A Biography* (New York: Harper and Row, 1931), pp. 231–267.

legislation. The speed amazed Wadsworth. Apparently Major General Crowder, the Judge Advocate and Baker's principal adviser on manpower, had for fifteen years been awaiting such a moment. Still the draft needed refinement and defense.[54] Wadsworth more than carried his weight in the committee and on the senate floor. He strongly supported the committee's majority report and took strong exception to the plea of Democrats for volunteerism. Wadsworth argued:

> Under the volunteer system the Government has to take nearly every able bodied man who comes forward. That means that many are taken who would be of more value to the country in other tasks than those of the trenches.
>
> The Confederates were wiser than the Federals in their military policy in the Civil War. They took up conscription a year earlier than we, not only because they needed men, but because military leaders formulated their policy. The comparative success of the Confederacy in the first years of the war was due to this wiser military policy—in part of course; in part, too, to their being on the defensive.
>
> The burdens of this war should fall equally on everybody capable of bearing that burden. We should not only be fair and democratic in this ideal of service, but we should so contrive our defensive system that it would be employed in the most efficient way. That is why we advocate the selective draft—selection of the best material for the particular duty.[55]

The country was in a patriotic mood and gave the President the draft legislation he sought.

Wadsworth did yeoman service on Military Affairs. When necessary he spoke for the army. In June of 1918 he called for the drafting of eighteen-year-olds and in the following months called for an army 6,000,000 strong.[56]

A non-partisan posture and respect for Chairman Chamberlain and Secretary Baker did not stop Wadsworth from criticizing Democrats. "The atmosphere here in Washington is not very pleasant," he wrote Root in

54. Wadsworth, Jr., *Reminiscences*, Ch. XI, *passim*. See Daniel R. Beaver, *Newton D. Baker and the American War Effort* (Lincoln: University of Nebraska Press, 1966), p. 33. Wadsworth's contention that Crowder had the draft law firmly in mind prior to April 7 is not inconsistent with Beaver's account. Although Beaver does not allude to Crowder's fifteen years of consideration, he does note that the Judge Advocate General initiated and administered the drafting of the bill.

55. *New York Times*, Apr. 24, 1917.

56. *Ibid.*, June 26, July 7, 1917.

the summer of 1917. "There is an undercurrent of dissatisfaction and suspicion." Wadsworth thought the administration "remote and secretive."[57] The antidote would be public criticism to which Chairman Chamberlain and Wadsworth would be principal parties.

Throughout the summer and fall of 1917 Wadsworth initiated a practice of informally inspecting various cantonments. Perhaps out of a mixture of nostalgia and duty, he would for the rest of his life enjoy tramping around army bases. Wadsworth loved soldiering. Generally satisfied with the quality of leadership of cantonments and the spirit of troops, throughout the fall he became particularly sensitive to shortages of guns, blankets, and clothing. By December of 1917 others became sensitive to these military shortages. Public hearings and executive sessions of the Military Affairs Committee revealed increasing lags of production. By then it was apparent that the military forces were not only short of supplies but that crucial weapons of war such as certain artillery pieces, tanks, and airplanes were non-existent.[58]

Adopting Wadsworth's method of field testing, in January four or five members of the committee visited a Bethlehem Steel plant in Pennsylvania where the Crozier "split-tail" field artillery pieces were being manufactured. To the horror of the committee members, six months of tooling had produced no guns, although the manufacture of fifty to one hundred per month by then had been anticipated. Following an executive session of the Military Affairs Committee, General William Crozier was fired, in part at the suggestion of the committee. Wadsworth and his colleagues, however, were soon convinced that the problem of production snarls needed stronger remedy than the shifting of personnel. The firing of General Crozier would not resolve tank production problems, nor explain the manufacturing of "liberty" motors which fitted no airplane, American or foreign.[59] Coincidental to the committee's restlessness over production problems, certain War Production Board personnel also demanded changes. Of that large operation, basically responsible for weapons problems of particular concern to the Military Affairs Committee, Bernard Baruch expressed the most exasperation. From his desk, charged with procuring raw materials, he noted of the board, "No one has a plan and all seem too tired to do anything except to criticize."[60]

57. J.W.W. to Elihu Root, Aug. 13, 1917, Wadsworth MSS.

58. Wadsworth, Jr., *Reminiscences*, Ch. XI, *passim*; J.W.W. to James W. Wadsworth, Sr., Dec. 20, 1917, Wadsworth MSS.

59. Wadsworth, Jr., *Reminiscences*, pp. 203–217.

60. Margaret L. Coit, *Mr. Baruch* (Cambridge, Mass.: Houghton Mifflin Co., 1957), pp. 164–9.

On January 21, Chairman Chamberlain initiated legislation demanding reorganization of war production, that sweeping powers be granted to a war cabinet intended to be superior to the Secretary of the Navy, the Secretary of War, and other officers of the government, except the President. A national debate ensued. Majority Leader Hitchcock defended, less strongly than Chamberlain, the legislation. Baker adamantly defended the WPB as constituted. Wilson defended the Secretary of War. Wadsworth, the principal Republican voice in what was becoming a national *cause celèbre,* applauded Chamberlain, insisting that "every citizen who has an interest in his country wants to see us really effective in the war." In addition to criticizing artillery, tank, and airplane motor tangles, the young New Yorker called for increased ship construction, mine development, improved transportation and manufacturing facilities. A single agency was necessary to coordinate the production efforts of industry and various government agencies. For several weeks Wilson and Baker continued to deny that executive inefficiency affected production and the procurement of war material. The pressure on the President mounted. General Wood, having returned from the "front," seemed to relish describing the lack of airplanes, the breakdown of American ordnance, and the necessity of American troops to use British small arms, French machine guns, and Italian trucks. As if to mollify, yet chastise, the President, Wadsworth commented: "This is not time for partisanship. We need men of vision, ability and courage" to coordinate the industrial effort.[61] Finally, the President capitulated and, without waiting for a congressional mandate, gave the chairman of the War Industries Board unilateral control over production and procurement of war material. By spring Wadsworth saw a "turning of the corner toward greater efficiency."

If Wadsworth wanted centralization of industrial purchasing, he was less enthusiastic about centralization of food production. He saw Food Administrator Herbert Hoover as too aggressive in seeking controls regarding the elimination of wastes, the punishment of profiteering and uncooperative farmers, and the stabilization of prices. He was sure that the extensiveness of such controls would threaten farmers, and thus depress production. Eventually, he feared, the government would have to appropriate millions and millions of dollars. "It is a state socialism run wild." Although Hoover received the power sought, Wadsworth had little to fear. The Food Administrator proved almost as supportive of the farmer's independence as was the farmer-politician from the Genesee Valley. Paradoxically, in a

61. Wadsworth, Jr., *Reminiscences,* Ch. XI, *passim; New York Times,* Jan. 21, Feb. 5, 6, 1918; Beaver, *op. cit.,* pp. 91–93.

year's time, Wadsworth would urge the Food Administrator to mandate a price increase for wheat in order to increase its production.[62]

6

The conservative New Yorker needed no committee assignment to speak out on finances. Never one to take senate floor privileges lightly, Wadsworth, on September 6, 1917, spent two hours supporting the Finance Committee's war revenue proposals against the designs of his radical colleagues. Western Senators Norris, LaFollette and Borah, not satisfied with the $1,000,000,000 tax increase over 1916, wanted approximately 50 percent more. While favoring "the utter and entire conscription of wealth," Wadsworth urged caution in view of the likely extension of the war beyond 1918. A tax increase beyond the committee's recommendation, he feared, would threaten further industrial development necessary to carry on a prolonged war. He thought England's heavy tax program was no pattern at all for American revenue for "we are still a new country" and still in need of pouring profits back into industrial corporations. Contrary to Senator Borah's contention, Wadsworth thought the corporations were not "storing away" their profits. Not surprisingly, Senators Harding, Weeks, Smoot, and Lodge urged on their conservative colleague with appropriate questions and helpful bits of information. Wadsworth's conclusion portended a conservatism which would prevail in America:

> My humble judgment is that [this tax bill] goes just far enough, just about what these industries and fortunes will bear in the first year of war. At the very best, with due respect to the members on the Committee on Finance, it is largely experimental. Neither they nor I nor any other Senator can tell exactly what the effect is going to be, but I do believe most sincerely, Mr. President, that it is wiser for us to proceed slowly, so that we shall not make it impossible for us to proceed with lightning and irresistible speed in that day and year when America shall strike the decisive blow.[63]

Wadsworth and his conservative colleagues carried the day, the test coming on an amendment offered by Senator LaFollette to raise the maximum of

62. *New York Times*, July 12, 1917.
63. *Congressional Record*, Vol. 55, 65th Congress, 1st. Session, Sept. 6, 1917, p. 6679.

graduated excess profits taxes from 60 percent to 70 percent. The House of Representatives sustained the Senate action.

Nor did Wadsworth need direct committee responsibility to discuss prohibition of alcohol, although the issue frequently came before the Agriculture Committee. "As a war measure, Senators, this bill is a fake," the New Yorker commented as he took up the fight against wartime prohibition. The Senator hung his charge on the bill's provision to continue prohibition after the war. The act amended the Conscription Act of 1917 so as to forbid the sale of alcoholic beverages at or near army camps and naval bases.[64] On the prohibition issue he saw hypocrisy everywhere. A colleague's remarkable peroration in defense of prohibition was followed by a whispered comment, "Jim, come over to my office, and I'll give you a drink." Jim never believed that the nation was dry. The movement to him was largely the work of the Anti-Saloon Leaguers and Bible-belt churchgoers. Both capitalized on the war to dry up America and make her sons morally and physically capable of fighting. Pressure for prohibition, during and after the war, was intense and most politicians succumbed. Wadsworth did not and in time would be punished by defeat at the polls.[65]

The same constitutional grounds which undergirded Wadsworth's opposition to prohibition explain his anti-woman suffrage position. He viewed both issues as responsibilities of the states, not the national government, an interpretation quite consistent with his general fear of intrusion by the federal government. Alice felt much the same way. As president of the National Anti-Suffrage Association, she embellished the constitutional grounds with various evil and far-out consequences of woman suffrage—the encouragement of pro-German, pacifist, and Socialist demands, further resistance to the draft, and the general denigration of self-government. Alice, however, did not have hundreds of thousands of constituents to answer to. Soon not a few of her husband's demanded his resignation from the United States Senate. Such constituents viewed him as a principal architect of a Republican-Democratic effort to defeat the amendment.[66]

In the spring of 1918 Wadsworth attempted to recoup political losses he had suffered in the state organization two years previously, by seeking a Republican candidate of his conservative stance for the governorship. Although flirting with the candidacy himself, he soon supported Attorney General Merton E. Lewis' bid to oppose Whitman in the primary. But again Whitman had the patronage and the power, and carried the direct

64. *Congressional Record*, Vol. 56, 65th Congress, 2nd. Session, Aug. 21, 1918, pp. 9641–44.

65. Wadsworth, Jr., *Reminiscences*, pp. 220–7.

66. *New York Times*, Nov. 23, 1917, Mar. 11, July 20, 27, 1918.

primary. And again the United States Senator retreated to Washington and looked to "larger events," meanwhile letting political nature take its course. The political yield proved abundant. Governor Whitman's defeat by Alfred E. Smith in November made Wadsworth the state's "first" Republican. At the same time the Republican ascendency in the Congress brought him into the chairmanship of one of its "first" committees, that of Military Affairs.

In the mid-1960s Wilson scholars in the Library of Congress were patronizingly amused by discovery of Wadsworth's diary impression of the President as "Mephistophelean" (fiendish), "Machiavellian," and a "veteran lecturer, not a President." "Good old Waddsy," exclaimed one, scornfully, about the youthful senator. Others concurred and rather dismissed him. Their attitude was understandable. Wilson was not the things Wadsworth called him. Also, during the Wilson presidency, Wadsworth was not an auspicious figure. Yet, in those Wilson years he was the same person as before and after.

In appearance he was youthful, possessing an athletic physique. His facial features were well-proportioned and handsome. By the time of his senatorial years, his hair line had receded considerably, without, however, the appearance of baldness. He possessed a confident bearing, tall and almost soldierly. Some observers thought his bearing aristocratic, and correctly so, for he was at ease and "unflappable" in most any company. His security, in turn, made it easy for him to think on his feet. Few men seemed so uninhibited in the use of their intelligence. Some listeners thought him brilliant, which he was not. He usually spoke without notes in low key, and manifesting sincerity. And, as always in his life, Wadsworth appeared quietly affable. Never a back-slapper, he was engagingly pleasant. People liked James Wadsworth, at close or long range. Some columnists even called him "Jimmy" in print, something which those close to him usually did not do for all their affection for him.

Wadsworth's ideological stance in 1916 was as constant as his physical appearance. As a rear-guard conservative defense against Wilson's leftward move in 1916, it did justice to Elihu Root's prescriptions against the New Freedom over the previous three years. Wadsworth opposed increased taxes, the reduced tariff, the Adamson eight-hour day for railroad workers, the Ship Purchase bill, and most vociferously, prohibition and woman suffrage. Aristocratic and conservative continuity from Root to Wadsworth in the United States Senate was nearly total. Although some peers of Root and Wadsworth accepted parts of progressivism such as woman suffrage, the two New Yorkers stood together in opposing it. Also, Wadsworth, like Root, favored preparedness. Both were not averse to using federal power for national defense.

V

"Mr. Chairman"

"**Y**ES, SIR, BOYS," observed the obese Senator Boies Penrose from Pennsylvania, "the country's going to get tired of going to school to Professor Wilson and just naturally play truant. Then they'll begin calling us to get them out of trouble." [1] If Wadsworth doubted what his powerful friend said, he did not doubt it after October 25, 1918. On that day, against the advice of friends, Woodrow Wilson broke the truce of non-partisan war effort and asked the country to return Democratic majorities to the Senate and the House. "Truly this man is a strange man," wrote Wadsworth to James Sheffield on the following day. "He conceded the Republicans are pro-war and, in the next breath says they are anti-Administration." [2] Wadsworth was astounded by the President's move. Indeed, many Republicans in the Congress had supported the war effort more than Democrats, especially in the House. In that body, faithful Julius Kahn of California, the ranking Republican on the Military Affairs Committee, was the administration's most ardent preparedness supporter.

On November 4 the voters "swapped horses" and elected a Republican Sixty-sixth Congress. Prior to its convening, Wadsworth ascended from the fourth-ranking Republican position on the Military Affairs Committee to its chairmanship. Francis Warren of Wyoming, the ranking Republican, preferred to assume the chairmanship of Appropriations. John Weeks of Massachusetts was defeated at the polls and the third-ranking Republican, James H. Brady of Idaho, died. Not a few Washington observers noted that when the Sixty-sixth Congress convened, young Wadsworth, the senior senator from the most populace state in the Union, would answer to "Mr. Chairman." And with Democrat Alfred E. Smith's election as governor of New York, Wadsworth was that state's ranking Republican. [3]

Military affairs were foremost in Wadsworth's mind in the winter of

1. Robert Douglas Bowden, *Boies Penrose* (Greenburg Publishers, 1937), p. 244.
2. J.W.W. to James Sheffield, Oct. 26, 1918, Sheffield MSS, Sterling Library, Yale University, New Haven, Conn.
3. James W. Wadsworth, Jr., *The Reminiscences of James W. Wadsworth, Jr.* (Columbia University: Oral History Research Office, 1952), Ch. XVI, *passim.*

1918–1919. Thinking it about time to "see something of the army that had been doing the fighting," just five days prior to the armistice he boarded a troop transport for Southampton, England. In mid-ocean, however, word of peace was received, and upon the ship's arrival England was in a state of ecstatic celebration.[4]

Despite the celebration of peace, Wadsworth's immediate mission was military and he made the most of it. In London, General Pershing's liaison officer escorted him for ten days as he checked out army personnel and installations. Most rewarding was his visit with General John F. O'Ryan, the Twenty-seventh Division commander, who had crossed the channel to look after 3,000 of his wounded in British hospitals. After England, Wadsworth spent two weeks along the front from the Swiss border to the Channel. Then to Paris, where, among other diversions, he looked into the estate matters of his late beloved Aunt Neelie. More importantly, long conversations in Paris with the American Expeditionary Force commander, General John Pershing, revealed military unhappiness with the recent armistice. The high military command of the three Allied powers preferred absolute destruction of the enemy to a surrender which left enemy military forces intact to fight another day. Also, Pershing feared that the enemy population was unaware of the serious defeat of their military forces and that one day a demagog might invoke the myth of German invincibility.[5]

Although Wadsworth's brief European tour was mainly military, its implications for peace were more significant. In London on a foggy November 20, he called on Lord Balfour, Britain's renowned foreign minister. Although very cordial, Balfour wanted to know what was implied in the League of Nations proposal so elusively described by the American president, and whether or not the new Republican congress would be hostile to Wilson in his conduct of foreign policy. Also, the foreign minister inquired as to why the President was coming to Europe. Wadsworth could only surmise. He was no more sure of the League's design and purpose than the foreign minister. He was certain that the Republican congress would cooperate with the President, and that Woodrow Wilson was coming to Paris "to use his influence as the head of a great country to achieve the best ends." More specifically, in regard to the League question, the Senator noted that his countrymen, while a "hard headed people," were "imbued with some pretty high ideals; that they would rejoice if an effective international instrument could be created." The closing repartee between

4. *Ibid.*, Ch. XIII, *passim.*
5. *Ibid.*, pp. 231–234.

Wadsworth and the great foreign minister was prophetic. The former referred to the skepticism of many Americans about the League, the latter was sure that "whatever was done, it [must] be done quickly." [6]

Soon the fears of both Balfour and Wadsworth were sustained. The skepticism of Americans about the peace treaty and the League soon took the form of Republican resolutions introduced in the Senate of the United States, that of Philander Knox being most critical of the President. Knox wanted Wilson's extraordinary war powers withdrawn and any league of nations project deferred.[7] Confusion reigned in American quarters. Even Henry White, the only Republican among the American peace commissioners who arrived in Paris in early January, had doubts, due in most part to his ignorance of the President's peace plans. White, wanting to talk, and knowing that Wadsworth was still in France, called him to his Paris apartment. The New Yorker was astounded to hear that the commission had not conferred with the President, either on board ship or in Paris.[8] Yet, having in the past described to Root and others Wilson's secretive ways, Wadsworth should not have been surprised.

In early January, 1919, Wadsworth returned home. As the chairman-designate of the Military Affairs Committee, his first concern was the establishment of a permanent military policy based on universal military training. The press, however, was more interested in his views on the Versailles negotiations. His response to peace queries was firm. He wanted an immediate settlement of vital war issues—the establishment of national boundaries, the extent of indemnities and reparations, the disposition of German colonies, the forms of government in the new nations, the elimination of famine, the destruction of the enemy's military capacity—all to be settled prior to the formation of a League of Nations.[9] Among his Senate colleagues Wadsworth was not a League advocate.

Most Republican senators, like Wadsworth, had reservations about the League Covenant supported so strenuously by the President, for a variety of reasons: the President's call for a Democratic congress in 1918, his avoidance of Senate representation on the Peace Commission, his lack of communication with the Senate Foreign Relations Committee, and his attempt at stifling senate comment upon his return from Paris in June. Wads-

6. *Ibid.*, pp. 236–240; James W. Wadsworth, Jr., *Diary*, Nov. 20, 1918, Wadsworth MSS, Library of Congress, Washington, D.C.

7. Jack E. Kendrick, "The League of Nations and the Republican Senate, 1918–1921" (Chapel Hill, N.C.: University of North Carolina, 1952), Ph.D. dissertation, Ch. II.

8. Wadsworth, Jr., *Reminiscences*, pp. 236–240; *New York Times*, Dec 22, 1918.

9. *New York Times*, Jan. 26, 1918.

worth, like Lodge, the chairman of the Foreign Relations Committee, was a "strong reservationist." Indeed, he was much influenced by the aristocratic and conservative Lodge, and on March 4, 1919, gladly signed his "round robin" resolution which questioned the Covenant's constitutionality and called for its extensive consideration prior to any senate ratification.[10] In September, the New York senator appended his own reservation—there were fourteen in all—to the treaty. His reservation provided that, should the economic boycott article (Article XVI) be invoked against a covenant-breaking nation, the United States reserved the right to trade with the nationals of that country. Wadsworth feared the consequences of the article for nationals who might be aliens living in America. His New York constituency was, of course, full of hyphenated Americans, such as Italian-Americans, who might well fall under the article.[11]

When the Senate voted on the League Covenant in November, most Democrats joined with "irreconcilable" Republicans—those unalterably opposed to any League—to defeat the League with reservations. Then, the reservationists joined with the irreconcilables to defeat the League without reservations.

When the Senate again voted on the League in March of 1920, the League to Enforce Peace feared that Wadsworth would defect to the irreconcilables, and with some justification.[12] In January of 1920, the Peace League and other League of Nations sympathizers had worked feverishly for a compromise on a reservation regarding the League's most contentious article, Article X. Article X provided for military and economic sanctions. As a compromise which would be acceptable to the two major parties was worked out, Wadsworth's vote became particularly important. Senator Kellogg thought "we can give . . . [the League with the re-written reservation] 34 or 35 votes; and we are assured that there are 29 Democrats . . . and probably 30." "I think Senator Wadsworth is in some doubt," Kellogg wrote to the elder statesman, Elihu Root. "He has great confidence in your judgment . . . [and you might] give him your legal opinion of this subject."[13] Root, who had suggested the new reservation to Article X, wanted

10. Kendrick, op. cit., Ch. II, passim.
11. Ibid., Ch. VI, passim; Henry F. Holthusen, James W. Wadsworth, Jr., A Biographical Sketch (New York: G. P. Putnam's Sons, 1926), pp. 134–6; Congressional Record, Vol. 58, 66th Congress, 1st Session, Sept. 19, 1919, pp. 5617–5622; New York Times, Sept. 20, 1919.
12. Polls by Rev. William short, Executive Director of the League to Enforce Peace, and Gus Karger of the Cincinnati Times-Star, Gilbert Hitchcock MSS, Library of Congress, Washington, D.C.
13. Frank B. Kellogg to Elihu Root, Mar. 12, 1920, Elihu Root MSS, Library of Congress, Washington, D.C.

it to succeed, yet he would not pressure his young successor: "You wanted me to write to Wadsworth. I hesitate to do that, because when a man is engaged in an excited controversy I do not think that volunteer advice from the outside is ordinarily welcome or useful. I have a very warm friendship and great admiration for Wadsworth, and I am very certain of his friendship for me." [14]

Wadsworth, however, did support the new reservation to Article X. And even though on March 19 some Democrats bolted their party to support the League with the revised reservation regarding Article X, the necessary two-thirds vote for ratification of the treaty was not forthcoming. The League was dead. Wadsworth's position as a strong reservationist in the spring of 1920 probably reflected that of his constituency and most Americans. More importantly, it reflected his own belief in American sovereignty. Family heritage such as that of the Lodges and the Wadsworths, so tied to the nation's founding, particularly prohibited their descendents from supporting an Article X without reservations. Besides, Wadsworth viewed Article X in the League Covenant as unconstitutional. Only the Congress has the war-making power. Again, one sees the impingement of familial and ideological influences on the young senator from New York. Although Wadsworth's cosmopolitanism by the mid-1920s would start him on a trek to a pragmatic internationalism which would reach significant proportions in the 1930s, for the rest of his life he would contend that Article X in the League Covenant threatened America's sovereignty and was unconstitutional. (Not all political leaders of Wadsworth's station were so cosmopolitan. Indeed, some, like the Tafts of Cincinnati and Hamilton Fish of New York, pursued more the nationalist route to American sovereignty.) Interestingly, four decades after the Covenant's defeat, Henry Cabot Lodge, a grandson of the elder Lodge, and James Jeremiah Wadsworth served as ambassadors to the United Nations, an international organization devoid of an Article X.

2

On January 28, 1919, Wadsworth reported to senate colleagues on his observations of the AEF. Perhaps, as the chairman-designate of Military Affairs, the New York senator felt compelled to speak at length. It was his longest senate address to date. Putting his remarks in the context of Euro-

14. Elihu Root to Frank B. Kellogg, Mar. 13, 1920, Elihu Root MSS.

pean conditions prior to American entry, Wadsworth explained how America became involved, what divisions first embarked for Europe, and where American divisions engaged the enemy. With a sense of the romantic he described the American doughboy—"a hometown boy . . . a source of wonder to his officers . . . arduous in his training . . . dashing in courage . . . superlatively patient . . . cheerful." He deplored supply shortages which endangered American troops. Yet, in spite of shortages, the AEF had "managed to go ahead with ever-increasing strength." No two divisions, the New Yorker stressed, better acquitted themselves than his own Twenty-seventh National Guard Division from New York and the Thirtieth from Tennessee. In detail Wadsworth described their attack against the enemy at Canal du Nord in the towns of St. Quentin and Cambrai, on the Hindenburg line. Then the chairman-designate revealed his lifetime aspiration for the future:

> Senators may remember that I have always been an earnest advocate of universal military training. I believe that we shall have to have it before we ever get a genuine military policy in the United States, so as to be provided with an army that can respond to any emergency—that together with a General Staff. If we are to have a system of universal military training, I hope it will be so arranged that the men selected for that training at a certain age shall be trained in areas marked geographically, and that when they have finished their training they shall be organized into regiments and divisions whose headquarters for administrative pur- pose shall be each in a given locality . . . such as a state, or a group of small states; . . . that they shall be completely federalized; that they shall be under the orders of the Federal Government.[15]

The third session of the Sixty-fifth Congress, sitting from December 7, 1918, to March 3, 1919, had been a lame duck Democratic session. Re- publicans chafed to take control—the Democrats had held it for a decade— and so impeded the Senate's business in order to force a special session upon adjournment of the Sixty-fourth Congress. Wadsworth helped by filibustering with the army appropriations bill. Despite Democratic efforts to bring to a vote the general deficiency bill, which Republicans thought too expensive, and the army appropriations bill, with which Wadsworth agreed, the New York senator would not yield the floor. He insisted that on March 4 the President call a special session of the Congress to consider

15. *Congressional Record*, Vol. 57, 65th Congress, 3rd Session, Jan. 28, 1919, p. 2200.

deficiency and army appropriation bills, bills denied a vote only by the Republican filibuster. Wadsworth ran out the clock.[16] Wilson, of course, would be in no hurry to convene a congress run by Republicans.

To move the wheels of government, Wilson had to succumb. On May 19, 1919, he convened the first session of the Sixty-sixth Congress. Wadsworth, now chairman of Military Affairs, moved to the front row of the senate chamber, third from the left. The congenial Harding, by mutual agreement, moved into the fourth seat. While the nation awaited great senate debate on the ratification of the Versailles Treaty, Wadsworth quietly prepared for hearings on national military policy. First, however, the army bill, held over from the lame duck session, had to be disposed of. As chairman, the young New Yorker handled the committee's legislation on the floor. His Albany experience, of course, served him well and he quickly learned to hold his own against queries from his colleagues, even from tough and craggy Kenneth McKellar of Tennessee. There were some painful moments. On the army appropriations bill to sustain a 400,000-man army, the chairman carefully explained that the requested appropriation was $100,000,000 less than needed because that amount had been unexpended in the previous fiscal year and would be carried over. McKellar questioned the new chairman's logic and method of handling the appropriation bill. In a barrage of questioning, Wadsworth faltered—"Oh, I beg the Senator's pardon; let me see"—particularly when McKellar noted that the Military Affairs Committee of the "other body" had seen no need to carry over the $100,000,000. Republican Walter Edge of New Jersey kindly suggested that as a matter of bookkeeping the Senate "perhaps should have the $100,000,000 lapse and reappropriate it, separating it in the items as the committee thinks it should." "The Senate, of course," replied the young chairman, "is the master of the situation."[17] Wadsworth's integrity, however, was not questioned, nor could one suspect that he was a big spender, even for the army.

On an evening late in the summer of 1919 Wadsworth crossed Lafayette Square, passed the White House, and entered the Willard Hotel on Pennsylvania Avenue, to address the Military Training Camps Association. The speaker was an anomaly to most of his audience. One young colonel, John McAuley Palmer, "was greatly impressed by him—at first by his youthful vigor, for he was barely forty-two years old, a very young man to head one of the great Senatorial Committees." But, wrote Palmer, "I was even more impressed by what he said. He spoke with great earnestness."

16. *Ibid.*, Mar. 3, 1919.
17. *Ibid.*, June 23, 1919.

Wadsworth, of course, was quite earnest about the establishment of a permanent military policy, the first business before the Military Affairs Committee. He described the agenda before the committee, and noted its attempt to search out the range of divergent recommendations regarding the nation's military organization and policy. "Some of you," he concluded, "may be called before us. If so, you should remember that the American people, through their Congress, have a right to your frank opinions, without reference to the opinions of any other person."[18]

Colonel Palmer had reason to listen well to the speaker of the evening. Nobody in the audience had more desire to talk frankly about military policy and nobody welcomed more Senator Wadsworth's entreaty to do so. Colonel John McAuley Palmer, a descendent of prominent military and political personages of the same name, currently served as chief of the War Plans Division of the General Staff of the United States Army. At the outbreak of war he, with a special committee of three other officers, prepared a plan of national military policy, based on universal military training. The plan in part served as a basis for military organization during the war. Palmer also drew up plans for the first expeditionary division dispatched to France, and in France he served as General Pershing's first Assistant Chief of Staff. After the armistice he was again assigned to the General Staff in Washington.[19] Unknown to Senator Wadsworth, Colonel Palmer and a coterie of fellow officers unalterably opposed the "Prussianistic" military policy views of the senior officers who served General Peyton March, the Chief of Staff. Some weeks were to elapse before the chairman of the Military Affairs Committee and the War Plans staff officer would meet across the committee table.

On July 26, 1919, Wadsworth formally announced the formation of a senate Military Affairs sub-committee to outline a long-range permanent military policy. The committee, with himself at the head, was comprised of Senators Sutherland, New, Frelinghuysen, Chamberlain, Thomas and Fletcher, all sympathetic to the concept of universal military training.[20]

On Thursday, August 7, 1919, at 2:00 P.M., Chairman Wadsworth convened the Military Affairs sub-committee "to consider the various proposals looking toward the permanent reorganization of the military policy of the country." On several days of each week, for eight months, three

18. John McAuley Palmer, *America In Arms* (New Haven, Conn.: Yale University Press, 1941), p. 158.

19. *Hearings, Sub-Committee, Committee on Military Affairs, United States Senate*, 66th Congress, 1st and 2nd sessions, pp. 1173–6.

20. *New York Times*, July 27, 1919.

Republican and three Democratic senators met in the Military Affairs Committee rooms off the northwest corner of the senate chamber to hear the advocates of this or that military policy. True to his word, the young chairman received any manner of military witnesses, the Chief of Staff, former Chiefs of Staff, the Secretary of War, former Secretaries of War, a variety of military association lobbyists, and a gamut of army and national guard officers. The chairman noted that three bills pertaining to military policy had already been introduced:

The first one was introduced by Senator [George E.] Chamberlain, Senate Bill 2691, to provide for universal military, naval, and vocational training and for mobilization of the manhood of the Nation in a national emergency; another bill introduced by Senator [Henry S.] New to create a separate department of aeronautics, defining the powers and duties of the director thereof, providing for the organization, disposition, and administration of a United States Air Force, creating the United States Air Reserve Force, and providing for the development of the civil and commercial aviation; a third bill introduced by myself, at the request of the War Department, to reorganize and increase the efficiency of the United States Army and for other purposes.[21]

Appropriately, General Peyton C. March, Chief of Staff, United States Army, testified first, in defense of the War Department's proposal. For two days General March elaborated on the War Department proposal, which called for the recruitment of a regular army of 510,000 officers and men into 21 divisions, the improvement and enlargement of the General Staff for planning, the instituting of universal military training of men between nineteen and twenty-one years of age for a three-month period, the attachment of trainees on a reporting basis to regular army divisions for a period of two years, and the replacement of automatic promotion by a selective promotion system. If implemented, the policy described by General March would result in an immediate war-strength army of 1,250,000 at a cost of $900,000,000.[22]

In subsequent testimony Secretary of War Baker,[23] General Pershing,[24] and high-ranking officers of the Washington military establishment gen-

21. *Hearings, Sub-Committee*, p. 3.
22. *Ibid.*, pp. 33–110; *New York Times*, Aug. 8, 1919.
23. *Hearings, Sub-Committee*, pp. 147–214; *New York Times*, Aug. 19, 1919.
24. *Hearings, Sub-Committee*, pp. 1571–1705; *New York Times*, Nov. 2, 6, 1919.

erally concurred in General March's defense of the War Department bill. Opposition came from high-ranking officers outside the establishment and from lower-echelon personnel within the War Department. Wadsworth himself was uneasy about the proposal, questioning its advocates about "Prussian" implications of a large standing army, and telling reporters only that it was a "step" in the right direction. General O'Ryan of the New York Twenty-seventh was the first to seriously criticize the March bill. He thought such a large army, five times the size of the pre-war army, wasteful, undemocratic, ineffective, and obsolete. He wanted to de-emphasize the regular army, and enhance the universal military service concept by having trainees, after three months of basic training, serve in a national reserve army unit for three years. Young citizens, of course, would have the option of serving in a national guard unit. General Leonard Wood, frequently out of sorts with the Washington hierarchy, also thought a 510,000-man regular army too large and, like O'Ryan, called for an organized reserve.[25] Former Secretary of War Stimson followed suit, insisting that a regular army should be just large enough to man foreign garrisons and serve as a nucleus of a citizen army.[26]

By October 7, Chairman Wadsworth had severe doubts about the March bill. Too much articulate testimony had contradicted it. Too many high-ranking officers had seemed pained when defending it. On the evening of that day the sub-committee sat in a corner of the Senator's panelled living room and finally decided to write its own bill, to reject the War Department's. It was not easy. All realized that great policy legislation was not to be home-made, that it normally was constructed in the appropriate departments of the executive branch.[27] In this case, however, the War Department could hardly write a bill contrary to that of its Chief of Staff. Uncertainty prevailed.

Two days after their evening session, Colonel Palmer appeared before the sub-committee. Wadsworth had suggested his appearance because of side comments by younger officers: "He can tell you some things." The committee was skeptical.

Hardly had Palmer begun his testimony before he rejected the War Department bill and advocated in its place legislation to create a citizens army. The advantages of his substitute bill were manifold. Particularly, it would emphasize citizen as well as professional military leadership, reducing professional personnel to a "determinable minimum," and would

25. *Hearings, Sub-Committee*, pp. 511–541; *New York Times*, Sept. 3, 1919.
26. *Hearings, Sub-Committee*, pp. 1237–1255; *New York Times*, Oct. 17, 1919.
27. Wadsworth, Jr., *Reminiscences*, pp. 303–11.

infuse public opinion into the determination of military policy. As if to demonstrate the incongruity of military professionalism in democratic government, Palmer revealed that General March had gagged the War Plans Division which recommended the citizens army. In two days, Palmer destroyed the March effort. The committee was fascinated. His differences with March were significant and much to the sub-committee's liking. Palmer wanted a regular army of 280,000 men, for garrison and training purposes rather than a standing army; universal military training of six months' duration as a basis for a citizens army; service of all trainees in an organized reserve for five years; the division of the country into sixteen corps areas for mobilization and training programs; the utilization of volunteer veterans in the citizens army; the utilization of reserve officers on a par with regular army officers; the retention of historical military designations for various divisions.[28]

The sub-committee wanted Palmer on its staff. Secretary of War Baker, however, was reluctant to cross his Chief of Staff. Having called Wadsworth to his office, he pointed to the adjoining Chief of Staff's office and commented: "You have put me in a . . . hot spot." Yet Baker respected the Senator's request, and would concur; his own doubts about the March bill were growing. The Secretary of War, however, suggested that the request for Palmer not be in the official record and that Wadsworth tear up his letter asking for Palmer.[29]

Palmer went to work for Wadsworth, assisted by Colonel John W. Gulick, both of whom were instructed by Secretary Baker that they were to operate independently of the War Department. Certainly Baker could not officially sanction Palmer's point of view, even though a growing number of officers now did.[30] Most significant was Colonel George C. Marshall's identification with the Wadsworth-Palmer citizen army philosophy. Serving in Washington as General Pershing's aide-de-camp, Marshall became closely associated with both Palmer and Wadsworth as the reorganization bill was hammered out. Years later, Marshall saw much of the Palmer family. He would always think Palmer's organizational efforts were never properly appreciated. During the weeks of late winter, 1919, Marshall and Wadsworth developed a highly durable friendship. At the time of Wadsworth's death in 1952, Marshall gave the former Military

28. *Hearings, Sub-Committee*, pp. 1173–1232.
29. Wadsworth, Jr., *Reminiscences*, pp. 309–311; *New York Times*, Nov. 17, 1919.
30. Palmer, *op. cit.*, pp. 158–160.

Affairs chairman one of his finest eulogies. Wadsworth came to believe that Marshall, with Root, was one of the two greatest Americans of the twentieth century.[31]

Now the subcommittee turned to executive sessions, putting flesh on the Palmer skeleton of army reorganization. Wadsworth and Palmer worked well in tandem. Both agreed that national guard and organized reserve officers should be members of the Army of the United States and equal in status to regular army officers. Wadsworth called the former "part-time soldiers," the latter, "all-time soldiers." Both felt strongly that the national guard should come under the army clause of the Constitution, not the militia clause, in order to make federalization of the guard constitutional. When Wadsworth questioned the political feasibility of telling forty-eight states where their guard units would fit into the various corps areas, Palmer responded that states would agree if regular army officers and national guard officers made such determinations together. Both agreed that in addition to garrison and expeditionary missions, the regular army would aid corps area commanders in the training of the UMT recruits for the national army. Also, Wadsworth and Palmer supported a single promotion list rather than the discriminating practice of promoting only as openings occurred in various branches of the army.[32]

On January 26, the full Senate Committee on Military Affairs, by a 9–5 vote, reported a bill, two Republicans and three Democrats voting Nay. The bill provided for universal military training of all eligible youths between eighteen and twenty-one years of age, for four months, in training centers in nine corps areas. Following their active service, trainees would constitute three organized reserve divisions in each corps area and would participate in one two-week maneuver annually. In addition to the reserve divisions, each corps area would maintain two national guard divisions and one regular army division. UMT alone would provide an organized reserve of 2,000,000 men after a period of five years.[33]

Democrat Kenneth McKellar led the opposition. It is "militarism run mad," he exhorted, "a militarism of the ultra-German type, a militarism never dreamed of by our forefathers, a militarism that is wholly unnecessary, a militarism that may be subversive of our democratic institution, a militarism that cannot be defended, a militarism that is wholly unjustified when we look at our history and our future." More precisely the com-

31. Forrest C. Pogue, *George C. Marshall* (New York: Viking Press, 1963), I, 213–215.
32. Palmer, *op cit.*, pp. 160–168.
33. *New York Times*, Jan. 27, 1920.

mittee's minority report viewed the legislation as lodging too much authority in the Chief of Staff, as too costly, as basically undemocratic, and as harmful to the national guard.[34]

McKellar was not alone in criticizing what the Military Affairs chairman said in defense of the reorganization legislation. Senators Kirby, Lenroot, and Nelson pursued Wadsworth on the senate plan, as did the Democratic leader, Gilbert Hitchcock. But McKellar was most persistent regarding the size of the General Staff, the appointment of commissioned officers as assistant under secretaries of war, War Department control over industry, the proliferation of generals of the army, and, of course, the cost.[35]

McKellar's complaints on cost were mostly "smoke."' Wadsworth thought the reorganization cheap at a very maximum of $700,000,000. After all, the indebtedness of the recent war was $25,000,000,000. When Philander Knox, of Pennsylvania, asked about a future war, the young chairman was prophetic:

> Mr. President, I am not sure that I know it but I suspect it. One cannot know about these things. Everybody realizes that the world is in an unset condition. . . . The spirit of nationalism [is] . . . more rife and rampant over the world today than ever before. . . . We cannot tell what is going to happen. We do not want these catastrophes to overtake us. They are horrible things. War itself is a horror. . . . I believe from the bottom of my heart, Senators, that it is the duty of this government and this country to give its young men a chance for their lives if it is going to ask them to fight for the country.[36]

Universal military training was anathema to America. The nation had just fought the last war. The President, although sympathetic to UMT, would not intervene. In the House, Democrats, sensing the mood of the country, beat the Republicans, and caucused against it, 160–17.[37] Senate Democrats were about to follow suit. The pressure on the senate Republican leadership was too much. "Jim," exclaimed an excited Frelinghuysen one morning, "Lodge says that the Democrats have decided to oppose universal training as a party issue. What can we do? He says that

34. *Ibid.*, Feb. 1, 1920; Arthur A. Ekirch, Jr., *The Civilian and the Military* (New York: Oxford University Press, 1956), pp. 200–205, for brief description of Senate debate and pressure group opposition to universal military training.

35. *Congressional Record*, Vol. 59, 66th Congress, 2nd Session, Apr. 1920, pp. 5824–5883.

36. *Ibid.*

37. *New York Times*, Feb. 10, 1920.

we Republicans cannot afford to take up that gauntlet." [38] The chairman capitulated and salvaged what he could. By quickly amending the legislation, with an invaluable assist from Colonels Palmer and Gulick, voluntary training was substituted for compulsory training. Frelinghuysen rushed to the floor with the amendments. Democrats, although anxious to defeat any Republican military policy bill, were caught by surprise. Minority Leader Hitchcock and McKellar squirmed, to Wadsworth's amusement. Hitchcock got the floor. "I shall be delighted to have the Senator amuse himself at the way we squirm, but I would like to have him amuse himself . . . [on] his own time." [39]

The Senate passed what now became known as the Wadsworth bill. Interminable Senate-House conferences began. Weeks elapsed. House conferees, at first suspicious of the volunteer citizen army concept, became convinced that the scheme should be incorporated in their legislation. Although late in their conversion, they successfully urged their House to support it.[40] The House approved the measure. The nation had a permanent and long-range military policy. As finally signed by the President on June 4, the new policy of army organization divided the nation into nine corps areas, each assigned one infantry division of the regular army, two of the national guard, and three of the organized reserves. Joint committees of the General Staff, representing regular and reserve officers, determined where the various state guard units fitted into the corps's twenty-four guard divisions. The regular army would stand at 280,000 men and 17,043 officers. The guard would be federalized in times of emergency. Corps training areas were officered by men from the three types of divisions. Ultimately, however, with military budget-cutting in the 1920s, what meager appropriations were forthcoming would go to the maintenance of regular army divisions, and not to the guard or the organized reserves. The rise of the citizens army would come only with the passage of the Burke-Wadsworth Act in 1940 as war clouds moved across the Atlantic.[41] Legislation to establish a department of aeronautics, supported by both Senators New and Wadsworth, had been dismissed immediately upon its introduction early in the reorganization hearings, and would not be successfully introduced until after World War II. Appropriately, Wadsworth's son-in-law, Stuart Symington, was to serve as the Air Force Department's first secretary.

38. Palmer, *op. cit.*, p. 170.
39. *Congressional Record,* Vol. 59, 66th Congress, 2nd Session, Apr. 1920, pp. 5242–9321, *passim.*
40. Palmer, *op. cit., pp.* 172–175; *New York Times,* May 27, 1920.
41. Palmer, *op. cit.*, pp. 174–176.

Few aristocratic and conservative tenets so affected the life of James Wadsworth as did that of military preparedness. Colonel Jeremiah Wadsworth, who sent Wadsworth's great grandfather into the Genesee Valley, had been Washington's Commissary General. Wadsworth's grandfather died heroically at the Battle of the Wilderness. His father was a major general's aide in the same war. Little wonder that Wadsworth had strong military propensities leading to army enlistment in the Spanish-American War; to formation, in Geneseo, of a cavalry troop of the national guard; to readily accepting service on the senate Military Affairs Committee during the Great War. All were a prelude to a legislative career almost unparalelled in its contribution to the nation's military policy in the first half of the twentieth century. Of civilian influence on the army, from 1900 to 1950, probably only Elihu Root's and Henry L. Stimson's equalled that of Wadsworth. Aside from the National Defense Act of 1920, we will note Wadsworth's authorship of the conscription acts of Word War II, draft extension, national service bills and attempted universal military training. By 1947 he would be "Mr. National Defense."

The making of the nation's foreign and military policy was perhaps never so important in the twentieth century as in 1919 and 1920. The spawning of Naziism and fascism were, in part, rooted in the political lethargy of the American senate. Had Wadsworth and his colleagues accepted both the League Covenant and universal military training, World War II might still be dormant.

Far more prophetic than his colleagues in recognizing the nation's future military needs, Wadsworth was one among many who feared the League Covenant of the Versailles Treaty. Yet he made amends for his nearly isolationist position in 1919. Throughout the 1920s he supported American participation in the World Court. Less than two decades later, as a congressman, he would stand very nearly alone among his fellow Republicans in decrying the isolationism of the Neutrality Acts, 1935–1937.

3

The League Covenant and national military policy were great issues during the transition period from war to peace, of far more long term significance than the emotionally-charged issues of the moment, woman suffrage and prohibition of alcohol. Yet Wadsworth's strong position that only states should have constitutional authority to determine their own policies regarding suffrage and prohibition would in time end his senate career. Prior to that bleak far-off November day of defeat in 1926, the young senator stood firmly in opposition to both the suffrage and pro-hibition causes.

October 19, 1918, was "Get Wadsworth Day" in the nation's capital. Just as the President of the United States rebuked those few "wilful" members of the United States Senate who filibustered against much needed legislation to arm American merchant ships, so suffragists rebuked those thirty-four "wilful" men who early in the month defeated the suffrage amendment to the Constitution. How dare James Wadsworth obstruct the processes of democracy? Off to the steps of the senate office building marched the suffragists, their banners proclaiming:

> Senator Wadsworth's regiment is
> fighting for democracy abroad.
> Senator Wadsworth left his regiment
> and is fighting against democracy
> in the Senate.
> Senator Wadsworth could serve his country best
> by fighting with his regiment abroad
> than by fighting women.[42]

By late 1918 the tide was turning in the suffragettes' favor. Until then the antagonists prevailed, and with them the New York senator. Up to then, Alice Wadsworth also prevailed. On July 1, 1917, she had been elected president of the National Association Opposed to Woman Suf-frage, to succeed Mrs. Arthur M. Dodge, who resigned her office when the organization moved its offices from New York City to Washington.[43] Alice's anti-suffrage activity in the second half of 1917 brought her nearly as much press coverage as all of the Senator's activity.

Alice was busy. Her correspondence with women leaders cried for genuine tranquility, not agitation at home in a time of war. "Surely," she wrote Mrs. Horace Brock, chairman of her organization's executive com-mittee, "the qualities of leadership most needed at this time are strength, health, and fairness of vision, a direct and uncomplex method of thought and action." [44] To the President of the United States she deplored "they who prattle of democracy and strive to force the will of the few upon the

42. *New York Times,* Oct. 19, 1918.
43. *Ibid.,* July 1, 1917.
44. *Ibid.,* July 2, 1917.

vast majority; they who shout of patriotism and defame the good name of their country." Specifically, Alice scorned the President for pardoning suffragists who illegally picketed the White House, wealthy suffragettes who martyrized themselves by going to the "work house" rather than pay their fines.[45] Her letter hurt. Suffragette leaders were quick to agree and to deplore the picketing by some in their ranks.[46] Alice pushed her offensive. Next she laid the victory of suffragettes in achieving the vote in New York State to Germans and pacifists, to an assortment of radical anti-war protesters, and to those who supported the Socialist candidate for mayor of New York City, Morris Hillquit.[47] Frequently, she entertained sympathetic congressmen. It was the only important political role of her lifetime and brought her a happy moment on October 2, 1918, when the Senate turned down the amendment. "Our faith in the wisdom and integrity of the United States Senate is justified," declared Alice after the vote. "We have held all along that if there was no desertion of fundamental principles we could not lose. . . . Thirty-four men . . . retained their sanity. . . . Millions of American women admire their courage." [48]

Suffragettes, however, were relentless. They pushed on local fronts, and New York, where Wadsworth was their chief target, was no exception. "By a majority of more than 100,000," reported Carrie Chapman Catt, the President of the National American Woman Suffrage Association, New York "had enfranchised its women in November, 1917; in the winter of 1918 the Legislature had called upon . . . [Wadsworth] by resolution to vote for the [Susan B. Anthony Amendment]. In September of 1918 his party, meeting in State Convention, had called upon him to vote for the amendment. . . . This action had been taken at the request of the State . . . and in 1919 his Legislature had again called upon him to support the amendment. Women knew of no stronger expression of public demand that could be made." Turning to history, the national feminist leader continued, "they found no mandate so completely given any Congressman at any time to persuade him to sacrifice his individual inclination to the public demand." [49] Wadsworth did not surrender.

He and John Weeks of Massachusetts spelled each other in stalking the senate chamber in order to prevent unanimous consent action to receive

45. *Ibid.*, Sept. 9, 1917.
46. *Ibid.*, Oct. 14, 1917.
47. *Ibid.*, Nov. 19, 1917.
48. *Ibid.*, Oct. 2, 1918.
49. Carrie Chapman Catt and Nettie Rogers Shuler, *Woman Suffrage and Politics, The True Story of the Suffrage Movement* (New York: Charles Scribner's Sons, 1926), p. 335.

a favorable suffrage committee report.[50] Cynically, many Republican senators supported Wadsworth and Weeks, wanting no action on the suffrage amendment. Republicans could take the credit when they constituted the congressional majority some weeks hence.

When the final senate debate came on June 4, 1919, early in the Sixty-sixth Republican Congress, Wadsworth was a lonely battler. John Weeks, whose defeat for re-election was attributed to suffragette opposition, was not there. The New York senator premised his opposition to woman suffrage on constitutional grounds: "The people of the several states when they organized their governments and adopted their constitutions, delegated certain powers to their legislatures and to their executives." The determination of the franchise was not the least of such powers. Furthermore, Wadsworth's computation of voting figures showed that in those states which had voted on the franchise issue in preceding years, 1,300,000 were against it and 254,000 for it. He was sure that the proponents of the amendment were using the amendment process to get woman suffrage without any direct voting by the people (usually only the federal congress and state legislatures vote on constitutional amendments). Such a process, Wadsworth felt, was "whittling away the sense of responsibility of individual citizens." He likened the amendment to other recent manifestations of paternalism, "a system such as was the curse of Germany." [51]

Lodge and George H. Moses, staunch New England conservatives, stood with Wadsworth as did five other Republicans. Twenty Democrats, almost all southern, also voted against the suffrage amendment.[52] But, the die was cast. For fifty years the National American Woman Suffrage Association had fought for the franchise. On the day of Wadsworth's suffrage defeat, they assembled at a gala gold-pen signing ceremony.

Wadsworth opposed prohibition on the same constitutional grounds as those on which he fought woman suffrage. He thought both were state responsibilities. If anything, he felt more strongly about national prohibition of alcohol since it would be essentially a negative amendment, all others being positive in terms of the rights and responsibilities of citizens. Also, many in Wadsworth's social class found it about as repugnant for men to be denied the use of natural spirits as it was for women to engage in political dialogue. Yet Wadsworth's principal interest was a strict construction of the Constitution. Even in national defense matters, where the New Yorker wanted an efficient centralization of the military, he moved

50. *Ibid.*, p. 336.
51. *Congressional Record*, Vol. 58, 66th Congress, 1st Session, June 14, 1919, pp. 616–618.
52. *New York Times*, June 5, 1919.

vigorously only when Colonel Palmer pointed to the army clause as a firm constitutional base.

The Anti-Saloon League had been around about as long as the National American Woman Suffrage Association and, like the suffragettes, capitalized on the reform spirit of the Progressive years. The war gave the prohibitionists an added advantage. They argued persuasively that grain should be used only for necessary food products, not for "booze." Shortly after the declaration of war, the Congress amended the food control bill to prohibit the use of grain and other foodstuffs in the manufacture of beverage alcohol. Under the law, provision to produce beer and wine was left to the President.[53] Many prohibitionists, of course, did not want beer or wine around any more than they did the more potent spirits. By constitutional amendment they wanted prohibition of all alcoholic beverages. Boies Penrose, the burly anti-prohibitionist from Pennsylvania, hoped the Anti-Saloon League would get so bogged down denying hyphenated Americans their beer and wine that they would drop the idea of constitutional amendment. They did not. On August 1, 1917, the Eighteenth Amendment passed the Senate overwhelmingly, 65–20. Penrose and Lodge took the lead in opposing the legislation. Wadsworth was one of eight other Republicans to vote with them.[54] By January 16, 1919, enough states approved the amendment to force its implementation one year later.[55]

Suffragettes and prohibitionists would not forgive James Wadsworth. The least they wanted was his political "scalp." Two days before Wadsworth's anti-suffrage address to the Senate on June 4, 1919, his own state party organization dispatched across the state a "secret steering committee" to determine the possible effect of his anti-suffrage and prohibitionist positions on Wadsworth's campaign for re-election and generally on the Republican cause in the state.[56] The Senator was not without friends. Will Hays, the Republican national chairman, studiously avoided any interference. Barnes, the old Albany warhorse, cajoled party stalwarts to stand up. The New York Times expressed indignation: "Is Mr. Wadsworth to be punished for his integrity and his independence? Is a re-nomination which he has deserved from the Republicans to be withheld at the demand of the coteries of one idea?"[57] By late June, the Association Opposed to Prohibition re-

53. Herbert Asbury, The Great Illusion, An Informal History of Prohibition (Garden City, N.Y.: Doubleday and Co., 1950), p. 130.

54. New York Times, Aug. 2, 1917.

55. O. T. Barck and Nelson M. Blake, Since 1900 (New York: The Macmillan Co., 1959), p. 265.

56. New York Times, June 3, 1919.

57. Ibid.

ported confidently that the Senator would be re-nominated and re-elected.[58]
Time was on Wadsworth's side. His performance as chairman of the
committee charged with legislating military policy was creditably viewed
by the press. The feminist and prohibitionist threat began to fade. When
Miss Garret Hay, national Republican committeewoman and chairman of
the Women's Division of the National Committee and of New York City's
League of Women Voters, kept up a studied tirade, fellow women party
leaders supported their senator.[59] He more than met them half way. At
Delmonico's, in mid-February, he assured four hundred women party
leaders that suffrage and prohibition were accomplished facts. With a
touch of exaggeration, he noted that America needed women's voting,
for the nation needed the participation of all segments of society. They
cheered.[60] A week later Miss Hay sat quietly in the rear of Carnegie Hall
where an unofficial Republican state convention, with three cheers, elected
the Senator a delegate-at-large to the forthcoming national convention. On
the following night, at a dinner held in Wadsworth's honor, 1,200 faithful
Republicans from across the state applauded mightily when Ogden Mills
declared that at stake in Wadsworth's re-election was the principle of
keeping a man of courage in office. In reply, Wadsworth dispassionately
centered on the prohibition issue, detailing his opposition—its misuse of
the amendment process—and counseled a wisdom that sounded well to
Republicans at the moment, but was not to be sustained in the coming
years. "At whatever hazards," cautioned Wadsworth, "[the Constitution]
must enjoy the respect and claim the devotion of an overwhelming majority
of the people. And so it [would be] wise for all of you, and especially for
those who hope for great things from the amendment, to exercise moderation rather than fanaticism, reason rather than hysteria. The last word
has not been spoken and until it is we must move in the spirit of fair
play, which results in public contentment, so essential to orderly conduct
of government." [61]
In April, New York Republicans confirmed at the polls the support
state leaders gave Wadsworth in February, and forecast his renomination
and re-election in the fall. They elected him one of four delegates-at-large
to the National Republican Convention.[62] The senior senator survived the
feminist and prohibitionist onslaught, including attacks by the powerful
New York League of Women Voters and the equally powerful Anti-Saloon

58. *Ibid.*, June 22, 1919.
59. *Ibid.*, Dec. 8, 1919.
60. *Ibid.*, Feb. 13, 1920.
61. *Ibid.*, Feb. 21, 1920.
62. *Ibid.*, Apr. 7, 1920.

League. He was honest, youthfully handsome, articulate, wealthy, and conservative, all important attributes in 1920. Besides, he was the senior senator and the chairman of one of the Senate's important committees. Not surprisingly, on May 24, leaders at a luncheon given by Nicholas Murray Butler selected Wadsworth to lead them at the Republican national convention.[63]

4

Not long before the 1920 National Republican Convention in Chicago, Harriet Wadsworth Harper, the Senator's sister, visited Jim and Alice at their home in Lafayette Square. James, as Harriet called her brother, was close to his sister and was most anxious to reciprocate the hospitality she and her husband always extended at their beautiful home in Virginia fox-hunting country, just west of the capital district. The Senator escorted his sister to the family gallery in the Senate. James lingered, and pointed out for Harriet the great and near-great. Fifty years later, still living in the beautiful Plains, Virginia, Harriet remembered so well Jim pointing to the handsome junior senator from Ohio, Warren Harding, and commenting: "That's presidential timber." [64]

In the 1920 Republican race, however, Wadsworth was not a Harding man, even though the two had been intimate, having come into the Senate together. When Harry Daugherty, Harding's indefatigable manager, described to Wadsworth and Barnes, late one January night in the latter's New York apartment, how Harding would be nominated at the Republican convention as a "dark horse" with strong second and third choice commitments, the two New York leaders stared in disbelief.[65] At heart, Wadsworth wanted Governor Frank Lowden of Illinois to be president. A self-made man, with an excellent record as congressman and governor, Lowden was then the most conservative of the other leading candidates, Leonard Wood, Hiram Johnson, and Herbert Hoover. Unfortunately, a senate investigation of campaign expenditures which revealed that both Lowden and Wood forces spent what seemed to be exorbitant sums in their pursuit of the presidency, dimmed their chances. Even at that, Wood

63. *Ibid.*, May 25, 1920.
64. Conversation with Harriet Wadsworth Harper, summer 1967.
65. J.W.W. to Mark Sullivan, Mar. 2, 1935, Wadsworth MSS.

was the strong man in the convention. He was incorruptible. When Boies
Penrose phoned his headquarters from his Pennsylvania sick bed to offer
him the presidency in exchange for three cabinet positions, Wood emphatically refused the deal. Among the old guard, Wood was handicapped
by the Roosevelt mantle which he proudly wore. Johnson, who had bolted
the party in 1912 to be T.R.'s Bull Moose running-mate, had little chance.
Hoover was tainted by his association with the Wilson administration and
was too intellectual for Republicans in 1920. To many delegates the
atmosphere of Hoover's Blackstone Hotel headquarters "was more that of
a college seminar."

Daugherty was right. Harding was nominated at Chicago, but with
little help from his senate seat-mate who thought him "presidential timber."
Although leading the New York delegation, Wadsworth had only limited
control over it. He and Charles D. Hilles, the New York national committeeman, managed, for maneuvering purposes, to hold most of the state's
delegation together on the first ballot. But on succeeding ballots, the delegation quickly deserted their "favorite son," Nicholas Murray Butler, and
jumped on what they hoped would be a Wood or a Lowden bandwagon.
Wadsworth had some influence in deflecting several ballots from Wood
to Lowden. By the fourth ballot Lowden's New York delegation strength
increased by six, whereas Wood lost three votes. The fact that T.R.'s sister,
Mrs. Corrine Robinson, said that Wood deserved her brother's mantle
surely further motivated Wadsworth to help the Lowden cause. One
Harding biographer attributes to Wadsworth the role of leading a "flying
squadron" to defeat Wood by gradually feeding Lowden votes from the
New York delegation. By the end of the fourth ballot, however, the New
York delegation, like the convention, was deadlocked.[66] Lodge, the convention chairman, recessed the convention for the night.

That night, Friday, June 11, 1920, George Harvey's suite on the thir-
teenth floor of the Blackstone Hotel, shared with Will Hays, became
infamous in American political history. There in a smoke-filled room,
party bosses—a Senate cabal—allegedly decided upon Warren Harding
at 2:00 a.m., and passed the word that when the morning balloting resumed, his votes were to be gradually increased until he was nominated.

Wadsworth, a frequent visitor to the suite where George Harvey,
editor of the North American Review, acted as master of ceremonies,
disputed the myth. "One thing I am certain of," he wrote author Mark
Sullivan, "and that is that the men who gathered in the famous smoke-

66. New York Times, June 11, 1920; see Robert K. Murray, The Harding
Era, Warren G. Harding and His Administration (Minneapolis: University of Minnesota Press), Ch. I, passim.

filled room were not affirmatively in favor of Harding. I was in and out of that room several times that night. It was a sort of a continuous performance with no definite affirmative decision reached." To Wadsworth, the 1920 Republican convention was one of the most unbossed of the eleven he attended in his lifetime. "The crowd in Harvey's room were like a lot of chickens with their heads off."

What Daugherty had described to Wadsworth and Barnes six months previously came to pass. Out of deadlock, the convention turned to the amiable senator from Ohio. Many delegates remembered Harding well. He had nominated Taft at the 1912 convention and presided well as temporary chairman of the 1916 convention. And important Republicans, like Wadsworth, said he was presidential timber.[67]

Actually, after Wadsworth left the Harvey suite between 1:00 and 1:30, it is very likely that those remaining—Senators Curtis of Kansas, Brandegee of Connecticut, Lodge of Massachusetts, Smoot of Idaho, and McCormick of Illinois—did determine to support Harding. It is ironic that as they did so, Wadsworth encountered his Ohio colleague wandering alone in an upstairs corridor. Harding knew Wadsworth did not favor his nomination. Jim had told him so several times. They talked. Harding inquired of his chances. Wadsworth offered little encouragement. Only George Aldridge and a fellow Rochesterian were supportive in the New York delegation. "Do you think I will gain . . . in the New York delegation?" asked Harding. "I haven't the slightest idea," replied Wadsworth.[68] Harding felt a show of some increased strength might put him over. The senators parted. From the corridor, Harding wandered into the Harvey suite and there was informed by Harvey that he was likely to be nominated.[69]

On the following morning several who had participated in the conversations in that smoke-filled room told their delegations that the Wood-Lowden deadlock would be permitted through four more ballots and then Harding would be given a "play."[70] Wadsworth did not so inform the New York delegation, and throughout the morning he received no intimation of a leadership strategy to put Harding over.[71] During the afternoon recess

67. J.W.W. to Mark Sullivan, Mar. 2, 1935, Wadsworth MSS; Wadsworth, Jr., *Reminiscences*, pp. 270–271; Alden Hatch, *The Wadsworths of the Genesee* (New York: Coward-McCann, Inc., 1959), p. 212.

68. Wadsworth, Jr., *Reminiscences*, p. 271.

69. Wesley M. Bagby, *The Road to Normalcy, The Presidential Campaign and Election of 1920* (Baltimore: The Johns Hopkins Press, 1962), p. 90.

70. *Ibid.*, p. 92.

71. Wadsworth, Jr. *Reminiscences*, p. 271; J.W.W. to Mark Sullivan, Mar. 2, 1935, Wadsworth MSS.

Harvey and some of the senatorial leaders switched from Harding to Will Hays as the best candidate to break the Wood-Lowden deadlock. Harvey and Senator Brandegee tried to get the Connecticut delegation to lead the way but failed. Instead, Connecticut led the swing to Harding.[72] By the ninth ballot the swing began in full stride and New York jumped on the bandwagon. Quite contrary to press reports, Wadsworth did not direct the New York delegation to abandon Wood and Lowden. It is likely that he so urged them, but unnecessarily, for by the tail end of the ninth ballot, it was clear to all that Warren Harding was about to be nominated. To the end, however, certain of the strong men in the New York delegation stood by their candidates—H. L. Stimson, for Wood; Fiorello LaGuardia, for Lenroot; Herbert Parsons, for Lowden; Nathan Miller, for Hoover; and Bert Snell, for Coolidge. Wadsworth had little compunction about leading the switch to Harding.[73] He thought Harding had a good grasp of America.

During the final moments of the ninth convention ballot which put Harding over, Wadsworth moved quickly to a low-ceilinged room beneath the speaker's platform to caucus with party leaders on the vice presidency. There Wadsworth, with his junior colleague, William Calder, and Medill McCormick of Illinois, Jim Watson of Indiana, and a few others, tried to put over Irving Lenroot, a Wisconsin liberal, in order to give the ticket some balance. Before that strategy could be worked out, a voice from the center aisle spontaneously nominated Coolidge. The Massachusetts governor, in September of 1919, caught the public's imagination with a telegram to Samuel Gompers, the head of the American Federation of Labor, regarding the Boston police strike. To Gompers, who was seeking relief for the strikers, Coolidge had wired: "There is no right to strike against the public safety by anybody, anywhere, any time." As with Harding, the delegates could think of no reason not to nominate Coolidge.[74]

Following the convention, Wadsworth looked after his own political fortunes. In late July he had little difficulty being nominated by an unofficial Republican state convention at Saratoga, despite firm opposition by the League of Women Voters and the Women's Christian Temperance Union.[75] Also, William H. Anderson continued his reckless Anti-Saloon outbursts. The latter probably helped the young senior senator. *The New York Times,* although about to support the state Democratic ticket, admired the way Wadsworth called Anderson "a reckless agitator" trying to "destroy

72. Bagby, *op. cit.,* p. 94.
73. *New York Times,* June 13, 1920.
74. Wadsworth, Jr., *Reminiscences,* p. 276; J.W.W. to Mark Sullivan, Mar. 2, 1935, Wadsworth MSS.
75. *New York Times,* July 24, 1920.

popular government." [76] Aside from prohibition and Anti-Salooners, Wadsworth had to contend with the American Federation of Labor and the war veterans. The former did not like their New York senator's support of the Esch-Cummins bill which turned the nation's railroads back to private industry,[77] and the veterans did not appreciate Wadsworth's fight against the bonus.[78] But, as in the July convention, the September primary opposition was slim. Wadsworth's plurality was close to 180,000 votes against a WCTU leader, Ella A. Boole, and Bronx Tax Commissioner George H. Payne. Wadsworth's victorious running mate was the Republican candidate for governor, Nathan Miller, a former judge of the Court of Appeals. In the general election, Ella Boole bolted the party and ran on the Prohibition ticket.[79]

For six weeks Wadsworth criss-crossed the state, ignoring Ella Boole and his Democratic opponent, Lieutenant Governor Harry Walker. He directed most of his fire against the Wilson administration for its abortive League of Nations fight; its Underwood-Simmons tariff, which again threatened the nation with depression; its high tax programs;[80] its little concern for farm security;[81] and generally, its centralization of government. Democrats taunted Wadsworth with T.R.'s 1914 description of him as a disloyal and archaic Republican.[82] The opposition dragged up what they could. In addition to describing him as "a political pre-Adamite," it noted that he possessed "a stagnant, reactionary, and hunker past" and meager intellectual equipment. Specifically, the opposition pointed to his support of the New York Central's interests when he sat in the Speaker's chair, while at the same time, he opposed the five-cent subway fare in New York City. As senator, it chided him for diverting Niagara Falls water to aid private power, and accused him of opposing Brandeis's appointment to the Supreme Court on racial grounds. Of course, suffragettes and prohibitionists daily reminded citizens of his record on the Eighteenth and Nineteenth Amendments. Wadsworth blandly denied all charges.[83] A host of Republicans jumped to his defense, among them Elihu Root, Charles E. Hughes, W. H. Taft and, of course, Warren Harding.[84]

76. *Ibid.*, July 26, 1920.
77. *Ibid.*, Oct. 4, 1920.
78. *Ibid.*, Aug. 7, 1920.
79. *Ibid.*, Sept. 15, 1920.
80. *Ibid.*, Oct. 3, 1920.
81. *Ibid.*, Aug. 6, 1920.
82. *Ibid.*, July 28, 1920.
83. *Ibid.*, Oct. 21, 1920.
84. *Ibid.*, Oct. 1920, *passim.*

Unquestionably, the senior senator was hurt by the charges of suffragists and prohibitionists. His plurality of 471,000 was only half that of Warren Harding. Still, he carried every county in the state. Ella Boole, the Prohibitionist, received 160,000 votes. The whole Republican slate won in New York. Miller, however, barely defeated the popular incumbent governor, Alfred Smith. It was a Republican era. The Harding Era had begun.

VI

The Harding Era

1

THE MORNING of Wednesday, November 3, 1920, brought to Wadsworth a satisfaction he would seldom again experience. Re-elected by a half-million vote plurality, his state and the nation also went Republican by large margins. In New York, only Alfred E. Smith came close to defeating his Republican opposition. Wadsworth's old Tammany friend lost the governorship to Nathan Miller by less than 50,000 votes. Then too, Wadsworth's beloved Senate would be well ensconced in Republican hands by a twenty-vote plurality. The re-election of close associates, such as James E. Watson of Indiana, George H. Moses of New Hampshire, and Boies Penrose of Pennsylvania, would give the Republicans in the Senate an authority reminiscent of McKinley days. Only in the South did Democrats really win, from whence came Cox's 127 electoral votes.[1]

On March 4, Washington would indeed be a Republican city; the situation boded well for Wadsworth's future. The senior senator from the most populous state, newly endorsed by his great constituency, he would fit well into the councils of the national leadership, particularly the ruling Senate elite and, of course, its Military Affairs Committee over which he would continue to preside.

James Jeremiah Wadsworth, reflecting in 1968 on the Senator's career, was sure that his father had wanted and expected Harding to appoint him Secretary of War.[2] And Bessie Christian, the Senator's residence secretary, reports that William J. "Wild Bill" Donovan, the World War I commander of the famous Sixty-ninth Division, told Wadsworth that the job was his for the asking.[3] Either the Senator would not ask or the stories are off the mark. Certainly it made sense for the new president to appoint his old

1. *New York Times*, Nov. 3, 4, 1920.
2. Conversation with James J. Wadsworth, Washington, D.C., July 11, 1968.
3. Conversation with Bessie Christian, Ocean City, Maryland, 1962.

134

friend. Few Republicans were as knowledgeable about military affairs as was the chairman of that committee in the Senate. And Harding had "tremendous respect" for his senate colleague.[4] However, former Senator John W. Weeks of Massachusetts, having served on the Senate Military Affairs Committee, and having been a valuable adviser to Harding during the campaign, got the position. In fact, Wadsworth helped him get it, first by discouraging the appointment of General Leonard Wood and, secondly, by assuring Harding of Weeks's excellent qualifications, adding, "I would like to have a dollar for every Army officer and every member of Congress who during the last two months has expressed the hope that Weeks could put his hand to this big task." [5]

On Monday, December 5, Harding returned to the senate chamber, but to repose only briefly in his seat beside his colleague from New York. Soon the beloved Vice President, Thomas Marshall, accompanied the President-elect to the dais to the applause of the chamber. The atmosphere was joyous. On departing, Harding said to the great Progressive, La Follette, "Now, Bob, be good!" La Follette bantered, somewhat ominously, "I'll be busy making you be good." [6] Jim had little opportunity to talk to his seatmate. He would have liked to see him "behind closed doors."

Wadsworth's desire to "closet" Harding was not in his own interest but on behalf of the eminent Elihu Root. The young senator wanted so much to see his predecessor in the first cabinet position, that of Secretary of State. "Mr. Root was here the other day," wrote Wadsworth to James Sheffield, "and I had a most delightful hour with him. He enlarged upon his views and I knew positively that he and Harding are very close together in their ideas. I begged him to talk to Harding just the way he talked to me and I have no doubt he did so at Marion last Monday." [7] Root did discuss foreign affairs with Harding at great length, but no appointment was forthcoming. Nor was Wadsworth successful during his own visit to Marion, even with the Republican organization of New York backing Root's candidacy. Harding had turned to Charles Evans Hughes for the position, an appointment probably least appreciated by his New York visitor. The President-elect thought Root too old and too "ultra conserva-

4. Charles D. Hilles to Harry Daugherty, Mar. 5, 1923, Hilles MSS, Sterling Library, Yale University, New Haven, Conn.

5. Robert K. Murray, The Harding Era (Minneapolis, Minn.: Minnesota Press, 1969), pp. 102–103.

6. Belle and Fola La Follette, Robert M. La Follette (New York: The Mac-Millan Co., 1953), p. 1020.

7. J.W.W. to James R. Sheffield, Dec. 16, 1920, Wadsworth MSS, Library of Congress, Washington, D.C.

tive." He probably also thought him too pro-League of Nations and much too independent for the senate establishment which, under Lodge's "direction," anticipated making foreign policy. Wadsworth, of course, could not gainsay Hughes's ability.[8]

On the surface, Wadsworth had little to show for his trip to Marion. Aside from failing on the Root appointment, the New York senator was unable to place his good friend, Charles D. Hilles, in as Secretary of the Treasury. Nor did he put over Robert Bliss as Assistant Secretary of State.[9] When, during an after-dinner walk in Marion with Harding and Senator Harry S. New of Indiana, Wadsworth protested the appointment of Harry Daugherty as Attorney General, Harding stopped him in his tracks, exclaiming, "Harry Daugherty has been my best friend from the beginning of this whole thing. I have told him that he can have any place in my cabinet he wants, outside of Secretary of State. He tells me that he wants to be Attorney-General and by God he will be Attorney-General." [10] The New Yorker succeeded only in his support of Weeks.

While Senator Wadsworth worked at influencing the President on the appointment of policy makers in the administration, with very limited success, he steered clear of lesser patronage positions, relying heavily on the New York national committeeman, Charles D. Hilles, to secure for the state its appropriate share of such positions. At times Wadsworth got involved, as when annoyed by the downstate patronage machinations of Senator Calder, State Chairman George Glynn, Westchester Republican leader William L. Ward, and Manhattan leader Samuel Koenig. "I have sound reasons for believing that my colleague [junior Senator Calder] has an understanding with Sam Koenig," Wadsworth wrote to James Sheffield. "Certainly Sam has been very thick with him this spring. I have noticed it upon several occasions." Their tampering with appointments to the Northern District of the United States District Attorney's office offended Wadsworth and he spoke to "Glynn about it pretty emphatically." [11]

As noted previously, Jim Wadsworth slipped away from the March 4 inaugural ceremonies to call upon Newton Baker and found him in his

8. Phillip C. Jessup, *Elihu Root* (New York: Dodd, Mead & Co., 1938), pp. 414–417.

9. James W. Wadsworth, Jr., *The Reminiscences of James W. Wadsworth, Jr.*, (Columbia University: Oral History Research Office, 1952), pp. 280–281; J.W.W. to James R. Sheffield, Dec. 16, 1920, J.W.W. to Ray Baker Harris, Apr. 2, 1934, June 20, 1938, J.W.W. to Charles D. Hilles, Nov. 26, 1935, Wadsworth MSS; *New York Times,* Dec. 20, 1920.

10. Wadsworth, Jr., *Reminiscences,* p. 281; J.W.W. to Ray Baker Harris, June 20, 1938, Wadsworth MSS.

11. J.W.W. to James R. Sheffield, July 14, 1921, Wadsworth MSS.

inner office shining his shoes. That evening most of Washington society, probably including Alice and Jim Wadsworth, attended an inaugural ball at Edward Beale McLean's large downtown mansion. Consistent with his folksy conception of the presidency, Harding vetoed a formal ball but took advantage of the hospitality of his wealthy Ohio friend. McLean, known as "Ned" to Harding and his associates, had given his wife, Evelyn Walsh, the famous Hope Diamond as a wedding gift. The great stone surely glittered at the McLean affair.

"The Ohio gang" and associates—the Hardings, the McLeans, the Daughertys, the Jesse Smiths, the Charles Sawyers, the Charles Forbeses, the Albert Laskers, and the Albert Falls—were much too coarse for patrician society in Washington. Their poker diet was quite in contrast to the cuisine of the Nicholas Longworths, the Theodore Roosevelts, Jr., the Henry Fletchers, the Medill McCormicks, the Charles Daweses, the Frederick Haleses, and the James Wadsworths. Alice Roosevelt Longworth, the former president's daughter and wife of the Speaker of the House, best captured something of patrician reaction to the "Ohio crowd's" life style in her *Crowded Hours:*

> Though violation of the Eighteenth Amendment was a matter of course in Washington, it was rather shocking to see the way Harding disregarded the Constitution he was sworn to uphold. Though nothing to drink was served downstairs, there were always, at least before the unofficial dinners, cocktails in the upstairs hall outside the President's room and guests were shown up there instead of waiting below for the President. While the big official receptions were going on, I don't think the people had any idea what was taking place in the rooms above. One evening while one was in progress, a friend of the Hardings asked me if I would like to go up to the study. I had heard rumors and was curious to see for myself what truth was in them. No rumor could have exceeded the reality: the study was filled with cronies, Daugherty, Jess Smith, Alec Moore, and others, the air heavy with tobacco smoke, trays of bottles containing every imaginable brand of whisky stood about, cards and poker chips ready at hand—a general atmosphere of waistcoat unbuttoned, feet on the desk, and the spittoon alongside.

(Of course, as Robert Murray points out, Alice's husband, Nicholas Longworth, was frequently at "Harding's poker table in that very study and even Alice had been known to take a hand.")[12] The non-patrician supe-

12. Alice Roosevelt Longworth, *Crowded Hours* (New York: Charles Scribner's Sons, 1933), p. 324; Murray, *op. cit.,* p. 521.

riors in the President's cabinet, Charles Evans Hughes and Herbert Hoover, were also uncomfortable with the White House social milieu. The former's sense of asceticism and the latter's Quaker religion did not square with "wet" White House poker sessions. On occasion, the Secretaries of the Treasury and of Agriculture, Andrew Mellon and Henry Wallace, respectively, joined the poker sessions as did Will Hays, the Postmaster General, but with decreasing frequency.

Patricians, and society-conscious Washingtonians generally, were lacking in the Congress during the Harding era. "In my time," notes one contemporary observer, "the Congress was not filled with very social-minded people. There were a few [who] would go along with the cabinet group, but the cabinet group largely went along with the diplomatic group. You learned to know the ambassadors from foreign countries pretty well and their wives but the Congressional crowd—or most of them—stayed on Capitol Hill." "Conspicuous exceptions," noted the observer, "were the Longworths and the Wadsworths—they went around in the social world a good deal." [13]

Ironically, Alice and Jim became much attached to the younger Theodore Roosevelt generation. With "Father's" [T.R., Sr.] passing in 1919, inter-family wounds seemed to heal. Jim's intercession at the suggestion of Corrine Roosevelt Robinson led in part at least to the appointment of Leonard Wood as Governor General of the Philippine Islands. The Theodore Roosevelts, Jr., and the James Wadsworths saw much of each other during the Harding years. (Young Ted, hopeful of following in his father's footsteps, came into the administration as Assistant Secretary of the Navy.) They were frequently seen together at Washington dinner parties. At times, the two couples joined to host social functions, as in the fall of 1921 when they gave a dinner dance at the Montgomery Country Club. Frequently young Ted joined Nicholas Longworth and Jim on their brisk walks in Rock Creek Park. So intimate was their association that on one occasion Jim suggested to Ted that he talk to Nick about his drinking, especially since he probably would become his party's majority leader in the House. And some time later, in 1924, Jim told Ted to quit acting like a "kid" if he expected to be elected governor of New York. Indeed, Jim and Alice were practically part of the Roosevelt family circle, and Jim became Ted's political mentor.[14] The Franklin Roosevelts, of course, were indisposed because of Franklin's paralytic condition. His recovery of health

13. James S. Curtis, *The Reminiscences of James S. Curtis* (Columbia University: Oral History Research Office, 1951), p. 140.

14. Theodore Roosevelt, Jr., *Diary*, Oct. 1, 1921 to May 7, 1922, Theodore Roosevelt, Jr., MSS, Library of Congress, Washington, D.C.

in the late 1920s, accompanied by feverish Democratic party commitment, did not result in resumption of the easy relationship between Franklin and Jim that existed during World War I days.

2

When the Senate convened in special session on March 5, 1921, Wadsworth, as chairman of one of its great committees, shared power and prestige with approximately a dozen colleagues, "a group of strong personalities, of hard fighters and forceful speakers" such as Henry Cabot Lodge, the rapidly aging majority leader; Albert B. Cummins of Iowa, the president *pro tempore*; Hiram Johnson of California, the former Bull Mooser; William E. Borah, the old "irreconcilable"; Charles Curtis of Kansas, the future vice president; Robert La Follette of Wisconsin, who was to make the President "be good"; Reed Smoot of Utah, the high tariff advocate; and Democrats David L. Walsh, Oscar W. Underwood, Joseph T. Robinson, Claude Swanson, Carter Glass, and John Sharp Williams. Calvin Coolidge, the new vice president, was tolerated. His Yankee quaintness harmonized exactly with the mahogany desks, each with cuspidor, the aged leather-backed chairs, the old clock on the rear wall, and the niches containing busts of the previous vice presidents.

The conservatism of Normalcy, generally quite apparent in the presidency and the great executive departments, excepting Agriculture, was soon found lacking in the Senate of the United States, to Wadsworth's discomfort. Lodge was old. Penrose was dying. La Follette, Johnson and Borah, all "wild asses of the desert," [15] countervailed the articulate and conservative Wadsworth. The latter, of course, went down the line in support of the Mellon tax programs, the elimination of nuisance taxes, a gradual reduction of normal and surtaxes on individual income, and the repeal of the excess profits tax. When Democrats and the western Republicans stymied the eastern Republican attempt to cut them, Wadsworth exclaimed: "What are you going to say to these people. . . . The patriotic taxpayer would stand for anything in war time . . . but the war is three years behind us and the people are looking to Congress to pass a revenue bill that will reflect a permanent policy. . . . The enemy is no longer facing us; we are not in a desperate situation; we do not have to raise $10,000,000,000

15. Robert S. Allen, *Washington Merry-Go-Round* (New York: Blue Ribbon Books, Inc., 1931), Ch. 8, *passim*.

in a year and a half with which to whip the Germans."[16] On revenue
legislation Wadsworth and fellow conservatives lost. Although some nuisance taxes were ended, the excess profits levies were raised and the income
and corporation taxes and surtaxes remained unchanged.

Nicholas Murray Butler, a frequent Wadsworth correspondent, called
La Follette and his associates "disintegrating forces." "Our organization,"
he lamented, "sadly lacks genuine leadership and faith in party principle."
Butler was distressed by La Follette's success in defeating the administration tax reduction legislation. "It is a mistake to sit still," he concluded,
"and to say that these gentlemen . . . will kill themselves by their conduct. Once upon a time that might have been true, but in the present state
of disorganized leadership this is not true. They need to be pounded all
the time."[17]

Butler could hardly accuse Wadsworth of not pounding the senate
liberals "all the time." In the following year Wadsworth again took an intense interest in taxation. He refuted Democratic leader Gilbert Hitchcock's contention that high surtaxes and excess profits taxes are paid by
rich men who can well afford it. On the contrary, explained Wadsworth,
"it is paid by the rich man or the rich corporation in the first instance and
then inevitably, in whole or in part . . . it percolates down through the
body politic, and rests its heavy hand directly or indirectly, upon every
man, woman, and child in the country." In reply, Hitchcock wondered
why, if Wadsworth was right, the corporations so fervently fought the excess profits taxation. The conservatives, however, had little success in effect-
ing significant tax reduction before the Republican victory in the 1924
presidential campaign.[18]

Wadsworth greatly admired the conservatism of the executive branch.
He applauded the Harding-appointed Railway Labor Board which, during
the 1922 business slump, approved the 12 percent wage cut. When the railroad "shopmen" struck in protest, Wadsworth further applauded the issuance by Judge Louis H. Wilkerson, at the request of the Attorney General,
of the most sweeping anti-labor injunction ever written. It enjoined the
union from supporting the strike by expending funds, picketing, communi-
cating, loitering, trespassing, obstructing, or in any way hindering the
movement of inspectors, passengers, and workers. Much of Washington

16. *Congressional Record*, Vol. 61, 67th Congress, 1st Session, Nov. 21, 1921,
p. 7100.

17. Nicholas M. Butler to J.W.W., Dec. 14, 1921, Butler MSS, Columbia University Library, New York, N.Y.

18. *Congressional Record*, Vol. 62, 67th Congress, 2nd Session, Dec. 20, 1921,
pp. 570–572.

was appalled by the severity of the injunction. Hoover and Assistant
Secretary of the Navy Theodore Roosevelt, Jr., expressed outrage in the
President's cabinet. The Attorney General, although "flabbergasted" by the
reaction in the cabinet, stuck to his guns. Most members of Congress were
reticent to discuss the injunction. Not so Wadsworth. He publicly supported the Attorney General, trusting that his efforts would "go a long way
toward restoring railroad transportation to its normal condition." [19]

Federal aid to education, anti-lynching legislation, and the child-labor
amendment were clear congressional issues on which Wadsworth could
hone his conservatism. Here he was the anvil. Without the slightest hesitation, he voted against the establishment of a federal department of education. "No matter what safeguards are put in such a measure," he wrote
the president of the National Education Association, "I am convinced that
in the long run the Federal Government, through its contribution to the
States, would assume control over the educational activities of the country."
Wadsworth recognized that some states had inferior education. Yet he
would "rather have forty-eight varieties of teaching with inefficiency here
and there than to see educational efforts in America confined in a Federal
straight-jacket." [20] Nearly a half-century would pass before America could
wipe away constitutional cobwebs sufficiently to elevate education to
cabinet status.

The New York senator was equally adamant about the Dyer anti-
lynching bill, even though he felt lynching "is a ghastly disgrace to the
country, no matter where, or how it occurs." Wadsworth viewed its provision to fine those counties where lynchings are committed as impossible.
"This is utterly outside the powers of the Federal Government," he wrote
one constituent.[21] The view of such northern Republicans caused black
Americans to repudiate the Republican party in droves throughout the
1920s.

On the child-labor amendment to the Constitution, Wadsworth parted
company with his majority leader. When the conservative Lodge asked
for unanimous consent to bring the amendment before the Senate, it having passed the House, Wadsworth objected. "This Amendment," he told
his colleagues, "goes further towards extending the central authority than
even the 18th." Why, "we'll have imperial government with provinces
instead of sovereign states." [22] Lenroot's plea that the Republican platform
of 1920 committed the party to the amendment went unheeded by Wads-

19. New York Times, Sept. 2, 1922; Murray, op. cit., pp. 255–257.
20. J.W.W. to Miss Olive M. Jones, Feb. 27, 1924, Wadsworth MSS.
21. J.W.W. to Prince C. James, Oct. 17, 1923, Wadsworth MSS.
22. New York Times, May 30, 1924.

worth. In fighting the amendment, he also faced strong opposition from women in his party. Wadsworth was determined. He thought it "unnecessary . . . to duplicate the inspection and administrative work" in all the states. Secondly, three or four states "already have Child Labor laws as strict or stricter than the one proposed in the Amendment." Thirdly, Wadsworth thought if there must be an amendment, then the Constitution should be amended simply by granting power to Congress to pass legislation regulating the employment of persons under a certain age. Lastly, and most telling, Wadsworth believed the child-labor amendment would establish a precedent for numerous comparable amendments which would only clutter up the Constitution.[23] Even Ralph Pulitzer of the *New York World* worried about a cluttered-up Constitution and went after it "tooth and nail." [24] Despite Wadsworth's and Pulitzer's objections, most senators supported their respective party platforms and voted for the amendment. The *Christian Science Monitor* lamented that Wadsworth "who has never been anything but stodgily regular breaks away from this party doctrine when it comes to protecting children." [25]

Wadsworth was sure the child-labor amendment would be ratified by the necessary three-fourths of the states, especially considering the ease with which the Eighteenth and Nineteenth Amendments had been adopted. And what of the seventy other proposed amendments pending in the Congress, he asked. Whereas progressives a decade previously feared the unamendability of the Constitution, now conservatives saw the pendulum swinging to the other extreme. To stem the tide, Wadsworth and Representative Finis J. Garrett of Tennessee proposed an amendment on amendments, principally stating that "at least one house in each of the legislatures which may ratify shall be elected after such amendments have been proposed; that any State may require that ratification by its legislature be subject to confirmation by popular vote; and that until three-fourths of the States have ratified, or more than one-fourth of the States have rejected, or defeated a proposed amendment, any State may change its vote." [26] In addressing the Lincoln Dinner at the National Republican Club on February 12, 1923, Wadsworth noted that of the thirty-eight states in which legislatures ratified the Nineteenth Amendment, five of the states had constitutions forbidding legislative ratification of federal amendments and of the thirty-eight states, thirty-four had legislatures elected

23. J.W.W. to Mrs. Pauline Sabin, Nov. 10, 1923, Wadsworth MSS.
24. Mrs. Pauline Sabin to J.W.W., Dec. 8, 1924, Wadsworth MSS.
25. *Christian Science Monitor*, Apr. 15, 1924.
26. *Virginia Law Review*, Vol. IX, No. 1, Nov. 1922.

THE HARDING ERA 143

prior to the submission of the Nineteenth Amendment. The Wadsworth-Garrett amendment would, Wadsworth explained, correct such inequities and place the vital process of constitution-building closer to the people. Furthermore, the Wadsworth-Garrett amendment would not prevent state legislatures from rescinding their action, so long as it was done prior to final ratification. Wadsworth pointed to California, Massachusetts, Ohio, and New York as states where the people, one way or another, were superseded by their legislatures on the important processes of constitutional amendment.[27]

Senator Thomas J. Walsh of Montana differed with Wadsworth. He thought the New Yorker unduly pessimistic: "I can point the Senator to a dozen provisions of this constitution, and point him to evils which might ensue, but they never have ensued. And we have been under the operation of this constitution for a century and a third." Yet Walsh saw merit in the resolution, if amended to mandate that the citizenry rather than the state legislature vote on all amendments. Wadsworth was sorry. Although the Walsh amendment was adopted by the Senate Judiciary Committee, he thought it smacked of centralization, the government telling the people what to do.

The Wadsworth-Garrett resolution, now called the Walsh-Wadsworth-Garrett resolution, had the support of *The New York World* and *The Florida Times-Union*.[28] But lethargy prevailed. Many conservative "drys," such as upstate Republicans, wanted the Eighteenth Amendment and were glad the existing constitutional processes made it possible. Liberals, normally happy to have people speak, as Wadsworth was recommending, knew from the Progressive Era experience that they could now move the federal government to act by processes other than constitutional amendment. H. L. Mencken, the *American Mercury's* editor, thought Wadsworth had something, only he wanted a wholly revised constitution submitted to the people, as is done periodically by New York State. With an eye to the Eighteenth Amendment, like Wadsworth he feared the infringement of the people's rights. He could not prophesy the nature of revision. "But, of this I am certain," he editorialized, "that a free people, asked to give up their ancient liberties, ought to have a fair chance to say yes or no, and not be rooked of them by a process suggesting that whereby a three-card monte man operates upon the husbandmen at a county fair." [29]

27. Speech of Senator Wadsworth at the Lincoln Dinner of the National Republican Club, Feb. 12, 1923, Wadsworth MSS.
28. *Congressional Record*, Vol. 62, 67th Congress, 2nd Session, July 25, 1922, p. 10610; *Florida Times Union*, Mar. 14, 1924; *New York World*, Mar. 27, 1924; *The Troy Times*, Feb. 26, 1924.
29. *The American Mercury*, Vol. 12, Nov. 1927, p. 287.

3

Wadsworth's first commitment in government service was to the military, and in the 1920s it was an awesome responsibility for the New Yorker. His patronage problems, his desire to help restore conservative economics, and his drive to inhibit the amending process were secondary to his struggle to protect the military. Aside from the expected trials of congressional oversight of the National Defense Act of 1920, Wadsworth and the military proponents were handicapped by pacifist and economy-minded attitudes which swept the nation. The very implementation of the National Defense Act was a particular burden, involving as it did the creation of nine corps areas in the country with its components of one regular army division, two national guard divisions and three reserve citizen divisions. Given the resistance of certain purely militarist types in the War Department to the concept of minimal regular forces and an expansible citizens army, Wadsworth kept a wary eye on General Staff activity. Understandably, he was somewhat relieved when his friend John W. Weeks, a former colleague on the Military Affairs Committee, was appointed Secretary of War.

On the morning of June 6, 1921, Wadsworth faced one of the significant challenges of his long legislative career, saving the army from drastic budget cuts. He felt confident. As a Republican, newly returned to the Senate, he faced a Republican senate serving under a Republican president. Carefully noting how his committee had consistently reduced War Department requests for annual appropriations since 1919, he again noted his request of $335,000,000 for fiscal 1922 as the appropriation necessary to achieve the required 175,000 troops. But mid-western isolationists, led by Senators Borah of Idaho and King of Utah, were unwilling to compromise. Nor were Democrats, particularly under the leadership of another midwesterner, Gilbert M. Hitchcock of Nebraska, interested in aiding the New Yorker in directing the new administration's War Department legislation. Was the $335,000,000 military aid request, asked Hitchcock, "accompanied by any formal estimate?" "The new Secretary of War could not possibly have made them up," replied Wadsworth.[30]

Following the Hitchcock-Wadsworth colloquy, Borah questioned the administration's sincerity. Wadsworth reported that the House figure of

30. *Congressional Record,* Vol. 61, 67th Congress, 1st Session, June 6, 7, 1921, pp. 2145–2183.

150,000 regular troops was an average between the high and the low army figure at the beginning and the end of the fiscal year 1922, and that it would bring about a reduction to 120,000 men by the end of the year. Borah retorted that Weeks would then come around for deficiency legislation to keep the army up to 150,000. Wadsworth bristled, "if . . . [the Senator] does not trust the Secretary of War, I do." Then Hitchcock wondered why 120,000 troops would not suffice. Wadsworth shot back: the army "will be so attenuated, so starved of men, that by the end of the year they would not be fit to take the field or do any effective work for any purpose." Borah suggested cutting the army to 100,000. The chairman could only reply: "and protect [whom]," before the Idahoan retorted: "Yes . . . the best protection in the world, Mr. President, for the United States right now is not a man in uniform but is a contented citizenship." On it went, with Borah and Hitchcock alternating. Hitchcock was sure that nine out of ten soldiers were doing little. They train, Wadsworth noted, to use automatic rifles, grenades, rifle grenades, etc. When Hitchcock asked what caused the House to think 120,000 troops would suffice, Wadsworth replied, "I do not feel competent to speculate in such a wild field." Borah concluded that the House was closer to the people. By now the Idaho statesman would agree to fewer than 100,000 troops. When the New Yorker pleaded for common sense, Borah replied sarcastically: "Nobody has any common sense except the Military Affairs Committee and the Army." [31]

For three days the debate ensued, with tough James Reed, Democrat from Missouri, and the old Progressives, Robert La Follette and George Norris, relieving Borah, and with Senate Military Affairs committeemen Lenroot, Fletcher, Frelinghuysen and Warren aiding Wadsworth.

On June 7 the Senate supported Wadsworth's 175,000-troop bill on a test vote, 34 to 30, but on the following day reversed itself and supported the 150,000 figure by a 36 to 32 vote. Most eastern and industrial state senators supported the larger army. Most Democrats and non-eastern Republicans sided with Borah and company. [32] Further disheartement came to Wadsworth in 1923 when the Congress cut the regular army to 125,000 men, at which figure it stayed throughout most of the decade. [33]

Most Americans were little concerned about troop reductions in the 1920s. A decrease of defense expenditures from 58.2 percent of the national

31. Ibid.
32. Ibid.
33. Ibid.

budget in 1919 to 14.17 percent in 1923 seemed natural. Oswald Garrison Villard, generally too liberal and sophisticated for Americans, represented well their feeling about the army. He longed for the days of the Indian fighter, General Nelson A. Miles, who surely would have opposed a reserve force of 95,000 officers, a regular army of 250,000 men, summer camps for training 50,000 citizens, and certainly any universal military training. For all their shortcomings, Villard thought "the old time soldiers seemed to us the wiser and truer patriots." [34]

Some voices outside the Congress and the army did fear troop reduction—the American Legion and the Citizens Military Training Association. Surprisingly, the pacifist *New York Globe* joined such great papers as *The New York Times, The New York Tribune, The Washington Post,* and *The Chicago Tribune,* in editorial protest. The *Review of Reviews* and the *Scientific American* tried to shore up the army.[35] In or out of government, however, Wadsworth was the army's most visible patron.

Although Wadsworth and western Republicans were opponents on military appropriations, they allied to fight the bonus. He and Borah were principal opposition leaders in the contest. Both opposed it from its inception in the newly formed American Legion in 1920. Even in the Wilson administration "adjusted compensation" legislation—land settlement, home purchases, vocational training or bonds—passed the House, only to be buried in the Senate Finance Committee. Harding, opposed to the bonus, withstood the veterans' pressure until 1922 when Republican Joseph Fordney of Michigan re-introduced his legislation. Basically, the bill provided for issuing paid-up twenty-year endowment certificates or policies. On March 23, the bill passed the House overwhelmingly, with a great cheer from the gallery accompanying each "yea" vote. When, in August, the legislation reached the senate floor, Wadsworth opened the opposing arguments. Carefully he noted what the United States had already done for veterans—at the outbreak of war raised the pay by 100 percent; at discharge expended $270,000,000 for an average of $60 per soldier; and of far less importance, allowed each veteran to take home an "entirely new outfit of clothing." He was precise about the clothing: "a pair of shoes, a pair of olive drab breeches, an olive drab shirt, an olive drab hat, and his choice of raincoat or slicker." These things, he noted, were done so that American doughboys would have the best comforts enjoyed by other soldiers.

When Senator Overman wondered why the United States matched

34. *Nation,* Vol. CXX, June 3, 1925, p. 618.
35. *Literary Digest,* Vol. 22, Mar. 18, 1922, p. 10.

the Canadian pay but not the Canadian bonus, Wadsworth thought "the two things are based on entirely different principles." [36] Not to be diverted, the New York senator made clear his two principal objections: first, the wrongness of buying patriotic service and, second, the lack of supportive revenue. Democratic leader Hitchcock reminded Wadsworth that had he not repealed the rich man's excess profits tax, there would have been sufficient revenue. The New Yorker gave his stock answer to the tax repeal charge: retention of such a tax would "percolate down" and affect all Americans, rich and poor. On August 30, the Senate passed the bonus legislation, 47–22. With an impressive state paper Harding vetoed the bill, noting, as Wadsworth had, the lack of supporting revenue. The House overrode the President's veto. The Senate sustained it, but by only four votes. [37]

Throughout 1923 and 1924 veterans' organizations pressed the Senate to override the President's veto of the bonus. Wadsworth was happy that he had taken a firm stand in 1920. In 1924 he could say: "I promised to vote against it." One veterans' organization, the Genesee Valley Post No. 194 of the American Legion, accused Wadsworth of being the beneficiary of military compensation in view of the military tract in western New York possessed by his ancestors. "The fact is," replied Wadsworth, "that not one acre of land now or ever possessed by the Wadsworth family accrued out of grants from the Government, state, or nation." [38]

To those sympathetic to Wadsworth's bonus position, he encouraged contact with newly elected senators, such as New York's Royal S. Copeland, whose attitudes were in doubt. [39] It was of little use. In March of 1924 the House overwhelmingly passed the bill, 355 to 54, and the Senate, including Senator Copeland, followed suit, both houses holding firm in overriding President Coolidge's veto.

Reaction to Wadsworth's firm stand on the bonus issue varied. One Massachusetts newspaper noted that there "were some real men in the National Senate on Monday. Among these we find James W. Wadsworth, Jr., of New York, easily the outstanding figure of the Alignment in the upper house. A minority Senator—Democrats took the New York state house in 1922—in a state peculiarly opposed to the Administration, with every political tradition dictating otherwise, we find Senator Wadsworth voting to sustain the President." [40] "If you run for office again," wrote one

36. *Congressional Record*, Vol. 64, 67th Congress, 4th Session, 1922, p. 11863.
37. *New York Times*, Aug. 28, 1922.
38. J.W.W. to Walter F. Martin, Apr. 7, 1924, Wadsworth MSS.
39. J.W.W. to Roger W. Thompson, Jan. 3, 1924, Wadsworth MSS.
40. *The Dedham Transcript*, May 24, 1924.

constituent, "a substantial part of my bonus will be spent in seeing that
you join ex-Senator Calder in the 'has beens.'" "If," replied Wadsworth,
"you are included among the great majority of veterans whose bonus,
ordinarily, would be in excess of $50.00, you won't get any cash at all to
spend against me. You will receive a paid-up insurance policy maturing
twenty years later." Wadsworth explained that after two years he might
borrow a little but by then Wadsworth's campaign would be over. In the
meantime the New York senator hoped they would meet and figure out
their prospects, "mine for staying in office and yours for getting me
out of it." [41]

Despite agonizing over troop reductions, narrow military types in the
War Department, and the bonus bills, Wadsworth would not have traded
his Military Affairs Committee chairmanship. He proudly watched the
"New Army" evolve. For one thing, Pershing was Chief of Staff and committed to the concept of a small regular army, to be reinforced in time of
war by citizen forces. And Secretary of War John W. Weeks represented
well the Wadsworth committee point of view. "Whereas in the past,"
Weeks noted in 1922, "citizen forces have been completely extemporized
or materially organized upon the occurrence of an emergency, the new
plan provides that they shall be allocated territorially, that their officers
and men shall be assigned to local units, and that as funds become available provision shall be made for the training of these officers and men."
Even with limited appropriations the Secretary of War saw that regular
army officers were assigned to the "organization, administration, and development of the National Guard, the Organized Reserves, the Reserve
Officers' Training Corps, and the Citizens' Training Corps." As prescribed
by the law, the eighteen national guard divisions and the twenty-seven
skeletal organized reserve divisions were "as far as practicable" recon-
structed on the basis of the "great combat divisions which won such high
distinction during the World War." To strengthen the organized reserves,
the Reserve Officer Training Corps on college campuses were developed.
In 1921 approximately 90,000 students completed a year's training. Also,
each of the nine corps areas had one or two summer camps for a month's
citizens' training. In the first year 40,589 applications were received and
11,085 young citizens, ranging in age from sixteen to thirty-five years, were
trained. In addition to developing the nine corps areas, the General Staff
organization in Washington was "divided into two categories: First, duty
of mobilizing the manhood and the resources of the nation and their prepa-

41. Lawrence M. Woolley to J.W.W., May 20, 1924, J.W.W. to Lawrence M.
Woolley, May 21, 1924, Wadsworth.MSS.

ration, training, concentration and delivery to the field forces, and, second, the use of the military forces for the national defense, i.e., actual employment of the armed forces against the enemy." [42]

Wadsworth did not confine his military affairs activity only to Washington. Where possible he tramped around army cantonments in and out of the country. Following a Caribbean trip in 1923, he submitted to the Secretary of War his findings of needs: batteries on Tobago Island, sixteen-inch batteries at both ends of the Canal, searchlights to make antiaircraft guns effective, expanded officers quarters, an improved water supply, etc. The chairman missed little, in or out of the country.[43] When the Twenty-sixth Infantry Regiment at Plattsburgh made Miss Marian Davis an honorary colonel, Wadsworth expressed the hope to Secretary Weeks "that such honorary colonelcies will not become customary in the Army." [44]

Wadsworth's relationship to the military cannot be concluded without reference to the controversial Brigadier General William ("Billy") Mitchell, the nation's foremost advocate of military air power in the decade following World War I. It was inevitable that their paths cross. Aside from their interfacing on military matters—Mitchell was Assistant Chief of the Army Air Service—the two had in common acceptance in high social circles, mutual friends such as the Frank McCoys, the Joseph Davieses, the Benedict Crowells, and the George Marshalls, and a love of horses. Most importantly, Wadsworth was impressed by Mitchell's testimony before his committee in 1919 that "in this country, our Army Aviation is shot to pieces and our Navy Aviation does not exist as an arm." Wadsworth had been annoyed by Navy Department reaction to Mitchell's charges, including that of Assistant Navy Secretary Franklin D. Roosevelt. The navy, in fact, had discontinued its aviation division, and Roosevelt challenged Mitchell's emphasis of aviation's importance by declaring it only an "adjunct to the Navy." [45] Contrariwise, Wadsworth supported Senator New's unsuccessful attempt at legislating a separate air force. More successfully, in the early 1920s, the chairman of the Military Affairs Committee salvaged appropriations for maintaining something of an air arm in the army. Also, he and Mitchell collaborated in constructing federal legislation, the Wadsworth-Winslow bill to license pilots, inspect aircraft, and supervise air

42. *Review of Reviews*, Mar. 1922, pp. 285–290.

43. J.W.W. to John W. Weeks, Apr. 16, 1923, Wadsworth MSS.

44. J.W.W. to John W. Weeks, Apr. 7, 1924, Wadsworth MSS.

45. Wadsworth, Jr., *Reminiscences*, pp. 323–331; Burke Davis, *The Billy Mitchell Affair* (New York: Random House, 1967), pp. 58–64.

posts. Not infrequently, the two discussed air policy in the Military Affairs Committee rooms in the capital.[46]

Soon Mitchell and Wadsworth saw more of each other. The former sought out the latter in his office and on occasion Wadsworth visited the general in his home and was impressed by his wife. But as Mitchell's case for the air service strengthened with the successful experimental air bombing of the German warship *Ostfriesland* and the old *USS Alabama,* Wadsworth thought his criticism of Navy and War Department leadership inordinate and his behavior erratic. He thought Mitchell "operated" too strenuously. He resented his talk of political advancement—that the air issue might bring him into the Senate from Wisconsin. Wadsworth and Mitchell gradually parted company.[47]

As Mitchell became particularly controversial in his public and personal life, Wadsworth was little surprised to receive a call from Mrs. Mitchell expressing concern about "her husband's mental and nervous condition." The general's wife also approached General Pershing with her husband's problems. Not long thereafter, War Secretary Weeks arranged for Mitchell to undergo observation at Walter Reed Hospital and subsequently prescribed a "long sea voyage" to study "the potentiality of air power in the Far East." Mitchell continued to break into print with his criticism of America's air power. About six weeks after his return to the United States, he appeared before the House Committee on Military Affairs and berated the General Staff of the War Department for burying his report. Immediately following Mitchell's testimony, Secretary Weeks called Wadsworth to report to him and his committee that the War Department had received the report only four days before Mitchell made his statement to the House Committee. From that day on, reports Wadsworth, "none of the pro-Mitchell agitation was exploited in the Senate." Eventually, Mitchell's violent denunciation of the military services resulted in his court martial for insubordination and his resignation. For all of his disdain for Mitchell's tactics, Wadsworth could not gainsay his expertise as a flier, and horseman, and as correct in much of his contention about the value of air power. History has borne him out as justified in his demands for an adequate air arm. Still, Wadsworth concluded in his memoirs: "He was not a hero in my mind." [48]

46. See Henry Ladd Smith, *Airways, The History of Commercial Aviation in the United States* (New York: Russell & Russell, Inc., 1965), p. 97 for general discussion of Wadsworth interest in air legislation; Isaac Don Levine, *Mitchell, Pioneer of Air Power* (New York: Duell, Sloan & Pearce), p. 191.

47. Wadsworth, Jr., *Reminiscences*, pp. 323–331.

48. *Ibid.*

Wadsworth's reaction to the Mitchell affair characterized generally his position in the capital city during the Republican era. Powerful, and sought out by ambitious people like Mitchell, Wadsworth responded to attractive personalities and heard out divergent views, but recoiled at unconventional behavior and fended off radical ideas. His support of the army, his forte in Washington, while vigorous, was conventional. It earned him the gratitude of secretaries of war, chiefs of staff, and rising officers, and if not of incautious officers like Mitchell, certainly those like Colonel George C. Marshall, Lieutenant Colonel Lesley McNair, and Major General Hugh A. Drum.

4

On October 22, 1921, Wadsworth entered one of the holy of holies in the Senate, the Foreign Relations Committee. To succeed Philander Knox of Pennsylvania, whose recent death had created the vacancy, the young senator from New York gave up his Agriculture assignment. In a sense he had arrived.[49] The majority leader, Henry C. Lodge, presided over the great committee. The Senate elite were among the committee membership— Republicans William E. Borah, the great "irreconcilable"; Hiram Johnson, the former Bull Mooser; George H. Moses, who called westerners "wild asses"; Irvine I. Lenroot, whom Wadsworth wanted to be Harding's running-mate; and Democrats Joseph T. Robinson, the future majority leader; Oscar W. Underwood, presidential contender; and Thomas J. Walsh, soon to be the great oil investigator. On call of the taciturn chairman, the prestigious committee gathered in its high-ceilinged, four-room suite on the Capitol's main floor. Only the Committee on Appropriations had more rooms.

At the moment Foreign Relations appealed to Wadsworth. There he would relate to agenda items of great national importance. The committee had great power, as evidenced by its recent confrontation with Wilson on the League issue. Wadsworth's hand in the authorship of several of the Lodge reservations to the League Covenant, and his recent opposition to the Colombian treaty, had already brought him into the Foreign Relations orbit.

In a great debate in the spring of 1922 on ratification of the long-delayed Colombian treaty, the Thompson-Urrutia Treaty, to provide $25,-000,000 for America's part in the 1903 Panamanian revolt, the New

49. *New York Times*, Oct. 20, 1921.

Yorker "bedded" with such Republican progressives and liberals as William Borah, Hiram Johnson, Robert La Follette, Charles McNary, George Norris and Miles Poindexter. Wadsworth's motives, however, differed from theirs. They resented giving the money to enhance American oil interests in Colombia. Borah opposed it for that reason, but also thought the treaty would impeach "for all time" the honor of two great Americans, Theodore Roosevelt and John Hay. Wadsworth viewed the treaty as a form of blackmail and harmful to our relations with other South American nations. Here Wadsworth alluded to provisions in the treaty providing for free Colombian tolls and the right of that nation to transport war goods through the canal. Most importantly, the New Yorker, like Borah, resented the implied censure of former Secretary of State John Hay, his father-in-law.

"Mr. President," announced Wadsworth during the debate, "I do not intend to discuss . . . the incidents that occurred in 1903. At that time I was very familiar with them. I learned them from the lips of a man who bore an important part in them. Having learned all the facts from him, I have been firmly convinced all these years that the Government of the United States bore its part in that incident in an absolutely honest, straightforward and unassailable manner. . . . I am not sufficiently nimble-footed to change my position." [50]

Wadsworth and Borah differed only on their great Americans, the former making no reference to Theodore Roosevelt. Four hours of argument changed few votes. Wadsworth and company lost, 69 to 19.

Although the tariff was more a Finance Committee consideration than a Foreign Relations agenda item, it had foreign affairs implications. Wadsworth's role was small in the stop-gap tariff legislation of 1921, other than voting for it. The permanent legislation in 1922 was more sweeping and affected products of many of Wadsworth's constituency.

Gloves interested Wadsworth most in the great tariff debate—warp-knit gloves, lisle gloves, ordinary knit gloves, and work gloves. To stop Gloversville's depression, the New York senator talked the Finance Committee into placing a 100 percent duty on gloves and took the floor to defend the committee action. Resenting references to a glove manufacturer as one "filling his pockets and bloating his bank account and making him inordinately rich . . . a familiar piece of tactics," Wadsworth described what had happened to the industry in two years. He stressed that one-tenth of the employees were denied full-time employment. Democrats let Wadsworth's unimpressive statistic pass, but protested loudly his conten-

50. *Ibid.*, Apr. 21, 1921; *Congressional Record*, Vol. 61, 67th Congress, 1st Session, Apr. 20, 1921, p. 472.

tion that the 100 percent tariff on gloves would reduce prices. Minority Leader Hitchcock did not believe it. Wadsworth responded: "In certain cases, . . . [it could]. When the foreigner has had a monopoly and commanded our markets, named his own price and had no competition, time and time again it has been shown that the imposition of a duty in protection of the American article has resulted not only in a vast increase in the production of the American-made article but a decrease in the prices of all the articles."[51]

Hitchcock still did not believe it. "That is the most extraordinary contradiction of his bill," the minority leader summarized his confusion. "The whole theory of the bill," he noted, "is to protect American industries from disastrous competition by raising the duties, so as to compel the goods to be sold at higher prices. Now the Senator is arguing that as a result of the raising of the duties the goods will be sold at lower prices." Wadsworth and Hitchcock deadlocked, the former arguing for a 100 percent duty to eliminate foreign monopoly and reduce domestic prices, the latter seeing a reduction of prices through foreign competition.[52]

Wadsworth's "Gloversville schedule," with some duties reaching 119 percent, was too much, even for Republicans. Majority Leader Lodge and nineteen Republicans bolted, insisting that the duties on gloves not exceed 75 percent. Only fifteen Republicans and one Democrat stayed with Wadsworth and the Finance Committee.[53] Even at that, the concept of protection was well preserved indeed. Generally, the average Fordney-McCumber duty was 38.5 percent. More serious than the concept of protection per se was the failure on the part of either Hitchcock or Wadsworth to recognize the changed economic role of the United States as a creditor nation. As Professor Robert Murray points out, however, the Fordney-McCumber Act's defect of denying debtor nations a market was seen only years later.[54]

Wadsworth played only a small role in debates over ratification of treaties emanating from the Washington Disarmament Conference, perhaps because the conference addressed itself largely to naval disarmament and Far Eastern affairs, both of marginal interest to the New Yorker. Certainly he encouraged Ted Roosevelt's participation as a principal aide to Secretary of State Hughes at the conference,[55] and publicly, he supported the great power naval ratio for capital ships: 5:5:3:1.7:1.7. The new For-

51. *Congressional Record*, Vol. 62, 67th Congress, 2nd Session, 1922, p. 10472.
52. *Ibid.*, pp. 10435–11144, *passim*.
53. *New York Times*, July 20, 21, 25, 26, 27, 28, 1921.
54. Murray, *op. cit.*, p. 279.
55. Theodore Roosevelt, Jr., *Diary*, summer 1921, *passim*, Theodore Roosevelt, Jr. MSS.

eign Relations Committee member did speak at length on the Disarmament Treaty on Noxious Gases. Although voting for ratification of the treaty, he did not think it was worth the paper it was written on. But here Wadsworth spoke as chairman of Military Affairs. First, he noted that the weapon's awesomeness was over-emphasized. Of America's 258,000 casualties in World War I, only 1,421 died from gas. Actually, he observed, shrapnel was far more deadly and cruel. Secondly, Wadsworth was sure that all nations would "continue . . . [their] research under government auspices, for no nation will dare take a chance." And in the United States, Wadsworth anticipated industrial research under private auspices. To an assembly of chemists, some months previously, he had made clear that to rely only on government-sponsored research is "to starve the nation of the spirit of initiative without which it cannot defend itself anywhere at any time." The Treaty on Noxious Gases passed unanimously in the Senate.[56]

For all of his apparent nationalism, to wit, opposition to the Colombian Treaty, his support of prohibitive tariff schedules, and his reference to the Washington Arms Conference gas treaty as a "scrap of paper," Wadsworth appeared as no "irreconcilable," largely because of his adamant support of the World Court. For such support *The New York Times* numbered him among the international-minded wing of the Foreign Relations Committee. The definitive historian of the United States involvement in the World Court has placed him with Senators Porter J. McCumber and Frank B. Kellogg as the only three Republicans on the Foreign Relations Committee who did believe in "international cooperation." His defense of the Court in December of 1923 marked the beginning of his trek to his internationalist stance of the late 1930s.[57] Even so, the trek was a slow one. He tied several restrictive reservations to American participation in the Court. In fact, certain pro-Court individuals in the administration were somewhat relieved when, in 1925, Wadsworth transferred from the Foreign

56. *Journal of Industrial and Engineering Chemistry*, Vol. 13, May 1921; *New York Times*, Mar. 30, 31, 1921; see Thomas H. Buckley, *The United States and the Washington Conference, 1921–1922* (Knoxville, Tenn.: The University of Tennessee Press, 1970), pp. 124–125, for evidence that American members of the Washington Conference's Subcommittee on Poison Gas opposed the prohibition of gas and that the final report of the subcommittee did not recommend prohibition. Secretary of State Hughes, however, presented a united front with the British and the French in favor of its prohibition.

57. *New York Times*, Dec. 2, 1923; Denna F. Fleming, *The United States and the World Court* (New York: Russell & Russell, 1945), p. 41; see Donald R. McCoy, *Calvin Coolidge, The Quiet President* (New York: The Macmillan Co.), p. 185: Professor McCoy lumps Wadsworth with the "powerful anti-internationalist forces."

Relations Committee to the Finance Committee.[58] His quick reaction to the Bok Peace Plan also demonstrated his lingering nationalism. When asked about the plan providing for the country to enter the World Court immediately and to participate in certain phases of League work, the Senator announced, "I have not read it and that probably indicates my interest in it." [59]

One Wadsworth commitment in foreign affairs became obvious, the defense of the eminent, late John Hay. Just as he fought the Colombian Treaty which brought the little nation $25,000,000 for the apparent misdeeds of T.R. and his Secretary of State in the "taking of Panama," so he fought for the return of the Isle of Pines to Cuba, as Hay had advocated.

About the size of Rhode Island, with a population of 4,250 Cubans and 700 Americans, the Isle of Pines stood off the southern coast of Cuba. Secretary of State Hay signed the Hay-Quesada Treaty on July 2, 1903, recognizing Cuba's sovereignty over the island, which had been occupied by American troops during the Spanish-American War. The Senate, however, ratified only that part of the treaty they liked, the establishment of a naval base at Guantánamo. "Matters have come to such a pass with the Senate," announced Hay at that time, "that it seems absolutely impossible to do business." All presidents and secretaries of state from 1903 to 1925 sought ratification without success.[60] Ratification finally came on March 14, 1925, and Wadsworth played no little part in achieving vindication for his father-in-law. He argued against Borah, now the Foreign Relations chairman, James Reed of Missouri, and Royal S. Copeland of New York that the Isle of Pines had been historically Cuban, that the island was never considered American, and that it had never been important to the national defense. His opponents failed to convince the Senate that American interests were too entrenched to be dislodged now.[61] To a degree, Wadsworth's effort was a faint beginning of the Good Neighbor Policy.

Perhaps the development of immigration policy and specifically the Johnson Act of 1924 best typified Wadsworth's attitude regarding foreign

58. New York Times, Mar. 6, 1925.

59. Ibid., Jan. 8, 1925; Syracuse Post-Standard, Jan. 10, 1924, was particularly critical of his stand on the Bok plan: "Even tho a Senator secure in the confidence of his own superior intelligence . . . he [Wadsworth] should at least make a pretense."

60. New York Times, April 23, 1925.

61. Congressional Record, Vol. 67, 69th Congress, 1st Session, March 11, 1925, p. 116–140. Also see Document No. 66, 68th Congress, 2nd Session, "Paper Relating to the Adjustment of Ownership of the Isle of Pines," noting Wadsworth's defense of the Cuban claim.

relations. While on the one hand he represented the nation's Anglo-Saxon bias in restricting the immigration of southern and eastern Europeans, on the other hand he sought to liberalize quota expansion to cover wives and children of immigrants already established in the new world. Of Wadsworth's Anglo-Saxon bias there was little question. "I believe with you," he wrote a Buffalo constituent, "that the general racial status of the people of the United States should not be allowed to change by reason of the large influx of peoples from the Mediterranean region. The 1890 basis would give us a larger number, proportionately, from northern Europe, which, I think would be a good thing." Yet, when Senator Reed of Pennsylvania conceived of "providing for admission of immigrants upon the so-called national origins plan," using the 1920 census, Wadsworth concurred, dismissing his much more discriminatory 1890 base.[62] In fact, his foreign views in the mid-1920s nearly defy categorization.

In 1925, Wadsworth traded his Foreign Relations assignment for one on the Finance Committee. His abiding interest in national defense made the whole business of the Military Affairs Committee more important to him. His conservative economics drew him to the Finance Committee as a second assignment. There his mission was to perpetuate his Sumnerian beliefs. That made the new assignment seem vital. On the Foreign Relations Committee, no particular commitment seemed to guide him as, for example, guided Borah toward the irreconcilable position and guided Kellogg into the internationalist camp.

5

Much of Washington was on the fringe of "the Harding scandals." One had only to breathe the air to encounter "the Ohio gang" and unsavory associates—Harry Daugherty, the Attorney General; Charles R. Forbes, head of the Veterans' Bureau; Jesse Smith, "lobbyist" and "fixer"; Thomas W. Miller, Alien Property Custodian; Albert Fall, Secretary of Interior; and others of their ilk. Wadsworth spent no little time extricating associates from the effects of their misdeeds and malfeasance in high places.

As mentioned earlier, Wadsworth urged Harding not to take Daugherty into the President's cabinet, and once Daugherty was in, warned

62. J.W.W. to Dilworth M. Silver, Apr. 9, 1924, Wadsworth MSS; David Mickey, "Senatorial Participation in the Shaping of Certain United States Foreign Policies." (University of Nebraska, 1954), Ph.D. dissertation (University Microfilms) Ch. III.

Harding about his activity in "the green house on K Street." Socially, the Daughertys and the Wadsworths traveled in quite different strata. They seldom met except through their mutual contacts with the President. Daugherty must have felt unwanted around Wadsworth and resented the distance between them. "Wadsworth is a man I like very much," he unloaded to Charles D. Hilles, New York's national committeeman, "but he has a wrong measure of the Attorney General, taken from the *New York World* or conversations with people like the Roosevelts." In fact, Daugherty was tired of easterners like Wadsworth and other New Yorkers who "want someone to kiss them every night." After all, "people west of New Jersey could get along without them." The Attorney General rambled to a conclusion: "I like Wadsworth, but while he is a very wonderful man in my estimation . . . yet I have seen men quite as big as Jim Wadsworth but of course at a very great distance." [63]

Daugherty's letter revealed a man out of his depth, especially when prescribing on the official stationery of his office, even in confidence, that Wadsworth and his kind "can all go to hell." His pique seemed clear: "I have never heard Jim Wadsworth," he exclaimed, "stand up in the Senate and say that . . . [he] knew the Attorney General to be a man of forty years' experience as a lawyer, a man of good character and a great deal of energy." [64] Hilles was appalled. He could only reply that Jim Wadsworth had not even defended the President of the United States in the Senate. "In fact," concluded Hilles, "as I drove away from your apartment the other night with the President, the President remarked to me that he did not know how Wadsworth felt about him, but that he had tremendous admiration for Wadsworth." [65]

Daugherty's real pique with Wadsworth was probably due to the New York senator's reaction to certain of the Justice Department's war fraud cases. Since taking office, he had been accused of laxity in such prosecutions. When he did move in early 1923, Wadsworth took the strongest possible exception to the Justice Department's action regarding cost-plus war contracts let by the former Assistant Secretary of War, Benedict Crowell.[66] During the war, Crowell was principally responsible for the work of the Emergency Construction Committee in the War Department and, therefore, frequently appeared before the Military Affairs Committee. Wadsworth admired his ability and commitment. Now, the Justice Department sought cost-plus indictments against Crowell and six associates closely

63. H. M. Daugherty to C. D. Hilles, Mar. 2, 1923, Hilles MSS.
64. *Ibid.*
65. C. D. Hilles to H. M. Daugherty, Mar. 5, 1923, Hilles MSS.
66. J.W.W. to H. M. Daugherty, Feb. 28, 1923, Wadsworth MSS.

identified with the Emergency Construction Committee. Aside from the alleged illegality of letting contracts without bid, a gamut of additional charges was included in the bill of indictment, one of which accused Crowell of owning stock in the parent company of the construction firm which received War Department contracts. Of the several hundred cost-plus contracts involved in the indictment, totalling $80,000,000, Crowell allegedly diverted $11,000,000 to his friends.[67]

Upon indictment of Crowell and his six associates by a special war frauds grand jury, Wadsworth moved to defend the former assistant secretary. "I beg leave," he wrote Daugherty on February 28, 1823, "to enclose herewith two letters addressed to you, the first one signed by Senator Frelinghuysen, Senator Fletcher, former Senator Chamberlain and myself, and the second signed by Senator New and Senator Sheppard. Attached to these is a letter addressed to me by the President of the Cleveland Trust Company of Cleveland, Ohio, together with certified copies of letters passing between the company and Mr. Benedict Crowell." Wadsworth had done his homework well. The first two letters described Crowell's exemplary service during the war as the Senate Military Affairs Committee observed it. It resented the treason implications, and noted that Crowell had severed "his connection with the Crowell-Lundoff-Little Company in March, 1918, two months before the alleged transaction." The letter from President F. H. Goff of the Cleveland Trust Company confirmed the same. Wadsworth "begged" the Attorney General to read the enclosures "with care" and noted, "I am keeping for my own files copies of these enclosures."[68] Daugherty's reply to Wadsworth, written the day after his homily to Hilles, took note of the enclosure, insisting, however, that justice must be done, but "if I conclude that a mistake has been made or a wrong done I will not hesitate to have the indictment nolled." He ominously explained, however, that cost-plus "contracts are illegal, and in this conclusion . . . [the Justice Department seems] to have the support of the Supreme Court of the United States."[69]

67. New York Times, Jan. 9, 23, 27, Feb. 27, 1923: associates indicted were William A. Starrett, former chairman of the Emergency Construction Committee, Clarence W. Lundoff, president of Lundoff-Bicknell Construction Co., Morton C. Tuttle, a former member of the committee, Major Clair W. Foster, formerly with the Corps of Engineers, John W. McGibbons, a bonding company representative, and James W. Means, former secretary of the committee; Murray, op. cit., pp. 297–298.

68. J.W.W. to Harry M. Daugherty, Feb. 28, 1923, F. H. Goff to J.W.W., Feb. 3, 1923, J.W.W., J. S. Frelinghuysen and Duncan U. Fletcher to H. M. Daugherty, Feb. 15, 1923, Wadsworth MSS.

69. Harry M. Daugherty to J.W.W., Mar. 3, 1923, Wadsworth MSS.

Daugherty ignored Wadsworth's plea, and sustained indictments which in time would prove groundless. Ironically, while prosecuting Crowell for taking the taxpayers' money, the Attorney General, unknown to Wadsworth and the public, apparently had had his hand in the government till. Jesse Smith, Daugherty's man Friday, had just received $200,000 in Liberty Bonds for expediting the Alien Property Custodian's favorable adjustment of a claim for 47 percent of the stock of the American Metal Company. Fifty thousand dollars worth of the bonds were cashed and deposited in Daugherty's brother's account.[70]

Fortunately, while Wadsworth did all he could for Crowell and associates within the government, Crowell was well defended by legal counsel on the outside. Frank Hogan, a well-known New York attorney, and H. L. Stimson, Wadsworth's friend from 1910 campaign days, charged the administration with turning a policy difference (on cost-plus contracting) between the Wilson and Harding administrations into criminal prosecution. Both counsellors defended before the Supreme Court of the District of Columbia the right of the Wilson administration to expedite military cantonment construction through cost-plus contracts. A Daugherty assistant, E. McCullough, former Ohio congressman, charged the defendants with heinous crimes. Justice Adolph H. Hoehling reserved decision.[71] Three months later, on January 30, 1924, he decided against the government, the fourth war frauds case lost by the Justice Department. Justice Hoehling noted that Secretary of War Baker had approved the cost-plus contracting as a necessary war action and that the Justice Department's facts did not support its conclusions. Furthermore, the indictment bill was so poorly drawn that the defendants were lost as to answering the charges. Stimson emphatically proclaimed the complete exoneration of his clients, Crowell and associates.[72]

Daugherty and his assistant prepared to appeal the host of adverse court decisions which dismissed the war fraud indictments. While doing so, the tables turned; a congressional investigating committee was exposing malfeasance in the Justice Department itself. Yet few now were as aware of that malfeasance as was Wadsworth.

On Thursday, March 6, 1924, William J. ("Wild Bill") Donovan, United States District Attorney in Buffalo, called Wadsworth, seeking advice. Fearing a frame-up by certain members of the "Ohio gang," Donovan wondered how to handle a Buffalo lawyer who informed him of a client who heard "a lot of stuff about Jesse Smith" from Smith's former wife,

70. Murray, op. cit., pp. 480–481. Although indicted for bribery, two hung juries failed to convict Daugherty.

71. New York Times, Oct. 4, 5, 10, 1923.

72. Ibid., Jan. 31, 1924.

Roxie Stinson. Apparently, when in an amorous mood, Roxie told the client about Jesse Smith's "dealings in stock, his close relations with Daugherty," and produced documentary evidence to substantiate her charges. Mal Daugherty, the Attorney General's brother, had gotten wind of the leak and threatened both the client and Roxie with prosecution for violating an Ohio illicit relations law if they did not "shut up." Donovan, wondering where the sordid information should go, asked Wadsworth. The Senator mulled over Donovan's problem and on the following day advised that the attorney, Henry Stern by name, and his client, whose name was A. L. Fink, come to his Washington office. Upon their arrival Wadsworth called Senator Smith W. Brookhart, then the chairman of a select committee investigating the Attorney General. Brookhart asked Wadsworth to send them right over.[73]

Fink's lover Roxie soon appeared before the Brookhart committee, "a slim, still handsome woman set against the fleshly background of Senators." "With her testimony," writes one of Harding's biographers, "Washington's backstairs gossip became black headlines across the country: the little House on H Street; the little Green House on K Street; Jess's shadow relationship with Daugherty. She told of deals and payoffs, suitcases of liquor, stock certificates and thousand-dollar bills—everything she could remember that Jess in his boastfulness or his anxiety had told her, even to the 'they' who were out to get him." [74] It was not long before newsmen discovered that Roxie's presence on the stand emanated from Wadsworth's office. Wadsworth hardly reveled at the discovery. "What a nasty mess it is!" he wrote his father. "My slight contact with it made me shudder as one does when one is compelled to pick up a piece of filth." However, he recognized the hearsay quality of the evidence and thought it possible Daugherty was innocent of the crimes charged against him.[75]

Wadsworth never forgave Daugherty for the Crowell indictment and his appeal of its dismissal by the District Court. With the Attorney General's resignation, following the Brookhart investigation and Coolidge's demand, the New York senator again went to the aid of the former Assistant Secretary of War. Following a lengthy conversation about the matter with the new Justice Department head, Harlan Stone, Wadsworth put into writing the latter's two alternatives: Stone must either "give up pressing

73. Memorandum dictated by Colonel William J. Donovan, Mar. 16, 1924, J.W.W. to J. W. Wadsworth, Sr., Mar. 22, 1924, Wadsworth MSS.

74. Francis Russell, *The Shadow of Blooming Grove, Warren G. Harding in his Times* (New York: McGraw-Hill Book Co., 1963), p. 618; Murray, *op. cit.*, pp. 476–477: although less sensational, Murray corroborates Russell's description.

75. J.W.W. to J. W. Wadsworth, Sr., Mar. 22, 1924, Wadsworth MSS.

the appeal" or go ahead with it and assume responsibility even though there was no evidence to show guilt of conspiracy. He warned that the Circuit Court would probably "decide against the government" and "I find it very difficult to believe that you as a lawyer and as Attorney General, can sponsor such an act." [76] On January 30, 1925, the new Attorney General announced that he had directed that the appeal of the decision of Justice Hoehling of the Supreme Court of the District of Columbia, sustaining the demurrer, not be prosecuted. The Crowell case was closed.[77]

Only a few days after Wadsworth sent Stern and Fink off to the Brookhart Committee, he again encountered the effects of Harding scandals. In the wake of the famous Elks Hill and Teapot Dome oil revelation, craggy Democrat McKellar attacked Secretary of the Treasury Mellon for his illegal, "pecuniary" interests in various enterprises, and freshman Democrat C. C. Dill of Washington demanded the resignation of the Assistant Secretary of the Navy, young Theodore Roosevelt. Dill accused Roosevelt of being a director of Sinclair's Mammoth Oil Company, of having carried the order to the President requesting the transfer of certain oil reserves from the Navy Department to Interior, and of having used Marines to remove competing oil claimants from the oil reserves. Wadsworth called Dill a "sniper" for attempting to besmirch the character of an honorable man. He waxed warm in defending not only a friend but a political asset in New York politics. He described Roosevelt's patriotism, his experience of being gassed in the war, and noted that his ties with Sinclair oil enterprises were severed prior to the Teapot Dome lease. Further, Wadsworth noted that Roosevelt had not carried the transfer order to the President, but, on the contrary, once aware of the action, secured a modification that the Interior Department grant no leases without Navy Department permission. Wadsworth probably was correct.[78] Editorial comment applauded his defense of Roosevelt. The Times concurred: "Mr. Roosevelt is a public-spirited man, born and bred in an atmosphere demanding patriotism and devotion to country. He has his ideals, and they are high ones, with respect to public service." [79] Wadsworth's political asset, soon to be his party's candidate for governor of New York, was saved. Fall, whom Wadsworth had thought to

76. J.W.W. to Harlan F. Stone, Jan. 15, 1925, Wadsworth MSS.
77. New York Times, Jan. 31, 1925.
78. New York Times, Apr. 1, 1924; Congressional Record, Vol. 65, 68th Congress, 1st Session, p. 5268; Lawrence Madaras, "The Public Career of Theodore Roosevelt, Jr." (New York University, 1964), Ph.D. dissertation, p. 209: Madaras corroborates Wadsworth's point of view; Burle Noggle, Teapot Dome, Oil and Politics in the 1920s (Louisiana State University Press, 1962), pp. 19–21: Noggle makes no mention of such efforts on Roosevelt's part.
79. New York Times, Apr. 2, 1924.

be a good senator and Secretary of the Interior, was convicted of accepting a $100,000 bribe for leasing naval oil and was sentenced to one year in jail.

By the summer of 1923 Harding was painfully aware of the misconduct of his cronies; and he was ill—his blood pressure was at 175. For the latter reason and not the former, as frequently contended, he decided on a western speaking tour that would take him to Alaska. Setting out on June 20, he soon wearied and became "nervous and distraught." Upon his return from Alaska the President suffered a heart attack and was put to bed in San Francisco. On the evening of August 2, he died from a brain hemorrhage. The nation mourned. "Little have we thought of his burden," noted Wadsworth, "the aggregate of the innumerable desires of all of us. He has left us secure and happy above all other peoples." [80]

To a large degree Harding did leave the people "secure and happy," notwithstanding the evidence of problems: the sickness of agriculture, the bonus pleas of veterans, labor troubles and third party threats. Undoubtedly life was more satisfying to Wadsworth than to most Americans. Indeed, life was comfortable on Lafayette Square. There, and in the finest drawing rooms of Washington, he chose his company, and he and Alice were always well received. When Coolidge became President, he and Grace received the Wadsworths at the White House. On one occasion Reverdy accompanied his parents to a family luncheon and recalls well the President's feeding table scraps to White House "hounds." [81] The Boss was frequently in residence at 1732 K Street, not distant from the Hay House. Porter Chandler, a cousin, recently educated at Oxford and Columbia Law School, was brought by Harlan Stone into the Criminal Division of the Justice Department, to the Senator's delight.[82] Almost when he pleased, Jim got back to the Genesee Valley, either to their great home at Hampton Corners, or to Hartford House. And of course he was always welcome at the Homestead, south of the village. The pace of the Congress slowed in the 1920s, between the feverish periods of World War I and the Great Depression. "Alice, Evelyn, Joan Whitney (my niece) and I have just returned from a six-week trip to Panama and the West Indies," he wrote satisfyingly in 1923. Family life was comforting, whether at some distant point, or in Washington or in the valley. When the children were not

80. *New York Times*, Aug. 5, 1923; Murray, *op. cit.*, p. 440.

81. Conversation with Reverdy Wadsworth, Geneseo, N.Y., 1969.

82. J.W.W. to Harlan Stone, July 9, 1924, Wadsworth MSS: "He [Porter Chandler] still has his heart set on going to Washington in the autumn and working in some capacity in your department. You and I, as I recollect it, have already discussed this."

present, they were well accounted for. In 1924 Evie married a pleasing and attractive young man from Baltimore, W. Stuart Symington. In the following year she presented her father with his first grandchild. Jerry followed his father's footsteps and entered Yale, and "little Reverdy" did the same by enrolling at Fay School.

His growing seniority and his Military Affairs chairmanship, in addition to representing the most populous state in the Union, afforded Wadsworth great prestige. Ideologically, his conservatism prevailed, although threatened by mid-western Republicans and an increasing number of liberal Democrats. Quietly articulate, and generally considered to possess a superior intellect,[83] the New Yorker was taken seriously. He was "no shaker," no William Borah. He was no architect of numerous great measures. Nevertheless, Wadsworth contributed consistently to the construction of military affairs legislation and bills in areas of specific interest, such as foreign relations, finance, and agriculture. When, in early February of 1923, senate Republicans sought help for their aging majority leader, Henry Cabot Lodge, Wadsworth and Lenroot were suggested to represent conservative and liberal interests, respectively. Lodge squashed the idea, however, noting emphatically that he and Curtis, the Republican whip, with the assistance of James Watson of Indiana, could lead the Senate majority.[84]

83. Robert C. Pell, *Reminiscences of Robert C. Pell* (Columbia University: Oral History Research Office, 1951). Pell, defeated by Ogden Mills in a House of Representatives race, noted that Mills and Wadsworth were the intellectual superiors of the "Republican organization."

84. *New York Times,* Feb. 4, 6, 1923.

Father and son in Washington, 1925, one year prior to the death of the former. *By permission of the Library of Congress.*

Wadsworth with his political mentor, William Barnes, at the White House, about 1921. *By permission of the Library of Congress.*

Walking in Rock Creek Park with Speaker Nicholas Longworth, about 1925.

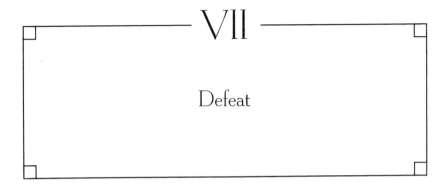

VII

Defeat

1

WADSWORTH always had an eye on New York politics. He vied for influence over the Republican state organization with those party leaders who hovered around the governor, when Republican, or the federal crowd downstate. Usually the Wadsworth element represented upstate interests and maintained a conservative ideological stance. By 1922, Barnes, Wadsworth's political patron, had lost his power as a principal catalyst of the upstate conservative faction. Indeed, he was even losing his newspaper, *The Albany Evening Journal*.[1] Wadsworth's principal allies were Charles D. Hilles, national committeeman, and Nicholas M. Butler, both from downstate but with decided conservative leanings. Other New Yorkers attending Wadsworth were young T.R., Jr., and James Sheffield, a fellow Yaleman who aspired to be Wadsworth's junior senator, but settled for the ambassadorship to Mexico.

The downstate Republicans particularly annoyed Wadsworth and his associates. William Calder, Brooklyn-bred, and that city's Building Commissioner before entering Congress, was privately unacceptable to Wadsworth. Not infrequently, the two got into patronage squabbles. Calder's support emanated from Samuel Koenig, the Manhattan chairman; William L. Ward, the Westchester leader; and Ogden Mills, the new congressman from Manhattan's 17th congressional district.

Nathan Miller, the governor, up for re-election in 1922, would have preferred a United States senatorial candidate other than Calder but feared downstate reprisal if he was not renominated. Wadsworth and Hilles would

1. Charles D. Hilles to Dwight Morrow, Aug. 29, 1924, Hilles MSS, Sterling Library, Yale University, New Haven, Conn. Hilles notes that Wadsworth was embarrassed by Barnes's financial status and by the latter's idea of having the state chairman buy $12,000 worth of *Albany Evening Journal* subscriptions.

have supported Sheffield, except for his lack of public exposure and his "traction" interests. Yet he would have been preferable to Calder, who, they felt, had not grown in the Senate and was generally unacceptable to the American Legion, "drys," women, and intellectuals. Besides, he had no "forensic ability." [2]

The principals in the New York 1922 campaign were Governor Miller and his opponent, the former governor, Alfred E. Emith. The United States senatorial candidates were William Calder and his Democratic opponent, Royal S. Copeland, former Health Commissioner of New York City. The Democrats made a clean sweep of it. Smith carried the slate with a 387,000-vote plurality. Aside from his genuine popularity in a fast-urbanizing state, Smith had the issues: demand for governmental reorganization, the executive budget, water power control, and a consistent position on prohibition enforcement.

"You are the only man I see in sight," wrote the defeated Miller to Wadsworth after the election, "to lead the Republicans of New York and the State of New York back where they belong." [3] Some Republican congressmen from New York did not see Wadsworth as their savior. They attributed recent Republican defeat to a loss of contact with the people. Their spokesmen, Luther Mott of Owego and Hamilton Fish of Putnam County, petitioned State Chairman Morris to seek Republican support of state-wide primaries, the short ballot, home-rule, price reduction, water power control, rent reductions, minimum wages, and "the removal of our courts from political domination." [4]

Actually, Republicans Mott and Fish feared what Miller advocated, that Wadsworth would lead the party. Thus they called for a democratization of the state committee. Wadsworth was not impressed by the Mott-Fish petition. "Each and every [recommendation]," he wrote Chairman George K. Morris, "is strictly a State of New York matter," and not the particular business of congressmen. Furthermore, noted Wadsworth, "several of the items were taken almost directly from the Democratic platform." Wadsworth, through Morris, lectured "Mott and Fish, et. al.," on political division of labor, noting that state legislators, federal congressmen, and county chairmen all have different constituencies and responsibilities that necessitate staying out of each others' way. [5]

Wadsworth was for an expression of opinion by writing to individuals

2. Charles D. Hilles to William M. Butler, Sept. 11, 1922, Hilles MSS.

3. Nathan Miller to J.W.W., Nov. 10, 1922, Wadsworth MSS, Library of Congress, Washington, D.C.

4. Hamilton Fish, et al., to George K. Morris, Dec. 18, 1922, Wadsworth MSS.

5. J.W.W. to George K. Morris, Dec. 18, 1922, Wadsworth MSS.

but was not for official intrusion. There was none. Throughout 1923 Wadsworth held the party reins. Morris consulted him on state matters, as did Hilles on federal problems. It was Wadsworth who informed the President of political conditions in New York. On occasion, when reporting to the President, he was accompanied by Hilles, Morris, and Theodore Roosevelt.

While keeping a knowing eye on New York politics and while performing his senatorial role, Wadsworth functioned also as a national political figure. Nineteen twenty-four might well mark the high point of his political influence.

Some New York Republicans considered Wadsworth presidential timber, but the Senator could only label as "more nonsense" a *New York World* clipping, "Tom Toms Beat for Wadsworth Boom next year." [6] Young Ted Roosevelt thought Wadsworth had a presidential chance, as did devotees from around the state. Many "Wadsworthmen" wanted him to have at least complimentary support in the 1924 National Republican Convention, hoping to hold the delegation together. Wadsworth disabused such strategy: "There is one thing I could not stand and that is playing the part of a favorite son as a piece of political strategy." [7]

Wadsworth was for Coolidge for President and had been since he assumed the presidency on August 2, 1923. Both he and Hilles pushed early for Coolidge's nomination. Hilles assured William Howard Taft that Wadsworth would be no candidate, that he would not lend "himself to any plan to divide the field." Nor would Weeks, Hoover, or Butler. Hilles thought Watson of Indiana, Lowden, Pinchot, and Hughes were unlikely candidates, for a variety of reasons. Only La Follette worried the national committeeman. "Some of our friends," he wrote Taft, "are apprehensive lest La Follette will remain out of the convention and become a candidate on an independent ticket." If such were to happen, Hilles feared that no candidate would achieve a majority and the election would be thrown into the House of Representatives, where the states are evenly divided between Republicans and Democrats. [8]

Wadsworth's political leadership was sorely tested in 1924, most generally as related to the forthcoming National Republican Convention of the same year. He easily passed the initial test on January 14, when state leaders chose him to head the seven delegates-at-large. [9] Then, selected in

6. *New York World*, Aug. 6, 1923.
7. J.W.W. to William Boardman, Dec. 18, 1923, Wadsworth MSS.
8. Charles D. Hilles to W. H. Taft, Oct. 16, 1923, Taft MSS, Library of Congress, Washington, D.C.
9. *New York Times*, Jan. 15, 1924.

the spring to be variously the convention's temporary and permanent chairman, he wound up being neither. When the President finally decided upon Representative Theodore Burton of Ohio as temporary chairman, and when Wadsworth's own idea of a far-westerner as permanent chairman was accepted, the New Yorker gladly stepped down.[10] A third test came on June 8, during the early hours of the convention when Westchester County and New York City leaders tried to replace Wadsworth with William L. Ward as the delegation's chairman. Ward, basing his campaign on Wadsworth's failure to achieve the permanent chairmanship, failed to achieve either the chairmanship or Hilles's spot on the national committee.[11]

Coolidge's nomination was not contested during the convention. On the vice presidential nomination, the only contest, Wadsworth spent considerable time, discussing candidates with a collection of politicos gathered first in Secretary of War Weeks's room, and then in National Chairman Butler's office. Among the leaders gathered there were Speaker Longworth, Ted Roosevelt, Hilles, Senator Harry New and presidential advisor Frank W. Stearns. Various candidates were eliminated. Charles G. Dawes was seen as a "wild man." The President did not like Charles Curtis's congressional voting record. Governor Frank Lowden of Illinois would not accept the nomination. Governor Arthur M. Hyde of Missouri had a Ku Klux Klan record. Major General James G. Harbord was viewed as a militarist. On the second day, at a conference of eastern representatives, Wadsworth pushed Harbord, who led until National Chairman Butler vetoed his candidacy. Butler favored former Governor Herbert Hadley of Missouri until it was discovered that "his lungs were not in shape." By the end of the second day Longworth expressed disgust at Butler's lack of direction, not sure whether he was laying "some deep scheme" or was "simply a plain boob." Butler finally said Borah was the man, but Wadsworth and Roosevelt knew he would not accept it. On the third day, during a meeting of the New York Caucus, Butler said it would be either the liberal Kenyon or the conservative Burton. In a New York factional fight, with Wadsworth, Hilles, and Mills favoring Burton, and Hayward, Davenport, and Koenig supporting Kenyon, Burton won, but to no avail, for the convention, including many New York delegates, did not want either. On the second ballot, Wadsworth "threw the entire delegation to Lowden." By the end of the second ballot, Lowden did not have the nomination and would not have accepted had he won. The convention recessed. In inter-

10. *Ibid.*, May 28, 1924.
11. *Ibid.*, June 9, 10, 1924.

vening conferences among the leaders, Dawes emerged the man. On the next ballot he was nominated.[12]

The forthcoming election of a governor in 1924 was central to New York politics in the eighteen months preceding the election, another test of Wadsworth's leadership. The stakes were high, for were the Republicans to carry the State House, Wadsworth's influence over both state and federal patronage in New York would probably assure his own re-election in 1926 and a bright political future.

For some months prior to the governorship race, young T.R. quietly badgered Wadsworth for a chance to run. He dreamed, understandably, of following in his father's footsteps—at Harvard, in military service, in the New York Assembly, as Assistant Secretary of the Navy, and as Governor of New York. And even the presidency was possible. Wadsworth told Roosevelt that New York politics were too messy "at present," that he should stay out, and certainly he should avoid any active candidacy.[13]

Wadsworth's political savvy warned him against converting T.R.'s dream into reality. His protégé, whom he had recently told to act more like a leader, was too much of a contrast to the giant incumbent, Governor Alfred E. Smith. Smith had grown mightily since those Assembly days in 1906 when as only one Tammany liege, he looked up at the powerful young Speaker Wadsworth. Since then he had gone a steady route to power, as Democratic Assembly leader, Speaker, sheriff of New York County, president of the Board of Alderman, governor and contender for the Democratic nomination for the presidency. Then too, Roosevelt was tainted with the Teapot Dome scandal, and his brother Archie with Sinclair's oil manipulations. And perhaps young Ted was too wet to hold the rural voters. Wadsworth would need a strong candidate with whom to confront downstate leaders who were trotting out their own candidates. The Manhattan and Kings County leaders were not enamored of having the upstater, Wadsworth, run things.

As Wadsworth was lunching with the Theodore Roosevelts in the summer of 1924, young Ted excused himself momentarily and Jim turned to Eleanor and said, "I am sure you would like to see Ted nominated this fall. So would I. I believe he would make a superb run against Smith, but it isn't in the cards now. Eddie Machold is going to get it. He has done some splendid work for the party for years and the boys all love him. He

12. Theodore Roosevelt, Jr., *Diary*, June 10, 11, 12, 1924, Theodore Roosevelt, Jr. MSS, Library of Congress, Washington, D.C.; *New York Times*, June 14, 1924; J. G. Harbord telegram to J.W.W., June 13, 1924, thanking J.W.W. for his support for Harbord for Vice President, Wadsworth MSS.

13. Roosevelt, Jr., *Diary*, 1923–24, *passim*, Theodore Roosevelt, Jr., MSS.

is entitled to it." [14] Henry Edmund Machold, an attractive downstater, had served as chairman of the party's state Executive Committee and for several terms as a successful Speaker of the Assembly. He seemed the ideal candidate, acceptable to most factions, and would undoubtedly have been nominated by the state Republican convention, had he not withdrawn at the last moment. Machold wanted the governorship and would have run against any Democrat except Smith. Once Smith decided to again serve the Democracy, Machold studiously avoided the nomination. The field opened. Candidates standing in the wings appeared on stage: William Hayward, Guy B. Moore, Judge Arthur S. Tompkins, Hamilton Fish, and, of course, Theodore Roosevelt, Jr., and five others. Some said, "let James do it," thus making it eleven.[15]

Wadsworth and State Chairman Morris, sensing the possible volatility of the forthcoming state Republican convention, took control and muscled T.R. to nomination on the first ballot. "As the son of his father," editorialized the New York Times, "he was brought forward mainly as a figure-head, and a second-rate choice figure-head at that." The New York paper noted, however, that T.R. would get a "fair hearing." [16]

On the day after Republicans adjourned their convention in Rochester, Democrats convened in Syracuse. There they nominated Smith by acclamation. In 1922 he had defeated the incumbent Governor Miller by 400,000 votes and, after two years of building a national reputation as an outstanding governor, worried little about Wadsworth's candidate. "We will have four solid weeks," he croaked nasally, "to show the people of this State that you cannot rub out the record nor nominate a myth in Washington and a name in New York and get away with it." [17]

Wadsworth criss-crossed the state for Roosevelt in 1924, defending the national administration and noting how the Republican legislature in New York saved the state from Smith's "legislative foolishness." His vigor belied his conservatism and identified him with the liberalism of the candidates. "Senator Wadsworth," reported the New York Sun, "is taking the leadership of his party from the group of elder statesmen who have dominated it for the last ten years, and almost liberalized it to match the progressive ideas advocated by Al Smith." [18]

Roosevelt, meeting the liberal demands of New York, pleaded for

14. Mrs. Theodore Roosevelt, Jr., Day Before Yesterday (New York: Doubleday, 1959).
15. New York Times, July 27, 1924.
16. Ibid., Sept. 26, 1924.
17. Ibid., Sept. 27, 1924.
18. New York Sun (citation misplaced).

farm cooperatives, a bonus for veterans, a forty-eight-hour work week for women, and the elimination of the KKK's intolerance.[19] Smith frequently stumped New England for the Democratic presidential nominee, John W. Davis, but when in New York State, he defended his system of executive budgeting and his consolidation of executive departments. Smith also pointed to his labor record, an impressive one which included the creation of an industrial council, the restoration of a Bureau of Women, the strengthening of the Workmen's Compensation Law, and the passage of a new childrens' act.

Smith, a national figure who knew the New York scene better than anyone, most of all Theodore Roosevelt, Jr., presented too much competition. Also, the "drys" split over the "wet" Roosevelt, not a few "sitting on their hands." Coolidge's popularity—he carried New York by 400,000 votes—did not help T.R. Smith's plurality was a very safe 140,000.[20]

Wadsworth blamed young T.R.'s defeat on New York City. He thought the party there had lost its fighting spirit. "For years," he wrote a New York City Republican, "I have contended that this is due, in great part, to the fusion habit in which it was indulged." He was right. Roosevelt went to New York City with a possible majority only to lose the city to Smith. Had Republicans in the city boroughs held the line for Roosevelt as they did for Coolidge, he would have won.[21] But a new day had dawned. Urban New York voted for the man, not the party, a portent of change in America. Normalcy was passing. Shortly Wadsworth would discover anew the impact of urbanism on New York politics, as he faced his own struggle for survival, the 1926 campaign for re-eletion to the United States Senate.

2

On March 4, 1925, at a moment before high noon, a remarkable event in the history of the vice presidency took place. It was the way in which Vice President-elect Charles F. Dawes accepted his new office. Distin-

19. Lawrence Madaras, "The Public Career of Theodore Roosevelt, Jr." (New York University, June 1964), Ph.D. dissertation, p. 230.

20. Ibid., pp. 230–242.

21. J.W.W. to Charles M. Pepper, Esq., Nov. 20, 1924, Wadsworth MSS; also, see J.W.W. to James M. Lown, July 19, 1924, Wadsworth MSS. Aside from lethargy of Republican organization in N.Y.C., Wadsworth thought Archibald Roosevelt's identification with H. Sinclair's oil operations was harmful to his brother's gubernatorial campaign.

guished persons crowded into the Senate chamber. President Coolidge sat directly facing the Vice President. Wadsworth occupied his front row seat, now only three removed from the majority leader. "What I say on entering this office," began Dawes, following his installation, "should relate to its administration and the conditions under which it is administered." Without precedent, the Vice President, pumping his arms and shaking his finger at gasping senators, indicted the body for its Rule XXII, the Senate's filibuster provision. In condemning the august Senate for its almost unlimited debate rule, a two-thirds vote being required to cut off debate, Dawes touched the great body's vitals. "Who would dare," concluded the Vice President, "to contend that under the spirit of democratic government the power to kill legislation . . . should . . . ever be in the hands of a minority or perhaps one Senator." [22] Before the Senate caught its collective breath, Dawes further incensed his new charges by insisting that time not be wasted installing new senators four at a time. "Bring them all up," he shouted.[23] Ten years before, at his own installation, Wadsworth had been depressed by the herding effect of oath-taking by fours!

Afterwards, senators spouted pent-up rage. "His melody of voice, grace of gesture, and majesty of presence were only excelled by his modesty," burst out the sarcastic Democrat James A. Reed of Missouri. "I have an opinion . . . but do not care to express [it]," commented the usually tolerant Republican George Norris of Nebraska.[24] Wadsworth felt differently. While disagreeing with the Vice President's conclusions, he thought the speech itself to be well written and inoffensive. "The manner in which it was delivered," he later confessed to a constituent, "was one of the most extraordinary things I have ever seen in or out of a legislative body. The members of the Senate who heard it kept very quiet. The galleries literally rocked with laughter. [And the herding of new Senators into the well] . . . following the conclusions of General Dawes's speech . . . [was] equally extraordinary." Wadsworth's sense of propriety gave way to that of charity. "I was not mad. I was sorry. . . . General Dawes is an exceedingly able man and a very delightful man as I happen to know through long acquaintances with him. The Senate will get used to him and he will get used to the Senate. And all will be well." Dawes was unperturbed. "I have had my say," he told the press. "Let [the Senators] . . . have theirs." [25]

22. Paul R. Leach, *That Man Dawes* (Chicago: The Reilly and Lee Co., 1930), pp. 242–244.

23. *Ibid.*, p. 246.

24. *Ibid.*, pp. 249–250.

25. J.W.W. to Ellsworth Buck, March 9, 1925, Wadsworth MSS; Leach, *op. cit.*, p. 251.

In retrospect all was well. Four years later Dawes would leave the Senate with the affection and gratitude of its members. He was a different breed from most vice president. Dawes had had vast legal, political, military, and government experience. He was a strong personality, frequently independent of powerful leaders, including presidents. His conservatism, independence, establishmentarianism, and commitment to public service were much like Wadsworth's. He held Wadsworth in high esteem. "In now recalling my judgments of Senators," he wrote in his memoirs, "among others the name of James W. Wadsworth, of New York . . . come to my mind. Viewed from any angle, not only as a Senator but as one qualified for constructive leadership in the public interest—mental or moral—military or civil—in Congress or out—I regard him as most unusual." [26] Elsewhere, in describing his vice presidential experience, Dawes commented on the thoroughness with which Wadsworth (and David A. Reed of Pennsylvania) approached any subject, and on his ability to "hold the attention of the Senate." [27]

On the subject of senate rules Wadsworth could not have disagreed more with Dawes. While the Vice President demanded a change in Rule XXII allowing unlimited debate, the New Yorker fought to retain the rule. Wadsworth was thankful that unlimited senate debate reduced the volume of legislation. "Under House rules," he noted, "a measure of utmost importance can be put through with scarcely any debate at all. When this is done the Senate generally has to revise the measure considerably. The Senate can do this on account of its liberality of the rules governing debate. Of course, a large number of people are impatient while the Senate is doing it. But I am wondering if we should legislate in impatience or with deliberation." [28] One-half century later critics of Rule XXII, including Wadsworth's son-in-law, Senator Stuart Symington of Missouri, still inveighed against the Wadsworth position of "due deliberation."

Wadsworth's high political status, in and out of the Senate, was maintained during the Sixty-ninth Congress. A senior senator, he retained his Military Affairs Committee chairmanship and moved onto the important Committee on Finance. In addition, he served on the Republican Steering Committee and the important Committee on Committees. Aside from holding the confidence of the Senate's presiding officer, the New Yorker

26. Charles G. Dawes, *Notes as Vice President, 1928–1929* (Boston: Little, Brown and Co., 1935), p. 82.

27. *Ibid.*, p. 108.

28. J.W.W. to Frank E. Rupert, March 9, 1925, Wadsworth MSS. See Neil MacNeil, *Forge of Democracy: The House of Representatives* (New York: D. McKay, 1963) for opposite position—that the House of Representatives is a more deliberative body because of strong committee deliberation and usage.

placed high with the leadership in the "other house." The new Speaker of the House of Representatives, Nicholas Longworth, had long been devoted to Wadsworth. Not infrequently, the New York senator advised the Cincinnati congressman on his Washington moves. Because of his seniority, his affinity with congressional leadership, and his reputation for intelligence and legislative capability, *Time Magazine* placed the New Yorker on its cover on December 28, 1925. In the same year certain Buffalonians boomed his name as the next presidential candidate.[29]

Wadsworth brushed aside the slight presidential bee. He as quickly brushed aside the more plausible suggestion that he succeed Secretary of War John Weeks upon the latter's death. Realistically, Wadsworth saw that any political advancement hinged on his own re-election in 1926, no little task, given the strength of Al Smith's Democracy in New York and the potency of upstate dry Republicans. Ever mindful of that forthcoming exercise, Wadsworth turned to the detail of senate performance. It was at times exacting. In one month during the Sixty-ninth Congress, Wadsworth received more than 10,000 communications, introduced 21 bills, received 1,041 callers, made 22 visits to various departments, and completed 2,301 telephone calls. The work load was little enough by the Senate's mid-century standards but a sizeable load for the quiet days of Calvin Coolidge.[30]

Of the great issues in the Sixty-ninth Congress which interested Wadsworth particularly, military, constitutional, agricultural, financial, and international, those pertinent to military affairs took precedence. So fundamental did Wadsworth see that committee's activity that he did all of his senate work in his private office adjoining the committee's suite on the Capitol's main floor. There on Fridays, the chairman convened his committee to shepherd the National Defense Act through its early days of implementation. It was not easy. The era's penchant for economy and the usual clamoring for rivers and harbors "pork" projects left little in the general War Department appropriations bill for retaining an army of 118,500 enlisted men and 12,000 officers. In addition, the committee was threatened by Budget Bureau cuts. Wadsworth was annoyed that, in conversation with Coolidge, the Chief Executive purposely "kept away from the subject." Wadsworth wrote to fellow committeeman Hiram Bingham, "I intend to discuss the matter publicly."[31] He did so on September 9, 1925, at the dedication of a Gettysburg battlefield monument commemorating the forty-one New York Civil War commanders. "That coun-

29. *Time Magazine*, Dec. 28, 1925, pp. 7–8.

30. Henry F. Holthusen, *James W. Wadsworth, Jr., A Biographical Sketch* (New York: G. P. Putnam's Sons, 1926), p. 184.

31. J.W.W. to Hiram Bingham, Aug. 26, 1925, Wadsworth MSS.

try," spoke Wadsworth, "which sends its young men upon the modern battlefield, undisciplined and untrained, comes perilously near committing murder." After detailing the strain imposed by the administration's rigid economy, "40,000 men of the Regular army living in rickety, wooden, wartime cantonments with leaky roofs and sagging floors," the Military Affairs chairman noted that any further reduction would "break" the system.[32] Such public positions helped somewhat. The army managed to maintain itself close to the 118,500 figure required by law, even though, by the session's end, the Secretary of War had to beg for $2,500,000 to do it. At least no evidence points to the President's asking Wadsworth what the Naval Affairs chairman was asked: "All this seems to cost money. What investigations have you made that will save money?"[33]

No little of Wadsworth's time in 1926 was spent on legislation aimed at reuniting aliens with their wives and children who were barred from entry to the United States by the recently passed immigration quota act. The President, in a message to the Congress, suggested such legislation and, of course, given the millions of immigrants in New York City, Wadsworth's sponsorship of a relief bill was good politics. The New York senator was not just moved politically, however. He recognized the cruelties imposed by the 1924 Johnson Immigration Act. His good friend Henry Curran, Ellis Island's Commissioner of Immigration, described to him many instances of immigrants who came to America intending, once established, to send for loved ones, only to be denied that possibility by the new act. Wadsworth's legislation would correct that situation and would also permit entry, beyond the quota, of aliens in Europe who served in the American military forces.[34]

Bill number S 2245, "A Bill to Amend the Immigration Act of 1924," brought Wadsworth's mail to flood stage, most of it opposed. Typically, a shoe salesman from Ogdensburg was not moved by Italians "crying" for their wives and relatives. "Well, all I can say," he wrote scathingly, "is if they and their posterity does not make any better Americans than those that are over here of their like, and I mean native born as well, it will be just as well for the country at large to keep them in their own nation." The shoe salesman bemoaned the presence of hyphenated Americans, concluding that "one hundred percent American voters" amounted to "more than all the damn foreign voters combined, and a whole lot over."[35] Even

32. "A Plea for Preparedness," Wadsworth address at Gettysburg, Sept. 10, 1925, Wadsworth MSS.
33. Frederick Hale to J.W.W., July 21, 1925, Wadsworth MSS.
34. *New York Times*, Dec. 19, 1925, Jan. 8, 12, 22, Feb. 5, 6, Mar. 6, 30, Apr. 8, 10, 1926.
35. W. Sherwell to J.W.W., Feb. 27, 1926, Wadsworth MSS.

the articulate editor of *The World's Work*, Arthur Page, protested to Wadsworth, wondering why Jews, when separated, always have to reunite "on this side of the Atlantic." [36]

Wadsworth reacted coolly to criticism of S 2245. He suggested that Curran behave accordingly. He answered the protest mail assiduously and courteously. ("Please do me the courtesy of believing that my proposal is the result of a deep conviction on my part that this great country should not unnecessarily inflict hardships upon innocent people." [37]) He agreed to a maximum of 35,000 extra quota entries.[38] He ignored charges of political motivation. (Of course, the Republican leader of the 15th Assembly District, New York City, thought the bill would mean thousands of votes.[39]) Wadsworth got only half a loaf, the admission of aliens who served in the armed forces.

Wadsworth persisted with the main thrust of S 2245, the admission of relatives of non-military aliens, even as a lame-duck senator, and finally got senate action in December of 1926. When his colleagues tried cavalierly to set the legislation aside, he made one of those rare senate speeches that change votes.[40] By a margin of two, his bill carried, but to no avail. The House demurred. A year and a half elapsed before President Coolidge signed legislation admitting relatives of aliens who had entered America prior to 1924. Even then, entries fell within the quota structure, but at least they were given priority.

Wadsworth could be moved by important circumstances of human beings who were not his constituents. When Miss Sophie Loeb, president of the National Child Welfare Commission, asked the New Yorker to sponsor legislation to care for some one thousand children of destitute mothers in the District of Columbia, he did so with enthusiasm. "When it comes to children," he told the District committee, "it is a theory and a principle with me that the best place for a child is in a home." [41] Specifically, Wadsworth's bill provided for a Mothers' Aid Bureau of five members to allocate money to mothers who had previously sought relief

36. Arthur Page to J.W.W., Mar. 2, 1926, Wadsworth MSS.

37. J.W.W. to C. H. Barclay, May 27, 1926; J.W.W. to Henry H. Curran, Jan. 22, 1926, Wadsworth MSS.

38. *New York Times*, Dec. 17, 1926.

39. Republican Leader, 15th Assembly District, to J.W.W., Apr. 8, 1926, Wadsworth MSS.

40. *New York Times*, Dec. 17, 1926.

41. *New York Evening World*, undated clipping; *Hearings*, "Mothers' Aid in the District of Columbia," 1926, Wadsworth MSS.

from District philanthropies. The legislation was not unlike the New York State provision. Wadsworth successfully countered opposition, primarily from Senator Capper of Kansas, who contended that such funds should be handled by the District's Board of Charities.[42]

Given his sympathy for the immigrant separated from his family and for the homeless child in the District of Columbia, one might expect that a constitutional amendment prohibiting child labor would gain Wadsworth's support. Certainly not. Twice the Supreme Court had turned down anti-child labor legislation as perversions of federal power. Wadsworth saw the constitutional amendment in the same light. Besides, he believed, albeit erroneously, that child labor conditions in the country were not horrendous. He thought even the conservative owner of the Gannett newspapers exaggerated child labor canditions. Of the "one million little children" a Gannett editorial pleaded for, Wadsworth saw 600,000 "working on farms with their parents," and of the remaining 400,000, most were delivering newspapers or shining shoes or tending store for a few hours. Most important to Wadsworth, child labor legislation was a state responsibility, and all states except one had restrictive legislation.[43]

A new education bill to create a federal department of education was the last straw to Wadsworth. Coming on the heels of seventeen years of federal bureaucratization, from the Federal Trade Commission to the Volstead Act, he thought the specter of federalization of education awesome. In the face of pressures from the National Education Association and southern constituencies seeking federal financial aid, Wadsworth solemnized: "If we continue to take power and transfer it to Washington, we shall destroy those qualities. Our local Governments would dwindle to the vanishing point, and we shall find the average man becoming a servant of the Government instead of its master. Let us remember that our country is a Federal Union of States, not an empire. Realizing, as we must, the dangers of a bureaucracy, irresponsible and remote from our view, let us pause and survey our situation before we yield to its inducements."[44] Even Robert Wagner, who was to succeed Wadsworth and epitomize the philosophy of centralization, drew back from support of the education bill. On this Wadsworth was quite in tune with his times.

Mrs. Charles Sabin, New York Republican committeewoman, questioned whether Wadsworth's adamant fear of centralization was in the

42. J.W.W. to Edward F. Brown, June 25, 1926, Wadsworth MSS.
43. J.W.W. to constituent, Nov. 16, 1924, Wadsworth MSS. Wadsworth refers to Gannett editorial in letter.
44. *New York Times,* Mar. 10, 1926.

Republican tradition. Wadsworth explained that occasional Republican support for a "strong central government" had always been only with constitutional sanctions under the commerce clause, the army clause, or clauses authorizing a national currency. "But in recent years, the federal government has gone far beyond these limits." For this, he blamed Democrats and especially Woodrow Wilson. "Today," he affirmed, "the Republican party is not in favor of further centralization." [45]

Much of the nation in 1926 wanted firm presidential action to intervene in a six-months-old coal strike. Wadsworth did not. When his junior colleague, Democrat Royal S. Copeland, demanded a senate resolution to press Coolidge to act, Wadsworth said it would be a "mere gesture," that the President was alive to the seriousness of the situation. [46] Wadsworth continually fought against the resolution though it finally passed, with the aid of twenty-six Republicans. He was of course delighted that Coolidge ignored the resolution and that miners and operators finally settled the matter "without governmental interference." [47]

Agriculture, the sickest of America's industries in the 1920s, warranted, to Wadsworth, little more interference than the coal situation. While supportive of the Fordney-McCumber Tariff and the Capper-Volstead Act (to legalize cooperative buying and selling) as a means to control farm surpluses he fought the Farm Credit Act and the Good Roads Act as expensive and paternalistic. He opposed the McNary-Haugen scheme for the federal government to buy certain surplus commodities for dumping overseas. "And if the government is to guarantee farmers against all losses," he sardonically noted, "due to such causes as over-production or slowing down of demand, it will have to protect other people who produce things and want to be assured of a profit." [48] Wadsworth saw the answers to the farmers' problems largely in tax reduction by local government and, more importantly, in diversification. He felt that northwest farmers, like those in the Genesee Valley, should raise several grains and a variety of fruits. Such farmers also would do well to raise lambs and dairy cattle. Furthermore, Wadsworth was confident "that agriculture has turned a corner and is making steady progress along the road of prosperity." [49] Although proud of his farming heritage and livelihood, Wadsworth was not a member of the Senate's "farm bloc."

45. J.W.W. to Mrs. Charles H. Sabin, Mar. 8, 1926, Wadsworth MSS.

46. J.W.W. to Francis C. Ott, Feb. 8, 1926, Wadsworth MSS.

47. J.W.W. to William O. Coleman, Apr. 4, 1926, Wadsworth MSS; *New York Times*, Feb. 10, 1926.

48. J.W.W. to William Pitkin, Dec. 19, 1925, Wadsworth MSS.

49. J.W.W. to A. Eugene Bolles, Aug. 27, 1925, Wadsworth MSS.

By the time of the Sixty-ninth Congress, centralization of the federal government was anathema to Wadsworth. It became a favorite theme. The aggregate of centralizatoin even in this Republican era was almost beyond his belief. To a rapt audience of Republican women he painted the dire consequences—"a great imperial government in Washington overlapping the power of the people themselves, in their several states and communities, manned by an army of bureaucrats, remote, often irresponsible, gaining more and more strength from its own momentum and clothed finally with the power to regulate the life of every person in the Republic." To fellow valleymen in Caledonia, New York, he swore to stop the flood of legislation which merely compounded the centralization.[50]

Almost always, Wadsworth's congressional efforts, outside of military and foreign policy, related to his fears of over-centralization, whether his concern at the moment was the great coal strike of 1926, the proposed child labor amendment, federal aid to agriculture, or the creation of a department of education.

4

No Republican among some eight hundred perspiring delegates at the 1920 national convention fought the Eighteenth Amendment more fiercely than James Wadsworth, at a time, reported Leonard Wood's biographer, "when non-conformity was regarded as akin to sacrilege." [51] Largely as a result of the New Yorker's stand, the Chicago platform builders referred only obliquely to prohibition enforcement: "Without obedience to law . . . our American institutions must perish." [52] Just eight months previously the Congress had passed the Volstead Act to implement the dry amendment.

Wadsworth loathed prohibition and all the hypocrisy and criminality it conjured up. While supportive of the Volstead Act as a necessary enforcement evil, his caustic reference to the whole dry effort brought down upon him the wrath of the National Women's Christian Temperance Union. Its president, Ella A. Boole, as a New York temperance senatorial candidate in 1920, opposed the "wayward" Wadsworth. At the polls, the

50. "Extract from Address by Senator Wadsworth at the Luncheon of National Women's Republican Club." N.Y. City, Feb. 12, 1926, Wadsworth MSS.

51. Hermann Hagedorn, *Leonard Wood, A Biography* (New York: Harper and Brothers, 1931), p. 354.

52. *New York Times,* June 4, 1920.

Senator brushed her and her dry cohorts aside. With the help of the Anti-Saloon League, however, they would defeat him yet—in six years.

Most upstate newspapers were critical of Wadsworth's anti-prohibition stand, except *The Buffalo Commercial* which applauded him for braving the jeers of the Anti-Saloon League and its bellicose state superintendent, William H. Anderson.[53] Wadsworth believed the Republican position on prohibition hurt his party. "The masses of people," he wrote a Brooklyn politico in 1923, "look upon us as the illiberal overpuritanical party, and as long as we bear such a reputation, we are going to be hurt at the polls."[54] To his friend, Ambassador James Sheffield, who had complained of searches for incoming liquor on the high seas, he wrote more forcefully: "How the world must despise us for making such asses of ourselves."[55] Many of Wadsworth's correspondents disagreed. One suggested that if he did not like the prohibition he could "go to Timbucktoo or Borio-boola-gha [sic] or somewhere else."[56]

Wadsworth and New Yorkers did not go to "Timbuckktoo." On May 31, 1923, they repealed the state's enforcement code, the Mullen-Gage Act, leaving the "Feds" the impossible enforcement job, with four federal courts handling cases of two hundred state and local courts. With the states' abandonment of enforcement, Wadsworth more than ever felt that the national prohibition effort "bedevilled our politics, multiplied corruption, and made hypocrites of millions."[57]

While national prohibition enforcement was impossible on annual appropriations of less than ten million dollars, the Anti-Saloon League shouted hosannas and elected large dry majorities to Congress in 1924. By the same pressure they got enforcement into the 1924 Republican platform. In the following year county WCTU presidents in New York convened to plan Wadsworth's defeat in 1926. So bitter were the temperance presidents about Wadsworth's betrayal that they contemplated supporting the wet Catholic, Al Smith, the then-likely Democratic senatorial candidate.

WCTU threats to Wadsworth were nothing as compared to those of the Anti-Saloon League which sought not only to eliminate the New York senator from politics but to "terrorize" the whole Republican party in New York. Chastising the party for the wet "Wadsworth-Barnes-Brown brewery bunch" which led it, League Superintendent Anderson, in late 1925, announced "war to the knife against Wadsworth." "The League

53. *Buffalo Commercial*, Apr. 24, 1922, Wadsworth MSS.
54. J.W.W. to Frank J. Price, Feb. 22, 1923, Wadsworth MSS.
55. J.W.W. to James E. Sheffield, May 9, 1923, Wadsworth MSS.
56. L. T. Brackett to J.W.W., Sept. 17, 1923, Wadsworth MSS.
57. J.W.W. to Edward W. Brown, Nov. 16, 1924, Wadsworth MSS.

asked no quarter last year [when Wadsworth put up the weak Roosevelt against the wet Smith] and will give none next year." [58]

The year 1926 broke with battle lines rapidly forming. By February 25, Anti-Saloon counsel Orville Poland threatened third party opposition to wet candidates of the major parties, especially the Republican Wadsworth.[59] The League's *Reform Bulletin* laid down a barrage of accusations alleging Wadsworth's illicit aid to wet elements. Wadsworth categorically denied influencing the appointment of prohibition agents. Next, he faced men of the cloth. "What sort of prohibition do you expect," a Washington minister cried to his congregation, "when prohibition agents are largely secured on the advice of such dripping wet Senators as those from Connecticut and New York.'" Showing disdain, Wadsworth informed the Methodist minister that his statement "was reckless." [60]

Other than girding to defeat Wadsworth, New York drys in 1926 concentrated on the Wales-Jenks bill, legislation to re-establish prohibition enforcement in New York. At hearings on the legislation, drys outnumbered wets one hundred to one and hissed Assemblyman Cuvillier who had introduced legislation which repealed the original enforcement law. While in Washington, far from the scene of battle, Wadsworth must have enjoyed Cuvillier's retort to the drys: "Shakes—that's what you are. You show yourself in your true light when you hiss." [61]

State enforcement legislation did not have a chance in New York. The state Senate, with its strong wet contingent, would not hear of it. Even the normally dry Assembly turned it down. Wadsworth pressure was blamed for that. Attention in the legislature turned to a referendum to let the people determine whether or not the federal enforcement act should be modified to permit states to determine intoxication levels of alcohol. Confident of a wet vote in New York, Wadsworth supported the referendum. The question was: when? If held in June of 1926, the drys would complain because farmers would not get to the polls in normal numbers. Then, too, a June vote would be expensive. More important, some New York City Republican leaders thought a June vote would be less injurious to the Republican candidates in the fall. "In any event," wrote Wadsworth to a Buffalo leader, "we cannot postpone this thing much longer," concluding that wets are entitled to this "gigantic petition." Wadsworth and the Republican leadership finally settled for a November referendum.[62] As the

58. Unidentified newspaper clipping, Wadsworth MSS.
59. *New York Times,* Jan. 25, 1926.
60. J.W.W. to Rev. Clarence T. Wilson, Mar. 16, 1926, Wadsworth MSS.
61. *New York Times,* Mar. 4, 1926.
62. J.W.W. to Fred A. Bradley, April 10, 1926, Wadsworth MSS.

New York Times explained it, a November referendum permitted Republicans to nominate a slate of drys and wets. "Sometimes, however, a political party can be clever to a point of its own undoing," editorialized the *Times,* concluding that "Republicans will be forced out of their silence." [63]

Dry voices, seldom silent, were raised in organized anguish. Fearing Wadsworth's wet leadership in national Republican councils, especially in the 1928 Republican convention, every conceivable dry organization in the state, ranging from the WCTU, the Prohibition party, and the New York Conference of the Methodist Church, to the Anti-Saloon League and the League of New York State's Women's Committee for Law Enforcement, jointly declared their intention to "select a candidate for the United States Senate . . . who will draw the votes of independent Republicans and secure the collective and individual support of those who are opposed to the continuation of the leadership of Senator Wadsworth." [64]

Wadsworth braced for the dry assault. From the recesses of New York City's Metropolitan Club, cousin Herbert Wadsworth "trembled" at the backlash of the present "fool laws" and suggested to "my dear Jim" a banner proclaiming the rights of personal liberty. Tell them, he urged, "if howlers can make a law that *I shall not,* they can equally well make a law that *I shall.*" [65] [Author's italics] Across town, from Morningside Heights, Columbia's President Butler put the same thing to Wadsworth more legalistically: "It is the business of law not to regulate private and personal habits but public activities and institutions. Therefore," concluded Butler, "the liquor traffic and the saloon come properly under legal control, while the private habits of individuals do not." [66] By June, Wadsworth had sent his "line" on the prohibition question to the party leaders. In short, he noted that the framers of the Constitution did not intend that private and personal habits be regulated, that a prohibition amendment should confer upon the Congress the power to freely legislate "upon the liquor traffic", that the Volstead Act could be modified to legalize the sale of wine and beer without violating the Eighteenth Amendment, and that permanent solution of the alcohol problem would come with repeal of the Eighteenth Amendment and the substitution of a system of local option such as prevailed in the Province of Quebec. [67]

Bolstering wet arguments was only one facet of Wadsworth's anti-

63. *New York Times,* Apr. 9, 1926.
64. Peter H. Odegard, *Pressure Politics, The Story of the Anti-Saloon League* (New York: Columbia University Press, 1928), p. 102.
65. Herbert Wadsworth to J.W.W., Apr. 23, 1926, Wadsworth MSS.
66. N. M. Butler to J.W.W., May 26, 1926, Wadsworth MSS.
67. J.W.W. to Clyde H. DeWitt, June 4, 1926, Wadsworth MSS.

prohibition work. He anxiously looked after the leadership of the Association Against the Prohibition Amendment. He watched the Prohibition party increase its efforts. He withstood daily Anti-Saloon League attacks. He listened to senate colleague, William E. Borah, view the "wet referendum" in New York as nullification of the Eighteenth Amendment.[68] He opposed the President's executive order authorizing the use of the injunction by local officials in the enforcement of the amendment. He interceded on behalf of a Catholic priest indicted for carrying a case of ale in his car.[69] He gave extensive explanation for his 1919 vote in favor of the Volstead Act. Then, most unhappily and most significantly, on June 7, 1926, Wadsworth received news that the state's dry organizations had joined to nominate Frank W. Cristman as an Independent Republican candidate to oppose him in November.

Cristman had served one year in the Assembly and two in the New York Senate before being defeated for renomination in 1916 by a nephew of Theodore Roosevelt. Now, as the dry candidate for the United States Senate, he would siphon off enough Republican votes to bring down the "leader of the wets." Wadsworth's defeat, noted the *Reform Bulletin*, "would be the greatest loss the wets could suffer."[70] It mattered little to the drys what Democrat would win. Some Republicans lamented. "Courage without brains," editorialized the partisan *Chicago Daily Tribune*, "is not very profitable in a deliberative body, and we think that just now the combination which Senator Wadsworth represents is too rare and too valuable to be sacrificed."[71]

5

"Everybody in politics," noted the Washington columnist, Frank Kent, "recognizes that the fight between Al and Jimmie is the main bout of the 1926 program."[72] Although a direct confrontation between Smith and Wadsworth was speculative throughout 1925 and much of 1926, there was little doubt of the high stakes of their respective campaigning. Each would test the dominance of his voice in their state and in the national councils

68. Associated Press story, July 18, 1926, Wadsworth MSS.
69. J.W.W. to Oliver D. Burden, Aug. 26, 1926, Wadsworth MSS.
70. Odegard, *op. cit.*, p. 102.
71. *Chicago Daily Tribune*, June 7, 1926, Wadsworth MSS.
72. Frank Kent, "Result May Bear Upon Presidency," Jan. 16, 1925 (newspaper clipping), Wadsworth MSS.

of their respective parties. With re-election as a wet Republican from the Empire State, Wadsworth would reach heady political heights. With a large win in New York, Smith would be assured of his party's presidential nomination.

Wadsworth's warm association with Smith, to span a half-century, suffered temporary strain as the 1926 contest approached. On election day, 1925, from his Main Street office in Geneseo, Wadsworth pondered his relationship with Al. "I write this letter," he wrote to Smith, ". . . as the only means of protesting against your persistent misrepresentation of my words and thoughts. I may add that this is the only letter of the kind I have ever felt called upon to write since I have been in public life." [73]

At issue between Wadsworth and Smith was a $100,000,000 bond amendment for public construction in New York State, just that day supported by the state's voters. Ten months previously the Governor, addressing New York realtors in Wadsworth's presence, made a plea for support in November of the bond, twice voted for by the Republican legislature. "You are here tonight as influential a Republican as I know," said Smith publicly to Wadsworth, "and now that we have got him here, in the language of our old friend, Jimmy Oliver, 'Where is he?'" Wadsworth, in reply, hedged, noting that there must be a comprehensive plan for financing state improvements, "no matter who is running the state." [74] Smith took Wadsworth's comment to be a public commitment to the bond drive. Wadsworth subsequently interpreted his remarks differently, insisting to national committeeman Charles Hilles that he had said that "the thing which should be done above all else was the drawing up a comprehensive and definite plan for state construction before the money was obligated." [75]

By the summer of 1925 Smith saw Wadsworth as the Republicans' "big gun" dragged into a scheme to "get" the Democratic governor by discrediting the bond issue, especially since the public was so supportive of the Governor's other two major programs, the elimination of railroad grade crossings and the consolidation of state agencies. [76] Wadsworth could not "travel" with the Republican legislature and the Governor on the public buildings bond issue. He felt such borrowing excessive. He did support the grade crossing bond, although grudgingly. More enthusiastically, he supported Smith's program for the consolidation of state agencies and deplored any Republican opposition to it. [77]

73. J.W.W. to Alfred Smith, Nov. 3, 1925, Wadsworth MSS.
74. New York Times, July 10, 1925.
75. J.W.W. to Charles D. Hilles, July 10, 1925, Hilles MSS.
76. New York Times, July 10, 1925.
77. J.W.W. to Elihu Root, Aug. 30, 1925, Wadsworth MSS.

The two "wets," 1926. Photographed from the original
in the Wadsworth Farms office, Main Street,
Geneseo, New York.

Wadsworth (seated, center) in the House of Representatives restaurant with, from left to right, New York Supreme Court Justice John F. Carew, Congressman George H. Tinkham of Massachusetts, and Minority Leader Bertrand Snell. *By permission of the Library of Congress.*

"You are not as clear as you state," Smith wrote in answer to Wadsworth's election-day letter, "on what was said in the adjoining room after the Realtors' dinner." Smith reminded Wadsworth that he showed no hostility to the public building program and, in fact, asked if there was any objection to it. Smith reiterated that the Republican suggestion that the Governor submit to the vote of the people a specific plan for the public buildings was ludicrous and impossible. Also, Smith wondered why prominent Republicans, such as former governor Nathan Miller, waited a year and a half before attacking it. "However," he concluded, "the people of the state have approved . . . the project and I am satisfied that it is right." [78]

The public buildings bond dispute marked only the beginning of contention between Smith and Wadsworth, although by November of 1925 neither was sure who would comprise the slate to be elected a year hence. Columnist Frank Kent thought Smith might add impetus to his presidential movement by "walking in to the Senate over the prostrate body of the Republican state leader." [79] The *Rochester Democrat and Chronicle* editorial writers suggested that Wadsworth beat Smith for the governorship and head for the White House.[80] The *New York Sun* wanted both of New York's "heroes" to be taken care of, by exchanging seats.[81] Like the *Sun*, *The Daily News* wanted both in office, but in their current positions.[82]

While the public speculated about what offices their heroes would seek in 1926, by the summer of that year Republican leaders knew that Wadsworth wanted to return to his prestigious senate seat. Thus they began their search for a gubernatorial running mate, a candidacy which Nicholas Murray Butler thought would "have several dubious and difficult characteristics," given Wadsworth's wet position.[83] Ogden Mills, Manhattan's blue stocking congressman, agreed with Butler but stood ready to accommodate the Republican leadership if they wanted a downstater on the slate.[84]

The downstate condition of the Republican party bothered Wadsworth in late 1925, as did the adamant dry element within the party upstate. Of the three Republican Assembly seats lost in 1925, two were in New York City and one in neighboring Westchester County. Also, the

78. Alfred Smith to J.W.W., Nov. 7, 1925, Wadsworth MSS.
79. Kent, *op. cit.*
80. *Rochester Democrat and Chronicle*, Apr. 2, 1924.
81. *New York Sun*, Apr. 7, 1925.
82. *New York Daily News*, Nov. 8, 1925.
83. Nicholas M. Butler to Ogden Mills, Aug. 25, 1925, Mills MSS, Library of Congress, Washington, D.C.
84. Ogden Mills to Nicholas M. Butler, Sept. 8, 1925, Mills MSS.

decisive mayoralty win for Democrat Jimmy Walker in New York City confirmed Republican slippage there. Wadsworth attributed the loss to the city's views of the state's Republicans as "illiberals," dry "bigots," and "Klan flirters." [85] Henry L. Stimson, from his law office deep in Manhattan, expressed to Wadsworth fear of "the adverse effect that such disintegration in the party may have upon your fortunes in 1926." [86]

Shortly after the beginning of the new year of 1926 Nicholas M. Butler was assured by Wadsworth that he would seek re-election. And, to dispel any public doubt, he informed the Columbia University president that he would "find some way to re-announce his wicked intentions." [87] In effect, Wadsworth did so by convening the state's party leaders in New York City to develop strategies for Republican success in 1926. These strategies included full backing for downstate county chairmen (under fire for disarray during the 1925 city campaign and for hedging on the prohibition move), and sufficient Republican support of Governor Smith's legislative program, so as not to discourage his possible retirement from the State House.[88] Wadsworth wishfully thought Smith was tired of the governorship and might resist Democratic persuasion to seek a fourth term. He noted to his friend James Sheffield in Mexico that some Democrats favored Franklin D. Roosevelt's candidacy for governor, "but the poor fellow is pretty badly crippled and I doubt if he would undertake the task." [89]

The *New York Times* disapproved editorially of the Republican strategy of ignoring prohibition, of Wadsworth's telling anti-prohibitionists that "though he is a wet, he is a Republican before he is a wet." [90] The strategy did not work. A better strategy proved to be a more candid wet expression by Wadsworth and firm Republican support of the November referendum. In the meantime, state leaders brought county leaders into line for Wadsworth and the referendum. National committeewoman Sabin worked on the women county leaders, thirty-three vice-chairmen, and claimed Wadsworth support by all but two. She told the women of Coolidge's high regard for Wadsworth and how Speaker Longworth described him as "by far the ablest man in the Senate today." [91] By May, the success of the refer-

85. J.W.W. to Sara Schuyler Butler, Dec. 8, 1925, Wadsworth MSS.

86. Henry L. Stimson to J.W.W., Apr. 9, 1925, Wadsworth MSS.

87. J.W.W. to Nicholas M. Butler, Jan. 8, 1926, Butler MSS, Columbia University Library, New York, N.Y.

88. *New York Times,* Jan. 16, 18, Feb. 3, 1926.

89. J.W.W. to George W. Pepper, J.W.W. to James Sheffield, Oct. 19, 1925, Wadsworth MSS.

90. *New York Times,* Feb. 12, 1926.

91. Mrs. Charles H. Sabin to J.W.W. (undated), Hilles MSS; *New York Times,* Mar. 13, Apr. 14, 1926.

endum strategy proved illusionary. Prohibitionists talked of reviving their party. By May also, the strategy of seeking presidential support for Wadsworth was attempted but failed. Coolidge was silent.

The Tammany delegation in Congress refused to accept Wadsworth's candidness on his wet position. "Isn't it a fact, Senator," wrote twenty-one Tammany Democrats into the Congressional Record, "that it was not until that ecclesiastical-political Klan cast you into the political discard by nominating Cristman against you that you formally declared yourself on the all-absorbing question of the hour." [92] With great hyperbole the delegation, led by Representative John Carew, accused Wadsworth of supporting the infamous Volstead Act. The Republican leadership in the House cried shame at the Democrats for their deed. Some doubt was raised as to whether the Democrats signed the letter. One Tammanyite, Emmanuel Celler, commiserated with the New York senator over the "phraseology." Democrat John O'Connor added to the hyperbole when he noted that Wadsworth's friends in the House proposed to strike the letter from the Record. O'Connor said that he might feel inclined to concur, "if you are really repentant and want to forget your dry past, or if your modesty impels you to suppress it." [93] In acid reply Wadsworth said that what O'Connor did was "of no importance to me." [94] Although the incident was closed, Wadsworth would hear much of his support of the Volstead Act.

The prohibition issue was closely related to the selection of Wadsworth's gubernatorial running mate. Republican leaders thrashed about determining criteria—wet or dry, upstater or downstater, high or moderate political status. Each criterion related to the larger issue, the Eighteenth Amendment. (For example, if the candidate were of only moderate status, wet voters might vote for Wadsworth because Republicans would have assured Smith's re-election). The leaders of both parties thrashed about in their consideration of candidates. Wadsworth would have buried the political hatchet in support of the eminent Charles E. Hughes but Hughes sought judicial appointment. Nicholas M. Butler was attractive to Wadsworth and to New York City but he enjoyed behind-the-scenes politics and saw the Wadsworth candidacy as a burden. State Supreme Court Justice George F. Thompson would have been an attractive running mate to match the emerging Democratic candidate, Justice Robert Wagner of the same court, but instead he pushed fellow Justice J. C. Cropsey. Cropsey was dry and Wadsworth blocked his candidacy. Congressman Hamilton

92. *Congressional Record,* Vol. 67, 69th Congress, 1st Session, June 9, 1926, pp. 10467–11640.

93. John J. O'Connor to J.W.W., June 11, 1926, Wadsworth MSS.

94. J.W.W. to John J. O'Connor, June 12, 1926, Wadsworth MSS.

Fish was interested but accused Wadsworth of "political buncombe and sheer hypocrisy" in his call for repeal. Wadsworth would gladly have taken his old conservative friend Charles D. Hilles, but the national committee-man's associates discouraged his candidacy, insisting to Hilles that he not be made a goat. Cornell President Jacob Schurman and Ambassador James Sheffield lacked sufficient stature to face Al Smith.[95]

"It looks very much today," wrote Ogden Mills on September 17, "as if the Republican Convention that meets a week from Monday will nomi-nate me for Governor, and reluctant as I am to consider it . . . I may have to do so in order to save Wadsworth, and prevent a defeat that might well result in the disintegration of the Party in the State." Although highly im-modest, Mills was intelligent and articulate, moderately dry and from downstate—sufficient credentials to earn Wadsworth's support at the forth-coming convention.[96]

As Republicans agreed upon Ogden Mills as their gubernatorial can-didate, Democrats seemed equally slow in the selection of their nominee. Although not constrained on the prohibition issue—Tammany was indeed wet—some Democrats wanted a deal with Republicans whereby the parties would confront Wadsworth and Smith with weak candidates. Claude Bowers, editor of the *New York Evening World,* took credit for scotching the deal by exposing it in his editorial columns. He notes in his oral memoir at Columbia University that, although Smith would not have tolerated a deal, Tammany leader George Olvaney would have, and needed to be "smoked out." "The business of barter and trade between party organiza-tions is greatly exaggerated," editorialized Bowers, "but there is enough of it to satisfy the cynic and the scoffer." Bowers warned that the people would turn against both Tammany and Smith if it did not put forth its strongest possible senatorial candidate. When Olvaney did not move, Bowers pleaded again in the *World* that "Democrats . . . subordinate everything to the one idea of finding the strongest consistent running mate for Al Smith." Shortly thereafter, Olvaney and Smith passed the word that New York Supreme Court Justice Robert Wagner, former president *pro-tem* of the state senate, was their man to face Wadsworth. Wadsworth was disap-pointed. He had hoped somewhat for an arrangement, noting, however, that "the open urging or admission of a deal to trade votes" would have been fatal. Although he viewed Wagner as "the strongest man . . . [Democrats] can put up in . . . the City," he found some solace in his

95. *New York Times,* July, Aug., Sept., 1926, *passim.*

96. Ogden Mills to Robert M. Washburn, Sept. 17, 1926, Mills MSS. When Republicans captured the State House in 1920, they re-established the convention system as New York's method of nominating state-wide candidates.

own ability to hold some wet Democratic votes in New York City, and in Wagner's limited exposure upstate.[97]

On August 4, Wadsworth opened his campaign, appropriately enough, in the prestigious old Fifth Avenue Hotel. There, where conservative New Yorkers loved to congregate, more than 1,000 partisans, mostly from the Republican Business Men, Inc., cheered their senatorial candidate. It was little wonder. Wadsworth appealed to both their conservative and wet tastes. They enjoyed being reminded of what recent Republican presidents and the Republican Congress had accomplished; the establishment of the executive budget, federal tax reductions, the adjustment of foreign debts, the reduction of the national debt, and the introduction of real protection into the tariff legislation. For another day, the speaker would save the accomplishments of good Republican leaders during Wadsworth's current term: immigration restriction, the establishment of the Aeronautics Bureau, treaty-making with Germany, the advocation of the World Court, the fight against McNary-Haugenism, and the passage of the National Defense Act, steered through the Senate by Wadsworth. Although last in his opening campaign address, prohibition was first on Wadsworth's mind, and he made the most of it.

On prohibition, Wadsworth went to the Constitution, noting that police powers were local and not national functions, that the federal control of personal habits would have been abhorrent to the Republic's founders. More specifically, the amendments were to protect the rights of citizens. "In all this list," he concluded, "we find them . . . saying to the Government "thou shalt not.' . . . It remained for one . . . the Eighteenth Amendment, to mar the symmetry of structure, to introduce a . . . subversion of fundamental principles and threaten the stability of the Federal Union of States." The audience rose as one to applaud their speaker and to applaud him again when Macy's Herbert Straus, Nicholas M. Butler, and editor Arthur Brisbane of the *Evening Journal* saw pressing need for his re-election. Brisbane predicted that a half-century later Americans would be proud of Wadsworth's conrtibution to the transition from war to peace.[98]

By the middle of August Wadsworth had addressed the dominant issues of the campaign. The wet issue so overshadowed others, however, that great papers, like the *Chicago Daily News*, supported both Wadsworth and Smith. On closer view, of course, the principals were far apart.

97. Claude Bowers, *Reminiscences of Claude Bowers* (Columbia University Oral Research Office, 1954); *New York Evening World*, July 29, Sept. 4, 1926; J.W.W. to John M. Harlan, July 24, 1926, Wadsworth MSS.

98. *New York Times*, Aug. 5, 1926; "Speech at Republican Business Men's Dinner," New York City, Aug. 4, 1926, Wadsworth MSS.

On Labor Day Smith could recite his efforts on behalf of labor—widows' pensions, workmen's compensation, shorter working hours, reduced gas rates. Wadsworth could boast authorship of little social justice legislation, other than legislation to permit relatives of aliens to enter the country and "Mothers' Aid" in the District of Columbia. In another speech, Wadsworth's conservatism showed when contending that laborers most admired those Americans "who can take a licking with a smile." [99]

As prohibition dominated the issues of the campaign, so too did it affect the organization of the campaign. While most Republicans who were asked served on the senatorial Campaign Committee, not a few declined. Israel T. Deyo of Binghamton thought Wadsworth not sufficiently in favor of law enforcement. Others found weak excuses. For example, Mrs. Eugene Meyer, Jr., of Westchester County, swore off membership "on political committees for one year." Even faithful Charles D. Hilles wondered if his name should be included, on the grounds that State Committee Chairman Morris and the executive chairman were not including their names. Wadsworth quickly disabused Hilles of his concern and added his name. The inclusion of such distinguished New Yorkers as Theodore Roosevelt, Jr., Charles E. Hughes, Henry M. Taft, Nicholas M. Butler, Colonel William J. Donovan, Lloyd C. Griscom, and Elihu Root served to compensate for the dry defections. [100]

By the middle of August, State Chairman Morris felt the dry protests upstate. He suggested that Wadsworth discuss other important issues than prohibition. [101] Wadsworth got mixed advice. One reporter for the *New York Herald Tribune* suggested to Wadsworth that he stress the prohibition issue in order to give the modificationists a head start before the drys woke up. [102] The most vitriolic of counsel came from Hamilton Fish. He scored Wadsworth publicly for dictating Republican policy, calling the forthcoming referendum a fraud. Wadsworth privately called Fish a "faker." [103]

Suffragists and the Ku Klux Klansmen joined the prohibitionists in their opposition to Wadsworth, although the former did so without benefit of the League of Women Voters. The League, formed by the suffragists

99. "Speech to be delivered by Senator James W. Wadsworth, Jr., at Labor Day celebration," Sept. 6, 1926, Wadsworth MSS.

100. J.W.W. to Elihu Root, July 10, 1926, Root to J.W.W., July 13, 1926, Israel R. Deyo to J.W.W., July 28, 1926, J.W.W. to C. D. Hilles, July 28, 1926, Wadsworth MSS; *New York Times*, Sept. 3, 1926.

101. William Hoppin to J.W.W., Aug. 13, 1926, Wadsworth MSS.

102. John E. Nevin to J.W.W., July 22, 1926, Wadsworth MSS.

103. *New York Times*, Sept. 1, 1926; J.W.W. to William G. Means, Sept. 14, 1926, Wadsworth MSS.

after the women won the vote, took no part in the campaign as an organization. Many of its members, however, supported Cristman or Wagner. The pro-Wagner support was an attempt to make their opposition to Wadsworth "two-fold." The Ku Klux Klan, at first offering aid to the patrician, Protestant, Republican senator, turned with a vengeance on Wadsworth when he spurned both their aid and their dry entreaties. *The Fellowship Forum*, the eastern Klan organ, urged New York's 2,000 Klansmen to vote for "Cristman, that bold, fearless, clean and courageous candidate" and at the same time "wing a bird which does not at present fly in harmony with good citizenship." Besides Wadsworth's wet record, the Klan was distressed by his attempt to tamper with the immigration quotas "when every red-blooded American was striving to prevent the destruction of the splendid 1924 Immigration law." The Klan, however, was of limited political force in New York, as compared to Pennsylvania and western states. Still, as Wadsworth campaigned in the Southern Tier, the large Klan letters painted on many barns demonstrated some KKK strength.[104]

By convention time Wadsworth and the Republican leadership had determined upon Congressman Ogden L. Mills of Manhattan as its gubernatorial candidate. In retaliation for engineering a wet slate and only a moderate enforcement plank, drys denied Wadsworth 81 delegates out of the 1,317 delegate votes cast. Most delegates, however, enjoyed Judge Thompson's invitation that they "leave the sidewalks of New York" for "that furrow turned by God, the Genesee Valley," the home of James Wadsworth.

While Republicans convened at Madison Square Garden, Democrats met in Syracuse. There Franklin Roosevelt, in the keynote address, while noting Wadsworth's charm, tagged him as the greatest example of "Bourbon reaction that the state had ever produced." Smith had his way in platform and slate. As expected, on prohibition the Democrats opposed the Volstead Act and called for a resounding "yes" vote on the referendum. Robert Wagner was nominated to oppose Wadsworth.[105]

Robert F. Wagner, like Smith, came from the sidewalks of New York and, also like Smith, represented a new urban progressivism. Reared in a tenement basement on the upper East Side, when he was ten years of age he rose at 4:00 o'clock in the morning to deliver newspapers. He differed

104. *New York Times*, Sept. 20, 26, 1926.

105. In addition to Wadsworth, the Republicans nominated Seymour Lowman for Lt. Governor, Albert Ottinger for Attorney General, and Vincent B. Murphy for Controller. Besides Smith, the Democratic slate of lesser candidates consisted of Edwin Corning for Lt. Governor, Benjamin Stolz for Attorney General, and Morris Tremain for Controller.

from Smith in his formal education. Wagner attended the College of the
City of New York and graduated with honors. Like Smith, he was a
protégé of Tammany Boss Murphy, moving from the Assembly to the
Senate, where he was elected majority leader in 1911. In 1919 Wagner was
elected to the state Supreme Court.[106]

Smith's comments on his running mate's nomination ended all "deal"
talk. "I have a great deal of respect for the senior Senator from New York,
for his integrity and for his family," said Smith, "but I don't care to see him
remain in the United States Senate, because he does not fairly represent
in my opinion, the progressive thought of the state." That Wagner was no
paper candidate was immediately apparent as he challenged the "reactionary policy that has characterized the whole public life of Senator
Wadsworth" and his political sincerity and intellectual candor.[107]

By contrast with Democratic exhortations, Wadsworth's acceptance
speech was an epistle of equanimity. "We see a vast multitude with faces
uplifted; in their features we note the stamp of confidence and determination and in their eyes the light of never perishing hope. An optimistic, an
adventurous and restless people, we are, cooled and steadied in great crises
by an extraordinary quality of self-restraint inherited from the fathers and
long since become a tradition." Wadsworth ascribed such equanimity to
the Republican transition from war to peace, to the new budget, the tariff,
the reduction of federal taxation, the settlement of foreign debts, the reduction of the national debts, all great Republican measures. As for criticism
of Wadsworth by Franklin Roosevelt and Wagner, the senior senator
pointed to his support of workmen's compensation to illustrate the absurd-
ity of their charge that he was reactionary. Rather than opposing workmen's compensation, as chairman of the Republican Steering Committee
Wadsworth saw the Cummins Longshoremen's bill through to passage, just
as some years previously, as Speaker of the Assembly, he had supported the
first workmen's compensation legislation enacted in the State of New
York. While silent on prohibition in his acceptance speech, as if not to
surface latent opposition, Wadsworth made implicit reference to it. Man's
fallibility, he noted, impelled him "to search for the truth all the more
diligently. And I shall not boast that I have always lived up to this ideal
of service. All I can say is that during all these years I have had it before
me. I shall hold it there always. I must do so, for above all else I want to be
able to look you in the face as I work and when I have finished, I want to

106. J. Joseph Huthmacher, *Senator Robert E. Wagner, and the Rise of
Urban Liberalism* (New York: Atheneum, 1968), Ch. 1–4, *passim*.
107. *New York Times*, Sept. 28–Oct. 4, 1926.

go to my home and be able to say to those who have given me a precious tradition, that I have not knowingly betrayed it."[108]

Throughout his legislative career Wagner reflected a social consciousness consistent with his probing criticism of James Wadsworth during the 1926 campaign. Although reaching for political issues to put him on the political offensive, Wagner quite naturally questioned Wadsworth's support of vast Republican primary expenditures in Pennsylvania and Illinois, his vote against the Adamson Act, his opposition to Louis Brandeis on the Supreme Court, his silence on the Harding scandals, his vote against the Federal Farm Loan Act, and his reluctance to restrain coal operators in the great coal strike of 1926. Just as naturally, Wagner pointed to general press criticism of Wadsworth's opposition to the Federal Reserve Act, income tax legislation, war profits taxation, tariff reduction, woman suffrage, and the direct primary. Wagner hit hardest, however, at Wadsworth's record on prohibition, trying to prove that the senior senator had come only lately to the wet position. Although grateful to Cristman for deflecting dry votes from Wadsworth, Wagner understood well the need to secure wet Democratic votes, downstate and upstate, which might go to the popular senator. By late October Wagner approached demogoguery. He talked of Wadsworth's "double dealing" on prohibition; how he voted against the Eighteenth Amendment, yet for the Volstead Act; how he now claimed a wet position, yet would not advise Republicans how to vote in the referendum.[109]

Wadsworth's campaign was almost wholly defensive. Forced by Wagner and the urban centers in the state to demonstrate the welfare aspects of his record and his opposition to the Eighteenth Amendment, Wadsworth had difficulty gaining the offensive. Although limited by comparison with Wagner's welfare stand, Wadsworth's record was, for that day, plausible. He justifiably pointed to his efforts on behalf of workmen's compensation for longshoremen, civil service retirement legislation, mothers' aid in the District of Columbia, post office pay raises, retirement benefit for army and navy nurses, and the admission of wives and children of immigrants into the country. Noting that his opponent ignored his welfare efforts, Wadsworth concluded: "Judge Wagner had better learn what has been going on at Washington before he tells the people about it." Still, Wagner's criticism was telling. Wadsworth was on sounder ground in answering the charge that he was a "fake wet." Indignantly, he argued

108. "Acceptance Speech," Madison Square Garden, 1926, Wadsworth MSS.
109. Huthmacher, *op. cit.*

that with the adoption of the Eighteenth Amendment in 1919, his "reverence for the Constitution" impelled him to support some kind of enforcement legislation. Thus, he voted for the Volstead Act over the President's veto, as the most practical legislation.[110] Quite correctly, Wadsworth pointed to his courageous record of opposition to the Eighteenth Amendment throughout the 1920s. At the height of the Anti-Saloon League's power, in 1923, he dared to call the Eighteenth Amendment "a fundamental error" behind the prevalent corruption and hypocrisy in the country. And, although hesitant to recommend a stand on the November referendum, by campaign's end he publicly declared his intentions to support it.

By late October, Wadsworth had made 86 speeches, averaging 35 minutes per speech, in 44 counties. He did it in a blue bus, lent to him by Mayor John W. Stevens of Fulton. In no other way could Wadsworth have covered so easily 2,500 miles.[111] "You'll love rambling and roaring through the country in our big bus," he wrote AHW. "It's great, and so comfortable—much more so than an ordinary car. And it makes 50 miles an hour just as easy." [112]

The Wadsworth campaign rolled like the blue bus, smoothly most of the time. Years of party service and loyalty brought in IOUs from the Niagara Frontier to the Finger Lakes country, through the Mohawk Valley to greater New York. The Wadsworth Club of Erie County alone distributed 317,00 pieces of literature, 16,000 posters, 350 signs, and 16,654 letters.[113] The upstate headquarters in Syracuse, under long-time associate Frederick Hammond, emulated the Erie County activity on an even larger scale. Remnants of William Barnes's organization in Albany made its last ditch effort in that county for years to come. W. W. Hoppin, manager of the Wadsworth campaign committee, operated out of the Hotel Belmont in New York City. From the road, Wadsworth lent words of encouragement and advice to various centers of Wadsworth campaigning. "You should get some man of the Jewish faith," he wrote to Hoppin, "to work in and out of the headquarters from now to election day—a man who can reach the Jewish people of the lower and upper East side and in the Bronx,— man who is one of them, can mingle with them and work for us. . . . And I think you should have an Italian-American doing the same kind of

110. *New York Times*, Sept. 28–Oct. 4; *New York World*, Sept. 28–Oct. 4, 1926.

111. *Ibid.*; also see Wadsworth campaign speeches, Oct. 7 (Glens Falls), Oct. 19 (Rochester), undated speeches, Wadsworth MSS.

112. J.W.W. to Alice Hay Wadsworth, Friday (undated), 1926, Wadsworth MSS.

113. Frank A. Born to J.W.W., Oct. 30, 1926, Wadsworth MSS.

work among the Italians—a good mixer." [114] To Mrs. Sabin, who saw the candidate's campaign biography to press, Wadsworth wrote, "If Holthusen [the author] needs more help I can arrange it through a friend of mine in Buffalo a little later on." [115] Wadsworth also looked after the testimonials— from Hughes, Root, Charles Dawes, Herbert Hoover, and an assortment of senators. Wadsworth particularly appreciated Root's recollection that ex-Vice President Marshall viewed Wadsworth as the Senate's most competent member.[116] Wagner, however, had a field day with the Hughes testimony, noting the elder statesman's inconsistent suggestion that Wadsworth be re-elected for the same reason that Smith should be defeated—long tenure in office.[117] Coolidge's testimony was of limited value. The best Wadsworth aides could do was to quote a week-old statement of the President that as a United States senator, Wadsworth "is not excelled in the Senate of the United States," and to note that Wadsworth, not Cristman, had been invited to the President's Adirondack retreat, White Pine Camp.[118] The President probably had serious doubts about the New York senator's wet position.

Franklin Roosevelt's wife, Eleanor, loomed large as a problem in the campaign, so much so that nearly a half-century later, Stuart Symington still expressed shock at her behavior.[119] Apparently, Eleanor's evil deed consisted of reminding the public that in 1914 her Uncle Theodore said, "it is rarely that a public man champions the right of big business to do wrong as openly as Mr. Wadsworth." When Wadsworth's friends insisted that T.R. was referring to the elder Wadsworth, Eleanor corrected them. "I feel it is incumbent," she said, "on me to defend the truth of these quotations as I had them looked up and have given them to a number of people." Other caveats of Eleanor's hardly assuaged the Wadsworth family, e.g., "We all of us have incidents in the past we would least prefer to remember, and isn't it amusing that father and son should have the same tendencies." More devastatingly, if less publicly, Eleanor, on one occasion, shrugged Wadsworth off as "a country squire of the 17th century in politics . . . in the 20th century . . . [with a] Marie Antoinette type of mind." [120]

114. J.W.W. to W. W. Hoppin, Oct. 3, 1926, Wadsworth MSS.

115. J.W.W. to Mrs. Charles H. Sabin, Aug. 30, 1926, Wadsworth MSS.

116. E. Root to Merwin Hart, 1926, Wadsworth MSS.

117. *Rochester Democrat and Chronicle*, Oct. 28, 1926.

118. Unidentified newspaper clipping, Wadsworth MSS; *New York World*, Aug. 30, 1926.

119. Conversation with Stuart Symington, summer 1968; while Symington would not identify Eleanor Roosevelt, the author readily deduced that she was the subject of criticism in the conversation.

120. *New York Times*, Oct. 16, 1926; Joseph P. Lash, *Eleanor and Franklin* (New York: W. W. Norton and Co., 1971), p. 310.

The Cristman candidacy, however, was Wadsworth's real problem. Backed by the Anti-Saloon League, the WCTU, most of the rural press, the Protestant clergy and the remnants of the Prohibition party, Cristman saw his goal in sight—to stop Wadsworth and blunt the national repeal movement. The prohibition stakes were high, however, and as the campaign progressed, drys enlarged their anti-Wadsworth repertoire. In addition to alleging Wadsworth's connections with unsavory liquor interests, drys charged him with excessive drinking. The origin of the charge, which reached New York City and other areas of the state, was traced to the Genesee Valley and to one Mrs. Edward Whitney of York. Wadsworth got an admission of Mrs. Whitney's role in the smudge campaign from her husband. Mr. Whitney expressed surprise that it had gone so far. Following the conversation, Wadsworth attempted to still the rumor with a certified letter of complaint to the Whitneys. Prohibitionists in the valley seemed as rabid as any in the state.[121]

As the election approached, the abuse Wadsworth suffered increased. The Reverend Clinton Howard, the "dry orator" of Rochester, chose Geneseo's Village Hall as the place to attack "Referendum Jim" as unstable as "a reed shaken in the wind" and as a "tin soldier" for failing to accompany Geneseo's cavalry troop to the Mexican border and for resigning from the troop in order to avoid service in France.[122] Contingents from the State Police barracks and Troop M restrained the local citizenry. From across the state, on New York City's east side, Wagner demagogically scored his opponent for legislating plutocracy in a way to cause "the blood of the bravest and the brains of the best . . . to perish within the lifetime of children now living."[123] Wadsworth, "hoarse, white, exhausted," spoke in a far quieter vein to the cheers of Rochester's partisans in the "big auditorium" in Rochester. Tears, streaming down the Boss's face, portended the election returns.[124]

6

Shortly before 11:00 A.M. on election day Wadsworth and AHW voted in a loft over a blacksmith shop in Groveland Station. The scene,

121. J.W.W. to Edward Whitney, July 10, 1926; J.W.W. to Mrs. Charles W. Sabin, July 10, 1926, Wadsworth MSS.

122. New York Times, Nov. 2, 1926.

123. Rochester Democrat and Chronicle, Oct. 31, 1926.

124. Alden Hatch, The Wadsworths of the Genesee (New York: Coward-McCann, Inc., 1959), p. 223.

repeated by rural folk across the state, confirmed the Boss's foreboding. More than 190,000 upstaters, mostly Republicans, defected to support the dry Cristman. Had Cristman not run, Wadsworth would easily have gotten enough votes to cover Wagner's plurality of 125,000 votes. Wagner was exuberant. "Here I was a poor immigrant, coming to this country at eight years of age, and America . . . gives me the highest office possible. . . . I hold no grievance," Wagner concluded, "against . . . James Wadsworth, who, to my mind, has conducted a very fair campaign against me." [125]

Regrets for Wadsworth's defeat were effusive. "Even his opponents will regret . . . his retirement," noted the pro-Wagner *New York World*.[126] "I am profoundly disappointed and grieved," wrote Nicholas Murray Butler. The *World* attributed the defeat to Smith's "progressive and alert leadership." Butler blamed the drys and the mid-term tide running against Republicans across the country.[127] Both the *World* and Butler were right. Smith's and Wagner's progressivism, particularly when contrasted with Wadsworth's consistent conservatism, appealed more to New York's evolving urbanism. Yet, had Cristman not run, Wadsworth undoubtedly would have been returned to the Senate.

As noted, Wadsworth's aristocratic strain was reflected by his commitment to principles—constitutionalism, responsibility, republicanism, conservatism, sovereignty, preparedness, anti-statism, and internationalism. Yet the idea of commitment to principle itself loomed perhaps largest among his conservative and aristocratic manifestations. Such was most dramatically illustrated in his wet sacrificial stance in 1926. On the issue he was a conservative twice over, adhering to a basic belief and deploring statism resulting from the amendment. The aristocratic strain was reflected by the political courage of his sacrifice. Howard Smith, Virginian and powerful (and conservative) chairman of the House Rules Committee in the decade following Wadsworth's tenure on the committee, captured the meaning of the act. He eulogized Wadsworth profusely to the author and when asked why he did so, stared incredulously and referred to the principle sacrifice of 1926.

Had Wadsworth been re-elected to the United States Senate, he might have been his party's presidential candidate in 1928. Columnist Frank Kent and son-in-law Stuart Symington believed so even if the Senator did not. Wadsworth did uniquely meet, almost without exception, what Clin-

125. *New York Times,* Nov. 3–4, 1926.
126. *New York World,* Nov. 3–4, 1926.
127. Nicholas M. Butler to J.W.W., Nov. 3, 1926, Butler MSS.

ton Rossiter much later considered the many criteria for presidential suitability. And to compensate for exceptions, Wadsworth's political base was the nation's largest state; his "establishment" connections were superb; and a 1926 senatorial victory might well have made his wet status an attractive presidential qualification in 1928.

Far from leading to the presidency, Wadsworth's political demise in the weeks following his defeat was pronounced. "It seems to be agreed," noted one columnist, "that he is a much diminished figure and certainly he is no longer regarded or referred to as the party boss [in New York]." [128] Henceforth, Wadsworth and Hilles shared Republican authority with Ogden Mills. The downstate aristocrat did his best to downgrade the defeated senator, and when Hoover became President in 1929—Mills had worked hard for him while Wadsworth was indifferent—Mills overshadowed the Geneseoan. But Wadsworth had his lieges, like Hilles, and his demise was short-lived. [129]

128. Frank R. Kent, "The Great Game of Politics," political column from unidentified newspapers, Wadsworth MSS.

129. Ogden Mills to George Morris, Dec. 6 and Dec. 30, 1926, Mills MSS; Judith Stein, "The Birth of Liberalism in New York State, 1932–1938" (Yale University, 1968), Ph.D. dissertation, Ch. I, *passim.*

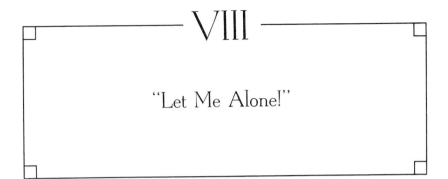

VIII

"Let Me Alone!"

1

At 12 o'clock noon on Monday, December 6, 1926, Vice President Dawes convened the "lame duck" session of the Sixty-ninth Congress. Then the chaplain prayed: "Help us this morning to realize that Thy grace is always sufficient. Grant to each one in the engagement of grave responsibilities to recognize dependence upon Thee." Wadsworth had witnessed many a convening session of the Senate of the United States. This was to be his last. Yet he was no lame duck, "a defeated Senator who sits tamely down after election and twiddles his thumbs." On the contrary, he seemed more brisk than ever. "In the one month that has elapsed in the present session of Congress," reported the *New York Evening Post*, "Senator Wadsworth has already accomplished as much as many a Senator in the whole term."[1]

The *Evening Post* referred particularly to Wadsworth's almost single-handed effort to defeat ratification of the Geneva Gas Protocol of 1925, and to secure amendment of the 1924 immigration legislation. Americans expected quick action on the gas treaty, negotiated in Geneva on June 19, 1925, and presented in the Senate at the opening of the session. Signed by twenty-nine representatives to the League of Nations conference, including the American, the treaty was exactly similar to Article V of the Washington Arms Conference treaty of 1922. Wadsworth had grave doubts about it. Having viewed as worthless the 1922 Washington Arms convention prohibiting the use of gas, he opposed gas prohibition even more vehemently now. On him devolved the responsibility for leading the opposition in the Senate, with no little help from David Reed of Pennsylvania. He had redoubtable opposition, vigorously led by the Foreign Relations Committee chairman, William Borah, and a Democratic leader, Thomas

1. *New York Evening Post*, undated clipping, Wadsworth MSS, Library of Congress, Washington, D.C.

201

Walsh of Montana. "I count the country lucky," Wadsworth informed his colleagues in the Senate, "that the . . . [1922] treaty has not yet been ratified in such a fashion as to compel the United States to adhere to its provisions." Wadsworth built his case well. "It should be remembered that when war breaks out, the treaties and conventions perish." He noted that although the Hague Convention of 1907 forbade the use of poison gas, Germany, a party to that convention, ignored it in 1915. "And, were we fighting for our life," he confessed "[we too] would seize any . . . military effective . . . weapon." [2]

The debate was Wadsworth's last important senate floor effort as Military Affairs chairman. He exploded the myths of the cruelty of gas. He noted that information which had not been available in 1922 demonstrated a contrary view. Of World War I weapons, gas was the least cruel. Of "70,000 gas casualties from the 224,000 total wounded," only 200 died on the field of battle, quite in contrast to the number of 34,248 killed "as the result of high explosives, bullets, bombs, and shrapnel wounds." He examined his data from many angles. Out of 100 Americans hit by bullet, shell, or shrapnel, 24 died. Of 100 gassed, two died. Of the 76 remaining of those who suffered from the gun-fire wounds, many were maimed for life. Of the remaining 98 who were gassed, practically all recovered. As for tubercular consequences of gas asphyxiation, there were reported only 173 cases of tuberculosis in 1918 among the 70,552 gas casualties.[3]

Borah, not often made uncomfortable in senate debate, admitted that treaties are broken in self-defense; more damaging to his fight for the protocol, he argued that even with senate ratification the United States could develop its gas arsenal. Wadsworth responded incredulously: "I do not see how we could look the rest of the world in the face." Borah ignored the response. Walsh spelled the Foreign Relations chairman. Then Borah took on David Reed of Pennsylvania, no easy task. Reed had charts all over the well of the Senate, largely to corroborate Wadsworth's opposition. The Senate went into executive session and defeated the treaty. A half-century later some Americans would agonize over the treaty's non-ratification in 1926, not, however, without still confronting many of the Wadsworth arguments.[4]

Wadsworth succeeded equally in swaying the Senate in amendment of the Johnson Immigration Act of 1924. As noted in the previous chapter,

2. *Ibid.*; also, *New York Times*, Feb. 7, June 3, 1922, June 6, 8, 1925; *Congressional Record*, Vol. 68, 69th Congress, 2nd Session, 1926, pp. 143–151.

3. *Congressional Record*, 68, 145.

4. *Ibid.*, pp. 145–146; *New York Times*, Oct. 12, 1970.

the New Yorker was concerned for aliens from eastern and southern Europe who were frequently denied reunion with loved ones by the act. By quiet persuasion, he achieved amendment to the act permitting the reuniting of alien families, only to have the legislation struck down by presidential veto. In time, after the New Yorker's retirement from the Senate, the legislative amendment did pass.

Supply bills regarding the military were, of course, the least difficult for Wadsworth. Eight years as chairman of the Military Affairs Committee paid off. Just prior to adjournment on March 4, he got appropriations for the construction and maintenance of barracks, officers' quarters, and hospitals, and a needed "bump" in the promotion lists.

The McNary-Haugen bill particularly kept Wadsworth far from "lame" in his closing senate days. For years the New York senator, who represented four times as many farmers as did Senator McNary of Oregon, smarted under the price-fixing demands of McNary and western farmers. Most offensive to Wadsworth, the McNary-Haugen bill, which had been defeated in 1924, was advocated even more vigorously in February of 1927. Under the law, the government was to compute the parity price of seven basic commodities, using for purposes of comparison the prosperous agriculture years, 1910–1914. The government, through the Agricultural Export Corporation, would then buy surplus commodities at the parity price and sell them on the world market at whatever price it could get. To cover the loss involved, farmers were to pay an equalization fee, or tax, on every bushel of wheat or other items they sold. But the fee so paid, it was assumed, would be less than the benefits derived from the domestic price. A Federal Farm Board of twelve members was to oversee the act's implementation.[5]

Wadsworth spoke at length against the farm bill. "With great hesitation," he noted, "I inject a personal note into my discussion. I am in this farming business myself, and I should hate to have any Federal Board manage my business for me. I should hate to have to take my share of the tax burden that is to be imposed upon the producers of this bill that is to become law. I should hate to have to encounter the annoyances, the restrictions, the red tape, and the delay which every producer of wheat, for example, will necessarily encounter if the board ever puts into operation the provisions of this bill with respect to that crop."

5. Theodore Saloutos and John D. Hicks, *Agricultural Discontent in the Middle West, 1900–1939* (Madison: University of Wisconsin Press, 1951), Ch. XIII, *passim*; John D. Hicks, *Republican Ascendancy, 1921–1933* (New York: Harper and Brothers, 1960), p. 198.

In detail Wadsworth described how heavy would be the hand of government on the shoulder of every wheat farmer in the country. "The imposition of the equalization fee and the necessary surveillance by government will establish the greatest bureaucracy ever known in this country. I am wondering," he continued somewhat emotionally, "how a farmer will feel when, having prepared his ground and sowed his seed and then harvested it and threshed it, he takes it to the local mill—where a great deal of wheat goes—the local flour mill, which exists in the typical village in all wheat growing states, and there offers it for sale. It is his property. It has been produced on land owned or rented by him. It has been produced with his labor." [6]

Wadsworth's avoidance of monetary benefits to farmers under the proposed legislation was not lost on his colleagues. Frank Gooding of Idaho reminded him that a farmer would gladly take the trouble Wadsworth described to get "32 cents more in his pocket for a bushel of wheat than he will get under this bill." (Indeed, the price of wheat had declined 85.5 cents per bushel in the previous seven years.) But Wadsworth did not believe the farmer would get 32 cents more, and he would not be diverted by Gooding's questions about the farmers' present low price predicament. "The thing I dread," he concluded, "in this proposition in addition to the constitutional objections which have been mentioned, and the thing that appalls me most is that it represents another attempt to take out of the hands of men the right to conduct their own business in their own way; and if I had my say about it, as a man engaged in these businesses as a serious undertaking, I would vote to take out of this bill every farm product which I raise and say, 'Let me alone!' " [7]

When the vote on the McNary-Haugen bill came, Wadsworth was dejected by the 51 to 43 margin of victory for its proponents, and by the House passage. He was elated, however, by Coolidge's quick veto. The President agreed with him that the bill asked the government to do what the government had no right to do. "It called for price fixing, for an improper delegation of taxing power, and for the creation of a vast and cumbersome bureaucracy." More specifically, Coolidge saw that, with the bill's price-fixing provisions, farmers would overproduce to take advantage of the higher prices.[8] Throughout the twenties Wadsworth had consistent answers to the farmers' plight: reduced local taxation, co-operative management of surpluses, and diversified farming.[9] Of course, eastern farmers like Wads-

6. *Congressional Record*, 68, 3431–3432.
7. *Ibid.*, p. 3433.
8. Hicks, *op. cit.*, p. 199.
9. J.W.W. to J. A. Livingston, May 7, 1926, Wadsworth MSS.

worth did not have the transportation and storage costs which many western farmers found burdensome. Also, few farmers anywhere had behind them a century and a half of access to fertile lands like those in the Genesee Valley.

On February 18, 1927, Wadsworth rose to defend Ambassador James R. Sheffield against charges of manifesting a hard-line and pro-oil interest bias in his relations with Mexican officials. The incident was an appropriate one for the closing of his senate career. It contained several Wadsworthean elements—Ivy League associations, political camaraderie, hard-line internationalism, big business bias and Republican loyalty.

On August 26, 1924, President Coolidge had appointed James Rockwell Sheffield Ambassador to Mexico. He was politically deserving and an intimate friend of prominent New York and national party leaders, particularly Wadsworth. Aside from having Yale in their backgrounds, Sheffield and Wadsworth both tied their political fortunes to their party's conservative segments. While in lucrative New York City law practice, Sheffield consistently served his party over the years and earned the gratitude and the association of James Wadsworth. His political reward, although unsought—was the Mexican ambassadorship.[10]

Sheffield's tenure as ambassador from 1924 to 1927 marked a watershed in United States-Latin American relations, "for he was the last articulate exponent of traditional policies prior to those advocates of new departure whose efforts came to fruition in the Good Neighbor Policy."[11] In this he was one with Wadsworth, his constant correspondent and defender.

Important during the Sheffield tenure in Mexico, and offensive to many Americans, particularly to the ambassador, was that country's recent revolution and attendant expropriation of foreign-owned land, radicalization of the labor movement, and rampant anti-clericalism. In regard to the expropriation of foreign land, more than fifty percent of which was American-owned, a 1923 Bucareli Conference of Mexican and American representatives somewhat eased Sheffield's job when he appeared in Mexico a year later, but not much. The conference brought agreement that the United States would accept Mexican bonds for expropriated lands, that Mexico would limit the size of its various expropriations, that a special commission would negotiate claims of American citizens against the revolutionary government, and most importantly, that the nation's new consti-

10. James J. Horn, "Diplomacy by Ultimatum. Ambassador Sheffield and Mexican-American Relations, 1924–1927" (State University of New York, Buffalo, N.Y., 1969), Ph.D. dissertation, pp. 18–43.
11. Ibid., p. i.

tution would be interpreted so as to protect Americans against the expropriation of land they had purchased and developed before the 1917 revolution. Still, the crude, socialistic and anti-Christian aspects of the new Mexican regime were repugnant to Sheffield. He, like Wadsworth, had sat at William Graham Sumner's feet at Yale and absorbed much of the great teacher's Social Darwinism. Sheffield carried the "white man's burden" to Mexico, and with it an arrogance prevalent in his class. While in Mexico, he was much more comfortable with the foreign colony, Mexico's upper classes, and the old Mexican leaders than with the new revolutionary crowd. He resented particularly President Plutarco Calles. When Calles, almost immediately upon Sheffield's arrival, told the ambassador that foreign capitalists could pay higher taxes and wages, Sheffield just as quickly warned Calles against it. Compulsory unionization of all employees, including those hired by American employers, also offended Sheffield. The ambassador, with more justification, was offended by the Mexican government's repression of the Catholic Church and also by its interference in the internal affairs of Nicaragua. Sheffield's known concerns and warnings seemed to Calles contrary to the guarantees of former Secretary of State Hughes that the United States would respect the revolution. Calles was right, for Sheffield's hard line was translated into a public warning from Secretary of State Kellogg. The Mexican response to the Kellogg lines was loud and clear. Calles and the Mexican press now said the Bucareli Conference lacked treaty force. Both Calles and his country's press seemed to say that Mexico would confiscate any American land, even that purchased prior to the revolution.[12]

Sheffield's correspondence with Wadsworth increased perceptibly when Kellogg recoiled from the Mexican reaction to the hard line suggested by the ambassador and when the Secretary of State called in "old Mexican" hands for new policy determinations regarding Mexico. Particularly was Sheffield angered by conciliatory State Department notes sent directly to Calles, bypassing Sheffield. "Just at the moment," he wrote Wadsworth on March 4, 1926, "the papers are full down here of what they consider an affront on the part of the Department of State to me." Expressing the hope that the President and the Secretary of State would help him with a statement of confidence, Sheffield asked Wadsworth about senate reaction and concluded: "I have sought no credit for anything I have done but I have tried to be a red-blooded American south of the Rio Grande just as I have always tried to be north of the Rio Grande, and whether I go back in a pullman car berth or in a pine box, I shall not change my point of view as to my duty as American Ambassador." [13]

Indeed, Sheffield did not change his point of view. Very likely, assurances from Wadsworth that he had the confidence of the State Department made him more adamant. "My good friend [Undersecretary of State] Joe Grew," Wadsworth wrote Sheffield, "assured me . . . that the Department . . . had the highest regard for you." [14] Still, the ambassador was uneasy. Wadsworth again assured him. "I have . . . talked very recently with Secretary Kellogg," he wrote to Sheffield. "He gave me most emphatic and explicit assurances that he was entirely satisfied with the work of our Ambassador to Mexico." [15]

Sheffield kept up a barrage of messages to Kellogg and the President, while at the same time urging Wadsworth to get his point of view to the Senate, and asking Nicholas Murray Butler to talk to important Republicans around the country. To all, in various ways, Sheffield urged Mexican negotiations by ultimatum, convinced as he was that the hard-line approach would bring Mexico around and make military intervention unnecessary. By February of 1927, Republicans such as William E. Borah, and Democrats such as Thomas J. Heflin of Alabama, had had enough of Sheffield's line. Aside from their fear of military intervention—Woodrow Wilson had tried that unsuccessfully—they doubted whether the procurement of oil was worth it, especially given the recent oil scandals of the Harding administration. The press also was grumbling.[16] When Heflin inferred on the floor of the Senate that the Sheffield line might well "blunder" the country into war, Wadsworth retorted: "I resent the innuendo that he has been faithless to his trust." [17] To make matters worse for Sheffield, President Calles requested from Coolidge a third party from America with whom to negotiate. He also sent to President Coolidge some previously intercepted communications between Kellogg and Sheffield which well documented the latter's hard line.[18]

It was little wonder that talk of Sheffield's resignation filled the air. Sheffield himself talked of resigning. "I secretly cherish," he wrote to Wadsworth on December 3, 1926, "the hope that things may be in such shape that I may properly ask to be relieved before summer—this of course

13. James R. Sheffield to J.W.W., Mar. 4, 1926, Wadsworth MSS.
14. J.W.W. to James R. Sheffield, Mar. 25, 1926, Wadsworth MSS.
15. J.W.W. to James R. Sheffield, Apr. 12, 1926, Wadsworth MSS.
16. Horn, *op. cit.,* pp. 158–189.
17. *Congressional Record,* 68, 4124.
18. Horn, *op. cit.,* pp. 158–189; Howard F. Cline, *The United States and Mexico* (Cambridge, Mass.: Harvard University Press, 1965), p. 210.

in strictest confidence—because I have a fortieth reunion at New Haven at the same time my boy has his triennial and I am inclined to think that we had better both be there to keep our eyes upon each other." [19]

Sheffield's hope to resign was fulfilled "before summer" of 1927. The President had not asked for it. In fact, he publicly applauded Sheffield's service, as did Wadsworth. Several months following his resignation, Sheffield summed up for Wadsworth in a paragraph his experience and his expectation regarding the future of United States-Mexico relations. It symbolized well the old diplomacy:

> I consider the appointment of Ambassador Morrow wise. I know him intimately and regard him highly. Of course, the Mexican Government will attempt to flatter and deceive him, and they may get away with it for a time. But eventually, I believe, Dwight will see through the deceit and hypocrisy and understand the real hostility and Bolshevic tendencies that in reality control their national policies. Any American Ambassador can make himself popular with the Mexican Government if he is content to simply utter mild protests, with expressions of sympathy, for what they are outwardly attempting to achieve. But no American Ambassador with red blood in his veins can ever be popular with the Mexican Government who stands up for the rights of American citizens in that country. The Indian in their make-up is predominant![20]

To the end of Sheffield's service in Mexico, Wadsworth remained loyal, doing what he could to defend him. President Coolidge also defended him, at the same time attempting to avert the dangers Sheffield seemed to stir up there. In time, however, the country and Wadsworth learned from the Sheffield experience that hard-line, special-interest diplomacy in the Americas was passé. Soon Ambassador Dwight Morrow would successfully take a friendly tack in United States-Mexican relations, one tolerant of the latter's recent revolution. For Wadsworth, the Sheffield affair seemed to mark the end of his chauvinism in foreign affairs. His trek to internationalism was pronounced by the middle 1930s.

On March 3, as the sun broke through the Senate's great glass skylight, Wadsworth engaged in his last filibuster, joined by a frequent supporter, David Reed of Pennsylvania. For more than thirty hours the two, with some help from like-minded senators, foiled a vote on appropriations to continue the life of the Campaign Fund Investigation Committee, a

19. James R. Sheffield to J.W.W., Dec. 3, 1926, Wadsworth MSS.
20. James R. Sheffield to J.W.W., Nov. 3, 1927, Wadsworth MSS.

select committee to look into the election of a colleague, Frank L. Smith of Illinois. Permitting only direly needed deficiency legislation, their tactics were grist for Dawes's campaign against unlimited debate.[21]

Yet the filibuster, because it succeeded, justified to Wadsworth his defense of unlimited debate. He filibustered because he thought it was dangerous to give a roving senate committee *carte blanche* to investigate where it pleased. He doubted the special committee's propriety in investigating the Illinois election of its United States senator. For one thing, he questioned the charge of excessive campaign expenditure. He thought Smith's campaign expenditure of $250,000 was not excessive and that the $125,000 contribution of utility magnate Samuel Insull did not mark the purchase of the senate seat. No state or federal law was violated, and the New Yorker felt the Senate wrong in denying Smith his seat pending the findings of the select committee. Wadsworth succeeded. The Campaign Fund Investigating Committee was denied its appropriations.[22] It should also be noted, however, that Smith eventually was denied his seat in the Senate.

Senator Pat Harrison of Mississippi thought the New Yorker's pro-Smith effort destroyed in three days his splendid record of twelve years in the Senate, and that he wrote "his name black in the Senatorial pages of the State of New York." The remark, however, did not accord with the general feeling of Democrats and Republicans alike. In the session's closing hours, senators from both parties surrounded the Wadsworth desk, expressing "deep regret" that his twelve years of service were ending. He was clearly the most conspicuous of those retiring. Following adjournment, *sine die*, at high noon, members of the Military Affairs Committee repaired to their committee suite, where Democratic leader Joseph Robinson spoke warmly and presented him with "a silver service."[23]

Appropriately, the military in Washington were most effusive in regretting Wadsworth's retirement. "The entire War Department, and every officer and soldier," wrote Secretary of War Davis, "feels deep regret that today you terminate your service with the United States Senate."[24] General Charles P. Summerall, the army's Chief of Staff, was more explicit: "The entire service has from the first looked upon you as the best friend it has ever had in public life."[25]

21. *New York Times,* Mar. 3, 4, 5, 1927.
22. *North American Review,* Dec. 1927; *New York Times,* Mar. 4, Nov. 27, 29, 1927.
23. *New York Times,* Mar. 4, 5, 1927.
24. Dwight F. Davis to J.W.W., Mar. 2, 1927, Wadsworth MSS.
25. General Charles P. Summerall to J.W.W., Mar. 4, 1927, Wadsworth MSS.

2

Family and friends, always important to Jim Wadsworth, seemed more so in the interlude between his congressional careers. Even in the most hectic of times, both were an integral part of his life. At the height of the 1926 campaign Jim and the Wadsworth clan had returned to Hartford House to celebrate the Boss and Louisa's fiftieth wedding anniversary. It was an elegant affair, duly recognized by President Coolidge and recorded on the society pages of great newspapers. It contrasted starkly with the Boss's death only weeks later, on Christmas eve of 1926. At the Wadsworth residence on K Street in northwest Washington, Reverdy played gin rummy with Louisa downstairs while Jim, his sister Harriet, and his wife, A.H.W., stood the death watch over the Boss on the second floor. "The dear old Boss," wrote Jim to Craig Wadsworth in Lima, Peru, "was such a forceful, understanding, generous person, and so influential in every day of our lives that, honestly, his going has left a tremendous void." Jim described to Craig how the Boss contracted pneumonia from tramping around Harriet's new cow barn at The Plains, and how he peacefully expired. "The funeral services," he concluded, "were at St. Michael's Sunday afternoon. They were very beautiful and impressive, the church being packed by people from Geneseo and the surrounding country. The troop turned out an escort which I was delighted to find pleased my mother immensely." [26]

If "Mother," Louisa, was now the matriarch, she was so only in name. Jim really presided over the family, from beautiful rambling Hampton House, just across the valley from Mt. Morris. He now spent less time in Washington.

On a beautiful fall day in 1970, Jerry, from his Geneseo Main Street office, mused about his relationship with his father some forty years previously. Both had occupied the same Main Street office—Jerry at the roll top desk; "Father" at the flat top by the window—and they had discovered each other, if only briefly. The year was 1927. They both were now committed to the valley. Up to this time the Senator's legislative career and Jerry's isolation in boarding school and Yale had frequently separated them. Now, when not tied to office accounts, correspondence, and records, farm talk prevailed. Frequently politics and "repeal" surfaced in their con-

26. J.W.W. to Craig W. Wadsworth, Jan. 7, 1927, Wadsworth MSS; also see *New York Times*, Dec. 25, 26, 27, 1927; conversation with Reverdy Wadsworth, autumn 1970.

versation. Nostalgia welled as Jerry recalled the period. It had been a fleeting one. Soon he went to Albany as his county's assemblyman, and his father returned to Washington to membership in "the other House." Even during that 1927 interlude, politics and "repeal" efforts were to separate Wadsworth from Jerry and the Main Street office.

The valley seemed full of Wadsworths at that time. With the coming of spring Louisa returned from Washington to Hartford House, and shortly thereafter Reverdy returned for the summer from St. Mark's. Evie and Stuart Symington were raising their young family in Rochester, just north of the valley. The Homestead Wadsworths, south of Geneseo, and cousin Porter Chandler, who lived on the valley flats across from Hartford House, although quite independent of Jim's wing of the family, nevertheless frequently saw much of the Hampton occupant.

Jerry had come home to stay in the summer of 1927. In June he was graduated from Yale and married Harty Tilton, the daughter of a socially prominent New York family. Harty has been described as "peppery and pretty with big hazel eyes and a strong will of her own." As the Boss had done for Jim, the Senator bought a farm for Jerry, the Haines Farm, located on a hilltop between the valley and Lake Conesus. Jerry renamed it "More Lands." There he and Harty settled and seriously farmed and stayed "put" except when Jerry was off on a repeal trip (with the Crusaders), or politicking (especially after his election to the Assembly), or particularly when they went off on their delayed honeymoon in late 1928.[27] For several weeks Jerry and Harty toured Europe, after crossing on the liner *Paris*. En route, they met Jerry's boyhood friend, Henry Cabot Lodge, and his new bride. In Paris, the two couples met again. While the girls recovered from their travels, young Cabot and Jerry went rabbit hunting in Melun. (There the hunt was quite different from riding to the hounds in the valley. Blood-sucking ferrets are placed in rabbit holes to scare them from their protective abode.) Soon, however, the Jerrys were again settled in More Lands.[28]

Much of the time the Senator—once a senator, always a senator—was deep in farming. In addition to the some 1800 acres adjacent to the Hampton estate, he now overlooked 4000 acres inherited from the Boss and more than 7,000 acres he had purchased recently from Herbert Wadsworth, several miles up the valley in Avon. It took an annual payroll of from

27. Alden Hatch, *The Wadsworths of the Genesee* (New York: Coward-McCann, Inc., 1959), p. 225.
28. William J. Miller, *Henry Cabot Lodge* (New York: James H. Heineman, Inc., 1967), pp. 85–87.

thirty to forty hands and a half-dozen foremen to handle the total of approximately 13,000 acres of land, 75 percent of which was used to raise beef. (As many as 700 head of young beef were shipped at a time to the Street farm at Canawaugus Crossing.) The remaining acreage was devoted to dairy farming and to the growing of truck goods, mostly wheat, corn, beans, and peas. Wadsworth was, indeed, glad to have Jerry back home.[29]

Washington was equally the home of the Wadsworths. Louisa spent winters at the K Street home until her death in 1932. With the razing of the Hay-Adams home on Lafayette Square, Jim and A.H.W. made 2800 Woodland Drive, N.W., their residence for more than a decade. They frequently visited Harriet and Fletcher Harper, at Friendship Farm, The Plains, Virginia, just west of the District of Columbia. Jim especially enjoyed Harriet's fine swimming pool. He was also fond of the horses there, although not as much as were Harriet and Fletcher. Like the Homestead Wadsworths in Geneseo, the Harpers devoted much of their life to horses. For decades Fletcher was master of the Orange County Hunt, Virginia's finest. Years later, at age seventy, Harriet won a hundred-mile endurance ride. At eighty-eight she was still riding daily.[30]

Wadsworth's senatorial defeat hardly at all affected his or A.H.W.'s

29. Conversation with Reverdy Wadsworth, spring 1970, and Tom Coyne, February, 1975. Also, see Gary Lane Fowler, *The Effects of Land Management in the Genesee Valley: A Study In Methodology* (M. A. Thesis, Syracuse University, 1957). Of the some 13,000 acres of the Senator's farms, approximately 6,700 were rented to tenants or lessees. James Wadsworth's tenancy system, with that of William P. Wadsworth's, south of the village, made the system the only one of its kind in the Northeast and the largest and one of longest duration (of comparable size) in the country. The system was particularly unique in that tenants or lessees paid the taxes on the farm, were required to put all of the farms' manure back into the soil, and in the early days had to clear so much land annually and put a specified percentage of their land in to wheat. Such tenancy leases had changed little through various periods of farming since the Wadsworth lands encompassed 70,000 acres in 1811—the subsistence farming period, 1789–1825, the cash grain farming from 1825 to 1850, and the dairy, beef, and crop diversification farming from 1850 to the 1930s. While the leasing arrangement had its "feudal" aspects, similar to the operation of the Rensselaers, Livingstons, and the Cortlandts in the Hudson Valley, it proved successful. In fact, Gary Lane Fowler concluded that the William P. Wadsworth tenant lands (under leases similar to James W. Wadsworth tenant farms) had comparable or higher indexes of land utilization than other types of farms in the valley. One explanation was that the Wadsworths were ever present to see that the provisions of the leases were adhered to. Then, too, Senator Wadsworth believed the provisions of the leases aided high utilization, especially the commitment to the land and the valley instilled by the payment of taxes. Of course, the alluvial deposits in the valley floor provided rich soil which farmers were quite willing to lease, especially with so little available to buy. Also, many farmers thought leasing cheaper than purchasing.

30. Alden Hatch, *op. cit.*, p. 107; also conversations with Harriet Wadsworth Harper, The Plains, Va., summer 1967.

Washington associations. The relationships of some Washingtonians seem permanent irrespective of what political office, if any, might at the moment be occupied. Jim was such a resident of the nation's capital. He belonged. Aside from his recent political office, his father had chaired the House Agriculture Committee, and his father before him had been military governor of the District. Even before the nation had a capital, Jim's ancestor, Jeremiah, served closely with the nation's founder for whom the capital was named.

Alice and Jim's Washington associates in the 1920s were select—the Charles G. Dawses, the Henry L. Stimsons, the Theodore Roosevelts, the Walter B. Howes, the Medill McCormicks, the Hiram Binghams, the Elliot Wadsworths, the Nicholas Longworths and certain distinguished military families, i.e., the George C. Marshalls, the Frank McCoys, the John Palmers and the John Pershings. Yale was frequently common to their backgrounds, except for military friends.

Although Wadsworth and his Washington circle of associates were ensconced in the stream of decision makers, like people everywhere, backfence gossip entered their lives. Alice was appalled by the commercial traffic besieging Lafayette Square. Jim wondered why Alice Longworth called her daughter Paulina ("My God, what a name"). Nicholas Longworth confided to Jim that before Representative Maurice ("Crummy") Crumpacker killed himself, he had thought that Longworth, Secretary Mellon, and Senator David Reed were plotting against his life.[31]

Not infrequently social and political obligations took the Wadsworths to New York City where their social circle included the Charles Sabins, the Elihu Roots, the James Sheffields, and a number of members of the Union League and the Metropolitan Club. There they frequently saw the Payne Whitneys. (Alice's sister, Helen, had married Payne.) Alice and Helen enjoyed shopping. Once, Alice took Helen to Harzof's, the notable rare book and manuscript dealer. Being an old customer, Alice was left alone by Harzof, but the brazen proprietor could not resist trying to sell Helen some Lincoln and Hay manuscripts from the Herndon-Weik collection. Eying the bejewelled Helen, he exhorted: "Buy the collection and give it to Yale! It's yours for one hundred thousand dollars."

"I've just given Yale two million dollars . . . and they haven't even thanked me," snapped Helen.

"For Christ's sake, woman," said Harzof, "you might wait until they lay the cornerstone."

"I haven't got a penny," retorted Helen.

31. Nicholas Longworth to J.W.W., Aug. 18, 1927, Wadsworth MSS.

"What the hell do you do with all your money?" replied Harzof in disgust, "buy diamond-studded toilet seats?" [32]

James Wadsworth was not averse to making money and invested some time and money in Colonial Western Airways, a subsidiary of the Colonial Air Transport, Inc. Colonial Western operated an air express and passenger business from Boston to Cleveland by way of Buffalo, and from New York to Montreal, the two routes intersecting at Schenectady. He was particularly attracted to the venture by its president, General John F. O'Ryan, the former commanding officer of New York's National Guard, and by the "monopolistic features of our proposed enterprise." [33] In addition to investing $10,000 in the company, Wadsworth served on the company's board of directors. Throughout much of 1927 and 1928 he backed O'Ryan in intra-company squabbles and used his prestige to recruit subscribers in Boston, Cleveland, and Buffalo. "Thanks for your influence with Eliot Wadsworth [in Boston]," wrote one officer of the company. "I was able to start with him the endless chain idea to get 20 men for $5,000 each." [34] In Cleveland, Wadsworth's friend Benedict Crowell took an active interest in the new organization. Jim was less a prophet in his own Genesee Valley country. "I regret to state," wrote William Hickok, the belt manufacturer, "that after looking over the proposed layout of the Colonial Airways Company I am not interested in same." [35] By 1929 Colonial Western Airways and Colonial Air Transport were under the holding company, Colonial Airways, and covered 967 miles with 20 planes. The parent company received the first large government air mail contract. In the same year Colonial Airways was absorbed by Aviation Corporation, another holding company, headed by bankers Harriman and Lehmann Brothers. With absorption of Colonial Western into the Aviation Corporation complex, Wadsworth's interest waned.

3

As expected, any opposition to Wadsworth's retirement from politics would die hard. Followers would not think of it, nor did the former sena-

32. David A. Randall, *Dukedom Large Enough* (New York: Random House, 1962), pp. 22–23.

33. John F. O'Ryan to J.W.W., June 29, July 5, 20, Dec. 3, 7, 22, 1927, Wadsworth MSS.

34. Lawrence L. Driggs to J.W.W., April 7, 1928, Wadsworth MSS.

35. William Hickok to J.W.W., July 28, 1927, Wadsworth MSS.

tor. James J. Lyons, a faithful upstate supporter, talked of a senate campaign in 1928, or "any candidacy which you may see fit to accept." [36] Wadsworth had a uniform reply for devotees like Lyons:

> Honestly, I have been unable thus far to make any definite political plans for 1928. For the present, I am up to my neck in work here, as a result largely of my father's death last Christmas. I travel about some, meet a good many people and hear a good many suggestions, most of them friendly, but it is quite impossible to estimate exactly the political situation which will confront us a year from now. I don't know whether my candidacy for any important office would be practical at that time; so many things may happen in the interim. One thing is pretty certain, and that is that I shall be in some kind of a political fight whether I am a candidate for office or not. You will understand, of course, that I cannot, in good conscience, abandon, in any degree my views on prohibition. The real truth is I feel more deeply on that subject than any other and am determined to remain in that fight regardless of other considerations.[37]

Wadsworth's political ambition was well contained. He took in stride various suggestions, dismissing most out of hand. Far less naïve than most who exhorted him on, to those who suggested the presidency his response was brief and firm: "I would not think of being a candidate for that high office." [38] More plausible was the suggestion of Lowden supporters that Wadsworth be a vice presidential candidate in 1928. The New Yorker was fond of Lowden but, with Coolidge still considered the likely candidate, presidential and vice presidential politics were little discussed in early 1927. The New Yorker's possible appointment as governor general of the Philippine Islands was talked about. Nicholas M. Butler suggested he forget it. "It is my desire," he wrote, "that you go back to the Senate in 1928." [39] "I can't possibly go out there," assured Wadsworth. "My roots here at Geneseo, domestic and business, are far too deep in the ground." [40]

Domestic and business roots aside, Wadsworth kept channels open to local and state politics. Much of his local politics file for 1927 and 1928 is filled with dozens of hand-written notes from Florence Knapp of Syracuse. Having served for years as vice-chairman of the Onondaga County Republican Committee and having been, in 1924, elected as the first

36. James J. Lyons to J.W.W., May 31, June 14, 1927, Wadsworth MSS.
37. J.W.W. to James J. Lyons, June 7, 1927, Wadsworth MSS.
38. J.W.W. to Birch Helms, May 24, 1927, Wadsworth MSS.
39. Nicholas M. Butler to J.W.W., Aug. 31, 1927, Wadsworth MSS.
40. J.W.W. to Nicholas M. Butler, Aug. 31, 1927, Wadsworth MSS.

woman secretary of state in New York, Mrs. Knapp had numerous contacts with Wadsworth. She had always supported him faithfully and constantly filled his ears with political news from Albany and Syracuse, much of it trivial. By 1928, however, her correspondence with Wadsworth was unnatural, at times hysterical. Extremely upright in appearance and reputation, Mrs. Knapp suffered the horrendous experience of being convicted of illegally paying some $27,000 to members of her family during the conducting of the 1925 census by her department in Albany. Humiliated by the exposure of two trials, she pleaded with Wadsworth to believe a conspiracy was plotted against her. He did not believe her but was sorry for her situation and sought the advice of Fred Hammond, his 1926 Syracuse campaign manager, about seeking leniency in her behalf.[41]

On September 1, 1928, Wadsworth wired State Supreme Court Justice Stephen Callaghan, pleading for "clemency" for Mrs. Knapp, "in view of what she has already gone through and her condition which I cannot help believing is unstable."[42] Attorney General Albert Ottinger also sought clemency. Justice was done, however. Mrs. Knapp was committed to thirty days in the Albany County jail.

Wadsworth maintained many political contacts around the state. His personal political stake demanded it. His interest in the party's course on prohibition also demanded it. He burned to influence that course. Throughout the spring of 1927 he and Nicholas Murray Butler hammered out a wet plank for the state Republican convention, to be convened in the fall. It wasn't easy. Most upstate delegates wanted a dry plank. Some wets in the party, such as William D. Guthrie of New York City, wanted an amendment of the Eighteenth Amendment which would give Congress authority to liberalize the constitutional limitations. Butler disagreed with Guthrie. He thought that national drys, such as Borah and Carter Glass, saw no alternative to repeal but prohibition. "It is there, in my judgment," he wrote, "that the issue should be put and kept. The public mind is moving toward repeal with astonishing rapidity." Butler thought the party stood "where the Whig Party stood in 1854 and that in 1927 it has the same choice between courage and cowardice that the Whig Party had then."[43] Wadsworth was about as adamant. The view of both men permeated party circles like fat in a fire. Hamilton Fish viewed their ideas as menacing "to Republican success in the State and the Nation." Putting repeal into the

41. See numerous undated hand-written letters, Florence Knapp to J.W.W., J.W.W. to Fred W. Hammond, Aug. 28, 1928, Wadsworth MSS.

42. Telegram, J.W.W. to Supreme Court Justice Stephen Callaghan, Sept. 1, 1928, Wadsworth MSS; *New York Times,* Sept. 5, 1928.

43. Nicholas M. Butler to Courtland Nicoll, Sept. 7, 1927, Wadsworth MSS.

Republican state platform would, according to Fish, "mean the loss of 500,000 Republican votes."[44] Why, even Al Smith was not talking repeal. Fish had the ear of delegates to the Republican state convention more than Wadsworth and Butler. Thus, the 1927 convention was silent on prohibition. Fish was right on Smith's stand in the state's Democratic party. The Democratic party in New York was also officially silent on prohibition. The Governor was not going to ruin his 1928 presidential chances with southern drys just to please Tammany wets.

Wadsworth was not deterred. Having failed to influence New York Republicans, he headed for the 1928 National Republican Convention. "I fully expect," he announced in late 1927, "to be one of the seven delegates-at-large."[45] Further, he announced his intention to help wipe out the Eighteenth Amendment at the convention. The idea of Wadsworth being a delegate-at-large made Fish, upstate drys, and the Anti-Saloon League apoplectic. With the support of county chairmen, however, and with Lafayette ("Lafe") Gleasons's adept handling of the state committee—he ruled any dry discussion out of order—Wadsworth was elected a delegate-at-large.[46]

Wadsworth's interest in the National Republican convention was not confined only to his lively concern about an anti-prohibition plank. The slate also attracted his attention, especially after Coolidge issued his famous "I do not choose to run" statement on August 2, 1927.

Politicians across the country did not know what to make of Coolidge's statement. Democrats like Claude Bowers of New York joked about it. He said that pancakes would be flat in 1928 without the Vermont sap running.[47] Republicans like George Moses of New Hampshire were more serious. "Remember Benjamin Harrison," he wired Wadsworth, on the day of the announcement.[48] Moses remembered how Harrison withdrew from the presidential race in 1892 and then turned on those who threw their hats into the ring. Moses, who really would have liked to see Wadsworth in the White House, wanted at least to head off the quickly developing boom for Commerce Secretary Herbert Hoover.[49]

Like most Republicans in the country, Wadsworth would have "gone forward" happily with four more years of Calvin Coolidge, and so told the President. Becoming convinced, however, that Coolidge meant what he

44. New York Times, July 1, 1927.
45. Ibid., Nov. 29, 1927.
46. Ibid., Feb. 24, March 10, 1928.
47. McCoy, op. cit., p. 384.
48. George M. Moses to J.W.W., Aug. 20, 1927, Wadsworth MSS.
49. George M. Moses to J.W.W., Aug. 6, 1927, Wadsworth MSS.

said, he plunked for Vice President Dawes for the Republican nomination. Dawes had always been a Wadsworth favorite. Their aristocratic and ideological similarities made their relationship highly congenial.

Strangely and unnecessarily, Wadsworth was strongly urged to support Dawes by the Democrat, William Sulzer, the former New York governor who had been deposed from his high office by impeachment through the efforts of Tammany chieftan Charles Murphy. "Your strongest candidate is General Dawes," Sulzer wrote Wadsworth. "It looks as if the business interests of the country will nominate him." Sulzer applauded the Dawes camp's apparent strategy to push forward "favorite sons" in several states, holding him back as a dark horse to be run later in the convention. Sulzer's memo to Wadsworth supporting Dawes trailed off with rather disjointed comments on how Smith dominated much of New York's Republican party; of how Wadsworth lost the 1926 election by walking into Smith's trap; and of how Wadsworth should run for the Senate again if not nominated for the vice-presidency. (He said he would tell Wadsworth about the Smith trap in due time.[50])

Sulzer's prattling did not move Wadsworth. He did not respond to the memorandum. He saw for himself how well Dawes stacked up against the several contenders: Commerce Secretary Hoover; Senator James E. Watson of Indiana, an important senate Republican; former Illinois Governor Frank O. Lowden, Wadsworth's 1920 choice; former Ohio Governor Frank B. Willis; Senator Charles Curtis of Kansas, the senate majority leader; and Senator Guy Goff of West Virginia. In the scramble for delegates in the country, Dawes, of course, had some substantial support. His political assets of courage and ability, however, did not compensate for the opposition he incurred by his independence while a vice president, by his loyalty to Frank Lowden, also of Illinois, and by his support of McNary-Haugenism, anathema to eastern Republicans. In spite of Dawes's McNary-Haugen stance, Wadsworth thought him the strongest candidate, and was one of five in the New York delegation who stayed with him until the Hoover machine gained majority support, at which time he "gracefully" moved to make the New York vote for Hoover unanimous.[51]

Repeal, of course, was Wadsworth's real mission at the national Republican convention in Kansas City. But dry barricades there were impregnable. The wets, deeply disorganized, were no match for the smooth Republican leadership, particularly Interior Secretary Hubert Work and Senators Simeon D. Fess and William E. Borah. The New York wets

50. Undated memorandum, Walter Sulzer to J.W.W., Wadsworth MSS.
51. McCoy, op. cit., p. 385–386; New York Times, June 14, 1928.

could not even get a minority report onto the convention floor, and when Nicholas Murray Butler offered a substitute for Borah's plank, he lost, although Senator Walter Edge thought "the chorus of ayes for his plank were quite as loud sounding . . . as the opponents."[52]

The Republican prohibition plank quoted Washington and Lincoln on constitutionalism, and concluded: "The people, through the method provided by the Constitution have written the Eighteenth Amendment into the Constitution. The Republican Party pledges itself and its nominees to the observance and vigorous enforcement of this provision of the Constitution."[53]

For all the courage of Wadsworth, Butler, and other "renegades," Edge thought their disorganization to blame for the Republican shilly-shallying on the great issue. While calling Republican drys "cowards," Edge also admonished Wadsworth. "When we have another convention," he wrote, "be prepared to go through with it in a really organized way. You and I [will] have the cross on our backs as members of the Republican Party for all time if we don't do so." In the meantime Edge suggested that Wadsworth "insist on being a candidate for renomination and reelection to the Senate from New York."[54] Wadsworth admitted that Edge was right on "our lack of preparation and organization" and that he was tempted to take his advice on the senate race.[55]

For a moment Wadsworth did consider Edge's suggestion regarding a senate race but soon realized that his New Jersey friend did not know the New York situation. Faithful Nat Elsberg, from his Broadway law office, did. "Those with whom I have spoken," he wrote Wadsworth, "say this is not the year for you to try it." Wadsworth readily agreed—he was too wet.[56]

Given the Republican enforcement plank, Wadsworth did not know how he could go on the stump for Hoover, although the presidential candidate wrote him that the organization "will want to press you into many different avenues of labor."[57] Wadsworth believed that something of a repeal statement in Hoover's acceptance speech might make it easier to go on the stump. He asked his friend William "Wild Bill" Donovan, in the Justice Department, to use his influence with Hoover to make such a

52. Walter Edge to J.W.W., June 18, 1928, Wadsworth MSS.
53. *New York Times*, June 15, 1928; *Current History*, Aug. 1928, p. 798.
54. Walter Edge to J.W.W., June 18, 1928, Wadsworth MSS.
55. J.W.W. to Walter Edge, June 23, 1928, Wadsworth MSS.
56. N. A. Elsberg to J.W.W., July 12, 1928; J.W.W. to N. A. Elsberg, July 13, 1928, Wadsworth MSS.
57. Herbert Hoover to J.W.W., June 19, 1928, Wadsworth MSS.

statement. "My hope," he wrote Donovan, "is that . . . [Hoover] will not close the door against the modification [of the Eighteenth Amendment] and thus throw upon the Republican workers the burden of defending the existing prohibition situation."⁵⁸ Donovan agreed, but had little influence.⁵⁹ On August 5, before 60,000 partisans, Hoover declared against repeal and stood for rigid enforcement. Furthermore, he made the issue the campaign's central point, describing prohibition as "noble in motive and far-reaching in purpose."⁶⁰ (Thus, for posterity, the ill-chosen phrase "the noble experiment" would haunt the memory of Herbert Hoover.)

Having turned to national politics to make up the ground he lost on the prohibition issue in the 1927 state Republican convention, Wadsworth tried again at the 1928 state Republican convention held in Syracuse. Again, he and Butler failed to move the upstate Republicans. Like the national counterpart, the convention went dry. Still, Wadsworth dutifully hit the campaign trail in 1928 for the state and national party slates.

Unenthusiastic about his presidential candidate, Wadsworth really "reached" when campaigning for Hoover. He berated William Jennings Bryan for his 1896 Democratic 16–1 campaign and applauded the Republicans for staying with the gold standard in that McKinley year. He scolded Woodrow Wilson for his League of Nations, and praised Republicans for defeating it in the Senate. He criticized Democratic tariffs and thanked Republicans for their protectionism. Specifically, he denounced Smith for favoring 1920 as a basis for immigration quotas rather than 1890, thus threatening the current high proportion of Anglo-Saxons in the country. Then he outlined Hoover's many qualifications for high office, his training and reputation, his executive experience from food administration to cabinet head and to food supplier during the "terrible Mississippi floods in 1927."⁶¹

4

"You ought to be President of the United States and I hope you will take that as coming from our hearts and as indicating to you our readiness and desire to fight elbow to elbow with you." Thus concluded Captain

58. J.W.W. to William J. Donovan, July 12, 1928, Wadsworth MSS.
59. William J. Donovan to J.W.W., July 20, 1928, Wadsworth MSS.
60. New York Times, Aug. 6, 1928.
61. Speech delivered by J.W.W. at Livonia, N.Y., Aug. 1, 1928, Wadsworth MSS.

W. H. Stayton, chairman of the Association Against the Prohibition Amendment, on May 21, 1927, in a brief note offering Wadsworth "anything you want me or this Association to do for you now or at any time." [62] Wadsworth thanked his correspondent, in turn offering his aid to "your organization and all others who believe that the situation has become unbearable. Please keep me informed about developments . . . I may be able to be of some use." [63] The exchange was prophetic. It brought together the country's foremost wet lobbyist and its foremost wet Republican.

W. H. Stayton, a naval captain, aristocratic in background and bearing, almost single-handedly and largely at his own expense, founded the AAPA. With friends, over a Shoreham Hotel luncheon, he began his trek to repeal on November 12, 1918, in part to rescue the wet fight from "the representatives of the traffic." Of some thirty or forty anti-prohibition organizations which emerged in the twenties, the AAPA was most powerful, achieving 720,000 members by 1927. Stayton did it, seldom deterred in his efforts by naval service and by his subsequent presidency of the Baltimore Shipping Company. But for all the AAPA membership and its pressure group strategies—lobbying for state enforcement repeal, advocating anti-prohibition referendums, opposing dry candidates, distributing press copy, spawning state wet organizations—1927 saw the country still bone dry.[64]

Out of numerous conferences in the late summer and fall of 1927, Wadsworth and Stayton determined upon an elite conference on an anti-prohibition drive, to be convened in Wadsworth's Washington residence in mid-winter. Only the most influential wets with impeccable credentials would be invited, such as ex-Senator Oscar W. Underwood, Elihu Root, Pierre S. DuPont, and General Lincoln C. Andrews. Stayton did the organizing, assiduously consulting with Wadsworth at each step.

62. W. H. Stayton to J.W.W., May 21, 1927, Wadsworth MSS.

63. J.W.W. to W. H. Stayton, May 28, 1927, Wadsworth MSS.

64. Dayton E. Heckman, "Prohibition Passes: The Story of the Association Against the Prohibition Amendment" (Ohio State University, 1939), Ph.D. dissertation, pp. 5–14; Andrew Sinclair, Era of Excess (New York: Harper Colophon Books, 1964, originally published by Harper & Row in 1962 under title Prohibition: Era of Excess), pp. 338–340; Herbert Asbury, The Great Illusion (Garden City, N.Y.; Doubleday & Co., Inc., 1950), p. 314; for work which views the repeal effort as a conspiracy by the wealthy class which sought repeal to have taxes shifted from them to liquor interests, see Fletcher Dobyus, The Amazing Story of Repeal (New York: Willett, Clark & Co., 1940); see James W. Wadsworth, The Reminiscences of James W. Wadsworth (Columbia University Oral History Research Office, 1952), p. 357: Wadsworth states that the AAPA was largely a fact-finding and educational effort and was not an organization to lobby or support wet candidates. Heckman and other sources indicate strong lobbying and political efforts by AAPA.

Although the AAPA staff did necessary logistical work for the conference and Stayton put his full weight behind it, Wadsworth kept the upper hand. He gave final approval to the list of participants and the letter of invitation they received. And when, a few days before the conference, Stayton announced his own AAPA policy at a Union League dinner in New York, Wadsworth wrote one of the invited participants that "we shall most certainly discuss his suggestion [the substitution of the Quebec Plan of local control for the Eighteenth Amendment] at our meeting in Washington, and I think we can make it apparent in a perfectly good-natured way that there may be a wiser policy. Thus far, I have found him quite amenable to suggestions, provided they are spoken to him direct." [65] Also, Wadsworth assured one of the conference participants, Grayson M. P. Murphy, that he, Wadsworth, not Stayton, would preside at the meeting. [66]

Form-like letters of invitation were not sufficient to induce all invited guests to attend the conference. Stayton, whose former naval rank and social standing helped, personally sought out certain of the guests to invite. Wadsworth contacted the more prestigious of those invited. In his personal contact he became quite specific about the meeting. "All will agree," he wrote Elihu Root, "that the time is ripe to put forward a definite program, preferably under the auspices of Captain Stayton's organization, enlarged to meet the nationwide situation." [67] Almost without exception all who were invited attended except Elihu Root, whose physicians insisted that he go to bed, not to Washington. "Please give my kind regards and good wishes to the gentlemen present . . . and say that I drink to their health." [68]

For two days, December 12 and 13, 2800 Woodland Drive in Washington was the scene of serious yet congenial dedication to strike down prohibition. [69] In a sense, the conclave marked the real beginning of counter-reformation of decades of the prohibition reform effort. Few at the conference disagreed that the state of morals was a grave concern, that public apathy toward prohibition was disappearing, and that the time had arrived to act. Reorganized with the backing of Wadsworth's imposing guests, the AAPA would countervail and defeat the Anti-Saloon League. A half-century later, in 1970, Jerry still remembered his father's excitement over the meeting.

65. J.W.W. to Grayson M. P. Murphy, Dec. 2, 1927, Wadsworth MSS.
66. *Ibid.*
67. J.W.W. to Elihu Root, Nov. 8, 1927, Wadsworth MSS.
68. Elihu Root to J.W.W., Nov. 30, 1927, Wadsworth MSS.
69. *New York Times*, Dec. 13, 1927; Heckman, *op. cit.*, Ch. 1, *passim.*

The conclave discussed the essential machinery for strengthening the AAPA. Being instructed to appoint two committees for the purpose, Wadsworth selected Colonel Julian Codeman, William Bell Wait, Senator Walter Edge, and Austin G. Fox for the program committee; and Pierre DuPont, Edward S. Harkness, and Charles S. Sabin to serve on the organization committee. Wadsworth and Stayton were to serve on both, *ex officio*. The committees were to report to a meeting of the group within a month's time.[70]

Again in early January, Wadsworth opened his home to the distinguished wets. In regard to the organization's purpose, the gathering pushed hard for outright repeal as the association's ultimate objective. Pragmatically, however, it viewed as a more plausible immediate objective the elimination from the Volstead Act of any mention of beers and wines and the permitting of states to define intoxicating liquors. A precise approach to repeal was unattainable and was left to a final determination by a strong executive committee. In regard to the association's organizational program, the group appointed the board of directors and the executive committee, and selected a president. The board of directors was large and honorific, with few executive responsibilities. Actually it never met. Much more important was the executive committee, which consisted of four pre-1928 members and seven new appointees. Four of the executive committee members were intimate friends of Wadsworth, Henry H. Curran, Benedict Crowell, Grason M. P. Murphy, and Charles H. Sabin. Wadsworth was elated that Curran was chosen as the new president of the organization. Curran, former president of the Borough of Manhattan and Commissioner of Immigration, Ellis Island, was devoted to Jim Wadsworth.[71] With such leadership established, the Geneseoan turned to other matters—the valley farms and Republican politics.[72]

Almost by force of habit when the position of Secretary of War was discussed in the press or among interested persons in the 1920s, Wadsworth's name came up. It had been mentioned previously when Harding had built his cabinet in December of 1920 and again in 1926 upon the death of Secretary Weeks. Nineteen twenty-eight was no exception. "In my opinion," wrote General John J. Pershing, prior to the election, "the next President could do nothing finer than select you for the portfolio of Secretary of War. No man in my time has ever held the position of Chair-

70. William H. Stayton to J.W.W., Nov. 1, 1927, Wadsworth MSS.
71. J.W.W. to Charles H. Sabin, Dec. 13, 1927, Wadsworth MSS.
72. Heckman, *op. cit.*, Ch. 1, *passim*.

man of Military Affairs in the Senate with such ability as you did. The army itself would rejoice mightily if this could happen." [73]

Wadsworth's response to Pershing was profuse and realistic. He wrote warmly of his affection for Pershing and the army and of his appreciation of the general's suggestion. Besides a senate tenure, he noted that the only "other office which has appealed to me for a long time is that of Secretary of War. . . . If the position were offered to me, free of embarrassing conditions, I would accept it and be grateful for the opportunity for service." But Wadsworth did not for a moment expect the nod. While agreeing with Pershing that Hoover would be elected, he noted that Hoover "is doubtless aware that I had hoped for the nomination of General Dawes." Concluding that Hoover bore him no "personal ill will," he was sure that Hoover could not "deny the reasonable claims of those who have helped to put him in high office." Then, bravely: "I have no right to be a candidate or claimant for appointment in Mr. Hoover's administration." [74] Wadsworth put it more succinctly to his son, Jerry, following Hoover's landslide victory over the wet Catholic, Smith: "Don't expect anything from that crowd." [75]

From day to day in early January 1929, the press speculated on and frequently supported the Wadsworth appointment, as did such Republican stalwarts as Senators David Reed of Pennsylvania and Hiram Bingham of Connecticut, but "politics" prevailed. Hoover turned to one of his convention floor managers, Congressman James W. Good, for the war post. [76]

Following the settling of the Hoover administration, Wadsworth concentrated again on farming and the politics of repeal. Indeed, seldom during the Hoover years were his political endeavors separated from the great issue of repeal. The endeavors, however, were not at the cost of his farming enterprise. As noted, while the former senator and Jerry frequently discussed politics and the wet issue in their Main Street office, their conversation usually turned to farming.

From the Main Street office, and occasionally from his Washington residence, Wadsworth kept up a steady stream of correspondence, with wets and drys alike. Nicholas Murray Butler and Wadsworth enjoyed commiserating, and together fighting the drys. Again in 1930, their wet attack

73. John J. Pershing to J.W.W., Aug. 7, 1928, Wadsworth MSS.

74. J.W.W. to John J. Pershing, Aug. 11, 1928, Wadsworth MSS.

75. Conversation with James J. Wadsworth, Sept. 1970; in 1974 Jerry qualified the statement, remembering that his father was alluding particularly to Ogden Mills and company when he referred to "that crowd."

76. New York Times, Jan. 12–21, 1929, passim.

in the Republican state convention, as in the two previous conventions, failed.[77] The difference in 1930 was that Wadsworth refused to be a delegate. By then he wanted outright repeal of the Eighteenth Amendment, a return of all liquor control to the states, leaving the federal government only the duty of restricting interstate liquor shipments into dry states.[78]

Wadsworth struck where he might be most effective, notably at the national chairman of the Women's National Committee for Law Enforcement, the foremost women's dry organization in the country, and at Simeon Fess, the national Republican chairman. While doing so, Pierre duPont, now thoroughly committed to the activity of the Association Against the Prohibition Amendment, appeared before the House Judiciary Committee, accompanied by Jerry who delivered his father's message. Jerry could not resist also speaking for himself. Although only twenty-four years of age, in a strong vibrant voice he declared: "Young people cannot be stifled in the folds of sumptuary rule. It is an intellectual claustrophobia. . . . As for drinking among young people, I assert, not claim, that it has grown by leaps and bounds. By the time I entered Yale, the pastime was so taken for granted it was not even discussed. We young people are rebellious but we are fair. We would not force Drys to drink [as] they have tried to force us to abstain. If there are 99 personal Drys in a room with one man who wanted a drink, they have no ethical right to snatch his glass away. We don't want the saloon but we want the God-given right of conducting our private lives without legislative interference."[79] His father was proud.

Wadsworth's attack upon Mrs. Henry W. Peabody of the Women's National Committee for Law Enforcement was private and largely in self-defense. In a lengthy personal letter she had charged Wadsworth and New York wets with "disloyalty" and with being "Bolsherkers." She pleaded with him to "turn right about face" and "give New York State one chance to clean up."[80] Wadsworth was courteous but firm, concentrating on the inaccuracy of her statement that New York did not meet its binding obligation in the Eighteenth Amendment to set up state machinery for carrying out its concurrent obligation. He pointed out that the decision, U.S. vs Lanze, 260 U.S. 377 (1922) Supreme Court of the United States, "explained the purpose of the concurrent power paragraph to the effect that the intention of the concurrent clause was simply to make it clear that the Eighteenth Amendment did not take away from the states the power which

77. *Ibid.*, Sept. 26, 1930.
78. *Ibid.*, Sept. 25, 1930.
79. *Time Magazine*, March 10, 1930.
80. Mrs. Henry W. Peabody to J.W.W., Oct. 1, 1929, Wadsworth MSS.

they have always possessed in regard to Prohibition within their several jurisdictions." Furthermore, he noted that the debates in the Congress on the Eighteenth Amendment did not indicate any intention to bind the states. Warming to a conclusion, he reminded her that states with enforcement laws—Pennsylvania, Illinois, Indiana, Louisiana, and Florida—were more crime-ridden than New York. "I fear our disagreement is complete and incurable," he closed.[81]

His correspondence with Simeon D. Fess, chairman of the Republican National Committee, was a public matter. Buoyed up by the Wickersham Commission report, a study made at the President's request, Wadsworth demanded that the Republican party support the right of. the people, through state conventions, to vote on repeal of the Eighteenth Amendment. Aside from the rightness of the action, it would be good politics. "And may I point out to your practical mind," he wrote, "that were the Republican National Convention to urge upon Republican members of Congress the submission of this matter to the people of the states, thus evidencing its desire to consult the people and accept their verdict, grave embarrassments to Republican candidates in the next Presidential election would be avoided." [82]

Fess, like the President, whose bidding he did, was shaken by the Wickersham Report. Of the eleven commissioners who wrote it, two favored repeal, five wanted revision and government monopoly of the liquor traffic, two favored revision and further trial, and only two supported the Hoover and Fess status quo positions. "I assume," replied Fess sarcastically, "that the letter was written in good faith, although it has the element of propaganda. . . . In reply to your specific recommendation that the Republican party recommend repeal of the Eighteenth Amendment, I am stating it to you that I shall use my influence to prevent the party from committing a fatal blunder in asking for the repeal of the Eighteenth Amendment." [83]

Much of Wadsworth's correspondence during the Hoover years was with his very close friend, Henry H. Curran, the AAPA President. By 1929 Wadsworth relented and accepted appointment to its board of directors and the executive committee. There, education, lobbying and campaign strategies for the final *coup de grâce* on the Eighteenth Amendment were worked out. Most of the Wadsworth moves, such as an article for the *North American Review* and his letter to Fess, were part of the

81. J.W.W. to Mrs. Henry W. Peabody, Oct. 7, 1929, Wadsworth MSS.
82. J.W.W. to Simeon D. Fess, Nov. 12, 1931, Wadsworth MSS.
83. Simeon D. Fess to J.W.W., Nov. 14, 1931, Wadsworth MSS.

strategy. Indeed, the AAPA drafted both the *Review* article and the Fess letter.[84] Also, the AAPA lobbied in the Congress for various repeal resolutions. Some of them, such as the Beck-Linthicum Resolution, came close to passage.[85] In 1932 Wadsworth showed much interest in the association's preparation for influencing the national Republican convention. Again he wrote the chairman of the National Republican Committee. This time he likened him to the boy who "stood on the burning deck," awaiting the word from the father, now "faint in death below." With impressive AAPA statistics he pointed to defections of Fess's fellow Ohioans from the dry effort: the Ohio delegation in the House of Representatives, the Republican candidates for governor and senator in Ohio, the Republican national committeeman from Ohio, the Republican governor of Ohio. He deplored "the counsels of timid souls, the mental contortionists" who called for adoption of a law enforcement plank at the forthcoming Republican convention. Wadsworth did not want to "seem importune" but wanted Fess to have a "few helpful facts . . . for the consideration of the distinguished Committee of which you are Chairman." More specifically he wanted a plank at least to support a national vote via amendment conventions in the states.[86] Fess did not bother to reply. When three wet women from Ohio made the same plea personally, he quickly remarked, "I'm against it."

Prohibition was the central issue at the 1932 Republican convention in Chicago. To be sure, economic depression gripped the attention of the nation more than prohibition but Republicans were beyond doing much about that at Chicago. With close to 13,000,000 Americans unemployed, with the bottom dropped out of the stock market, with banks failing by the thousands, with hundreds of farms being foreclosed daily, the national gloom permeated the Republican convention. The prohibition problem was almost a welcomed diversion. Carl Hallauer, a young Republican leader from Rochester, described to author Alden Hatch its impact on the New York caucus:

It was frightfully hot in that overcrowded room. We sat there on little funeral-parlor chairs dripping with sweat. Things were in a rough state for the Party. At first the discussion was how to dump Hoover, because we knew he was a liability. But we also knew that he would be nominated. Ogden Mills, Secretary of the Treasury, represented President Hoover on the delegation, and he held it in line.

84. Dobyns, *op. cit.*, pp. 14–15.
85. Sinclair, *op. cit.*, pp. 373–4.
86. J.W.W. to Simeon D. Fess, April 1932, Wadsworth MSS.

Then we took up prohibition. Nicholas Murray Butler made an excellent speech favoring repeal. Wadsworth followed him with a brilliant exposition of the subject. It was factual and profound, but at the same time truly moving. I still remember the feeling he gave you of complete sincerity.

After he finished, Wadsworth said to Mills, 'Ogden, you represent the President. I want to say that it's going to be difficult to re-elect Hoover, but repeal is the vital question. We can't win without it.

"The Democrats right here next week are going to nominate Frank Roosevelt. I knew him when he was Assistant Secretary of the Navy. He will have a wet plank. If we don't have a wet plank, he will get in, and if he does we won't get rid of him until he dies. And thrift will never be heard of again."

Mills said, "I'm so convinced you're right Senator, that I'm going to call the President."

He did, and argued for half an hour over long distance. When he hung up he said, "Mr. Hoover says it's got to be a dry plank." [87]

In reality, the Republican plank was not dry but rather wet-dry. Although Fess and Borah were still very dry, Mills and the platform committee hedged and supported a plank calling for the "submission" of the prohibition to the people, but with no recommendation. Hiram Bingham, Nicholas Butler, and Wadsworth, of course, wanted repeal but lost their substitute plank. Following the defeat of the submission plank, Mills said to Wadsworth: "This ought to teach you a lesson. You better give up." [88]

Actually, in the submission plank, Wadsworth achieved from Mills what he had asked of Fess a year previously. But by 1932 even a moist Republican platform was not enough for America. The country wanted repeal and the Democrats gave it to them. Once the wet Franklin Roosevelt won, its coming was only a matter of time.

The significance of Wadsworth's role in the repeal effort is difficult, if not impossible, to determine. Explanations of repeal are manifold and include the antics of such prohibitionists as Bishop James Cannon, Assistant Attorney General Mabel Walker Willebrandt, and Ella Boole, Wadsworth's 1920 prohibitionist opponent; the destruction of dry myths which had connected such "sins" as prostitution and venereal disease with alcohol; and the revelation in an increasingly urban society that virtue did not reside only in dry rural America. [89]

87. Hatch, *op. cit.*, p. 232.
88. *Ibid.*, p. 233.
89. Sinclair, *op. cit.*, pp. 400–416.

Of the waves that washed away the solid rock of prohibition, few Americans made as many as the scion of Geneseo. Few waves were as substantial as his campaign against the fanatical Ella Boole in 1920 and the dry Cristman in 1926. No American helped so much to reconstitute the AAPA as the effective wet interest group in the country. And no significant political figure addressed his countrymen so often on the subject as did Wadsworth. In the early 1960s the powerful Howard Smith, chairman of the Rules Committee in the House of Representatives, reminisced fondly about the long life of James Wadsworth and remembered best his wet fight, and his sacrifice of his senate seat for the cause.

6

Nineteen thirty-two was a momentous year in Washington and the nation. More divisive than repeal was the great depression. The life savings of millions were wiped out. The unemployed were hungry. Government and charity ran out of their last relief funds. Fathers took to the roads in search of jobs and food. The country was sullen.

Leaders in government and the great political parties thrashed about for solutions. Although flexible by standards of previous presidents who confronted economic crises, Hoover's obduracy to federal relief was as rigid as his opposition to repeal. The public demanded change. Democrats could not lose, not that their party and presidential candidate called for great change. Indeed, Franklin Roosevelt, as David Burner recently has written, called for economy in government; "hedged on the tariff; . . . ignored labor;" and "hailed agriculture in the most general terms." Still large portions of hinterland and urban America wanted a change in the presidency and elected Roosevelt overwhelmingly.[90]

Wadsworth witnessed much of the agony of depression politics from his residence in Washington. Little did he think, however, that soon he would watch personally, from the halls of Congress, the Democratic ascendency. He did, beginning on March 4, 1933. Since his defeat in 1926 Wadsworth aspired to high political office, particularly the Senate of the United States. However, too many Republicans across the state would not forgive him his wet stand, and, as the great depression deepened, his conservatism precluded senatorial nomination, let alone election.

90. David B. Burner, *The Politics of Provincialism* (New York: Alfred A. Knopf, 1968), p. 251.

But on a summer's day in 1932, while counseling party leaders in the comfortable Republican Committee rooms of the Union Trust Company in Rochester, opportunity knocked, not mightily, except for what Wadsworth would make of it. Carl Hallauer, a young Bausch and Lomb official, and Harry Bareham, the Monroe County chairman, urged the former senator to run for the House of Representatives. If he were to consent, the party could avoid a damaging intra-party contest for the nomination between the incumbent Archie Sanders and the vigorous though relatively unknown challenger, Nathan C. Shiverick.[91] Shiverick, Reverdy Wadsworth's godfather and for twenty years manager of Herbert Wadsworth's Avon estate, agreed to withdraw from the race if Wadsworth were to run.

The "primadonna" complex of senators and former senators frequently makes a lesser office unappealing to them. Such was not the case with Wadsworth. Assignment in "the other House" posed no threat. He was far too secure in status and commitment to public service. Besides, there was good precedent for stepping down. From the White House, John Quincy Adams descended to the House of Representatives. In the presence of Hallauer and Bareham, Wadsworth pondered the feelings of A.H.W. and Jerry and begged leave to think over the offer.

A.H.W. immediately sensed Jim's enthusiasm for a return to legislative life. "Jimmy, I'd go ahead," she urged. That left Jerry. At More Lands Wadsworth found him mending fences. The two adjourned to the More Lands office and over bourbon old-fashioneds Jerry too urged his father to run. Magnanimously, Wadsworth asked Jerry to make the race. "I could have had it," Jerry has told author Alden Hatch. "Father would have stood back and pushed me forward." But Jerry who had been elected to the Assembly only a year previously, deferred to his father. A week later Wadsworth returned to the bank rooms. With a bit of Wadsworthean arrogance, seldom manifested, he answered their queries: "Fellows, if you think its good for the Party and the Nation, I'll do it." [92]

Wadsworth reveled in being back in the thick and turmoil of politics. He easily picked up the campaign trail. It was like old times. And his ideas had not changed much. He advocated a 25 percent reduction in federal expenditures. He insisted that government not compete with business. He recommended the abolition of all unnecessary governmental activity. He wanted no federal aid to state and local governments. Specifically, he chastised the federal government for its expensive Agricultural Marketing Act.[93]

91. Hatch, *op. cit.*, pp. 234–235.
92. *Ibid.*, pp. 234–236.
93. *Rochester Times-Union*, Aug. 4, 1932.

Wadsworth sounded a conservative, though wet, clarion call in his congressional campaigning. Of course Democrats, from Franklin Roosevelt down to Daniel A. White, his own Democratic opponent, frequently sounded a similar call. Their liberalism was far more marked after the election than before.

While much of America put Democrats in office in 1932, New York's 39th Congressional District, West Rochester and the Genesee Valley, sent Wadsworth to Washington. His Democratic opponent, from Medina, carried only the Rochester wards. Ernst R. Clark, a Law Enforcement candidate, pulled few votes. The Geneseoan won by a comfortable 10,000-vote plurality. His election was an anomaly.[94] Few freshman Republicans would accompany him into the House well for installation on March 4, 1933.

94. *Rochester Democrat & Chronicle,* Nov. 3, 4, 5, 1932. *See* Appendix B for map of Wadsworth's congressional district, 1933–50.

IX

"Reform Is a Terrible Thing"

1

COLUMNIST Mark Sullivan thought Wadsworth "perhaps the one most important person who emerged . . . in the recent election."[1] Walter Lippmann saw his return to public life as an "example of high promise."[2] "Almost every day, and on every hand, in Washington," noted the *New York Times* columnist, Arthur Krock, "candid speculation about Mr. Wadsworth can be heard among all types of Republicans."[3] Certainly Washington Republicans did welcome back James Wadsworth. Indeed, the Roosevelt onslaught so reduced their numbers in "town" as to make any freshman Republican a novelty, let alone the former senior senator from New York. And Wadsworth looked particularly good next to surviving but lackluster Republicans who assumed their party's leadership on the hill—fellow New Yorker Bertrand H. Snell, the minority leader; Robert Luce of Massachusetts, the chairman of the Republican Conference; and Chester Bolton of Ohio, the chairman of the Republican Congressional Committee; along with an unglamorous lot of senators such as Charles McNary and Simeon Fess, respectively the minority and assistant minority leaders. The colorful senate Republicans James Watson, George Moses, and Reed Smoot had suffered defeat in the recent election, and the liberals, Hiram Johnson, Robert La Follette, Jr., and George Norris were *persona non grata* to most Republicans.

Like Krock and Sullivan, some Republicans expected Wadsworth's leadership in Congress to make him their standard-bearer in 1936. Generally, they expected either that his leadership of the Republican wet bloc

1. *Chicago Sunday Telegram*, Nov. 20, 1932.
2. Unidentified news clipping, Nov. 11, 1932, Wadsworth MSS, Library of Congress, Washington, D.C.
3. *New York Times*, Jan. 8, 1933.

in Congress would be broadened, or that his possible senatorial or gubernatorial candidacy in 1934 would lead to an active race for the presidential
nomination in 1936. Such thoughts were aided by the recent deaths of
Calvin Coolidge and Dwight W. Morrow, whom Republicans had looked
at longingly as presidential contenders. (Practically all Republicans felt
that Hoover's overwhelming defeat in 1932 disqualified him.) Political
observers were particularly impressed by the diversity among those Republicans who looked to Wadsworth for leadership, such as the sophisticated
Republican congressman from Old Westbury, New York, Robert Bacon,
Jr., and the much less sophisticated Mrs. Mabel Willebrandt, the former
dry crusader. Interestingly, many of the new congressman's followers
feared most the competition for presidential nomination thrown up by his
fellow New Yorker, Ogden Mills, the former Secretary of the Treasury.[4]

"Jim's ears must be burned off by now," commented one reporter about
the laurels heaped on the New Yorker early in 1933.[5] But although self-
assured as always, Wadsworth reentered Washington with his usual lack
of bombast. He had no interest in trying to bypass the seniority system.
Instead, he basked quietly in the reception given by old friends on the
hill, Republicans and Democrats. Some, of course, received him well for
his expected leadership in the Republican party; others, because he was
one Republican who fought the drys. Some accepted him for continuing
the Wadsworth tradition of service in Washington. Many Washingtonians
just liked Wadsworth for his quiet gregariousness. Without question, the
New Yorker enjoyed being back in his Woodland Drive home early in
1933. Not yet burdened by the trials of the leviathan New Deal, and not
yet pegged as its obstinate critic, his life was serene for the moment, despite the depths of depression which marred the landscape for him and
all America.

The joy for Wadsworth of again being on the Washington scene was
enhanced by repeal of the Eighteenth Amendment. Although the repeal
effort had moved like the proverbial tortoise through the twenties, at times
immobile, as in 1926 when New York's upstaters voted for Cristman, in
1933 it bounded to a successful end. The Democratic sweep in 1932, with
its undaunted repeal plank, did it. When the lame duck Congress convened after the election, both houses voted overwhelmingly for the repeal
of the Eighteenth Amendment. Now the wets were supreme and, as Andrew Sinclair has noted, as fanatical for repeal as the drys had been for

4. Unidentified news clipping, 1933, Wadsworth MSS.
5. Ray Tucker, unidentified news clipping, 1933, Wadsworth MSS.

the original amendment.[6] They would accept only outright repeal. Wadsworth was not yet in the House of Representatives, but fellow New Yorker, Emmanuel Celler, spoke for him and wets across the land: "Let us flee from prohibition as one would from a foul dungeon, from a charnel house."[7] In passing the Twenty-first Amendment, Congress gave the drys only one concession. Liquor would not be permitted in states which prohibited it.

To make sure that rural drys would not obstruct ratification of the Twenty-first Amendment in the states, wets had insisted that the states vote on ratification by state conventions rather than by rurally-dominated legislatures. Wadsworth wanted even more assurance that the states would ratify. In March of 1932 he had urged that the Congress direct that delegates be elected by congressional districts rather than by the more rurally-drawn lower house districts of the states. It was ironic that one whose life epitomized American ruralism now expressed shock at such over-rural representation. "It is well known," he argued emphatically, "that the rotten borough exists in many of the states, some of them surviving from pre-revolutionary days. In these states, the rural population enjoys a representation in the lower house of the State Legislature far greater proportionately than the urban districts. Many years must elapse and terrific political battles must be fought before these situations can be cured. Were conventions of the people in the states to be based upon such representation the verdicts of these conventions might run absolutely contrary to the will of the people. I think we should not risk such a result."[8] But the Congress did risk such a result. It did as Wadsworth would want on any other occasion. It let the states determine the selection of delegates to ratifying conventions.

The New York Legislature acted to have its delegates to the state convention elected at large. Over dinner in late March 1933, Wadsworth and Al Smith drew up a tentative bipartisan slate. To their mutual satisfaction, Al would chair the convention and Jim would serve as vice chairman, and each named the faithful wets of his respective party to go on the slate of 150. Because the Democrats dominated the State House and the Legislature in Albany, they understandably dominated the slate.[9]

Preparation for the repeal convention brought Smith and Wadsworth

6. Andrew Sinclair, Era of Excess, A Social History of the Prohibition Movement (New York: Harper & Row, 1962), Ch. 21, passim.
7. Ibid., p. 366.
8. J. W. Wadsworth Memorandum, March 25, 1932. Wadsworth MSS.
9. J.W.W. to Alfred E. Smith, March 24, 1933, Wadsworth MSS.

together in a way reminiscent of Assembly days. Lurking behind their common repeal efforts was a shared uneasiness about Franklin Roosevelt. Foreshadowings of their future venture against the thirty-first president were apparent. As their relationship warmed, Wadsworth confessed his pleasure at their recent conversation which gave him a "chance to say some things . . . [to Smith he had] never said before."[10]

The drys across the state put up a slate to oppose the wets in the special election on May 23. Placid-faced, but burning, E. A. Boole, Wadsworth's 1920 Prohibition opponent, pleaded with the W.C.T.U. members to give up their gold and silver and their jewels to raise money to fight the Smith-Wadsworth slate.[11] But their day was done. The pendulum had swung; drys were in great disrepute. They lost by a ratio of 20 to 1.

The New York repeal convention was a happy and satisfying affair. It convened in Albany's ornate assembly chamber, home to both Smith and Wadsworth. At 11:35 A.M. on June 27, 1933, Governor Herbert Lehman, the temporary chairman, led the state's leaders of repeal from the Speaker's rooms into the chamber. In his address, Governor Lehman paid particular tribute to Smith and Wadsworth and to J. D. Rockefeller and Elihu Root, the other noted apostles of repeal in New York. Following Smith's nomination and election, Elihu Root was elected honorary president of the convention. Smith graciously introduced the eighty-eight-year-old statesman, noting that truth and honor had followed him through his distinguished career. The acclaim, one of the last accorded to him, was loud and warm.[12] Wadsworth beamed. "You would have been delighted at Senator Root," he later reported to a former senate colleague. "The old gentleman made a fine speech, gossiped with everybody, paid strict attention to the proceedings and had the time of his life."[13]

Then followed Wadsworth's nomination and election as vice president of the convention. "No introduction is needed; he is no stranger to this rostrum," commented Smith as he welcomed him to his side. "How times have changed! Think of you and me on the same ticket," replied Wadsworth, to the appreciative laughter of the audience. The Geneseoan quickly turned to the business at hand: "It had been a long battle," he stated, "[but] life is contention." Expectedly, he noted the error of the Eighteenth Amendment. More interestingly, he reminded the delegation that the last time such a convention was elected by the people was 145 years before, to ratify the Constitution of the United States. With a note

10. *Ibid.*
11. *New York Times,* April 20, 1933.
12. *Ibid.,* June 28, 1933.
13. J.W.W. to J. S. Frelinghuysen, July 11, 1933, Wadsworth MSS.

of exaggeration, he said he was sure that the constitutional "fathers" would be pleased that the people of the state and not the legislature had elected them. Indeed, he concluded, the "fathers" expected that all substantive amendments would be ratified by conventions rather than by state legislatures. Had such been the case regarding the Eighteenth Amendment, he believed it probably would not have been written into the Constitution. There was no doubt in his mind that the people in the several states would now elect conventions to do what New York was proceeding to do, ratify the Twenty-first Amendment.[14]

The New York convention ratified the Twenty-first Amendment without a dissenting vote. Other states would ratify with much less ease, but would ratify. While Wadsworth knew they would, he feared that Republican leaders across the country would let the Democrats lead the fight and get the credit. "This has been a great and continuing disappointment," he wrote to Reed Smoot of Utah, "for I had hoped that our Republican leaders would have recovered from their timidity. . . . As one of your old friends I would not like to hear it charged that you had swung the State into a place of utter solitude."[15] Smoot, steering clear of the fight, personified the ostrich-like Republican leaders Wadsworth was describing. At exactly 5:32-½ (New York time) on December 5, 1933, bone dry Utah repealed, and as the thirty-sixth state to do so, brought prohibition in the United States to an end.

Not all New Yorkers expressed glee at repeal. From Rochester, Frank Gannett, the powerful owner of a chain of New York and out-of-state newspapers, saddened by its acceptance, pleaded for moderation. Wadsworth assured him that repeal in New York would be moderate. He personally urged local option upon the state Liquor Control Board. Gannett could keep rural patches of New York dry and would do so for years to come. By and large, however, the citizens of no state so thirsted for repeal as did New Yorkers, and Wadsworth was no exception.[16]

2

"You may be interested to know that I like the House of Representatives," Wadsworth wrote to former Senator Frelinghuysen. "There are

14. *New York Times,* June 28, 1933.
15. J.W.W. to Reed Smoot, Sept. 30, 1933, Wadsworth MSS.
16. J.W.W. to Frank E. Gannett, Oct. 23, 1933, Wadsworth MSS.

a lot of very good and agreeable men there especially among the younger men on the Republican side. They have not yet emerged into prominence but they are good material for the future. We Republicans, of course, don't amount to a row of pins, being outvoted 3 to 1. But it is rather fun to watch the huge Democratic majority hanging sometimes by a mere thread and . . . to see conservative Democrats quietly expressing their concern over some of the radical measures which Roosevelt has made them put through. The atmosphere of the House is one of rough and tumble as compared with the Senate. One gets the very clear impression that one does not amount to very much! There is little chance for acquiring a swelled head there, especially if you are in a helpless minority. I have been trying to persuade Hiram Bingham to come to the House from his home district in Connecticut and I have also been after Jim Watson. Why don't you try it? Really it is well worth it." [17]

Thus Wadsworth summed up his feeling after the famous First One Hundred Days. It was an honest reflection. Republicans in the Seventy-third Congress did not amount to a "row of pins." "The Republican side . . . [did look] pitiful," agreed one House Democrat, Wilburn Cartwright of Oklahoma, "mostly empty seats as they had been well thinned out in the previous election. The few remaining members were afraid to squawk." Another Democrat did not pity the Republicans, commenting happily: "A few years ago you had to use the whole house for your caucus—now you can hold it in a phone booth." [18] As small as the caucuses were, Wadsworth dutifully attended and loyally supported Minority Leader Bertrand Snell. He brushed aside as "unfair" stories that the wet Republican bloc would advance him for the Republican leadership. Usually Wadsworth eschewed attention. On one occasion, when cloakroom talk turned to his 1936 presidential possibilities, he retreated hastily.[19]

Just as dutifully, the freshman congressman accepted assignment to the Banking and Currency Committee although he would have much preferred Military Affairs. There were no vacancies on the latter, and besides, fellow New Yorker Walter Andrews from Buffalo already sat on the committee. In addition to the Banking and Currency Committee, Wadsworth had appointments to the committees of Elections and Public Lands. The Elections Committee made some jaunts investigating the election of colleagues. He rather enjoyed Public Lands, which he held until 1937, because of his own western experience from 1911 to 1915.

17. J.W.W. to J. S. Frelinghuysen, July, 1933, Wadsworth MSS.

18. James T. Patterson, *Congressional Conservatism and the New Deal* (Lexington, Ky.: University of Kentucky Press, 1967), Ch. 1, *passim*.

19. *New York Times*, Jan. 12, 1933.

Wadsworth's House experience was not like that of the old Senate days when he quietly presided over the much smaller Military Affairs Committee in a great suite off the Senate. "There were twenty-five of us [on Banking and Currency]—a mob," he wrote a downstate friend. "The Chairman, Henry B. Steagall, talks all the time and confusion reigns." He did note the presence of a few good men, Republicans of course, who "will have to stand guard" against "crazy" proposals likely to be thrown at the committee. To prepare himself to talk intelligently from the bottom of the table, he asked Charles Sabin, chairman of the board of the New York Guaranty Bank, to "jot down some of your ideas about our banking system." [20]

The atmosphere of the House was indeed "one of rough and tumble as compared to the Senate." James Bryce's classic description of the House in *The American Commonwealth,* although antedating Wadsworth's tenure by a quarter of a century, was still largely valid:

> When you enter, your first impression is of noise and turmoil, a noise like that of short sharp waves in a Highland loch, fretting under a squall against a rocky shore. The raising and dropping of desk lids, the scratching of pens, the clapping of hands to call the pages, keen little boys who race along the gangways, the pattering of many feet, the hum of talking on the floor and in the galleries, make up a din over which the Speaker with the sharp taps of his hammer, or the orators straining shrill throats, find it hard to make themselves audible. Nor is it only the noise that gives the impression of disorder. Often three or four members are on their feet at once, each shouting to catch the Speaker's attention. Others tired of sitting still, rise to stretch themselves, while the Western visitor, long, lank, and imperturbable, leans his arms on the railing, chewing his cigar, and surveys the scene with little reverence. Less favorable conditions for oratory cannot be imagined.[21]

In quite another important aspect the House differed from the "other body," especially as Wadsworth had known the Senate in the 1920s. In the previous decade the Senate and, only to a lesser degree, the House, were comprised of members who prided themselves on being independent of the President. Key Pittman of Nevada warned Franklin Roosevelt that "during the long Republican regime . . . Congressmen have grown individualistic, they have lost the habit of cooperation, they have grown un-

20. J.W.W. to Charles H. Sabin, March 24, 1933, Wadsworth MSS.
21. James Bryce, *The American Commonwealth,* Vol. 1 (New York: The Macmillan Co., 1912), p. 145.

accustomed to discipline." Wadsworth respected that congressional independence and would have hoped Pittman was right.[22] Pittman, however, was wrong. Given the conditions of the country in 1933 and the adept manner of Roosevelt's leadership, Congress was anything but rebellious. To Wadsworth's fascination and horror, the House, during the First One Hundred Days of the Seventy-third Congress, passed fifteen key bills with only forty hours of debate. And in the case of the important emerging banking legislation, of particular interest to Wadsworth as a new member of the sponsoring committee, the New Yorker watched in disbelief the bill's passage after less than one hour's debate. In much of the New Deal legislation in that important period, Congress gave the President more than he asked for by way of tax, currency, collective bargaining, and minimum wage legislation. Congressmen, even many Republicans, seemed infected by F.D.R.'s charm and popularity. "I like him very much," wrote home the senate Republican leader, Charles McNary.[23]

Wadsworth did not like Franklin Roosevelt, even though occasionally they had seen each other socially and had swum together in Rock Creek Park. He cared little for him socially and not at all politically. Instead, Wadsworth sided with Representative James Beck of Pennsylvania, Harding's and Coolidge's former Solicitor General, in preparing some kind of assault on the New Deal.[24] Thus far, Republicans were woefully disorganized. And while Wadsworth approved of Snell's attack, chiding the administration for the nation's growing indebtedness and for its huge expenditures, he wanted a more effective attack on the New Deal.[25] For one thing, he was sure ten-minute speeches would not have sufficient effect. He preferred three first-class speeches on a measure such as the National Industrial Recovery Act rather than a dozen very brief comments. "A man had to be a genius at 'staccato utterance' to even hold the attention of the weary members with such a speech."[26] To speak only meaningfully in the House was Wadsworth's mission for years to come. As an individual congressman he made it work. He usually took the House floor only when granted a reasonable time allocation, and only when he felt prepared to say something worthwhile. In time his remarks were so anticipated that frequently someone called for a quorum, often over the Genoseoan's protests. Comments for the *Congressional Record* were of little interest to

22. Patterson, *op. cit.*, p. 1.
23. *Ibid*, p. 8.
24. J.W.W. to James M. Beck, Sept. 1, 1933, Wadsworth MSS.
25. J.W.W. to A. B. Houghton, July 12, 1933, Wadsworth MSS.
26. J.W.W. to James M. Beck, Aug. 15, 1933, Wadsworth MSS.

him. Unfortunately little of Wadsworth's example brushed off on Republican colleagues. Still, in future years colleagues remembered him for the way the House listened when he spoke. Invariably he spoke simply, yet in depth, usually by combining his specialization efforts in the House in the areas of finance, government control, foreign affairs, and military affairs with his almost innate conservatism.

3

On January 30, 1933, Wadsworth went to Topeka, Kansas, the heartland of America, and there, at the GOP's annual Harvest Day shebang, enunciated his conservatism. While Topeka had its old Bull Moose Progressives, traditional Republicans there had their day with James Wadsworth. He talked their language of classical economics. The root of America's problems, he explained, lay in World War I and its consequent destruction of property. The borrowing of money by people and governments to compensate for the destruction of production was excessive and contagious. Everybody borrowed, here and abroad. "The simple life was pooh-poohed, a new era dawned." Finally, by the summer of 1927, he noted, "one of the attenuated tottering props underneath . . . the economy . . . snapped, the whole mass crashed down through the flimsy financial structure underneath and crushed the world with its inert weight." Wadsworth blamed no one government, certainly not the Republican administrations of the 1920s. Instead, he blamed the "inevitable penalty of human passions." He saw no answers in the many "nostrums proposed over the three years of Depression." In fact, the New Yorker believed that such government "nostrums" as price fixing, trade controls, and farm supports would interfere with the economic law. He did agree with Hoover's moratorium on German reparations and European debts. Both should be forgiven in order to start again the "tide of the world" which would make America prosperous. It wasn't easy, however, for Wadsworth to forgive the foreign debts.[27]

In essence, Wadsworth at Topeka reflected the bias of traditional Republicans. He deplored domestic indebtedness and government interference. He insisted that private enterprise be kept free, and he exhorted all to have faith in the economic law. It seemed as if he remembered well William Graham Sumner's lessons on Darwinism taught him at Yale. (At

27. Speech delivered at Topeka, Kansas, Jan. 30, 1933, Wadsworth MSS.

least, like Sumner, Wadsworth's actions were consistent with his words. As Sumner did then, the New Yorker now favored tariff reductions and trade reciprocity.)

On March 11, just seven days after Roosevelt's fateful inauguration as president, Wadsworth again pointed to the world debacle as the cause of America's suffering. Now he spoke as a member of the Congress's loyal opposition to the national Columbia Broadcasting System audience from Washington's Shoreham Hotel. For a moment he was gripped by a strange interlude, as indeed was the nation. For once he supported a Democratic president. Never again would he do so, at least not on the great domestic issues of the day. Clinging to his belief in the economic law of sound currencies and balanced budgets, he applauded the new president's actions in declaring a bank holiday and in requesting congressional action on an economy bill. In the case of the former, he supported the "dictatorial" powers which the Congress gave to the President to "open" the banks on a sound currency basis. In regard to the latter, he was elated by the President's early implementation of the Economy Act which effected a 15 percent cut in pensions for veterans and the salaries of federal employees. Wadsworth closed his address in full support of the President: "Events are placing upon the shoulders of the President of the United States a tremendous burden of responsibility. He will carry that responsibility much more easily if the people of the country, the great army of Americans, conform to necessary discipline and stand united in support of his measures. I am confident the people today welcome the opportunity —this opportunity to serve." [28]

Wadsworth soon regretted his words. Little had he dreamed that in the hundred days between early March and the middle of June the President would push fifteen major laws to enactment, most of which appalled the Geneseoan. On March 20, he gladly supported the President's request for 3.2 percent beer but such support practically ended his honeymoon with the President. Roosevelt's extended honeymoon with the vast majority of the Congress, however, mostly with Democrats, brought forth such landmark programs as the Civilian Conservation Corps, the Federal Emergency Relief Administration, the Agriculture Adjustment Administration, the Tennessee Valley Authority, the Truth-in-Securities Act, the abrogation of the gold standard, the National Recovery Administration, and the second Glass-Steagall Act (not to be confused with the 1932 act by the same name). Through the first third of the one hundred days, Wadsworth clung to the "utter stagnation of international trade" as the cause of the depression, and sought answers in the improvement of trade by reducing

28. Copy of address over the Columbia Broadcasting System by James W. Wadsworth, March 11, 1933, Wadsworth MSS.

tariffs, by forgiving many inter-governmental debts, and by maintaining sound currencies.[29] The New Dealers, however, viewed America's problems as basically internal and soluble by vigorous domestic programs.

By early May, Wadsworth cried for a stop to the New Deal parade of domestic legislation. When John Rankin of Mississippi asked him what general policy "would . . . meet that overwhelming burden that confronts the people of the world," Wadsworth replied, "Let economic law take its course." During the debate, however, Wadsworth admitted that recent tariffs had been excessively high. Whereupon, the scholarly Hatton W. Sumners of Texas wondered if now government should not aid others in order to counteract the long-standing tariff "interference with the operation of natural law."

The dialogue was classic. Sumners and Wadsworth represented the elite and powerful of their respective parties. "The galleries cannot hear us," said Sumners, "so we might as well talk about this thing. . . . Here is my opinion: with agriculture prostrate and almost bled white, should we not give it a blood transfusion [with price supports, etc.]? Would not that be the evolution of natural law?" "No," answered Wadsworth, "that is not the evolution of natural law. I do not think the pending measures [AAA and farm relief] constitute blood transfusions. I speak the point of view of a farmer. That has been my life and the life of my father before me." The discussion then ranged quietly over the pending regulatory proposals. Wadsworth became adamant. "I do not want my business regulated by the Secretary of Agriculture or any one else. If I am not fit to conduct it, then I deserve to lose it, and I hope that Uncle Sam will never be dressed up as a nurse girl to take care of people who cannot run their business."[30]

By June 16, 1933, the New Deal had ground out its program of the one hundred days, ignoring, of course, Wadsworth and the Republicans. His opposition was almost total. By late June he particularly feared the permanency of many New Deal programs, such as the NRA which he thought had been passed as a temporary measure. "If the attempt is made," he said on the House floor on June 17, "to make the [NRA] plan permanent, we will find ourselves on the verge of a great fundamental constitutional contest, revolving [around] the proposal that individualism shall not be our dominant trait as a nation but that we shall be a regimented people."[31]

Aside from his opposition to the regulatory and permanency aspects of

29. J.W.W. to W. Douglas Ward, Apr. 4, 1933, Wadsworth MSS.

30. *Congressional Record*, Vol. 77, 73rd Congress, 1st Session, 1933, pp. 2830–4.

31. *New York Times*, June 18, 1933.

the NRA, by the fall of 1933 Wadsworth did not think it was working. "I cannot identify the slightest benefits from the NRA movement in this rural region," he wrote to Representative James M. Beck on September 1. "Further, it is having no beneficial effect among merchants and business concerns in the smaller cities and villages." Specifically, he noted that Genesee valley employers had already paid the minimum wage but now were hurt by the maximum hours restriction for "it is impossible for them to put on a second shift." As for local farmers, they were "getting nothing out of it except the immediate prospect of paying more for their supplies." [32]

The fall of 1933 was politically a long one for Wadsworth and most Republicans. Democrats happily digested the measures of the one hundred days, and the country generally seemed content. Aside from northwestern farmers, who nearly revolted, people were grateful. Conditions were improving. Banks were open. Employment rose. People ate. Homes were saved. Construction was up. Yet many Geneseoans, like Wadsworth, feared the New Deal's success. They feared its constitutional implications and were ready to do battle to save the Constitution. Their congressman spoke for them. From his Geneseo office he put pen to an address to be delivered to young Republicans in Baltimore, Ohio. "Frankly," he wrote, "I anticipate the oncoming of [a] great contest. If and when it comes, into what political alignments shall our people fall? Can we hope that the Democratic Party as a National organization will throw the weight of its influence against the [New Deal] movement? Will it be faithful to the philosophy of its great founder, Thomas Jefferson, or will it yield to the political temptation of the hour? Let us hope, sincerely, that the old Democratic Party will refuse to sell its birthright for a mess of political pottage. It will serve its country mightily if it does so refuse." [33]

When the Seventy-third Congress again convened on January 3, 1943, Wadsworth offered the New Dealers no support. Rather he was primed to fight them. He thought the agriculture program was weak in three respects. The Thomas Amendment to the AAA pushed inflation at a time when sound currency was desperately needed. The Frazier bill provided for immense loans to the farmers to be "piled on top of the present huge National debt." And the regulation of farm prices by enforcing a policy of scarcity was undemocratic. He still plunked for "the opening up of foreign markets" as a way out for agriculture. Of the three elements in the agriculture program, its inflationary element disturbed him most.

32. J.W.W. to James M. Beck, Sept. 1, 1933, Wadsworth MSS.
33. Speech presented before Young Republican League, Baltimore, Ohio, Oct. 18, 1933, Wadsworth MSS.

244 THE GENTLEMAN FROM NEW YORK

"The President's suggestion of devaluing the dollar," he complained to a constituent, "amounts to putting the government in charge of the amount of currency which shall be in use from time to time, rather than to let the demands of industry and agriculture work their automatic control." [34] Wadsworth, of course, was right. F.D.R. was not averse to experimenting with currency control.

By the second session of the Seventy-third Congress the NRA was anathema to Wadsworth. In regard to the Civilian Works Administration, a program to give relief money in exchange for some work, the Geneseoan wondered if "a straight out dole [might not] . . . be better." And he felt that any amount spent on a proposed St. Lawrence waterway would be a waste of money.[35] Wagner's proposed Industrial Disputes bill, the forerunner of the famous Wagner Labor Relations Act, was evil to Wadsworth, outlawing as it would the company union. "I do not want the government to tell people just exactly how they shall bargain, and through what agencies." [36]

Two bills particularly earned Wadsworth's attention in the spring of 1934, the Securities and Exchange bill and the Veterans' Pension bill.

No proposed legislation upset large business interests in the country more than the Securities and Exchange bill, sent to Capitol Hill by the President on February 9, 1934. Essentially, the bill was intended to protect investors from insider's manipulation of the securities market, and to reduce the speculation on the market by increasing the margin requirements. Financiers protested that the regulation required to implement the legislation's objectives would greatly inhibit the Exchange. "Besides," noted Richard Whitney, the president of the New York Exchange, "the Exchange is a perfect institution." Moderates like James Forrestal (of Dillon, Reed) and Robert A. Lovett (of Brown Brothers), seeing the inevitability of such legislation, came to work with the administration in the hope of getting a law satisfactory to Washington and to Wall Street.[37]

Wadsworth, whose congressional specialization in finance and his newly-achieved seat on the Interstate and Foreign Commerce Committee brought him close to the Securities and Exchange Commission legislation, took a middle position on the bill, between that of Whitney and Forrestal. After some weeks of committee hearings, he ventured particular exceptions to the bill: the forbidding of investment by members of the Exchange, the

34. J.W.W. to Mark Kling, Jan. 2, 1934, Wadsworth MSS.
35. J.W.W. to O. Edwin Risley, Jan. 17, 1934, Wadsworth MSS.
36. J.W.W. to John J. Scully, March 30, 1934, Wadsworth MSS.
37. Arthur W. Schlesinger, Jr., The Coming of the New Deal (Boston, Mass.: Houghton Mifflin Co., 1958), Ch. 29, passim.

requirement that a list of all stockholders accompany proxies, the rigidity of margin requirements, and the provision that "no loans may be made by a broker except . . . [those that] are collaterated by securities listed on the stock exchange."[38] In late April, on the floor of the House, he added two more concerns, the *carte blanche* authority of the Securities and Exchange Commission to determine what securities might be listed by the Exchange, and bookkeeping requirements frequently duplicating the state formats. Democrats chided the New Yorker for failing to note recent floor amendments to the bill. Wadsworth did admit with "pleasure" that the committee had effected certain changes in the bill—the reduction of margins, the permitting of Exchange members to invest on the market, and the dropping of the requirement that the names of all stockholders (*e.g.*, 160,000 in ATT) be submitted with proxy forms sent to shareholders.[39]

On two points Wadsworth was adamant in his opposition to the S.E.C. legislation. He viewed Section 2 as "a speech" which emphasized the evils in the present system for one purpose only, to force a favorable Supreme Court decision. "I have never seen anything quite like it. . . . It has no place in a statute of the United States." Secondly, he felt that the banks should not come under the margin requirements; that if they were loaning too much money for speculative purposes, the Federal Reserve Board had, under the 1933 Glass-Steagall Act, authority to control them.[40] Furthermore, Wadsworth's modest experience as a director of the Geneseo bank demonstrated that rather intimate relationships between banker and borrower made margin requirements unnecessary. The banker, unlike the broker, knew what a sound loan would be for a borrower. The New Dealers had their way. The act passed, 281 to 84, with the Geneseoan in the negative. The President signed the landmark act on June 6, 1934.

Wadsworth took much interest in the Independent Offices Appropriation bill, vetoed by the President on March 26 and passed over the President's veto shortly thereafter. It was the President's first severe jolt in the Congress. Ironically, the President vetoed the bill principally because it restored many of the 1933 Economy Act cuts which Wadsworth and the Republicans had applauded so heartily.[41] But Wadsworth, patron of the armed services, could not understand continuing the 15 percent cut in veterans' pensions when the President had encouraged a 10 percent increase in wages across the country. Furthermore, Wadsworth viewed the

38. J.W.W. to W.G. Andrews, March 3, 1934, Wadsworth MSS.
39. *Congressional Record,* Vol. 78, 73rd Congress, 2nd Session, 1934, pp. 7713–15.
40. *Ibid.*
41. *New York Times,* March 22, 23, 27 and 28, 1934.

15 percent increase in the cost of living as more than justification for the restoration of veterans' pensions. Wadsworth also took the President to task for opposing the bill because it restored 29,000 "presumptive pensions" of World War I veterans and the pensions of Spanish American War veterans. The New York congressman agreed that pensions for disability, "presuming" to be service-related, should be reviewed, but not "cruelly" cut off before review. He also felt that the administration should restore all pensions of Spanish-American War veterans at 75 percent of the original pensions without any review because of the sparseness of medical records of such veterans.[42]

Wadsworth's actions demonstrated that when he was put to a choice between saving money or aiding the veteran, he frequently chose the latter. The President and the Director of the Budget fumed at a Wadsworth memorandum justifying the congressional action. Roosevelt described him as "not wholly correct or sincere."[43] Douglas called his support "wilfully deceiving."[44] The strong language of the President and his budget director apparently stemmed from the credibility the Wadsworth memorandum cost the administration with the New York Times. The great paper had supported the President on the issue and Louis Wiley, its managing editor, personally asked the President for clarification of the Wadsworth memorandum. Lewis Douglas intended to reply to Wiley, but if he did, his answer is lost to history.[45] At any rate the Geneseoan gladly helped put down the President.

Few other Republicans in the House of Representatives hit the President and the New Deal as soon and as meaningfully as did Wadsworth. Bertrand Snell, the Republican minority leader, and Hamilton Fish, the blue-stocking congressman from Dutchess County, New York, talked more but had less national impact than Wadsworth. Snell was a tough floor leader of his party in the House but lacked any charisma. Fish was too loud and controversial to gather much support beyond his district. John Taber of Auburn, New York, was on his way to becoming a New Deal critic, but as yet he lacked the seniority to attract national attention. Robert Luce and Chester Bolton held important committee positions, but they

42. James W. Wadsworth, "Statement Concerning Passage of Independent Offices Appropriation Bill over Presidential Veto," Franklin D. Roosevelt MSS, Franklin D. Roosevelt Library, Hyde Park, N.Y.

43. Franklin D. Roosevelt to Lewis Douglas, May 11, 1934, Franklin D. Roosevelt MSS.

44. Lewis Douglas to Franklin D. Roosevelt, May 11, 1934, Franklin D. Roosevelt MSS.

45. Franklin D. Roosevelt Library staff reports that no reply from Douglas to Wiley is in Franklin D. Roosevelt collection.

were so inconspicuous that they were practically ignored by the press. Joseph Martin of Massachusetts and Clifford Hope of Kansas did share anti-New Deal honors with Wadsworth.

The National Radio Forum invited Wadsworth to sum up the Republican position in a broadcast arranged by the *Washington Star* for April 2, 1934. He struck hard at the centralization of New Deal government, particularly as typified by the National Recovery Administration and the Agriculture Adjustment Administration. He struck painstakingly at the New Deal's undemocratic, centralist, regulatory, and permanent programs. At least some of his radio and newspaper audience applauded him for his words:

> In view of the combination of events rapidly unfolding before our very eyes, there can be no doubt whatsoever that we are face to face with a tremendous issue. What is to be done about this program which seeks the abandonment of the American conception of liberty under a Constitution; which challenges the Tenth Amendment by putting the Federal Government in the possession of complete authority over these matters which that Amendment reserves to the States and the people; which spells the end of the Federal Union of States; which sets up a government imperial in character, ruled by a huge bureaucracy and controlling the daily lives of millions of people—tells them, in fact, how they shall earn a living?
>
> If this program is to become permanent, if this new philosophy is to prevail, then, indeed, our children will exist as subjects in a land where their forefathers have lived as masters.[46]

Although fearful for the nation's future under the New Deal, by late spring of 1934 Wadsworth could not believe the people would sustain the administration. "I agree with you," he wrote Theodore Roosevelt, Jr., "the tide is turning. More and more people are waking up to what this whole thing means. Sending that little tailor in Jersey City to jail the other day for charging thirty-five cents for pressing a suit of clothes instead of the forty cents dictated by the [NRA] code represents a fine spectacle."[47] In fine spirits and form, Wadsworth, on June 11, drove over to Geneva, New York, from Geneseo to deliver the Hobart College Phi Beta Kappa address. Again he filled his listeners' ears with the evils of the new paternalism in Washington.

46. *Washington Evening Star*, Apr. 21, 1934.
47. J.W.W. to Theodore Roosevelt, Jr., Apr. 24, 1934, Wadsworth MSS.

4

That Wadsworth intended to strike at the New Deal after its first year was attested to by his heavy involvement in the formation of the American Liberty League. Indeed, he was the single Republican in prominent political office to help organize it. More than any group of Americans, the Liberty League existed to stem the New Deal tide. In actuality the organization was conceived in the mind of John Jacob Raskob, former national chairman of the Democratic party. While commiserating one day with R. R. M. Carpenter, a retired DuPont vice president, about the Roosevelt leadership, he suggested that the DuPont and General Motors groups be induced to "organize to protect society from the sufferings which it is bound to endure if we allow communist elements to lead the people to believe that all businessmen are crooks." [48] The proposed organization shortly took solid form when Raskob's mentor, Al Smith, for some time disenchanted with Franklin Roosevelt, agreed to help and in turn sought the aid of the Geneseo Republican. Wadsworth and Smith served as the first directors of the organization. Its executive committee consisted of John W. Davis, the 1924 Democratic candidate for president; Jouett Shouse, former executive chairman of the Democratic National Committee; Nathan I. Miller, former Republican governor of New York; Irenee DuPont, the well-known Delaware industrialist; along with Wadsworth and Smith. At its first organizational meeting in late August of 1934, Wadsworth gladly nominated Jouett Shouse as president of the League. Shouse, who was duly elected, had worked closely with Wadsworth in the Association Against the Prohibition Amendment. At the second meeting of the League's executive committee, on September 4, Wadsworth was instrumental in having his old friend from AAPA days, Captain William Stayton, elected executive secretary of the organization. [49]

Shouse's announcement that the League's intentions were to "teach the necessity of respect for the rights of persons and property" and "the duty of government to encourage individual and group initiative and enterprise" fooled few people as to its unannounced aim, to bring about the defeat of Franklin D. Roosevelt. Because the leadership was avowedly

48. Frederick Rudolph, "The American Liberty League, 1934–1940," *American Historical Review*, LVI, No. 1, Oct. 1950, pp. 19–33; also, George Wolfskill, *The Revolt of the Conservatives, A History of the Liberty League* (Boston: Houghton-Mifflin Co., 1962), Ch. 1 and 2.

49. Minutes of meetings of Directors of American Liberty League, Aug. 28, Sept. 4, Sept. 18, 1934, Wadsworth MSS.

anti-Roosevelt and because it emphasized so much the rights of individuals rather than their equality, the League shortly became suspect. Even though Roosevelt feigned support of the League's aims for the rights of individuals, he taunted the organization "for having failed to advocate the other seven or eight commandments." The President felt the war from the right. "All the big guns," he wrote Ambassador Bill Bullitt in Moscow, "have started shooting—Al Smith, John W. Davis, James W. Wadsworth, DuPont, Shouse, etc. Their organization has already been labeled the 'I Can't Take it Club.' " [50] While the contest between Roosevelt and the League was grim, it was not without its lighter moments. When the President heard that sophisticated Wall Streeters were actually evincing interest in the new organization, he laughed for ten minutes.

Throughout the fall of 1934, Wadsworth assiduously attended the meetings of the League's executive committee. As in AAPA days, he and Shouse counseled Stayton in his oversight of organizational details, including the League's growth plans to encompass women and the younger New Deal antagonists. Mrs. Charles Sabin, another associate from the repeal days, was placed on the board of directors,[51] and Jerry's colleagues in the recent repeal organization of young people, the Crusaders, were recruited into the League's ranks. In addition to ringing in former repeal associates, the League proceeded to establish state divisions and national chapters of businessmen, farmers, laborers, and lawyers.

Unlike the AAPA, however, membership in the Liberty League went little beyond 75,000. No labor or farm divisions were ever established. In fact, the League seriously lacked grass roots support. Its membership was largely drawn from the well-known business and industrial interests of the East and the North and some Jeffersonian Democrats, particularly from the South. Also, even though a million dollars was spent to proselytize people to the League's idea of the American way, its enunciations were too Darwinistic and smacked too much of "romantic individualism, the worship of success and the high value of personal power and prestige" to appeal to any large numbers of Americans. At times, League spokesmen bordered on arrogance, as when a Wisconsin member said for publication: "The farmer without anything north or south of his neck . . . needs a prod in the pants and not a pat on the back." [52]

50. Schlesinger, Jr., op. cit., pp. 486–7, passim.
51. Minutes of American Liberty League, Aug. 28, 1934, Wadsworth MSS.
52. Rudolph, op. cit., passim. For excellent accounts of support of the League by Jeffersonian Democrats, see Wolfskill, op. cit., Ch. 7; D. R. McCoy, Landon of Kansas (Lincoln, Neb.: University of Nebraska Press, 1966), pp. 268–9. McCoy particularly emphasizes the role in the Liberty League of Henry Breckenridge,

Some League members grumbled about the League being too mealy-mouthed. J. Howard Pew, of the Sun Oil complex, complained to Wadsworth that the League would "not establish itself unless it demonstrates wisdom enough to find the right side of these controversial issues." While more sophisticated than the Wisconsinite, Pew nevertheless wanted war on "the socialization of industry" and the "nationalization of property." Pew was right about the League's non-controversial rhetoric. The League was trapped. If it talked about the New Deal as the Wisconsin member or Pew talked, depression victims would scorn it.[53] If it talked about the New Deal in philosophical terms, its rhetoric, while well-sounding, offered no solutions to the same victims of the great economic crisis.

The League had no more loyal supporter than Wadsworth. When its fortunes were particularly low in early 1935 because it had not gathered its expected support, he wrote and traveled to forestall the League's collapse. Also, he did his bit at recruiting affluent businessmen. In the late spring of 1935 he assured Ernest Woodward, the Jell-O magnate from LeRoy, New York, that the General Foods chairman, Edward Hutton, should not "still" be perturbed about the "failure of the League to push a vigorous campaign." He noted Stayton's success with executive management, adding: "We had an excellent meeting of the advisory committee in Chicago. . . . They came from several states and proved to be fine people —all ready to go. Finally, my faith is restored. I think the effort well worth while." A month later he was still imploring Woodward to stick with the League.[54]

Ideologically, Wadsworth was comfortable with the League, and as it became even more critical of the administratoin, he turned to the right with it. Usually, however, he eschewed the irrational rhetoric of many League members. Quite exceptional was his comment to a downstate associate: "I have always contended that the average man would rather live

---

President Wilson' Assistant Secretary of War, in encouraging disaffected Democrats to oppose Roosevelt. Also see Arthur Schlesinger, Jr., *The Politics of Upheaval* (Boston: Houghton-Mifflin), Ch. 28, p. 520. Raskob and the duPonts were prepared to support Governor Eugene Talmadge against F.D.R. Also see Robert J. Comerford, "American Liberty League" (St. Johns University, 1967), Ph.D. dissertation, "Introduction." Comerford is less hostile to the American Liberty League, noting that most League members had a liberal outlook in the previous era of reform but that they looked reactionary because their opposition to F.D.R.'s change in the balance of power coincided with business disenchantment with the New Deal.

53. J. Howard Pew to J.W.W., Jan. 4, 1935, Wadsworth MSS.

54. Ernest L. Woodward to J.W.W., June 22, 1935, J.W.W. to Ernest L. Woodward, June 24, 1935, Ernest L. Woodward to J.W.W., July 11, 1935, and J.W.W. to Ernest L. Woodward, July 15, 1935, Wadsworth MSS.

on half rations and be free than to gorge himself at the table of his master." [55]

Normally, Wadsworth was a calming influence among excited Leaguers. When a Ku Klux Klan leader called on him at the House office building to offer the League all the Klan's membership, power, and "channels of communication," Wadsworth emphatically refused, recalling with some feeling the Klan's vigorous support of Cristman in the New York 1926 senate campaign. And when he subsequently realized that the Klan leadership had so convinced Irenee DuPont of the need for a League-KKK coalition that the latter publicly "blurted" out its desirability, Wadsworth "hustled to stop" the union. [56]

By mid-1936 the League had directed an alarmingly long list of strictures at the New Deal, from charging it with endangering the Constitution, excessively centralizing government, engaging in dangerous economic planning, basing regulation on false economic theories, and retarding economic recovery, to the regimentating of agriculture, threatening private enterprise, unbalancing the budget, subjecting banks to political control, and impairing the credit of the United States. So severe and so partisan were the charges that the cumulative rejection of the League— Landon viewed it as the "kiss of death"—caught up with the League's executive committee. At its June 1936 meeting, almost to a man it favored disbanding so that its presence in the forthcoming presidential campaign would not embarrass those who just as adamantly hoped to defeat the New Deal. Wadsworth took exception to the executive committee. "I am convinced," he wrote Stayton, "that were we to liquidate and abandon our organization at this hour our actions would be taken by every cheap demagogue in the country as an acknowledgment of failure; that Mr. Roosevelt and his lieutenants would seize such an opportunity to point with pride at the death of an organization which dared to disagree, on fundamental grounds, with the major policies of the New Deal; that our departure from the field would bring discouragement to other organizations which, following in our footsteps in a general way, have endeavored to protest against the undermining of American institutions." More specifically, he detailed his opposition to disbandment: it would cause a nation-wide sensation; it would be acceding to smearing demagogues; it would deny the country an important teaching voice; it would make impossible its reconstitution. In response to Stayton's question about how the organization would exist without harming the Republican cause, the New York congressman was

55. J.W.W. to William Hard, July 5, 1935, Wadsworth MSS.
56. J.W.W. to Charles D. Hilles, Sept. 5, 1935, C. D. Hilles MSS, Sterling Library, Yale University, New Haven, Conn.

almost clairvoyant. "I think we should answer that we began as a non-partisan organization and that we intend to maintain ourselves as such; that we have never intended to espouse the cause of a political party nor of individual candidates; that we have not spent and will not spend a single penny for the support of any party or any candidate in the election; that none of our members are pledged, directly or indirectly, to vote for or against a party or candidate; that all members of the League, regardless of prior or existing political affiliations, are utterly free to speak and vote as they please in this presidential election; that the League will continue patiently, persistently and unselfishly its efforts to bring to the people certain fundamental truths, and that having done so, the League will be content if it shall have impressed upon the people the seriousness of the issues which confront them." Wadsworth warmed to his conclusion: "No, my dear Captain, I am utterly opposed to dissolution. We have a right to look the world in the face." [57]

Wadsworth's position carried the day. The League did not disband. But the New Yorker felt the weight of influential Americans who could not accept the League's extreme criticism of the New Deal. They questioned the logic of his argument that because the League claimed non-partisanship it was non-partisan. The eminent and conservative New York Times columnist, Arthur Krock, a friend of Wadsworth, could not square the non-partisan stance with its whole partisan history. Further, Krock noted, the League's recent "dinner in Washington . . . was so opulent, so unrepresentative of any elements save those which would be attacked as personally disgruntled or selfishly interested, that Alfred E. Smith's speech was turned into a New Deal asset, according to both Democratic and Republican politicians." Krock damned the League for losing its head, noting that even when Franklin Roosevelt attempted to balance the budget and when he vetoed the bonus bill, both actions favored by the League, the organization still could not praise the President.[58]

Wadsworth, in a letter to the Times, manfully questioned Krock's "assertion" that the League spoke 'for Governor Alfred Landon or Colonel Frank Knox, the respective Republican candidates for president and vice president. "It obviously does not." The Geneseoan admitted that the League was opposed to the "present regime," insisting, however, that "Mr. Krock's article is not required to acquaint the American public with that

57. J.W.W. to William H. Stayton, June 19, 1936, Wadsworth MSS. Also see Wolfskill, op. cit., p. 139.

58. New York Times, Aug. 7, 1936. See Schlesinger, Jr., The Politics of Upheaval. Schlesinger writes that F.D.R. dated the revival of his popularity in 1936 from the Liberty League dinner in Washington's Mayflower Hotel in late January.

fact." Also, Wadsworth resented the charge that the League had "lost its head within the last few months and unjustly criticized the Roosevelt administration." He finished his letter: "Every expression from the League is a matter of record. Its publications from its inception have analyzed in a factual way the legislative and executive record of the New Deal. No fact it has adduced has been controverted. No argument it has voiced has been answered." [59] Krock was upset by the Wadsworth response. In conversation with Stuart Symington in New York City a few days later, he warned Wadsworth's son-in-law of the adverse impression in Washington accruing to the League and to Wadsworth. When Symington followed up his conversation with a query for more information, Krock merely reiterated his concern and affection for the Senator and hoped that Symington would say nothing to Wadsworth about their conversation. [60]

Franklin Roosevelt carried every state but Maine and Vermont in the 1936 election. The League had failed. Apart from not making any dent in Roosevelt's re-election, it failed to get any conservatives elected to the Seventy-fifth Congress. Four years later it expired. In retrospect, the reasons for defeat are manifold: it was too conservative and too partisan; it failed to grasp the change affecting American politics; it misjudged Roosevelt's great popularity; it worried more about what the New Deal would become than what it really was; it offered no alternatives. Basically, it was a class agency. Most of the League's leaders expired politically with the League's passing, except Wadsworth. Of its significant leaders, only he survived in public office. James Beck, Philadelphia's very conservative and compelling congressman, was powerful in the movement but left the halls of Congress in 1934. Wadsworth remained until 1951. [61]

Undoubtedly, Wadsworth kept plutocratic company in the American Liberty League. John J. Raskob, Irenee du Pont and J. Howard Pew were surely more interested in the fate of General Motors, E. I. du Pont de Nemours & Company, and the Sun Oil Company at the hands of the New Deal than its threat to the liberty of Americans. But Wadsworth's role was more truly gentry-elite than plutocratic. His anti-statist struggles in a half century of legislative life lent credence to the fervor with which he gave leadership and loyalty to the American Liberty League. He viewed it as no temporary political device. He feared for the very life of America because of the New Deal's endangerment of its constitution and institutions. He saw its plan of economic planning, regimentation, political control, impairment of credit, and deficit spending as frightful; few other

59. *New York Times,* Aug. 8, 1936.
60. Arthur Krock to W. S. Symington, Aug. 19, 1936, Wadsworth MSS.
61. Comerford, *op. cit.,* Ch. 3, *passim.*; Wolfskill, *op. cit.,* Ch. 10, *passim.*

members of the League saw it in that light. His fears were the basis of his pleas to Stayton and the *New York Times* for the League's retention far beyond the presidential election of 1936.

5

In spite of Democratic gains in the House of Representatives in the mid-term elections of 1934, Wadsworth won re-election handily by a 5–4 margin and entered the Seventy-fourth Congress with an almost aberrant enthusiasm. For one thing, the Democratic gains seemed to him to necessitate even more his crusade against the New Deal. Secondly, he questioned the ability of his party's leadership in the House to relate to conservative Democrats, particularly southerners. "I wish you could hear them in the cloak room," he told one Republican audience. He described how one prominent Democratic member asked him what Thomas Jefferson would do if he were to witness Roosevelt's enlargement of the federal government. Wadsworth replied that Jefferson would gladly go "back" to the day when that government which governed least governed best. "Not at all," replied the Democratic colleague, "He would run . . . to Massachusetts and dig up Paul Revere" and warn the people.[62]

Wadsworth became fond of those southern Democrats from Virginia and Georgia who increasingly joined him in his anti-New Deal efforts. The New Yorker spent no little time empathizing with his southern brethern. From that relationship a southern Democratic-Republican coalition appeared, embryonic, to be sure, but at least alive. To a Virginian he wrote: "I too have noted how Congressman [Howard] Smith has stood up to a lot of this insanity, [and] . . . have you noticed how the Georgia representatives also are behaving in very much the same way."[63] He seemed to work the southern vineyard in the House, leaving much of the Republican leadership to the conservative triumvirate of New Yorkers Bert Snell, John Taber, and Daniel Reed.

Wadsworth again sought a constitutional amendment to mandate that at least one house of a state legislature ratifying a constitutional amendment be elected after the amendment's passage in Congress. Also, he wanted a prohibition against changing votes once one-fourth of the states defeated an amendment. Wadsworth, and Nicholas Murray Butler, still

62. *New York Times*, May 23, 1934.
63. J.W.W. to Thomas Atkinson, Jr., April 10, 1935, Wadsworth MSS.

smarted at the ratification of the Eighteenth Amendment in 1919. While Democrats in the House showed some appreciation of Wadsworth's efforts, they had bigger fish to fry.

The New Yorker did not like either the Democrats' indifference to his amendment bill or their bigger fish. By the spring of 1935, the Democratic leadership in the Congress and the President had drifted to the left. Wadsworth, having voted "nay" on a dozen domestic issues prior to June of 1935, e.g., a $4,800,000,000 relief appropriation, voluntary retirement of Supreme Court justices at seventy years of age, a $500,000 appropriation to eradicate pests, a program to lessen war profits, and extension of TVA, hardly believed it possible that there could be more legislation to oppose. Yet it was only beginning.[64] The bulk of the "Second New Deal's" legislation came in the second one hundred-day period in the summer months of 1935. It was centered around four landmark bills: the social security bill, the Wagner labor measure, banking legislation, and a public utility holding bill.

Wadsworth had no doubt that the President would get his social security program. "All its features," he wrote Jerry in early January, "are lumped in one bill which we shall not be able to amend. It means a new era in this country, for, having once taken the step, no future Congress will ever repeal these pension and compensation laws. Too many votes will be involved. More than that, a great class of pensioners, having been built up over the country, you will find them organizing themselves and bringing almost irresistible pressure for an increase in the pensions and compensations and for a reduction in the minimum age." [65]

The social security legislation did have "lumped" within it three important elements—aid to unemployables, a pay-roll tax for state implementation of unemployment insurance, and an exclusively federal system of old-age pensions. Wadsworth fought the legislation as best he could. Admitting that he was "old-fashioned" and "very, very lonely" in the House of Representatives, he feared the vast federal financing and administration of the program. "In what sort of country shall our grandchildren live? Shall it be a free country or one in which the citizen is a subject taught to depend upon government?" When the Democratic spokesman, John McCormick, asked Wadsworth, almost increduously, whether or not he opposed unemployment compensation (the section of the bill with great-

64. New York Times, record of roll call votes of New York area congressmen, 1934, passim. For accounts of the second "One Hundred Days," see William Leuchtenburg, Franklin D. Roosevelt and the New Deal (New York: Harper & Row, 1963), Ch. 7, and Arthur M. Schlesinger, Jr., The Politics of Upheaval, Ch. 21–23.
65. J.W.W. to J. J. Wadsworth, Jan. 21, 1935, Wadsworth MSS.

est immediate implication), the Geneseoan replied, to the applause of Republicans: "Under Federal auspices, yes." [66] The President signed the act on August 14, 1935. In that summer, Roosevelt heard far more clearly the appeals of the left—Father Coughlin, Dr. Townsend, Huey Long—than the Wadsworth appeal of the right. If the right influenced him at all, it was to move leftward.

"The Wagner Labor Disputes Bill went through the House, as you know," Wadsworth wrote Charles Hilles on June 20, 1935. "It went through with a wild whoop. We could not even get a roll call on final passage—a disgraceful performance." [67] His only solace was that the Court would surely strike it down, as only a month previously it had struck down the National Industrial Recovery Act as an invasion of intra-state commerce. Ironically, the Court's action regarding the NIRA made the Wagner Act "must" legislation for the President. To replace 7a of NIRA, the new act established a National Labor Relations Board with authority to conduct elections of their bargaining agents by employees, to restrain employers from interfering with union activities, and to require employers to bargain in good faith with union leaders. The act, when signed on July 5, would stand as the hallmark of Robert Wagner, Wadsworth's victorious opponent in 1926.

The Banking Act of 1935 was of only cursory interest to Wadsworth, although like other major bills of the second one hundred days, he opposed it. The law marked a significant shift toward centralization of the banking system and to federal authority over banking. More germane to Wadsworth, primarily because of his membership on the Foreign and Interstate Commerce Committee, was the Public Utilities Holding Company bill. Public utilities magnates, such as Samuel Insull, had a bad image in America and as Roosevelt moved leftward in 1935 it was natural that he should take them on. The Public Utilities Holding Company bill proposed to break them up. The legislation was a neo-Brandeisian blow at bigness.

Samuel Rayburn and Wadsworth, from the well of the House, led their parties in fighting, respectively, for and against the legislation. Rayburn, chairman of the Foreign and Interstate Commerce Committee, documented thoroughly the manipulative behavior of vast electrical empires. Wadsworth took exception. He chided the chairman for giving the impression that all electrical concerns were equally guilty of monopolistic wrongdoing. Wadsworth was sure, for example, that Associated Gas and Electric

66. *Congressional Record*, 79, 74th Congress, 1st Session, April 17, 1935, pp. 6060–1. See Leuchtenburg, *op. cit.*, p. 147.

67. J.W.W. to Charles D. Hilles, June 20, 1935, C. D. Hilles MSS.

was not guilty. "Does not the gentleman think that he ought to yield at this point?" asked Rayburn. The gentleman from New York did. To the applause of his supporters, the chairman of the Committee explained that he was describing in what an evil manner some uitilities operated and that "there is nothing in the charge or the law of many of the others to keep them from doing the same thing." Wadsworth was undaunted. For forty minutes he continued to argue that the great electrical utilities of the country had reduced their prices, maintained their wages, kept up their employment, and looked solicitously after their subordinate operating companies. Wadsworth lost to Rayburn but not without some consolation. Sixteen of twenty-seven New York Democrats joined the Republican spokesman in rejecting the "death sentence" which would have practically wiped out all electrical holding companies. As a compromise, the final version of the bill eliminated only public utility holding companies more than twice removed from the operating units.[68]

On August 27th the first session of the Seventy-fourth Congress came to an end. It was apparent by late July that the President had asked for and would get a package of legislation at least equal to that which had emanated from the famous First One Hundred Days in the spring of 1933. Fundamentally, the Second One Hundred Days program differed from the first in its Brandeisian approach, its distinct anti-corporation, anti-business, and anti-upperclass flavor, as illustrated by the Wagner Act, the public utility holding measure, the banking bill, and the Wealth Tax Act of 1935. The revenue act was particularly irritating to the upper classes. It increased significantly the estate, gift, and capital taxes, levied an excess-profit tax, and raised the surtax to the highest rates in history.

Wadsworth was never more anguished and depressed by presidential leadership than in mid-summer of 1935. When in the Senate under the Democratic President Woodrow Wilson, he had seen nothing like this. He had been much bothered by Roosevelt's performance at the close of the First One Hundred Days in 1933, but he viewed the early New Deal acts as emergency legislation and quite temporary. Subsequent to 1935, Wadsworth would still be offended by domestic programs of Roosevelt and Truman, but such programs would be cushioned by increased Republican strength in the Congress, by the resistance of southern Democrats, and by Wadsworth's own increased interest in military and foreign affairs. An outpouring to an old Texas friend, Edward Bolton, in mid-summer of 1935 reflects the depths of the Geneseoan's feeling about the Democratic president as Roosevelt reached the high point of his congressional domestic

68. *Congressional Record*, 79, 10369, 10371, 10372; J.W.W. to D. R. Sanders, March, 1935, Wadsworth MSS.

support in his long White House tenure. The letter is also revealing of
the brewing resistance of southern Democrats:

> I often lie awake, appalled at what is going on. It is due entirely to
> the idiosyncracies of one man. That man has impaired to a large extent,
> the moral fibre of millions of our people. He has put an immense class of
> dependents upon government. He persists in the belief that government
> should be supreme over the individual and plan his life. He has no
> contempt for ne'er do-wells and loafers. He rejoices when government
> feeds and clothes them. By the same token, he is jealous and suspicious of
> the successful. At times he becomes vindictive and seeks to injure the
> people whom he calls over-privileged. Seldom, if ever, does he think any-
> thing through. As a result he often finds himself in a tight corner, from
> which he ducks as skillfully as he can and generally at the cost of break-
> ing his word to somebody. His unreliability in this respect was thoroughly
> understood at Albany while he was governor of New York. It may be of
> interest to you to know that Republican leaders in the state legislature,
> after extensive experience with him, reached a tacit agreement that no
> one of them would confer with the governor on a public question unless
> a third person were present. What was so well known at Albany is now
> becoming well known at Washington. All the sensible Democrats here in
> Congress are sorely disturbed. One trouble is their majority is too large
> and thus the conservative Democrat is not in a position to lead a success-
> ful bolt in the House or in the Senate. There are too many sheep being
> driven in the other direction. These conservative Democrats know just
> as well as you and I do that our institutions are menaced. They cannot
> stop their leader. It is too late. They could have stopped him two years
> ago but they did not realize at that time the sort of man he is and
> they were intent upon making his administration a great success in order to
> secure re-election for him in '36. A curiously desperate frame of mind
> pervades the Democrats in Congress. They know that Roosevelt is slip-
> ping very, very badly and that they are slipping with him. Instead of
> trying to save something for the country by blocking his crazy program
> they have determined in their desperation to hang together, else they
> might hang separately. In other words, they are going through with him
> to the bitter end. All these bills that you hear about are going to pass.
> Congressional leaders took the bear by the tail back in 1933. From month
> to month they went on while the pace increased hoping that the animal
> would slow down pretty soon. Now the pace is faster than ever and they
> can't let go. I do not get any political satisfaction from this situation. It is
> too serious.[69]

69. J.W.W. to Edward R. Bolton, July 25, 1935, Wadsworth MSS.

What Wadsworth said to Bolton privately he dressed up for public presentation to former National Recovery Administration Director Hugh Johnson at the University of Virginia's Institute of Public Affairs. There, an audience of 6,000 men and women applauded the New Yorker's conclusion that the President, in his departure from his 1932 platform, was "leading the country to the brink of a great decision as to whether the country should change the Constitution to enable the continuation of his New Deal policies." Johnson, an able New Deal defender, denied Wadsworth's contention that the Supreme Court's recent anti-NRA decision proved Wadsworth correct in his assessment of the New Deal. He argued the contrary. Pointing to Wadsworth and the Court, Johnson noted that "the wreckage and the ruin of this hour are proof positive that we have come to an end of an era and that the old Bourbon formula of government of, by, and for the wise, the good and the beneficent has got to be modified if our political and economic systems are to continue to exist." [70]

In contrast to Wadsworth's "wretched summer" in Washington, his return to the valley and Hartford House was a welcome respite. For some three years, since Louisa's death in 1932 and the gutting by fire of the Hampton estate in the same year, Jim and AHW had devoted attention to the scraping of the great home's woodwork and paper down to the original finish. The restoring of the woodwork and the matching of the original paper was completed in time for the one hundredth anniversary of the ancestral home. On September 21, 1936, six hundred guests attended a "centennial party." Villagers and elite alike revelled in the idyllic setting of vast and well-groomed gardens out of doors and the muted elegance of the redecorated interior. Many of the Boss's heavy Victorian pieces of furniture were replaced, whereas many of the original furnishings installed by the pioneer builder James Samuel Wadsworth were retained. Most striking was the library's beautiful white mahogany paneling rescued from the razed Hay home on Lafayette Square in Washington.

The celebration, centered in a huge tent at the north end of Hartford House, with bandstand and dance floor, marked the first important event of the Genesee Valley's social season, antedating by a week the opening of the valley hunt.[71]

Even in the bucolic setting of Hartford House, Wadsworth could not shake visions of the New Deal encroachment. Although escaping there much of the influence of the second New Deal, he had only to step out of

70. Address prepared for Univ. of Virginia's Institute of Public Affairs, delivered on July 12, 1935, Wadsworth MSS. New York *Times,* July 13, 1935.
71. *New York Times,* Sept. 22, 1935.

Rear of Hartford House, overlooking the Genesee Valley.

Interior of Hartford House, showing the paneling
from the Hay home in Washington, D.C.

Hartford House to feel the impact of the AAA crop control. More importantly, he feared its pervasiveness across the nation. And he saw no end to it. It was "a senseless violation of supply and demand." When finally the AAA came to control potato production, he announced his intention to raise all the potatoes he wanted to and to "sell them wherever I please." As with the depression generally, Wadsworth blamed the agriculture problem on "economic nationalism." What was needed, he felt, was an elimination of tariffs, embargoes, restrictions, and quotas, not their retention. He prescribed again and again international trade and a balanced budget as the best antidote for agriculture.[72]

Even Franklin Roosevelt called a halt to further New Deal legislation after the Second One Hundred Days. He viewed 1936 as a time of healing, not, however, without reminding the country of his good work in the previous year, and of the evils of the American rich. Although his annual message to the Congress in 1936 was caustic, he recommended no new reforms and indeed suggested certain cuts in government spending. Wadsworth was not impressed by the nibble to cut some spending. He viewed the occasion of the presentation of the annual State of the Union message as a "political rally" with the President's appearance the "signal for a prolonged burst of handclapping, lusty cheers, and triumphant hoots from the great throng of his supporters." Nor was Wadsworth impressed by the President's extolling of "his achievements without limit," and his excoriating "his opponents without mercy."[73] In regard to the nibble to cut spending, the Geneseoan soon saw that it did not square with the budget message submitted to the Congress on January 6, 1936. The President, in his budget message, did not recommend cuts in the regular budget in order to balance it, nor could he predict what the relief expenditure would be.

Through all the New Deal atmosphere Wadsworth felt a ray of warm light with the Supreme Court's 1935 decision to throw out the AAA. He was particularly warmed by its argument that "among the powers delegated in the Constitution there cannot be found any power to regulate farm production."[74]

The 6 to 3 adverse court decision, coming unexpectedly in January of 1936, intruded on the President's breathing spell regarding new legislation. He, of course, burned as did other important New Deal adherents. Justice Harlan Stone, in a biting minority decision, criticized the Court for

72. *New York Times,* Sept. 25, 1935.
73. *Congressional Record,* 79, 33405.
74. *Ibid.,* pp. 1182–3.

its "tortured construction of the Constitution" and reminded it that "courts are not the only agency of government that must be assumed to have the capacity to govern." Governor George Earle of Pennsylvania meant to disparage the Court when he declared that the six-man majority was "committed to the policies of the Liberty League." [75] Wadsworth agreed with Earle on the Court's Liberty League stance but saw nothing at all disparaging about it.

No sooner had the Court turned down the AAA than Roosevelt's agricultural advisers put together a new farm law that would permit the Agriculture Department to pay farmers for curtailing production, with the hope that it would not displease the Court. The bill, called the Soil Conservation and Domestic Allotment Act, paid farmers for sowing soil-enriching grasses and legumes instead of "soil-depleting commercial crops." When an Indiana farmer urged the bill's passage as a "duty we owe our farmers," Wadsworth saw price-fixing in any form as "a wretched violation of economic law that simply cannot be put across." Then he likened production control to a "toy balloon." Wherever you push the thumb of control, the balloon will bulge out someplace else, until you will have "1,000 thumbs and you will have to attempt to push in every single square inch of the balloon and the balloon will burst." [76] Despite Wadsworth's efforts, the administration got its so-called Conservation Act, a stop-gap measure which curbed production until the second AAA was passed in 1938. Reform, to Wadsworth, was indeed "a terrible thing."

By 1936 Wadsworth's opposition to the social welfare state came close to the ultimate classic economic position of the day. The relief afforded millions of Americans by various New Deal programs was almost totally rejected. To Wadsworth the programs represented the abyss. As he had fought Wilson's New Freedom, now he rejected the apex of the New Deal domestic efforts, and subsequently would oppose as strenuously Harry Truman's Fair Deal.

On the eve of the 1936 Republican convention, Wadsworth demanded a balanced budget, reduction of relief expenditures, the replacement of "made work" by minimal direct cash relief payments, state care of the permanently unemployed, the stabilization of currency by international agreement, the elimination of federal control of wages and hours, the retention of the Supreme Court as currenty constituted, the elimination of

75. William E. Leuchtenburg, *op. cit.*, pp. 170–1.
76. J.W.W. to Roy A. Porter, Feb. 6, 1935, Wadsworth MSS.

parity payments in agriculture, the development of foreign markets to aid agriculture, the retention of protective tariff levels until international agreement made tariff adjustment possible, and the elimination of public electrical power.[77]

77. Press interview, unidentified news clipping, June 1, 1936.

X

The Old Guard and the Young Turks

1

THAT the political wheel of fortune turns was aptly demonstrated when Wadsworth visited Albany's capitol hill on January 6, 1933. In recent years he had been only a defeated United States senator, his voice stilled in the councils of government and his party. Now, newly elected to national office at a time when Republicans almost everywhere staggered under the recent Democratic onslaught, he found Republican leaders in the state capital rushing to his side. "I am quite certain," said one, "that we would be only too happy to follow Congressman Wadsworth as our leader if he would only let us." [1]

Correspondents at Albany's annual Legislative Correspondents' dinner, New York's counterpart to the Washington Gridiron dinner, put to song their hopes that Wadsworth would lead:

OH, JIMMY!

(Air: "Please")

Please, come and be our leader—
   Oh please, you can see we need a
      New Strain of good Geneseo stock.
You are the one to do it—
   Oh please, come and see us through it—
      Oh please, take our party out of hock!

1. *New York Times,* Jan. 7, 1932; Judith Stein, "The Birth of Liberal Republicanism in New York State, 1932–1938" (Yale University, 1968), Ph. D. dissertation, *passsim.* Miss Stein notes that Wadsworth, C. D. Hilles, and Ogden Mills were the principal Republican leaders in the 1920s and early 1930s. Although Henry L. Stimson and Charles Evans Hughes were important Republicans, they addressed themselves to foreign rather than domestic affairs.

Once there were guys as chairmen
Who steered us over bumps;
Now only poor to fair men—
We sure are in the dumps!
Oh please, be our Uncle Waddy—
Oh please, be our Sugar Daddy,
And please, save us from this crop of chumps.

Once our leaders served us well—
Men like Platt and Ben Odell—
They were men who packed a punch!
One grand old bunch!
Now we have Nick Butler, Snell,
Maier and Kracke—what the hell!
You can see how we need help![2]

Some Republicans, generally the more conservative and upstate ones, may have had good reason to seek Wadsworth's leadership. W. Kingsland Macy, the state Republican chairman from Long Island, was re-organizing the party, and not to their liking. Although in 1930 Wadsworth's good friend Charles Hilles had put Macy in as chairman, by 1932 the latter turned on his benefactor. He forced Samuel S. Koenig, always loyal to Hilles and Wadsworth, out of the New York County chairmanship and replaced him with the younger and more liberal leader, Charles Mellon, Jr. Then, in 1933, Macy and Mellen did what upstate leaders had always considered bad business. In New York City they fused the party with numerous reform groups, disenchanted Democrats, and the business community, to support a recently-defeated congressman, Fiorello LaGuardia, for mayor.[3] LaGuardia's history of Republican irregularity was particularly attractive to fusionists. Macy went with him and got a winner. And with him he got eleven Republican assemblymen from the city. For his victory, upstate Republicans might have forgiven Macy his fusion efforts. Certainly drastic Republican surgery was needed downstate and it made sense for the state chairman to do all that was necessary to advance his party in the city, especially with the opportunity afforded by the recent Tammany-Walker scandal. (An investigation of New York City Magistrates Court by Judge Samuel Seabury revealed great wrong-doing.) But

2. Albany Legislative Correspondents' dinner program, Feb. 13, 1933, p. 11, Wadsworth MSS, Library of Congress, Washington, D.C.
3. Stein, *op. cit.*, Ch. III, *passim.*

then, Macy attacked Assembly Speaker Joseph McGuinnies and the clerk of the Assembly, Frederick Hammond.[4]

McGuinnies and Hammond were Wadsworth-Hilles men. Indeed, Frederick Hammond had run Wadsworth's campaign office in Syracuse during the 1926 campaign. Macy's moves against McGuinnies and Hammond had at least two clear purposes: to break Wadsworth's new influence on the party, and to blunt the impact of his conservative ideology. Such a victory, on top of the LaGuardia election, would, so Macy thought, bring the party to a more competitive position with Governor Lehman's "Little New Deal." The Geneseoan knew well what was happening. When Erie County's surrogate, Louis B. Hart, an old friend, suggested to Wadsworth that Macy have his way on Assembly reorganization— ("Jim, this is another era.")[5]—a reply from Wadsworth came forthwith. Macy's success downstate notwithstanding, Wadsworth thought the chairman "a curiously unbalanced man and peculiarly susceptible to the spotlight temptation." He reported to Hart that for months he and Hilles and numerous upstate Republicans had not been able to deal with Macy. Wadsworth described in detail how Macy had worked on the greater New York county chairmen to defeat McGuinnies as Speaker when the Assembly convened in January of 1933. They all had refused. "He lost his nerve there," added Wadsworth, "but as he had to beat somebody in order to show his importance he jumped on Hammond." After that, Wadsworth, absorbed with Washington matters, stayed out of the intra-party fight until it got slanderous. "The thing was so vicious . . . ," he wrote Hart, "that I got mad on Hammond's account." Wadsworth then attended a meeting of county chairmen in Utica and defended both McGuinnies and Hammond, in Macy's presence. He also helped form a committee to examine Macy's accusation that McGuinnies and Hammond practiced "invisible government." Macy, correctly perceiving the outcome of the committee's investigation, refused to serve on it. "One is tempted to believe," concluded Wadsworth to Hart, "that he [Macy] belongs in a mad house!" He was sure that to give him his way would be cowardice. "Louis," Wadsworth said finally, "it is just this kind of cowardice, evidenced during several years past, which has been the undoing of the Republican Party. Its leaders have not stood up."[6]

4. *Ibid.*; Warren Moscow, *Politics in the Empire State* (New York: Alfred A. Knopf, 1948), p. 74; Arthur Schlesinger, Jr., *The Crisis of the Old Order* (Boston: Houghton-Mifflin Co., 1957), p. 394; Arthur Mann, *LaGuardia Comes to Power, 1933* (New York: J. B. Lippincott Co., 1965), Ch. III.

5. Louis B. Hart to J.W.W., Dec. 28, 1933, Wadsworth MSS.

6. J.W.W. to Louis B. Hart, Jan. 2, 1934, Wadsworth MSS.

The Geneseoan stood up to Macy but only with partial success. In early January the Republican caucus in the Assembly retained McGuinnies as speaker but kept Hammond as clerk only with the understanding that it would be his last term in that office.[7]

Following the rather bruising caucus fight over the clerkship, political embers smoldered in the party, erupting again in the gubernatorial race in 1934. Macy had determinatoin. For the race he trotted out the eminent Samuel Seabury, who had devastatingly revealed the Walker scandals. National Committeeman Hilles pleaded with Wadsworth himself to make the race. From May to October, upstate Republicans and party conservatives from New York City urged the Geneseoan to run.[8] Wadsworth was interested, as much to beat Macy as to win against Lehman. He cheered any anti-Macy effort, such as the forming of a committee of 300 to select strong Republican legislative and congressional candidates across the state rather than leaving the effort to the state chairman. (Macy was enraged by the maneuver.) Hilles thought Wadsworth would make the gubernatorial race, but the congressman finally thought better of it. Nicholas Murray Butler put the situation accurately when he gave him two good reasons not to run: he probably could not defeat Lehman, and he shouldn't risk losing the floor of the House of Representatives as a good anti-New Deal platform.[9] Wadsworth agreed, and so informed Hilles.[10] Hilles then compromised with downstate Republicans on Robert Moses, former Secretary of State under Al Smith, as the party's candidate to face Lehman. The convention nominated Moses, and in the process followed the upstate edict that Macy be replaced in the chairmanship by Melvin Eaton of Chenango County, a leader who would listen to the "real" leaders of the party, James Wadsworth and Charles D. Hilles.[11] Macy's political career was ended but not without solid achievements. While LaGuardia, as mayor, did not help Macy build his party in New York City, he undoubtedly helped build good government there. And, although Moses lost to Lehman in 1934, he gave the Republican Party a more liberal image than would have any candidate nominated by the upstaters.[12]

7. Stein, op. cit., Ch. III; New York Times, Dec. 10, 1933.

8. J.W.W. to C. D. Hilles, Sept. 7, 1934, C. D. Hilles to J.W.W., Sept. 10, 1934, C. D. Hilles to L. T. Vernon, Nov. 1, 1934, Hilles MSS, Sterling Library, Yale University, New Haven, Conn.

9. Nicholas Murray Butler to J.W.W., Sept. 10, 1934, Butler MSS, Columbia University Library, New York, N.Y.

10. J.W.W. to Nicholas M. Butler, Sept. 12, 1934, Butler MSS.

11. New York Times, Oct. 5, 1934.

12. Stein, op. cit., Ch. III.

Wadsworth was re-elected to the House by a comfortable 13,275-vote plurality in 1934. His opponent, David A. White, carried only the urban centers in the 39th District. Wadsworth and Hilles would continue for a while to dominate New York Republican politics but the times were closing in. The like of W. Kingsland Macy would return to fight them on more fronts than the state party organization.

2

While Hilles and Wadsworth successfully silenced Macy, the November 1934 state-wide elections did not bode well for their continued leadership of the party. Lehman was handily re-elected governor. Democratic voting strength increased across the state. The Assembly went Democratic for the first time since 1913. Even Monroe County went Democratic. Hilles, in a weak moment, admitted that the election gave the New Deal a mandate in the state. Now McGuinnies' leadership of the party in the Assembly was sacrificed. Irving Ives, a Hamilton College graduate and a Chenango County assemblyman, pushed for the minority leadership. Wadsworth and Hilles stuck with McGuinnies but to no avail. State chairman Eaton polled county leaders and saw the futility of staying with McGuinnies. Republicans wanted new leadership. Ives had solid support from central New York and the Southern Tier. Eaton and Ogden Mills, the former Secretary of the Treasury, supported him. Wadsworth and Hilles lost. Jerry, of course, as a member of the Assembly and his father's son, supported McGuinnies to the end. Although McGuinnies' defeat marked no great revolt in the party or in the Assembly as Macy had originally intended, it did indicate the party's move away from the right.[13]

Throughout 1935, Democratic proposals in the Assembly received much Republican support. The Ives Republican leadership paved the way for considerable bi-partisan support of Lehman's "Little New Deal" programs. More importantly, however, Republicans, like Democrats, perceived that people were demanding such programs as unemployment insurance, a broadened workmen's compensation, jury trials in labor injunction cases, and accountability by public utilities. Given their recently-acquired modernism and the fact that 1935 was an off-election year, —"Franklin wasn't running"—Republicans again took control of the Assembly in January of 1936.

Following the election of 1935, New York Republicans made their

13. *Ibid.*, Ch. IV, *passim; New York Times,* Jan. 2, 3, 1935.

plans to organize the Assembly. As a Republican oasis, the lower house in Albany was important. Beyond city government, it was practically the only source of power and patronage for New York Republicans. Democrats were entrenched in the state senate, the governorship, and in Washington. State chairman Eaton would support his fellow Chenangoan, Irving Ives, as Speaker. Except for six Erie County rebels, Republicans were not interested in a replay of the 1934 leadership fight. Besides, Ives was respectable enough to conservatives like the Wadsworths even though they had supported McGuinnies in his fight against Ives a year previously.

Jerry was interested in the majority leadership, the Assembly's number two position. Both his father and Hilles, hoped he would be appointed, both to assure his political future and, more importantly, to assure their voice in the changing councils of the state party. Jerry was a formidable candidate for that position. He possessed many of the same attributes which launched his father's political career thirty years previously—youth, intelligence, education, physical attractiveness, important associations, commitment, and self-assurance. And the majority leadership might well have taken Jerry into the speakership and beyond, as it had his father.

Two candidates vied with Jerry for the leadership position: Leonard Hall of Nassau County and Oswald D. Heck of Schenectady. Because Hall came from Long Island, he was eliminated early. (In the recent election, the downstate Assembly districts had elected only three Republicans to the Assembly.) Jerry was not hurt by his opposition to Ives for the leadership post in 1934 because Heck had also been with the conservatives in that fight. Some thought Jerry was aided by his rural constituency which had enabled him to support controversial anti-New Deal positions.[14]

By mid-November Wadsworth was optimistic about Jerry's chances. Ives had called the Congressman in Washington to report that he had not decided which of the two candidates to support, contrary to some press reports that Heck was favored over Jerry.[15] By late November, the press reported that Jerry had pledges from more than fifty of his colleagues.[16] An ominous sign, however, portended Jerry's defeat. Eaton deferred to the downstaters' desire to have an urbanite in the leadership position, specifically Heck. And, although Ives complained about Eaton's interference with his organization of the Assembly, the fellow Chenangoans apparently agreed on Heck. Jerry could not hold his pledges. Heck was appointed. In a show of harmony, the new majority leader asked Jerry to sit at his

14. *New York Times*, Nov. 13, 1935.
15. J.W.W. to C. D. Hilles, Nov. 15, 1935, Hilles MSS.
16. *New York Times*, Nov. 26, 1936. Jerry, in conversation with the author in 1972, recalled that he had more than fifty pledges.

side. The Congressman was disappointed but understanding.[17] "These things happen in politics," he wrote Fred Hammond, "and I am glad to say that Jerry is taking it exceedingly well and has determined to work harder than ever in the Assembly this winter."[18]

Jerry's presence was felt in the 1936 session of the Assembly. It had about it a Wadsworthian constancy like that of his father and grandfather. Although the young Turks, as the new Republican leaders came to be called, avoided direct attacks on the New Deal, they did strike at the proliferation of programs and taxes. When Governor Lehman presented to the legislature an eight-point social security package, which would bring to the state twenty million dollars of federal funds, Jerry, as chairman of the Public Relief and Welfare Committee, said "no" and made it stick. Speaker Ives was ambivalent. The Lehman package had much that would appeal to the urban areas where Ives needed Republican assemblymen. Yet the package, which provided for the lowering of the pension age to sixty-five, and aid for dependent children, the blind, crippled children, etc., marked a proliferation of legislation and smacked too much of state and federal paternalism. At the same time Ives was conscious of the influence of Townsendites in the state, many of them very conservative on all other matters but very vociferous about the need for government aid to older people. Fearing the upstate, middle class Republican oldsters who were almost as zealous about old age pensions as they were about prohibition, Ives leaned toward support of the governor's social security program. Jerry insisted to Ives and Republicans, however, that the Lehman bill was unnecessary, that his own "Wadsworth bill" before the legislature reduced the age of eligibility for the old age pension from seventy to sixty-five years. Furthermore, his bill did not carry Lehman's four-million-dollar price tag. In fact, a million-dollar surplus in the Welfare Department meant that his bill would cost nothing in higher taxes. The Wadsworth bill seemed more consistent with Republican commitments. Even the young Turks who supported some New Deal programs sought to avoid excessive governmental paternalism and accompanying costs. The Wadsworth bill passed both houses.[19]

Governor Lehman took to the radio airways to explain what Republicans had done to his social security program. He stressed that the New Deal in New York was in peril. Twenty million dollars of federal aid to the state's helpless citizens, the young, the crippled, the aged, was to

17. *New York Times*, Nov. 19, 1935, Jan. 2, 1936.
18. J.W.W. to Fred W. Hammond, Jan. 2, 1936, Wadsworth MSS.
19. Stein, *op. cit.*, Ch. IV.

be denied because the Republican assembly feared matching the federal grant with only $4,000,000 from the state. Eyes were on Jerry. It was his committee and his advice which licked the Lehman bill. He had called it "just another New Deal boon-doggle," which would bring "further federal dictatorship." Now he jumped, precipitously, to the Republican defense: "There can be no such thing as social security in this world of ours today." [20]

Democrats were gleeful. They repeated Jerry's unfortunate remark again and again as typifying the callous Republican view, ignoring his important qualification that government should make an "honest attempt to alleviate the suffering of those who through no fault of their own, find themselves destitute." Macy's Republican holdovers, too, were pleased. The former state chairman got revenge, wiring the Governor to say that Jerry's comment was the "most reactionary and tory doctrine ever enunciated by the party of Abraham Lincoln, Theodore Roosevelt and Charles Evans Hughes." Urban county leaders Kenneth Simpson of New York County, John Crews of Kings, Warren Ashmead of Queens, and Edwin Jaeckle of Erie commiserated over Jerry's statement. *The Knickerbocker Press* expressed regret. The Livingston County assemblyman was hurt politically. The image of an old guardsman marked his youthful countenance. More importantly, the furor buried much of the good work he had performed as chairman of the Public Relief and Welfare Committee, notably the drawing and passage of legislation to make permanent the state relief programs. In the quiet of the governor's office a year after the furor, Lehman commended Jerry for his forthrightness and his principled position on the state's relief programs. [21]

3

James Wadsworth did not take seriously perennial presidential booms on his behalf. Nevertheless, he and his family never quite shook the White House aspirations which occasionally had possessed them in the mid-1920s. Stuart Symington, as late as 1968, still recalled that distant family hope. The prods for Wadsworth to think seriously of the White House again for 1936 came from numerous sources. [22] "Whenever I have

20. *Ibid.*, p. 102.
21. *Ibid.*, Ch. IV. Jerry mentioned Governor Lehman's comment in conversation with the author in 1972.
22. Conversation with Stuart Symington, summer 1968.

been in Washington in the last year," wrote an influential friend in 1933, "and politics was the subject of discussion, your name was always mentioned as the logical one to be the candidate."[23] The *New York Post,* the *Washington Post,* and the Philadelphia papers noted presidential stirrings on the Congressman's behalf. Not infrequently, comment alluded to the similarity of backgrounds of Roosevelt and Wadsworth, both hailing from a "long-established, well-to-do, landholding aristocracy of upstate New York." The press noted the likeness of their estates, Roosevelt's on the Hudson, Wadsworth's on the Genesee. The chairman of the Massachusetts Republican State Committee was sure that a Wadsworth-McNary ticket would be the "strongest possible" for 1936.[24]

On April 23, 1935, eighty prominent eastern Republicans, including National Chairman Henry P. Fletcher, assembled in Philadelphia allegedly to initiate a Wadsworth boom.[25] A few days later a public relations firm in Philadelphia expressed interest in building Wadsworth's image among the 12,000,000 Negroes in the country.[26] Simultaneously, the *New York Sun* editorialized that if he were to run, he would have an even chance against F.D.R.[27] The Geneseoan took the Philadelphia ploy with proper reticence. "That dinner," he wrote an upstate newsman, ". . . was private . . . and most of the guests were old friends of mine whom I had served in the field artillery. . . . There was no political significance to it whatsoever and no boom was started at the dinner."[28]

By late 1935 Wadsworth seemed surprised and annoyed by any presidential boomlet. When the *St. Louis Globe-Democrat* featured a lengthy article on his "dark horse" possibility, he noted to a Missourian the implausibility of his candidacy.[29] He had more difficulty putting down former Senator Joseph I. France of Maryland. For two hours he talked him out of starting anything like a movement. "He left somewhat depressed," Wadsworth wrote Hilles, "but not entirely suppressed."[30]

As the convention approached, politicos interested in Wadsworth were getting wiser and, by 1936, pushed his vice presidential candidacy. Again, Wadsworth followers met in Philadelphia. There they planned for

23. Charles B. Claiborne to J.W.W., Dec. 21, 1933, Wadsworth MSS.

24. Press Clipping Scrap book, Wadsworth MSS.

25. *New York Times,* Apr. 24, 1935.

26. Joseph V. Baker to J.W.W., Apr. 31, 1935, Wadsworth MSS.

27. *New York Sun,* Mar. 30, 1935.

28. J.W.W. to Milo Shanks, May 10, 1935, Wadsworth MSS.

29. J.W.W. to James A. Potter, Jan. 10, 1935, Wadsworth MSS.

30. Confidential memorandum, J.W.W. to C. D. Hilles, Jan. 17, 1936, Wadsworth MSS.

Wadsworth, Alfred E. Smith, and James W. Davis, caricatured as organizers of the American Liberty League, 1934. Facsimile drawn by Gordon Miller from unidentified newspaper clipping.

Hearst Newspaper cartoon, 1934. *By permission of the Library of Congress.*

eastern states to send uninstructed delegates to the forthcoming national convention in Cleveland so that such delegates might trade their first place votes for Alfred M. Landon of Kansas, "if he enters with commanding power from the West," with assurances that western delegates would support Wadsworth for the second place. Wadsworth was wet and conservative, two things Landon was not. Yet, like the Kansan, he was pro-farmer. Many Republicans expected that a farm push in the South and the West, with both Landon and Wadsworth appealing to eastern business interests, would bring the party more votes than Roosevelt with his labor-urban support. Republican leaders from Pennsylvania, New Jersey, New York, and Massachusetts, by controlling more than 25 percent of the total delegate strength, were confident of putting over their Landon-Wadsworth ticket.[31]

In April of 1936 Wadsworth journeyed westward to address the John Marshall Club of St. Louis, Missouri. Although the Wadsworth camp was wise to view their leader as a vice presidential candidate, and were smart to provide exposure for him in St. Louis, the Geneseoan knew more than they about how vice presidential nominations are consummated.[32] He knew that vice presidential nominations come from a "psychological situation arising after the head of the ticket is nominated." He knew they could not be planned. As he had witnessed numerous times, presidential candidates had made the decision at the last moment for a variety of reasons, or nominations might come from the floor without any planning, as when a delegate from Oregon jumped up and nominated Calvin Coolidge at the 1920 convention.

Wadsworth took lightly the vice presidential efforts made on his behalf. "I have been nominated," he wrote Jim Watson, "for Vice President in three separate college conventions, once to run with Landon, once to run with Knox, and once to run with Vandenberg. I am expecting any moment that some college will nominate me for Vice President to run with Borah. Then, if still another would only nominate me as Vice President to run with Dickinson the list would be complete."[33]

In terms of whom Wadsworth wanted for President, he agreed that the Republican candidate should be a westerner "who can bind that region together, and still be acceptable to the East."[34] He was pleased that Borah took himself out of the running—"The man does not seem to have any conception as to where a dollar comes from, how it is earned and how it

31. New York Times, Feb. 4, 1936.
32. St. Louis Globe Democrat, Mar. 11, 1936.
33. J.W.W. to James E. Watson, May 12, 1936, Wadsworth MSS.
34. J.W.W. to Oscar W. Johnson, Apr. 9, 1936, Wadsworth MSS..

is spent." [35] The Geneseoan liked Frank Knox, and liked particularly his strong conservative *Chicago Daily News* editorials.[36] Senators Arthur Vandenberg and Lester J. Dickinson were not discussed much by Wadsworth in his correspondence or among Republicans, at least as compared to Landon. In the spring of 1936 Landon seemed in the forefront and Wadsworth was favorably disposed toward him, at least until Nicholas Murray Butler reminded him of the Kansan's Bull Moose background. Wadsworth then began to wonder whether or not Landon could stand up to New Deal intrusions into a Republican administration.[37]

Landon came up fast as the Republican front runner. Just one year before the convention, fellow Kansan William Allen White had had serious doubts about him as a contender. Still, there was a paucity of candidates and Kansas' national committeeman, John D. M. Hamilton, sounded out Republican sentiment around the country. To Hamilton's pleasant surprise, Wadsworth's fellow New Yorker, Bertrand Snell, and former senate confidant, George Moses of New Hampshire, thought well of Landon as a candidate. By the fall of 1935, his candidacy gelled. He seemed to meet the necessary criteria for 1936; he was a westerner, free of Hoover identification, and a successful oil businessman. Most importantly, his ideological "innards" seemed right. They satisfied western Bull Moosers. And, although eastern conservatives like Wadsworth, Hilles, J. Henry Rorback of Connecticut, and David Reed of Pennsylvania had doubts, some eastern financial leaders like Ogden Mills, Eugene Meyer, and Winthrop Aldrich, saw him as safe. Many Republicans knew how to read polls and primary returns, and Gallop's December 1935 survey put the Kansan way ahead of other contenders. Borah was too rancorous, Vandenberg, too narrow, Knox, too wild a promiser, and Hoover was too much stigmatized by the Great Depression. Although Landon himself entered no primaries, where associates entered him he did well, especially in Massachusetts and New Jersey. By convention time, contenders Borah and Knox were out of the race, and Herbert Hoover and Vandenberg were "out of sight." [38]

That the grass roots of presidential politics are the county and state organizations was well illustrated by the State of New York. There, leaders of urban counties who were constantly chipping away at the Wadsworth-

35. J.W.W. to William M. Calder, Feb. 3, 1936, Wadsworth MSS.

36. J.W.W. to Dennis T. Flynn, May 15, 1935, Wadsworth MSS.

37. J.W.W. to C. D. Hilles, May 29, 1936, Wadsworth MSS.

38. Stein, *op. cit.*, Ch. VIII, *passim;* George H. Mayer, *The Republican Party, 1854–1964* (New York: Oxford University Press, 1964), pp. 436–445; Donald R. McCoy, *Landon of Kansas* (Lincoln University of Nebraska Press, 1966), p. 251.

Hilles influence pushed for Landon. Wadsworth and Hilles did not know for whom to push. They wanted a westerner, but were doubtful of Landon's "inner strength" and were dead set against Borah. While Wadsworth and Hilles liked Borah's opposition to a centralization of the power of government, they did not understand his aversion to a concentration of corporate power. Wadsworth was satisfied that Hamilton Fish would get nowhere in the New York delegation peddling the Borah candidacy.

Wadsworth kept silent on his presidential choice, as did Hilles. The Geneseoan, of course, also kept quiet about any vice presidential aspirations he might have harbored. "No one of us," he wrote his good Erie County friend, W. G. "Ham" Andrews, "especially myself, can afford for one moment to give the impression that he is a candidate for anything." [39]

Wadsworth was not quiet on the subject of New York's representation on the Resolutions Committee of the national convention. In the late spring he agonized over the make-up of the committee. He was pleased that former Vice President Dawes and former United States Senator David Reed were to serve. He wished to serve on the committee and help them write a platform that would "emphasize the preservation of the American system of government and the liberty of the individual." [40] "It should," he wrote a downstate friend, "defend the Supreme Court and the Constitution. On fundamentals it should be utterly courageous." Thinking of Ogden Mills's "dry" stance on the committee four years previously, Wadsworth was certain of one thing. "It is this," he informed Charles Hilles, "that the New York delegation must not be represented on the resolution committee at Cleveland as it was represented at Chicago in 1932. Get me?" [41]

Hilles, however, could not swing his good friend Wadsworth onto the Resolutions Committee. There were several objections within the New York delegation, "the freshest of which is that Jerry offended them by his course respecting Social Security." [42] Other grounds for opposing Wadsworth were manifold—his "wet" history, his Liberty League leadership, and, perhaps most importantly, disaffection in various regions of the state with the Wadsworth-Hilles influence. In addition to downstate opposition, Wadsworth lost much of his grip in such upstate areas as Buffalo, Syracuse, and even parts of the Southern Tier. By convention time, his influence within the state seemed confined to only his congressional district

39. J.W.W. to W. G. Andrews, Apr. 20, 1936, Wadsworth MSS.
40. J.W.W. to George T. Adee, May 16, 1936, Wadsworth MSS.
41. J.W.W. to C. D. Hilles, Apr. 29, 1936, Hilles MSS.
42. C. D. Hilles to J.W.W., May 26, 1936, Hilles MSS.

and portions of the surrounding districts of Daniel Reed, John Taber, and W. Sterling Cole. About Wadsworth's only consolation over the failure to receive the Resolutions assignment was Taber's appointment to represent the New York delegation. Taber worked well with such conservatives as David Reed, Hiram Bingham, George Moses, and Walter Edge, all defeated Republican senators, in their attempt to press upon the presidential candidate a platform much to Wadsworth's liking.

The denial of a seat on the Resolutions Committee portended further defeat for Wadsworth at the hands of the young Turks. As national leaders became convinced that Landon would be nominated on the first ballot, not a few delegates earnestly looked to Wadsworth as vice presidential timber.[43] Unfortunately, the New York Central "Special" train carrying the New York delegation to Cleveland turned into a "last mile" ride for the Geneseoan. The politicos concluded that Wadsworth's presence on the ticket would jeopardize the carrying of New York State for both state and national tickets.[44] Too fresh in the minds of urban delegates were the congressman's Liberty League efforts and Jerry's social security fight. Also, many rural leaders could not yet forgive Wadsworth his "wet" efforts. As the New York delegation, now strong for Landon, sealed Wadsworth's fate, the Geneseoan "motored" to Cleveland with his wife.

The Cleveland convention, of course, was not a satisfactory experience for Wadsworth. He did, however, thoroughly enjoy his stay at the residence of Benedict Crowell, an old friend from World War I Washington days. And, through John Taber, his platform ideas were aired in the Resolutions Committee. In addition, the upstate New Yorker was always accorded a certain deference. Still, the New York State Republican convention delegation denied him a Resolutions Committee seat or even a mention of vice presidential support. The young Turks took over the delegation and unashamedly jumped aboard the Landon band wagon. Wadsworth had no choice but to concur.[45]

As the convention closed, Wadsworth still had not quite felt the full impact of his Cleveland defeat. In fact, he even thought his party might turn to him to run for governor, in spite of his "wickedness." Walter "Ham" Andrews of Buffalo was talking him up.[46] Hilles soon disabused Wadsworth, noting Andrews' impolitic side.[47] Hilles expected "the new

43. New York Times, Apr. 13, 1936.
44. Ibid., June 8, 1936.
45. Ibid., June 9, 1936.
46. Ibid., June 6, 1936.
47. C. D. Hilles to J.W.W., July 16, 1936, Hilles MSS.

leadership" to come up with a candidate to be nominated in the forthcoming state convention. The young Turks did; they not only put across William F. Bleakley, a Supreme Court justice, as the candidate, but humiliated the Geneseoan in the process.

State Chairman Melvin Eaton suggested to Wadsworth that "as balm for the Cleveland episode" he should serve as chairman of the state convention's Resolution Committee. Wadsworth was reluctant, but agreed, only to find that urban representatives on the Resolutions Committee opposed him for the chairmanship. Angered by the insult, he fought it through to a vote, losing by 24 to 15. The contest was a rout for Hilles, Wadsworth, and Eaton. The downstate forces felt the action was essential to demonstrate their control of the party in the state.[48]

The old guard at once commiserated over the assault but to little avail. When James Sheffield heard what had happened, he wrote consolingly to Wadsworth: "If the 'Old Guard' has to be set aside, and the golden days of its leadership including George Aldridge, Elton Brown, Will Barnes, yourself, and Charles Hilles forgotten, then political history must be rewritten with the truth left out." [49]

Wadsworth had aplomb. He hit the campaign trail. After all, "Franklin" was the real enemy. "I have been on the stump almost continuously for the last few weeks," he wrote Sheffield on October 19, "and shall respond gladly to any cry for help that reaches my ears from now until election day. And, if I am re-elected, I shall go right ahead in my obstinate way contending for the things that you and I believe in." [50]

The Geneseoan was easily re-elected to his own seat in the 39th congressional district by a plurality of 25,179 votes, 11,928 more than in 1932. Only rural constituencies, like those of Wadsworth's district, and the majority of New York assemblymen seemed to stay Republican.[51]

Although the New York Assembly went Republican, its ideological cast differed considerably from the previous Assembly, as did the Republican State Committee and the Republican leadership in the state Senate. The state committee went on record, with only Jerry dissenting, favoring Republican support of more liberal policies. Aside from bolting the executive committee resolution, Jerry battled the Assembly Republicans' support of Ives for the speakership. His influence with five assemblymen forced Ives to withdraw in favor of Oswald Heck.[52]

48. New York Times, Sept. 29, 1936.
49. James Sheffield to J.W.W., Oct. 8, 1936, Wadsworth MSS.
50. J.W.W. to James Sheffield, Oct. 19, 1936, Wadsworth MSS.
51. New York Times, Nov. 21, 1936.
52. Stein, op. cit., Ch. V; New York Times, Jan. 6, 7, 1936.

Jerry now had several reasons for fighting Ives. For one thing, he questioned his integrity and ability. Also, he might have harbored a hurt for being passed over for the majority leadership in the previous year. "One looks with a kind of sorrowful admiration on Jeremiah Wadsworth," editorialized the New York Times. "A brilliant and attractive figure, with his father's courage, he was the solitary voice against liberalization. His private resentments at Albany, if he had them, are but a trifle. It would be a serious loss to politics if so promising and able a man should have to waste himself in fighting tendencies and necessities of the times." [53]

That Jerry intended to fight the times was soon apparent. As chairman of the Assembly's Public Relief and Welfare Committee, he again fought the Governor's welfare package. But in less than one week into the new session, the Lehman program passed, 115–20. Jerry's conservative support dwindled from a vast majority of Assembly Republicans in 1936 to nineteen in the beginning of the 1937 session. The Democratic governor got all he wanted: old age pensions; aid for the blind; maternal and child health care; aid for dependent children. And if there were doubts about the "Little New Deal's" arrival in New York, Republicans in the Legislature dispelled them by supporting minimum wage legislation and a miniature Wagner Labor Act.[54]

One test of true conservatism is persistency. A month did not elapse before Jerry again offered up himself for the cause. Franklin Roosevelt had created a great stir in the country with his proposal that, under certain conditions, he be allowed to appoint additional Supreme Court judges to a maximum of fifteen. Democrats and Republicans alike generally resisted the idea as a threat to constitutional government, in effect making the Court a pawn of the President. Jerry felt it appropriate that the legislature of the President's home state memorialize the Congress to deny the President his plan. Two hours after he introduced a resolution in the Assembly, Thomas C. Desmond introduced a concurrent, though less caustic, resolution in the Senate. "Since then," Jerry wrote his father, "the newspapers have carried 'dope stories' to the effect that [State Republican] Chairman Murray, Speaker Heck and other of our nebulous minds called 'the leaders' have decided that it would not be wise to make such a partisan affair of it. I have, therefore, in writing, offered to withdraw my resolution and am now awaiting a reply from Mr. Heck. I have no particular interest in

53. New York Times, Jan. 14, 1936. In conversation with the author in 1972, Jerry reported that Ives had inquired of his financial condition and offered him certain lulus. Jerry interpreted such an offer as sign of lack of integrity.

54. Stein, op. cit., Ch. V; New York Times, Feb. 11, 1937.

having the resolution bear my name anyway. It seems to me that I have been in the headlines enough for one session already." [55]

The Assembly leadership lost little time in taking Jerry up on his offer to withdraw the resolution. They quietly concluded that fighting the President in the councils of government in his home state was no way to liberalize the party. "I have decided," Jerry told the press, "to withhold the resolution." Senator Desmond did the same thing. [56]

The Wadsworths, father and son, were now the "Old Guard," even to their protégés. When Erie County Chairman Edwin Jaeckle and gubernatorial candidate Bleakley had forced Eaton out as chairman, Wadsworth helped put across William Murray of Oneida. [57] But Murray was with the young liberals, the young Turks, in reading the election results. He fought Jerry on the Lehman social security program and the Supreme Court resolutions. New York County Chairman Kenneth Simpson, beholden to Hilles and Wadsworth for his initial election, also turned liberal. By working closely with the radically viewed American Labor Party in 1937, he helped push LaGuardia again into the New York City mayor's seat, along with a slate of solid Republicans. Thomas Dewey, a rising young attorney who ran for District Attorney only because LaGuardia headed the ticket, was launched on his career. [58]

By late 1937 the party's liberal wing controlled the state Republican party. Whether converted to liberalism or liberally inclined prior to their political assent, they meant to compete with the Democrats on New Deal grounds. They were the vanguard of a new eastern establishment. There were the workers and there were the leaders. Edwin Jaeckle of Erie County, Kenneth Simpson of New York, J. Russell Sprague of Nassau, John R. Crews of Kings, State Chairman Murray, and former chairman Macy constituted the workers. The leaders were Speaker Oswald Heck, Senate Minority Leader Perly Pitcher, Mayor LaGuardia, New York District Attorney Dewey, and briefly, Congressman Hamilton Fish. LaGuardia was interested only in New York City and cared little for Republican organization, even in the city. He felt he could run on a laundry ticket and win. Dewey ascended quickly into the leadership. [59]

Dewey appeared on the scene at the right time, just as the young Turks replaced the old guard. Although Chairman Murray maintained

55. James J. Wadsworth to J.W.W., Feb. 15, 1937, Wadsworth MSS.
56. *New York Times*, Feb. 16, 1937.
57. *New York Times*, Feb. 12, 15, 16, 1937.
58. Stein, *op. cit.*, Ch. V.
59. *Ibid.*, Ch. VI.

some loyalty to Wadsworth, Simpson saw to it that the executive committee of the party, over which he presided, made the significant decisions. Murray was to linger on as nominal state chairman until 1940, when Jaeckle forced his resignation. Ogden Mills, never close to Wadsworth but counted an important old guardsman, died in 1937. Wadsworth himself concentrated more on congressional matters, frequently as an escape from the rebuffs of his state party. Hilles, the mainstay of the old guard, was forced out as national committeeman in 1938, after twenty-six years in that position. To Hilles, Wadsworth could only understate his distress: "With you as National Committeeman," he wrote, "I have always felt comfortable." Feeling "adrift" without Hilles, he concluded: "Those thoughtless people who mouth the word 'liberalize' and seek to capitalize it for their own advantage, are very apt to try to push someone utterly unfit for the place. Jaeckle and Ham Fish and Macy and others of their ilk will be bellowing about it, mark my words, and some of our less courageous leaders will join in the uproar."[60] Kenneth Simpson, considered "fit" by Jaeckle, was duly elected national committeeman by the state committee. A few conservative county chairmen, such as Rolland Marvin of Onondaga, Robert Roberts of Madison, Philip Elting of Ulster, T. Broderick of Monroe, and Frank Cook of Livingston, would stay on into the Dewey era but without influence.[61]

Not surprisingly, Dewey won the nomination for governor in 1938. Jerry, always ambitious, wanted to be lieutenant governor. Some upstaters thought Dewey might be charitable and balance the ticket with the young conservative. Dewey probably had cut the downstaters' umbilical cord to the old leadership, and Jaeckle, from Buffalo, would not have accepted the rebuilding of the Wadsworth power in his own backyard. At any rate, when Lehman decided to run again for governor, Dewey all the more disassociated himself from the old guard. Frederic Bontecou, a conservative from Poughkeepsie—and short, like Dewey—was given the second spot. The remainder of the Dewey slate was all liberal. They almost beat the Democrats. Lehman squeaked through with only a 64,000-vote plurality. Such a close race entrenched Dewey all the more in the party leadership. The conservatives, including Jerry, met in Syracuse for a post mortem and to plan the party's rescue. It was an illusionary conclave.[62]

60. J.W.W. to C. D. Hilles, Sept. 27, 1937, Hilles MSS.
61. Stein, op. cit., Ch. VIII; Barry K. Beyer, "Thomas E. Dewey, 1937–1947: A Study in Political Leadership" (Univ. of Rochester, 1962), Ph.D. dissertation, Ch. III.
62. Stein, op. cit., Ch. X; Beyer, op. cit., Ch. III, VI, IX.

Ironically, while the Wadsworths' political fortunes in the state party ebbed, the elder Wadsworth grew in national stature. As the next chapters will demonstrate, his forthrightness and influence regarding the repeal of the 1935–1937 neutrality acts and his sponsorship of military legislation launched a new and esteemed congressional career. And while his domestic conservatism was constant, the public image of James Wadsworth during the war years was more and more tied to his foreign and military affairs activity.

As the 1940 presidential campaign approached, newspapers and political figures occasionally referred to the New York congressman as the Republican party's hope for the presidency. "James Wadsworth, Jr.," editorialized the Charleston, South Carolina News and Courier, "is a better Democrat than is James Farley, Franklin Roosevelt or any Northern leader of the Democratic party. He defends the rights of states. His whole career has been one of straightforward and outspoken faithfulness to principles of government regardless of their consequences." The St. Louis Globe-Democrat also stressed his presidential possibilities.[63] While a poll of twenty-five Democratic members of Congress showed Senator Arthur Vandenberg to be the expected Republican nominee over Senator Taft, the preponderance of the congressmen polled supported Wadsworth. The reason they usually gave for favoring his prospects was that he was the "greatest statesman of the Republican party."[64]

To entreaties that he enter the race, the New Yorker had a firm and realistic reply. "My course," he wrote an interested Missourian, "has been such as to put me in opposition to a great many groups. Believe me that in many instances I have enjoyed the experience, but there are others who have not and who remember me accordingly. This is true especially of my own state, where, to be perfectly frank with you, I am regarded too much of a reactionary."[65] Almost invariably and with a sense of pride, Wadsworth then pointed to his political scars and closed his letter by noting the independence his House seat afforded him.

On January 24, 1940, Wadsworth announced publicly that he would lead a national drive for Frank Gannett of Rochester for president.[66] Gannett, the owner and publisher of seventeen important papers, most of

63. Charleston, S. C., News & Courier, 1936; St. Louis Globe–Democrat, Oct. 19, 1939, Wadsworth MSS.
64. New York Herald Tribune, Nov. 14, 1939.
65. J.W.W. to Claude E. Sowers, May 13, 1936, Wadsworth MSS.
66. New York Times, Jan. 25, 1940.

them in New York, was a consistent anti-New Deal critic, and had given vigorous leadership to the fight against Roosevelt's government reorganization Supreme Court proposals. Yet he hardly deserved the deference of a presidential nomination. His candidacy was unalterably tied to anti-Dewey politics within the state Republican party.

Dewey, ever tightening his grip on the state party, aspired to the presidential nomination. A number of his critics in the state—the Wadsworths; Thomas E. Broderick, the Monroe County leader; Mayor Rolland B. Marvin of Syracuse; Senator Joe R. Hanley of Wyoming County, the Senate majority leader; Queens Borough President George Harvey—saw in the Gannett candidacy a chance to at least deal Dewey's presidential hopes a body blow.[67]

Gannett seemed unaware of the political swirl surrounding his candidacy. "Good news," he naïvely wrote Wadsworth in early 1940, "continues to come in from all sections and I know our chances of winning are improving. . . . Victory will mean much for all of us and, I am sure, save America from disaster." He was profuse in thanking Wadsworth for leading the drive.[68]

Wadsworth was not naïve in his support of Gannett. Undoubtedly, he too saw the merit in foiling Dewey's presidential efforts and at the same time loosening the "little man's" reins on the party. Also, Wadsworth was aware that his own leadership over dissident Republicans would be enhanced by his role in the Gannett campaign. Then, too, Wadsworth appreciated the fact that the "bone dry" Gannett, whose papers deluged much of New York, had remained fairly neutral in the 1926 senatorial contest.[69] Also, a favor for Gannett in 1940 might enhance Jerry's future press "image" in the Gannett newspaper chain.[70] Perhaps most important, Wadsworth and Gannett were equally conservative. The congressman did appreciate Gannett's many anti-New Deal efforts, particularly his fight against the "court-packing" proposal.

Because Wadsworth sincerely believed in Gannett's aversion to the New Deal, and because the Congressman had a history of bold action, he could say with as much honesty as is possible in American politics: "Mr.

67. *Ibid.*, Jan. 17, 1940.

68. Frank Gannett to J.W.W., Jan. 30, 1940, Wadsworth MSS.

69. Conversation with J.J. Wadsworth, summer 1968. See Henry W. Clune, *The Rochester I Know* (Garden City, N.Y.: Doubleday & Co., Inc., 1972), pp. 379–380. Clune states that the opposition of the Gannett newspapers in 1926 helped defeat Wadsworth in his senate race. Conversation with Blake McKelvey, City of Rochester Historian, November 1972: McKelvey recalled to the author that Wadsworth headed the Gannett campaign with great distaste.

70. Author's conversation with Carl Hallauer, summer 1968.

Gannett's candidacy is genuine. Most assuredly it is not put forward as a gesture or an attempt to stop some other candidate. Neither he nor his supporters have entered, directly or indirectly, into any sort of agreement which tends to deprive his candidacy of complete independence." [71]

The Gannett candidacy within the New York party got something of a boost when Dewey, in April of 1940, moved to dislodge Kenneth Simpson as Republican national committeeman. Although Simpson, as the New York County leader, started Dewey on his political way, the former proved too "erratic and often arbitrary" for his protégé. In early 1939, for example, Simpson had made a blistering anti-Hoover speech just as Dewey was courting the ex-president for 1940 presidential support. After that Dewey told an Albany legislative correspondents' dinner that he wished Simpson would develop a "permanent case of laryngitis." Getting Simpson off the national committee would assure the permanency of the laryngitis.[72] Gannett jumped to Simpson's defense and Wadsworth, although no friend of the latter, questioned the legality of Dewey's move. "This is not," the Geneseoan wrote former Assembly Speaker Joseph McGuinnies, "a question of the survival or purging of Kenneth Simpson. . . . It is a question of orderly and legal procedure. The State Committee has urged the State Chairman to call the delegates together for the purpose of electing a National Committeeman. I'm sure you will agree with me that the State Chairman has no jurisdiction whatsoever over national delegates." [73] Again, as with the Gannett candidacy, Wadsworth's fight against the Simpson ouster was complex. While no one could question his belief in "orderly and legal procedure," the Geneseoan's support of Simpson coincidentally brought the New York County chairman into the Gannett camp.

Legal or illegal, Dewey had his way. The state chairman convened the New York delegates and by a 55–37 vote deposed the national committeeman. He was replaced by the staunch Dewey supporter, J. Russell Sprague of Nassau County.[74]

In the national convention itself, Wadsworth, a delegate to the convention, duly nominated Gannett. The newspaper publisher, of course, stood no chance against the major contenders, Dewey, Robert Taft, and Wendell Willkie.[75]

71. J.W.W. address, delivered over CBS, May 1, 1940, Wadsworth MSS.

72. Moscow, op. cit., pp. 75–79; Stein, op. cit., Ch. X.

73. J.W.W. to Joseph McGuinnies, Apr. 24, 1940, Wadsworth MSS.

74. New York Times, June 13, 1940. Jerry told the author in 1972 that Sprague proved to be a superb State Republican Chairman. He also noted that Dewey proved to be an outstanding governor.

75. New York Times, June 26, 27, 1940.

Gannett, at his best showing, received a total of thirty-three votes on the first ballot. He blamed Wadsworth. "My manager," he wrote following the convention, "thought it best not to poll my full strength on the first ballot but we know now that was the wrong procedure." [76] Gannett thought, as a starter, he had the support of one hundred delegates in thirty states. The degree of similarity between Gannett and Wadsworth in domestic conservatism was matched only by the degree of difference in political subtlety and reality. Gannett lived in a political dream world. Not so Wadsworth.

The newspaper publisher did, however, receive seventeen votes in the New York delegation. The support of those seventeen delegates may well have encouraged the twelve other delegates who supported a candidate other than the powerful Dewey. At any rate, Dewey lacked the support of twenty-nine votes in his own delegation. The District Attorney needed those twenty-nine votes. With them he would have demonstrated to the national convention his solid home support, and on the first ballot would have been close to receiving 400 votes, only 101 votes shy of the nomination. As it was, Dewey slipped on succeeding ballots and the contest turned into a race between Wendell Willkie and Ohio Senator Robert Taft. The former had gained fame as president of the Commonwealth and Southern power facility when he secured for his company a demanded price from the government for subsidiaries taken over by TVA. By clever management of the convention, he gained the nomination on the third ballot.

Wadsworth was not disappointed by Wendell Willkie's nomination. After the second ballot, he dropped his support of Gannett and shifted to the Hoosier. He lost little time in offering his service to the presidential candidate. "It is good to have your assurance," replied Willkie, "that you will help in the coming campaign. There is no man in public office for whom I have more respect than you and I am going to call upon you frequently." [77]

76. Frank Gannett to Francis S. Murphy, Aug. 7, 1940, Gannett MSS. O.T. Barck, Jr., and Nelson M. Blake, *Since 1900: A History of the United States in our Times* (New York: The MacMillan Co., 1965), pp. 574–576.

77. Wendell Willkie to J.W.W., July 10, 1940, Wadsworth MSS.

XI

"Let Us Be Calm"

1

WITHIN a month in early 1937 two of Wadsworth's warmest and most inspiring associates passed away, Frederic Kernochan on January 9, and Elihu Root on February 7. Fred had been young Jim Wadsworth's roomate during eleven years of schooling, at Fay School, St. Mark's, and Yale. He was the best man at Wadsworth's wedding and the godfather of his eldest child. Thrown together by their respective families, they were immediately attracted to each other and were fiercely loyal friends for more than fifty years. "Ours was a flawless friendship," wrote Wadsworth to a mutual associate. He noted that he had been acquainted with Fred "for a longer period than with any other person now alive, except my sister, Harriet." Of the hundreds who mourned at Kernochan's bier—he had been the presiding judge of the Court of Special Sessions in New York City—few were so personally affected as Wadsworth. No longer would they meet as they had at least once a year to "resume at exactly the spot at which we left off." The richness of their relationship, rooted in very early beginnings—"we spent each summer together"— intensified with each passing year.[1]

Interestingly, Kernochan was a Democrat, and the son of a "Cleveland Democrat." Differing party affiliation among young scions failed to affect the closeness and meaning of their association. Fred Kernochan was close to Franklin Roosevelt. Such triangular relationships were common among closely knit eastern aristocrats. While Wadsworth and Kernochan perennially "resumed" their relationship, Kernochan and the President enjoyed intermittent good fellowship. Kernochan frequently was included in a small party, including Kermit Roosevelt and Vincent Astor, which accompanied the President on sailing respites off Long Island or the Ba-

1. J.W.W. to Edwin B. King, Jan. 18, 1937, Wadsworth MSS, Library of Congress, Warshington, D.C.

hamas. Roosevelt often played the prankster's role at Kernochan's expense. On one trip to the Bahamas the President conspired with the colonial governor to have a disreputable island character formally call on the presidential party and present to the self-conscious Kernochan a many-ribboned scroll dubbing him "Honorary Commissioner of the Mud." Thereafter, Kernochan was so addressed by the President.[2]

Both Wadsworth and Roosevelt appreciated Kernochan's loyalty and courage. Not infrequently the New York jurist took on Tammany for its common practice of charging judges $1,000 to keep their seats on the bench. For exposing the Hall publicly, Kernochan was denied advancement on the bench.[3]

On July 8, 1939, Wadsworth gladly gave the dedicatory address at the Frederic Kernochan Memorial, a 250-boy camping unit at the Ten Mile River Scout Camp, Narrowsburg, New York. "Knowing the handicaps," Wadsworth said of Kernochan on that occasion, "which must face boys brought up in crowded city districts, he wanted to do something to widen their vision and develop their decent instincts." He then related something of Kernochan's skill in the art of human relations, his years of devotion to scouting, and the sensitivity with which he handled cases on the New York City bench. Although Wadsworth knew Kernochan far better than did the President, both were in agreement as to his sterling character.[4]

Elihu Root had been Wadsworth's "father confessor" for years. Wadsworth, on the other hand, was in awe of him. He nearly worshipped him. Next to his own father he relied on the sage of Clinton for advice, political and otherwise. And Root thought Wadsworth the best upstate New Yorker to serve in the United States Senate. Their almost innate conservatism sealed their relationship.

Wadsworth felt privileged to give the principal address, on June 6, 1938, at an impressive Root memorial service at the 1938 Constitutional Convention. Because Wadsworth's role in state political affairs was diminishing, he particularly appreciated the assignment. It marked something of his acceptability by New York politicos and, more significantly, it enhanced his public image as the protégé of the great statesman.[5]

Wadsworth recounted to the convention delegates the legacy their fellow New Yorker had left his country: liberty premised on the doctrine of states rights. Recognizing that Elihu Root occasionally saw the need to expand some federal control, Wadsworth emphatically concluded: "But

2. *New York Times*, Jan. 10, 11, 1937.
3. *Ibid.*
4. *New York Times*, July 19, 1939; Wadsworth address, Wadsworth MSS.
5. *New York Times*, June 7, 1938.

never did he modify his conviction . . . that the Federal Government would collapse into utter demoralization, and that liberty would be lost, if the people in the several states and in their communities abandoned their responsibilities." While Democrats probably fidgeted at the enunciation of Root's conservative doctrine, Wadsworth spoke from the heart. His words were not partisan trapping. Indeed, the great statesman had implanted on the Geneseoan's mind the teaching of Jefferson, the goodness of keeping government local.[6]

Wadsworth would miss the warmth of the old relationships which he had enjoyed with Kernochan and Root. At the Constitutional Convention he surely felt the lack of old associates. For the most part the delegates were a new breed, too enamored by Governor Lehman's "Little New Deal" to warm to the Geneseoan. Steadily, Wadsworth's circle of associates in the state had narrowed, with friends now more centered in the Genesee Valley and Washington. There, on the farms and in the House of Representatives, warmth came in large quantity. Wadsworth responded to it. He was heartened when a House Democrat from Pennsylvania refused to give a Syracuse Democrat pointers for a forthcoming debate with Wadsworth. Contrariwise, the western Pennsylvania congressman, Robert Allen, suggested that the New York Democrats launch a "Wadsworth boom for President." "I will tell you quite frankly," wrote Wadsworth gratefully to Allen, "that your letter . . . goes beyond anything I have ever experienced in the way of bringing me encouragement to go on with this job in which you and I are engaged."[7]

Besides the House of Representatives, the family and farms consumed much of Wadsworth's time and effort. The Jerrys, the Symingtons, A.H.W., and Reverdy were much on his mind. He constantly inquired after their health. And when possible he enjoyed having them around. Over Christmas holidays and during long summers, the family frequently gathered at Hartford House. (Years later, James Wadsworth Symington, Chief of Protocol during the Lyndon Johnson presidency, cherished the memory of long visits to the "big house," and particularly did he prize intimate conversations with his grandfather.[8]

Wadsworth was serious about his farming. He and Jerry kept up a running correspondence on conditions of the various farms, especially the buying, feeding, sheltering, and selling of beef. Few details missed their attention. "The last heifer sent to the Orchard Farm by our friend Jim

6. Ibid.

7. Robert G. Allen to Henry S. Fraser, Oct. 31, 1939, J.W.W. to Robert G. Allen, Nov. 1, 1939, Wadsworth MSS.

8. Conversation with J. W. Symington, Washington, D.C., summer 1966.

The Wadsworth family: Alice and James W. in center;
Evie and Stuart Symington, upper left; Jerry and Harty Wadsworth,
upper right; Reverdy and Eleanor Wadsworth seated at front.

Hanna is no good. She was shy one quarter when she arrived and need-less to say has not improved since. It is easy to see she will never pay her way. Better rass [sic] your friend . . . about her. Otherwise everything is O.K." Some letters later Wadsworth and Jerry were still concerned about the heifer with the "shy quarter." Finally Howard Gott, one of the farm managers, was told to "take a good look at the heifer and then go over and see Jim Hanna." [9]

2

Although in the late 1930s Wadsworth gradually lost his influence in the state Republican leadership, the opposite, as noted, was true in the House of Representatives during the same period. For some time in mid-decade, he had complained about the Snell leadership. Then, in the first week of January, 1937, he called upon the Republican Conference to move the leadership to action. He sensed support among most of the House Republicans, although Snell, of course, was displeased. In a second con-ference he specifically suggested that the minority leader appoint a policy committee of nine members "to give serious consideration to major legisla-tive problems . . . and to report to the Conference from time to time recommendations as to what attitude the Republicans should take upon them." [10] The New Yorker felt that such an organized effort was the least that the eighty-nine House Republicans could do for seventeen million Americans who had voted for their ticket in 1936. Snell had no recourse but to appoint such a committee. "In the nature of the case he had to make me chairman," Wadsworth wrote to Jerry, "and just to make it entirely pleasant he put Ham Fish on it and two Townsendites, Ralph O. Brew-ster of Maine and James W. Mott of Oregon." Wadsworth was pleased by the remaining committee members: Charles A. Wolverton of New Jersey, Dudley A. White of Ohio, Earl C. Michener of Michigan, Charles A. Halleck of Indiana, and Melvin J. Moss of Minnesota. He felt that the committee gelled well except for Fish, Brewster and Mott, who talked "interminably." [11]

Hamilton Fish, like Wadsworth, descended from a line of distin-

9. J.W.W. to J. J. Wadsworth, Mar. 15, 1937, Wadsworth MSS.

10. Resolution by Wadsworth in House Republican Conference, undated, Wadsworth MSS.

11. J.W.W. to J. J. Wadsworth, Feb. 11, 1937, Bertrand Snell to J.W.W., Jan. 26, 1937, Wadsworth MSS.

guished Americans. His grandfather served as Secretary of State in the Grant administration. Wadsworth and Fish had for years been at odds in the state Republican organization and in the House. Within the state party, Fish was at the moment allied with the downstate leadership in dissipating the Wadsworth-Hilles leadership. His recent effort in that course had been the introduction of a resolution in the state committee calling for the liberalization of the Republican party, a resolution which only Jerry voted against. Now he asked the Republican Conference in the House of Representatives to pass the same resolution. As he described the support of the New York State committee for the resolution with but one dissenting vote, he "glared" at Wadsworth. But House Republicans were a different breed from those who served on the New York State committee. "A whole parade of men followed . . [Fish to the well of the House] when he finished speaking," wrote Wadsworth to Jerry, "and gave him the devil." Somewhat overwhelmed, Fish withdrew his resolution.[12]

Fish stayed on the Republican Policy Committee until early August when he walked out in protest against Wadsworth's appointment to the New York World's Fair Commission. Fish had wanted the coveted appointment—only one House Republican was to be appointed—and the Republican Conference had recommended him. But Speaker Bankhead would not hear of it. Possibly the Democratic leader was turned off by Fish's unending attacks on the administration, particularly regarding its foreign policy. Republican leader Snell was reluctant to bow to the Speaker, but when Bankhead said that the Fair Commission of six would then be without a House Republican, Wadsworth was appointed.[13]

Wadsworth made something of the Republican Policy Committee. Within a week of its organization, he got through the Conference a position paper on the administration of the social security program. The statement represented, for the first time in years, a united Republican position on a major issue. As widely reported in the press, it proposed significant changes in the social security program, i.e., disallowing expenditures of social security funds for government operating expenditures, keeping payroll taxes at 2 percent for at least five years, increasing pensions for those retiring within the next ten to twenty years, and beginning the payment of pensions in 1939 instead of 1942. The Democrats in the House took little heed of what some eighty Republicans said, but at least were more aware of their presence. The Policy Committee followed up its position on

12. J.W.W. to J. J. Wadsworth, Feb. 5, 1937, Wadsworth MSS.
13. New York Times, Aug. 10, 1938.

the social security program with papers on the President's attempt to eliminate the Comptroller General and to "pack" the Supreme Court.[14]

Republicans faced a dilemma in the House of Representatives: whether to take a strong partisan position and antagonize Democrats, or to adopt a "strategy of silence" and effect a bi-partisan alliance with conservative Democrats. Wadsworth was so intent on repealing the New Deal that he was more prone to partisanship, as evidenced by his drive to form a policy committee. Still, he fluctuated between the two strategies. Policy statements were forthcoming, and throughout 1937 and 1938 the New Yorker's reputation in the House as the most severe and articulate Republican critic of the New Deal steadily grew. At times, however, Wadsworth lapsed into the "strategy of silence."

The Supreme Court issue of 1937 illustrated the strategy dilemma facing Wadsworth and Republicans in the House. The New Yorker had been enraged by Roosevelt's "horse and buggy" comment about anti-New Deal court decisions. Also, he became alarmed when, in the President's January State of the Union address, Roosevelt called upon the judiciary "to do its part in making democracy successful." [15] Upon hearing that, the Policy Committee commended the Court for guarding "our liberties" and for serving as a "great balance wheel conducive to orderly progress." "We shall resist to the end," concluded the report, "any and all attempts to discredit, undermine, or destroy [the Court's] integrity or its independence." [16] When the President, one month later, asked the Congress for authority to appoint an additional judge for every federal judge who attained age seventy, Republicans were indeed ready to "resist to the end." [17] Various qualifications of the President's proposal, a limit of fifty appointments and a maximum of fifteen on the Supreme Court, etc., made it no less blatant to Republicans.

For all the temptation to strike partisan blows at the administration on the Court issue, Republican leaders chose the "strategy of silence." Sufficient Republicans and Democrats counseled such an approach that even rabid New Deal critics like Wadsworth concurred. "If we are to win [the Court fight]," he wrote a Rochester Republican, "we must do it with Democratic votes in the House and the Senate. A group of bitterly earnest Democrats is already at work on the problem. They have urged

14. Resolution re Comptroller General, Social Security, and Comptroller General, early 1937, Wadsworth MSS.

15. New York Times, Jan. 7, 1937.

16. Report, Policy Committee Report on Supreme Court, Jan. 25, 1937, Wadsworth MSS.

17. New York Times, Feb. 6, 1937.

that we Republicans refrain from taking united party action for the time being."[18] Interestingly, on the very day Wadswort wrote a similar letter to Jerry, the latter introduced, in the New York State Legislature, a strong resolution opposing the Roosevelt plan. Jerry quickly withdrew his resolution. Important Republican spokesmen outside the Congress, like Alfred Landon, Herbert Hoover and National Chairman John Hamilton, also were quiet on the issue.[19]

Wadsworth, however, did encourage the citizenry to speak up and to pressure their congressmen to defeat the plan. He was extremely pleased by Frank E. Gannett's well-financed National Committee to Uphold Constitutional Government which directed a large-scale letter-writing campaign against it.[20]

Although at first discouraged about chances to defeat the Court proposal, by late February Wadsworth was cautiously optimistic and dropped his veil of silence. In response to an upstate Central Trades and Labor Council query, he noted that the administration no longer pretended that fifteen justices were needed to do the work. More importantly, he pointed to the precedent of Court servility inherent in the proposal. If Americans blamed the Court for blocking "their program . . . why not blame the Constitution?" he asked. "Let us proceed in orderly fashion," he typically concluded.[21]

The President wanted a quick decision on the Court proposal but could not get it. The Senate deliberated for weeks. Each passing day cost Roosevelt votes. The House waited. By late spring, the national dialogue was hurting the President. Then, a series of incidents brought final defeat to the bill. The Court itself, by close decisions, upheld the constitutionality of the Washington Minimum Wage Act, the Frazier-Lemke Mortgage Act, and the Wagner National Labor Relations Act,

18. J.W.W. to Thomas Broderick, Esq., Feb. 11, 1937, Wadsworth MSS, J.W.W. to J. J. Wadsworth, Feb. 11, 1937, Wadsworth MSS; Joseph Boskin, "Politics of an Opposition Party: the Republican Party in the New Deal Period, 1936–1940" (University of Minnesota, 1959), Ph.D. dissertation, Ch. IV, passim; James T. Patterson, Congressional Conservatism and the New Deal (Lexington, Ky.: University of Kentucky Press, 1967), pp. 109–19; Donald R. McCoy, Landon of Kansas (Lincoln: University of Nebraska Press, 1966), pp. 356–8. McCoy notes that Democratic Senator Burton K. Wheeler was principally responsible for asking Republican leaders to be silent on the Court issue.

19. J. J. Wadsworth to J.W.W., Feb. 15, 1937, Wadsworth MSS: See Chapter X, "The Young Turks and the Old Guard."

20. J.W.W. to Thomas Broderick, Esq., Feb. 11, 1937; J.W.W. to Frank E. Gannett, Esq., Feb. 18, 1937, Wadsworth MSS.

21. Buffalo Evening News, Mar. 8, 1937.

all New Deal measures. On June 2, Associate Justice Van Devanter retired, giving the President an opportunity to make a liberal appointment, the first opening since F.D.R. took office. On July 14, Roosevelt's loyal lieutenant in the Senate, Joseph Robinson, died, and on the funeral train home from Arkansas the Democrats decided to tell the President that the bill had no chance. Then, in early July, Hatton Sumner rose in the House and gave the bill what Wadsworth thought was the *coup de. grâce*. The Texas Democrat spoke so scornfully of the bill, and with such authority, that untold numbers of Democrats defeted from administration ranks. For the current session the plan was dead. The President was defeated. Still, Wadsworth admonished the historian James Truslow Adams that "We must not forget that the man in the White House will use all his power and all his tricky adroitness to accomplish his purpose at some time during the remainder of his term. . . . He is mad with bitterness and vindictiveness." [22]

Wadsworth had not been comfortable with the strategy of silence invoked in the early weeks of the Court fight. It was too incongruous with his idea that there should be strong Republican policy statements on the great issues, and with his great desire, following the Court defeat, to attack the President. Most House Republicans agreed with him, although Francis Case of South Dakota urged the New Yorker to be more constructive and less negative in his criticism of the President.[23] Wadsworth agreed with Case that "we can at least . . . avoid the appearance of being merely partisan." [24] The New Yorker's authorship of the several Policy Committee papers issued early in 1937 was restrained compared to his highly partisan personal statements on important domestic issues." [25]

Nineteen thirty-eight dawned as a significant year for Wadsworth. The Court issue encouraged southern Democrats and conservative Republicans to join in further strikes at the New Deal. They did so successfully regarding executive reorganization, revenue, relief, and anti-lynching legislation. Roosevelt had his triumph in 1938—the second AAA, the Fair Labor Standard Acts, the temporary National Economic Committee—but anti-New Deal signs were clear. Particularly in the

22. J.W.W. to James Truslow Adams, July 18, 1937, Wadsworth MSS; James W. Wadsworth, Jr., *The Reminiscences of James W. Wadsworth, Jr.* (Columbia University Oral History Research Office, 1952), pp. 423–5.

23. Francis Case to J.W.W., Feb. 3, 1937, Wadsworth MSS.

24. J.W.W. to Francis Case, Feb. 4, 1937, Wadsworth MSS.

25. *St. Louis Globe Democrat*, Oct. 22, 1938; *New York Times*, Nov. 7, 1937.

House Rules Committee there seemed to develop a Republican-Democratic coalition which would obstruct the New Deal movement for years.[26]

Often Republicans and southern Democrats in the House sought Wadsworth's counsel regarding the coalition. And frequently Republican leaders outside the Congress sought his services. He gladly represented his party at what probably was the largest mid-term meeting of the party ever held. Before 20,000 partisans in one of Homer Capehart's cornfields outside of Washington, Indiana, he described Democratic programs as "orgies of extravagance," the cause of "the Roosevelt Depression," and an attempt to take the word "thrift" from the English language. He exhorted his party again to "save the country." [27]

Republicans did gain stunning victories in the fall elections in state houses across the country, the United States Senate, and especially the House of Representatives, winning there 169 seats. Wadsworth easily won re-election in his own 39th congressional district and eagerly anticipated the convening of the new Congress.

Bert Snell, Republican leader in the House, was growing hard of hearing and despaired of any chance ever to be elected Speaker. He did not stand for re-election from his Potsdam, New York, district.[28] Wadsworth's friends in the House urged him to seek election to the leadership position. "I will admit to you," the Geneseoan wrote to Hilles, "that such an undertaking intrigues me immensely." Although publicly, and among most House members, Wadsworth showed disinterest in the position, his correspondence and reports of conferences at Hartford House and in Washington revealed his intense desire for the job.[29]

Hilles, however, was discouraged about the prospects. He reported that Carl Mapes of Michigan would have western support, that New England would vote for Joseph Martin of Massachusetts, and that many freshman Republican congressmen from around the country would feel obligated to the latter because of his chairmanship of the Republican Congressional Campaign Committee.[30] Still, Wadsworth was not dis-

26. Patterson, *op. cit.*, Ch. 6, *passim;* William E. Leuchtenburg, *Franklin D. Roosevelt and the New Deal, 1932–1940* (New York: Harper & Row, Inc., 1963), Ch. 11.
27. *New York Times,* Aug. 28, 1938; "Speech at 'Cornfield Conference'," Aug. 27, 1938, Wadsworth MSS.
28. Joseph Martin (as told to Robert J. Donovan), *My First Fifty Years in Politics* (New York: McGraw-Hill Book Co., 1960), p. 81.
29. J.W.W. to Charles D. Hilles, Aug. 18, 1938, Charles D. Hilles MSS, Sterling Library, Yale University, New Haven, Conn.
30. Charles D. Hilles to J.W.W., Aug. 23, 1938, Charles D. Hilles MSS.

couraged. A few congressmen outside the New York delegation made modest efforts to persuade members to support him. Within the New York delegation, Daniel Reed, Sterling Cole, Clarence Hancock, and Ham Andrews gathered together what support they could.[31] But Martin's influence, even in New York, was too much, especially with the ardent support of downstaters like Hamilton Fish. (Fish even got some Martin votes in upstate districts adjacent to Wadsworth's.) Bert Lord, an old friend of Wadsworth from Chenango County, refused the Geneseoan's invitation to serve on his campaign committee. Wadsworth, however, stayed in the race to the end.[32] Aside from Martin's position as the Republican congressional chairman, his more moderate ideological position helped to put him over. Despite recent New Deal setbacks and the revival of Republicanism, Wadsworth was too partisan, too insistent on the New Deal's repeal, and too much tied to rural America, to assume congressional leadership in his party in an age of urban-industrialism.

At the meeting of the Republican Conference in the House on January 2, 1939, Wadsworth finally moved to make unanimous Martin's election as the minority leader.[33] The Geneseoan would not again contend for the position. Martin's middle-of-the-road ideology and consummate political and organizational skill assured him re-election as leader for two decades, twice ascending to the speakership. Wadsworth's congressional role, however, was not diminished by Martin's victory in 1939. In a *Life* poll of fifty-three correspondents in that year, the New Yorker was rated second only to Martin as the most able Republican in the House. Of all members of the House, he was viewed as the most intelligent.[34] Over the next several years House members would rate him their most able colleague.[35] Such deference was not owing to his anti-New Deal stand, a futile effort; rather, it was because he turned his

31. *New York Times*, Nov. 16, 1938; J.W.W. to Bert Lord, Nov. 25, 1938, Bertrand Lord MSS, Columbia University Library, New York, N.Y.

32. Telegram, Hamilton Fish to Bertrand Lord, Nov. 16, 1938, Daniel Reed to Bertrand Lord, Nov. 25, 1938, Bertrand Lord to W. Sterling Cole, Dec. 3, 1938, Bertrand Lord to J.W.W., Dec. 3, 1938, Bertrand Lord MSS.

33. Martin, *op. cit.*, p. 82. At the close of his life Martin commented about Wadsworth: "For a moment it looked as though I might be opposed by Representative James W. Wadsworth, Jr. of New York, whom I regard to this day as one of the most distinguished men of my time in Congress."

34. *Life Magazine*, Mar. 20, 1939, pp. 14–17. Wadsworth was also described as among the laziest, perhaps because he loathed writing speeches, or because he spent considerable time in Geneseo running the farms. Stuart Symington took strong exception to the allegation.

35. *Pageant Magazine*, Aug. 1946, pp. 12–13.

attention more meaningfully to foreign and military affairs at a time when darkening war clouds made these matters essential.

3

The great depression and the ensuing debate over the federal government's role in ending it so absorbed the nation that foreign affairs took a back seat. Yet the lives of Americans were as much threatened by foreign conflagrations as by domestic conditions at home. During the decade of the 1930s, Japan violated numerous treaties by occupying Manchuria, bombing Shanghai, and proceeding with the occupation of much of Southeast Asia. In 1935 Mussolini's divisions overran Ethiopia, Hitler denounced the Treaty of Versailles, and, in 1936, marched his troops into the Rhineland. Shortly thereafter, Mussolini and Hitler formed the Rome-Berlin Axis to give their countries a freer hand in dominating Europe and challenging France and England. Spain was in civil war, with Germany and Italy supplying war material to Franco, a fascist revolutionary, and with Russia providing some aid to shore up the Republican government. Yet most Americans remained either unconcerned or repelled by the world state of war.

Important leaders, in and out of Congress, gave credence to a rampant isolationism for a variety of reasons. Historian Manfred Jonas describes the varieties of isolationists: foreign oriented, belligerent, timid, radical, and conservative. The "foreign oriented," like Father Charles E. Coughlin, were isolationists out of sympathy for Nazi Germany. The "radical," like Norman Thomas, were isolationists to facilitate the establishment of a socialist order. "Conservative" isolationists, like Herbert Hoover, saw war as the final blow to world order. The most important isolationists were the "belligerents" and the "timid." The former, like Senators Hiram Johnson and William E. Borah, and Representative Hamilton Fish, believed that the American tradition of isolation had served the country well since the days of Washington. The "timid," like Senators Arthur Vandenberg and Gerald P. Nye, wanted peace so badly that they would willingly sacrifice traditional American rights to achieve it. Senator Nye of North Dakota was perhaps foremost in leading the isolationists in the Congress. A special committee of the Senate which he chaired set out to prove true a *Fortune Magazine* contention that the country's leaders and munitions makers took the nation into World War I, prolonged that war, and generally "disturbed the peace" of the world.

As an upshot of the Nye investigation and the developing isolationism, Congress, in 1935, passed the first of several neutrality acts.[36]

The Neutrality Act of 1935, a temporary stop-gap which was to operate until February 29, 1936, provided that when war broke out, the President was to recognize its existence and, through a Munitions Control Board, prohibit the shipment of any arms to belligerents. The act also provided that no American vessels should carry implements of war to belligerent nations and that the President should warn American citizens that any traveling on belligerent ships would be done at their own risk. So popular was the legislation in the House of Representatives that the Rules Committee rushed it through the House with only perfunctory debate and with no amendments. Of sixteen speakers on the bill, Wadsworth was one of three who opposed the legislation. Specifically, the New Yorker deplored the harm complusory embargoes on arms shipments would afford the world's weaker nations. He pointed to the likely effect of such legislation on Ethiopia in her struggle against Mussolini's heavily-armed contingents. He noted that had France employed such an embargo in 1776, American independence might not have been achieved. To a chorus of isolationist contention, mostly "timid," that the Congress was only protecting America against possible foreign involvement and was asserting its constitutional right to advise on foreign policy, Wadsworth responded: "I appreciate perfectly well the high ideals that move the good people who support this measure, but it seems to me we should be more realistic about what America will do in the future when trouble breaks out in the world." Only Foreign Affairs Committee Chairman Sam D. McReynolds and Republican Harold Knutson of Minnesota stood with Wadsworth on that fateful day in August. The Senate offered no opposition to the bill, except for the half-hearted attempt by James Hamilton Lewis of Illinois to postpone the action until the next Congress. Very few Americans seemed clairvoyant about the act. The President saw dangerous implications in it but signed the law to avoid an inevitable overriding of a presidential veto.[37]

36. See Robert A. Devine, *The Illusion of Neutrality* (Aurora, Ill.: Quadrangle Paperback, 1968), Ch. 4–7, *passim*, Selig Adler, *The Uncertain Giant* (London: Collier Books, 1969), Ch. VII–VIII, *passim*; Donald F. Drummond, *The Passing of American Neutrality, 1937–1941* (Ann Arbor: University of Michigan Press, 1955), *passim*; William L. Langer and S. Everett Gleason, *The Challenge to Isolationism, 1937–1940* (New York: Harper & Row, 1952), Ch. I, *passim*; Manfred Jonas, *Isolationism in America, 1935–1941* (Ithaca: Cornell University Press, 1966), Ch. II and III.

37. *Congressional Record*, Vol. 79, 74th Congress, 1st Session, Aug. 23, 1935, pp. 14358–14361; *New York Times*, Aug. 24, 1935; Devine, *op. cit.*, p. 115.

In February of 1936 Congress extended the Neutrality Act for fourteen months, and several amendments were added to it. No loans or credits were to be extended to any belligerent nation; the act was not to apply to American republics in war with a nation outside the hemisphere; and the President could extend the embargo to other countries that might become belligerents.[38]

One year later, in March of 1937, the House moved to make permanent the arms embargo. Again, certain changes and amendments were incorporated into the Neutrality Act; the President was granted more discretion as to when he could proclaim a state of war; Americans were prohibited from traveling on belligerent ships; the legislation applied to civil wars (as in Spain); the President could prohibit belligerent ships from using American ports; and, most importantly, the President could use his own discretion in prohibiting, for a period of two years, the export of non-combatant goods to belligerents except on a cash and carry basis (meaning that they must be paid for in advance and shipped in foreign vessels). Again the Senate and its coterie of isolationists drew up the bill and launched its passage. Only fifteen dared to oppose it.[39]

Unlike the Senate, the House engaged in protracted debate on the 1937 neutrality legislation. Republicans led the assault, usually contending that the bill's cash and carry provision gave the President too much discretionary authority. Others, like Charles A. Eaton of New Jersey, feared the harm the cash and carry provision could do to the shipping industry and the economy in general. Only a few hardy souls like Wadsworth advocated complete repeal of the neutrality legislation.[40]

On the last day of extended debate, Wadsworth alone opposed the bill, and stood almost alone on the final vote. Again, as he had done two years previously, he deplored the harm done to weaker nations by the act. More specifically, he viewed the act as a denial of America's freedom to act in defense of liberty. "Mine is a voice crying in the wilderness," he said, "[but] to me [the bill] means surrender of an ancient and precious tradition, the sacrifice of an ideal." He was prophetic and somewhat eloquent. The House listened. "The struggle for liberty," he reminded his colleagues, "has been going on . . . for centuries. . . . As we look across the world today it is apparent that in many great areas the struggle will have to commence over again." A dialogue ensued. Luther Johnson of Texas probed. He asked if the New Yorker opposed all neutrality legislation. Wadsworth hedged. "I would not go further than

38. Devine, op. cit., pp. 157–158; New York Times, Feb. 18, Apr. 30, 1936.
39. Devine, op. cit., pp. 186–193; Adler, op. cit., p. 182.
40. Devine, op. cit., pp. 186–188.

the present law and I would extend that for one year." "Why extend it for a year," asked Johnson, "if it is wrong in principle?" As "an experiment for a short time," answered Wadsworth, "I have no faith in it as a permanent law." Johnson pushed harder. Farmer-Laborite Paul John Kvale of Minnesota, who frequently "paired" with Wadsworth on voting, jumped to the New Yorker's defense. He noted that although he and Wadsworth differed in nine out of ten issues, "as a former Senator, as the author of the National Defense Act, and as a former Chairman of the Military Affairs Committee of the Senate, I have a very high regard for his views, and I think the gentleman has made a contribution to this discussion." The House applauded. Johnson was unabashed. He resumed the debate, noting in particular the bill's potential for peace. The final vote was 376 yeas and 13 nays. Some voted nay only because the bill was too discretionary. Seldom had Wadsworth stood so alone.[41]

As world conditions deteriorated in late 1937, internationalists began emerging and taking public stock of isolationists' assaults. In Chicago, on October 5, 1937, the President launched what historians generally described as a trial balloon of contemplated action. "When an epidemic of physical disease starts to spread, the community . . . joins in a quarantine of the patients in order to protect the health of the community against the spread of the disease." [42] The trial balloon failed. In response, isolationists tried to pass a Ludlow Amendment which would require a public referendum on a declaration of war, except in case of invasion. Other internationalists emerged into public view. Henry L. Stimson, the eminent Republican who had previously made known his distaste for the neutrality acts, now wrote to the New York Times that he viewed the Ludlow resolution as a final blow at the authority and direction of the government in foreign affairs. Wadsworth, distressed by the Ludlow attempt, was delighted at the Times letter and so wrote his old friend. "Most certainly you have rendered a public service of tremendous value in straightening out the muddled thinking which seems to obsess too many people." In closing, Wadsworth noted that he still carried the little gold match box inscribed, "J.W.W., Jr., from H.L.S., Nov. 10, 1910." Later, when Stimson came into the President's coalition cabinet, he and Wadsworth again renewed their very close ties.[43]

With Europe approaching the brink of full-scale war in late 1938 —Chamberlain had capitulated to Hitler on Germany's occupation of

41. *Congressional Record,* Vol. 81, 75th Congress, 1st Session, Mar. 18, 1937, pp. 2384–2403; *New York Times,* Mar. 19, 1937.
42. Devine, *op. cit.,* p. 211.
43. J.W.W. to Henry L. Stimson, Jan. 6, 1938, Wadsworth MSS.

Sudeten Czechoslovakia, and Jews were being persecuted in Germany—administration leaders became particularly anxious about the restrictive neutrality legislation. Watching both European disintegration and American opinion polls, the President talked of the unfairness of neutrality, unfair to the victims of aggression. He treaded lightly, though, since the country was basically anti-interventionist. Many distrusted him, especially after his Supreme Court fight and his recent attempted purge of "disloyal" Democrats. Key Pittman, chairman of the Senate Foreign Relations Committee, advised caution and suggested that the President let him handle repeal; but Pittman could not do it. Senator Elbert D. Thomas of Utah then took hold of the issue and advocated that the embargo be lifted against the victims of aggression.[44] Stimson wrote another letter to the *Times* defending the Thomas proposal.[45]

With Hitler's invasion of the remainder of Czechoslovakia in March of 1939, the President and his spokesmen in and out of Congress became braver about seeking repeal of the neutrality legislation. Both the Senate Foreign Relations Committee and the House Foreign Affairs Committee conducted hearings on the subject. Before the Senate committee Stimson was most outspoken, supporting revision that would result in aid to victims of aggression, the Thomas Amendment. Wadsworth appeared before the House committee and urged as a minimum measure the repeal of both the automatic arms embargo against all belligerents and the discretionary cash and carry policy for all other commerce. He also favored, but considered less important, the repeal of the restriction on Americans traveling aboard belligerent vessels. Few witnesses were as outspoken as Wadsworth; he was much more blunt in his comment than any administration spokesman dared to be.[46] With many Democrats still half in the non-interventionist camp, the President and his representatives walked gingerly in their effort to achieve repeal.

"These [neutrality] rules," warned Wadsworth, "tie the hands of the government and in doing so create the widespread impression that the warnings and protestations of our government prior to an outbreak need not be respected." By repealing the arms embargo and the cash and carry provisions of the law, the New Yorker was sure that the aggressors would "take notice." Administration leaders quietly applauded Wadsworth.[47] Under-Secretary of State Sumner Welles expressed appreciation. "Personally," he added, "I share very fully the views which

44. Devine, *op. cit.*, pp. 312–325; Adler, *op. cit.*, pp. 212–215.
45. *New York Times*, Mar. 7, 1939.
46. *New York Times*, Apr. 12, 1939; Devine, *op. cit.*, p. 241.
47. *Ibid.*

you have expressed. . . . I hope that your testimony will be widely published." [48]

The neutrality issue in the summer of 1939 was complex and divisive. Positions varied, ranging from support of outright repeal and numerous forms of quasi-embargo to rigid prohibition of any shipment to belligerent nations. Key Pittman could not get a majority of his Senate committee to agree on any one position. Sol Bloom, the acting chairman of the House Foreign Affairs Committee, had even less control over his committee. In fact, Bloom stepped aside and let Luther Johnson, Wadsworth's antagonist of two years before, take over. Now Johnson was for some kind of repeal. [49]

While Congress wandered over the neutrality landscape, Wadsworth increased his public speaking on the subject. His often stated fear was that war would break out before the Neutrality Act was repealed, thus shutting off aid to Great Britain and France. He spoke well of Roosevelt's and Secretary Hull's decision not to support the present embargo provision; he did so even within the walls of the New York Republican Club. By mid-summer of 1939 he loomed large as an advocate of repeal. [50] The *London Times* took favorable note of his long and consistent opposition to the legislation. [51]

However, non-interventionism, if not isolationism, still prevailed in America. Republican John M. Vorys of Ohio succeeded in amending proposed legislation in order to permit only the sale of defensive implements of war. Wadsworth was one of the few Republicans to argue against it and to vote against it. He took to the air to point out how the amendment would threaten "liberty the world over." [52] The administration, still reluctant to incur the opposition of isolationist Democrats or partisan Republicans, again thanked the New Yorker. "What you said," wrote Welles this time, "should bring home with great clarity and force to the American people the fundamental fact that what is really at stake is the peace and security of the United States itself." [53]

But Wadsworth was annoyed. Although appreciative of Welles's plaudits, the New Yorker wanted some administrative firmness on repeal. He was sick when, in late June, Congressman Allen of Pennsylvania secured surprising House support for repealing all the neutrality legisla-

48. Sumner Welles to J.W.W., Apr. 29, 1939, Wadsworth MSS.
49. Devine, *op. cit., pp.* 269–273.
50. *New York Times,* June 10, 1939.
51. *London Times,* June 29, 1939.
52. *New York Times,* July 13, 1939.
53. Sumner Welles to J.W.W., July 3, 1939, Wadsworth MSS.

tion except for the Munitions Board, only to have the White House pass the word that complete repeal was going too far and might be potentially dangerous. "The whole thing," Wadsworth wrote a New York intimate, "has been wretchedly managed by the administration and by the Democratic leaders in the House."[54]

The administration had good reason to call off a vote on the Allen Amendment and a host of alternatives calling for something less than total repeal. The State Department and the President did not know how the Senate would react, especially the die-hard isolationists who could always resort to the filibuster. Vice President Garner finally told the President he did not have the votes to get anything like repeal of the Neutrality Act. The administration, resignedly, let the Congress go home.[55]

The neutrality repeal picture changed with Germany's invasion of Poland on September 1, 1939, followed by the general outbreak of war in Europe. Now the President acted. He called the Congress into special session. Still fearing the isolationists, he masterfully proclaimed neutrality while at the same time recommending cash and carry policy regarding all material, contraband and non-contraband. Wadsworth, too, was cautious. "I do not believe," he wrote a repeal friend in New York City, "it would be wise for me, known as a pretty partisan Republican, to indulge in any public statement regarding the Neutrality Act until the President makes his official recommendation to the Congress."[56]

Congressional debate intensified. Isolationists knew what the President was up to and threw all they could at him and repealers like Wadsworth. For a while the New Yorker got more than a thousand letters a day, practically all against repeal, and for a while isolationists like William E. Borah and Charles Lindbergh dominated the headlines.[57]

The administration, at last, was galvanized into action. Whereas Wadsworth previously talked repeal in the State Department offices, usually in that of Under-Secretary Welles, and less frequently in that of Secretary Hull, now he was *persona grata* in the White House. The President gladly received him as he did such prominent repeal Republicans as Alfred Landon, Frank Knox, Henry L. Stimson, and William A. White.[58] The latter headed the Non-Partisan Committee for Peace through Revision

54. J.W.W. to William M. Chadbourne, July 5, 1939, Wadsworth MSS; Devine, *op. cit.*, pp. 271–272.
55. Selig Adler, *op. cit.*, pp. 212–214.
56. J.W.W. to William M. Chadbourne, Sept. 12, 1939, Wadsworth MSS.
57. J.W.W. to F. M. O'Connell, Esq., Oct. 11, 1939, Wadsworth MSS.
58. *New York Times*, Sept. 26, 1939.

of the Neutrality Act. Stimson conferred with Wadsworth. "On this question of the embargo," he wrote him, "I hope and think that there are no differences of viewpoint between us."[59] There were none. Both agreed on the need for complete repeal of the embargo. Both also agreed that if there was to be anything less than total repeal, the Merchant Marine should be as little restricted as possible as to where it might carry its goods. "Frankly," Wadsworth answered Stimson, "I do not like any part of this surrender of our neutral rights, but assuming that there is no way of stopping it entirely, I am urging that the surrender be confined [only] to our commerce with belligerents in Europe.[60]

By mid-October the isolationists' attempt to stir up anti-repeal sentiment ran out of steam; European disintegration was too appalling. Wadsworth's mail and that of fellow repeal congressmen fell off. Also, the isolationists ran out of money. Henry Ford, who had talked of spending much money on the isolationist cause, reneged.[61] Repeal spokesmen, seeing repeal in sight, spoke on. Wadsworth addressed numerous groups in New York and out-of-state audiences in Chicago and St. Louis. Newspaper and public opinion polls began shifting in favor of the President's position. Also, internationalist lawyers, important businessmen, and prominent Republicans such as Senator Robert A. Taft of Ohio were coming around.

Throughout October, the Senate was the center of attention. An air of expectancy prevailed there as the debate began. Vice President Garner let the isolationists in the upper chamber talk until they ran down. Administration spokesmen spoke minimally and avoided any suggestion that their measure was intended to aid England or France. This strategy confused the isolationists. Their number dwindled in the Senate; Borah and his bloc could not mount a filibuster. Following days of futile isolationist efforts to amend the proposed neutrality revision legislation, the Senate passed the measure, 63–30.[62]

Now the scene shifted to the House of Representatives which had been biding its time while the public riveted its attention on "the other body." James Farley, however, had kept his eye on the House and became alarmed at isolationist strength there, especially among certain "foreign oriented isolationists," e.g., Irish Catholics. Floor debate there began on October 31, limited by the Rules Committee to only ten hours. Isolationists, especially Hamilton Fish, bitterly criticized the Rules Committee for

59. Henry L. Stimson to J.W.W., Oct. 12, 1939, Wadsworth MSS.

60. J.W.W. to Henry L. Stimson, Oct. 14, 1939, Wadsworth MSS.

61. Devine, op. cit., pp. 299–302.

62. "Schedule of Wadsworth Speeches," Wadsworth MSS; Devine, op. cit., pp. 312–325.

its gag rule. Because of the rule, the House jammed all of its bitterness and divisiveness on the issue into three short legislative days. The isolationists' most cogent argument was that too great a revision of the neutrality legislation coming after the outbreak of war would be un-neutral in itself. Wadsworth had expressed the same fear as he sought repeal before the outbreak of war. Administration spokesmen Luther Johnson of Texas and James P. Richards replied that because war had broken out the Congress needed to do "what [it thought was in] the best interests of the country." Replacing the arms embargo with the cash and carry safeguards would accomplish that. Now some members even advocated outright repeal. Tough Dewey Short of Missouri replied angrily: "First, we furnish munitions; second, we furnish money; and, finally, we furnish men." [63]

The House debate reached its climax on November 2. On that day the House voted on two proposals, the first a compromise measure which would prohibit the sale of arms or ammunition, but would permit the export of defensive war implements such as aircraft and coastal artillery. The House rejected it. Then it proceeded to debate repeal of the full arms embargo.

Every gallery seat was filled. The House members stayed on the floor or milled about in the cloak rooms. Senators availed themselves of floor privileges. The chief protagonists on the great issue closed the arguments. The summations of varieties of isolationists, of course, revealed nothing new. It had all been heard before, if not over the past four years, certainly in recent weeks in the Senate or most certainly in recent days in the House. Yet excitement prevailed. The age of inter-war isolationism in America was about to expire, although its death rattle would last until the day the Japanese attacked Pearl Harbor.[64]

Only James Wadsworth and Sam Rayburn brought the huge House assemblage to its feet applauding on the last day of congressional debate. The Democratic side allotted more time to the New York Republican than to any of its spokesmen, including Majority Leader Rayburn and Speaker Bankhead. "Mr. Speaker," began Wadsworth, deliberately and, as usual, unpretentiously, "it is with hesitation that I address the House upon this subject. I am perfectly aware of the fact that I have done so on many occasions in the past. I doubt if I can add much." The New Yorker reiterated his opposition to practically all of the standing neutrality legislation, especially attempts at "establishing rigid rules governing the conduct of the Government of the United States in the face of unpredictable

63. Devine, *op. cit.*, pp. 325–328.
64. *Ibid.*, pp. 328–331.

events." He deplored, as he had so often before, the sad consequences such legislation afforded Ethiopia and the Spanish loyalists as they "reached to find a weapon with which to defend themselves." He regretted the President's need to grasp at a technicality to aid China, in reference to Roosevelt's avoidance of implementation of the Neutrality Act on the ground that the Sino-Japanese War was undeclared. The New Yorker disparaged the pending Senate cash and carry provision of the neutrality bill. Like its predecessor bill, it was complex and confusing, but at least it did not distinguish between contraband and non-contraband of war, an impossible task. At the same time he noted that the bill provided for keeping American ships out of war zones. Wadsworth was sure that the proposed repeal of the embargo would not bring the war to American shores. To those who feared reprisals Wadsworth was provoked to scorn. "If," he said, "we are ever to frame the foreign policy of the United States upon the theory that we cannot . . . [act to protect our] own Government, . . . [and] our own country, then, by heaven, we would better crawl into a hole and pull the hole after us."

Wadsworth closed, not with a plea for repeal, but for an embracing quiet:

> Let us be calm. What we must do, of course, is keep our heads steady and keep our feet on the ground [and] put our house in order. . . . It needs it. Nothing is gained for us or in the interest of peace and liberty by exciting enmity. Perfect our defense. Command respect. I think Theodore Roosevelt expressed it very well when he said, 'Speak softly and carry a big stick.' " [Applause, the members rising.][65]

The final vote came on instruction to House conferees to retain a full arms embargo. It lost by a 243–181 vote.

Charles Ross of the *Washington Post* thought "there was no more striking episode in the neutrality debate than the ovation given James W. Wadsworth." He thought the House applauded two things, "the excellence of the speech and the manifest intellectual honesty of the speaker." "To hear him and observe the effect on the House," continued Ross, "was like sitting in the Supreme Court chamber and seeing the Court snap out of boredom when a lawyer like the late Newton D. Baker, after the legalistic verbosities of lesser lights, began to cut to the heart of an issue with plain English." [66] The press reaction to Wadsworth's address was nearly

65. "Let us be Calm" speech, Nov. 2, 1939, Wadsworth MSS.
66. *St. Louis Post Dispatch*, Nov. 6, 1939.

unanimous in its praise. Pearson and Allen, in their syndicated column, called it brilliant, "not only the best in the House, but [it] topped anything in the Senate." Furthermore they thought it changed votes, an almost unknown occurrence in the House.[67] The New Yorker's correspondence also reflected admiration for what he said. Joseph Tumulty, a voice of the Wilsonian past, was ecstatic. He praised the Republican for the "notable part" he played in sustaining the President. "What you did . . . ," he wrote, "in this matter is characteristic of you—always doing the forthright, decent thing. I do not know any man in either party for whom I have a greater respect and esteem than you."[68]

The extraordinary praise puzzled Wadsworth. "The funny thing about the speech," he wrote Al Smith, "is that I have made practically that same speech at least three times upon the floor of the House of Representatives in the last three years."[69] The Geneseoan, of course, was warmed by the outpouring. Because so few Republicans in the Congress supported him, he appreciated hearing from such party members as Stimson and William Allen White. The exchange with White was most interesting. After a half-century of being at ideological loggerheads, the Old Bull Mooser and the Republican standpatter embraced. "It is odd," wrote the appreciative White, "that you and I have trudged along in politics in this country for forty years and never have found agreement until we joined in trying to repeal the embargo. They say you made a swell speech." The famous editor then wondered how western Republicans, with their Greenback, Granger, and Populist tradition could join with the eastern Republican crowd, in 1940, to beat the "opportunist" President.[70] Wadsworth replied warmly, noting that he and the *Emporia Gazette* editor had more in common than the repeal of neutrality and a distrust of the President. They had the same neighbors. "I find there is no difference," wrote Wadsworth, "between the fundamental thinking of a farmer in the Genesee Valley in Western New York and a farmer in Iowa or Kansas." Both believed, he noted, that "liberty, a thing of the spirit, is infinitely more precious than mere material security."[71]

Wadsworth's internationalism, manifested by his neutrality repeal efforts in the mid-1930s, was consistent with the cosmopolitan aristocratic strain of such twentieth century secretaries of state as John Hay, Elihu Root, and Henry L. Stimson.

67. *Buffalo Courier*, Nov. 7, 1939.
68. Joseph P. Tumulty to J.W.W., Nov. 17, 1939, Wadsworth MSS.
69. J.W.W. to Alfred E. Smith, Nov. 30, 1939, Wadsworth MSS.
70. William Allen White to J.W.W., Nov. 23, 1939, Wadsworth MSS.
71. J.W.W. to William Allen White, Nov. 27, 1939, Wadsworth MSS.

4

Consistent with Wadsworth's support of cash and carry trade with belligerents was his fight for preparedness legislation. In 1938, prior to the repeal of the neutrality acts, the New Yorker had defended the administration's $1,120,000,000 naval construction bill to provide a two-ocean navy. Most Republicans assailed the bill as part of a plan either to involve America in foreign wars, or to help Britain save her empire. A portent of isolationists' problems in the three years to follow was the vigorous applause accorded Wadsworth's address on the bill. Spelling out the nature of aggression in Europe and Asia, he concluded that force ruled the world. In quick succession applause accompanied his staccato-like style of quiet speech: "We as a Nation have never supported the philosophy of force. [Applause] . . . It is incumbent upon us to shape our course in such fashion as to make this generation of Americans and future generations in this beloved country safe. [Applause] Safe; safe against force. [Applause]" Specifically, the New Yorker advocated the two-ocean navy to protect the Western Hemisphere. "No one else is going to protect it for us," he concluded.[72] Wadsworth carried few Republicans with him on the bill. Again, Sumner Welles expressed appreciation. "What you so eloquently said," he wrote, "I personally believe . . . and I cannot help but feel that your address will prove greatly enlightening to public opinion in our country and most beneficial in its results."[73] For every letter like Welles's, however, opposing mail abounded. "By what right," wrote a constituent clergyman, "do you use the word 'Christian' when you are willing that we expend a great amount of money to blow the fathers, the sons, the husbands of a foreign people to pieces. Battleships have never settled anything yet, but love, Christian love, has changed a whole world. Why not try it?"[74]

Early in 1939 Wadsworth again did yeoman service for the administration's defense program. As chairman of a newly-appointed Republican Conference committee to study the national defense problem, he influenced his party to assume a less partisan position on preparedness. In the course of House debate on an Army Air Corps expansion bill Wadsworth unveiled the Republican position. In short, his party defended the Monroe Doctrine, called for the establishment of an impregnable defensive shield

72. *Congressional Record*, Vol. 83, 75th Congress, 3rd Session, Mar. 15, 1938, pp. 3413–4; *New York Times*, Mar. 16, 1938.
73. Sumner Welles to J.W.W., Mar. 16, 1938, Wadsworth MSS.
74. Rev. Clifford W. Hilliker to J.W.W., May 16, 1938, Wadsworth MSS.

at the one hundred and eightieth meridian in the Pacific Ocean, pointed to the need to make effective American defensive forces "far out in the Atlantic Ocean," instructed the House on ways to strengthen the Panama Canal, and, most importantly, supported the administration's request to "bring [the Army Air Corps] total to a maximum authorized strength of 5,500 [planes]." The Republicans' only caveat was that the "authorized strength be reached by annual increments over a period of 3 or 4 years" to ease both the payment and planning of production. The House demurred on the Republicans' view and overwhelmingly passed the legislation.[75] "I at once recognized your skillful hand," Henry L. Stimson congratulated Wadsworth, "when the report of the minority came out deciding not to oppose an adequate defense. It would have been a catastrophe if they had taken an isolationist position." [76] Wadsworth's influence on dissipating the isolationists' anti-preparedness stand in the House is difficult to assess. Indeed, Hitler's increasingly vicious repression of German Jews and his sabre-rattling in connection with his occupation of Czechoslovakia in 1938 and 1939 alarmed even some isolationists. Besides, "belligerent" isolationists saw certain preparedness legislation as a means of truly keeping America out of foreign wars. Before the year 1940 was over, military and naval appropriations in the Congress would reach a total of $17,000,000,000.

Wadsworth was conscious of the dollar mark on American defense spending. In late 1939 and throughout the following spring, he at times appeared ambivalent, on the one hand demanding immediate action to improve the military establishment, yet, on the other, insisting that the nation avoid the process called "deficit financing." He chastised Roosevelt for saddling the country with a $44,000,000,000 debt as a starting point if war were to come. "I am not an economist," he told the Economic Club of Detroit, "but . . . [am aware] that two plus two equals four, that what goes up must come down, that interest runs on Sunday as well as the other six days in the week, that heavy debt cramps enterprise and spreads fear. I am appalled at the prospect." [77] While the Geneseoan intermittently chastised the President for foolish domestic expenditures, his principal interests became military ones. General George Marshall, the new Chief of Staff, wrote to say the "analysis of the military problem in your Detroit speech is . . . without error. . . . Matters of financial policy are outside my province and I make no comment." Marshall closed by asking his old

75. *New York Times*, Feb. 15, 1939; *Congressional Record*, Vol. 84, 76th Congress, 1st Session, Feb. 14, 1939, pp. 1375-6.

76. Henry L. Stimson to J.W.W., Feb. 15, 1939, Wadsworth MSS.

77. "National Defense," Feb. 12, 1940, Wadsworth MSS.

friend to come to Fort Myer for a late Sunday breakfast to "talk . . . over military matters and prospects in general." [78]

It is not difficult to imagine what Wadsworth and the Chief of Staff discussed over breakfast in February of 1940—the air corps, ordnance procurement, military garrisons, enlistments—and possibly they reminisced. Their association went back almost a quarter of a century to the time when Marshall served as Pershing's aide-de-camp and befriended Wadsworth, then the young chairman of the Senate's Military Affairs Committee. At that time, Wadsworth was sponsoring and shepherding through the Senate the National Defense Act of 1920 which established, in all its basics, the army which Marshall now headed. The two men were committed to the "citizen army" concept built into the 1920 act. Both regretted that the Congress had not passed universal military training which was intended to provide citizen reserves called for in the act. Still the skeleton of nine corps armies with regular army, national guard, and army reserve divisions was intact. And although the regular army divisions in the corps areas were undermanned, Marshall apparently felt that the 17,000 additional men he requested of the Congress in 1940 would bring the regular army to fairly adequate strength. [79]

The regular army was thought of as an initial shield which would hold off a potential enemy during a period of wartime mobilization. It was expected that conscription would be implemented sixty days after a declaration of war and that prior to that time a "Civilian Volunteer Effort" would be launched. The whole scheme was known as the "Protective Mobilization Plan" and no evidence reveals Wadsworth's or Marshall's displeasure with it. [80]

Grenville Clark, a member of the prestigious New York law firm, Root, Clark, Buckner and Ballantine, and a small group of men meeting at the Harvard Club in New York City thought otherwise. The group, the Executive Committee of the Second Corps Area Military Training Camps

78. George C. Marshall to J.W.W., Feb. 16, 1940, Wadsworth MSS.

79. Samuel R. Spencer, Jr., "A History of the Selective Training and Service Act of 1940 from Inception to Enactment" (Harvard University, 1951), Ph.D. dissertation, p. 84. Wadsworth's correspondence in this period reveals a similar lack of concern about military manpower needs. See Forest C. Pogue, George C. Marshall, Ordeal and Hope, 1939–1942 (New York: Viking Press, 1965), pp. 56–58. Pogue argues that Marshall favored conscription for years but for political reasons he did not advocate it. He quotes Marshall: "No one had to tell me how much it [conscription] was needed—I knew that years before—but the great question was how to get it. It wasn't for me to establish a reputation because I asked for selective service legislation." p. 57.

80. Spencer, Jr., op. cit., Ch. II, passim.

Association, represented the ultimate in eastern wealth and influence. Their meeting on May 10, 1940, was to plan a fitting observance of the twenty-fifth anniversary of the Plattsburgh movement in which they had all participated. Clark suddenly interposed that the world situation was too serious to plan a parade or a dinner, that as the Plattsburgh movement had met a need for officers prior to the first world war, the MTCA should now launch a movement for the training of much-needed manpower. Clark argued that the Officers' Reserve Corps, established after the first world war, continued to provide trained leadership but not trained manpower. His suggestion was indeed a bold one, that there be a peacetime compulsory selective service and training act.[81]

Clark and his associates formed a nation-wide National Emergency Committee of approximately 1,000 members to establish contact with key members of the Congress and the executive office, to publicize the need for conscription, and to begin the drafting of necessary legislation. The bulk of the effort was assumed by a small executive committee centered in Manhattan. That the NEC, and Clark particularly, had influence was demonstrated by its successful contact with such persons as Wadsworth, General Marshall, and the President. In fact, Clark, through his long-time association with Franklin Roosevelt and Supreme Court Justice Felix Frankfurter, was able to suggest the appointment of Henry L. Stimson and Robert Patterson (fellow members of the New York Bar) as Secretary and Assistant Secretary of War in 1940. In the public relations effort, the NEC provided the press with appropriate copy at just the right times. Most importantly, the Clark associates, with the aid of retired General John Palmer and Wadsworth, drafted the conscription bill, frequently consulting with War Department personnel in the process.[82]

The NEC was not alone in considering conscription legislation. The President had given much thought to a combination of military and vocational training, an impractical scheme which never got off the ground. The Joint Army and Navy Committee on Manpower, under War and Navy Department auspices, for years had considered selective service legislation. Its proposal, however, unlike that of the NEC, was not a peacetime bill, but was to be implemented sixty days after emergency mobilization. The NEC bill also differed from the Joint Committee bill in specifics of age range, pay, length of training, and deferments. The NEC wanted to draft those in the 21–45 age group. The Joint Committee placed emphasis on the 21–31 age group. The NEC favored a token payment of five dollars

81. Spencer, Jr., *op. cit.*, pp. 7–9; Pogue, *op. cit.*, pp. 56–57.
82. Spencer, Jr., *op. cit.*, pp. 103–127; Pogue, *op. cit.*, p. 57.

per month. The military favored regular army pay. In regard to length of training, the New Yorkers, as the Clark group came to be known, called for six months of training as opposed to the Joint Army and Navy Committee plan of eighteen months. On deferments, the NEC and Joint Committee bills were comparable, except that President Conant of Harvard advised the New Yorkers to defer certain scientists.[83]

It was fortunate for the fate of the NEC bill that the President appointed Stimson Secretary of War, coincidentally on the day the bill was introduced in the Senate. For one thing, Stimson accepted the War assignment on the condition that the President would support a peacetime draft. For another, the War Department, including General Marshall, was cool to peacetime conscription prior to Stimson's appointment. Because of the isolationist climate still prevailing in the country and because it was an election year, the President did not immediately support conscription and would not do so until mid-summer. And although War Department personnel consulted with the New Yorkers on the bill, the Department was nearly moribund from twenty years of financial starvation. As noted, even George Marshall, in February of 1940, was satisfied with asking Congress to support only 17,000 additional men in the regular army. It took Stimson's prodding of the President and his direction of the War Department to bring both to support peacetime conscription.[84]

Wadsworth's ties to the proposed selective service and training act were innumerable. Because Clark recognized the Geneseoan's influence, ability, and commitment to national defense, he relied on him for advice and to shepherd the bill through the House.[85] On the draft issue and other matters Stimson relied on Wadsworth as his principal liaison in the House of Representatives. General Palmer, the NEC's principal military adviser, had admired Wadsworth from the day of his sponsorship of the National Defense Act of 1920. In fact, he dedicated his definitive book on military policy, *America in Arms,* to Wadsworth.[86] Marshall, the Chief of Staff, and Wadsworth were on intimate terms and in close touch. The President, although diametrically opposed to Wadsworth's ideas on domestic policy, liked the Geneseoan personally and, at Stimson's suggestion, frequently

83. Spencer, Jr., *op. cit.,* Ch. IV *passim.*

84. Spencer, Jr., *op. cit.,* Ch. V, *passim;* Henry L. Stimson and McGeorge Bundy, *On Active Service in Peace and War* (New York: Harper & Brothers, 1947), pp. 345–348 and 377–379.

85. Spencer, Jr., *op. cit.,* pp. 160–161.

86. John McAuley Palmer, *America in Arms, The Experience of the United States with Military Organization* (New Haven, Conn.: Yale University Press, 1941).

consulted him on military matters, especially after war broke out.[87] Aside from Wadsworth's relations with important people, no person in elective public office, other than the President, matched his experience with the development of American military policy. It was natural that his role in the passage of the first peacetime conscription legislation would be significant.

With France falling before the German *blitzkreig* in June 1940, and with congressmen anxious to leave Washington for the national conventions, the New Yorkers moved rapidly to get their bill into the congressional hopper before adjournment. They wisely tried for bi-partisan sponsorship but with so little administration support that Democratic leaders would not put their names on the bill. Clark hurriedly did what he could. House sponsorship was no problem, for Wadsworth gladly sponsored the bill there. In the Senate, Henry C. Lodge of Massachusetts was approached, but while considering the sponsorship, got miffed at Clark for approaching Edward R. Burke of Nebraska. Whereupon, Lodge suggested that Burke's name alone go on the Senate bill. It did. On June 20, the Nebraska senator introduced Bill S 4164 before senate adjournment. Simultaneously, the wire services and 2,000 newspapers were provided with copies of the bill. On the following day, Wadsworth put HR 10132 into the congressional hopper.[88] Thus was born the Burke-Wadsworth bill.

The public was caught rather unaware by the quick action to introduce the selective service bill. As yet the NEC had ground out little press copy. Certain of Clark's associates discussed the bill, as did *New York Times'* Colonel Julius Ochs Adler with Princeton alumni. A *Times* editorial defended the idea. Wadsworth probably was the first political figure to discuss the draft at length. He did so before the Women's National Republican Club. Noting adequate appropriations in Congress for naval and military equipment expansion, he viewed voluntary recruitment of manpower as inadequate. "I submit," he concluded, "that the only absolutely certain way of getting the men in sufficient numbers and at the right time and at the right place is through a selective draft system. More than that, I cannot conceive of any more democratic method of preparing our defense. A selective draft system is founded upon the principle that every man owes a duty to defend his country."[89] The President said he liked the *Times* editorial but emphasized his own

87. Spencer, Jr., *op. cit.*, pp. 393–394.
88. *Ibid.*, Ch. V, *passim.*
89. "Get Ready Now," Speech before Women's National Republican Club, June 15, 1940, Wadsworth MSS.

proposal to place young men and women in training schools.[90] Wadsworth thought the President mad to suggest such a thing. "Frankly," he wrote a constituent, "I have never known of such a system being put into effect in any country upon the face of the earth—not even in Germany." [91]

Hardly was Stimson settled in the War Department when the President suggested that Marshall be permitted to implement the Civilian Volunteer Effort. Clark, who seemed intuitive in influencing people at critical moments, convinced Stimson to fight the CVE on the ground that Burke-Wadsworth opponents would seize upon the volunteer effort as sufficient, or at least worth a good long test before resorting to conscription. Undoubtedly, it would have killed the bill until the next Congress.[92]

The Senate hearing on the conscription legislation began on July 2 and preceded those in the House by one week. Senator Morris Sheppard, the chairman of the Senate's Military Affairs Committee, opened the hearings with a strong supportive letter from General Pershing. He then called upon Wadsworth who reminded the chairman that the two of them had supported peacetime conscription as far back as 1920:

> Mr. Chairman, perhaps you will let me reminisce for just a moment. Perhaps you and I are the only persons at this table who can remember things that far back. In 1920 we served on the Committee on Military Affairs of the Senate in the preliminary consideration of the National Defense Act of that year. The bill we reported to the Senate contained in it provisions for compulsory military training. We had to drop that provision; could not get anywhere with it. Perhaps that is the best description of our predicament, and I may remind you, Senator Sheppard, you and I supported that bill at that time, and the answer that was given to us was, "Oh, well, there will not be any more wars." That is all. [Applause][93]

There followed a host of advocates, among them Senator Burke, Clark, Dr. James Conant, president of Harvard University, Colonel William "Wild Bill" Donovan, former commanding officer of the "fighting 69th," and General Palmer. Like Wadsworth, General Palmer referred to the origins of the present measure in the Defense Act of 1920, empha-

90. New York Times, June 18, 1940; Spencer, Jr., op. cit., pp. 188–193.
91. J.W.W. to E. Willoughby, Esq., June 21, 1940, Wadsworth MSS.
92. Spencer, Jr., op. cit., pp. 183–197.
93. Hearings before the Committee on Military Affairs, United States Senate, Seventy-Sixth Congress, Third Session on S 4164, p. 6.

sizing the advantage of the "citizen army" concept over the "expansible standing army" favored by the Joint Army and Navy Committee. The New Yorkers closed their case on July 5 and awaited the War Department testimony to be given in the following week. The War Department was moving away from the expansible army concept, but Clark was dismayed to learn over the weekend that the Joint Committee would oppose the Burke-Wadsworth Bill on several grounds: that the bill was neither permanent nor temporary, that its age limits were too wide, that its training period of eight months was too short, that its provision for home defense was unnecessary, and that it was the work of amateurs and should be replaced by the Joint Committee's bill. Again Clark called Stimson and rescued the bill, not that its replacement would have been a catastrophe. The New Yorkers had won their big point when the War Department came around to compulsory peacetime training. Stimson brought together important parties favoring conscription, listened to their respective points of view, and informed them that the Burke-Wadsworth bill, with certain modifications, would be the War Department bill. The New Yorkers and the War Department agreed to remove the home defense item, support a one-year training period, accept the army pay scale, and eliminate the concept of any draft substitutions. Thus, when the Senate hearing convened, the War Department's representatives were favorable in their comment, noting the agreed modifications. Foes, however, came in droves, among them Major George Fielding Eliot, Hanson W. Baldwin, Norman Thomas, Oswald Garrison Villard, Walter Lippmann, and General Hugh Johnson. Their criticisms ranged from the dictatorial aspects of peacetime conscription, the measure as a step toward war, and the bill's lack of necessity, to the measure's being merely a result of British propaganda and Wall Street profit makers. Many of the military analysts favored a small mechanized army of 400,000 to 500,000 men over a mass army of millions.[94]

Opponents of the bill seemed to be making headway, particularly in view of the President's relative silence. Because the President was silent, Stimson and Secretary of the Navy Knox were also quiet. As a result, administration leaders in the Congress did not get behind the bill. The President was waiting for a consensus to develop. Isolationism was not dead. Congressional approval of cash and carry legislation and increased appropriations for the army and the navy were quite different from peacetime conscription.

On July 10, at his press conference, the President finally, though

94. *Ibid., passim;* Spencer, Jr., *op. cit.,* Ch. VI, *passim.*

only mildly, supported the bill. His support, however, was sufficient to bring Secretaries Stimson and Knox before the Military Affairs Committee. They, of course, corroborated the advocates' positions.[95]

Throughout July the President made no further public statement on the bill. He sensed unhappiness about the measure among even Democrats in the Congress. He noted to associates that while he liked Jim Wadsworth personally, Democrats in the House complained that only Wadsworth's name was on their side of the bill. And, of course, Burke's arch conservatism cooled New Deal Democrats in the Senate. The President toyed with the idea of having the names of Democratic leaders put on the bill but Clark got to Stimson and squelched the idea. The NEC leader correctly saw that the country was familiar with the Burke-Wadsworth Bill and would be confused by another name.[96]

While the President dallied on the bill, Democratic leaders became less and less enthusiastic about it. Finally, after continual prodding by Stimson, the President, at his August 2 press conference, unequivocally supported the Burke-Wadsworth Bill. He followed his press conference statement with strong letters to key congressmen supporting the bill. Still, amendments and delaying tactics threatened it. The principal modification, the Maloney Amendment, called for trying the volunteer approach until January, 1941. If passed, the amendment would cost the army months of valuable time. The amendment picked up support. Again the President equivocated. Now he appeared to be awaiting Wendell Willkie's speech accepting the Republican presidential nomination.[97]

Perhaps Wadsworth's most important contribution to the bill's ultimate passage was his influence on Willkie's position. On July 24 he had written a lengthy letter to the presidential candidate, describing the bill, the responsible compromises currently being worked out, the necessity of its enactment, the expected implementation of the measure, and the effect of the bill on the future security of the country. In closing, Wadsworth reminded Willkie that the "bill did not originate in the White House. The President had nothing to do with it from its inception. As you may remember, he indulged in a wild dream to the effect that every boy and girl in the United States . . . should be sent to a federal vocational training school with Sidney Hillman and such like in charge. I happen to know that he clung to that idea for a long time and that

95. Wadsworth, *Reminiscences,* pp. 433–444; *New York Times,* July 11, 1940.
96. Spencer, Jr., *op. cit.,* p. 394.
97. *Ibid.,* Ch. X, *passim.*

it was with the greatest reluctance and hesitation that he finally consented to support the bill." Wadsworth then wisely pointed up Stimson's influence on getting the President to support the bill. By strong inference, Wadsworth urged Willkie's support.[98]

"I was very appreciative of your letter," Willkie wrote Wadsworth on August 5. "It is the most instructing thing I have read about the selective draft. I think you will be satisfied with what I say on the subject in my acceptance speech."[99] Wadsworth and advocates of the draft bill were indeed satisfied. "I cannot ask the American people," Willkie said in Ellwood, Indiana, on August 17, "to put their faith in me without recording my conviction that some form of selective service is the only democratic way in which to secure the trained and competent manpower we need for national defense."[100]

With both presidential candidates firmly behind the Burke-Wadsworth bill, the Maloney Amendment failed in the Senate. But Congress found it hard to take that final step to peacetime conscription. The Senate in a 44-43 vote narrowly defeated an amendment proposed by Carl Hayden of Arizona to try the volunteer approach for at least sixty days before implementing compulsory conscription. Following the defeat of the Hayden Amendment the bill went to the House. On instructions from Wadsworth and majority leader Rayburn, the House Committee on Military Affairs had conducted hearings awaiting the Senate action, intending to substitute the Senate bill for that of the House. With the Senate bill in hand the House engaged in two days' debate prior to a vote.[101]

The pressure on House members mounted. Isolationists, antimilitarists, non-interventionists, and an assortment of right- and left-wingers demanded the bill's defeat. To neutralize their drive the NEC proposed to demand an investigation of subversive influence in the conscription campaign. Wadsworth opposed the NEC request as too late and too theatrical. The NEC dropped the idea.[102]

The first day of the House debate was a repetition of the national dialogue which had ensued all summer. Wadsworth's personal foe, Hamilton Fish, led the attack. Chairman Andrew May of the Military Affairs Committee led the defense. Tension broke when a member of the gallery shouted: "American conscription is American fascism."[103]

98. J.W.W. to Wendell Willkie, July 24, 1940, Wadsworth MSS.
99. Wendell Willkie to J.W.W., Aug. 5, 1940, Wadsworth MSS.
100. *New York Times,* Aug. 18, 1940.
101. Spencer, Jr., *op. cit.,* Ch. XII, *passim.*
102. *Ibid.*
103. *Ibid.*

Summation speeches came on the second day. All seats were filled when Wadsworth gave the principal closing address for the advocates of the bill. The Geneseoan confessed that he too should have been aware of Hitler's threat, but now that his aggressive designs were obvious, America must adapt its military policy. "It is not an attempt to establish a permanent policy in the United States," he assured the House. "It is meant to meet if it is possible to meet it, the immediate future and to put the country in a position to meet the situation promptly. In my humble judgment, we cannot afford to indulge in a 'wait and see' policy. Others have indulged in that and they have perished." [104] Throughout Wadsworth's address he was interrupted by applause and at his conclusion the entire House rose in a great and spontaneous ovation. The bill was passed but not without change, for Fish at least got adoption of the Hayden Amendment. It died, however, in conference. Final passage and presidential signature on the nation's first peacetime conscription act was thus assured. Wadsworth was quietly ecstatic. He immediately wrote to Grenville Clark:

It is about time that I saluted you. . . . I hope you do not object and that you will retaliate appropriately. As you have read in the newspapers this morning, or heard over the radio, the Senate and House conference finished their work on our bill last night. Ham Andrews reported the result to me over the phone and I confess I rejoiced at the news. Our only real set-back was in the matter of the age range. We wanted the forty-five year maximum. The Senate asked for the thirty-one year maximum. The conferees have settled upon the thirty-five year maximum—an obvious compromise. Perhaps we got a little the worst of it, but after all twenty-one to thirty-five is not so bad. And as I look back over this bitter battle I am really somewhat astounded that our bill has not suffered more. As a matter of fact, it comes out practically intact so far as fundamentals go. . . . The tumult and the shouting are subsiding, and I find myself possessed of a moment in which I can write to you calmly and dispassionately. I have one thing in my mind just now, and that is admiration for and gratitude to you and those who worked with you in starting this thing and carrying on the battle so bravely. Your emergency committee has performed a vital public service. It performed it unselfishly and with a vision not often possessed by any group in these hectic days. You paid me a high compliment in asking me to introduce the bill, and what is much more important, you gave me a chance to serve in a great cause.

104. *Congressional Record,* Vol. 86, 76th Congress, 3rd Session, Sept. 4, 1940, pp. 17383–6; Spencer, Jr., *op. cit.,* p. 471.

I rejoice at the opportunity, and not the least part of my satisfaction is my better acquaintance with you and your fellows. Perhaps we shall get a chance to serve together again some day. If so, I shall volunteer for the draft.[105]

Wadsworth and Stimson exchanged letters in like vein. The roles of the three were essential to the passage of the Burke-Wadsworth bill, as were those of the President, Wendell Willkie, General Marshall, and Senator Burke. More important than the roles of individuals was the act itself.

In subsequent years Stimson would view the passage of the act among the two or three important events prior to America's entry into the war. The act provided the country with the nucleus of a sizeable army of 1,650,000 at the time of the Pearl Harbor attack. It made possible the development of new training techniques to be immediately employed and on a large scale. It gave impetus for the manufacture of weapons to supply a mass army. It geared the country psychologically for war.[106]

105. J.W.W. to Grenville Clark, Sept. 12, 1940, Wadsworth MSS.
106. Spencer, Jr., *op. cit.*, Ch. XIII, *passim.*

XII

"Mr. National Defense"

1

A T 4:00 P.M. on a leisurely Sunday at Harriet's home, "The Plains," forty-five miles west of Washington, Wadsworth put in a call to Secretary of War Stimson. He wanted to confirm a meeting they were to have on the following day. "I'm sorry," answered Mrs. Stimson. "The Secretary's not here. He's had to go to the White House in a hurry." "Is there some trouble?" asked Wadsworth. "We just got the news a few moments ago that the Japanese have bombed Pearl Harbor," answered Mrs. Stimson.[1] That attack by the Japanese sealed the fate of Wadsworth, no less than that of untold numbers of Americans. For the duration and to the decade's end, he would author and watch over defense and related legislation with even greater fervor than in the years prior to Pearl Harbor. His commitment would earn for him the appellation, "Mr. National Defense."[2]

The war indeed affected the congressional and personal life of James Wadsworth. The two lives were frequently meshed as one. Associates were often those in military roles who had vital interests in congressional affairs. Frequently, Wadsworth called upon ranking War Department personnel such as Secretary Stimson, Assistant Secretary Robert Patterson, General George Marshall, the Chief of Staff, former Secretary Dwight W. Davis, who returned to the Department for the war years,[3] and General John Palmer, the War Department's principal postwar policy planner. Except for a minimal partisanship nationally and in New York politics, and some necessary comment on domestic measures coming before the House, Wads-

1. James W. Wadsworth, Jr., *The Reminiscences of James W. Wadsworth, Jr.* (Columbia University Oral History Research Office, 1952), pp. 444–5.
2. Beverly Smith, "Mr. National Defense," *Saturday Evening Post*, Mar. 18, 1947.
3. Harvey Bundy, *The Reminiscences of Harvey Bundy* (Columbia University Oral History Research Office, undated).

worth contained his politics for the duration, one of the few Republicans to do so.

Military associates were not confined only to the Pentagon. He was in frequent touch with generals in the field—Lt. General Hugh Drum, Commander, First Army; Lt. General W. H. Haskell, Commander, New York National Guard; Lt. General Leslie J. McNair, Commander of Ground Forces, United States Army; Lt. General Patton, Commander, Third Army, European Theatre; Lt. General Robert C. Richardson, Commander, Army's Hawaii Department; and Maj. General Frank McCoy (retired). Wadsworth was very close to the Patton family. Following a visit with them in their Fort Benning home, the Congressman collected regimental insignia for the General's son, and later he commiserated with Mrs. Patton when that same son had academic troubles at West Point. Subsequently, he followed the movements of both the General and his Third Army. Following the famous incident in which Patton slapped one of his hospitalized men, Wadsworth offered immediate support. The General thanked him for his unfaltering friendship. Reverdy, a lieutenant in Patton's Third Army, continually informed his father of the General's amazing courage and exploits. When, five days after V-E Day, the General deplaned in Germany for a happy reunion with the touring New York congressman, he suggested that when Wadsworth returned to Washington, he fight the "Goddamn Russians." It was like Patton to follow one admonition with another. The other, with the concurrence of Reverdy, who was present, called for a halt to the army's non-fraternization policy. He noted that the "prick was mightier than the sword." In the following year, Patton cautioned Wadsworth against any precipitous American disarmament. He noted that a vocal minority of Americans had urged it after every war as a way to produce peace, but the fact that the United States had fought ten wars in two hundred years proved to Patton that "the gentlemen who advocated . . . [it] are liars." To the end, Wadsworth defended Patton. "He is," the New Yorker wrote, "really a great soldier—a remarkable mixture of intellectual culture, profane humor, and a deepseated love of God and of His son, Jesus Christ."[4]

Wadsworth's containment of politics was felt in the highest councils. He and Harry Truman, both personally committed to Dr. Frank Buchman's Moral Re-Armament movement, valiantly tried to get the move-

4. J.W.W. to George Patton, Mar. 14, 1941, J.W.W. to Mrs. George Patton, Mar. 29, 1941, J.W.W. to Mrs. George Patton, Sept. 7, 1943, June 1, 1944, George S. Patton to J.W.W., Feb. 22, 1944, Aug. 21, 1945, J.W.W. to J. F. Weller, Apr. 4, 1944, Wadsworth MSS, Library of Congress, Washington, D.C.; Alden Hatch, *The Wadsworths of the Genesee* (New York: Coward-McCann, Inc., 1959), pp. 273–4; conversation with Reverdy Wadsworth, summer 1967.

ment's workers deferred from the draft. He used his influence with General Marshall to get the Distinguished Service Medal for Woodrow Wilson's Assistant Secretary of War, Benedict Crowell, for rendering twenty-five years of service to the army.[5]

Old friends were, of course, not sacrificed for new war associates. He and A.H.W. frequently met them for dinner at the Alibi or the Racquet Club in Washington, and certainly even war could not cause Wadsworth to sacrifice his relationships with his family. On the contrary, as in most American homes, war drew the family closer. He was proud of Reverdy, who rose from private to major. He was no less proud, and concerned, about Jerry, physically ineligible for war service. When Jerry's reports of life with Buffalo's Curtiss-Wright Corporation fell off, his father showed concern.: "What are your problems? . . . How are you getting on with the Curtiss high command? . . . I can't disguise the fact that I'm hungry for a report from you."[6] Wadsworth and A.H.W. saw much of Evie. Frequently she accompanied Stuart to town where, as president of the Emerson Electric Manufacturing Company, he had government business. On one occasion Wadsworth interceded to see that his son-in-law appeared before the Military Affairs Committee to clear himself of charges that Emerson Electric was getting "fat" on gun turret contracts. Stuart Symington adulated his father-in-law.[7] The frequency of their visits, however, did not preclude some friction between the New Deal Democrat and the stand-pat Republican. Stuart "blew-off" one night and apologized to his father-in-law the following day. "If there is any guilt," answered Wadsworth graciously, "I should be charged with 60% of it." At some length he explained how they were both "born arguifiers" and talked "a little louder" as the time passed.[8] It was typical of Wadsworth to be so solicitous of Symington's feelings. He was delighted when Stuart was permanently located in Washington as the government's Surplus Property Administrator.

"Jimmy" Wadsworth Symington, the younger son of Evie and Stuart, eloquently described to the author his grandfather's kindly solicitude. From his State Department office—he was President Lyndon Johnson's Chief of

5. *New York World Telegram,* June 4, 1943; J.W.W. to George C. Marshall, July 14, 1945, Walter G. Andrews to J.W.W., July 25, 1942, Wadsworth MSS.

6. J.W.W. to J. J. Wadsworth, May 18, 1943, Wadsworth MSS.

7. Statement of W. S. Symington, president of the Emerson Electric Mfg. Co., St. Louis, Mo., before House Military Affairs Committee, July 28, 1941, Wadsworth MSS; although evidence supports the warm personal relationship between Wadsworth and Symington, caveats about it have been expressed to the author by Bessie Christian and some members of the family.

8. W. S. Symington to J.W.W., Jan. 17, 1942; J.W.W. to W. S. Symington, Jan. 20, 1942, Wadsworth MSS. Symington reported to the author that the argument was over a military and not a political matter.

Wadsworth in the Hartford House library, 1946, with a statue of his grandfather, General James S. Wadsworth, in the background. *By permission of the Library of Congress. Photograph by Ollie Atkins,* The Saturday Evening Post.

Alice Hay Wadsworth.

Harriet Wadsworth Harper, 1930. Portrait in Hartford House.

Wadsworth with son Reverdy during World War II.

Protocol at the time—he remembered vividly and fondly how his grand-father wrote to him in boot camp at Paris Island. One particular letter was four typewritten pages in length and was filled with family news, sage advice, reminiscences, and was revealing of the congressman's pride and belief in soldiering. In part, he wrote:

> You are learning a lot about fellers. There are all kinds of them. Scarce any two are alike. Some are quick, some are slow. Some are square, some are slick. Some want to learn and do. Others want to learn and can't. Some do not care about learning anything. But way down under-neath you will find something good in pretty nearly all of them. Patience is what is needed in sizing up dependably a big gang of youngsters. You know, I envy you. I wish I could look back on the experience you are having. When I saw that my assistance was needed to make sure that the Spaniards were defeated in 1898 I went into a field artillery outfit, sup-posedly on active duty in time of war, and, literally, I did not know a thing except how to ride and care for a horse. I certainly did not know how to take care of myself. Neither did anybody else in the outfit, despite the fact that four-fifths of them were college graduates. Very smart—elite. The Spaniards saw us coming and surrendered. We spent the sum-mer in Puerto Rico, eating and drinking everything we could get hold of. Sloppy from top to bottom. Half our horses died on the picket line and half the men were sick. I held up pretty well until, aboard the transport coming home, I insisted upon eating three rations (all at once) of spoiled beef. I lost thirty-seven pounds. Looking back on it years afterwards I realize that I had been a rotten soldier—just no good. Why? Because I had had no boot training. Nobody had in those days except in the tiny regular Army, Marine Corps and Navy. That's why I have been a crank about training ever since.[9]

Wadsworth and Wendell Willkie enjoyed a political love affair dur-ing the war years. The bond was a pragmatic internationalism and, second-arily, a desire to foil Tom Dewey's White House ambitions. Wadsworth sat up one night reading Willkie's *One World* and told the author how much he liked it. Willkie was equally pleased by Wadsworth's war role. In June of 1942, the titular leader exorted the Republican state organiza-tion in New York to seriously consider Wadsworth over Dewey as their candidate for governor.[10] Willkie's statement brought to Wadsworth a rash

9. J.W.W. to J. W. Symington, Dec. 20, 1945, Wadsworth, MSS; conversation with author, January 1968.

10. *New York Times*, June 14, 1942.

of favorable correspondence and considerable press support. Wadsworth made light of the alleged boomlet, writing one supporter, "If I have a public duty anywhere it is right here in Washington. If I can be actually useful close to the scene of action during this war it is here."[11] Willkie, however, did not make light of a Wadsworth candidacy. Of a large field of possible candidates, he truly favored Wadsworth, or possibly Assembly Majority Leader Irving Ives.[12] Dewey was nervous about Wadsworth's political moves in the early summer of 1942. "He feels," wrote a Dewey intimate, "that the Wadsworth family still holds against him the fact that Jerry was not nominated for Lieutenant Governor [in 1938]." The Dewey camp considered running Jerry for lieutenant governor this time but decided against it. Dewey did not need a Wadsworth on the ticket to get the nomination. "Between you and me," the elder Geneseoan wrote the Dewey intimate, "I wish that little man would cure himself of the habit of taking things so personally."[13] The Manhattan district attorney was nominated and elected.

The 39th Congressional District was all Wadsworth's in 1942. He stood unopposed, his first such experience, because, so the Monroe County Democratic Committee said, "he did not follow the Republican policy of blind stupidity and obstruction as advocated by . . . [Republican leaders] who stuck to the old party prejudices." Wadsworth was grateful, and yet amused. "I find myself," he wrote New York Senator James Mead, "endorsed by the Republicans, by the Democrats, and by the *New Republic*."[14]

The unanimity of Wadsworth's election brought him added status. The *New York Times* columnist Arthur Krock said he "now had the opportunity to be the real leader in the House—in command of the coalition of anti-New Dealers."[15] Wadsworth's own New York delegation seemed to prepare the ground for Krock's prophecy. They removed Daniel Reed, their senior Republican, from the very important Republican House Committee on Committees and appointed Wadsworth in his place.[16] While Wadsworth gladly led his delegation in the House, he continued to demur at partisan and coalition politics during the war years.

11. J.W.W. to Frank A. Lord, June 22, 1942, Wadsworth MSS.
12. Donald Bruce Johnson, *The Republican Party and Wendell Willkie* (Urbana, Ill.: University of Illinois Press, 1960), p. 208.
13. F. B. Lord to J.W.W., May 29, 1942, J.W.W. to F. B. Lord, June 5, 1942, J.W.W. to J. J. Wadsworth, June 19, 1942, Wadsworth MSS.
14. Democratic Press Statement; James M. Mead to J.W.W., J.W.W. to James M. Mead, July 13, 1942, Wadsworth MSS.
15. Hiram Bingham to J.W.W., Nov. 7, 1942, Wadsworth MSS.
16. Frank Crowther to Daniel Reed, Jan. 11, 1943, Lewis K. Rockefeller to Daniel Reed, Jan. 11, 1943, Reed MSS, Cornell University Library, Ithaca, N.Y.

In 1943 columnist Drew Pearson thought New York Republicans would put up Wadsworth for president. Pearson reasoned that the New Yorker had the status and that by 1944 the country would be ready for a conservative.[17] However, Wadsworth did not dream of leaving the House. He was happy to return to it. In 1944 the Democrats contended for his seat. Their candidate lost, two to one.

If observers had thought Wadsworth's support of the New Deal's foreign and military policy effected a change in his domestic record, that record would have set them straight. He proved as consistently conservative as ever, as witnessed by a sampling of his reaction to the domestic scene, in and out of Congress. In Congress he voted against placing beans, potatoes, oats, barley, rye, and apples under production controls, thus entitling their growers to parity price payments. He agonized over the firm federal wheat controls and was bothered particularly by the United States Department of Agriculture's inconsistent policies regarding them. He thought price-fixing of lamb and beef excessive and spoke against "these radically inclined youngsters" making policy in Leon Henderson's Office of Price Administration. In point of fact, Wadsworth admitted the need for some minimal price controls. However, he did not like New Dealers providing them.[18]

On other House matters, Wadsworth opposed the St. Lawrence Seaway, because it was "dreamy" and because the advancement of hydroelectric power, and not navigation, seemed the principal motive of proponents. "It would put government into business on a large scale," he wrote a constituent.[19] He opposed vigorously both the anti-poll tax and anti-lynching bills.[20] He thought both bills were state prerogatives and not those of the federal government. He supported the work of the Dies Committee on Un-American Activities even though Willkie told him, "as presently constituted it [is] terrible." "Despite some errors," wrote Wadsworth, "it has done an excellent job."[21] Consistent with his conservative

17. Pearson column, Oct. 2, 1943, Wadsworth MSS: Wadsworth wrote over column "completely false."

18. J.W.W. to H. M. Collamer, Apr. 2, 1941, J.W.W. to Roy A. Porter, May 29, 1943, J.W.W. to Wm. P. Walls, Nov. 18, 1942, J.W.W. to Ernest L. Woodward, Apr. 15, 1943, Wadsworth MSS; James W. Wadsworth, Jr., Diary, Mar. 15, 1945, Wadsworth MSS.

19. J.W.W. to William A. Wheeler, Dec. 1, 1944, Wadsworth MSS.

20. J.W.W. to Harry D. Williams, May 24, 1944, J.W.W. to George E. Ulp, May 31, 1943, J.W.W. to Prince C. James, Oct. 17, 1943, Wadsworth MSS.

21. Wendell Willkie to J.W.W., Feb. 21, 1942, J.W.W. to George H. Beckwith, May 21, 1943, Wadsworth MSS.

record on domestic matters, Wadsworth urged the retention of two pressure groups in which he had been active, the American Liberty League and the Repeal Associates. He thought the former might well be needed after the war "to restore private enterprise as the controlling philosophy underlying our economic system." He suggested that Repeal Associates might be transformed into an organization which "would be devoted to the preservation of our dual form of government under the Constitution." [22]

Wadsworth's activity during his long tenure on the important Interstate and Foreign Commerce Committee from 1933 to 1943 attracted national attention only in 1941. For almost a decade he had viewed warily what he thought to be a harmful intrusion by the Securities and Exchange Commission into the corporate life of America. Finally he acted. On April 14, 1941, he surprised both the financial community and the SEC by introducing certain amendments to the securities laws, "to put both dollars and men to work and thus fortify our free institutions." Wadsworth was sure that by moderating the SEC's requirements and intrusion the economy would again move forward. Specifically, he asked that the stock prospectuses be stripped to essentials, that stock brokers be permitted to advertise in the press, that registration of new stock issuances be simplified, that the waiting period between a request to issue stock and the actual issuance be reduced, that the exchange industry be consulted prior to the establishment of new SEC rules, that the SEC not make public charges of wrong-doing without proof, that the exchange industry have appellate access to the courts, and that the SEC change its mandate to protecting the industry as well as policing it. Actually, the stock exchange industry and the SEC had for months been negotiating changes in the laws.[23] But the New Yorker tired of waiting and launched his own investigation on which he based his recommendations. Much of the press supported his action. The *New York Times*, editorially, thought his suggestions "cut through the tangle of technicalities which seems to have enmeshed the SEC and the financial community in one long, interminable wrangle," and agreed that the SEC should "temper its rough hand." [24] The *New York Telegram's* financial editor appreciated Wadsworth's concern for the small corporation.[25]

By August of 1941, the securities industry and the SEC, as a result of Wadsworth's prodding and its own increased momentum of negotiation,

22. J.W.W. to Ernest L. Woodward, Jan. 26, 1942, J.W.W. to Elizabeth Livingston, Apr. 29, 1942, Wadsworth MSS.

23. Press release, Apr. 14, 1941, Wadsworth MSS.

24. *New York Times* editorial, Apr. 16, 1941.

25. *New York Telegram*, "Amendments to Securities Act Found Desirable on Basis of Past Experience," Apr. 15, 1921.

Two cartoon facsimiles drawn by Gordon Miller, the upper from an unidentified newspaper clipping, April 1941; the lower from the *Washington Evening Star,* February 6, 1941.

agreed on fifty-five of eighty-six proposed changes to the exchange regulations. Many of Wadsworth's suggestions were implemented. Remaining points of contention were largely others than those he recommended, namely, exemptions from SEC control, the handling of proxies, and the election of stock exchange officials.[26] Although Wadsworth soon after left the Foreign and Inter-state Commerce Committee which constantly watched over the Securities and Exchange Commission, he never stopped grumbling about stock prospectuses and registration statements, the SEC's authority, and the rigid proxy rules.

2

Domestic measures, such as amendments of the exchange acts, earned Wadsworth little staying power or stature. On the contrary, he floundered on them. In point of fact, the SEC by the war years was a well-established and welcomed institution.[27] The New Yorker's days in Congress probably would have ended inauspiciously had not foreign affairs and the war brought him forward. They did so periodically, as in early 1941 when the lend-lease debate stirred the country.

England, in 1940, stood alone. She was at her lowest ebb, desperately short of manpower, resources, and money. The President of the United States had done what he could. His administration achieved limited repeal of the neutrality legislation. It loaned England fifty over-aged destroyers. Such acts were insufficient. England needed aid short of war and the President wanted to give it to her. But various forms of isolationism still permeated much of America. For weeks, the President considered how to shore up Europe's last free land yet still enforce the neutrality laws. Non-interventionists, mostly Republicans like Fish, Vandenberg, Taft, and Hoover, watched his every move.

Then a solution evolved, one to aid England without violating the Johnson default act or the neutrality measures. England would not need to borrow any money, nor would the United States give her aid, both of which would have been illegal. The nation would lease to her, on loan, the war materials necessary to her survival. England would repay in kind following the war. Roosevelt conceived the idea while on a Caribbean cruise

26. *Business Week*, Aug. 16, 1941; *Nation's Business*, Oct. 1941; *Congressional Record*, Vol. 87, 77th Congress, 1st Session, Aug, 1941, p. 3090.

27. Ralph F. Debedts, *The New Deal's SEC: The Formative Years* (New York: Columbia University Press, 1964), p. 192.

in December of 1940. Upon his return, he confidently informed his policy makers of his decision. On December 17, he broke the idea to the press. On December 29, he addressed the people. Always, he emphasized the defensive nature of his proposal and insisted that it would not take us closer to war. Rather, the purpose was to keep America out of a "last ditch war for the preservation of American independence." [28] The idea was drafted into law and the President let it appear to originate in the House under the patriotic number HR 1776. If passed as introduced, it would give the President great power "to . . . transfer, exchange, lease, lend, or otherwise dispose of 'implements of war.'" He alone would direct an "arsenal of Democracy" which would change the world's balance of power. Historian Robert Osgood called it the "most extensive commitment made by an American President." [29] American opinion supported the idea. But vocal and volatile isolationists, mostly Republicans, did not. They feared the fate of America's peace, given the bill's passage. The President rightly feared the irreparable divisiveness they might cause America.

Among the few Republicans of note and influence who stepped forward to defend HR 1776 were Wendell Willkie, the titular head of the party, and Wadsworth. Both did so on January 18, 1941, before 1,600 Republican women at the National Republican Club in New York City. There Willkie warned against Republican isolationism and urged Republicans everywhere, especially in Washington, to carefully study Wadsworth's suggestions regarding the bill. The Geneseoan was in fine form. "I have rarely heard him," wrote Charles Hilles, "make a clearer, fairer, saner, more logical or more forceful presentation of a pending public question. He has an honest mind. He is a statesman devoid of showmanship." [30]

Recognizing the President's plan as startling, Wadsworth pleaded with his audience to submerge "old feelings" against the President and recognize that only he could exercise power in foreign affairs. Yet he insisted that limitations be cautiously imposed, limitations of time and of money. Furthermore, he urged that the Congress appoint an oversight committee which "shall consult frequently with the Chief Executive and afford him an opportunity to take them into his confidence." [31] Wadsworth made plain, however, his support of HR 1776.

28. Warren F. Kimball, *The Most Unsordid Act, Lend-Lease, 1939–1941* (Baltimore: The Johns Hopkins Press, 1969), pp. 120–125; James MacGregor Burns, *Roosevelt, The Soldier of Freedom* (New York: Harcourt Brace-Iovanovich, Inc., 1970), pp. 25–29.

29. Kimball, *op. cit.*, p. 130.

30. Charles D. Hilles to John Marshall, Jan. 21, 1941, Wadsworth MSS.

31. *New York Times*, Jan. 19, 1941. *Congressional Record*, Vol. 87, 77th Congress, 1st Session, Mar. 1941, pp. 192–4; J.W.W. to Charles D. Hilles, Jan. 22, 1941, Wadsworth MSS.

Wadsworth was committed to HR 1776 in word and deed. Unhesitatingly, he entered the old State Department building and conferred with Cordell Hull on strategies to effect the widest possible margin for the legislation. Hull reported Wadsworth's visit to Treasury Secretary Morgenthau, who in turn urged that Republicans, like Wadsworth, be included in White House conferences on the bill. The President vetoed an attempt at bi-partisan foreign policy.[32] Still, Wadsworth was heard. White House strategists considered his suggestion, and that of others, that the bill not go to the House Foreign Affairs Committee where Chairman Sol Bloom might bungle it or where the senior Republican, Hamilton Fish, could make a spectacle of himself. Wadsworth wanted the bill in the Military Affairs Committee. Rayburn liked the idea, but finally agreed with the Democratic leadership that the hue and cry from Foreign Affairs would not be worth it.[33]

Hearings conducted by the House Foreign Affairs Committee were the spectacle Wadsworth expected. Chairman Bloom and Hamilton Fish got into a shouting match. Bloom resented Fish's constant references to the "President's dictator bill" and Fish was angry because he could not invite his own witnesses. For a while the Republican minority on the committee met in another room.

Roosevelt was right about the divisiveness caused by Republicans. As the debate warmed up, they pulled out all the old shibboleths. Hamilton Fish kept referring to the "fascist bill" and the declaration of war. In the Senate chamber, Arthur H. Vandenberg, the "generalissimo" of forces opposing the bill, charged that HR 1776 would give the President authority to "make undeclared war . . . as he pleases." Hiram Johnson of California told the Senate he declined "to change the whole form of my government on a specious plea of assisting one belligerent." Senator Robert Taft of Ohio cried that only a "rubber stamp" Congress would pass such a bill. Outside the halls of Congress, the former Republican leader, Herbert Hoover, and the future leader, Thomas Dewey, both decried it. Basically the arguments of the opponents were two-fold: lend-lease would take us to war; it would give Franklin Roosevelt dictatorial powers.[34]

The administration forces kept their heads. They wrote a good bill and defended it before the congressional committee. Roosevelt personally counseled his spokesmen who appeared on the Hill. They stressed the

32. Kimball, op. cit., p. 142.
33. Ibid., p. 144.
34. Ibid., pp. 154–6; C. David Tompkins, Senator Arthur H. Vandenberg: The Evolution of a Modern Republican, 1884–1945 (E. Lansing: Michigan State University Press, 1970), p. 188.

measure as one of national defense, of buying protection, of supporting British sea power as a barrier to the invasion of America. They studiously avoided the broader foreign policy implications.[35]

Inordinate attempts were made at amending the nine sections of the bill. The President early agreed to four changes in the measure: a time limitation, a periodic reporting to the Congress, the prohibition of additional convoy powers, and consultation with the Army and the Navy Chiefs of Staff.[36] The first two were consistent with Wadsworth's recommendations. With such amendments, the bill was brought from the Foreign Affairs Committee to the floor for debate. Prior to the last day of debate, three additional amendments were voted in the House: the limitation of transfers of existing stocks of war, authority of Congress to terminate the powers granted by the bill, and a clause stating that the bill did not authorize the entry of American vessels into combat zones.[37]

Only one significant amendment was left unresolved on the last day of debate. Wadsworth hoped to unify the nation with a compromise formula, one which would give the President all the necessary authority to accomplish "all out" aid to Britain, yet fix a $7,000,000,000 limit on funds to be expended in the two-year period. The New Yorker was sure that friends of aid to Britain could not criticize the suggestion on the ground that it was inadequate. On the contrary, the pro-Communist, Vito Marcantonio, asked: "cannot . . . the suggestion be described as the sky is the limit?"[38]

The Democratic leadership decided against the Wadsworth amendment but carefully let down its author, arguing variously that seven times seven billions of dollars were given to the Allies in 1917 and 1918, that the limitation would not satisfy the critics, and that England might be misled by a specific amount, construing it as an absolute commitment. Then Speaker Rayburn went to the well of the House. He wanted to agree with Wadsworth, "whose patriotism and whose judgment we all admire, and who as a man we love," but he thought the bill protective enough of congressional prerogatives. Then majority leader McCormick agreed with the Speaker, outlining more specifically the built-in protections in the measure. Rayburn and McCormick had little difficulty in defeating the amendment, 38–122, and had much less difficulty defeating other amendments. In the final vote, the New Yorker voted for the bill, managing the concurrence of only twenty-four Republicans. Isolationist

35. Kimball, *op. cit.*, Ch. VI, *passim.*; Burns, *op. cit.*, p. 45.
36. Kimball, *op. cit.*, pp. 198–99; Burns, *op. cit.*, p. 46.
37. Kimball, *op. cit.*, pp. 202–204.
38. *Ibid.*, pp. 204–205; *New York Times*, Feb. 5, 6, 7, 8, 9, 1941.

Republicans in the Senate failed in attempts to further restrict the President. There, Senators James Byrnes, Harry Byrd, and Robert Taft agreed to passage if Congress were given the kind of close oversight Wadsworth had asked for. The bill was passed and signed by the President.[39]

"There is a good deal of wild-eyed curiosity amongst newspapermen and others," wrote Wadsworth to Jerry, "due to the fact that the President, in asking for a lend-lease appropriation of seven billion dollars, has used exactly the same figure as I proposed. . . . The newspapermen are saying, 'How come? Is Roosevelt bossing Wadsworth or is Wadsworth bossing Roosevelt?'" Wadsworth hardly bossed Roosevelt. Still the President deferred to the Geneseoan, giving some credence to his seven-billion-dollar suggestion. Also, he sent him one of the pens with which he signed the bill. "Your mother insists," Wadsworth concluded in his letter to Jerry, "that I tie a ribbon around it and keep it somewhere. Just now it is in my pen rack and quite indistinguishable from the other pens. In a day or two I shall not be able to identify it. So what the hell." [40]

Wadsworth scorned the President for his patronizing attitude, as revealed by the pen incident. Like many of his fellow Republicans, he too distrusted the President. "There is more prejudice against and distrust of Roosevelt among the minority here than I have ever noticed in the case of any other man," he wrote a fellow New Yorker. Still, he thought fellow Republicans "are blinded . . . to the extent that they cannot see the larger issue." [41]

It is difficult to measure Wadsworth's role in the passage of lend-lease legislation. With the President's support, it passed by a wide margin. More important than the Geneseoan's attempt at placing a seven-billion-dollar limitation on the lend-lease expenditures, was the impression that responsible Republicans like himself did support the concept of lend-lease. Thus, Wadsworth helped create the climate that enabled the President to play "consensus politics." Wadsworth, as a highly respected Republican, had played the same role regarding the "cash and carry" aid to Britain, and the conscription legislation of 1940. He helped to pave the way. He would do so again shortly in regard to the convoying of lend-lease material to Great Britain, and the final repeal of the neutrality acts.

Few Americans outside government did more to effect the consensus than Grenville Clark. Certainly he was most prominent and influential

39. *New York Times*, Feb. 9, 1941.
40. J.W.W. to J. J. Wadsworth, March 13, 1941, Wadsworth MSS.
41. J.W.W. to James B. Eveline, Feb. 11, 1941, Wadsworth MSS.

among those favoring American escort of lend-lease convoys and the final repeal of the neutrality legislation.[42] A member of Elihu Root's prestigious law firm and a prime mover behind the 1940 conscription legislation, Clark had intimate contact with the first rank of policy makers, particularly the President and Secretary of War Stimson. Not surprisingly, Wadsworth was his principal liaison with the Congress.[43]

In the spring of 1940 Clark submitted to the President a petition of more than 1,000 signatures of prominent Americans calling for the naval escort of American convoys to Europe. Surmising, however, that the President would not act without congressional authority, Clark urged Wadsworth to introduce in the Congress a supportive resolution. The request came as no surprise to Wadsworth, for he had already told Clark that a vote defeating Senator Charles N. Tobey's anti-convoy resolution would be purely negative. "I think," concluded Clark, "you would be performing the most important service of your career if you choose . . . to break the jam which is paralyzing our policy."[44]

Important interventionists felt the same as did Clark and Wadsworth about convoy escorts. To them, the lend-lease legislation was useless without them. Stimson and Knox pressed the President, as did Willkie. But to no avail. Roosevelt felt that public support was inadequate, that isolationism was still too rampant. The voices of cabinet members, and even Willkie, were muted by the President.[45] Wadsworth spoke publicly on the issue, almost immediately upon receipt of Clark's plea. "If we are going to manufacture for Britain," he told reporters, "as we have committed ourselves to doing, we must take such action as may be required to see that the products reach the destination."[46]

Wadsworth, like Clark, wanted congressional action, although he too thought the President, as Commander-in-Chief, could order the escorting of convoys by American naval forces.[47] Stimson, however, persuaded the Geneseoan not to introduce the resolution, but to give the President a chance to let favorable public opinion crystalize.[48] In mid-May, the Presi-

42. William Langer and S. Everett Gleason, *The Undeclared War, 1940–1941* (New York: Harper & Brothers, 1953), p. 425. In early April the President agonized over whether or not the public was ready for "so drastic a solution" as convoy escorts.

43. Note below prolific correspondence between Clark and Roosevelt and Clark and Wadsworth.

44. Grenville Clark to J.W.W., April 23, 1941, Wadsworth MSS.

45. J.W.W. to Grenville Clark, May 26, 1941, Wadsworth MSS; Langer and Gleason, *op. cit.*, p. 442.

46. *New York Times*, April 28, 1941.

47. J.W.W. to Charles D. Hilles, May 27, 1941, Wadsworth MSS.

48. J.W.W. to Grenville Clark, May 26, 1941, Wadsworth MSS.

dent permitted Stimson and Knox to mention publicly the need for neutrality repeal. Late in the month, the President himself discussed the matter. Wadsworth was pleased that Roosevelt called the German blockade of Atlantic sea lanes a national emergency.[49] On reflection, however, Wadsworth saw that firm executive direction was still lacking. Stimson thought that the President was awaiting a genuine incident on the high seas to justify his asking the Congress for neutrality repeal. If so, he found Hitler unaccommodating for the *Führer* warned Admiral Raider to keep his wolfpacks clear of American naval and merchant ships.[50]

Throughout the summer of 1941, neutrality repeal was discussed fervently in many quarters: the White House, the Departments of State, War and Navy, the congressional Democratic leadership, the national Republican party, a segment of a minority leadership in Congress, and a coterie of New York Republican interventionists. Not infrequently, Wadsworth was their liaison. He seemed to be in continuous contact on the issue with Lewis Douglas, a Roosevelt intimate, Henry L. Stimson, Speaker Rayburn, Grenville Clark, Wendell Willkie, and Charles Eaton, the ranking Republican on the House Foreign Affairs Committee.

All, however, awaited firm word from the President. Only Clark seemed determined to force his hand. "Needless to say," Wadsworth wrote Clark in late June, "I am in general agreement with the sentiments expressed, and yet so far as I can learn such a move if made, would receive less encouragement than would have been the case a month ago. In other words, I am convinced that the President would turn it down. In a general way and without going into any details I have talked this problem over with the Speaker, and with other people pretty high in the Administration. There is no doubt that for the time being at least we are stymied. By that I mean that were the resolution introduced it would not get out of committee, and hence there would be no debate or vote. Like you, I am holding it up my sleeve in the hope that perhaps someday we will get a reasonably green light."[51]

Wadsworth, Stimson, Clark, and others agonized over the fact that the green light did not come until late fall. Still they were not just helplessly awaiting the presidential nod. Rather, they helped move the consensus for which the President waited. By fall, a public debate on neutrality ensued, abetted by interventionists and by world events. By then the United States occupied Greenland and Iceland. The Germans had sunk the *Greer,*

49. J.W.W. to Mrs. Robert Woods Bliss, May 28, 1941, Wadsworth MSS.
50. Langer and Gleason, *op. cit.,* p. 458.
51. J.W.W. to Grenville Clark, June 25, 1941, Wadsworth MSS.

the Atlantic Charter had been signed, and the Gallop polls were favoring repeal. It was the last great neutrality debate and isolationists pulled out all the stops.[52]

By November the White House finally moved to legalize American shipments of goods to England. It asked Congress to repeal the neutrality acts to permit the movement of American merchant ships into combat zones. Isolationists were furious. The administration won repeal in the Senate, but victory in the House was by no means sure. The chips were down. The Democratic leadership selected Wadsworth, Majority Leader McCormick, and Speaker Rayburn to close the debate. The latter two stressed national security and the President's desire for the repeal of the neutrality acts. Wadsworth, consistent with his past positions on American foreign policy, going back to his support of the World Court in the 1920s, emphasized international law and the need to support the champions of freedom in the world. His defense was a microcosm of the thinking of those eastern Republicans who backed order and freedom in the world. In concluding his remarks he confidently advocated both:

But, Mr. Speaker, there is just one thing of which I am absolutely confident. We must not—and we might as well be realistic about this; it is a grim situation, and we must look it straight in the face—we must not, we cannot permit this world revolution to prevail, for if it should succeed, there will be no freedom. Here in our country we shall have to desert our form of government in order to marshall and regiment our people in a desperate attempt to prevent the spread of the revolution here. Freedom will be the safer in America if the attacks on freedom elsewhere are defeated.

When I speak of freedom, I mean those things of the spirit so much more precious than material things, things for which human beings have striven for centuries and centuries. At times the race seemed to have achieved its great objective only to suffer a set-back. Indeed a terrible set-back has occurred in recent years. Fearful disillusionments have over-taken people. Once again freedom is at stake.

On November 13 the House of Representatives amended sections two and three of the neutrality acts to permit American merchant ships to enter combat zones, and section six to permit the arming of American merchant ships. "No decision of greater importance has been made since the war," announced the *New York Times*. Repeal won, by 20 votes.

52. Langer and Gleason, *op. cit.*, Ch. XXIII, Ch. XXV, *passim*.

Twenty-two of the 211 Yea votes were Republican. Nine of the 22 were votes from the New York delegation which Wadsworth headed.[53]

The Geneseoan's influence over the new consensus and the twenty-two crucial Republican votes in the House is unknown. The vote did mark the last important impulse of isolationism and Wadsworth probably played a significant role in dissipating it. From his roll-top desk in the *Emporia Gazette* office in Emporia, Kansas, William Allen White, symbol of Republican interventionism, penned his thanks.[54]

3

As the War Department implemented the Selective Service Act, inducting over 600,000 men within a year of its adoption, Stimson and Marshall were glad to have Wadsworth in the House of Representatives. Aside from counselling the Pentagon leaders, Wadsworth was their staunchest defender in the House. Many congressmen felt that the Secretary acted too much like God, his logic was too cold, his character too strong. Many Republicans had a special dislike for him. Besides being an interventionist, he had defected to the Democratic administration. And Stimson, in turn, could not understand the behavior of most Republicans in the House. He often wondered why the right, mostly Republican, could not behave like Wadsworth on military and foreign policy (and why the left could not behave like Harry Hopkins).[55] Wadsworth gladly carried the War Department ball in the Committee Room and on the House floor. He also spent a great deal of time in the Secretary's office, ready to serve his old friend. He defended him unreservedly. When Washington rumors circulated that Wadsworth was to succeed Stimson in the War Department, he immediately commended the Secretary. Stimson replied to Wadsworth: "It was like you to write such a letter, and I appreciate it and thank you more than I can say."[56] Stimson was moved by his loyalty, as was George Marshall. Wadsworth attacked the *New Republic* for accusing Marshall of failing "in any way to awaken sleeping and decadent Army officers."

53. *Ibid.*, pp. 758–760; *New York Times*, Nov. 14, 1941; *Congressional Record*, Vol. 87, 77th Congress, 1st Session, Nov. 13, 1941, pp. 8870–1.

54. William Allen White to J.W.W., Nov. 18, 1941, Wadsworth MSS.

55. Henry L. Stimson and McGeorge Bundy, *On Active Service in Peace and War* (New York: Harper & Brothers, 1947), pp. 470–472.

56. J.W.W. to Henry L. Stimson, March 5, 1942, Henry L. Stimson to J.W.W., March 8, 1942, Wadsworth MSS; *Rochester Democrat and Chronicle*, Mar. 5, 1942.

Wadsworth suggested that the magazine's editors read the War Department's annual reports in order to understand that the army's high-ranking officers had sought modernization for years. Marshall thanked Wadsworth effusively for "losing his temper" at the magazine and hoped that he was "prepared to lose it quite frequently in the coming months to support the Army." [57] The *New Republic* had a point, though. The new army had not .yet shaken down. In time, the magazine would support vehemently both Marshall and Wadsworth on military policy.

Army advocates were quiet in early 1941, except for various moves to widen the draft age. Grenville Clark, seldom still, had not forgotten the 21–35 draft age range compromise accepted at the time the Congress passed the Burke-Wadsworth Act. Wadsworth was right in wanting to leave well enough alone. Congress would not change it.[58] Besides, more important problems loomed, such as the retention of draftees in the service beyond their expected stint of one year. The Geneseoan thought that only after one year's training were the draftees ready to test and sharpen the army's newly-manned units. "It would be most unwise to break up a well-trained division such as yours," he wrote Major General William H. Haskell, the Twenty-seventh Division's commanding officer.[59]

Isolationist sentiment lingered on in America. Untold millions opposed the extension of the draft. Mark Sullivan reflected an articulate anti-draft point of view in the country. Admitting the gravity of the world situation, he favored the maintenance of a voluntary permanent army of one and a half million men, in addition to a year's training of reserves between eighteen and twenty-one years of age. Wadsworth doubted that one and a half million Americans would volunteer, and feared that if they did, such a large permanent army would lead to a "military caste." The training of reserves to supplement the professional army was completely contrary to the citizen army concept of keeping the regular army small, to be used only as training cadre.[60]

In late summer, the draft renewal passed the Senate by a comfortable margin, but the House Republicans, and no few Democrats, were bent on defeating it. Besides voting against the bill, they tried to make it innocuous by adding amendments striking the preamble's reference to the "national peril", retaining the twelve-month training period, even if the

57. J.W.W. to *The New Republic*, Feb. 19, 1941, J.W.W. to George C. Marshall, Feb. 19, 1941, George C. Marshall to J.W.W., Feb. 21, 1941, Wadsworth MSS.

58. *Rochester Democrat and Chronicle*, May 16, 1941.

59. J.W.W. to General William H. Haskell, July 8, 1941, Wadsworth MSS.

60. J.W.W. to Mrs. Maude A. Glover, July 30, 1941, Wadsworth MSS.

draft were continued, and limiting to 900,000 the number to be drafted in any one year. Joseph Martin, Hamilton Fish, Everett Dirksen, and Dewey Short were the most vociferous Republicans to oppose the bill. The ranking minority member of the House Military Affairs Committee, Walter G. Andrews, a close friend of Wadsworth, supported the extension. He appealed to Republicans to pass it, as "the soundest course for the security of our country and its future." Democrats generally applauded Andrews, but only four or five Republicans did so.[61]

On the morning of August 12, Wadsworth rose and made what Congressman Joseph Clark Baldwin, of New York City, described as "one of the most brilliant speeches I've ever heard on the Republican side." In the presence of hushed though "crowded galleries," Wadsworth, poised as always and with his usual deep and pleasant voice, noted that only 640,000 men, one-half of one percent of the nation's people, had been drafted, and that contrary to his party's contention, the army would suffer by their release. In detail he described how units of the army, such as New York's Twenty-seventh National Guard Division, were only now coming to full strength. He ticked off other divisions only now ready to train as a team. He argued the logic of keeping the divisions intact to "fend off" the war that Germany and Japan seemed determined "to move toward America." He closed by asking his colleagues to have confidence that conscripted Americans would accept the sacrifice. "I have confidence in these men. I do not call them 'boys'. They are men. Take a look at them . . . they are men who will do their duty. American soldiers always do their duty when they know a great decision is made."[62]

A great decision was made. By a vote of 203–202 the House retained draftees and their units for eighteen more months. Republicans were surprised, but once realizing how close they came to defeating the dreaded draft, they demanded recapitulation. Speaker Rayburn ordered a re-vote. Stillness prevailed. No votes changed. Republicans again complained but to no avail. The bill was passed.[63]

Columnist Frank Kent attributed passage of the act to "those twenty other Republicans" who gathered around Wadsworth, "one of those all too rare birds in political life—a man of principle."[64] One can not be sure

61. *New York Times*, Aug. 12, 1941.

62. *Ibid.*, Aug. 13; *Congressional Record*, Vol. 87, 77th Congress, 1st Session, Aug. 12, 1941, speech in Wadsworth MSS; Joseph Clark Baldwin, *The Reminiscences of Joseph Clark Baldwin* (Columbia University Oral History Research Office, 1954).

63. Burns, *op cit.*, p. 120; *New York Times*, Aug. 13, 1841; Langer and Gleason, *op. cit.*, p. 574.

64. Unidentified news clipping, Aug. 1941, Frank B. Kent column, "The Great Game of Politics," Wadsworth MSS.

whether Kent was right. It is significant, however, that a quarter of the "other twenty" were New Yorkers loyal to the Geneseoan. Willkie sent a note of congratulations. Wadsworth replied: "I was in despair . . . one trouble in the House is that an overwhelming majority on the Republican side are so obsessed with the distrust and hatred of Roosevelt that they are blind to much more important considerations." [65]

The minutiae of military life seemed as important to Wadsworth as large policy matters. In the months prior to the Pearl Harbor attack, he and General Marshall discussed and exchanged correspondence on a gamut of matters. Illustrative of them was the New Yorker's concern for the One Hundred First Reconnaissance Regiment which included Geneseo's Troop M, stationed at Fort Devens, Massachusetts. Wadsworth watched them on late summer maneuvers in North Carolina and suggested that they not winter back at Devens. "That is pretty tough climate, as you know." Wadsworth wrote three pages of justification for his argument.[66] Marshall patiently explained why the regiment would have to return to Devens: it was within the area of the Sixth Army Corps, to which it was assigned; funds were not available for "construction of new housing" in the South; winter equipment was to be tested at Devens, etc." [67] Wadsworth still suggested that the One Hundred First and the One Hundred Fourth Reconnaissance Regiments at Indian Town Gap, Pennsylvania, be stationed together in the "deep South." [68] Marshall explained that the reconnaissance regiments are not organized to operate together, but with "an Army Corps." [69] Marshall usually did take Wadsworth's "field" concern seriously, as he did the old friend's ideas on "the eligibility" of certain types of enlisted men for commissions in the army. The Geneseoan was particularly concerned that certain non-commissioned officers over twenty-eight years of age be eligible for Officer Candidate School. Secretaries Stimson and Knox also listened to Wadsworth on small matters, such as the latter's concern that neither navy nor army personnel be eligible for re-enlistment bonuses in time of war.[70]

While Wadsworth enjoyed the atmosphere of soldiering and tramping around cantonments and fussing over military details, such as unit

65. W. Willkie to J.W.W., Aug. 14, 1941, J.W.W. to W. Willkie, Aug. 18, 1941, Wadsworth MSS.

66. J.W.W. to George C. Marshall, Sept. 24, 1941, Wadsworth MSS.

67. George C. Marshall to J.W.W., Oct. 7, 1941, Wadsworth MSS.

68. J.W.W. to George C. Marshall, Oct. 11, 1941, Wadsworth MSS.

69. George C. Marshall to J.W.W., Oct. 20, 1941, Wadsworth MSS.

70. J.W.W. to George C. Marshall, Dec. 2, 1941, George C. Marshall to J.W.W., Dec. 19, 1941, J.W.W. to Henry L. Stimson and Frank Knox, Feb. 2, 1942, Henry L. Stimson to J.W.W., March 9, 1942, Wadsworth MSS.

placement, pay scales, etc., large issues were his forte. Within a week after Pearl Harbor, A. J. May and Robert Reynolds, respectively chairmen of the House and Senate Military Affairs committees, invited Wadsworth to meet with them daily in the role of *ex-officio* member and counselor. The committee particularly wanted Wadsworth's advice on amendments to the Selective Service Act.[71] The New Yorker's first advice was to lower the draft age from twenty to eighteen.[72] The Democratic chairmen, however, were not wont to move without administration concurrence, and while Stimson fully agreed with Wadsworth that the draft age should be lowered further, he too awaited a presidential nod. Roosevelt again awaited the consensus. On June 9 he noted that legislation to lower the draft would not be needed for several months. Throughout 1940, the Military Affairs Committee, Stimson, and the Selective Service people became excited about the presidential inaction, especially with the draft boards' ever-increasing conscription of married men. Wadsworth acted. "The thing was so alarming that I made up my mind not to wait any longer," he wrote Grenville Clark on September 11, 1942. "So I put the bill in. Senator Chan Gurney evidently went through the same mental process but he introduced his bill a couple of days before mine went in."[73] The President still procrastinated. He reported to the press that the new draft legislation would be unnecessary until 1943. On October 12 the President relented. Within a month, the bill became law. The draft age was lowered to eighteen years.[74]

Wadsworth's significant effort to bring military and civilian needs into balance culminated in the National Service Act. Again, Grenville Clark played a large role. Almost from December 7, 1941, the New York City attorney thought that the whole country should be pulled together by a national compulsory effort, as in Britain, Australia, and Russia. Like many, he believed there should be some form of "manpower board" to coordinate the civilian productivity. While the administration, thinking along the same lines, established the War Manpower Commission in April of 1942, Clark concluded that both he and the administration had the cart before the horse and that what was needed was "a universal obligation for national service," a labor draft. Clark tested his labor draft idea on "a small group . . . whose judgment [he thought] exceptionally good,"

71. *Rochester Democrat and Chronicle*, Dec. 18, 1941.
72. J.W.W. to Henry L. Stimson, April 30, 1942, Wadsworth MSS.
73. J.W.W. to Grenville Clark, Sept. 11, 1942, Wadsworth MSS.
74. *New York Times*, July 16, Aug. 27, Sept. 7, 10, 25, Oct. 12, 1942; Roland Young, *Congressional Politics in the Second World War* (New York: Columbia Univ., 1956), pp. 68–70.

including Wadsworth.[75] Clark then approached the President. The President expressed interest and turned over Clark's letter to Selective Service Director Lewis Hershey "for his consideration." [76] Clark, encouraged by Roosevelt's quick reply, wrote a bill and sent it forthwith to the President. The President again expressed interest and again sent Clark's letter, and the accompanying draft, to Director Hershey. Clark kept Wadsworth fully apprised of the bill's progress in the administration. When he heard, in early summer of 1942, that the War Manpower Commission was studying it, he sent Wadsworth copies of explanatory letters he had sent to both War Manpower Commissioner McNutt and the President. Clark prodded the President. "I doubt," he wrote him, "whether there will be prompt action by the Commission not only to frame a bill but recommend it definitely to Congress . . . unless and until you tell the Commission that this ought to be done without delay." [77]

Wadsworth shared Clark's concern that the draft would be buried in the War Manpower Commission unless the President acted. He also suggested to Clark that a national ceiling be placed on wages "as a precursor if such an act is to be effective." Secondly, he suggested that the act provide for setting aside the "closed shop" and the "union shop" for the duration, that men drafted to work in a union plant not be forced to join the union. Even without wage ceilings or "a closed shop" prohibition, Wadsworth was willing to sponsor Clark's bill in the House, but he felt it useless to do so until after the fall elections.[78] In the meantime, Clark busied himself with the formation of a Citizen's Committee for the National War Service Act.[79]

On February 8, 1943, Wadsworth and Senator Warren Austin of Vermont introduced S 666 and HR 1742, "a bill to provide for the successful prosecution of the war through a system of civilian selective war service with the aid of the selective service system." In short, the bill called for the registration of all men between eighteen and sixty-five years of age, and all women between eighteen and fifty years of age. Following such registration, the President would specify the numbers of workers needed in critical industries and, through the War Manpower Commission, would call for volunteers. If sufficient volunteers were not forthcoming, the Selective Service System would draft qualified individuals. Certain citizens

75. Grenville Clark to Henry L. Stimson, Apr. 3, 1942, Wadsworth MSS.
76. Franklin D. Roosevelt to Grenville Clark, June 13, 1942, Wadsworth MSS.
77. Grenville Clark to Franklin D. Roosevelt, July 1, 1942, Wadsworth MSS.
78. J.W.W. to Grenville Clark, July 13, 1942, Wadsworth MSS.
79. Grenville Clark to J.W.W., Sept. 10, 1942, Wadsworth MSS.

would be exempt from the law: those subject to military conscription, women with children under 18 years of age, pregnant women, and state and local government employees. Persons guilty of violating the law would be subject to a $1,000 fine and imprisonment for six months.[80]

On the day of the bill's introduction, Wadsworth and Austin told the press what the bill would do: provide for total mobilization; cure the evils of employment imbalance, hoarding of labor, labor piracy, and employee absenteeism; remove confusion caused by illegal War Manpower Commission orders; encourage voluntary manpower commitments; protect family life and labor unions; preserve postwar re-employment and seniority rights; and utilize the Selective Service System's democratic system of "selection." The co-authors reiterated that the bill would not interfere with family life, labor organizations, or generally the nation's democratic processes.[81] The Citizens for the National War Service Act, the American Legion, the Navy and War Departments, and certain newspapers—the *New York Times*, the *New York Herald Tribune*, and the *Washington Evening Star*—defended the bill.[82] *The Chicago Tribune* opposed the bill, as did the American Federation of Labor and the Congress of Industrial Organizations.[83] The War Manpower Commission was quiet on the bill, even in the face of Wadsworth's vehement criticism of McNutt's "work or fight" order as "plain coercion and without legal authority." The President, too, was quiet, at the same time energetically conferring with McNutt on ways to increase industrial production without a "labor draft." Only War Secretary Stimson and Navy Secretary Frank Knox, in the administration, defended the bill publicly.[84]

On March 2, Wadsworth was the first witness before the Senate Military Affairs Committee hearing on the bill. As one-time chairman of the committee, he was received hospitably.[85] Great newspapers had reiterated editorially their support of the bill. Stimson appeared before the committee and described the bill as "essential to win the war."[86] But Chairman Reynolds opposed the bill, as did most of the Senate Military Affairs

80. *New York Times*, Feb. 9, 1943; Stimson and Bundy, *op. cit.*, p. 482.

81. "Joint statement by Senator Warren R. Austin of Vermont and Representative James W. Wadsworth of New York, re Proposed National War Service Act of 1943," Wadsworth MSS.

82. *Washington Evening Star*, March 1, 1943; *New York Times*, Mar. 2, 1943; *New York Herald Tribune*, March 3, 1943.

83. *Chicago Tribune*, Feb. 10, 1943; Stimson and Bundy, *op. cit.*, p. 482.

84. Stimson and Bundy, *op. cit.*, p. 482.

85. J.W.W. to J. J. Wadsworth, Mar. 1, 1943, Wadsworth MSS.

86. *Washington Evening Star*, Mar. 20, 1943.

Committee. Even the presence on the committee of the co-author, Warren
Austin, had little impact. Rather, the committee seemed more influenced
by labor's point of view. The steel workers and the united electrical
workers testified that the bill would lessen prôductivity, presumably by
lessening morale. The Brotherhood of Railway Trainmen told the Senate
committee that the bill would destroy labor unions by excusing workers
from union membership. Industry generally sided with labor. It pointed to
current high productivity and described possible evils to be wrought by
governmental interference.[87]

Similar testimony was presented to the House Military Affairs Committee. Appearing before it in late spring, Wadsworth predicted that the
war would be long and tough, and that the country needed the bill to
win it. Roosevelt and War Manpower Commissioner McNutt both edged
toward support of the bill by late summer.[88]

The civilian manpower situation worsened. McNutt desperately
urged the War Department to furlough thousands of men to go into the
copper mines. The War Department demurred. Stimson, by memorandum
and personal plea, pressed Roosevelt to openly support the Austin-Wadsworth bill. The President hesitated.[89] In private conversation with Wadsworth he showed a renewed interest.[90] In the September and October
Gallop polls, the majority of the people favored the bill.[91] Still the
consensus was not decisive enough for the President. The two congressional Military Affairs committees manifested continued coolness. In the
late fall of 1943, the President's special counsel, Samuel Rosenman,
suggested to Clark that "perhaps the best thing is just to coast along
until some definite decision is reached."[92] Clark asked Wadsworth
whether he should continue his efforts.[93]

Apparently, Wadsworth and Austin thought Clark's effort was worth
it, for the latter entered a period of feverish activity. He wrote a long
letter to the President, reviewing the bill's chronology and reminding
the President that Woodrow Wilson had continued "turning on the
heat" even when the tide turned. Clark launched a campaign to petition

87. *New York Times,* Mar. 10, 11, 27, Apr. 6, 7, 18, 1943.
88. *Ibid.,* July 6, 1943.
89. Henry L. Stimson, "Memorandum for the President," July 1, 1943, Wadsworth MSS; Stimson and Bundy, *op. cit.,* p. 482; J.W.W. to Grenville Clark, July
9, 1943, Wadsworth MSS.
90. *New York Times,* July 6, 1943.
91. *Ibid.,* Sept. 15, 1943.
92. Samuel I. Rosenman to Grenville Clark, Oct. 7, 1943, Wadsworth MSS.
93. Grenville Clark to J.W.W., Oct. 9, 1943, Wadsworth MSS.

Congress and the President. He prodded Stimson to pressure Marshall and Rayburn to get behind the bill. He itemized for Wadsworth these and other of his renewed efforts on behalf of the measure.[94]

On January 11, 1944, the President acted. In his State of the Union message, he advocated national war service legislation, but tied the bill to additional legislation on prices, taxes, and profits.[95] Wadsworth thought such strategy a mistake, for by tying it to other controversial measures, the President gave the "shrinkers" an out.[96] And labor leaders William Green and Philip Murray complained to the White House; the "undemocratic bill," they argued, would not prevent strikes or solve the present manpower problem. They thought the WMC's voluntary approach was succeeding.[97] The President again equivocated. The opportunity for passage was lost. Still, Wadsworth and Austin spoke in defense of the bill. With the nation's manpower nearly depleted, the armed services needed 900,000 men, and industry needed more than 1,000,000. They argued that only the selective service and the national war service legislation would provide necessary manpower to meet military and industrial needs.[98] Eminent Americans, like Walter Lippmann, agreed, but many congressmen were lukewarm at best and thought the President too late and too indifferent.[99] Even the congressional Military Affairs committees, throughout 1944, kept the bill from the floor.[100] Only the continued pressures of Wadsworth, Austin, Stimson, Knox, and Clark kept the legislation alive. Clark kept writing to the President. Stimson prodded him at every opportunity. Wadsworth and Austin tried to allay labor's fears. They talked "earnestly" to William Green and Philip Murray in Secretary Knox's office. "Austin and I tried our best to be friendly," Wadsworth wrote Clark, "to assure Green and Murray that we were not attempting to attack the labor movement, that we have no grievance whatsoever against labor unions, that our bill was never intended as an anti-strike measure, and that all we wanted was to get the 'low down' from them as to what they thought should be done to meet this very

94. Grenville Clark to Franklin D. Roosevelt, Dec. 30, 1943, Grenville Clark to H. L. Stimson, Jan. 6, 1944, Wadsworth MSS.

95. Roland Young, *op. cit.,* pp. 77–79; *New York Times,* Jan. 12, 1944.

96. J.W.W. to Grenville Clark, Jan. 31, 1944, Wadsworth MSS.

97. *New York Times,* Jan. 13, 1944.

98. *Congressional Record,* Vol. 90, 78th Congress, 2nd Session, Jan. 27, 28, 1944, Appendix, pp. 437–8.

99. Walter Lippmann, "An Act of Dedication," Jan. 5, 1944, Wadsworth MSS; *New York Times,* Mar. 12, 1944.

100. *New York Times,* Apr. 22, 1944.

critical situation." After two hours of discussion, Green had still clung to his fear of forced labor.[101]

Throughout 1944 the Congress considered drafting 4,000,000 4-Fs into critical industries. But Congress could not refute those like Wadsworth who felt it unjust to "pick out [the 4-F] and require him to perform a duty which is not required of other civilians, man or woman." Nor could the President.[102] To the horror of presidential speech-writer Rosenman, the President told him to secretly draft a war service bill statement for his State of the Union address to be delivered on January 6, 1945. He did not want to argue about it any more. This time, he did not equivocate.[103] He accepted Clark's admonition to "turn on the heat" as the tide of the war was turning.

The President spelled out military needs to justify the passage of the War Service Act: the production of ordnance supplies, tanks, heavy trucks, B-29s, cruisers, carriers, rockets, etc. Most emphatically he alluded to the manufacture of a new weapon, a possible reference to the A-Bomb. If a large new weapon system were to be quickly produced, certainly authority over the recruitment and control of its labor force would be required. Many congressmen had difficulty reconciling the President's ardent plea with his years of apparent indifference to the bill. Chairman May and the House Military Affairs Committee saw it only as a last resort act, to date unneeded.[104]

Yet the Commander-in-Chief had spoken, with strong public support by the war leaders, Henry L. Stimson and George Marshall. General Marshall mesmerized no few congressmen in a Library of Congress session on the bill. Congress debated earnestly. Two questions evolved: Were standards of service applicable to a soldier also applicable to a civilian worker? and were current voluntary controls over production adequate?

Wadsworth said yes to both questions. To the latter question, he pointed to years of waste and hoarding of valuable labor, the ineffectiveness and illegality of War Manpower Commission threats. To the question of equal obligation, he reiterated the bill's democratic principle, that all adults be treated equally. Recognizing labor and management's concern about federal regulation, he concluded: "When the life of our

101. J.W.W. to Grenville Clark, Mar. 29, 1944, Wadsworth MSS.

102. J.W.W. to Douglas S. Brown, Jan. 11, 1945, Wadsworth MSS.

103. New York Times, Jan. 7, 1945; Stimson and Bundy, op. cit., p. 485; Burns, op. cit., p. 432.

104. New York Times, Jan. 7, 1945.

country is at stake, we all must give up some elements of our freedom."
Wadsworth was persuasive.[105] His words, however, were somewhat
blunted by his subsequent proposed amendment to set aside the closed
and union shop for the duration of the war. On that he failed.[106] The
House did, on March 8, pass a limited National Service bill to freeze
workers in critical industries and to order certain workers into war jobs.[107]
The Senate demurred on the "labor draft." Its bill set ceilings on the
numbers of employees who could be hired and permitted those on old-age
assistance to work without loss of their retirement benefits.[108]

"The Senate kicked out our bill," Wadsworth wrote General Patton,
"and substituted something which . . . isn't worth the paper it is written
on. It misses the whole point, to wit: Every competent adult citizen
should be duty-bound under the law to serve in industry and agriculture
in support of the armed services wherever needed. They tell me I am
urging slave labor."[109] Austin, too, was appalled by the Senate action.
In the House-Senate conference on the two bills, he secured compromises:
the retention of the House provision on the work freeze, and the Senate
provision on employment ceilings.[110] Although wearied by conference
haggling, the House accepted the conference report by a close 167–160
vote.[111] The Senate did not.[112] The National War Service bill was dead.

Wadsworth's fight for the National War Service bill, like that of
Austin, Clark and Stimson, reached, as one historian has noted, "zeal
and patriotism of a high order." Certainly the War Manpower Commission's voluntary controls over industrial production were not working
well.[113] Had the war gone differently in 1945, the Austin-Wadsworth
bill surely would have passed and contributed mightily to the war effort.
But by 1945, the war condition, though still harsh, had turned in favor
of America and the Allies. The nation looked to victory. Wadsworth
himself looked to the post-war world.

105. *Congressional Record,* Vol. 91, 79th Congress, 1st Session, Jan. 30, 1945,
pp. 313–4.
106. *New York Times,* Feb. 1, 1945.
107. *Ibid.,* Feb. 3, 1945.
108. *Ibid.,* Mar. 8, 9, 1945.
109. J.W.W. to George S. Patton, Mar. 13, 1945, Wadsworth MSS.
110. *New York Times,* Mar. 22, 1945.
111. *Ibid.,* Mar. 28, 1945.
112. *Ibid.,* Apr. 4, 1945.
113. Stimson and Bundy, *op. cit.,* pp. 473–489. For good survey of National

Service legislation attempts, see Roland Young, *op. cit.,* pp. 76–88.

4

In January of 1944 Wadsworth convinced Speaker Rayburn and Minority Leader Martin of the need for a special "committee on post-war military planning." The three agreed, with others in the House leadership, that the committees on Military and Naval Affairs operated in narrow legislative fields, concerned primarily with immediate war operations, and not with long-range planning. Also, Rayburn and Wadsworth remembered well that lethargy regarding post-World War I military policy contributed to a dismantling of United States military forces in the 1920s. Wadsworth recommended that the committee be comprised of twenty-three members, seven each from the Military Affairs and Naval Affairs committees, and nine from the House at large who possessed "fresh and unprejudiced minds." Rayburn followed the advice and appointed to the committee some of the House's most eminent members. Wadsworth thought it wise that Rayburn appointed as chairman Clifford Woodrum, a ranking member of the Appropriations Committee. Of course the New Yorker was pleased to accept appointment as vice chairman of the committee. Woodrum relied heavily on Wadsworth for agenda items—recruitment and training policy, including universal military training; the organization of the reserve components; the problems of supply; the post-war functions and missions of the armed forces; and, perhaps most importantly, "a study of the development of unity of command as practiced during the war in order to determine to what extent unity of command may be developed.[114] Wadsworth in turn was counseled by his old friend, General John Palmer. The Geneseoan was pleased that Marshall had recalled the military policy expert to active duty to advise the Chief of Staff on post-war matters. It was reminiscent of 1919. "Wadsworth hinted." Palmer wrote to Marshall, "that he would like to have me serve with the special committee as I did with his Senate Military Committee after the last war." Palmer remained, however, in the Pentagon as the "military elder statesman," grinding out pertinent memoranda for Wadsworth and Marshall regarding aspects of agenda items.[115] Palmer was the committee's first witness. On April 24, he replayed his role of some twenty-five years earlier, placing military policy in historical perspective and noting President Washington's interest in

114. J.W.W. to W. Stuart Symington, Mar. 30, 1949, Wadsworth MSS; *Newsweek,* Apr. 3, 1944.
115. John M. Palmer to George C. Marshall, Mar. 10, 1944, Wadsworth MSS.

a citizen army based on universal military training. Committee members, however, thought better of approaching UMT in an election year and, after politely receiving Palmer's testimony, examined instead the possibilities of unification of the armed forces.[116]

Three days prior to the beginning of the special committee's hearings, Wadsworth and Woodrum called on the secretaries of war and navy in order to elicit their cooperation. As expected, both Stimson and Knox received the congressmen courteously and enthusiastically. To Wadsworth's and Woodrum's surprise, Knox "proceeded to express his definite opinion," wrote the New Yorker some years later to Secretary of the Air Force, Stuart Symington, "that the two Departments, War and Navy, should be combined in such a way as to assure better teamwork." The Geneseoan noted in his letter to Symington that had Knox lived to testify, he might well have silenced the opposition to unification by high-ranking naval officers. Unleashed by Knox's death, they forced the committee to shelve the unification proposal for the duration of the war, thus stymieing it for years. Still, the roots of unification were set in the Woodrum Committee and grew until the act was accomplished in 1947.[117] Wadsworth always defended the idea of unification and was saddened that Stuart Symington's role as the first Air Force Secretary in the Department of Defense was made more difficult by continued naval obstruction.

On unification, Wadsworth did succeed in his own bailiwick, the House. There, and before a special Senate-House "streamlining" committee on congressional reorganization, he was the first to detail specifically the reduction of House committees to sixteen, including the consolidation of the House Military and Naval Affairs committees into a single Armed Forces Committee. One year later, with the passage of the Reorganization Act of 1946, the New Yorker's recommendation regarding the formation of a House Armed Forces Committee was written into law.[118]

Universal military training was Wadsworth's first interest and he made the most of his post-war military policy committee membership in pushing it, after the 1944 election. Of course, Wadsworth had advocated universal military training very early in the war. Sympathetic reception

116. John M. Palmer to unidentified party, Apr. 18, 1944, Wadsworth MSS.

117. J.W.W. to W. Stuart Symington, Apr. 12, 1949, Wadsworth MSS; conversation with W. Stuart Symington, summer 1968; C. W. Barklund, *The Department of Defense* (New York: Praeger, 1968), pp. 38–49.

118. *Rochester Democrat and Chronicle*, Apr. 20, 1945; J.W.W. to John M. Palmer, Mar. 23, 1945; *Congressional Record*, Vol. 91, Apr. 2, 1945, p. 3006.

around the country to a syndicated *Washington Evening Star* article on UMT, and his own recollection that Congress moved too late on such legislation after World War I, convinced him to move. In mid-July of 1942, the New Yorker requested of Palmer that he be permitted to "sit in occasionally" on War Department conferences on the subject—to "learn" and "to be really useful when we have something to propose . . . to the powers that be in the War Department and to the Congress." Simultaneously he informed the press of his post-war plans to train one million men a year between the ages of eighteen and twenty-one, to be followed by five years of reserve service.[119]

Wadsworth's adamancy on the subject even took the eager General Palmer by surprise. It had not occurred to the War Department's "elder statesman" that such legislation could be introduced prior to the war's end.[120] When Palmer suggested that universal military training "will probably come in the form of one or more brief amendments to the Selective Service Act," Wadsworth took immediate exception. "The Selective Service Act is a temporary measure," he wrote Palmer. "Ours is to be permanent." He then sketched his outline of the bill.[121]

Wadsworth was not alone in envisioning permanent universal military training. Along with a *Washington Star* columnist, the American Legion and the Military Training Camps Association also saw the need for the post-war policy, and established quick liaison with their "old friend" in the House. Wadsworth relied on several quarters in the drafting of the UMT bill, but leaned most heavily on Palmer and Grenville Clark. Clark, like Palmer, was enthusiastic about the measure, yet hesitant. He feared that the bill's early introduction might hinder the passage of the National Service Act.[122]

On February 11, 1943, Wadsworth and Chan Gurney introduced post-war compulsory military training legislation in their respective bodies. The bills in the two houses were virtually identical, providing that when a youth reached eighteen years of age, or within three years thereafter, he be inducted into the army or navy for a training period of one year, followed by a four-year reserve status. The system was to go into effect six months after the war's end. Almost immediately upon the bill's introduction, however, Wadsworth soft-pedaled the measure for

119. *New York Times,* July 20, 1942; J.W.W. to John M. Palmer, July 20, 1942, Wadsworth MSS.
120. John M. Palmer to J.W.W., July 22, 1942, Wadsworth MSS.
121. J.W.W. to John M. Palmer, Aug. 24, 1942, Wadsworth MSS.
122. Grenville Clark to J.W.W., Jan. 20, 1943, Wadsworth MSS.

fear of prejudicing his National Service Act, viewed in so many quarters as immediately essential to the war's effort. The Geneseoan was not displeased by lack of congressional action on UMT in 1943.[123] "All we want," he wrote Lieutenant General Hugh A. Drum, "is to get the principle of Universal Military Training firmly established as a foundation upon which to rebuild our peacetime situation."[124]

In January of 1944 Chairman Andrew May of the House Military Affairs Committee introduced UMT legislation differing only in detail from the Gurney-Wadsworth bill. It provided for an eight-year reserve stint for trainees as compared to four years called for in the Gurney-Wadsworth bill. Although in subsequent months, and years, the May bill would share attention equally with the Gurney-Wadsworth bill, the New York congressman's role as the military spokesman in the House was undiminished.[125] Having co-authored the Burke-Wadsworth Act and national service legislation, in March of 1944 he successfully sponsored a House resolution to establish the special committee on post-war military policy.

The New Yorker had two reasons for wishing to establish the post-war policy committee, to focus attention on the need for universal military training, and to give it a bi-partisan cast. Before a Military Affairs Committee hearing in May of 1944, Wadsworth predicted post-war tensions in the world and emphatically demanded the universal military training as a minimum need for the country's safety.[126] Again the congressional leadership hesitated. While in 1943 UMT was sacrificed for consideration of the National Service bill, in 1944 it was buried in presidential politics. In addition, noted Palmer, "the War Department . . . needed time to prepare a sound case for presentation to the [post-war] committee." Still, as Wadsworth hoped, universal military training came into public focus. Pressure groups for it and against it emerged in public dialogue.[127] Largely to Wadsworth's credit, the presidential candidates did not publicly oppose UMT. In fact, Roosevelt privately approved it, and Dewey, the Republican candidate, at least agreed publicly

123. *New York Times,* Feb. 11, 1943; Robert Ward, "Movement for UMT, 1942–1945" (University of North Carolina, 1957), Ph.D. dissertation, Ch. II, *passim;* John M. Swomley, Jr., "A Study of the Universal Training Campaign, 1944–1952" (University of Colorado, 1959), Ph.D. dissertation, Ch. II, *passim.*

124. J.W.W. to Hugh A. Drum, Nov. 22, 1943, Wadsworth MSS.

125. *New York Times,* Jan. 27, 1944, Ward, *op. cit.,* Ch. II; Swomley, *op. cit.,* Ch. II.

126. Ward, *op. cit.,* Ch. II, *passim.*

127. Swomley, *op. cit.,* Ch. III, IV, *passim.*

with Wadsworth that the army's strength should be maintained after the war.[128]

Following the election, the UMT movement gathered momentum. Stimson and Wadsworth cajoled the leaders of organized labor. Labor, frightened by the labor draft in Wadsworth's National Service bill, was equally leery of UMT regimentation.[129] *The Christian Herald* featured statements of Wadsworth and Norman Thomas for and against the measure. The Geneseoan appeared on the American Forum of the Air to defend UMT as a peacetime measure. There he pointed to his citizen army concept, the damaging anti-military attitude of Americans in the 1920s, the democratic manner of Switzerland's military training, and the frightful demand on America to lead in the post-World War II world.[130] By December of 1944, 78 percent of the American people favored a post-war UMT program, but labor was not alone in being leery.[131] Perhaps there was no more articulate opponent than the noted news columnist, George Sokolsky. "Those who argue for a peacetime compulsory military service," he wrote in one of his syndicated columns, "suffer from a refinement of manners and delicacy of expression." He felt that the proponents of UMT distrusted the common people for there actually was no "prospective enemy" for a large UMT army to fight. He argued that Germany, Japan, and Italy would be reduced to rubble and that surely we would not contemplate warring against our allies. "Even," he cynically concluded, "such love and adoration as we Americans have bestowed upon Soviet Russia cannot lead to war."[132]

The Sokolsky column was too much for Wadsworth. "Frankly," he wrote the columnist, "I am at a loss to understand how you have reached the conclusion that any reputable person or group is urging a permanent conscripted army in time of peace." The New Yorker patiently explained that his measure called for training, not service. Sokolsky wasn't impressed. "I cannot for the life of me understand why it is necessary to take these steps that you advocate at the present time unless it is the assumption that the American people will not favor such measures

128. *New York Herald Tribune,* July 19, 1944; *New York Times,* July 20, 1944.

129. J.W.W. to Philip Murray, Dec. 6, 1944, J.W.W. to Thomas C. Cashen, Dec. 6, 1944, J.W.W. to Henry L. Stimson, Dec. 15, 1944, Wadsworth MSS.

130. *Christian Herald,* Nov. 1944; The American Forum of the Air, Nov. 28, 1944, Wadsworth MSS.

131. *Opinion News,* Dec. 5, 1944.

132. *New York Sun* (undated), "Who is the Prospective Enemy?" by George E. Sokolsky, Wadsworth MSS.

after the war is over."[133] Sokolsky was right, of course; Wadsworth did fear a post-war apathy similar to that which had occurred after World War I.

Chairman May of the House Military Affairs Committee, after numerous conversations with Wadsworth, reintroduced UMT legislation on January 3, 1945. It differed essentially from the previous proposals in that it required that the year of compulsory training be completed within a four-year period following the eighteenth birthday, to be followed by a six-year reserve requirement.[134] Wadsworth stumped for the bill, simultaneously agreeing with Stimson, Patterson, and Marshall, however, that its passage should be deferred until the National Service Act was disposed of. FDR had plunked hard for the National Service bill in his State of the Union message, and in ensuing months its attempted passage overshadowed the UMT bill and dissipated much of the energy of the military element in the congress and the executive branch. Then some of the budding United Nations advocates began urging international abolition of military conscription. Wadsworth helped put out that fire by getting assurances from Congressman Charles Eaton, a United States delegate to the United Nations Charter Conference in San Francisco, that an anti-conscription resolution would not be on the agenda.[135]

By late spring, 1945, Wadsworth demanded immediate congressional action on UMT. Friends of the bill were elated by the strong support given the bill by the new president. Harry S Truman was impressed by the measure and particularly by the support Rayburn and Wadsworth gave to it. From June 4 to June 19 the select Committee on Post-War Military Policy heard more than one hundred witnesses testify for and against the bill. In early July, the committee recommended that "the Congress adopt, as a matter of broad policy, a system of Universal Military Training for the critical years ahead." The committee stood ready to assist "the Committee on Military Affairs and . . . the members of Congress in their consideration of specific legislation on the subject." The Post-War Policy Committee suggested that certain features be considered in any system of universal military training: that training be for modern warfare, that it be in accord with technological developments, that it be "democratic," that it fit into the structure provided for preserva-

133. J.W.W. to George Sokolsky, Dec. 16, 1944, Wadsworth MSS; George Sokolsky to J.W.W., Jan. 15, 1945.

134. *New York Times,* Jan. 3, 1945; Ward, *op. cit.,* Ch. II; Swomley, *op. cit.,* Ch. III.

135. James W. Wadsworth, Jr., *Diary,* Jan. 10, 1945, Wadsworth MSS.

tion of the national guard, that it interfere as little as possible with "normal education," and that it not require military duty except "to meet a national emergency." [136]

Wadsworth was pleased by the Woodrum report and was particularly optimistic when President Truman forthrightly recommended its conclusions in one of his messages to the Congress. "The message," Wadsworth wrote Archibald Thacher, "has the effect of compelling the Congress to go at this thing seriously." [137] Again, in his January 1946 State of the Union message, the President called for passage of universal military training. But, as the Geneseoan predicted, 1946 was not unlike the year that followed World War I. The country wearied of war and the instruments of war. Shortly, rising tensions between East and West would again bring UMT demands to the fore, but for the moment America reverted partially to its "isolationist impulse." The best that Congress could do in May of 1946 was to extend the draft to provide at least a minimal army. [138]

As noted previously, Wadsworth, early in the war, was appointed to the Foreign Affairs Committee. "The men here in the House whom I regard as my best friends," he wrote on January 10, 1942, "ganged up on me and persuaded me to leave the Committee on Interstate and Foreign Commerce, of which I have been a member for ten years, and take a place on the Foreign Affairs Committee." [139] The appointment had many ramifications. It was the culmination of a decade of Wadsworth's effort in the foreign affairs field. It provided a forum which in three years brought him recognition by Democratic and Republican colleagues in the House as the member "who had the best grasp of Foreign Affairs," even over Sol Bloom and Charles Eaton, respectively the ranking Democrat and Republican on the Foreign Affairs Committee. [140] Most importantly, it marked a decisive move on the part of the House Republican leadership away from its traditional isolationist position. In appointing the Geneseoan, Joseph Martin and the Republican Committee on Committees deposed from the Foreign Affairs Committee the erstwhile

136. J.W.W. to Melvin J. Mass, July 5, 1945; UMT Report No. 857, July 5, 1945, Wadsworth MSS; Swomley, op. cit., Ch. IV.

137. J.W.W. to Archibald G. Thacher, Oct. 24, 1945, Wadsworth MSS.

138. Ward, op. cit., Ch. III.

139. J.W.W. to constituent, early 1943; New York Herald Tribune, Jan. 8, 1943.

140. Pageant Magazine, "What Congress Thinks of Congress," Aug. 1946.

isolationist Hamilton Fish.[141] Thus, the appointment had symbolic significance. Needless to say, it exacerbated the already bad relations between the two scions within the New York delegation.

Wadsworth's foreign affairs role, although less time-consuming than his military and national service legislation efforts, was probably more meaningful. Few, if any, Republicans in national elective office, so nudged the GOP from isolationism to a bi-partisan international foreign policy. America had been at war for only six months when Wadsworth had insisted that the country "more than any other nation, must take the lead in working out a [postwar] system in establishing an international organization." He cautioned, however, as a practical matter, against a repetition of Article X of the League of Nations Covenant, a provision mandating international sanctions against League violators. It had divided the public and brought Senate defeat of the Versailles Treaty in 1919 and 1920. Also, he urged, ideally, that only nations "devoted to liberty" should comprise any such international organization. Wadsworth's internationalism was a mixture of pragmatism and idealism.[142]

The New Yorker, of course, was not alone in nudging the Republican party. William Allen White was much concerned for the sake of the party and the nation and worked especially hard at bringing national non-elected party leaders such as Hoover and Landon into the international wing. He was anxious, for example, to work out any differences on foreign policy matters between Wadsworth and Hoover and carried to the former president some of Wadsworth's mild criticisms of Hoover's book, *The Problems of Lasting Peace*. Principally, while admiring the former president's description of the world's problems, Wadsworth felt his book was too short on solution.[143]

The more Wadsworth read about and thought through the problems

141. *New York Herald Tribune*, Jan. 8, 1943.

142. "University of Rochester Commencement Address," June, 1942, Wadsworth MSS; *Rochester Democrat and Chronicle*, May 13, 1942.

143. J.W.W. to William Allen White, Mar. 29, 1943, Wadsworth MSS. See Tompkins, *op. cit.*, Ch. XIV. Tompkins notes that Vandenberg's internationalism evolved gradually from Dec. 7, 1941, to his first clear-cut public statement in support of full-fledged American participation in a post-war international organization in January of 1945. Up to that point, he either distrusted the President for his "excessive secrecy" or cautioned internationally-inclined Republicans not to embrace internationalism lest they divide the Republican party and preclude the possibility of United States participation in a post-war United Nations. Also, Professor Tompkins points out that Vandenberg was genuinely concerned that planning for post-war internationalism be soft-pedaled until the Senate was assured its proper role in the working of such foreign policy.

of foreign relations, the more firm he became about America's role in establishing order and freedom in the world. He was indeed enamored of Willkie's *One World*.[144] He took an intense interest in reciprocal trade, post-war lend lease and rehabilitation programs, the potential Palestine problem, and executive agreements with foreign governments. The Palestine problem, the establishment of a separate Jewish state, defied categorization as an internationalist or isolationist issue. The New Yorker opposed its establishment, fearing the divisiveness which possibly would be caused by the divided loyalty of American Jews.[145]

Wadsworth's most significant foreign affairs effort during the war and immediate post-war period was his support of the United Nations concept, and specifically the Fulbright resolution which put the House of Representatives on record as favoring it. When the young congressman from Arkansas, William Fulbright, brought forward his important resolution in the spring of 1943, Wadsworth talked the author and the Democratic leadership—namely, Rayburn, McCormick, and Bloom—into postponing House action until Republican support was assured. The Geneseoan wanted a bi-partisan approach to post-war foreign policy, and not a repetition of the partisanship of 1919 which so devastated American participation in the League of Nations. Wadsworth was confident that forthcoming support of the United Nations by Republican leaders at a proposed party conference, to be held at Mackinac Island, Michigan, in September of 1943, would prepare the way for truly bi-partisan support in the House.[146]

The Democrats took Wadsworth's advice. House action on any U.N. resolution, including the Fulbright resolution, was held off in the summer of 1943. Republican leaders met at Mackinac in early September and took an historic step. They committed their party, albeit reluctantly, to support of American participation in some international organization following the war. It is ironic that the pre-war non-interventionists dominated the conference, to the exclusion of important internationalists like Wadsworth, and yet carried their party out of the isolationist camp. Arthur Vandenberg chaired the conference's post-war Foreign Affairs Committee and a year later dramatically announced his shift to internationalism. Most historical interpretation credits his actions with swinging the GOP to support a bi-

144. J.W.W. to W. Willkie, Apr. 1, 1943, Wadsworth MSS.

145. *Congressional Record*, Vol. 91, 79th Congress, 1st Session, Dec. 19, 1945, pp. 12386–7; J.W.W. to Jacob Keller, Feb. 29, 1944, Wadsworth MSS.

146. Haynes Johnson and Bernard M. Gwertzman, *Fulbright the Dissenter* (New York: Doubleday, 1968), p. 69, pp. 71–2.

partisan international foreign policy. The turn of Republican support, however, might well be seen in Wadsworth's efforts regarding the Fulbright resolution months before the Mackinac conference, and by his bipartisan support of the repeal of the neutrality acts several years before Vandenberg's public renunciation of isolationism.[147]

The *Washington Evening Star* thought Wadsworth's statement on the Fulbright resolution just prior to its passage the best "expression" on the subject in the House.[148] There, the Geneseoan answered specifically the charge of his fellow New Yorker, Daniel Reed, that passage of the Fulbright resolution would make the United States a slave of a super-government. "Rather," he noted, "I see in this resolution an assertion on the part of the House, perhaps for the first time in its history, an expression . . . as to what may be hoped and worked for in the world after this war is over." Wadsworth was a pragmatic internationalist. "I say," he said, "that there can be little hope for peace and decency in the world without the help of the United States. I hope that we take the leadership." Again, as he had noted a year and a half previously, he saw no inconsistency between what he now asked of the House members and what he had requested of his Senate colleagues some twenty-five years previously. Again, he warned the House against another Article X and expressed satisfaction that such a provision mandating international sanctions was not implied in the Fulbright resolution. It avoided, he stressed, the pitfalls of the League Covenant because it committed the country without giving the impression "to the world at large that we are to abandon our Constitutional processes."[149] The House supported the Fulbright resolution overwhelmingly and within weeks the Senate supported a similar measure, the Connelly resolution.[150]

Victory-Europe Day came on May 8, 1945. Soon Republicans were to dominate the Congress. Wadsworth would ascend to the House's powerful Rules Committee. Although foreign policy would continue to absorb his interest—he supported the United Nations Rehabilitation and Relief Administration and the continuation of a modified lend-lease program—he would inevitably, as would the country, turn to domestic problems.[151] As expected, he was a conservative in mid-century. But, in the interlude be-

147. *New York Times,* Sept. 3, 4, 6, 7, 8, 9, 12, 20, 1943.
148. *Washington Evening Star,* Sept. 22, 1943.
149. *Congressional Record,* Vol. 89, 78th Congress, 1st Session, Sept. 20, 1943, p. 7668.
150. *Congressional Record,* Vol. 89, Nov. 5, 1943, *passim.*
151. *New York Times,* Jan. 21, Apr. 18, 1944.

tween war and peace, he, like America, enjoyed the respite of "letting go." Other Americans danced in Times Square, ate what had been forbidden for four long years, drank to excess, or dreamed of the return of loved ones from the field of battle. Wadsworth went to Europe. Ostensibly, he went to settle the estate of dear Aunt Tillie, "a property in France [which] . . . consisted of a large chateau and 500 acres of land about twenty miles outside of Paris." In short order he left "the whole thing in the hands . . . of the Paris partner of Coudert Brothers in New York" and then celebrated the war's cessation by gathering together loved ones from American forces over Europe. The army gladly accommodated the congressman. They sent to him Reverdy; Tim Symington, a grandson; Bill Wadsworth, a cousin; John Hay Whitney, a nephew; and John Gott, the son of his general farm superintendent. The sight of Reverdy particularly moved him. "He is in fine shape," he wrote a close associate. "How he managed to come through without a scratch passes my comprehension. The stunt for which he got the Bronze Medal was, in my judgment, not as tough as some of the other things he had to go through, to wit: the Bastogne siege. . . . Following the Bastogne show and the failure of Von Rundstedt push, his Division went right on fighting until at the time of the surrender they were way down on the Austrian border. Of the thirty-nine officers in his tank battalion who started out on the campaign in October, Rev was one of nine who came through unscathed. I shiver and thank God." [152]

152. J.W.W. to Perry C. Buchner, June 18, 1945, Wadsworth MSS.

XIII

Conservative in Mid-Century

1

FRANK FORTUNE, the Washington reporter for the *Buffalo Evening News*, who covered Wadsworth in his "twilight years" from 1946 to 1951, described the Senator ("We always called him Senator") as "quite liberal." Fortune, of course, was recalling Wadsworth's bold stands, especially for a Republican, on military and foreign policy, not his record on domestic issues.[1] In fact, the *New Republic's* 1946 survey of congressional votes on major issues shows that only one House member in the New York delegation, John Taber of Auburn, and only twenty in the whole House of Representatives, equalled or surpassed Wadsworth in the number of votes against progressive domestic measures.[2] Wadsworth, of course, saw as highly consistent his military, foreign, and domestic positions. He believed that America needed not only an adequate military force to protect its heritage; it also needed an internationalist foreign policy to make the world "decent" and stable and thus lessen the need to use American fighting forces. In 1947, when America was turning to a post-war internationalist commitment, the members of the House, disagreeing almost totally with his stance on domestic issues, viewed Wadsworth as both its "ablest member" and the one who "has the best grasp of foreign affairs." [3] Harvard University conferred on him the honorary degree of Doctor of Laws.

On November 5, 1946, Wadsworth was returned to the House of Representatives by a safe 65–35 margin. Republican success in his 41st District was somewhat reflected in the country at large. For the first time since 1928, both houses of congress went Republican. In the House, fifty-

1. Conversation with Frank Fortune, Washington, Jan. 1968.

2. *The New Republic,* Sept. 16, 1946, Vol. 115, No. 11.

3. *Pageant Magazine,* Aug. 1956. See Neil Mac Neil, *Dirksen, Portrait of a Public Man* (New York: World, 1970), p. 145. Dirksen, in 1945, quoted columnist Ray Tucker as saying that "the ablest man in Congress was . . . Wadsworth of New York."

Senator Warren Austin and Wadsworth, co-authors of the defeated National Service bill. *By permission of the Library of Congress.*

Recipients of the honorary doctoral degree at Harvard, 1947. Front row, left to right: J. Robert Oppenheimer, Ernest Cadman Colwell, George Catlett Marshall, President James Bryant Conant, Omar Nelson Bradley, Thomas Stearns Eliot, James Wolcott Wadsworth, Jr. Back row, left to right: William Addison Dwiggins, George Henry Chase, William Holding Carter, Ivor Armstrong Richards, William Francis Gibbs, Frank Learoyd Boyden. *By permission of the Library of Congress.*

five Republicans were added to the Republican side, and Joseph Martin, who had been the Republican leader there since his defeat of Wadsworth for the position in 1937, was elected Speaker. Wadsworth was elected to the prestigious and powerful Rules Committee.[4] On the Rules Committee for his remaining four years in the House, Wadsworth, on great domestic issues, particularly on tax reduction, economy in government, and the decentralization of government, played coalition politics to the hilt. There conservative Republicans and southern Democrats allied to keep New Dealish legislation from the floor, and when they did permit the House to vote on certain bills, they frequently gave them closed rules, prohibiting any amendments from the floor. Democrats, of course, screamed about such "gag rules," rather as did the Republicans when the Democrats used the Rules Committee in similar arbitrary fashion in 1933.[5]

As a member of the Rules Committee, Wadsworth had to relinquish his Foreign Affairs Committee assignment. His interest now would be not with constructing bills but with policing them, determining which of hundreds of bills would go to the floor of the House. Prior to Wadsworth's elevation to the Rules Committee, Ham Andrews of Buffalo had strongly urged him to accept the chairmanship of the newly-organized Armed Services Committee. Such responsibility would have thrown Wadsworth into the minutiae of both army and navy legislation, quite in contrast to the oversight of all legislation he would engage in as a Rules committeeman. The Geneseoan might have been interested in the Armed Services assignment, and was appreciative of Andrews's generosity, but thought better of it. Andrews was the ranking Republican on the new committee and Wadsworth respected too much both the seniority system and his Erie County neighbor to accept the chairmanship if it came his way. "It ought not to be worked out that way. You must go along with the job."[6] In spite of Wadsworth's responsibility on the Rules Committee, he continued to interest himself in what he considered to be seminal domestic, military, and foreign policy legislation, such as the Taft-Hartley Act, universal military training, and legislation supportive of the United Nations.

As a House patriarch and a member of the Rules Committee, without responsibility for attending time-consuming committee hearings, Wadsworth stalked the House, effortlessly. He carried his large frame youthfully "with an athlete's swinging, slightly pigeon-toed gait." His hallmark

4. *New York Times,* Jan. 14, 1947.

5. Lewis J. Lapham, "Party Leadership and the House Committee on Rules" (Harvard University, 1953), Ph.D. dissertation, Ch. VI, *passim.*

6. J.W.W. to W. G. Andrews, Dec. 23, 1946, Wadsworth MSS, Library of Congress, Washington, D.C.

was his "tanned outdoor complexion, a bald, big-domed head, big ears and strikingly large, dark eyes." When he did approach the lectern now, noise subsided and almost always a member called for a quorum for all to "hear this." As he spoke with deep and pleasant voice, poised and relaxed, more members entered the chamber and "nobody slithered out." When not speaking, he was a good "floor man," listening, watching, counseling, frequently "napping" but with a "sixth sense," coming alive on large issues. Always, he roused himself. Colleagues were careful not to disturb him. Yet Wadsworth was not lethargic as the unknowing sometimes suspected. Once, when napping in the Republican cloak room, just off the House floor, he overheard a colleague describe Marshall as a "scoundrel." The Geneseoan immediately demanded a retraction and got it. More often he told a good story in the cloak room, or listened to one, laughing sometimes "until the tears rolled down his cheeks." [7]

As an esteemed House member addressing seminal legislation in the postwar years, Wadsworth's congressional years were full. Life outside the halls of Congress was comparably complete. He and AHW frequently had a quiet dinner at one of the District's older and more solid clubs and restaurants. Most generally, they frequented the Alibi Club, Martens, the Carlton, the 1925 F Street Club, the Racquet Club, and the Army and Navy Club and the Shoreham Hotel, seemingly in that order of preference. When AHW was in Geneseo and the Senator ate alone, he enjoyed most the Alibi Club. When together, they often ate there with a party of one or two couples, as the Dwight Davises, the General Frank McCoys, the Hamilton Andrewses, the Walter Howes, the Nicholas Roosevelts, the Warren Austins, or members of the family—the Jerrys, the Symingtons, Mrs. Henry Roosevelt, Ellie's mother. Frequently, the Wadsworths were guests at Washington dinners of social prominence, such as at the British Embassy, the Henry Luces, the Cornelius Blisses, the Forrestals. [8]

Wadsworth and AHW were reluctant guests. They were too secure and comfortable in their family circle or small groups of elite friends to splash in Washington society. AHW once prided herself on making it through a White House reception in twenty-five minutes. Lingering there with Washington's social set was, to her, uninviting. Her only official effort, year in and year out, was her annual call at the White House. But it was not like it was in the old days. At the turn of the century, it had been emptier of officials and more personal, as when she had lived across

7. Conversation with W. Sterling Cole, Jan. 1968; James W. Wadsworth, Jr., *Diary*, 1949–50, *passim*, Wadsworth MSS; Beverly Smith, "Mr. National Defense," *Saturday Evening Post*, March 8, 1947.

8. Wadsworth, Jr., *Diary*, 1945–48, *passim*.

Lafayette Square and went over to play with young Alice Roosevelt and the rest of T.R.'s "White House gang."[9]

AHW had much of Alice Roosevelt's (later Alice Roosevelt Longworth) independence, manner, and speech. She admitted that she probably "ruined" her husband many times by ignoring the rules of etiquette. Wadsworth's sister, Harriet, rather agreed, and so did Bessie Christian, the Senator's residence secretary. Yet AHW provided a warm home in old Georgetown and did succeed in giving the Senator "as much peace and quiet as possible." Rather than gad about the District, she preferred to ride quietly with her husband through the countryside, or go with him to a late afternoon movie. When not in Washington—during the summers, for instance—she watched over Hartford House in Geneseo.[10]

By choice, Washington after dark in the late 1940s was a quiet place to the Wadsworths. Usually, the Senator retired at 10:30 or 11:00 o'clock, after playing cards with AHW, reading some documents, or working on his scrapbook. On occasion, he retired much earlier for a good long sleep. Especially did he sleep "long" at Cornerways or Hartford House in Geneseo after vigorously overseeing the farms in the valley.

To repeat, however, Wadsworth's life was in no way lethargic. One night he happily endured the tomfoolery of Washington's prestigious Gridiron Club—its music, its skits—and in the presence of the nation's great and near-great, he rose, presumably at a late hour, to address the celebrated assembly. By tradition, only two persons address the Gridiron Club at its semi-annual celebration, the President and one from the opposing political party. It was not unlike Wadsworth, after properly chiding the spenders in government, to pay tribute to the press who honored the speaker by their invitation.[11] In simple eloquence, Wadsworth concluded:

> In the midst of all the confusion of thought and turmoil which characterizes this day, the correspondent is under a strain just as are many people in government. He asks us to join him in an hour of relaxation. I suspect that he needs that hour himself. Most certainly his guests welcome it and are most grateful. There is one phase of it which is particularly healthy and helpful. As you "kid" us you teach us not to "kid" ourselves. Please don't ever abandon this custom, else we perish. Tomorrow you will resume your task of telling the people what is going on in Washington. That's a large order these days. When you fill it let us in

9. Wadsworth, Jr., *Diary*, 1945–1948, *passim.;* undated clipping on life of and interview with Alice Hay Wadsworth, 1949.

10. *Ibid.*

11. *New York Times,* Apr. 9, 14, Dec. 9, 15, 1946.

on the secret. We are all so anxious to know. But be that as it may, you will live up to your high traditions of service to the country and give us the truth. It is the truth that will keep us free.[12]

2

No domestic issue immediately following the war concerned Wadsworth so much as that of price controls, and especially the price control on meat. Except for rent control, he felt that the Office of Price Administration should decontrol prices and get the country back to normal. OPA officials felt that the post-war scarcity of commodities would cause an horrendous inflation without a continuation of wartime controls. Contrariwise, pressure groups like the National Association of Manufacturers argued that decontrol would stimulate higher production, thus avoiding higher prices, and also avoiding the ever-expanding black market. Farmers, like Wadsworth, felt they needed relief, particularly because of their tax burden and the high cost of labor.

In the spring of 1946, Wadsworth made decontrol of livestock prices a mission. On several occasions, in late April and early May, he described the scandalous black market in meat, its origins, and its dreadful effect on the industry. With the aid of charts, he quietly detailed how the 1942 roll-back in prices in livestock and finished meat products had driven rolling beef stock from the Chicago yards and packing houses, away from federal expert graders and across the horizon to slaughter houses where beef sellers could get what the black market traffic would bear. Wadsworth's statistics were telling. He showed that since 1942, packing houses in the country had increased from 1,500 to 26,500 "today." Specifically, he noted the decline in purchases by the great houses in Chicago. "Here is the record given to me over the telephone by a man I have known for forty years and who is the soul of honesty. Armour and Company yesterday purchased 400 cattle, as compared to 2,000 three or four years ago; Swift, 300 as compared to 1,800; Wilson & Company, 250 as compared to 1,500." Whereas previously, 75 percent of the cattle coming into Chicago were slaughtered in the Chicago houses, now 75 percent were slaughtered outside of the center of the industry. The House was moved by the New Yorker's testimony and by a 127–117 teller vote agreed to decontrols on the livestock industry, but then reversed itself by a 139–122 roll-call vote, "a very strange sommersault." A few days later Wadsworth again decried

12. MSS of address, 1946, Wadsworth MSS.

the controls on meat prices and noted the "utter demoralization of the Chicago livestock market." As the Geneseoan left the well of the House, Speaker Rayburn publicly addressed his friend.[13] "If I had my way," he said, feeling administrative constraints, "I would have joined with the gentleman from New York in passing his amendment."[14] Eventually, on October 14, Wadsworth and Rayburn got their way. On that day the President gave up price controls on meat and all commodities.

Wadsworth's victory in the fight to get the government out of the meat-pricing business inspired him to further anti-New Deal-Fair Deal efforts in the domestic field. In the Eightieth Congress his domestic interests were three-fold: restraint of labor, economy in government, and decrease in the federal bureaucracy.

The Geneseoan gloried in the passage of the Taft-Hartley Act, the Republicans' major achievement in the Eightieth Congress, "a distinct step forward in curing a situation which was taxing the entire American people." He had been utterly demoralized by the post-war labor demands and strikes, especially in the coal and railroad industries. Aside from support of the Taft-Hartley bill, Wadsworth fought labor's attempts at getting "portal to portal" pay.[15]

To effect needed economies in government, as a member of the Rules Committee, and frequently as a speaker on the floor, the New Yorker stood against federal aid to the school lunch program, mental health research, medical education, and, most vociferously, federal aid to public education. "The harsh fact is," he wrote the editor of the *Instructor Magazine*, "that we cannot go much further with federal aid undertakings. . . . The habit has grown all over the country of looking toward Washington for money—money out of the federal treasury—on the theory that it won't cost the states or committees anything. 'Something for nothing.'"[16]

To get the federal government down to somewhat manageable proportion, Wadsworth supported reduction of various federal taxes, a decrease in Justice Department anti-trust prosecution, the abandonment of further building of TVA steam plants, and the localization of rent control. By and large, the Eightieth Congress agreed with Wadsworth's con-

13. *Congressional Record*, Vol. 92, 79th Congress, 2nd Session, pp. 3804–10, Apr. 16, 1946; Wadsworth, Jr., *Diary*, Apr. 17, 1946; *New York Times*, Apr. 18, 1946.

14. *New York Times*, May 4, 1946.

15. Clipping of either *Rochester Times-Union* or *Rochester Democrat and Chronicle*, July 29, 1947, Wadsworth MSS.

16. J.W.W. to Miss Mary E. Owen, Apr. 29, 1948, *Instructor Magazine*, Wadsworth MSS.

servative stance on domestic matters, and he was delighted. "Great God," he wrote a constituent, "have you been watching what the Congress has been doing . . . despite the protest of the President?" The Eightieth Congress acted "magnificently . . . despite world confusion and domestic difficulties which were inevitable following a great war." [17]

3

Wadsworth's support of the administration's foreign policy was quite different from his position on domestic issues. He went down the line in support of the United Nations, the United Nations Relief and Rehabilitation Administration, Greece-Turkey aid, loans to Britain, the Marshall Plan, Voice of America, cultural exchange, the admission of 200,000 displaced persons, and the extension of the reciprocal trade programs. He shuddered at the cost, however. "They give one puase," he wrote a conservative friend, "and yet I don't know what we can do about it. We have to take a stand, and if we do it promptly and vigorously at the outset we have a better chance of avoiding trouble in the future." To Republicans who questioned the constitutionality of it all, he gave soothing assurances. Under the common defense and general welfare clause, the expenditures were quite constitutional.[18]

More important than the soothing of constituents were Wadsworth's internationalist efforts in the Rules Committee and on the floor. Although the post-war Congress gave President Truman remarkable support in his various foreign programs, administration officials appreciated Wadsworth's leadership among Republican internationalists. The signal for his House speech on the $3,750,000,000 British loan brought 307 members to their seats to listen silently while he gave what he called "the picture as I see it." After describing British sacrifices in life and physical plant, he noted British need for working capital to get money to move Britain again. Resumption of the British plant, he noted, would accrue to the advantage of the United States "just as it would to the advantage of a town when a plant . . . which has suffered, through no fault of its own . . . is [with new capital] to start its machinery. . . . Every merchant up and down Main Street advantages by it." And Wadsworth, noting his unconven-

17. Eric Goldman, *The Crucial Decade, 1945–1955* (New York: Knopf, 1956), Ch. I–IV, *passim;* Wadsworth, Jr., *Diary,* 1947–1948, *passim;* J.W.W. to Frank S. Hayden, 1948, Wadsworth MSS.

18. J.W.W. to John Reynolds, May 29, 1947, Wadsworth MSS.

tionality, especially for a sound businessman, insisted on no collateral. Nor was the New Yorker concerned that the new socialist government would get the loan, convinced as he was that a healthy economic England would require less government control and not more. On the following day, Everett Dirksen pushed for collateral but lost, 138–97. In the final vote, following a reverently-received plea from Speaker Rayburn, 61 Republicans joined 157 Democrats to pass the legislation. The bill having passed the Senate, the President almost immediately signed it into law.[19]

When the Republicans took over the Eightieth Congress, Wadsworth became particularly important to the Truman administration in matters of foreign and military policy. As a member of the Rules Committee, he served as one of six from that paramount committee to serve also on the Committee on Expenditures in the Executive Department, a vehicle which Republicans expected to use to "investigate the Democratic administration." Clair Hoffman, the Democratic baiting chairman of the Expenditures Committee, and Wadsworth feuded throughout the Eightieth Congress, especially on military and foreign policy matters. For example, Undersecretary of State Dean Acheson and Assistant Secretary Will Clayton asked Wadsworth to see that Marshall, the new secretary, was spared Hoffman's "net." By and large, he was.[20]

Wadsworth's analogy of the advantage to both Main Streeters and the United States of restoring to productivity a Main Street plant and the British plant premised much of our foreign policy. Aid to Greece and Turkey in May of 1947 and the $5,300,000,000 first year's installment of aid through the Marshall Plan, signed on April 3, 1948, were acts of both political and economic containment of Russia.[21] Wadsworth, of course, supported both. He asked Acheson to have Marshall invite House Foreign Affairs Committee Chairman Eaton, a strong defender of the Greek Aid bill, to the White House. The Under-Secretary assured the New Yorker that it would be done. With the support of the prestigious Secretary of State and of Wadsworth and Minority Leader Rayburn, the last to advocate the bill in the House well, it passed. The New Yorker worked equally hard on the Marshall Plan program, noting in his diary confer-

19. *Congressional Record,* Vol. 92, 79th Congress, 2nd Session, June 1946, pp. 8857–8; J.W.W. to H. C. Taylor, June 26, 1946, Wadsworth MSS; *New York Times,* July 13, 1946.

20. Wadsworth, Jr., *Diary,* Jan.–Feb., 1947, *passim; New York Times,* Jan. 14, 1946.

York: Harcourt Brace & World, Inc., 1955), *passim; Congressional Record,* Vol. 93,

21. Joseph Marion Jones, *The Fifteen Weeks, Feb. 21–June 5, 1947* (New 80th Congress, 1947, p. 4611, p. 4742.

ences between himself, State Department personnel, and the House Republican leadership, which brought assurances of passage. On the last day of March 1948, the bill was passed, 329–71, indicating firm establishment of the nation's bi-partisan foreign policy, Wadsworth's goal for more than a decade.[22]

4

On June 15, 1944, the House Committee on Post-War Military Policy, which had been established at Wadsworth's suggestion, and on which he served as vice-chairman, reported its findings regarding unification of the armed forces. For several weeks, the committee heard pro and con testimony. In short, the War Department wanted a single department; the Navy Department counselled caution, without specifically opposing unification. The Woodrum Committee, being without authority to make recommendations, merely reported the general differences, noted the formation of a Joint Chiefs-of-Staff Special Committee on Reorganization, and suggested that no action be taken on unification until after the war. Between the war's end in September of 1945 and December of that year, the Joint Chiefs-of-Staff Special Committee report was submitted to the President. Although the report favored a single department, Admiral Richardson expressed serious reservations about the need for a separate air force, the contemplated power of the proposed Secretary of Defense, the single commander of the armed forces, and the threat to the full and free development of the navy. Also, in the fall of 1945 the Senate Committee on Military Affairs held hearings on a unification bill which reflected differences noted in the Joint Chiefs-of-Staff majority and minority reports.[23]

On December 17, 1945, President Truman, on his own, without specific advice from his Chiefs-of-Staff other than their divided report, recommended to the Congress a single department of national defense. His plan called for a single department with one cabinet-level secretary, a separate air force, a chief-of-staff of the armed forces, and an advisory joint chief-

22. Wadsworth, Jr., Diary, May 2, 1947; Jones, op. cit., passim; J.W.W. to Claude I. Hamilton, Mar. 3, 1948, Wadsworth MSS.

23. Lawrence J. Legere, Jr., Unification of the Armed Forces, Ch. V., "The Road to Unification: 1944–1947" (Washington, D.C.: Office of the Chief of Military History, Dept. of the Army, undated); C. W. Barklund, The Department of Defense (New York: Frederick A. Praeger, 1968), pp. 3–50.

of-staff. He carefully noted that "the Navy should, of course, retain its own carrier ships and water-based aviation . . . and . . . the Marine Corps should be continued as an integral part of the Navy."[24]

The navy balked at the President's message. As noted, had Navy Secretary Knox lived, unification might have come more painlessly, but now the navy demanded that its Marines operate all amphibious operations. The navy had ample opportunity to express itself before numerous committees in early 1946, and although its opposition softened as spring came in 1946, its position on its air and marine arms was firm. Finally in May the President committed War Secretary Robert Patterson and Navy Secretary James Forrestal to the following agreements: a single department of defense, a separate air force (with responsibility for essentially all land-based aircraft), and Marine responsibility for amphibious operations. Still differences persisted, particularly regarding interpretation of the agreement the President obtained. The navy saw more autonomy in its agreement than did the army. It insisted on prescribing in law the roles and missions of its air arms and the Marines. Finally, the President suggested delaying congressional action until 1947.[25]

Throughout 1946 Wadsworth actively supported unification legislation. His major effort, however, was in a related matter, the consolidation of the House committees on Military and Naval Affairs. Interestingly, the idea was fought most vociferously by his neighbor and usually devoted follower, W. Sterling Cole from the Southern Tier of New York State. When Congressman Cole, a ranking member of the Naval Affairs Committee, addressed the whole House on the wisdom of maintaining the committees' separation, Wadsworth immediately replied in kind, deploring Cole's suggestion as inconsistent with the recently-passed congressional reorganization bill which called for the consolidation of forty-eight standing committees into nineteen. Furthermore, he noted that if Cole were to have his way, a separate navy committee would again report out a separate navy bill "once more . . . [compelling the House] to legislate piecemeal on the problem of national defense."[26] Wadsworth's logic stood. The House consolidated its Naval and Military Affairs committees.

Actually, in 1946, Stuart Symington played a more important role than his father-in-law in unification. As Assistant Secretary of War for Air, he met on November 7, 1946, with Navy Secretary Forrestal, General Norstad, and Admirals Redford and Sherman and hammered out a series

24. *Ibid.*

25. *Ibid.*

26. J.W.W. to all members of House of Representatives, Dec. 21, 1946, Wadsworth MSS.

of agreements. Their agreement on unification was essentially based on the assumption that the President would make crystal clear the roles and missions of the naval air arm and the Marines. On this agreement, President Truman based his January 17, 1947, message regarding unification legislation.[27]

Hearings on the new bill began before the House Committee on Expenditures in the Executive Departments, on which Wadsworth sat as a member of the Rules Committee, and before the Senate Committee on the Armed Forces. Now Wadsworth was directly involved in the important measure. The bill faced tough sledding against navy air leaders and the tough anti-unification chairman of the Expenditures Committee, Clair Hoffman. Other navy men still believed that the new Secretary of National Defense should be a sort of assistant president, only generally concerned with the operations of the Navy Department.[28]

Wadsworth spent weeks prodding the chairman of the Expenditures Committee to move the unification bill, but Hoffman procrastinated. The Geneseoan also met unification opponents in the Rules Committee. When a bill to establish a uniform procurement procedure between the services was strenuously fought before the Rules Committee by former chairman Sabbath, former Naval Affairs chairman Carl Vinson, and Representative Ross Rizley, the New Yorker complained to Rules Chairman Leo J. Allen about the heckling of witnesses. Rizley wanted more time to study the military bill, complaining that he did not have a son-in-law who was Assistant Secretary of War for Air. Wadsworth asked for "order," "decorum," noting that he "didn't put him there—President Truman did," and, besides, "partisan politics do not enter the War Department." [29]

More importantly, Wadsworth worked on influential House members, like fellow Rules committeeman Christian Herter, to support the legislation and particularly to keep specific "roles and missions" out of the bill. Once "roles and missions" were spelled out, Wadsworth feared that next the Congress would determine the size of regiments.[30]

By late spring, Hoffman became disturbed by the virtually solid pro-unification front of the Navy and War Departments witnesses, and looked for opponents of the measure. He found them in ranking naval officers who, two years later, would figure in a sensational B-36 investigation which attempted to convict the new Air Secretary, Stuart Symington, of direct-

27. Legere, *op. cit.*, Ch. V, VI.

28. *Ibid.*

29. Wadsworth, Jr., *Diary*, Feb., March 1947, *passim; Rochester Democrat and Chronicle* or *Rochester Times-Union*, March 21, 1947, Wadsworth MSS.

30. J.W.W. to Christian A. Herter, May 5, 1947, Wadsworth MSS.

ing a lucrative "aircraft combine." To get the bill on the floor, Wadsworth finally offered an amendment which would assure the navy and the Marine Corps of their continued usefulness. Hoffman still would not move, whereupon the committee did an unusual thing. Against the chairman's wishes, it appointed a sub-committee to write the bill. Still, Hoffman, without the concurrence of Navy Secretary Forrestal or Admiral Nimitz, the Navy Chief-of-Staff, brought before the committee more unification opponents. When all of Hoffman's witnesses finished giving their testimony, he appointed his own sub-committee to write the bill. When, however, its bill was finally submitted to the full committee, Wadsworth and Representative John McCormick substituted their report and won approval to send what was essentially the President's bill to the floor.[31] There Wadsworth assumed majority leadership in the passage of the bill. Essentially he noted, as he frequently had before, the need for unification of the national military establishment, the general importance of the Secretary of Defense and his relationship to the army, navy, and air force departments, and the various agencies in the national defense establishment: the National Security Council, the Central Intelligence Agency, the National Securities Resources Board, the War Council, the Joint Chiefs-of-Staff, the Munitions Board, and the Research and Development Board.[32] Although the House expressed concern about civilian control over the CIA and its confinement to only military intelligence, the only amendment was that of W. Sterling Cole, who succeeded in getting the roles and missions of the naval air arm and the Marine corps written into the law. Fortunately, from Wadsworth's perspective, the White House brought pressure to bear on the House-Senate conference to keep "roles and missions" out of the law so as not to impair the authority of the Secretary of Defense and the President to administer the several departments, including the seemingly recalcitrant Marine and naval air officers.[33]

Navy Secretary Forrestal, long since won over to unification, was grateful to Wadsworth. "To your unfailing patience, tact and good sense," he wrote, "is due in very large measure the passage of the unification bill." [34] One year later Wadsworth would commiserate with both Forrestal, the then Secretary of Defense, and Stuart Symington, the then Secretary of the Air Force, for their never-ending problems with the naval high command. The New Yorker was convinced that the law clearly provided

31. Wadsworth, Jr., *Diary*, May 1947, *passim*.
32. *Congressional Record*, Vol. 93, 80th Congress, July 19, 1947, pp. 9397–8.
33. *New York Times*, July 20–31, 1947, *passim*.
34. James Forrestal to J.W.W., July 28, 1947, Wadsworth MSS.

for the latter's subservience to the Secretary of Defense and the President. Time would prove him correct.

As noted, Wadsworth's principal motivation for the establishment of the post-war Military Policy Committee was to proselytize for UMT. Although he pushed for a post-war UMT program only months after the war began, and sponsored specific legislation in 1943 and 1944, as the war ended in 1945 he got a broader forum for UMT in the form of the post-war committee. The committee recommended it and in 1946 the President supported it as he did again in 1947. In 1946, the best the President could get was the extension of the draft until March 31, 1947. And late in 1946 he appointed a nine-man Advisory Committee on Universal Military Training to work out a specific service plan.

When the Selective Service Act expired in March of 1947, effusive thanks went to Wadsworth for fathering the first bill in 1940. "No one can say," wrote Secretary of War Patterson, "what that gain [of 1,400,000 trained men by 1941] meant in lives and treasure saved in the course of the war." [35] But Wadsworth was depressed. The country was now without UMT or the selective service system. He feared a repetition of post-World War I lethargy. The Compton Advisory Committee on UMT on June 1 issued a 200,000-word report warning of "extermination" within seven years unless UMT was soon adopted. Wadsworth went on the stump. Friends of UMT, such as Archibald Thacher, and retired Supreme Court Justice Owen Roberts, formed a "National Security Committee." The opposition tightened, labor and religious leaders taking the lead. By fall the army pushed UMT to the hilt, dropping a call for a renewed selective service system, and setting up model camps to show the public how well trainees would be treated. [36]

In his January State of the Union address, the President pleaded for universal military training. Wadsworth admired him for it, although he thought his domestic demands sounded like a Sears, Roebuck catalog. [37] Actually, the polls favored UMT and the Armed Forces Committee of the House supported it unanimously. The Senate was favorably disposed, but Leo Allen, the chairman of the House Rules Committee, said "there would be no law." He could swing it because four Republicans and one

35. Robert Patterson to J.W.W., Mar. 31, 1947, Wadsworth MSS.

36. Robert David Ward, "The Movement for Universal Military Training in the United States, 1942–1952" (University of North Carolina, 1957), Ph.D. dissertation, Ch. V, *passim*; J.W.W. to A. G. Thacher, Oct. 13, 1947, A. G. Thacher to J.W.W., Oct. 9, 1947, Wadsworth MSS.

37. Wadsworth, Jr., *Diary*, Jan. 7, 1948.

Democrat voted with him. Wadsworth, in leading the six committeemen for the bill, could not bring Allen around.[38] He put Forrestal and Marshall, respectively, to persuading the Senate and House leaders, but to no avail. He frequently caucused in his office on how to pressure the Rules Committee UMT opponents, but without success. Finally the President, in desperation, dropped UMT and supported a new selective service act. Now Wadsworth, again recognizing UMT's precarious position, spent more time in the Pentagon, helping with the construction of draft legislation, while still keeping UMT hopes alive. Senator Gurney wanted to combine the selective service with a modified UMT. Wadsworth thought it unfair to give certain draftees brief universal military training and others years of service.[39] "There would be hell to pay under any such procedure."[40] When Allen's followers on the Rules Committee also refused to even give the draft legislation a rule, Wadsworth was beside himself. The committee stalled. "At the conclusion of the afternoon meeting," he noted in his diary, "I uttered an emphatic protest against these stalling tactics. Chairman Allen made no reply worthy of name and simply walked out of the room." Wadsworth went to Martin, and while the Speaker was unenthusiastic about the selective service bill, he assured Wadsworth that the bill would get a rule. After months of delay, the Rules Committee freed the bill for debate. Wadsworth, with Armed Services Chairman Andrews, led the House in support of the bill. It passed, with amendments killing a civil rights provision and reducing the service to one year. As finally signed by the President, however, the bill provided for twenty-one months of service for all men called up between the ages of eighteen and twenty-five. The New Yorker breathed a sigh of relief but universal military training seemed as far off as ever.[41]

5

On January 3, 1949, Wadsworth boarded the old "rattler" at Canandaigua and returned to Washington from his usual satisfying Christmas

38. Jim G. Lucas, "And Here is How it's Done . . ." (undated Scripps-Howard clipping).

39. Wadsworth, Jr., *Diary*, Apr. 1948.

40. J.W.W. to A. G. Thacher, May 4, 1948, Wadsworth MSS.

41. Wadsworth, Jr., *Diary*, Apr., May 1948; Ward, *op. cit.*, Ch. VII, IX; John M. Swomley, Jr., "A Study of the Universal Training Campaign, 1944–1952" (University of Colorado, 1959), Ph.D. dissertation, Ch. V, VI.

holiday in Geneseo. Time to think of those good recent days in Hartford House and on his farms was cut short by a busy itinerary and an agenda of important matters. Foremost was consideration of Democratic plans to amend the rules of the House so that after the Rules Committee "sat" on a bill for twenty-one days, the chairman of a standing committee would receive recognition by the Speaker to "call up" his bill. Wadsworth had grave misgivings. Such a twenty-one-day rule would place "enormous power in the Speaker and the chairmen of the standing committee." [42] Yet, many Republicans and Democrats alike could see the Democratic dilemma: either Speaker Rayburn would be given authority to recognize chairmen and get bills out of the Rules Committee or the newly-elected Democratic President would get little of the program he had promised to the American people. Harry Truman did not intend to have a "do-nothing" Congress stop him.

Wadsworth, of course, had no intention of accommodating Mr. Truman in meeting his campaign pledges, at least on the domestic side. He was horrified at the thought of the continuing Fair Deal march. Rather confidently he and fellow Republicans had expected to continue the working alliance on the Rules Committee with southern Democrats Eugene Cox of Georgia, Howard W. Smith of Virginia, and William M. Colmer of Mississippi. Ideologically, the southern gentlemen differed hardly at all from the Republican side of Wadsworth, Clarence J. Brown of Ohio, Leo E. Allen of Illinois, and Christian A. Herter of Massachusetts. The coalition would stem the tide. They would out-vote the Fair Deal side of the Rules Committee by seven to five. They had a vote to spare, for a tie vote on any bill would lose. But, because such confidence had been well founded, critics of the great committee thrashed about for ways to reform it, ranging from reducing its power to packing it with Fair Dealers. Recognizing the inevitability of some change, Wadsworth's associate, Christian Herter, had considered such "reforms" as forbidding the "Committee from considering substantive merits of committee reports" or letting the committee function as a "second thought" committee, "returning promptly a bill of which it disapproves to the sponsoring committee for reconsideration but with no power to hold the measure on a second request for a rule." Wadsworth wanted no such changes.[43] He and the Republican Steering Committee accepted another Herter proposal that "Calendar Wednesday" be made to work by

42. Wadsworth, Jr., *Diary*, Jan. 3, 1949.

43. Christopher Van Hollen, "The House Committee on Rules (1933–1951): Agent of Party and Agent of Opposition" (Johns Hopkins University, 1951), Ph.D. dissertation, pp. 251–253.

eliminating dilatory tactics on that day, a day intended for committees, alphabetically, to bring up bills not yet considered on the floor. Wadsworth recognized that "Calendar Wednesday" was "a rule which has been greatly opposed during the last few years." He felt that a workable "Calendar Wednesday" and the availability of the discharge petition (218 signatures for floor consideration) would bring the House under majority control. Of course, the discharge petition historically had been as unworkable as "Calendar Wednesday." So many times Wadsworth himself had said: "I never sign discharge petitions."[44]

The Republicans, however, did not have a chance to support their position on Rules. On the same January day when the first session of the Eighty-first Congress, a Democratic congress, convened, Rules Chairman Sabath introduced the twenty-one-day amendment and moved "the previous question," thus eliminating debate. By a 275-142 vote the Rules of the House were changed, a very uncommon occurrence. The grand coalition of Republicans and southern Democrats which Wadsworth had always so much appreciated was sorely threatened. For all the prestige and eminence of Wadsworth and his fellow Rulesmen, Mr. Sam could now pass them by. He would do so on eight occasions in the Eighty-first Congress.[45]

Wadsworth was to live unhappily with the twenty-one-day rule during his remaining days in the Congress. Although very close to Speaker Rayburn—the party lines had long since blurred—he greatly feared the power handed to the office of Speaker by the twenty-one-day rule. When one person replaced twelve as the maker of policy in that great parliamentary body, shades of "Czar" Reed and "Uncle" Joe Cannon, tyrannical speakers at the turn of the century, appeared in the chamber. Wadsworth also feared, of course, the onslaught of Fair Deal legislation and what it would do to his America.

Wadsworth was too experienced in large legislative and political matters to be seemingly perturbed by changes of the moment. As with the change in the Rules, he accepted his removal from the Committee on Expenditure in the Executive Department. (A minority member of the House may have only one committee assignment except for exempt committees such as the District of Columbia Committee.) Tradition was shattered when he, with all his seniority, asked for and received the last place on the District committee, normally considered a lesser

44. Wadsworth, Jr., *Diary*, Jan. 3, 1944.

45. Van Hollen, *op. cit.*, pp. 259–264; Lapham, *op. cit.*, pp. 187–237; James A. Robinson, *The House Rules Committee* (New York: The Bobbs Merrill Co., Inc., 1963), *passim*.

committee. He "wanted something more to do." [46] He rather enjoyed "chasing around the city in police cars." [47] Nor was Wadsworth perturbed when denied a vote on the Republican Policy Committee on which committee he had automatically sat because of his membership on the Rules Committee. ("Many will see it as a slap at the much abused [Rules] Committee." [48]) Wadsworth thought little of lesser status accompanying loss of a major committee assignment, appointment to a minor committee, and a denial of vote on the Republican Policy Committee. Early in the session, much of his time was devoted to conferences in Minority Leader Martin's office, assigning Republicans to the many fewer assignments available in the new Congress. [49]

Wadsworth braced himself for the Fair Deal onslaught. "If the party does not stand up unflinchingly against the trend toward the socialist state, the party will shortly have no reason for existence." He hoped a national leader would emerge. Dewey, he felt, "will not and cannot exercise such a leadership." Wadsworth would give his party two years to escape the fate of the Whig party "or else." Until then, Republicans in the Congress would carry the burden. "Pray for us." [50]

The onslaught came on January 5, 1949, when Harry Truman, his own president now, stepped to the rostrum of the joint session of Congress and demanded such Fair Deal measures as tax increases, Taft-Hartley repeal, increased minimum wages, expanded social security, extended rent control, stand-by wage controls, strengthened anti-trust laws, low-rent housing, a Fair Employment Practices Commission, and Universal Military Training. [51] Only for UMT was Wadsworth grateful. The other recommendations along with the President's suggestion that the government might build its own steel plants "opens up a vista at the end of which the socialistic state can clearly be seen." [52] And upon reading the President's January 12 economic report, Wadsworth thought it "terrifying" in its dimensions. "Apparently the government will be responsible for everything." [53] Aside from the growth of government, the burden of

46. Wadsworth, Jr., *Diary*, Jan. 7, 1949; *Washington Evening Star*, Jan. 29, 1949.

47. Alden Hatch, *The Wadsworths of the Genesee* (New York: Coward-McCann, Inc., 1959), p. 281.

48. Wadsworth, Jr., *Diary*, Jan. 25, 1949.

49. *Ibid.*, Jan. 10, 1949.

50. J.W.W. to Mrs. Charles Case, Jan. 18, 1949, Wadsworth MSS.

51. *New York Times*, Jan. 6, 1949.

52. Wadsworth, Jr., *Diary*, Jan. 5, 1949.

53. *Ibid.*, Jan. 12, 1949.

taxation to support it was viewed as staggering. To his friend Walter Sanders on the other side of the valley, he commiserated that Geneseo people felt about the Fair Deal as did those in Nunda. "It is high time. Do you and your neighbors realize what the Truman program means in the matter of expenditures by the federal government? Higher federal taxes, which, of course, are handed down to every man, woman and child in the country, directly or indirectly—four billion dollars of them. Then add three billion of social security taxes."[54] He feared for the people of Livingston County, and for their grandchildren.

Always a farmer, Wadsworth was particularly sensitive to federal intrusion into agriculture. Whether in the Rules Committee or on the floor, he fought anything which smacked of intrusion. When the Agriculture Committee sought legislation to aid farmers who were victims of disaster, Wadsworth supported the legislation but wanted assurances that such recipients were truly victims of "natural disaster" and not "economic disaster." He feared that Fair Dealers would use "economic disasters" as an excuse for much unnecessary federal intrusion.[55]

More compelling in the agricultural field was Wadsworth's fight against the Brannan Plan which would have eliminated marketing quotas, permitting perishables to be sold on the market for what the public would pay. If the market price did not bring a fair return to the farmer, the government would pay the difference out of the treasury. To Wadsworth, this was a step in the wrong direction. Aside from the two- to eight-billion-dollar annual cost, he felt such legislation, regulating production and guaranteeing prices at near parity level above the supply and demand level, would make the Secretary of Agriculture the "Master of Agriculture." Inevitably, "the operation of practically all farms in America would fall under government control." Farmers did not want to be told what they should grow and what they should be paid, he told the House. "They like to sit on the porch on a Saturday evening after supper," he said, almost nostalgically, "and gaze across their fields. . . . They like to sit there and plan freely."[56] Wadsworth wanted the Gore substitute for the Brannan Plan. Its provisions for flexible support, 60-90 percent, depending on the surplus available, "would prevent the piling up of surplus and it would not actually regiment the farmer."[57] Needless

54. J.W.W. to W. B. Sanders, Jan. 28, 1949, Wadsworth MSS.

55. *Congressional Record*, Vol. 95, 81st Congress, 1st Session, Feb. 21, 1949, p. 1460; Wadsworth, Jr., *Diary*, Feb. 21, 1949.

56. *Congressional Record*, Vol. 95, 81st Congress, 1st Session, p. 9837–41, July 20, 1949.

57. J.W.W. to Charles Chase, Aug. 10, 1949, Wadsworth MSS.

to say, he was pleased that by supporting the Gore substitute, the Democrats in the House continued the Eightieth Congress's farm program of flexible price supports. "This is the hardest blow that the administration has received."[58]

Repeal of the Taft-Hartley law was high on Truman's Fair Deal list. It came to Rules in the Lesinski bill, where Wadsworth fought it. The Republican Conference fought it. They wanted even more restrictions on labor than provided for in Taft-Hartley. On second thought, they felt it best to go no further than retaining Taft-Hartley restrictions, for if they did, a softer Senate position on labor might hurt House Republicans.[59] On the floor of the House, Wadsworth traced the history of the "original Wagner Labor Relations Act" (1935) and of the attempt in 1947 to balance the burden of responsibility between labor and industry. Wadsworth was satisfied that the Taft-Hartley bill of 1947 did create the balance, and without hurting labor's membership. "Believe it or not, I rejoice in that." Also, he noted, the 1947 act did not increase strikes. "It had exactly the opposite effect."[60] Nor did it decrease wages, as was prophesied. After some days of debate, Taft-Hartley repeal was defeated by 211-196. A close vote but "scarcely a Truman victory," Wadsworth noted, with satisfaction, in his diary.[61]

At 11:00 o'clock on August 17, 1949, Wadsworth entered the oval room of the White House to discuss with the President the establishment of the National Science Foundation. Truman wanted it badly and had reason to call in Wadsworth, a key to favorable Rules Committee action on the bill. Also, the President knew of Wadsworth's interest in research as a board member of the Carnegie Institute of Washington, and as an advocate of strong defense. Truman respectfully tried persuasion and Wadsworth replied in kind, reiterating the fears he had recently expressed to Cornell's President Day, fears of the bill's cost and its federalization of research. The President felt the Science Foundation was exceptional and should be supported. Wadsworth could only promise that he "would recite his views to the members of the Rules Committee," adding, "I am still deeply concerned about this flood of new commitments."[62] The President could have predicted the bill's fate. It received no rule from the committee and would not come to the floor until the next

58. Wadsworth, Jr., Diary, July 21, 1949.
59. Ibid., Apr. 12, 25, 1949.
60. Congressional Record, Vol. 95, op. cit., Apr. 26, 1949, pp. 5059–60.
61. Wadsworth, Jr., Diary, May 4, 1949.
62. Ibid., Aug. 17, 1949.

session, and then only under the twenty-one-day rule. Wadsworth would fight it in Rules and on the floor.

The White House meeting on the National Science Foundation proposal was a culmination of pressure on Wadsworth, primarily from Vannevar Bush, President of the Carnegie Institute of Washington, and James Conant, President of Harvard University, to support a rule for the bill. Bush was initially low-key. On June 27, 1949, he merely told Wadsworth that the legislation was much needed "to centralize and clarify federal support of university research and fellowships." [63] A month later, by army courier, he expressed unhappiness about news of the bill and a willingness to "interrupt his vacation and come down." [64] At the same time, President Conant urged action, noting that the armed services and the Atomic Energy Commission are not agencies "suitable for handling this type of [research] . . . , they both are too closely tied to security on the one hand and may be subject to arbitrary action on the other." [65] Wadsworth's response must not have been surprising to Conant, Bush, or the President. "From the beginning," he wrote to Conant, "I have entertained grave doubts as to the wisdom of the federal government's embarking upon an educational program of this sort. The constant multiplication of federal functions, the inevitable concentration of power, step by step, in the federal government, has given me deep concern for several years." [66]

As the National Science Foundation bill "aged" before the Rules Committee, Wadsworth's arguments against it developed further. On September 15, he said that the Foundation, a federal agency, could purchase its own real estate or lease it. Furthermore, the Foundation "will actually take over control on the highest level of education and research." By October 3, he noted that "no limit is placed upon the cost." [67] But Wadsworth could be persuaded, in part. By the middle of October he suggested to Bush, "it might be possible to insert in the bill an appropriate provision making it clear that it was not the purpose or intent of the Act to increase the sum total of expenditure being made in the field of scientific research by the several departments and executive agencies now operating in this field." [68] Budget Director Frank

63. Vannevar Bush to J.W.W., June 27, 1949, Vannevar Bush MSS, Library of Congress, Washington, D.C.

64. Vannevar Bush to J.W.W., Aug. 1, 1949, Vannevar Bush MSS.

65. James Conant to J.W.W., July 27, 1949, Wadsworth MSS.

66. J.W.W. to James Conant, Aug. 4, 1949, Wadsworth MSS.

67. J.W.W. to Ralph B. Mellon, Oct. 3, 1949, Wadsworth MSS.

68. J.W.W. to Vannevar Bush, Oct. 12, 1949, Wadsworth MSS; Wadsworth, Jr., *Diary*, Oct. 12, 1949.

Pace could not agree. "It is the [Budget] Bureau's view," he wrote Wadsworth, "based upon a careful restudy, that the pending bills and legislative history adequately meet the point which you have raised in your letter to Mr. Bush." [69] Wadsworth was disappointed, "I doubt that Mr. Pace has read the bill with care." [70] Wadsworth tried to fight it on the floor. Losing his battle there, he attempted to amend the legislation to confine the Foundation to basic research, an attempt to protect the applied scientific research of the armed forces. This amendment was lost as was another to deny the Foundation authority to purchase and sell property.[71] The bill passed but Wadsworth saw some improvement as the bill came from conference. The Foundation was not to "invade" fields of applied research unless so requested by the Secretary of Defense in connection with a national defense problem.[72]

Civil rights legislation was important to Harry Truman. Of the principal bills, Fair Employment Practices Commission, anti-poll tax, omnibus civil rights, and home rule in the District of Columbia, Wadsworth supported only the latter. Regarding FEPC and its police provisions to eliminate discrimination in employment, Wadsworth informed the executive secretary of the National Association for the Advancement of Colored People that "our best and only weapon for the achievement of this highly desirable objective must be the enlightenment and teaching of the individual to abandon his prejudices." As for the poll tax bill, Wadsworth fought it in Rules, and when it was brought to the floor under the twenty-one-day rule, he fought it there. "The Congress of the United States has no power whatsoever under the Constitution to forbid a state to employ a poll tax as a measure fixing the qualifications of its voters." On this point Wadsworth was sensitive. For support, he referred his correspondent to Section Two, Article One of the Constitution, which makes voting requirements a state function. Home rule for the District of Columbia differed, in Wadsworth's mind, from the FEPC and anti-poll tax bills. It clearly was a federal responsibility and as a member of the District Committee he supported it.[73] All civil rights acts, including the catch-all omnibus bill, failed, however, in the Eighty-first Congress.

Against domestic legislation in the Congress Wadsworth continued

69. Frank Pace, Jr., to J.W.W., Nov. 12, 1949, Wadsworth MSS.

70. J.W.W. to Vannevar Bush, Dec. 21, 1949, Wadsworth MSS.

71. *Congressional Record*, Vol. 96, 81st Congress, 2nd Session, Feb. 27, 1950, pp. 2414–5, Feb. 28, 1950, p. 2526; Wadsworth, Jr., *Diary*, Feb. 28, 1950.

72. Wadsworth, Jr., *Diary*, Apr. 27, 1950.

73. J.W.W. to John A. Cooke, Feb. 23, 1950, Wadsworth MSS; *Buffalo Evening News*, Feb. 22, 1950.

a consistent protest. He voted against rent control, public housing, social security, Brannan plan, anti-poll tax, anti-trust enforcement, gas regulation, minimum wage, Taft-Hartley, FEPC, and credit control legislation.[74] Yet Wadsworth did not parrot the notoriously conservative line of Pennsylvania's congressman, Robert Rich, who invariably grunted, "Where's the money coming from?" as Fair Deal legislation entered the congressional "hopper." Wadsworth's more refined approach was exemplified by his public housing position: "I would support such an undertaking," he wrote his friend Robert Moses of New York City, "in the belief that a number of our larger cities are not able . . . to assume the entire burden of construction. . . . The feature which I cannot stomach is that provision which authorizes the federal agency to pay out subsidies in support of the completed projects over a period of forty years." Wadsworth did not want the federal government and the Congress to be bound for forty years. In addition, such long-term commitments inevitably would affect the politics of multitudes—"Vote for so-and-so and Save Your Homes."[75]

Unlike Congressman Rich, Wadsworth saw a ray of hope. "I believe," he wrote a constituent, "that many of the recommendations of the Hoover Commission, if adopted, would save in the aggregate a great deal of money without reducing the number of functions performed by the government."[76] His hope and refinement were strained, however, by the spring of 1950. The accumulated effect of Fair Deal legislation was too much. For every bill successfully blocked, others broke through, mostly spending bills—for agriculture, education, social security, housing. He recounted to the House the road the country had taken to long-term deficit spending. Incensed by a bill providing for $50,000,000 in aid to rural libraries, Wadsworth rose on the floor to say:

Mr. Speaker, we have to stop, look, and listen. Only yesterday we increased the financial commitments of the U. S. government by 23 million dollars for several years to come.

Only the week before we increased the future financial commitments of the U. S. government to a minimum of 15 billion dollars a year, and it will not stop there. It will grow, once established.

I can remember a bill passed by the House last summer extending federal aid to states and municipalities to aid those states and municipalities to draft architectural and engineering plans for the building of local

74. *New Republic,* Nov. 14, 1949, Oct. 9, 1950.
75. J.W.W. to Robert Moses, June 25, 1949, Wadsworth MSS.
76. J.W.W. to Raymond H. Lambert, Mar. 16, 1950, Wadsworth MSS.

courthouses, city halls and sewage-disposal plants. It is called the advance planning bill. It costs 100 million dollars a year. What will be its fate in the Senate I do not know.

I think of another. There is now pending on the House calendar a bill to grant federal subsidies to medical colleges, dental colleges and nurses training schools—permanent. Two hundred and fifty million dollars a year it will cost. That came out of the Committee on Interstate and Foreign Commerce.

We cannot go on this way. We must call a halt somewhere. It is time to do it now. You and I know deep in our hearts that the states of this Union, 48 splendid subdivisions of this federal union, are amply able to see to it that their people have adequate library service. They do not need to come to Washington and we do not have the money with which to pay them.[77]

6

As Wadsworth ended his congressional years with ringing pleas for domestic conservatism, he also ended them in the cause of internationalizing our foreign policy. He supported forthrightly the President's new Secretary of State, Dean Acheson. As a "red scare" appeared on the horizon and a constituent questioned Acheson's loyalty, Wadsworth jumped to defend both his loyalty and integrity. "There is not the slightest trace of communism in his mental operations," he wrote.[78] He loathed Republican Conference action late in the Eighty-first Congress denouncing the Secretary of State.[79] He supported the Korean intervention when Republicans like Taft were issuing caveats about the war there.[80] He supported the Point IV program even though he had serious reservations about guaranteeing, without conditions, bank investment in backward countries.[81] He successfully urged the Republican Conference in the House not to criticize the administration's Yugoslavia aid bill and took charge of the bill on the floor.[82] He supported communication with the Russians under favorable circumstances.[83]

77. *Rochester Times-Union*, Mar. 11, 1950.
78. J.W.W. to W. H. Whitney, Jan. 26, 1949, Wadsworth MSS.
79. Wadsworth, Jr., *Diary*, Dec. 14, 1950.
80. *Ibid.*, June 27, 1950.
81. *Ibid.*, June 1, 1950.
82. *Ibid.*, Dec. 11, 12, 1950.
83. J.W.W. to Thomas H. Alvord, Mar. 1, 1950, Wadsworth MSS.

Perhaps the genius of American politics was marked by Wadsworth's ability to support the Truman administration in its foreign policy while adamantly fighting its domestic policy. It marked a sophistication shown by few fellow Republicans. Yet it came easily to Wadsworth. It evolved over a half-century of public service. As he had questioned the centralization of Theodore Roosevelt's New Nationalism, a half-century later he questioned the centralization of Harry Truman's Fair Deal. Wadsworth's feeling for internationalism in foreign policy evolved over a shorter period. Not until the 1930s did he firmly espouse the internationalists' view, but once committed, he met the isolationists and non-interventionists of that period with the same vigor with which he met them two decades later.

Wadsworth did more than support the administration's foreign policy. He became positive and even visionary, quite in contrast with his approach to domestic politics. He employed his influence in two causes particularly, Moral Re-Armament and Atlantic Union. The former received far less of his attention than the latter.

Wadsworth liked "old" Frank Buchman, the Moral Re-Armament founder. He felt if Buchman could just get his movement started it might work.[84] Moral Re-Armament, known as MRA, was a loosely organized and highly idealistic international attempt at applying the morality of all religions to the problems of the world. "It's the good road," said Buchman, "of an ideology inspired by God upon which all can unite. Catholic, Jew or Protestant, Hindu, Muslim, Buddhist and Confucianist —all find they can change, where needed, and travel along this road together." Many people of Wadsworth's influence in this country, such as Harry S Truman, Philip Murray, Admiral Richard Byrd, and abroad, such as Robert Schuman and Ludwig Erhard, appreciated its unifying and encompassing spirit. "Moral Re-Armament," said Buchman in a 1949 address, "has the tremendous uniting power that comes from change in both East and West. It gives the full dimension of change. Economic change. Social change. National change. International change. All based on personal change." Part of MRA's success in attracting influential support, aside from its movement's moral and unifying theme, was its assiduous attention paid to people like Wadsworth.[85] They "begged" Wadsworth to attend their 1949 conference at Coux, Switzerland. Wadsworth declined but not without calling on Speaker Rayburn "to have four or five members" attend.[86] In time, Wadsworth saw the movement

84. Conversation with J. J. Wadsworth, July 11, 1968, Washington, D.C.

85. Basil Entwistle and John McCooks Roots, *Moral Re-Armament: What is it?* (Los Angeles: Pace Publications, 1967), *passim.*

86. Wadsworth, Jr., *Diary,* May 31, 1949.

as somewhat naïve. Ten years later his son, Jerry had a comparable experience with MRA. When serving as United States representative to the Disarmament Conference at Geneva, he too was studiously attended by MRA "for awhile."[87] The momentary interest of both father and son in the movement marked their willingness to explore channels which might lessen the world's tensions.

Atlantic Union was another matter, taken far more seriously. "It aims," Wadsworth wrote to eighty-five of his House colleagues on August 18, 1949, "to permit timely, fruitful exploration of the possibilities of finding a less costly and more effective way to peace by uniting the Western union countries through the principles of free federal union which the 13 states promised in our constitution." On behalf of Congressmen Hale Boggs (Democrat from Louisiana), Clifford Davis (Democrat from Tennessee), Walter H. Judd (Republican from Minnesota), and George A. Smathers (Democrat from Florida), he pleaded for support of a resolution submitted on July 26, of which he was the chief sponsor. Wadsworth contended that by convening an "Atlantic Convention" the United States would take the offensive, "without writing any blank checks." To even consider union, he felt, "would rouse immediate, invigorating hope." Furthermore, as a regional federation, it would strengthen the U.N. and would not be subject to Soviet veto. Wadsworth noted the strong support of the Senate and of the newly-formed Atlantic Union Committee, a private organization.[88]

The idea of an Atlantic convention was not new. It was first suggested in 1939 in *Union Now*, an interest group magazine committed to world union. No attempt was made to implement the proposal for ten years. By 1949 the idea had the active support of Clarence K. Streit, founder and president, Federal Union, Inc.; Estes Kefauver, United States Senator from Tennessee; Will Clayton, former Under-Secretary of State; Owen J. Roberts, former Justice, United States Supreme Court; and Robert Patterson, former Secretary of War.[89] The latter two were particularly close to Wadsworth. Both Roberts and Patterson had strongly supported Wadsworth in his UMT efforts. On behalf of the group, Will Clayton, on July 15, asked Wadsworth to introduce the Atlantic Resolution. Wadsworth gladly did so, only suggesting that distinguished mem-

87. Conversation with J. J. Wadsworth, July 11, 1968, Washington, D.C.

88. J.W.W. to 85 colleagues in House of Representatives, Aug. 18, 1949, Wadsworth MSS.

89. Mrs. Chase S. Osborn, "How the Atlantic Convention Came to Be," *Freedom and Union*, Jan. 1962, pp. 12–13; also see Istavan Szent-Miklosy, "Development of American Thinking on an Atlantic Community, 1945–1962" (Columbia University, 1962), Ph.D. dissertation, *passim*.

bers from the "other side" join him.[90] Congressmen Boggs, Davis, and Smathers were quite distinguished Democrats.

On October 14 Wadsworth preceded former Justice Roberts in supporting the Atlantic Resolution before the Foreign Affairs Committee. Elihu Root's legal influence was apparent:

> My belief is that we cannot achieve anything approaching a stable peace unless we persuade a reasonable number of nations—and perhaps more may come in later—to subscribe to a code of law.
>
> The signing of treaties; the making of alliances, military and otherwise; and the subsidizing of other nations to help them to get on their feet, are all only temporary at best.
>
> Subsidization of other nations, no matter how much some of it has been necessary, cannot go on indefinitely.
>
> We must first build a foundation of law, secure adherence to it by the nations—then we can proceed.[91]

Throughout the second session of the Eighty-first Congress, Wadsworth supported Atlantic Union, frequently engaging in strategy meetings with Clarence Streit and Justice Roberts. On June 29, 1950, he sent 160 letters to his colleagues soliciting their support. Later in the summer, he and other leaders in the movement attended a State Department session on Atlantic Union. There Wadsworth reiterated the temporary nature of the Economic Cooperative Administration, military assistance and Point IV, although agreeing wholeheartedly that such measures must continue to be supported. Of the State Department personnel, Wadsworth felt that only John Foster Dulles was sympathetic. He thought Dean Acheson and Averell Harriman had a "narrow view."[92] Secretary Acheson did agree to study the Atlantic proposal more closely with a small congressional committee. Wadsworth was designated as a member, with Congressmen Judd and Boggs and Senators Edward J. Thye, J. William Fulbright, and Estes Kefauver.[93] Such was only "window dressing" however. Wadsworth still felt, and correctly, that Secretary Acheson and Ambassador Harriman were too "completely absorbed in our present difficulties . . . to be looking ahead."[94]

90. Wadsworth, Jr., *Diary*, July 15, 1949.

91. *Rochester Times-Union*, Oct. 14, 1949.

92. Wadsworth, Jr., *Diary*, Aug. 10, 1950.

93. Clarence K. Streit to Dean Acheson, Aug. 10, 1950, Atlantic Union Committee MSS, Library of Congress, New York, N.Y.

94. J.W.W. to Gerald B. Henry, Aug. 16, 1950, Wadsworth MSS.

Acheson's opposition to Atlantic Union was crucial. The President of the United States "had given a green light to the resolution to call a convention." "The little man" is for it, Roberts exclaimed to Streit, with one qualification, that Acheson did not object.[95] Hale Boggs and Walter Judd effected a strategy to bring Acheson around by having General Marshall work on him. Boggs and Clarence Streit believed that "our best hope of bringing the General around lies in . . . [Wadsworth using his] great influence with him to this end." In approaching Marshall, Streit reminded Wadsworth that in a 1947 speech on European economic cooperation, Marshall alluded to our early federal experience as a possible precedent for European unity.[96]

On November 2 Wadsworth talked at length with General Marshall, newly-appointed Secretary of Defense. He found his attitude toward Atlantic Union "distinctly encouraging—it certainly doesn't resemble that of the Secretary of State." Wadsworth explained to his old friend that the convention might not succeed in getting anywhere in the first few months but added that Atlantic Union was inevitable "and when I said that," Wadsworth reported to Streit, "he didn't deny it." Marshall felt that although France was moving on the same road, she complicated the situation with "proposals about German rearmament." Even though encouraged by Marshall's interest in Atlantic Union, Wadsworth thought it best not to ask him for a commitment to the resolution lest he appear too aggressive.[97]

In spite of sophisticated pressures on the State Department regarding Atlantic Union, it remained a hard "nut to crack." Assistant Secretary of State for European Affairs, George W. Perkins, wrote to Clarence Streit in December that America's allies felt that "we must devote our attention to the major military problems." Innocuously, he reported that "constant consideration is being given . . . to the nature of our political relationship with the friendly nations of the North Atlantic Area."[98] State Department obdurance, if anything, increased the commitment of Wadsworth and the Atlantic Union proponents. Throughout the winter of 1950–51 he kept his Union contracts alive. He was comfortable working with old friends like Patterson, Roberts, and Joseph Grew, former Ambassador to Japan. He

95. Clarence K. Streit, "Owen J. Roberts and Atlantic Union" *University of Pennsylvania Law Review*, Dec. 1955, p. 14; conversation of author with Clarence K. Streit, July 11, 1968, Washington, D.C.

96. Clarence K. Streit to J.W.W., Sept. 25, 1950, Wadsworth MSS.

97. Clarence K. Streit, "Confidential Summary of phone talk, Rep. James Wadsworth . . . with Secretary Marshall," Nov. 2, 1950, Atlantic Union Committee MSS; Wadsworth to Clarence K. Streit, Nov. 10, 1950, Wadsworth MSS.

98. George W. Perkins to Clarence K. Streit, Dec. 14, 1950, Atlantic Union Committee MSS.

took the cause to the public. "Literally," he told the New York State Bankers Association, "something better must be found than what's now going on." [99] He lived to see no real fruition of the movement. But then he was too experienced to have really expected much fruition. Just prior to his death, an advocate informed him of favorable action on the resolution by the Senate Foreign Relations Committee and that the State Department was now favorably disposed. Unaware of Wadsworth's terminal illness, his correspondent encouraged him to continue his good work for the cause.[100] Although another generation would see little fruition of the Atlantic Union concept as Wadsworth, Streit, and Roberts envisioned it, various cooperative actions such as NATO's non-military endeavors were built, in part, on early Atlantic Union thinking.[101] Wadsworth's own son, Jerry, who was to become the Ambassador to the United Nations in 1960, would see the western world still unready for Atlantic Union.[102]

7

When the second session of the Congress convened in early January of 1950, the Republican-southern Democrat coalition on the Rules Committee determined to repeal the twenty-one-day rule. On January 13, after a hearing on three bills, two of which were pending under the twenty-one-day rule, Congressman Cox resurrected a repeal resolution introduced almost a year previously. Surprisingly, it carried, 9–2, with Democrats Lyle of Texas and New Yorker James Delaney joining the coalition. Harry Truman was furious and determined "to do everything possible to have the motion beaten" on the floor. He succeeded but not before the country witnessed gyrations seldom seen even in the turbulent House of Representatives.[103]

The strategy of administration leaders in the House was to hold off action on the Cox repeal resolution until after a February 23 vote on legislation to establish a Fair Employment Practices Commission. With that legislation, hated so much by southerners, out of the way, southern Democrats would then be persuaded to support Speaker Rayburn and the administration on the retaining of the twenty-one-day rule. Cox, of course, saw through administration strategy and determined to get a vote on the

99. *Rochester Times-Union,* May 24, 1951.
100. Walden Moore to J.W.W., May 2, 1952, Wadsworth MSS.
101. Szent-Miklosy, *op. cit., passim.*
102. Conversation with J. J. Wadsworth, July 11, 1968, Washington, D.C.
103. Lapham, *op. cit.,* Ch. IX; Van Hollen, *op. cit.,* Ch. VIII.

repeal resolution before February 23 so that southern Democrats would support repeal of the twenty-one-day rule in order to have the Rules Committee stop FEPC from coming to the floor. On January 17, the coalition "moved" in executive session to instruct Chairman Sabbath to report the repeal resolution at once. Sabbath protested that it was his prerogative as chairman to report the resolution when he chose. In the ensuing committee fight, House Parliamentarian Lewis Deschler was called into the committee room. He reported that a majority of the committee could "work its will," whereupon Colmer called for a vote directing Cox to take the resolution to the House. Chairman Sabath then adjourned the meeting, bringing down his gavel so hard as to send its head "spinning into space with members dodging wildly." Sabath ran to the Speaker, and Mr. Sam, always shrewd, saw a flaw in the coalition strategy. If the vote on the repeal resolution came before the FEPC vote, many Republicans would have to vote against it in order to make possible voting for FEPC which could come up on February 23 only under the twenty-one-day rule. In 1948 the Republican platform declared strongly for civil rights and urban constituents did not hesitate to remind their congressmen, particularly Republicans, that a vote for repeal of the twenty-one-day rule would in effect be a vote against FEPC.[104]

Wadsworth was sure Rayburn knew what he was doing. He regretted the determination of southern Democrats to tie the twenty-one-day repeal resolution to FEPC. Stoically, however, he tried to save the repeal resolution. The great debate on the Rules change came on Friday, January 20. Chairman Sabath, a virtual prisoner of the coalition during his eleven years as chairman of the Rules Committee, released accumulated tensions. He saw the unholy alliance of reactionary Republicans and reactionary Democrats as an attempt to restore the days when "Czar" Reed was Speaker at the turn of the century. He talked about the three Democrats who ganged up with the Republicans, "leaving me, the Chairman, and the other real Democrats on the Committee in a minority." He argued that such an alliance made the twenty-one-day rule necessary.[105]

In the debate Wadsworth, of course, did not refer to the alliance. He took the high road, describing the "origin of this movement which finally resulted in its making by a vote of 9 to 2, this recommendation that the rules should be changed." He noted that in June of 1949 Republicans and Democrats alike on the Rules Committee became alarmed with the trend of legislation, leading to deficits of $1,800,000,000 in 1949 and $5,000,000,-

104. Wadsworth, Jr., *Diary*, Jan. 17, 1950; Van Hollen, *op. cit.*, Ch. VIII; Lapham, *op cit.*, Ch. IX.

105. *Congressional Record*, Vol. 96, 81st Congress, 2nd Session, Jan. 20, 1950, p. 7026.

000 in 1950. At that time, he noted, the committee was not thinking of FEPC or any particular legislation. When the Information Service revealed that actually the cost of all remaining commitments would reach $9,000,-000,000, the committee concluded that the twenty-one-day rule made it impossible for the "conveyor belt of legislation" to be turned off. For forty to fifty years, he argued, the determining of the aggregate effect of legislation was left to the Rules Committee. "That Committee could sit there and watch the trend and make its recommendations in one form or another—to the effect that we would better go slow because we are going too far and going too fast." Wadsworth said the condition of the House was chaotic. "All the old rule did was to permit the Committee . . . to screen . . . the great multitude of requests for future commitment—that is all." He concluded by assuring the House that the committee was not interested in power. Their job was a thankless one of being "hauled and pulled." [106]

Wadsworth's economy plea in the debate might have had impact—most House speeches do not—had not Republican Leo Allen exposed the real concern of the coalition: "whether or not the entire [Truman] Socialistic program will succeed or be defeated." [107] Speaker Rayburn caught that, left the rostrum, and noted that his dear friend Mr. Cox "winced" when Allen spoke. "Who won the election in 1948 anyhow?" he asked. By repealing the rule, he explained, four Republicans "can get two Democratic members of the Committee" and stop any program in the House.[108] In the roll call, 64 Republicans joined 171 Democrats to retain the twenty-one-day rule. At the end of that eventful day Wadsworth could only note in his diary, "In my judgment the party lost a remarkable opportunity . . . to stand up and be counted in favor of order in contrast to chaos." [109] A night's sleep did not help. "I am wondering now," he noted on the following day, "if any of the 64 Republicans . . . are proud of what they have done to the party and the country." [110]

8

Wadsworth's diary notations about the struggle to repeal the twenty-one-day rule were certainly not casual. Just as the struggle released eleven

106. *Ibid.*
107. *Ibid.,* p. 7027.
108. *Ibid.,* p. 7029.
109. Wadsworth, Jr., *Diary,* Jan. 20, 1950.
110. *Ibid.,* Jan. 21, 1950.

years of pent-up frustration in the breast of Adolph Sabbath, for Wadsworth it culminated a lifetime of identification with the South. Wadsworth always spoke warmly of how Lee had arranged to have his grandfather's body returned to Union lines after his death in the Battle of the Wilderness. Southerners in the House had befriended his father when, as chairman of the Agriculture Committee, he had fought T.R. on meat inspection legislation. Wadsworth himself lived in the South during his ranching days from 1911 to 1914. In 1938 he suggested to New York national committeeman C. D. Hilles that he do what he could to get Republican support for Eugene Tallmadge, Democratic candidate for governor in Georgia. During his own political career, southerners and the southern press spoke kindly of him. Wadsworth was comfortable with southerners. Fifteen years after his death, his sister, Harriet, from The Plains, Virginia, insisted that Jim was really himself a southerner. Her best source of such evidence was Howard Smith, erstwhile chairman of the Rules Committee in the early 1940s. "Howard Smith and Jim thought alike." [111] She knew because Mr. Smith was her congressman, attended her church, and not infrequently visited with Jim when he came to The Plains to stay with her.

Harriet was right. In many respects Jim was a southerner. When that "conveyor belt" of Fair Deal legislation started up in the spring of 1949, he appreciated the way that southern Democrats and Republicans stood together. He agreed with J. Harvie Williams of New York City that "on really fundamental questions a large majority of Southern Senators and Congressmen are in close agreement with a large majority of Republican Senators and Congressmen." He agreed that southern Democrats and Republicans would help each other in fighting things which they both disliked. But when Williams, long an advocate of coalition politics, suggested a formal combination of southern Democrats and Republicans in the Congress, Wadsworth, while sympathetic, could not agree. Emphatically, he said, "it would be quite impossible." He explained his reasoning at some length!

> The old political traditions are still too strong, and incidentally the seniority system has brought the Southern Democrats positions of power which they will not surrender even though the retaining of them appears to align them with the Democratic party. In other words I do not believe that the Southern Democrats will be willing to withdraw from some of their committee chairmanships and allow some Republicans to succeed them.

111. Conversation with Harriet Wadsworth Harper, Aug. 1967.

Wadsworth concluded, however, that the "two groups can swing a tremendous influence by voting together." [112] He was satisfied that the tendency was in that direction and he hoped it would grow stronger. Certainly Wadsworth was pleased by the tendency of Republicans and southern Democrats to work together on the Rules Committee, particularly in the effort of January 1950 to repeal the twenty-one-day rule. He was just as displeased that the sixty-four Republicans had abandoned the alliance.

Williams was not alone in thinking about coalition politics. In February of 1951 Senator Karl Mundt of South Dakota expressed concern to Wadsworth about a "serious political dilemma confronting both political parties of this country." Mundt felt that with the elimination, by the 1936 Democratic Convention, of the two-thirds rule for nominating presidential candidates, the southerners lost control of their party. The Democratic Party was no longer interested in such American concepts as "private ownership, individual initiative, states' rights and the dignity of the individual." Mundt thought a victory in 1952 of a government committed to such concepts was more important than the victory of any particular party. Mundt too proposed coalition and sought Wadsworth's advice.[113]

The seeking of Wadsworth's opinion about coalition by both Williams and Mundt was not unrelated. By 1951 Williams was in Washington organizing the American Good Government Society, an organization committed to coalition and staunchly supported by the Senator from South Dakota. Presumably Wadsworth responded to Mundt as he had to Williams two years previously. Although sympathetic to the cause of formal realignment, Wadsworth still saw it as impractical. He did not know how it could be done. In the two years since their initial correspondence on coalition, Harry Williams had devoted most of his time to the problem of coalition and gave Wadsworth the benefit of his findings.

Williams was quite equipped to discuss coalition politics with Wadsworth. John O'Connor had first filled his ears with coalition possibilities in 1938 when FDR successfully "purged" him in the Democratic congressional primary. O'Connor then ran as an independent Democrat and a Republican. He had had assurances from southern Democrats controlling the Congress that if returned to Congress with some Democratic support, he would remain as chairman of the Rules Committee. Unfortunately for the cause of coalition, he lost.

Williams saw real possibilities in coalition. He honed his arguments on long discussions with Republicans and Democrats alike. Wadsworth's old friend, Charles D. Hilles, former chairman of the Republican Na-

112. J.W.W. to J. Harvie Williams, Mar. 7, 1949, Wadsworth MSS.

113. Karl E. Mundt to J.W.W., Feb. 27, 1951, Earl E. Mundt to J.W.W., March 17, 1951, Wadsworth MSS.

tional Committee, and Josiah W. Bailey, United States Senator from North Carolina, were his principal advisers. Williams traveled throughout the South talking coalition. Albert Hawks, United States Senator from New Jersey, was interested and in early 1950 set up a conference attended by the patriarchs of the southern Democracy, Harry Byrd and Richard Russell, United States senators from Virginia and Georgia, respectively. Certainly the Republicans were not ignored. On one occasion, Williams boarded a train with Senator Mundt and headed for South Dakota, leaving at Cumberland, Maryland, only after exploring coalition possibilities. Clarence Brown, solid Taft Republican from Ohio, was intensely interested and, if necessary, was ready to sacrifice his seniority on the Rules Committee. Before long, leaders of the two groups were brought together. Clarence Brown and Williams were invited to Columbia, South Carolina, where Governor Byrnes introduced the Ohio congressman to Senator Bailey of North Carolina.

Wadsworth was right about the southern Democrats. Their seniority in the Congress, and thus their power in the party, was very important to them. Bailey asked the hard question. "Is the ground solid? We can't step over the line until the ground is solid." Byrd and Russell were not yet ready to give up on the Democratic convention. They hoped for restoration of the two-thirds rule.

But Williams had some answers by the time he and Wadsworth talked in April of 1951. Before creating the new coalition party, he suggested that Republicans elect public officials in the North but that Democrats operate in the South as a southern Democratic party, unaffiliated with northern Democrats. Nothing would change at the local level but everything would change in Washington. There Republicans and southern Democrats would constitute themselves as the official majority. In the committees of the Congress the senior member of the new majority would be chairman, be he Republican or southern Democrat. The coalition would be formalized. It would be dramatic. It would attract the attention of the press. Wadsworth listened. Surely he listened well. But there would be no time to reply. For the moment, he would "hurry off to the White House" to see Jerry "sworn" as Deputy Federal Civil Defense Administrator. Thereafter, his little time remaining—only a year—would be consumed by his chairmanship of the National Security Training Commission. Ironically, as Williams and Wadsworth talked coalition, essentially an anti-Fair Deal effort, Truman appointed Wadsworth and son to responsible federal offices, perhaps a tribute to Truman and to the Wadsworths.[114]

114. Conversation with J. Harvie Williams, July 11, 1968, Washington, D.C.; J. Harvie Williams, *Coalition Now!* (Washington: American Good Government Society, Inc., 1955), *passim.*

James Jeremiah Wadsworth, the mid-1950s.

Evelyn Wadsworth Symington,
about 1934.

James Wadsworth Symington, age 45.

XIV

"I Want to Go Home"

1

"THIS is to warn you that on Wednesday my retirement from the Congress will be announced," Wadsworth wrote Stuart Symington on May 27, 1950. He further said that Stuart knew the reasons —age seventy-three, and certain "signal smokes" (gastric ulcer), and "a lot of things to do at home where I can be my own master out in the fresh air."[1] The ulcer probably most inspired retirement. Wadsworth experienced severe pain and spent two weeks in the Doctors Hospital in Washington, "drenched with milk."[2] Two years previously he had suffered from a duodenal ulcer which had "passed out." Then too, Wadsworth wanted to spend more time with A.H.W. "We ought to be together at Geneseo, N.Y., taking drives to the farms or going on vacation trips together."[3]

Wadsworth's youthful appearance belied a need for retirement, as did his vigorous activity. Over the past Christmas holidays he had given twenty addresses. Upon returning to the second session of Congress, he threw himself into the "twenty-one-day rule" fight. Back from the hospital in February, he assumed his congressional chores and addressed himself to certain major issues—foreign policy matters such as the Atlantic Union resolution, domestic legislation such as the National Science Foundation, and the military, always the military. UMT still loomed on the horizon. In April he was elected president of the Capitol Hill Association, Inc., an organization to assume responsibility for building a new Republican Club in the capitol. Although Congressman James C. Auchincloss was to be chairman of the executive committee, "the working committee,"

---

1. J.W.W. to S. W. Symington, May 27, 1950, Wadsworth MSS, Library of Congress, Washington, D.C.

2. J.W.W. to Clarence L. Hay, Feb. 7, 1950, Wadsworth MSS.

3. Alden Hatch, *The Wadsworths of the Genesee* (N.Y.: McCann-Coward, 1959), p. 281.

Wadsworth did much to successfully launch the club.[4] Rather than considering the New York congressman a retiree, his good friend Ernest White suggested in the *Syracuse Herald American* that he run for governor. "I'm too old and too wicked," pleaded Wadsworth; besides "I have lost touch almost completely with state politics."[5]

As they had during his long political life, columnists treated Wadsworth kindly in retirement. (He never refused a reporter an interview.) Arthur Krock called him "the conscience of the House" and described his role in the great debate on draft extension on the eve of Pearl Harbor.[6] Walter Lippmann praised him as one of "the handful" of outstanding Americans who ran for lower federal office after having held higher office.[7] Elmer Davis singled out his sacrifice of his Senate seat in 1926 to Robert Wagner on the prohibition issue.[8] Vern Groop, of the Gannett News Service summarized his life and concluded that he was "one of the most respected elder statesmen in Congress."[9]

Reporters sought Wadsworth out for a retirement comment on personalities and legislative life. On listing outstanding congressmen, he preferred to pick "some no longer serving," all distinguished conservatives. He chose among Republicans Senator Philander C. Knox of Pennsylvania, formerly Taft's Secretary of State; Senator George Sutherland of Utah, subsequently a distinguished Supreme Court Justice; and Speaker Nicholas Longworth of Ohio, a Wadsworth intimate. The Democrats he listed as outstanding were Senator John Sharp Williams of Mississippi, a southerner who had befriended both Wadsworth and his father, and Speaker John N. Garner of Texas, who, like Wadsworth, was deeply offended by F.D.R.'s breaking the two-term tradition. He referred to the passage of the Burke-Wadsworth bill in 1940 as the highlight of his public life, and the renewal of the draft in August, 1941, as "the most dramatic."[10] Pinpointing for the Gannett News Service his principal observations of the Congress, he chose to defend the seniority system. He felt that election of committee chairmen would result in an "outcropping of personal ambition" and attendant resentment and bitterness.[11]

Personal expressions of gratitude must have moved Wadsworth, although he took them in stride. Stuart Symington wired, "It is a sad day

4. James W. Wadsworth, Jr., *Diary,* Apr. 4, 1950, Wadsworth MSS.

5. J.W.W. to Jacob P. Miller, May 6, 1950, Wadsworth MSS.

6. Arthur Krock, *New York Times,* June 2, 1950.

7. August W. Bennett to J.W.W., June 6, 1949, Wadsworth MSS.

8. Elmer Davis, WMAL Radio, Washington, D.C., May 31, 1950.

9. Vern Croop, *Rochester Times-Union,* May 31, 1953.

10. *Ibid.,* June 4, 1950.

11. J.W.W. to A. Vernon Croop, June 20, 1950, Wadsworth MSS.

for my country when the finest American I ever knew leaves its service." [12]
Old friend Archibald Thacher wrote that "no one . . . has ever given
so largely of his abilities to the military security of the United States." [13]
From the Senate, Lyndon B. Johnson wired: "May I add my congratulations to a man who has done so much for his country as a soldier, a statesman and at one time as a part-time Texan. The example of men like
James W. Wadsworth is an inspiration which those of us who now sit in
the Senate Chamber do our best to emulate." [14]

Exchanges of correspondence conjured up pleasant reminiscences of
Wadsworth's past. He recalled to J. H. Finnegan of Canton, New York,
his selection as Speaker of the Assembly in 1906, still insisting that T.R.
had nothing to do with it.[15] To Richard Templeton in Buffalo he stated
his belief that the contest at the 1910 state convention in Saratoga was
T.R.'s attempt to get back in the White House.[16] "Al Smith," he wrote
Bayard Swope, "brings back a lot of delightful memories. I was devoted to
that man. In my judgment he was the best product of democracy at its
best." [17] A most precious memory was that of association with "your grandfather," he wrote to Henry Cabot Lodge, Jr. "I was a youngster . . . but
he treated me with a generosity . . . that I have never forgotten." [18]
Whether the younger Lodge's grandfather would have condoned Wadsworth's memory of Wilson is questionable. "Looking back," he wrote
S. S. Menken, "I am not disposed to criticize unduly President Wilson or
President [F.] Roosevelt for their pre-war utterances. It may well have
been wise for them to move slowly and allow public sentiment to be mobil-
ized. . . . Had they been more prompt in forcing the issue the public
might have rejected their respective appeals. And that would have been
most distressful." [19] Wadsworth looked forward to recording his reminiscences. He was to be one of the first participants in Allen Nevins's oral
research project at Columbia University. "I am aware . . . however," he
wrote Fred Tanner, "that my recollections and indeed my papers, cannot
compare in importance with those of Henry Stimson, Elihu Root or George
Wickersham." [20]

If real public servants are the subjects of poetry, then Wadsworth

12. W. Stuart Symington to Wadsworth, May 30, 1950, Wadsworth MSS.
13. Archibald Thacher to J.W.W., June 13, 1950, Wadsworth MSS.
14. L. B. Johnson to Wadsworth, 1950, Wadsworth MSS.
15. J.W.W. to J. A. Finnegan, June 9, 1950, Wadsworth MSS.
16. J.W.W. to Richard W. Templeton, June 5, 1950, Wadsworth MSS.
17. J.W.W. to H. Bayard Swope, June 7, 1950, Wadsworth MSS.
18. J.W.W. to Henry C. Lodge, June 26, 1950, Wadsworth MSS.
19. J.W.W. to S. Starwood Menken, June 6, 1950, Wadsworth MSS.
20. J.W.W. to Frederick C. Tanner, June 26, 1960, Wadsworth MSS.

qualified. "I was just sitting there when he began to read the poem he had written about me," he said of John McSweeney, Democrat from Ohio. McSweeney claimed no particular talent but tried to do his "humble best" before the House, setting his theme by referring to James Whitcomb Riley's "The Old Man and Jim." After several improbable verses, he closed:

> "Well, good bye, Jim:
> Take keer of yourself!"
> Back to your stately mansion and
>   your rolling New York land
> We send you, Jim, with blessings
>   and friendly grasp of hand.
> We wish you countless happy years
>   of well-earned recreation
> As a partial compensation for your
>   service to our nation.
> So like your friendly Indian neighbors,
>   who have honored you as chief,
> We shall raise our hand sedately
>   and merely answer "how,"
>   and then say—
> "Well, good bye, Jim:
> Take keer of yourself!" [21]

Clarence Hay, Wadsworth's brother-in-law, could not be outdone by McSweeney. Attempting to draw on his own father's talent, he dashed off:

> You thought McSweeney's poem would be
>   the last of 'em brother
> For once you guessed it wrong and
>   brace yourself, here comes another.
> When anyone is plugging your career
>   I tell 'em, Mister
> You're speaking of the Statesman
>   who is married to my sister.
> So since no mother's son of 'em
>   can question that relation
> Just who can blame my thorax if
>   it shows a slight inflation

21. *New York Tribune*, Sept. 20, 1950.

You Wadsworths past and present
   are a damned good lot between you.
To close I'll just say, "Bye now
   Jim, take it easy, I'll be seeing ya." [22]

On September 21 George Marshall, newly appointed Secretary of
Defense, traveled to Rochester to join eight hundred persons paying tribute
to Wadsworth. It was a gala affair with old friends like George Marshall,
"Wild Bill" Donovan, and son-in-law Stuart Symington present. Tributes
came from across the nation. But it had its serious purpose. General Marshall, in his first statement in his new position, asked for universal military
training. Heaping praise on Wadsworth, the five-star general asserted that
"if Congress had passed the original Wadsworth bill [1920], I do not believe even a Hitler would have dared to provoke a second World War."
Describing the "truly magnificient service" Wadsworth rendered his country throughout much of the century, Marshall saw the establishment of
UMT as a fitting culmination of Wadsworth's career. [23]

Wadsworth, of course, responded warmly to Marshall's praise and his
plea for UMT. Humorous and urbane, he reflected seriousness by expressing fear that without UMT "we may be caught in a similar condition to
that which we were in during the early part of World War II." [24] Without
doubt, George Marshall and James Wadsworth were the nation's leading
advocates of universal military training, and each inspired the other in
his pleas.

The fall of 1950 was the twilight of Wadsworth's life. Soon public
responsibility and worsening health would close it out. "The winter wheat
has all been sown," he wrote old friend Henry Curran, former Chief
Magistrate of New York City, "and is coming up bright green. The third
cutting of alfalfa is in the barn and the meadow is storing up strength for
next spring. The silos are all filled with rich corn, chopped very fine. The
dairy cows and the beef steers are munching it. The lambs are all weaned
and sold and their mothers are putting on flesh to carry them through the
winter. The men are cleaning up dead trees, sawing and chopping them
into four feet lengths. They will keep me warm." [25]

Wadsworth had gone home. In one of his last and most meaningful
exchanges of reminiscences, Henry L. Stimson expressed the meaning of

22. Clarence L. Hay poem, Scrapbook, Wadsworth MSS.
23. *New York Times,* Sept. 22, 1950.
24. *Rochester Times-Union,* Sept. 22, 1950.
25. J.W.W. to Henry Curran, Oct. 10, 1950, Wadsworth MSS.

Wadsworth on his farms, 1946.
Photographs by Ollie Atkins,
The Saturday Evening Post.

home. "I was a dreadfully ignorant person," wrote the truly eminent Stimson, "and in want of friends and sponsors to help me along. You met me that evening [Buffalo, 1910], and took me down to the hospitality of your home in Geneseo, and for a couple of days you rested and cheered me up. Geneseo has ever since represented a sort of home and refuge to me, and as the years brought me your friendship and knowledge of the value of your wisdom and guidance, I have admired and . . . loved you." [26]

On Friday, December 22, 1950, the House said farewell to James Wadsworth and also, coincidentally, to his good friend, Earl Michener of Michigan. Both sides of the aisle were profuse in tribute. Speaker Rayburn led in the remarks, commenting on the attainment of Wadsworth's fine qualities, "he got some of that out on the bounding prairies of West Texas." [27] Wadsworth's response, described by himself as his "last feeble effort" was fittingly a discourse on the Bill of Rights and the sanctity of the individual. Appropriately, Wadsworth's last words for the House were a plea for the retention of states rights in spirit and deed as set forth in the tenth Amendment.

And then, finally, to make it absolutely clear that government derives all its power from the people, . . . [the fathers] ended up the Bill of Rights with the famous article 10, which reads: 'The powers not delegated to the United States by the Constitution, nor prohibited by it to the States, are reserved to the States respectively, or to the people.' In other words, "no more power unless we give it to you." That article 10 is the last word, the conclusive "thou-shall not," addressed to the Government. With it the story is complete. Down through the years some attempts have been made to trespass upon the sacred right of the citizen. They have failed, but similar attempts may be made in the future. They will fail if we teach our children and our grandchildren the real meaning and the vital importance of the Bill of Rights. I say teach our children and our grandchildren because I know as you all know, that liberty does not survive among a careless, uninformed people. It is earned first by the people themselves. Having earned it, they must watch over it lest it be taken away from them by a higher power. Let this thing be taught over and over again in our homes, our schools, our colleges. Telling an old story again and again may seem unnecessary but the history of the human race demonstrates that the truth cannot be told too often.[28]

26. H. L. Stimson to J.W.W., Oct. 18, 1950, Wadsworth MSS.
27. *New York Times,* Dec. 23, 1950.
28. *Congressional Record,* Vol. 96, 81st Congress, 2nd Session, Dec. 22, 1950, pp. 7006–8; A 7888.

2

The affairs of the military were still Wadsworth's first concern. Early in the Eighty-first Congress he deplored the continuous hauling and pulling among the services. Upon reading Defense Secretary Forrestal's first annual report, he realized that much more could have been accomplished had the 1947 unification act given him "absolute power."[29] "Uncle" Carl Vinson, Wadsworth's military counterpart across the aisle, did not agree.[30] Their differences, in part, stemmed from their military specialization. Vinson, now chairman of the Armed Services Committee, for years had been chairman of Naval Affairs, and rather feared army independence. Despite the opinion of the powerful chairman, Wadsworth, a few days later, dropped in at Forrestal's home and reported the feeling in the House in favor of amending the National Security Act to give the Defense Secretary more power.[31] Wadsworth found support for his position in the March 1, 1949, report of the Commission on Organization of the Executive Branch of Government. The Commission, known as the Hoover Commission, said the national military establishment was "perilously close to the weakest type of Department." Principally, it would strengthen the Secretary of Defense, by reducing the secretaries of the several services to the rank of under-secretary. Although little appreciable change would come in the Eight-first Congress, the ground work for increasing the Defense Secretary's authority was being laid.[32]

Stuart Symington, probably next to Forrestal himself, was most interested in and most affected by the unification problem. The navy airmen were getting to him. His father-in-law suggested that Navy Department attempts at influencing Congress to deny its air force seventy groups was illegal and should be reported to the Attorney General. Aside from being illegal, such attempts at influencing Congress were quite contrary to the spirit of unification.[33] As background on the origins of unification, requested by Stuart, Wadsworth described Navy Secretary Knox's strong support of unification, expressed to Wadsworth personally, only days prior to Knox's untimely death. Had he lived to give such testimony to the Congress in 1944, the cause of unification would have been far firmer.[34]

29. Wadsworth, Jr., *Diary,* Jan. 4, 1949.
30. *Ibid.,* Jan. 26, 1949.
31. *Ibid.,* Jan. 29, 1949.
32. *New York Times,* Mar. 1, 1949.
33. Wadsworth, Jr., *Diary,* Feb. 20, 1949.
34. J.W.W. to W. Stuart Symington, Apr. 12, 1949, Wadsworth MSS.

On May 27, Symington really felt the navy pressure. Representative James E. Van Zandt, Republican from Pennsylvania and a former naval officer, introduced Resolution 227 calling for a complete investigation of all military communications between military officials and any company or companies which received defense contracts. The Pennsylvania congressman charged that the B-36 bomber was manufactured by a company controlled by Floyd Odlum and that Air Secretary Symington cancelled contracts with four other companies in deference to the Odlum contract, even though flying men a year previously were ready to abandon the B-36. On the next day, Van Zandt called for an Armed Forces Committee hearing, reporting that Symington was planning to resign as Air Secretary in 1950 and become the head of an Odlum "aircraft combine." He reported that Symington had visited Odlum at his Palm Springs home on more than one occasion. Somewhat irrelevantly he noted that Symington's wartime gun turrets, manufactured in St. Louis, had been "unsatisfactory." [35]

Symington was enraged by the Van Zandt charge. He knew, of course, that the navy was opposed to the B-36. "The reason," he told his father-in-law in early April, was because "if the plane is right, which it now obviously is, there could be no justification whatever for the giant super carrier, which the Navy originally told the Congress could be built for $120,000,000." Furthermore, he said, the carrier never had the approval of the Joint Chiefs of Staff. But the viciousness of the Van Zandt charge surprised Symington.[36]

Wadsworth advised his son-in-law to "refrain absolutely from attempting to answer [Van Zandt's] charges through the press," but rather to "be content, for the time being with merely stating with some emphasis that the charges, etc., are false"; and to "express his entire willingness that the matter be investigated." Vinson had told Wadsworth that his committee would investigate, giving Symington opportunity to disprove the rumors.[37] Symington took his father-in-law's advice and bided his time. For the record he wrote to Chairman Vinson denying that he intended to resign as Van Zandt had charged.

Throughout June and July, 1949, Symington prepared for the hearing, putting key Defense people to work on the B-36 contractual arrangements. Wadsworth went over the text of his son-in-law's statement "slowly and carefully." He was confident that it would "demolish the charges and rumors leveled at the air force." He strongly suggested, however, that

35. Murray Green, "Stuart Symington and the B-36" (American University, 1960), Ph.D. dissertation, Ch. II, *passim.*

36. W. Stuart Symington to J.W.W., Apr. 11, 1949, Wadsworth MSS.

37. Wadsworth, Jr., *Diary,* May 26, 1949.

Symington's statement "should be presented toward the end of the hearings." He wanted others to "lay some stones, some of them in the very foundation itself, on the erection of the building clear up to the eaves. It is for you then to put on the roof covering the whole structure." The veteran congressman was insistent. "Put the stone-by-stone builders on first." He felt that Symington's summary was so fine it would cop the defense. "You ought to deliver that last smashing blow." [38]

Symington, of course, appreciated his father-in-law's advice. He demurred somewhat on his order of appearance. He was willing to let Messrs. Lovett and Patterson speak before him but not the air force people.[39] Vinson and Wadsworth pretty much had their way. Air Force Generals Kenney, LeMay, and Vandenberg preceded Symington, as did Lovett and Patterson.

On August 12, Symington read his forty-two-page statement before the Armed Services Committee. Essentially, he concluded that the B-36 was truly an intercontinental bomber, that it had no equal, and that national security was the only consideration in its purchase. In testimony he said that he knew who authored what became known as "the anonymous document" which inspired Van Zandt's charges. Drew Pearson already had told the country that it was one Cedric R. Worth. During the Symington testimony, Chairman Vinson asked Van Zandt to explain the similarity of "the anonymous document" and his original accusations made on the floor of the House. When he evaded, the doughty chairman reprimanded him. Late in August Representative Dewey Short (Republican from Missouri) asked that Worth be called before the committee. Upon his confession that he authored the document on advice of Navy Department personnel, the B-36 charge began to crumble.[40] The charge fell completely when, in early September, a navy inquiry brought a confession from Commander Thomas D. Davis that he had given much of the unsubstantiated evidence to Cedric Worth.[41] Symington, of course, survived the navy onslaught. The comfort and advice of his father-in-law during the tense months was simply another building block in their relationship.

Wadsworth was quietly ecstatic about UMT. So many times he came so close to seeing it enacted. His commitment was as great as ever. "You and I know," he wrote friend Archibald Thacher in February, 1950, "that no one of the three [armed services] nor any combination among them could possibly maintain this country's position for more than a few weeks."

38. J.W.W. to W. Stuart Symington, Aug. 8, 1949, Wadsworth MSS.
39. W. Stuart Symington to J.W.W., Aug. 9, 1949, Wadsworth MSS.
40. Green, *op. cit.*, Ch. XII, *passim.*
41. *New York Times*, Sept. 7, 1950.

He encouraged Thacher to urge his UMT Citizens Committee to "maintain its record" for UMT and the current draft law.[42] If Thacher and Wadsworth knew the country needed UMT and conscription, John Swomley, of the National Council Against Conscription, informed him that others thought differently. The American people thought "peacetime conscription is still a very unpopular thing," he wrote to Wadsworth, and said it reminded them "much more of European militarism than of freedom-loving, civilian-controlled America."[43]

During the summer hearings on draft extension, Wadsworth was impressed by the testimony of General Omar Bradley and Admiral Forrest Sherman that draft extension during the Korean War was essential, but could only conclude that "the functional error is the failure to establish a dependable citizen reserve."[44] He told the House that the UMT was the only answer. "I am wondering if we will ever get it," he recorded in his diary.[45] On June 30 President Truman signed draft extension legislation. With that legislation out of the way, Marshall and Wadsworth made their push for UMT.

Wadsworth, as in previous years, held out hope. Supreme Court Justice Owen Roberts reported to him that Truman decided to again recommend UMT.[46] Throughout early August General Bradley waited for final word from the President. Wadsworth became impatient. "I am tired of having legislation affecting the fate of the country prepared at the other end of Pennsylvania Avenue."[47] When, on August 8, Defense Secretary Louis Johnson publicly called for UMT, Wadsworth asked Congress to remain in session until it was accomplished. Furthermore, he suggested that Congress, and not the President, set the date for the implementation of UMT. "The Constitution provides that Congress shall have the power to raise and support armies."[48] All was in vain. While Wadsworth, and even Secretary Johnson, pressed, Chairman Vinson followed the President's suggestion that the legislation not be pressed in the Eight-first Congress. Wadsworth did receive Vinson's assurances, "absolutely," that he would do his level best to push UMT as soon as the new Congress convened. Clearly, with Wadsworth gone from the Congress by 1951, UMT would lose its first advocate. Its fate would be in Carl Vinson's hands.[49]

42. J.W.W. to A. G. Thacher, Feb. 18, 1950, Wadsworth MSS.
43. John M. Swomley, Jr., to J.W.W., May 12, 1950, Wadsworth MSS.
44. Wadsworth, Jr., *Diary*, July 24, 1950.
45. *Ibid.*, July 25, 1950.
46. *Ibid.*, July 27, 1950.
47. *Ibid.*, Aug. 8, 1950.
48. *Rochester Times-Union*, Aug. 8, 1950.
49. Wadsworth, Jr., *Diary*, Aug. 31, 1950.

In the fall of 1950, Patterson and Wadsworth exchanged correspondence on the crucial issue pertaining to UMT. The former Secretary of War preferred universal military service, not training for all young men at eighteen, "to continue for a two-year term."[50] Wadsworth agreed with his old friend that there should be no exceptions regarding college deferments but strongly disagreed with Patterson on universal military service for two reasons. First, he felt that Patterson's idea of two years of service would not "assure ourselves an adequate reserve force." Secondly, filling up the professional forces every year would mean that the United States had embraced the old European military caste system. Wadsworth did see difficulties in recruiting a standing force of something like three million men to meet the Korean crisis while UMT was launched. He recognized that the draft would have to be used but favored the establishment of UMT "as soon as we encounter what might be called a lull . . . in international tension." In short, Wadsworth wanted his citizen army.[51]

Upon taking over as Secretary of Defense, Marshall discovered that many Pentagon people thought like Patterson—they wanted to recruit through the draft. Wadsworth was happy that Marshall insisted that "these people look further ahead," toward a reserve citizen army based on UMT. Lovett supported him. By February, Marshall and Lovett had their Pentagon bill in Vinson's hand and, true to his word, Vinson wrote Wadsworth that "I plan to introduce a new bill . . . this afternoon." He enclosed a copy.[52]

Through the spring the bill had tough sledding. Although out of Congress, Wadsworth wrote to all members of the House in support of the legislation. Some responses were negative. Clair Hoffman, powerful ranking Republican on the Committee on Expenditures in the Executive Department, wrote that while it was not undemocratic to require young men to prepare themselves to defend their country, "it is equally obvious that no young American should be required to fight in a war which either politicians or military-minded men assume is our war, but in which, in reality, we are but remotely concerned."[53] With such reaction to UMT building up, Wadsworth referred to "the UMT mess." He blamed Truman. "We have a weak President and a hostile Congress."[54]

The opposition to UMT was so strong in the House that Chairman Vinson finally had to agree to limit the bill to endorsing the principle of

50. Robert T. Patterson to J.W.W., Oct. 17, 1950, Wadsworth MSS.
51. J.W.W. to Robert P. Patterson, Oct. 20, 1950, Wadsworth MSS.
52. J.W.W. to A. G. Thacher, Nov. 9, 1950, Carl Vinson to J.W.W., Feb. 28, 1951, Wadsworth MSS.
53. Clair E. Hoffman to J.W.W., Apr. 9, 1951, Wadsworth MSS.
54. J.W.W. to Julian A. Ripley, Apr. 11, 1951, Wadsworth MSS.

UMT and to prescribing a separate later vote on implementation by Congress. Essentially, the bill provided for the establishment of a National Security Training Commission of three civilians and two representatives of the military, who within four months after confirmation would submit implementation recommendations to Congress.

On June 19, 1951, President Truman signed the Draft-UMT bill which extended selective service until 1955, lowered the draft age to eighteen, and planned for a universal military training system for the first time in the nation's history. Immediately after signing the bill, the President nominated the members of the National Security Training Commission, which would have general supervision over the UMT program. Not surprisingly, Wadsworth was nominated, with Admiral Thomas Kinkaid, Lieutenant General Raymond S. McLain, William L. Clayton, and Dr. Karl T. Compton.[55] Clayton and Compton were old associates in the UMT struggle.

Wadsworth was obviously happy to serve on the National Security Training Commission, and when Truman designated him as chairman, he assured the Chief Executive he would do his "best." [56] Hurried on by the "signal smokes" and the four-month mandate to complete the commission report, he plunged ahead, invading the Pentagon, securing staff, getting information, consulting with members of Congress, and generally cutting red tape. "The other members of the Commission have left it up to me." Being an old hand around Congress and the Pentagon, Wadsworth was well received in his work. He was appalled to find the Navy and Air Force Departments so little prepared for UMT. Despite their slight preparation, the commission completed its preliminary report by September 1. Time was pressing. On September 10, Wadsworth went to the Emergency Hospital for an operation and remained there until November 1. "He would not quite say what was suspected, but he left no doubt in my mind it was cancer," Jerry reports.[57]

Defense Secretary Lovett was impressed by the report, agreeing that even though the Korean War situation imposed demands on the military manpower pool, eighteen-year-olds could be available to initiate UMT. Aware of his friend's sensitivity to "costs," Lovett assured Wadsworth that the comptroller of the Department of Defense would review the cost estimates of the program for possible reduction.[58]

On October 28, 1951, the report went to the Congress. Its declaration

55. *New York Times,* June 20, 1951.
56. J.W.W. to H. S. Truman, July 2, 1951, Wadsworth MSS.
57. Hatch, *op. cit.,* p. 286–7.
58. R. Lovett to J.W.W., Oct. 1951, Wadsworth MSS.

that "the return to frontier conditions demands a frontier response" essentially summed up its preamble. Specifically the commission report recommendéd that, upon reaching eighteen years of age, a young man receive six months of training in one of three armed services, that he be paid thirty dollars per month plus dependency allotments, that he not be subject to combat, that his moral welfare be supervised, that his training be almost entirely military, and that after his six months of training he serve in a reserve organization for seven and a half years.[59] Wadsworth successfully resisted pressures to introduce educational programs along with the military training. The idea smacked too much of indoctrination. Pointedly, the President thanked Wadsworth for the "splendid work" he had performed on the report, expressing particular appreciation for "working against the handicaps of serious illness."[60]

"We won't get this through without a fight," Wadsworth reported to the press while recuperating from the September operation. He seemed conscious that this was his last battle.[61] When Carl Vinson ·called for Armed Services Committee hearings on January 9, Wadsworth declared, "I'm going to get there if they have to wheel me in."[62]

On January 16, 1952, Wadsworth, now accompanied by his nurse, made his last appearance before a congressional committee. He was convinced that UMT could be substituted for the draft, providing world conditions got no worse during a two or three year period. Less persuasively, he noted that the country would save billions of dollars. Somewhat revealing of the report's tough sledding, he pleaded for a small start as soon as possible. Much of his testimony was given to explaining why the commission insisted on a six-month training period as opposed to two three-month periods.[63]

In early February Wadsworth bravely predicted approval of the commission's report. "It's rather difficult for opponents of UMT to fight this particular bill because it does nothing more than this same Congress told us to do" last year. Further, the bill did not start UMT. Such decisions were up to the Congress and the President. Wadsworth conceded that defeat of the bill would shelve UMT.[64]

"What a farce this bill is," screamed hard-bitten Dewey Short of Missouri, a ranking Armed Services Committee Republican, on the day

59. *New York Times*, Oct. 29, 1951.
60. H. S. Truman to J.W.W., Dec. 5, 1951, Wadsworth MSS.
61. *Rochester Times-Union*, Dec. 1951, Wadsworth MSS.
62. J.W.W. to L. C. Arends, Dec. 17, 1951, Wadsworth MSS.
63. *New York Times*, Jan. 16, 1952.
64. *Rochester Times-Union*, Feb. 3, 1952.

of decision. For thirty years he had been subjected to UMT propaganda and this was his valediction of opposition. He chastised the American Legion for threatening political extinction to those who opposed UMT. He described the legislation as "a radical departure from our American tradition." He mocked those who saw UMT precedent in little Sweden or Switzerland. He scorned the idea of matching "man for man with hordes in Russia, and on the continent of Asia." He was horrified by possible consequences of military rigidity on young developing minds. He wondered how character could be built in a barracks. He shrank at the cost. He decried the idea of some being trained for six months and their cousins being drafted for two years. Then Short reached his peroration, saying to his colleagues that he stayed "in this body" to defeat UMT. "Let us work for peace," he closed, "and not build up a military machine thinking only of war. War is not inevitable. We want to live and let live. But liberty is more precious then life itself and we shall die to preserve this liberty that is ours." [65]

Dewey Short carried the House. Had Wadsworth been there, he might have successfully rebutted his old colleague, but not likely. After all, Vinson and Rayburn were old UMT hands in the House. Vinson tried sugar-coating. He called for, and got, amendment to forbid UMT application while the draft was in effect and to set 1958 as a terminating date for the legislation. Rayburn took the floor and pleaded for passage in order to show the NATO nations that the United States was standing by them. The efforts of Vinson and Rayburn were to no avail. Republicans secured amendment to the bill which precluded changes that even the armed services felt necessary. Seeing the opportunity afforded by the confusion, Short moved to recommit the bill to committee, to bury it. [66]

By a vote of 236–162 UMT fell on March 5. Only coincidentally, Wadsworth had collapsed on the previous day and was rushed to the Emergency Hospital in Washington. "I don't believe I can make it this time," [67] he told Jerry.

Universal military training was dead. Appropriations to sustain the commission would not be cut drastically and the advent of a Republican

65. *Congressional Record*, Vol. 98, 82nd Congress, 2nd Session, p. 1634–2786, Feb. 28, 1952.

66. *New York Times*, Mar. 5, 1952; Robert David Ward, "The Movement for Universal Training in the United States, 1942–1952" (University of North Carolina, 1957), Ph.D. dissertation, Ch. IX, *passim*; John M. Swomley, Jr., "A Study of the Universal Training Campaign, 1944–52" (University of Colorado, 1959), Ph.D. dissertation, Ch. VI, *passim*.

67. Hatch, *op. cit.*, p. 289.

administration in 1952 would finish it off. Predictably, Speaker Joseph Martin and "Mr. Republican," Senator Robert Taft, would have no part of it. And Dewey Short would sit as chairman of the Armed Services Committee in the House.

On a quiet August morning, sixteen years after his deed, Dewey Short mused with satisfaction on the defeat of UMT. In the reflective peace of his home, adjacent to the Washington Cathedral, he spoke lovingly of "Jim" Wadsworth, recounting the intimacy of their association. "We would go off and 'strike a blow for liberty.'" But Dewey Short still felt "Jim" was wrong on UMT.[68]

It can be argued that history has sustained Short, but not with complete assurance. While in 1968 he expressed satisfaction, political activists in the Wadsworth family still saw merit in UMT. Symington, a member of the Armed Forces Committee of the United States Senate,[69] still thought it workable. Jerry, from his Federal Communication Commission office, felt its implementation might have avoided for America the burning of draft cards in the late 1960s.[70] And James Wadsworth Symington, Lyndon Johnson's Chief of Protocol, as he reflected on his grandfather and the long summers and "great" christmas holidays at Hartford House, saw merit in UMT in which all boys, whether from the ghetto or a "big house," would live and train and, if necessary, fight together to protect their country.[71]

3

"John! I want to go home!" wrote the recuperating Wadsworth to Representative Taber, on September 24, 1951, from his Emergency Hospital room in Washington.[72] All decisions on the UMT bill were made and he would return from Hartford House in January to defend the report before Congress. Meanwhile, Wadsworth was ready to forsake the Pentagon, what remained of Washington social life, assignments such as the chairmanship of the Loyalty Review board which Frances Perkins at the request of Truman had offered to him months previously, and the comfortable Washington homes of his family. The fall foliage

68. Conversation with Dewey Short, Washington, D.C., July 13, 1968.
69. Conversation with W. Stuart Symington, Jan. 1968.
70. Conversation with J. J. Wadsworth, July 11, 1968.
71. Conversation with J. W. Symington, Jan. 1968.
72. J.W.W. to John Taber, Sept. 24, 1951, Taber MSS.

of the Genesee Valley beckoned now even more than when he described the lure of his farms to Henry Curran a few months before.

Wadsworth left the Emergency Hospital for Hartford House in time for the Thanksgiving holiday, unable to fly on to Chicago for a portrait presentation sponsored by the livestock industry on November 25. On that day, the industry paid tribute to Wadsworth and placed his portrait permanently in the plush Saddle and Sirloin Club located adjacent to the great Chicago stockyards. Reverdy, representing his father, announced a surprise for the gathering. Switching on a tape recorder, his father talked warmly to his "cattle" friends for the last time. He spoke nostalgically of rural America, of the farmer who worked in soil and with livestock, of the wonderful freedom found only on the range and on the farm. Should the liberty of the men who live and work in "God's out-of-doors" be lost, then indeed "the citadel which our forefathers built will crumble into rubble." [73]

In mid-December Wadsworth was rushed to Strong Memorial Hospital in Rochester "for observation," to return to Geneseo two days after Christmas. As noted, he attended UMT hearings in Washington in January, and on February 13 "traveled alone on the 'old Rattler' to Geneseo to view his farms beneath their heavy blanket of snow for the last time." [74] Back in Washington, on March 4 he collapsed and was rushed to the Emergency Hospital. In late March members of the family gathered around, although Reverdy called reports of the children being summoned as "sensational." From Missouri, Symington tried to cheer his father-in-law and brought him up to date on his campaign for the Democratic senatorial nomination. "Truman controls the Pendergast machine and said machine is backing another candidate. It will be enjoyable." [75] Wadsworth's condition was not good. The cancer progressed. It took its seventy-four-year-old victim on a Saturday night, June 21, 1952, at 8:30 P.M.

A long, vigorous life, including a half-century of public service, evoked expected tributes, public and private. One sensed that the President's was more than perfunctory. He described Wadsworth as "a man of independent thought and action . . . a true patriot and outstanding servant." The President concluded that "every American enjoys greater security today because of . . . [his] long interest in military preparedness." [76] Truman's eulogy stemmed from personal observation of and con-

73. Hatch, op. cit., p. 290–91.
74. Ibid., p. 289.
75. W. Stuart Symington to J.W.W., Mar. 18, 1952, Wadsworth MSS.
76. Rochester Times-Union, June 23, 1952.

tact with Wadsworth. In April of 1945 Wadsworth had immediately offered the new President his service. Then too, Truman and Wadsworth had many mutual associations. Interestingly, the two, so apart in heritage and ideology, were very close to many who constituted the first line of the President's administration—George Marshall, James Forrestal, Dean Acheson, Robert Patterson, H. L. Stimson, and Stuart Symington. AHW and Evie both dashed off handwritten notes thanking the President. From his home in Leesburg, Virginia, General Marshall succinctly gathered his feelings: "I knew him since he was chairman of a military committee in 1919. I have always admired him tremendously and I felt he represented one of the finest types of legislator we have. His integrity and wisdom together made him outstanding, and his passing was a great tragedy." Of all the tributes, from those of Truman, Marshall, and Dewey to those of Gannett, Taft, and Barkley, that of Congressman W. Sterling Cole of Bath, New York, was probably most from the heart: "To me Jim Wadsworth was the personification of the ideal in public service. For nearly two decades he was my idol and served as an example which I sought to emulate." Cole had been Wadsworth's protégé and recipient of the American Political Science Association's first "Outstanding Congressman" award.[77] Sixteen years later, from his Washington law office, he recounted the spell of Wadsworth, speaking of one occasion when he had wanted to interrupt his mentor's address to the House just briefly to offer a factual aid, but "did not dare."[78]

The editorial pages of the great newspapers probably reflect the truest sentiment of a nation's reaction to the passing of a public figure. Papers such as the *St. Louis Post-Dispatch,* the *New York Herald Tribune,* the *Washington Star,* and the *New York Times* did Wadsworth's memory honor. The editorial themes, generally similar, varied in emphasis. The *Post-Dispatch* saw that the "keynote" of his record was "courage." It alluded particularly to the sacrifice of his Senate seat in 1926. The *Tribune* noted that "on domestic issues he was a consistent opponent of the New Deal; in international and military affairs he was a staunch champion of co-operation and preparedness." The *Washington Star* wrote that he "will be remembered longest for his work in behalf of preparedness," noting, however, that he "also labored constructively in foreign and domestic commerce, labor relations, interior affairs and agriculture."[79] The *Times* touched most of the bases of Wadsworth's

77. *Ibid.*
78. Conversation with W. Sterling Cole, Jan. 1968.
79. *St. Louis Post-Dispatch, New York Herald Tribune, Washington Star* clippings, undated, Wadsworth MSS.

life, describing it as one of strong convictions, expressed "even if they were unpopular," frequently regarded as ultra-conservative on domestic issues, far from conservative on the relationship of the United States to the rest of the world, "always championing . . . a strong United States . . . vigorous in its commitments," and one of "decisive leadership in the field of military manpower legislation." The *Times* concluded: "His life and his work illustrate the fact that real patriotism is no matter of party or group labels. In some cases he was more 'liberal' than the 'liberals.' His cause was the cause of his country and his interpretation of that cause was his own. We are stronger today for his enlistment in it." [80]

Overall, the June 1952 editorials on Wadsworth seemed to constitute a most appropriate definition of the conservative in mid-century—the intelligent, consistent opponent of the New Deal's and Fair Deal's centralization and deficit spending, who, with equal consistency and vigor, supported a strong defense and a large role for America in international affairs.

Yet Wadsworth was more than a conservative in mid-century. The various eulogies confirmed that he was rather uniquely a conservative in the American gentry-elite tradition as manifested by his principles of service, property, responsibility, constitutionalism, antistatism, military preparedness, and internationalism. He believed in and lived by these principles, never demagogically and certainly with very little thought to his public relations.

On Wednesday, June 25, notables from official and residential Washington attended private memorial services in the great Washington Cathedral. The Right Reverend Angus Dun, Protestant Episcopal Bishop of Washington and an old friend from early Albany days, conducted the services with Reverend Francis B. Sayre, Jr., the Dean of the Cathedral. (One might have wondered if Dean Sayre, Woodrow Wilson's grandson, was aware of Wadsworth's role in opposing the League of Nations, but such ironies are commonplace in Washington.)

Generals of the Army George C. Marshall and Omar Bradley accompanied the family in the Cathedral rites. With them also were Clark Clifford, former counsel to the President; Robert A. Lovett, Secretary of Defense; John W. Snyder, Secretary of the Treasury; Frank Pace, Jr., Secretary of the Army; and numerous high-ranking military personnel. Appropriately, Wadsworth's body was escorted by uniformed men from the various armed services. Frequent references were made in the service to Wadsworth's devotion to preparedness. One of the hymns was the familiar and majestic, "The Son of God Goes Forth to War."

80. *New York Times*, June 23, 1952.

Just shortly prior to the cathedral service, the House of Representatives interrupted debate on extension of the Defense Production Act to permit its members to pay homage to Wadsworth "across town." Speaker Martin and Republican Whip Les Arends led the delegation. From the Senate side, Minority Leader Robert A. Taft of Ohio, J. William Fulbright of Arkansas, and L. Everett Saltonstall of Massachusetts were prominent representatives. Following the services, the body was returned to Geneseo.[81]

Among the Rochester representatives at the Washington service was Carl Hallauer, the Bausch and Lomb executive who had worked so hard for a national Wadsworth ticket in 1936. As Hallauer descended the cathedral steps, he and Taft fell into conversation eulogizing Wadsworth. They spent a quiet time at dinner "with Martha" at the Taft home on 31st Street, N.W. They talked into the night about Wadsworth and politics. In the forthcoming Republican convention, only Hallauer in the New York delegation was to withstand Dewey's pressure and support Taft in his contest for the presidential nomination against Eisenhower.

At the stroke of 4:00 P.M. on Friday, June 27, the Reverend Walter Muir stepped to the altar of St. Michael's Episcopal Church in Geneseo to lead a host of representatives from the valley in their last tribute. From St. Michael's the funeral procession wound through the woods of Temple Hill "between the solemn ranks of the Geneseo Troop, now the Twenty-seventh Reconnaisance Company, New York National Guard."[82] The life of James W. Wadsworth, Jr., now stilled in the soil of the Genesee Valley, awaited the assessment of history.

81. *Rochester Times-Union*, June 23, 1952; *New York Times*, June 26, 1952.
82. Conversation with Carl Hallaner, 1968; Hatch, *op. cit.*, p. 292.

James Wolcott Wadsworth, Jr. Bust by Anna Dunbar, Buffalo, New York.
In Hartford House.

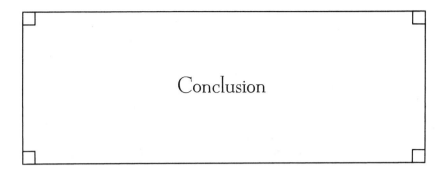

Conclusion

AQUARTER of a century has elapsed since James Wadsworth took his leave of the Congress of the United States. Today's historical assessments of him will vary depending upon one's historical school. Conflict-combative historians will see Wadsworth as Eleanor Roosevelt did, possessing a Marie Antoinette mentality. New left historians could as easily applaud his antistatism as they have Herbert Hoover's. Conservative historians could be enamored of his classical economic beliefs. New conservative historians would probably resent his inflexibility. This censensus historian views conflict as usually constrained in America and sees a healthy role played out by conservative gentry who bring to American politics an independence frequently different from leaders who come to office by way of the interest group or the party machine. Of course, in another quarter of a century and beyond, new assessments, based on new evidence and new schools of history, will emerge to view James Wadsworth and his contemporaries differently from assessments of today.

James Wadsworth was a gentleman and a conservative, as demonstrated by the convergence in his life of aristocratic and conservative tenets. As such, he possessed a confidence and integrity that were sometimes misinterpreted by lay observers and academicians as simplistic and reactionary behavior. To be sure, Wadsworth was not immune to simplistic and reactionary ideas but more often he was engagingly forthright, and very conservative. His uniqueness to historians was that he was so forthright and conservative in places of political action for so long. During that period which Eric Goldman calls "the Half Century of Revolution," Wadsworth's life has microcosmic value to historians.

James Wadsworth was more than an observer. Over his long political life he was a political participant and as such influenced events by commission as well as ommission.

415

The Half Century of Revolution marked a period of dramatic and urban growth in America, resulting in dire economic conditions which necessitated government response. That response essentially took the form of the Square Deal, the New Freedom, the New Deal and the Fair Deal. James Wadsworth loathed them all for their statist responses to domestic needs. In loyalty to what he perceived to be his commission, he articulated a conservative position on which liberals had to hone welfare and statist programs. And by occupying important seats in the two houses of Congress, he denied liberals votes and potentially powerful voices in places of power. Seldom has the Senate of the United States witnessed as dramatic a metamorphosis in one seat as when Robert Wagner replaced James Wadsworth. And there is no gainsaying that as the United States Senator from New York, Wadsworth opposed many needed reforms of the day or that Robert Wagner was more in tune with the needs of the day. Yet in the mosaic of American political life, Wadsworth's anvil role contributed to the political health of the nation. Indeed, one day his fear of the State may be viewed as prophetic.

Eric Goldman correctly perceives another side of the Half Century of Revolution—the move of the nation from isolationism to responsible internationalism. Indeed, the growth of American industrialism and its creditor status mandated an involvement of America in the community of nations. Here Wadsworth's role was importantly positive. Once he began his trek to internationalism in the mid-1920s, his commitment influenced considerably the repeal of the neutrality of the mid-1930s which prepared the way for America's entry into what Hugo L. Black has described as this nation's only justifiable war in this century. And concurrently important with Wadsworth's foreign affairs role was his authorship of the nation's conscription legislation for World War II. He unflaggingly maintained his strong internationalism and support for the defense of the nation in the postwar period, most significantly evidenced in his concept of the nation's role in the United Nations and the debate on universal military training. Of course, from the perspective of a quarter of a century, colored by the nation's Vietnam experience, Wadsworth's internationalist and military posture in relation to World War II can be viewed simplistically as leading to the morass of Vietnam. James W. Wadsworth's most significant legacy might directly relate to the nation's foreign and military policy as influenced by the two public lives he most touched—James J. Wadsworth, the nation's ambassador to the United Nations in 1960; and W. Stuart Symington, the Secretary of the Air Force in the Truman years and subsequently chairman of the Armed Services Committee of the Senate of the United States.

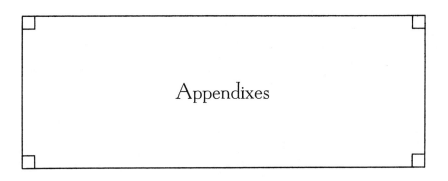

Appendixes

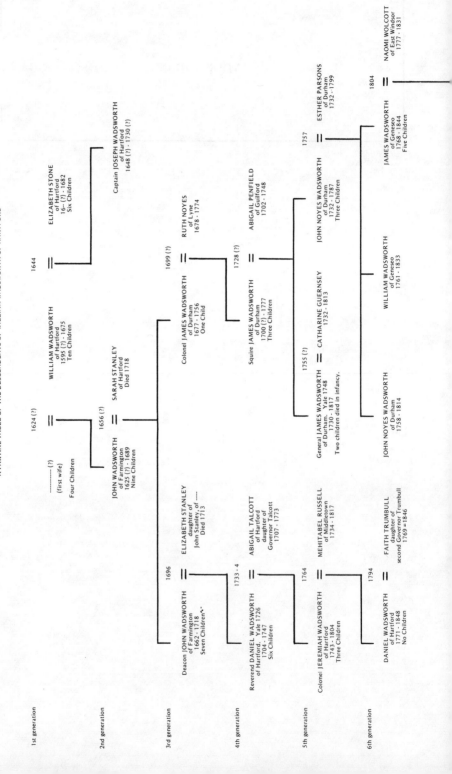

A PARTIAL TABLE OF THE DESCENDENTS OF WILLIAM WADSWORTH OF HARTFORD

1st generation

2nd generation

3rd generation

4th generation

5th generation

6th generation

WILLIAM WADSWORTH
of Hartford
1595 (?) - 1675
Ten Children

1644

ELIZABETH STONE
of Hartford
16-- (?) - 1682
Six Children

1624 (?)

----------- (?)
(first wife)
Four Children

JOHN WADSWORTH
of Farmington
1625 (?) - 1689
Nine Children

1656 (?)

SARAH STANLEY
of Hartford
Died 1718

Captain JOSEPH WADSWORTH
of Hartford
1648 (?) - 1730 (?)

Colonel JAMES WADSWORTH
of Durham
1677 - 1756
One Child

1699 (?)

RUTH NOYES
of Lyne
1678 - 1774

Squire JAMES WADSWORTH
of Durham
1700 (?) - 1777
Three Children

1728 (?)

ABIGAIL PENFIELD
of Guilford
1702 - 1748

Deacon JOHN WADSWORTH
of Farmington
1662 - 1718
Seven Children^

1696

ELIZABETH STANLEY
daughter of
John Stanley, of ------
Died 1713

Reverend DANIEL WADSWORTH
of Hartford. Yale 1726
1704 - 1747
Six Children

1733 - 4

ABIGAIL TALCOTT
of Hartford
daughter of
Governor Talcott
1707 - 1773

General JAMES WADSWORTH
of Durham. Yale 1748
1730 - 1817
Two children died in infancy.

1755 (?)

CATHARINE GUERNSEY
of Durham
1732 - 1813

JOHN NOYES WADSWORTH
of Durham
1732-1787
Three Children

1757

ESTHER PARSONS
of Durham
1732 - 1799

Colonel JEREMIAH WADSWORTH
of Hartford
1743 - 1804
Three Children

1764

MEHITABEL RUSSELL
of Middletown
1734 - 1817

JOHN NOYES WADSWORTH
of Durham
1758 - 1814

WILLIAM WADSWORTH
of Geneseo
1761 - 1833

JAMES WADSWORTH
of Geneseo
1768 - 1844
Five Children

1804

NAOMI WOLCOTT
of East Windsor
1777 - 1831

DANIEL WADSWORTH
of Hartford
1771 - 1848
No Children

1794

FAITH TRUMBULL
daughter of
second Governor Trumbull
1769 = 1846

7th generation

8th generation

9th generation

10th generation

11th generation

MARY CRAIG WHARTON
of Philadelphia
1812 - 1874

1834

JAMES SAMUEL WADSWORTH
of Geneseo
1807 - 1864
Six Children

CRAIG WHARTON WADSWORTH
of Geneseo
1841 - 1872
Two Children

EVELYN WILLING PETERS
1845 - 1886

1864

CHARLES F. WADSWORTH
of Geneseo
1835 - 1899
One Child

JESSE BURDEN
of Philadelphia
1840 - 1917

1876

JAMES WOLCOTT WADSWORTH
of Geneseo
1846 - 1926
Two Children

MARIE LOUISA TRAVERS
of New York
1848 - 1931

1913

FLETCHER HARPER
of New York
1874 - 1963

HARRIET WADSWORTH
of Geneseo
1881 -
No Children

1902

JAMES WOLCOTT WADSWORTH
of Geneseo
1877 - 1952
Three Children

ALICE HAY
of Washington
1880 - 1960

1924

W. STUART SYMINGTON
of St. Louis
1901 -

EVELYN WADSWORTH
of Geneseo
1903 - 1971
Two Children

1937

REVERDY WADSWORTH
of Geneseo
1914 - 1970
One Child

ELEANOR ROOSEVELT
of Washington
1915 -

1950

W. STUART SYMINGTON
of St. Louis
1925 -
Four Children

JANEY BELLE STUDT
of St. Louis
1928 -

1953

JAMES WADSWORTH SYMINGTON
of St. Louis
1927 -
Two Children

SYLVIA CAROLINE SCHAPP
of St. Louis
1932 -

1927

JAMES JEREMIAH WADSWORTH
of Geneseo
1905 -
One Child

HARTY TILTON
of New York
1906 - 1965

1965

HARRY ROOSEVELT WADSWORTH
of Geneseo
1941 -
Two Children

N. RAYE POPP
of Geneseo
1944 -

1948

TROWBRIDGE STRONG
of Philadelphia
1925 -

ALICE WADSWORTH
of Washington
1928 -
Five Children

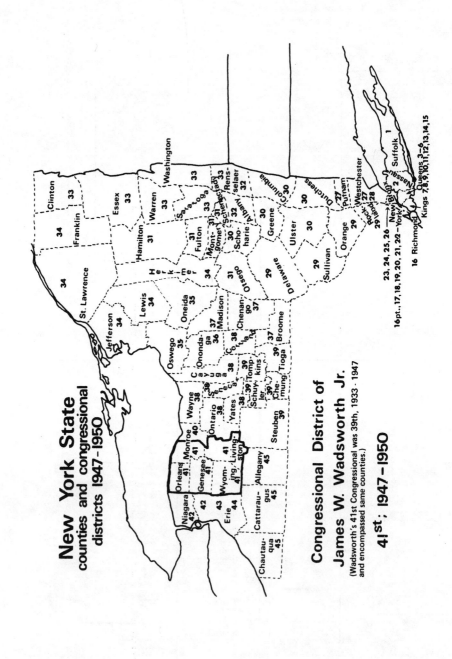

New York State
counties and congressional districts 1947-1950

Congressional District of
James W. Wadsworth Jr.

(Wadsworth's 41st Congressional was 39th, 1933 - 1947 and encompassed same counties.)

41st: 1947-1950

Clinton
Franklin 33
St. Lawrence 34
Essex 33
Warren 33
Washington
Hamilton 31
Jefferson 34
Lewis 34
Fulton 31
Mont-gomer 31
Saratoga 33
Schenectady 31
Rens-selaer 33
Herkimer 34
Oneida 35
Madison 36
Scho-harie 30
Albany 32
Columbia 30
Oswego 35
Onondaga 37
Cortland 38
Chenango 37
Otsego 31
Greene 30
Ulster 30
Delaware 29
Wayne 38
Ontario 38
Seneca 38
Yates 38
Tompkins 39
Schuyler 39
Che-mung 39
Tioga 39
Broome 39
Sullivan 29
Orange 29
Dutchess 29
Putnam 29
Rock-land 28
Westchester 27
Monroe 41
Orleans 41
Genesee 41
Wyom-ing 41
Living-ston 41
Niagara 42
Erie 42
43
44
Cattar-augus 45
Allegany 45
Steuben 39
Chautau-qua 45

New York 2
Bronx 23, 24, 25, 26
16pt., 17, 18, 19, 20, 21, 22-
16 Richmond
Kings 7, 8, 9, 10, 11, 12, 13, 14, 15
Queens 3-6
Suffolk 1

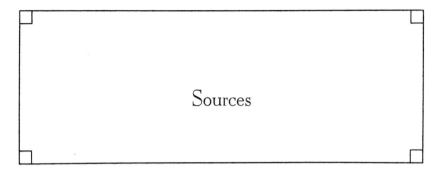

Sources

I T would serve no purpose to list here all of the materials used in the writing of this book. The notes are very complete and should be consulted for specific bibliographic information. The sources below are those which proved especially helpful to the author.

UNPUBLISHED SOURCES

Interviews

Members of the Wadsworth family have been completely cooperative and helpful. Most important was James J. Wadsworth, the Senator's elder son. As noted in the Introduction, he read the entire manuscript and discussed each chapter singly with the author. His suggestions were never obtrusive. Because he himself was so active politically during his father's congressional tenure in the thirties and the forties, his observations of his father's career during that period were particularly helpful. Although the Senator's second son, Reverdy Wadsworth, prior to his untimely death in 1971, answered the author's many questions and conscientiously offered comments on the manuscript, he had been too young during much of his father's political career to offer many observations. Other members of the family with whom the author talked at length were Evelyn Wadsworth Symington, the Senator's daughter; W. Stuart Symington, his son-in-law; Harriet Wadsworth Harper, his sister; James Wadsworth Symington, his grandson; and Porter Chandler, his cousin. The author also talked at length with Bessie Christian, who for a long period served as residence secretary to the Senator.

Political figures interviewed are too numerous to list completely. In regard to local politics, W. B. Sanders of Nunda and Thomas Slaight of Geneseo were most helpful. Regarding regional politics in the Genesee Valley, Carl Hallauer of Rochester offered many insights into the Senator's relationship with Rochester political leaders. At the congressional level, the author had lengthy interviews with Kenneth Keating, Helen G. Douglas, Dewey Short, Howard Smith, W. Sterling Cole, and the Senator's two immediate successors in the House of Representatives, Harold C. Ostertag and Barber B. Conable, Jr. Clarence K. Streit of Washington, D.C., talked to the author at length about Wadsworth's work on behalf of Atlantic Union. Two Buffalo newspaper reporters serving in Washington, Frank Fortune of the *Buffalo Evening News* and Lucian C. Warren of the *Buffalo Courier Express,* had observed Wadsworth closely in the 1940s and had many helpful comments on the Senator.

Manuscript Collections

The Wadsworth papers in the Library of Congress were, of course, the most helpful of the manuscript collections used in the project. It is fortunate that Senator Wadsworth selected wisely in deciding which of his papers to retain. My examination of other pertinent manuscript collections and of hundreds of printed sources convinces me that his selections were faithful representations of his life. The manuscript collection currently includes letters, speeches, clippings, a very helpful diary and a handwritten autobiography which covers the early political years of James Wadsworth. Wadsworth's faithful retention of pertinent documentation is also demonstrated by a perusal of the complete file of letters and documents for the interim period (1927-1932) between his Senate and House terms. Reverdy Wadsworth came upon the interim collection in the Senator's Main Street office in Geneseo and kindly turned them over to the author.

Very essential manuscript collections used in the project were those of Theodore Roosevelt, Theodore Roosevelt, Jr., Charles E. Hughes, Elihu Root, and William Howard Taft, all in the Library of Congress; the Franklin D. Roosevelt collection in the Presidential Library at Hyde Park; and the Henry L. Stimson and Charles D. Hilles papers, located in the Sterling Library at Yale University. Helpful collections in the Library of Congress were those of Gilbert Hitchcock, Ogden Mills, Vannevar Bush, and the Atlantic Union Committee. Additional collections consulted and used were the Herbert Parsons, Nicholas Murray Butler, and Bertrand Lord papers, all located at the Columbia University Library. The Regional Manuscripts Library at Cornell University holds the following collections which were used: the papers of Frank Gannett, W. Sterling Cole, Daniel Reed, and John Taber. Other collections consulted were those of Frank Higgins, Syracuse University Library; Henry C. Lodge, the Weidmer Library at Harvard; Jonathan M. Wainwright, New York Historical Library; Robert H. Fuller and George B. Agnew the New York Public Library.

Oral History

The author was extremely fortunate to have available "The Reminiscences of James W. Wadsworth, Jr.," one of the earliest and one of the most voluminous memoirs taped by the Oral History Research Office of Columbia University. Other helpful reminiscences in the Oral History Research Office were those of Beverely R. Robinson, William Stiles Bennet, Warren Isbell Lee, William H. Wadhams, Frederick C. Tanner, James W. Gerard, William S. Curtis, Robert C. Pell, Harvey Bundy, Joseph Clark Baldwin, Claude Bowers, William A. Prendergast and Westwood A. Todd. All pertained to the first two decades of Wadsworth's political life, with particular emphasis on the New York scene.

National Archives Materials

Although the author spent some days in the National Archives searching War Department and congressional committee files for helpful information regarding legislation identified with James Wadsworth, the results were meager. What was found is documented in the footnotes.

Doctoral Dissertations

Although dozens of dissertations were consulted, the following were most heavily relied upon. Herbert H. Rosenthal, "The Progressive Movement in New York State, 1906–1914" (Harvard University, 1955), was very useful for placing Wadsworth in the context of New York politics in the first decade. It supplemented nicely Wesser's definitive book (see below) on the Hughes governorship. Jack E. Kendrick, "The League of Nations and the Republican Senate, 1918–1921" (University of North Carolina, 1922), was extremely helpful on Wadsworths' role in the Senate fight against the ratification of the League Covenant. James J. Horn, "Diplomacy by Ultimatum: Ambassador Sheffield and Mexican-American Relations, 1924–1927" (State University of New York at Buffalo, 1969), was the best secondary source of the relationship between Wadsworth and Ambassador Sheffield during the Mexican-American problem in the 1920s. Also helpful on foreign affairs during Wadsworth's role on the Senate Foreign Relations Committee was David Mickey, "Senatorial Participation in the Shaping of Certain United States Foreign Policies" (University of Nebraska, 1954). Wadsworth's leadership role in the New York Republican party during the 1920s is well covered in Lawrence Madaras, "The Public Career of Theodore Roosevelt, Jr." (New York University, 1964). A very major supplement to secondary sources on prohibition was Dayton E. Heckman, "Prohibition Passes: The Story of the Association Against the Prohibition Amendment" (Ohio State University, 1939).

A number of significant dissertations covered Wadsworth's political career in the 1930s. A very essential work on New York politics during the period was Judith Stein, "The Birth of Liberalism in New York State, 1932–1938" (Yale University, 1968). A very helpful work on Wadsworth's important role in the Liberty League was Robert J. Comerford, "American Liberty League" (St. John's University, 1967). In its detailed coverage of the League it added considerably to Wolfskill's work (see below). Supplementing James Patterson's book on congressional conservatism in the 1930s (see below) was Joseph Boskin, "Politics of an Opposition Party: The Republican Party in the New Deal

Period, 1936–1940" (University of Minnesota, 1959). The most important
work on Thomas Dewey and his successful fight against the Wadsworth influence in the New York Republican party was Barry K. Beyer, "Thomas E.
Dewey, 1937–1947: A Study in Political Leadership" (University of Rochester, 1962). It is the only study of Dewey based on his papers in the University
of Rochester Library, which have since been closed to scholars. A number of
important dissertations covered Wadsworth's role in conscription and universal
military training, principally, Samuel R. Spencer, Jr., "A History of the Selective Training and Service Act of 1940, from Inception to Enactment" (Harvard
University, 1951); John M. Swomley, Jr., "A Study of the Universal Training
Campaign, 1944–1952" (University of Colorado, 1959); and Robert Ward,
"Movement for U.M.T. in the United States, 1942–1952" (University of
North Carolina, 1957). An important thesis on the Atlantic Union was Istavan Szent-Miklosy, "Development of American Thinking on an Atlantic Com-
munity, 1945–1962" (Columbia University, 1962). Two important disserta-
tions related to Wadsworth's Rules Committee assignment in the late 1940s
are Lewis J. Lapham, "Party Leadership and the House Committee on Rules"
(Harvard University, 1953), and Christopher Van Hollen, "The House Committee on Rules—1933–1951: Agent of Party and Agent of Opposition" (Johns
Hopkins University, 1951). Stuart Symington's service as Secretary of the Air
Force is covered in Murray Green, "Stuart Symington and the B-36" (American
University, 1960).

PUBLISHED SOURCES

Government Publications

The *Congressional Record* was of inestimable value in writing this biography. Particularly did the author appreciate the availability of bound volumes
of all of Wadsworth's Senate remarks. As was typical, Reverdy Wadsworth encouraged the author to take from the Senator's Geneseo Main Street office publications which might be at all helpful. In addition to the Senate remarks, the
author quickly picked up several volumes of congressional hearings, the most
important being the hearings covering the National Defense Act of 1920 of
which the Senator was the author.

Newspapers, Magazines and Periodicals

What would historians do without newspapers, and especially the *New
York Times*, with its index. Without attempting to list all newspapers used,
the following proved most helpful: *Livingston Republican, New York Herald
Tribune, Buffalo Commercial, Rochester Democrat and Chronicle, Buffalo*

Evening News, New York World, Washington Post, New York Evening Post, Washington Star, Syracuse Post-Standard, and *Chicago Tribune.* The following magazines were helpful: *Time, Life, Pageant, Business Week, Saturday Evening Post, The Nation's Business, McClures, Current History, Literary Digest, Review of Reviews, The Nation, North American Review, The New Republic.*

Needless to say, numerous issues of scholarly journals were essential, especially the following: *American Historical Review, New York History, American Heritage, Agriculture History, The Journal of American History, The American Political Science Review.*

Memoirs and Biographies

The following works were of general use to the author. Although superficial and based only on the Wadsworth papers, Alden Hatch's book, *The Wadsworths of the Genesee* (New York: Coward-McCann, Inc., 1959), was, of course, useful to the author. Henry F. Holthusen's work, *James W. Wadsworth, Jr., A Biographical Sketch* (New York: G. P. Putnam's Sons, 1926), was a campaign biography and very limited in its use to the author. Although Paul I. Wellman's *Stuart Symington: A Man with a Mission* (Garden City, N.Y.: Doubleday & Co., Inc., 1960) was a campaign biography, it is the only available book on Stuart Symington and portrays well Symington's relationship with his father-in-law. In view of Elihu Root's mentor role regarding James Wadsworth, Philip C. Jessup's two-volume work, *Elihu Root* (New York: Dodd, Mead & Co., 1938), and Richard W. Leopold's *Elihu Root and the Conservative Tradition* (Boston: Little, Brown & Co., 1954) were very helpful. The latter work was particularly useful in defining Wadsworth's conservatism. Henry L. Stimson was a life-long associate of Wadsworth's and therefore, Henry L. Stimson and McGeorge Bundy's *On Active Service in Peace and War* (New York: Harper & Brothers, 1947) was frequently referred to. Jerry Wadsworth's association with Henry Cabot Lodge took the author to William J. Miller's *Henry Cabot Lodge* (New York: James H. Heineman, Inc., 1967). For a picture of Rochester, three works were particularly important: Blake McKelvey's *Rochester: The Quest for Quality, 1890–1925* (Cambridge: Harvard University Press, 1956) and his *Rochester: An Emerging Metropolis, 1925–1961* (Rochester: Christopher Press, 1961); and Henry Clune's *The Rochester I Know* (Garden City, N.Y.: Doubleday & Co., Inc., 1972). The Genesee Valley is beautifully portrayed by Margaret Chanler's *Autumn in the Valley* (Boston: Little, Brown, 1934).

For background on the Wadsworth family, W. H. Gocher, *Wadsworth of the Charter Oak* (Hartford, Conn.: W. H. Gocher, 1904), dealt well with the Wadsworths' Connecticut ancestors. The best book on the Valley Wadsworths, and General James S. Wadsworth in particular, is Henry Greenleaf Pearson, *James S. Wadsworth of Geneseo* (New York: Charles Scribner's Sons, 1913).

James Wadsworth's father-in-law, John Hay, is well portrayed by two books: Tyler Dennett, *John Hay* (New York: Dodd, Mead & Co., 1934), and William Roscoe Thayer, *The Life and Letters of John Hay, Vol. II* (Boston and New York: Houghton Mifflin Co., 1916).

Important biographies related to Wadsworth's early political career in the first decade are Henry F. Pringle, *The Life and Times of William Howard Taft* (New York: Farrar & Rinehart, Inc., 1939), and Norman Hapgood and Henry Moskowitz, *Up from the Streets, A Life of Alfred E. Smith* (New York: Harcourt Brace & Co., 1927). There are a large number of helpful biographies and autobiographies which relate to Wadsworth's Senate years from 1915–1927. James W. Gerard's *The Memoirs of James W. Gerard* (New York: Doubleday, 1951) was important for understanding the Wadsworth 1914 senatorial campaign. A very essential work for understanding Woodrow Wilson's New Freedom and the general political context of Wadsworth's early Senate years is Arthur Link's multi-volume work on Woodrow Wilson, *Wilson, New Freedom; Progressivism and Peace* (Princeton: Princeton University Press, 1956–65). Henry F. Ashurst's memoir, *A Many-Colored Toga; The Diary of Henry F. Ashurst* (Tempe: University of Arizona Press, 1962), provides a worthwhile view of the Senate by one of JWW's colleagues in that body, as does Robert Douglas Bowden's *Boies Penrose* (New York: Greenberg, 1937). The voluminous work on Robert La Follette by Belle and Fola La Follette, *Robert M. La Follette* (New York: The Macmillan Co., 1953), is essential for understanding the United States Senate during the period. Three works cover nicely the social scene in Washington during Wadsworth's early Senate tenure: Jonathan Daniels, *Washington Quadrille* (New York: Doubleday & Co., 1968); David A. Randall, *Dukedom Large Enough* (New York: Random House, 1962); and Molly Berkley, *Winking at the Brim* (Boston: Houghton, Mifflin, 1967). Wadsworth's role on the Senate Military Affairs Committee made essential Daniel R. Beaver's *Newton D. Baker and the American War Effort* (Lincoln: University of Nebraska Press, 1966). The Washington social (and political) scene in the 1920s is vividly portrayed by Alice Roosevelt Longworth, *Crowded Hours* (New York: Charles Scribner's Sons, 1933), and Mrs. Theodore Roosevelt, Jr., *Day Before Yesterday* (New York: Doubleday, 1959). Hermann Hagedorn's *Leonard Wood, A Biography* (New York: Harper & Row, 1931) is important as related to the 1920 Republican Convention. Two recent biographies on Warren Harding proved helpful: Francis Russell, *The Shadow of Blooming Grove, Warren G. Harding and his Times* (New York: McGraw-Hill Book Co., 1968), and Robert K. Murray, *The Harding Era* (Minneapolis: Minnesota Press, 1969). The work by Robert Murray is, by far, the more sound of the two. Arthur Schlesinger's *The Crisis of the Old Order* (Boston: Houghton, Mifflin Co., 1957), an important, though biased, book on F.D.R. during that period, was frequently referred to. The Coolidge presidency is best covered in Donald McCoy, *Calvin Coolidge, The Quiet President* (New York: The Macmillan Co., 1967). In view of

Wadsworth's close association with Vice President Dawes, two works were particularly helpful: Charles G. Dawes, *Notes as Vice President, 1928–1929* (Boston: Little, Brown & Co., 1935), and Paul R. Leach, *That Man Dawes* (Chicago: The Reilly & Lee Co., 1930). A number of works cover the "Billy Mitchell affair," to which Wadsworth was tangentially related, particularly Burke Davis, *The Billy Mitchell Affair* (New York: Random House, 1967). Two books are particularly important as related to Wadsworths' 1926 senatorial campaign: J. Joseph Huthmacher, *Senator Robert E. Wagner, and the Rise of Urban Liberalism* (New York: Atheneum, 1968), and Joseph P. Lash, *Eleanor and Franklin* (New York: W. W. Norton & Co., 1971).

For biographies of the 1930s, Schlesinger's two works on the period were essential: Arthur Schlesinger, Jr., *The Politics of Upheaval* (Boston: Houghton, Mifflin, 1963), and *The Coming of the New Deal* (Boston: Houghton, Mifflin, 1958). Donald McCoy's *Landon of Kansas* (Lincoln: University of Nebraska Press, 1966) was helpful in portraying the context of the important 1936 campaign. In view of Wadsworth's aspiration to assume the Republican leadership in the House of Representatives, Joseph Martin's memoir (as told to Robert J. Donovan), *My First Fifty Years in Politics* (New York: McGraw-Hill Book Co., 1960), was particularly helpful. Arthur Mann's biography, *La Guardia Comes to Power, 1933* (New York: J. B. Lippincott Co., 1965), provided a portrait of a liberal New York colleague in the House of Representatives during the early New Deal years.

Because of Wadsworth's interest in military legislation in the 1940s, Forrest C. Pogue's biography, *George C. Marshall, Vol. I* (New York: Viking Press, 1963), was an essential work. Two biographies proved extremely worthwhile in understanding the nation's foreign policy in the 1940s: James MacGregor Burns, *Roosevelt, The Soldier of Freedom* (New York: Harcourt Brace-Jovanovich, Inc., 1970), and Haynes Johnson and Bernard M. Gwertzman, *Fulbright the Dissenter* (New York: Doubleday, 1968).

Special Studies and Monographs

Certain general works were used as constant references. Although a number of fine twentieth-century political histories are available, the author relied particularly on O. T. Barck and Nelson M. Blake, *Since 1900: A History of the United States in our Times* (New York: The Macmillan Co., 1965). The best survey of New York history is found in David M. Ellis, et. al., *A Short History of New York State* (Ithaca, N.Y.: Cornell University Press, 1957). A concise and penetrating work on New York politics is Warren Moscow's *Politics in the Empire State* (New York: Alfred A. Knopf, 1948). A fine general history of the Republican party nationally is George H. Mayer, *The Republican Party, 1854–1964* (New York: Oxford University Press, 1964). In regard to agricultural history, with which Wadsworth was constantly identified, Theodore Saloutos and John D. Hicks, *Agricultural Discontent in the Middle West, 1900–1939* (Madison: University of Wisconsin Press, 1951), was most

428 SOURCES

helpful. For local history, the only significant work on Livingston County history is Lockwood Doty's *History of Livingston County, New York* (Jackson, Mich.: W. J. Van Deusen, 1905).

Col. Vincent J. Esposito, *The West Point Atlas of American Wars, Vol. I* (New York: F. A. Praeger, 1959), makes important references to General James Wadsworth's Civil War role. An interesting portrait of Yale College during Wadsworth's student days is seen in Henry S. Canby's *Alma Mater, The Gothic Age of the American College* (New York: Farrar and Rinehart, 1936). The national political scene in the first decade is well covered in George Mowry, *The Era of Theodore Roosevelt, 1900–1912* (New York: Harper & Row, 1958). The New York political scene is thoroughly covered in Roscoe C. E. Brown, *History of the State of New York, Political and Governmental, Vol. IV* (Syracuse: The Syracuse Press, Inc., 1922). The Hughes administration is detailed in Robert F. Wesser's worthwhile monograph, *Charles Evans Hughes, Politics and Reform in New York, 1905–1910* (Ithaca, N.Y.: Cornell University Press, 1967). Essential to observing the origins of the Meat Inspection Act is Claude Bowers, *Beveridge and the Progressive Era* (Boston: Houghton, Mifflin, 1932), and Upton Sinclair's muck-raking work, *The Jungle* (New York: Harper & Brothers, 1905).

There are numerous monographs on matters in the 1920s related to Wadsworth's senate tenure. Two extremely helpful works on the general political context of the 1920s are John D. Hicks, *Republican Ascendancy, 1921–1933* (New York: Harper & Brothers, 1960), and David B. Burner, *The Politics of Provincialism* (New York: Alfred A. Knopf, 1968). Wadsworth's authorship of the Military Defense Act of 1920 is covered in detail in John McAuley Palmer's *America in Arms, The Experience of the United States with Military Organization* (New Haven, Conn.: Yale University Press, 1941). The most important work on the 1920 election is Wesley M. Bagby's *The Road to Normalcy, The Presidential Campaign and Election of 1920* (Baltimore: The Johns Hopkins Press, 1962). A number of works on the suffrage movement make reference to Wadsworth's anti-suffrage position. The most useful of these was Carrie C. Catt and Nettie R. Shuler, *Woman Suffrage and Politics, The True Story of the Suffrage Movement* (New York: Charles Scribner's Sons, 1926). The best monograph on the important Teapot Dome scandal of the 1920s is Burle Noggle, *Teapot Dome, Oil and Politics in the 1920s* (Baton Rouge: Louisiana State University Press, 1962). Wadsworth's interest in aviation legislation is referred to in Ladd Smith, *Airways, The History of Commercial Aviation in the United States* (New York: Russell & Russell, Inc., 1965). Three foreign affairs monographs helpful to understanding Wadsworth's senate role in foreign affairs are: Thomas H. Buckley, *The United States and the Washington Conference, 1921–1922* (Knoxville: The University of Tennessee Press, 1970); Denna F. Fleming, *The United States and the World Court* (New York: Russell & Russell, 1945); and Howard F. Cline, *The United States and Mexico* (Cambridge, Mass.: Harvard University Press,

1965). The largest national affair affecting Wadsworth's political life in the 1920s was the "noble experiment." Two monographs are essential to an understanding of prohibition: Andrew Sinclair, *Era of Excess* (New York: Harper Colophon Books, 1964); Peter H. Odegard, *Pressure Politics, The Story of the Anti-Saloon League* (New York: Columbia University Press, 1928). Of less help was Herbert Asbury, *The Great Illusion, An Informal History of Prohibition* (Garden City, N.Y.: Doubleday & Co., 1950). An extremely biased work which defends the "noble experiment" is Fletcher Dobyns, *The Amazing Story of Repeal* (New York: Willett, Clark & Co., 1940).

Regarding Wadsworth's House of Representatives tenure, James Bryce's *The American Commonwealth, Vol. I* (New York: The Macmillan Co., 1912) provided a classic description of the House of Representatives in a period just prior to Wadsworth's entry into that body. Neil MacNeil, *Forge of Democracy: The House of Representatives* (New York: D. McKay, 1963), is a fine recent history of the House of Representatives. The political context of the early 1930s is contemporarily surveyed in Robert S. Allen, *Washington Merry-Go-Round* (New York: Blue Ribbon Books, 1931). Two important surveys of the national political scene are William Leuchtenburg, *Franklin D. Roosevelt and the New Deal, 1932–1940* (New York: Harper & Row, 1963), and James T. Patterson, *Congressional Conservatism and the New Deal* (Lexington: University of Kentucky Press, 1967). The American Liberty League in which Wadsworth played such an important role is quite well analyzed in George Wolfskill, *The Revolt of the Conservatives, A History of the Liberty League* (Boston: Houghton, Mifflin Co., 1962). Two domestic issues in which Wadsworth was actively involved in the House of Representatives, currency and securities control, are described in John A. Brennan, *Silver and the First New Deal* (Reno: University of Nevada Press, 1969), and Ralph F. Debedts, *The New Deal's SEC: The Formative Years* (New York: Columbia University Press, 1964). A general survey of foreign affairs in the 1930s is covered in Selig Adler's *The Uncertain Giant* (London: Collier Books, 1969). The specific problem of isolationism with which Wadsworth contended is viewed in four important books: Manfred Jonas, *Isolationism in America, 1935–1941* (Ithaca, N.Y.: Cornell University Press, 1966); Robert A. Devine, *The Illusion of Neutrality* (Aurora, Ill.: Quandrangle Paperback, 1968); Donald F. Drummond, *The Passing of American Neutrality, 1937–1941* (Ann Arbor: University of Michigan Press, 1955); and William L. Langer and S. Everett Gleason, *The Challenge to Isolationism, 1937–1940* (New York: Harper & Row, 1952). Because of Wadsworth's important role in lend-lease legislation, the recent book by Warren F. Kimball, *The Most Unsordid Act, Lend-Lease, 1939–1941* (Baltimore: The Johns Hopkins Press, 1969), was important to this author.

The best description of repeal of the remaining neutrality legislation in 1940 is William Langer and S. Everett Gleason's *The Undeclared War, 1940–1941* (New York: Harper & Brothers, 1953). Wadsworth's participation in the construction of military legislation in the House of Representatives made essential the following works: Arthur A. Ekirch, Jr., *The Civilian and the Military* (New York: Oxford University Press, 1956); Lawrence J. Legere, Jr., *Unification of the Armed Forces* (Washington: Office of the Chief of Military History, Dept. of the Army, undated); and C. W. Barklund, *The Department of Defense* (New York: Praeger, 1968). The best work on Willkie's role in the Republican party in the 1940s is Donald Bruce Johnson, *The Republican Party and Wendell Willkie* (Urbana: University of Illinois Press, 1960). For background on the Congress during the Second World War, the author relied on Roland Young, *Congressional Politics in the Second World War* (New York: Columbia University, 1956). Wadsworths' contemporary in Republican internationalism, Arthur Vandenberg, is well covered in a recent book by C. David Tompkins, *Senator Arthur H. Vandenberg: The Evolution of a Modern Republican, 1884–1945* (E. Lansing: Michigan State University Press, 1970). For a survey of the 1945–1955 period, the author relied on Eric Goldman, *The Crucial Decade, 1945–1955* (New York: Knopf, 1956). Secondary materials on the Moral Re-Armament movement are sparse and the author had to rely on an in-house publication by Basil Entwistle and John R. McCooks, *Moral Re-Armament: What is it?* (Los Angeles: Pace Publications, 1967). For coverage of the Rules Committee on which Wadsworth served, James A. Robinson's *The House Rules Committee* (New York: The Bobbs-Merrill Co., Inc., 1963) was most helpful. In regard to the Republican-southern Democratic coalition, in which Wadsworth was active, some works provided important background. One work, an in-house publication by J. Harvie Williams, *Coalition Now!* (Washington: American Good Government Society, Inc., 1955), provided an ideological defense of the coalition. A more helpful general work was J. MacGregor Burns, *The Deadlock of Democracy* (Englewood Cliffs: Prentice-Hall, 1963).

Index

(James W. Wadsworth, Jr., is designated as JWW)

431

N.Y. caucus, Natl. Rep. Conv. (1932), 227–28
Halleck, Charles A., 290
Hamilton College, 268
Hamilton, John D. M., 275, 293
Hammond, Frederick, 196, 216, 266, 267, 270
Hampton House, 23, 27, 30, 83, 162, 210
Hancock, Clarence E., supports JWW for H of R leadership, 296
Hanley, J. R., 283
Hanna, James, 290
Harbord, James G., 168
Harding, Warren G.: 92, 105, 131–32; el. to U.S. Senate, 90; sits with JWW, 114; "dark horse" candidate for Pres., 128; JWW describes, 128; nominated for Pres., 130–31; visits Senate, 135; appt. C. E. Hughes, Sec of State, 135; appts Harry H. Daugherty, Attorney General, 136; conservatism in Presidency, 139; opposes veterans bonus, 146–147; relations with JWW, 157; admires JWW, 157; death, 162; scandals, 195
Harding, Mrs. Warren, "The Dutchess," 246
Harper, Fletcher, 212
Harper, Harriet Wadsworth, 5, 27, 128, 210, 212, 286, 320, 363, 390; horseback riding, 13
Harriman, W. Averell, 385
Harriman, E. H., 33
Harriman and Lehmann Bros, 214
Harrison, Benjamin, 217
Harrison, Byron (Pat), 209
Hartford House: 11, 13, 162, 210–11, 261, 288, 295, 363, 374, 409; centennial, 259; Christmas holidays, 394
Harvard Club, 310
Harvard University, 76, 169, 312, 314, 379
Harvey, George: 238; role in Rep. Natl. Conv. (1926), 129, 131
Harzof's, 213
Haskell, Lt. Gen. W. H., 321, 338
Hatch, Alden, 230
Hatch, Edward G., defends Otto Kelsey before N.Y. Senate, 63–64
Hawkes, Albert, approached on coalition politics, post WW II, 392
Hay, John: 15, 21, 27, 29, 93–94, 152, 155, 213, 307; described, 24; John Hay–Henry Adams relationship, 24n–25n
Hay, John, residence, Washington, D.C.: 212, 259; described, 94
Hay, Adelbert S.: 21; fellow Yale student, 15; death, 26
Hay, Clarence: describes C. E. Hughes, 99; poem on JWW, 397–98

Hay, Miss Garret; opposes JWW, 127
Hay, Helen, 27
Hayden, Carl T., amendment to Burke-Wadsworth bill defeated, 317
Hay-Quesada Treaty, 155
Hays, Will H., relations with Warren Harding, 138
Haywood, William, 168, 170
Hearst, William R., 56–57
Heck, Oswald: 280; defeats James J. Wadsworth for N.Y. Assembly Majority Leadership, 269; Speaker, N.Y. Assembly, 278; opposition to anti court packing, 279
Hedges, Job E., aids H. L. Stimson in 1910 campaign for N.Y. Gov., 81; runs for N.Y. Gov., 86
Heflin, Thomas J., critical of James R. Sheffield, 207
Hemlock Lake, 32
Henderson, Leon, 326
Hendricks, Francis, 35; supports JWW for NY Assembly Speakership, 37
Hershey, Maj. Gen. Lewis B.: receives Natl. War Service bill, 342
Herter, Christian H., 374; relations with JWW on unification
Hickok, William, 214
Higgins, Frank W.: 31, 34, 39–41, 43; selects JWW for N.Y. Assembly Speakership, 35; keep B. Odell as N.Y. Rep. Ch., 43–44; health declines
Hill, David Jayne: 88; suggested for NY Gov, 1908, 70
Hilles, Charles D., 85, 96, 129, 167–68, 184, 192, 200, 256, 267–68, 276–78, 280, 330, 390; JWW supports him for Sec of Treas, 1920, 136; oversees NY patronage (1920s), 136; describes JWW, 157; close association with JWW, 165; Assesses Rep Pres situation (1924), 167; his Natl Committeeman status threatened, 168; possible JWW running mate (1926), 190; picks W. K. Macy for NY Rep Ch, 265; sees New Deal mandate in NY, 268; loses Natl Com Membership, 281; advises J. H. Williams on coalition politics, 390–91
Hillman, Sidney, wants training in conscription leg, 315
Hillquit, Morris, 124
Hindenburg line, 113
Hinman-Green bill: 741, JWW opposes, 73; provisions, 73; defeated, 75
History: assessment of JWW, 415–16
Hitchcock, Gilbert M., 104; opposes JWW on tariff, 53; Natl Defense Act, 1920, 120–21; answer JWW on taxes: opposes JWW on mil appropriations, 1920, 144–145; opposes JWW on veterans bonus, 147

JAMES W. WADSWORTH, Jr.

The Gentleman from New York

was composed in 10-point Linotype Fairfield, leaded two points,
with the display type handset in Egmont Light
by Joe Mann Associates, York, Pennsylvania;
printed offset on Perkins & Squier 55-pound Litho
by Valley Offset, Deposit, New York;
Smyth-sewn and bound in Columbia Colonial Vellum over boards
by Vail-Ballou Press, Inc., Binghamton, New York;
and published by

SYRACUSE UNIVERSITY PRESS
Syracuse, New York 13210